Programmer's Guide to NetWare

The Communications Book Series

Author	Title	ISBN
Held/Sarch	Data Communications, Second Edition	0-07-027988-8
Fortier	Handbook of LAN Technology	0-07-021623-1
Cooper	Computer and Communications Security: Strategy for the 90's	0-07-012926-6
Kessler	ISDN	0-07-034242-3
Liebing/Knutson/ Day	NetWare Workstation Troubleshooting and Maintenance Handbook	0-07-607027-1
Liebing/Neff	NetWare Server Troubleshooting and Maintenance Handbook	0-07-607028-X

The Computing That Works Book Series

Brainerd	A Programmer's Guide to FORTRAN 90	0-07-000248-7
Birnes	High Level Languages and Software Applications Reference	0-07-005394-4
Birnes	PC Hardware and Systems Implementations Reference	0-07-005396-0
Ashley/Fernandez	Online Communications Software: A Professional's Guide	0-07-002463-4
Baker	C Tools for Scientists and Engineers	0-07-003355-2
Birnes	On-Line Programming Language Reference Guide	0-07-005395-2
Birnes	The Microcomputer Applications Handbook	0-07-005397-9
Buerger	LATEX: For Scientists and Engineers	0-07-008845-4
Byers	Inside the IBM PS/2 Systems	0-07-009527-2h 0-07-009525-6pb
Fernandez/Ashley	Assembley Language Programming for 80383	0-07-020575-2
Kliewer	EGA/VGA: A Programmer's Reference Guide, Second Edition	0-07-035099-X
Lecarme/et al	Software Portability: With Microcomputer Issues, Expanded Edition	0-07-036964-X
Morgan/McGilton	Introducing UNIX System V	0-07-043152-3
Ross	Data Exchange in the PC and MS DOS Environment	0-07-053923-5
Sheldon	Introducing PC-DOS and MS-DOS, Second Edition	0-07-056565-1
Sheldon	Hard Disk Management in the PC & MS Environment	0-07-056556-2
Simon	How to be a Successful Computer Consultant, Second Edition	0-07-057552-5pb 0-07-057554-1h
Smith	Advanced Programming and Applications in Turbo C	0-07-058708-6h 0-07-058707-8pb

For more information about other McGraw-Hill materials, call 1-800-2-MCGRAW in the United States. In other countries, call your McGraw-Hill office.

Programmer's Guide to NetWare

Charles G. Rose

McGraw-Hill, Inc.
1221 Avenue of the Americas
New York, NY 10020

To Lauren, who makes it all worthwhile.

1234567890

Cover design by Kate Hennessy Johnson. The editor for this book was Don Martin and the production supervisor was David B. Doering. It was composed in PageMaker 3.01 by Doering & Associates.

Library of Congress Cataloging-in-Publication Data

Rose, Charles G.
The programmer's guide to NetWare/ by Charles G. Rose, IV.
p. cm.
Includes index.
ISBN 0-07-607029-8 : $49.95
1. NetWare (Computer operating system) I. Title
QA76.76.063R67 1990
005.7' 1369--dc20 90-13210
CIP

For information about our audio products, write us at:
Newbridge Book Clubs, 3000 Cindel Drive, Delran, NJ 08370

Table of Contents

ACKNOWLEDGEMENTS

First and foremost, I would like to thank Vince Sondej for truly caring about this project. Without his efforts, you would not be reading this. Somewhere in Utah there are several thousand Post-It notes with my name on them. Significant thanks also go to:

Dave Doering, for the figures, layout, and typesetting; my appreciation for doing them all well in the five minutes he was given.

Don Martin, who is responsible for you not reading any little extraneous words anywhere in the text; I mean not one word will you find that is the least bit repetitive, redundant, or otherwise unnecessary. In the interest of being brief and concise, he has carefully removed redundancy everywhere and not one word is repetitive. Really.

Gamal Herbon for downloading literally megabytes of book.

Ed Liebing for inspiration, encouragement, and helping me get started.

Del Robins and Glenn Stephens at Novell for their help on NetWare 286/386 API compatibility.

Milt Anderson at Novell for shedding light on the AFP API, which remained dark until my talking with him.

Tom Brough, Tim Bird, and Lori Gauthier at Novell for their helpful advice and recommendations.

Cheryl Seeman at Novell for all her coordinating efforts and for helping me get the materials I needed.

Claudia Flowers and Theron Shreve at McGraw-Hill who helped make this book a reality from the corporate side.

Borland International, Zortech, and Microsoft Corporation for providing evaluation copies of their language products.

My cat, Muse, who sat on my lap and provided great company through many of the chapters; thanks to him also for explaining the VAP mechanism to me.

And a profound thanks to my wife, Lauren, without whose faith, support, and encouragement this book would not have been possible.

Appendices

FOREWORD

There are fundamental changes occurring in the computer industry. Network computing, using PCs, LANs, and servers, is challenging traditional centralized data processing architectures. Many if not most computer applications can be successfully moved from minicomputer and mainframe platforms onto PC LANs with significant cost savings and increased performance, flexibility, and growth potential. And the aggregate power of a LAN full of PCs and servers, if fully utilized, allows for the development of new applications and user interfaces that would be impractical if not impossible in the past.

As with all revolutions, some of the rules are now changed. The new network computing world requires new methodologies in implementing multiuser software applications. In some ways software design is more complicated. Data access synchronization becomes a much bigger issue. Decisions have to be made how to distribute the processing: where to cut the application into client and server pieces. Yet in other ways network computing simplifies software development, since each PC is supporting only one user.

This book covers the issues that must be dealt with and the system calls used to develop applications for Novell NetWare. As the pioneering and premier PC-based network computing environment, NetWare has evolved a rich (and often overlapping) set of DOS-extending system calls to handle the unique requirements of distributed processing. All of the system calls (even some I'd forgotten about) are described and explained, with examples. The challenge and opportunity comes in truly understanding and then exploiting the power of network computing.

Drew Major
NetWare architect

Introduction

The communications industry has proclaimed the 1990s the "Decade of the Local Area Network," the decade when software will be built to take full advantage of network resources.

Unlike applications imported from the DOS world, the software of the 1990s will exploit the multiuser resources available on the LAN. This new software is unlikely to be built, however, unless network programmers receive some sort of boost.

That is because, although LAN software steadily evolves toward distributed, client-server applications, toward groupware, toward distributed processing, as yet none has proved so compelling as to persuade companies to invest in LANs solely to reap the benefits.

One of the major reasons the industry doesn't produce better LAN software is a lack of programmer education. That clearly is the case with Novell Inc.'s NetWare.

Mainframe and minicomputer programmers have experience with issues raised by multiple users, but few if any of them have had the opportunity to program in an environment as highly distributed as a NetWare LAN.

Indeed, few have had the opportunity to even read about programming in such an environment. There are Novell Inc.'s NetWare Application Programming Interface (API) function-call references and technical overview, but there is no third-party source of direction and explanation that might prompt a developer to design as well as to program.

The *Programmer's Guide to NetWare*, therefore, is intended to provide a framework for design and a comprehensive coverage of the issues facing any programmer in the Novell NetWare environment. The book provides not only reference information but also illustrations of how to use the various API groups, including code examples for each. It is the hope of the author that the book also may inspire programmers to push the limits of LAN technology.

Coverage

Current through NetWare 386, the *Programmer's Guide to NetWare* covers beginning, intermediate, and advanced NetWare programming.

Each chapter begins with a discussion of theories, data structures and general information on an API group. The discussion covers design and implementation issues, the "why and where" of using the calls. After the individual function calls are presented in detail, each chapter concludes with a code example.

Each code example is written in C and will stand alone, i.e., it will not rely on any external libraries, such as the Novell NetWare C Interface Library. The C language was chosen for its popularity among developers. The example programs will be supplemented with discussions of the calls used and the operations performed.

Chapter one introduces the NetWare programming environment, the history of NetWare and such basic considerations in programming as how a NetWare function call is made, how registers are used, and what request and reply packets contain, among others.

Chapter two covers the Locking API (also known as the Data Synchronization API.) It provides an introduction to the environment and issues of multiple-user programming. Scenarios for locking are presented, as are pitfalls and ways of avoiding them.

Chapter three on the File Services API covers file-related calls. Explained are calls that allow the developer to copy files, examine or change their attributes, and erase or restore them.

Chapter four on Directory Services includes the calls that deal with volumes, directory handles, mapping drives, basic directory operations (create directory, remove directory, etc.) and security (directory trustee management).

Chapter five covers Novell's Transaction Tracking System. (TTS is only included in System Fault Tolerant (SFT) versions of NetWare.) The TTS provides a powerful mechanism for transaction-based fault tolerance; the developers of NetWare say it is one of the aspects of NetWare of which they are most proud.

Chapter six covers the Bindery, NetWare's database of information on users, servers, groups, queues, print servers and other "objects." Covered is how the programmer can interact with the Bindery to manage those objects and their associated "properties" and "values."

Chapter seven covers the Queue Management System (QMS) API. When a print job is sent to a file server, it goes first to a queue where it waits to be serviced. In NetWare 2.0a and below, the queue was a service only available to the file server, but with NetWare 2.1x, the queue services are available to any developer who wishes to take advantage of them. This chapter explains how the queue mechanism works and how to make use of it.

Chapter eight explains the calls involved in the printing process, showing how to capture an application's output to the LPT device and reroute it to a network printer as well as how to manipulate the associated flags.

Chapter nine covers the Connection and Workstation services which allow an application to attach, log into, and use the services of a file server. Also provided are calls that provide information on a user's workstation.

Chapter 10 is on Message Services which allow the developer to send messages between network nodes, as well as to maintain message "pipes" between workstations.

Chapter 11 covers the Accounting Services which allow users to record and track application and network use.

Chapter 12 explains how to use the Apple Macintosh-related calls that NetWare 2.15 brought to the Novell environment. This chapter discusses the AppleTalk Filing Protocol (AFP) calls and how they allow DOS and Apple format files to coexist on the same file server.

Chapter 13 explains the File Server Services API. These services provide the same statistical reporting and file server control capabilities that are available through the NetWare FConsole utility. Statistics about the file server cache, disk drives, TTS, and connection usage are available. Also covered are such server-control capabilities as "bringing a file server down" and enabling and disabling login.

Chapter 14 covers Communications Services, the low-level communication facilities of NetWare. Both the Internetwork Packet Exchange (IPX) protocol and the Sequenced Packet Exchange (SPX) protocol are covered.

Chapter 15 is on Diagnostic Services. These services allow the developer to query workstations, bridges, and servers for extensive information and statistics about their configurations and conditions.

Chapter 16 covers the Service Advertising Protocol (SAP) which allows programmers to build their own application servers and advertise them on an internetwork.

Chapter 17 presents the Value-Added Process (VAP) Services API, a powerful mechanism long shrouded in mystique and confusion. The issues surrounding building VAPs, as well as their structures and elements, are shown. Also, a sample VAP is built and a skeleton is presented from which programmers can build their own VAPs.

(VAPs are specific to 2.1x versions of NetWare. The NetWare Loadable Module was introduced in NetWare 386 and provides an easier way to build server-based applications while adding more features to the environment.)

Chapter 18 is on the user interface, a subject of increasing attention of late. As the look of the Graphical User Interface (GUI) slowly grows in popularity, the need for developers to focus on the environment they will use for presentation management increases apace. This chapter takes the most popular GUI for DOS, Microsoft Windows, and discusses how NetWare applications can be built to work in so demanding an environment.

Chapter 19 focuses on the character-based user interface. The C-Worthy user interface is used in system utilities like Syscon, Filer, and FConsole; this chapter examines how to use it to create network applications that really communicate with the user.

Chapter 20 discusses the exciting new world of object-oriented programming and how its concepts can be used in the NetWare environment. Design issues will be discussed and a C++ programming example provided.

This book would not be available without the help and cooperation of Novell. It is intended to supplement Novell's NetWare documentation rather than supplant it. In fact, for each API call, the Novell C Interface Syntax will be shown.

It is the author's sincere hope that this book will inspire developers to use the network services and resources to their fullest, designing network applications to exploit network services from the beginning rather than merely porting DOS applications to the network environment. As the awareness of network programming grows, so will the power of programmers' tools, which will in turn be reflected in the applications that are produced. Perhaps with the right combination of education, network resources, and programmers' tools, we can all make the 1990's the "Decade of the LAN."

1 Programming in the NetWare Environment

Welcome to the world of NetWare API programming! To acquaint you with programming in the Novell NetWare environment, we will begin with a bit of history, tracking the evolution of the LAN and Novell's role in making it a powerful alternative to mainframe or minicomputer processing.

Next, we will cover the NetWare Core Protocol API mechanism, compiler usage, the versions of NetWare, the workstation shell, request and reply packets and other facets of programming in NetWare.

History

Novell Inc., nee Novell Data Systems Inc. (NDS), was founded in the late 1970s. NDS built Z-80 based microcomputers running CP/M while supplying private-labeled printers, software, and other components. Then, in the early 1980s, NDS began to build networking products.

The original NDS file server was designed and built around the Motorola 68000 processor and supported a star topology. Individual cables were strung out from a central file server. The connections were made via RS-422 connections running at 232 kilobits per second.

The software for the server was created by a group of independent consultants recently graduated from Brigham Young University and calling themselves Superset.

Superset first received a six-week contract from NDS to develop a disk serving operating system that would support CP/M (and later, UNIX workstations). Having their contract extended several times, Superset built the base of the operating system that would become NetWare.

Unfortunately, NDS went bankrupt in the early 1980s. Safeguard Scientifics, the provider of much of NDS's startup capital, oversaw the reorganization into Novell, Inc. Around this time, the IBM PC was being introduced. One of the Superset consultants purchased a PC and immediately began writing "shells" that would allow these new machines to interact with the 68000-based file server.

The file server operating system continued to be built and was renamed ShareNet which became the name for the complete network system for IBM PCs. Included was a 68000-based file server with 256 kilobytes of RAM, a processor board, and a multiplexer board. NetWare Interface Cards (NICs) were placed in the machines to facilitate access to the file server.

With the release of the IBM PC/XT, ShareNet was renamed NetWare/S-net (S stood for Star which was the name of the topology used). As other compatible products were introduced, they would add a letter to the end of NetWare: NetWare/G incorporated Gateway's boards and others followed suit.

Next, Novell introduced NetWare/86 which incorporated file-serving capabilities, including such multiuser capabilities as security and data synchronization. (Previously, the server had simply responded to a workstation's request for reads and writes to parts of a disk.) This file-based model proved to be a critical part of Novell's philosophy in server architecture.

In 1984, Novell introduced its Independent Software Vendor (ISV) program, inviting vendors to write NetWare-aware applications. Besides offering a COBOL compiler that translated mini- and mainframe-based systems to the NetWare environment, Novell published its Application Programming Interfaces (APIs), documenting the many and varied calls that could be made to access network resources. The first APIs documented were for NetWare versions 4.0 and 4.6. In this book, we document which calls were introduced when and which versions of NetWare they will work with.

In 1985, Advanced NetWare version 1.0 was introduced; it was followed by Advanced NetWare 2.0, which included support for the Intel 80286 processor, in 1986.

System Fault Tolerance (SFT) was also introduced in 1986; this add-on provided protection for the file server. SFT Level I included "HOTFIX," a feature that allowed the server to detect a bad block on the hard disk and write the data to a different area, as well as read after write verification of data. SFT Level II provided the Transaction Tracking System (detailed in chapter 5) as well as disk mirroring and duplexing, which provided hardware redundancy for added protection against data loss.

In 1987, NetWare 2.1 was introduced, with SFT Level I capabilities built into the operating system. Level II capabilities were incorporated into a product called SFT NetWare. (Subsequent versions 2.11 and 2.12 provided fixes to the NetWare 2.1 software.)

Also in 1987, the Entry Level System (ELS) versions of NetWare starting appearing; these provided less-expensive versions of NetWare but with fewer features. (For example, ELS I allowed only 4 concurrent users.)

In 1988, NetWare for VMS running on the DEC VAX was introduced. This software allowed a DEC minicomputer to act as a Novell file server. Novell later generalized this idea by introducing Portable NetWare in 1989; this would allow any third-party hardware manufacturer to get NetWare running on its host environment.

In 1989, Novell shipped NetWare 2.15; this version allowed the Apple Macintosh computer to be used as a workstation on the LAN by providing support for the AppleTalk Filing Protocol (AFP). The AFP API was soon released and is documented in chapter 12.

In September 1989, Novell shipped NetWare 386, a product that takes full advantage of the 386 chip and provides increased performance and a host of new features.

The NetWare programming environment

The NetWare programming environment is fairly straightforward once you learn several concepts. This section will explain the areas of interest to the programmer and the concepts to be familiar with before attempting to program in the NetWare environment. (For more detail on the differences between the NetWare 286 and NetWare 386 environments, see appendix C.)

The workstation shell

The workstation shell is a program that must be loaded into memory before a user can log into a network. Users with Advanced NetWare 2.1 and above will know the shell by its two component programs, IPX and NET3. IPX handles the Internetwork Packet Exchange Protocol used to communicate with the file server and other workstations. NET3 is the interface between the network and DOS.

Users running versions of NetWare prior to 2.1x will know the shell as ANET3.COM, which combines IPX and NET3 in one file. In NetWare 2.1x, IPX must stand alone because it changes for each LAN adapter board and NET3 does not (NET2 and NET4 are available for DOS versions 2.x and 4.x respectively).

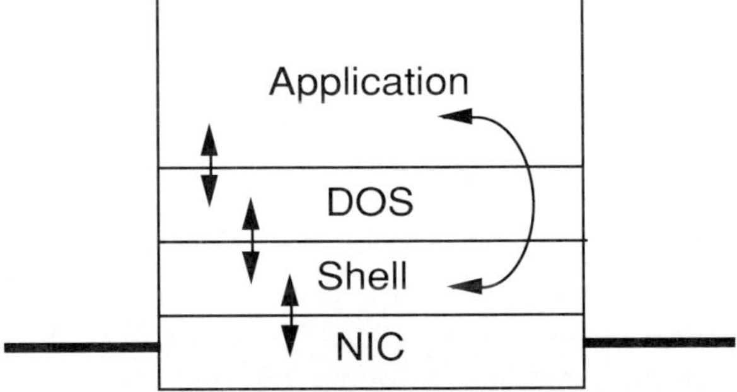

Figure 1: The relationship of the NetWare shell and DOS.

The purpose of the shell is to provide a seamless connection between DOS and the network. When the shell is loaded, a software connection is created and the closest file server is "attached" to the workstation. The first drive available— starting the scan with drive F:—is "mapped" to the LOGIN directory of the local file server (the DOS LASTDRIVE parameter is used in finding the first available drive). At this point, the user may execute the LOGIN program and log in to the file server.

By "mapping a drive" we mean using a logical drive letter to access some subdirectory on a file server. Most Novell users are familiar with the (server/volume:path) nomenclature used to describe the exact directory on a certain volume on a certain file server. For instance, if drive F: were mapped to FS1/SYS:PUBLIC, when you looked at a directory of F: you would see the files in the PUBLIC directory on the SYS: volume on file server FS1.

Drive mapping is a means of conveniently accessing the file server through DOS. The logical drive created is much like the one DOS creates in response to a SUBST command. The drive is considered logical, as opposed to physical, which would mean an actual drive existing in the local workstation. Instead, the NetWare shell fools DOS into thinking there are drives from F: to Z: (and actually beyond since temporary drives may use several punctuation characters for drive letters).

Here's how. What happens programmatically when the shell is loaded is that it patches several DOS interrupts.

Interrupts used by IPX.COM

08h	Clock - IPX gets timing information from here.
2Fh	DOS multiplex - when called, the shell checks to see if the interrupt is 7Ah. If so, the segment:offset address of the 7Ah interrupt is returned. This is used with the IPX mechanism (chapter 14) as well as with the Broadcast Inform mechanism used with the Message Services (chapter 10).
64h	Internal IPX interrupt (points to same location as 7Ah interrupt).
7Ah	IPX interrupt (commonly used, but new utilities should make a far call to this interrupt's location) (chapter 14).
F4h & F6h	Internal IPX interrupts.
Fxh	Others used in this range.

Interrupts used by NetX.COM (Net2, Net3 or Net4)

10h	BIOS Video (used by the message broadcast mechanism)
17h	BIOS Printer (for parallel printer redirection)
1Bh	Control-Break or Control-C (to preserve breaks during critical sections of the shell)
20h	Old program terminate interrupt (used to track tasks)
21h	DOS interrupt (most API calls go through here)
24h	Critical Error Handler (displays network errors)
27h	Terminate and Stay Resident interrupt (used to track tasks)
F5h	Used internally

The shell then interprets between workstation and file server. For example, if a user wishes to open a file on a network drive, the shell traps the user's open file request and itself sends a packet to the file server requesting that the file be opened. The server then sends a packet back to the shell informing it whether the request has been granted or not. The shell returns from interrupt 21h to the requesting program the appropriate DOS response. Figure 2 illustrates this process.

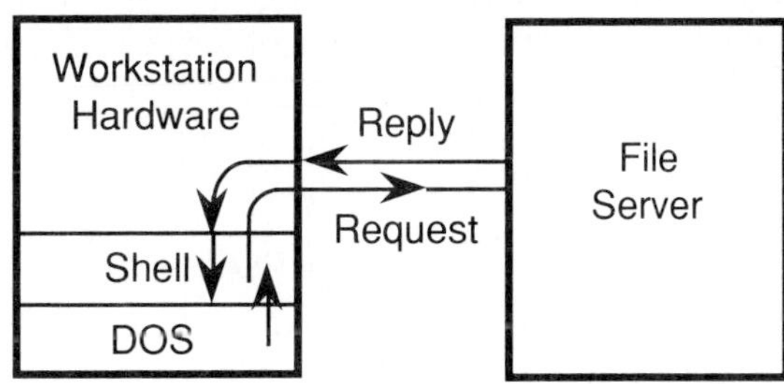

Figure 2: A request is sent and a reply received over the network.

The shell is critical in many ways to the programmer since it is the software that takes the information provided by the programmer in a function call and interacts with the file server for the response. Also, there are several tables in the shell that are used to keep information on drives, attached servers, and other pertinent details about the workstation's environment.

High-low format

Many of the numbers provided in request/reply packets are in high-low format, a carryover from the environment in which NetWare was developed, the Motorola 68000 processor environment. The Intel 80X86 family of processors store numbers in low-high format, i.e., an integer is stored with its least significant byte (LSB) first and its most significant byte (MSB) last. For example, the integer 0x1234 is stored as 0x3412. For a long (four-byte) integer, 0x12345678 is stored as 0x78563412. Often, a programmer will have an IntSwap and a LongSwap routine defined to swap from hi-lo to lo-hi format and back.

Because of the differences highlighted by these two processors, Novell is investigating other ways to provide transparency across different hardware platforms. A concept called Transparent Data Interface (TDI) allows a software layer to be established that converts data from its representational format to its hardware-specific format. This idea has become important with the release of Portable NetWare where any number of hardware platforms may need to be supported running NetWare.

Programming languages

NetWare applications may be developed in any language that can be linked with external routines, or in any language that has access to the registers and is able to call interrupt 21h. Assembly, C, Pascal, Fortran, BASIC, and many others will work well. Fourth-generation languages, such as dBase, Clipper, and Advanced Revelation also will work since they can call external C or Assembly routines.

This book will provide examples in C since it is the most popular language used today for development. C excels in flexibility, power, and portability, and is well known in the industry. Also, C structures lend themselves well to use as request/reply packets that may be sent to the file server for processing. They require a little more code space but they improve the readability of the program and are inherently self-documenting.

Compiler usage

Most of the examples in this book were written using Borland's Turbo C for its accessibility (low cost), its overall power as a C compiler, its continuing compatibility with the NetWare shells and operating system, its popularity in schools and colleges and Borland's support for object-oriented programming and commitment to supporting Windows in the future. Several examples take advantage of Turbo C's ability to access the registers from C (AX is _AX, AL is _AL, etc).

Although your compiler may not support this feature, any of the function-call level routines may be written in assembler.

Our choice of compiler does not mean the other compilers such as those from Microsoft, Lattice, Watcom, and Zortech are not appropriate; we have simply chosen Turbo C as an instructional tool.

Request and reply packets

Many of the function calls you will use when programming Novell networks will use only registers, but most require request and reply packets. If a file server needs 10 fields of information, it can't place them all in registers, so it uses a packet (also called a structure in this book since we often use C structures to code them). A packet is simply a group of fields to send to or receive from a file server. A buffer is the memory space that packet occupies (the terms are often used interchangeably).

For example, if you wish to get the flags associated with a print job, you would use the Get Default Capture Flags call. That would require a 63-byte packet for the file server to use when the call is returned. The registers AH, AL, and CX would be set to different values and the ES:BX register pair would point to the 63-byte packet that would be filled with information when the function call returned and the packet was received. Packets that are sent to the file server for the purpose of informing the file server about a call are called request packets whereas those sent for the file server to fill in are called reply packets.

In most function calls, there is a request and reply packet. All of the fields in the request buffer must be set up before making a call. And the size of the reply packet must also be specified. At the start of every packet is a WORD value that indicates the byte length of the packet. This value is set to the length of the packet minus two (its own length). THE REPLY PACKET LENGTH MUST BE SET BEFORE THE CALL IS MADE! If forgotten, this can be a source of much confusion.

It is difficult to say that certain register pairs are always used for certain tasks since there is no solid consistency among the calls. In many of the calls the DS:SI register pair contains the address of the request packet while the ES:DI pair contains the address of the reply packet. Some calls will use only a request or a reply packet; others calls will use different registers (such as the Get Default Capture Flags call) for holding the address of a particular packet. The diversity of styles is accredited to the task of supporting differing versions of the NetWare API as well as maintaining compatibility with some DOS calls.

We will demonstrate in our example programs several ways to make a NetWare API call. Often we will make a request buffer a C structure and make it global, calling it Request or Reply. This is done for the student of NetWare programming to illustrate the purpose of the structure and to make it more easily accessible. Real-world applications will often keep data private and pass addresses to it as well as adopting naming conventions for the request and reply packets that are used.

Data representation

In this book, we use the following names for unsigned data types:

- BYTE unsigned char
- WORD unsigned int
- LONG unsigned long

Digging in

Since the best way to learn how to program using the NetWare APIs is to dig in and try it, we will start with a simple example that shows what station, or connection number, you are currently logged in to on the network.

Here's the code to our first program, WHATMION.C:

```
/*                                                                    */
/* WhatMIOn  - Returns the station number user is logged in t        */
/*                                                                    */
/* by Charles Rose                                                    */
/*                                                                    */

#include <stdio.h>
#include <dos.h>

int GetConnectionNumber( void );

main()
{
        int station;

        /* Find out the station/connection number of the current user      */
        station = GetConnectionNumber();

        printf( "You are logged into station %d.\n", station );
}
int GetConnectionNumber( void )
{
        _AH = 0xDC;

        geninterrupt( 0x21 );

        return _AL;
}
```

The first two lines of the program include the stdio.h file, used for the printf() statement. Dos.h is included for geninterrupt(), which we will discuss below. The next line is the function prototype of the GetConnectionNumber() function.

Function prototypes are part of the ANSI C specification and are used to promote better error checking, monitoring elements such as prototype/function definition agreement and checking the numbers and types of parameters being passed by functions. Function prototypes will be used in all of the examples in this book.

Next, main() is declared and the int variable *station* is defined. GetConnectionNumber() is called, passing no parameters (the function parameters were defined void, meaning none are passed). The GetConnectionNumber function sets the AH register to DCh using the pseudoregister feature of Turbo C (AH is referred to as _AH).

Interrupt 21h is then called using the geninterrupt() function. Geninterrupt() immediately generates the interrupt specified, doing no register preservation, so the programmer should be aware that some registers could be destroyed. Using register variables or register optimization when using geninterrupt() and the pseudoregister variables is not recommended.

Finally, GetConnectionNumber returns _AL, the number of the current station which is placed in the variable station.

The program ends by printing the value of station to the screen.

You have written your first NetWare-aware program! The rest of the material covered in this book will build on a structure similar to this one.

2 Locking Services

One of the most significant benefits of using a LAN is having a central file facility, a single location where all users can effectively share information. However, as soon as two or more users seek access to the same file at the same time, problems arise. This chapter will explain the issues involved in data synchronization, or locking, that confront the developer when writing or amending programs for the NetWare environment.

The problems that arise in this multiuser environment may range from simple overwriting of data to a "fatal embrace" between users. In addressing them, the programmer may physically lock a file or group of files (file locking) or a portion of a file (record locking). Or the programmer may name the file or record to be locked (logical locking) and may even specify how many users may have simultaneous access (semaphore).

Whatever the choice, the programmer must pay a price in degraded network performance for each lock employed, so the most elegant programs will lock as little as possible for the least possible time. To that end, this chapter will cover the seven types of locking and the six functions available for the major types. Finally, we will develop a small database application to illustrate how record locking works. In addition, we develop a sample software metering program that shows how many users are in the sample program at once and limits the number of concurrent users.

Synchronization problems

A classic example of the need for data read/write synchronization is the following scenario: A mail-order consumer electronics company uses purchasing/inventory software that runs on a network. Users in the shipping and receiving departments read the inventory record for CD players, which says that there are 10 in stock. Shipping processes an order for two players and writes the new total, eight, back to the disk in the file server. Receiving, meanwhile, has just received another 10 units, so the user there adds that to the original 10 and writes 20 back to the server. Since receiving was last to write to the disk, its record (20 instead of 18) is the one that ends up on the disk.

With some kind of synchronization between the two users, an accurate stock figure could have been preserved. When shipping first read the record, the program should have prevented other users from modifying that file or record until shipping had amended it. Only then should the program allow receiving to read and amend it.

There are several ways to avoid this data-overwrite problem; no matter which way is chosen, the developer must be sensitive to the time a user must wait when working with a software application. The type of application involved affects the choice. If a file is seldom used, for example, file locking may be appropriate. If a file is often used, but it is rare that much record contention will occur, record locking may do. (In more complex cases, such as the case of an airline reservation system where there may be hundreds or thousands of users and several may need simultaneous access to the record of a particular flight, other methods will be necessary.)

Two reasonably simple methods of avoiding data overwrite are complete lockout and a read-modify-update cycle. In a complete lockout, any user attempting to access a locked file or record is told that the object is locked, try again later. In a read-modify-update cycle, a user reads and modifies data, but before it is written back to disk the original data is checked to see if another user modified it. If unchanged, the data is written; if changed, the programmer must decide whether to abort the operation, continue the operation with modifications or present the options to the user.

Avoiding a fatal embrace

A data overwrite corrupts data. A "deadlock" or "fatal embrace" does not; it just locks the system up on the user entirely. It occurs when two stations each have a lock on data the other one wants. For example, two users have records from a personnel system locked and on their screens. The first user has record 23, the second record 55. The first asks to also see record 55 and second asks to also see record 23. The two stations lock up, each waiting for the other to release a file, and if there is no timeout written into their systems, the stations will wait forever.

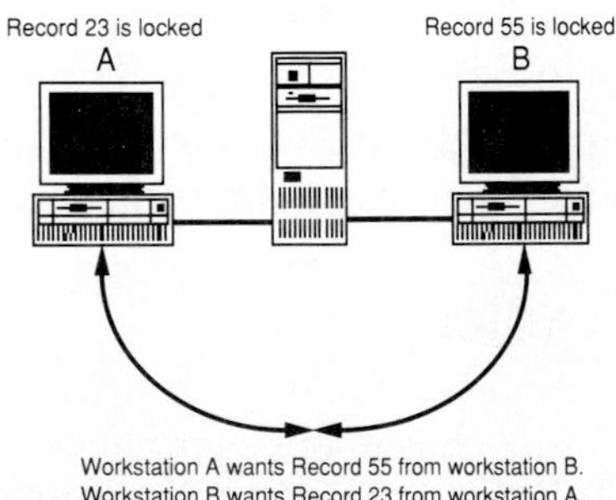
Record 23 is locked
A
Record 55 is locked
B
Workstation A wants Record 55 from workstation B.
Workstation B wants Record 23 from workstation A.

Figure 3: The Fatal Embrace--Workstation A cannot respond to a request from workstation B until it receives a response to its request from B.

Fatal embrace can be prevented by making use of NetWare functions and the Timeout Limit variable used in most locking function calls. This variable specifies the maximum time to wait for a lock to be released before returning to the program.

Buffering problems

Other synchronization problems may arise from high-level programming languages in which programmers write multiuser database applications. Programmers using such languages as C and Pascal must be aware that these languages may hold input and output data in an I/O buffer before writing it to disk. If a program waits to write data to the disk until it has a sufficient number of bytes to make writing worthwhile, the timing of locks and writes can be misaligned and data can be corrupted.

These buffering problems can be solved either by using low-level I/O routines that don't use buffering or by ensuring that the buffers are flushed immediately after any data is written. Buffers can be flushed by issuing an explicit call to flush them, by closing and reopening a file, or, in some cases, by performing a read after a write.

There are sources of buffering problems other than language. The developer should be aware that the operating system, the workstation, and the server may be involved in a certain amount of buffering. The file server, for example, performs "elevator seeking" on files to minimize disk head travel and thus improve performance. What this means is that the disk controller will use the most efficient path necessary to fulfill disk-access requests. So even when workstation A requests data before B does, if B is closer to the data, B may nonetheless receive the information first. Also, the workstation shell, NET3.COM, caches files in some cases. Programmers of time-sensitive applications should be aware of these facts.

Overlapping data

Another language-oriented problem arises when a programming language reads or writes blocks of data larger than desired. In some languages, data is read and written in 512- or 1024-byte blocks, and if the record size is, for example, 142 bytes, data in subsequent 142-byte records may be corrupted.

To see if this is happening, testing should be done with several users reading and writing records (the example program at the end of this chapter, TestLock, may be used in testing for this problem). As in any program testing environment, the more and varied the combination of tests, the greater the likelihood of uncovering difficult bugs. To correct such a problem, use lower level I/O routines that only write the size of block requested, or encode your own routines in a lower level language such as Assembler. In most cases, however, this won't be necessary.

File-extension problems

It is fairly straightforward to conceptualize how a locking system may work with records that already exist in a file. It's a more complex matter, however, when a developer has to lock records that haven't yet been added to a file.

Suppose, for example, that two users wish to add records to the end of a single file. If both update to the same location, data will be overwritten. The solution to this problem may lie in using a logical record lock for the last record, or a semaphore, or in locking the file completely.

Locking and system performance

The solution to any particular locking problem will lie mainly in the needs of the software application. How many users will be reading and writing to the same files or records or fields at once? Are there some read-only users? What are the performance requirements of the system? Performance requirements are particularly important. Those requirements include the number of concurrent users to be supported and the speed with which a request is to be processed. These can vary widely; a real-time telephone order processing system needs a much quicker response time than a mailing list management application, for example. In either case, however, the developer must balance data synchronization and protection against performance.

If a record is locked while one user is changing data on the screen, others will have to wait for that user to finish and save the record before they can modify it. Therefore, to improve performance with locking, try to minimize what has to be locked and how long it must be locked. Record locking instead of file locking is an example of this kind of minimizing. Field locking can be also performed if extreme circumstances warrant it.

One important performance factor to consider is just when locking actually occurs. The lock-read-modify-write-unlock cycle is called the update cycle, it is the time this cycle takes that should be kept to a minimum to improve performance.

To minimize update time, developers may allow one user read-write access while granting others read-only access, or they may give all users read access and update all users' screens immediately if any changes occur. (This is the approach taken by Borland's Paradox database management system.) These and other sophisticated methods of data synchronization are only as limited as the imaginations of the programmers developing them.

The best way to "performance tune" an application that uses locking is to test it under different circumstances. Simulate different user loads, for example, and anticipate the amount of system use at different times of day. In this light, some locking methods may seem well-suited while others may become impractical for meeting performance requirements.

Transactional processing

Users working with database applications often work with more than one file at a time. So when one record is saved, several files may need updating. In our multiuser scenario, these files will need to be locked; if even one is not, a fatal embrace may occur. To prevent this, several files are "logged," meaning the system adds them to a list of files to lock together.

When the program issues the call Lock File Set, the system checks to see if all of the files are unlocked. If just one file is unable to be locked, the call fails and returns, preventing the "fatal embrace."

The Locking Application Programming Interface

The NetWare Locking API offers seven different ways to synchronize data processing: DOS function 5C, automatic file locking, physical file locking, physical record locking, logical file locking, logical record locking, and semaphore.

It is important to distinguish physical locking from logical locking. A physical lock prevents calls to write to a range of bytes (record locking) or to a file (file locking). If a program makes a call to write to a file or record that is locked by another workstation, the call fails and returns an error code.

Logical locking does not impose a physical lock on the file. And if a program makes a call to write to a file or record that is logically locked by another workstation, but not physically locked, the system will allow the action.

Thus, for logical locking to succeed, all programs must conform to the same logical locking conventions and must check for logical locks before amending files.

In this section, we will describe the seven types of data synchronization, then provide detailed descriptions of the calls.

Locking with DOS function 5C

DOS function 5C was introduced by Microsoft in DOS version 3 and is meant to provide compatibility across different types of network operating systems. Novell began supporting the call, Control Record Access, with Advanced NetWare version 1.02. The call specifies a file handle and a byte range to lock, and sets a flag to either lock or unlock the byte range.

Automatic file locking

Automatic locking is performed by NetWare on new files that are copied to the network. At this level, files are set by NetWare to the default, nonshareable read-write, and the system arbitrates sharing violations by denying others access to a file once someone else has opened it. If a user tries to open a file that another user has locked, he or she will receive an "Abort, Retry" type of message (courtesy of the DOS Critical Error mechanism, Interrupt 24h), instructing the user how to proceed.

The program running in this case is not aware of any sharing violation and is not notified. The file in this case will remain locked until the user that opened it closes it. If a program needs to be notified of these sharing violations, the "Abort, Retry" messages may be trapped through a replacement of the default Critical Error Handler.

This is the simplest form of locking. It requires no work on anyone's part; everything is done by NetWare. This type of locking may actually be appropriate for an application that almost never has two people trying to access the same file. If the "Abort, Retry" message is sufficient warning to the user, then this may be the way to go.

A file may also be flagged shareable read-only (through the NetWare "FLAG" command-line utility) if the developer wishes to only allow shared read access to the file.

Physical file locking

When using physical file locking, it is the programmer's responsibility to make the calls to lock or unlock files. When these calls were created, they were designed to accept file control blocks (FCBs). This was done mainly because in 1983, when NetWare was introduced, it supported both CP/M as well as DOS. Also, under the early versions of DOS, there was no such thing as a file handle. DOS supported FCBs to maintain compatibility with CP/M. Beginning with version 2.0 of DOS, however, file handles were supported, and we see the same support in the physical file locking calls of NetWare versions 4.6 and later.

The FCB versions have not been documented for several years by Novell and, although they are supported through NetWare 386 (to maintain compatibility with older programs), Novell representatives say that by the end of 1990 the workstation shell will not support these FCB calls.

If a programmer wishes to use a straightforward, simple method of locking, and has few demands on the system, physical file locking presents a sound means of data synchronization.

Physical record locking

Physical record locking is the most sophisticated locking available under NetWare, with the system physically locking a byte range in a file. Actually this byte range may be a field in a record, or a subfield; the level of detail and complexity may be set by the developer. To describe the record, programmers specify the starting position in the file and the length of the record. NetWare then physically locks that range.

As with physical file locking, several of the calls now accept FCBs instead of file handles, but these calls will not be supported in the future.

Logical locking

Logical locking is based on an abstraction, an agreed upon "name" for a particular data item rather than a physical specification for one. A logical lock is represented by a string of characters that names a file or a record that a station wishes to lock. Other stations issue calls to NetWare to determine the status of the lock and to pass on the string containing the lock name. The file server responds to the workstation, indicating whether the lock is in use or free.

It is important to remember that since logically locked files can be written to by anyone, they require cooperation from all accessing stations to be successful. And it is advisable when using both logical and physical locks together not to lock a set of both types with a Lock Set call.

The logical file locking calls first appeared in NetWare version 4.0. The two calls, Begin Logical File Locking (C8h) and End Logical File Locking (C9h), provided a convenient method of locking all open files that were flagged as shareable. Instead of using the log call, as is common with other types of locking, the programmer would open all the files needing to be locked, call Begin Logical File Locking, perform the necessary I/O, and call End Logical File Locking.

As with the FCB-version of the physical locking calls, this mode has not been documented for the last few years although it has been supported; it will not be supported after 1990. The Log File call, used to log a group of files before locking them, provides a better, more consistent method of locking a group of files and is used with physical file locking, physical record locking, and logical record locking.

Semaphores

Semaphores are similar to record locks in that they lock based on a string, but semaphores allow more than one user to control the lock at a time. Semaphores are used when a programmer wants to allow access to an application, but wishes for no more than, for example, four users to have access at one time. The semaphore could be set up so that when the fifth station requested access, it would be denied. Both semaphores and logical locks extend the use of synchronization to network resources rather than specific files.

NetWare locking functions

There are six broad types of calls used in data synchronization. In each, an object is a physical file, a physical record, or a logical record.

Log (and *lock*) *object* is used when a developer wishes to build a list of entities to be locked as a set, or to lock each object as it is added to the list. Logged objects are added to a log table. The calls are Log File, Log Logical Record, and Log Physical Record.

Lock Set of objects is used to lock the set of objects built from the above call. The calls are Lock File Set, Lock Logical Record Set, and Lock Physical Record Set.

Release object releases a lock on a particular object, but doesn't remove it from the log table. The calls are Release File, Release Logical Record, and Release Physical Record.

Release Set of logged objects releases the locks on the objects in the log table, but doesn't remove them from the table. The calls are Release File Set, Release Logical Record Set, and Release Physical Record Set.

Clear object unlocks and clears the object from the log table. The calls are Clear File, Clear Logical Record, and Clear Physical Record.

Clear Set of logged objects unlocks all logged objects and clears the log table. The calls are Clear File Set, Clear Logical Record Set, and Clear Physical Record Set.

'Lock modes' and NetWare upgrades

When NetWare was upgraded from version 4.0 to version 4.6, some changes were made to several of the locking calls. However, developers had already written software to conform to the 4.0 specification. To handle this situation, version 4.6 included two new API calls: Get Lock Mode and Set Lock Mode (C6h).

These calls let applications change the "lock mode" from zero, which makes the Log and Lock calls behave differently (for physical file and record locking as well as physical file locking) from what they did with version 4.0. Also, the logical file locking call Begin Logical File Locking (C8h) is affected.

Programmers can now set the lock mode to 1, called the "Extended Lock Mode," which enables the APIs to function with the 4.6 extensions. When writing new programs today, one should use the extended lock mode; we will nonetheless provide documentation on how the old, 4.0-style calls work.

Calls in the Locking API

The following descriptions will include which versions of NetWare support which calls. Throughout the book, we'll explain fields within the calls only at the first mention of each field in each chapter. Appendix B contains a comprehensive, alphabetical listing of the fields for quick reference.

Get Lock Mode (C6h 00h) and Set Lock Mode (C6h 01h)

These calls are supported in NetWare version 4.6, in Advanced NetWare versions 1.0, 1.02, 2.0, and 2.1, and in NetWare 386 and later versions.

Registers in:
AH C6h
AL Function Code
00h = set to 4.0-style "compatibility mode"
01h = set to 4.6 and later "extended lock mode"
02h = return current lock mode

Registers out:
AL Current lock mode

A function can test for NetWare 4.6 and above (and therefore the capability of using extended lock mode) through the following code fragment:

```
MOV     AX, 0C601h        ;Put C6h in AH, 01h (extended mode) to AL
INT     21h               ;Attempt to set lock mode to extended
MOV     AX, 0C602h        ;Now get the current lock mode in AL
CMP     AL, 01h           ;Is the current mode 1?
JNE     BELOW_NET_4.6     ;If not, we're not NetWare 4.6 or above...
```

New programs should be written with the lock mode set to extended; Novell provided the compatibility mode to support those programs developed before NetWare 4.6. The default lock mode is 0. If the lock mode is set to 1, when a program terminates, or calls End of Job (D6h), the lock mode is returned to 0.

The NetWare C Interface format is:

```
int GetLockMode( void );
int SetLockMode( BYTE lockMode );
```

Physical file locking calls

File locking is perhaps the simplest form of locking, so we will continue our discussion of the API with it.

Log File (EBh) (ASCIIZ)

This call is supported in NetWare versions 4.0 and 4.6, in Advanced NetWare versions 1.0, 1.02, 2.0 and 2.1, and in NetWare 386 and later versions. It's the first call used with file locks. It places the location and the length of the file in a log table which resides on the file server. (A log table is unique to each workstation.)

The programmer has the option of immediately locking the file when this call is made. Most often, however, this call is used when placing a group of files into a log table to be locked later with Lock File Set.

Under lock mode 0, the compatibility mode, we use:

Registers in:

AH	EBh
DS:DX	Request Buffer Address

Completion Codes:

00h	No Error
FFh	Fail

Request Buffer:

File Path	1-255	ASCIIZ (max len is 255)

Under lock mode 1, the extended mode, we use:

Registers in:

AH	EBh
AL	Locking Directive
DS:DX	Request Buffer Address
BP	Timeout Limit

Registers out:

AL	Completion Code

Completion Codes:

00	Success
96h	Server Out of Memory
FEh	Timeout Failure
FFh	Hardware Failure

Request Buffer:

File Path	1-255	ASCIIZ (max len is 255)

The *Locking Directive* directs the call to either log or log and immediately lock the file. It may have one of two values with this call:

00 Log file
01 Log and lock file

Timeout Limit is the time the program will wait for a file to become available if another station has it locked. It is measured in clock ticks, where a tick is an eighteenth of a second (1/18), and may be set to 0 if no wait is desired.

File Path is a null-terminated string (ASCIIZ) that specifies the full pathname of the target file. Full paths may be specified as in SYS:USER\DJT\MYFILE.DAT or paths may extend the default directory. Assuming the default directory is SYS:APPS, setting *File Path* to WP\TEST.DAT would make the target file SYS:APPS\WP\TEST.DAT.

A non-existent filename can be locked to avoid opening a window of access between creation and locking of a new file.

The NetWare C Interface format is:

```
int LogFile( char *fileName, BYTE lockDirective,
   WORD timeoutLimit );
```

Log File (CAh) (FCB)

This call is supported in NetWare versions 4.0 and 4.6, in Advanced NetWare versions 1.0, 1.02, 2.0, and 2.1, and in NetWare 386. It provides the same function as the preceding one, but FCBs are used. This function, according to Novell, is supported through NetWare 386, but will not be supported after 1990.

Under lock mode 0, the compatibility mode, we use:

Registers in:

AH	CAh
DS:DX	Address of File Control Block

Completion Codes:

00h	No Error
FFh	Fail

Under lock mode 1, the extended mode, we use:

Registers in:

AH	CAh
AL	Locking Directive
DS:DX	Address of FCB
BP	Timeout Limit

Registers out:

AL	Completion Code

Completion Codes:

00	Success
96h	Server Out of Memory
FEh	Timeout Failure
FFh	Hardware Failure

The NetWare C Interface format is not supported.

Lock File Set (CBh)

This call is supported in NetWare versions 4.0 and 4.6, in Advanced NetWare versions 1.0, 1.02, 2.0, and 2.1, and in NetWare 386 and later versions. Once all of the necessary files are logged, Lock File Set is used to lock all of the files at once, thus preventing fatal embrace. This is an all or nothing call; either all files in the log set are locked, or none are. If one of the files can't be locked after the maximum timeout, the call will fail, having locked no files.

Under lock mode 0, the compatibility mode, use:

Registers in:

AH	CBh
DL	Mode (0 = No Wait, 1 = Wait)

Registers out:

AL	Completion Code

Completion Codes:

00h	Success
FFh	Failure

Under lock mode 1, the extended mode, use:

Registers in:

AH	CBh
BP	Timeout Limit (in 1/18th seconds, 0 = no wait)

Registers out:

AL	Completion Code

Completion Codes:

00h	Success
FEh	Timeout Failure
FFh	Failure

The NetWare C Interface format is:

```
int LockFileSet( WORD timeoutLimit );
```

When lock mode is set to 0, the shell may wait, depending on the value of *mode*, until the entire file table is clear before returning. With lock mode set to 1, the shell waits until the entire file table is clear, or until the specified timeout occurs, whichever comes first.

Release File (ECh) (ASCIIZ)

This call is supported in NetWare version 4.6, in Advanced NetWare versions 1.0, 1.02, 2.0, and 2.1, and in NetWare 386 and later versions. It's used when the developer wishes to unlock a specific file. The developer provides a null-terminated string containing the file path of the file to be unlocked.

Registers in:

AH	ECh
DS:DX	Request Buffer Address

Registers out:

AL	Completion Code

Completion Codes:

00h	Success
FFh	No Files Found

Request Buffer:

File Path	1-255	ASCIIZ (max len is 255)

The NetWare C Interface format is:

```
int ReleaseFile( char *fileName );
```

Release File (CCh) (FCB)

This call is supported in NetWare versions 4.0 and 4.6, in Advanced NetWare versions 1.0, 1.02, 2.0, and 2.1, and in NetWare 386. It performs the same function as the preceding call, but uses FCBs. This function, according to Novell, is supported through NetWare 386, but will not be supported after 1990.

Registers in:

AH	CCh
DS:DX	Address of File Control Block

Registers out:
AL Completion Code

Completion Codes:
00h Success
FFh Failure

The NetWare C Interface format is not supported.

Release File Set (CDh)

This call is supported in NetWare versions 4.0 and 4.6, in Advanced NetWare versions 1.0, 1.02, 2.0, and 2.1, and in NetWare 386 and later versions. It unlocks all files in the log table, but doesn't remove them from the log table. Any of the files that are still open at the time of the Release request become "detached." A detached file remains open but cannot be accessed without generating an error. A Lock File Set must be issued and accepted to reattach the logged files before any I/O can take place.

The next call to be discussed, Clear File, deals with removing files from the log table. This call requires only that the AH register be loaded with CDh and returns nothing.

Registers in:
AH CDh

Registers out:
none

The NetWare C Interface format is:

```
void ReleaseFileSet( void );
```

Clear File (EDh) (ASCIIZ)

This call is supported in NetWare version 4.6, in Advanced NetWare versions 1.0, 1.02, 2.0, and 2.1, and in NetWare 386 and later versions. It's used when a programmer has finished with a file and not only wants to unlock the file but also wants to remove it from the log table. Another related call, Clear File Set, unlocks and removes all of the files from the log table. As before, just the File Path is required for this function.

Registers in:
AH EDh
DS:DX Request Buffer Address

Registers out:
AL Completion Code

Completion Codes:
00h Success
FFh No Files Found

The NetWare C Interface format is:

```
int ClearFile( char *fileName );
```

Clear File (CEh) (FCB)

This call is supported in NetWare versions 4.0 and 4.6, in Advanced NetWare versions 1.0, 1.02, 2.0, and 2.1, and in NetWare 386. It performs the same function as the preceding call, but uses FCBs. This function, according to Novell, is supported through NetWare 386, but will not be supported after 1990.

Registers in:
AH CEh
DS:DX Address of File Control Block

Registers out:
AL Completion Code

Completion Codes:
00h Success
FFh Failure

The NetWare C Interface format is not supported.

Clear File Set (CFh)

This call is supported in NetWare versions 4.0 and 4.6, in Advanced NetWare versions 1.0, 1.02, 2.0, and 2.1, and in NetWare 386 and later versions. Clear File Set unlocks all files in the log table, and removes them from the log table. As with Release File Set, this call requires no parameters and returns none.

Registers in:
AH CFh

Registers out:
none

The NetWare C Interface format is:

```
void ClearFileSet( void );
```

Logical file locking calls

As stated earlier, these two calls will not be supported in versions of NetWare dated after 1990; they are covered here for the sake of completeness.

Note that these calls use logical locking, not physical locking. This means that if the current station has used this call to lock several files, another station can open and write to these files. For these functions to work, all stations using the application must use these calls to coordinate the synchronization process.

Begin Logical File Locking (C8h)

This call is supported in NetWare versions 4.0 and 4.6, in Advanced NetWare versions 1.0, 1.02, 2.0, and 2.1, and in NetWare 386. To use it, the programmer must first open the files marked shareable that need to be locked. Once this call is made, the file server places a logical lock on the shareable files currently open.

Under lock mode 0, the compatibility mode, use:

Registers in:

AH	C8h
DL	Mode (0 = No Wait, 1 = Wait)

Registers out:

AL	Completion Code

Completion Codes:

00h	Success
FFh	Failure

Under lock mode 1, the extended mode, use:

Registers in:

AH	C8h
BP	Timeout Limit (in 1/18th seconds, 0 = no wait)

Registers out:

AL	Completion Code

Completion Codes:

00h	Success
FEh	Timeout Failure
FFh	Failure

The NetWare C Interface format is not supported.

End Logical File Locking (C9h)

This call is supported in NetWare versions 4.0 and 4.6, in Advanced NetWare versions 1.0, 1.02, 2.0, and 2.1, and in NetWare 386. It releases files locked by the preceding call. If other stations are waiting to lock the files, the server grants locks first come, first serve. The station waiting the longest gets the locks first.

Registers in:

AH	C9h

Registers out:

AL	Completion Code

Completion Codes:

00h	Success
FFh	Failure

The NetWare C Interface format is not supported.

Physical record locking calls

Locking byte ranges within files is more powerful than file locking, since it doesn't completely exclude others from a file while a user has a record locked. Record locking gives developers and users more freedom and flexibility, but the developer must keep track of the start and length elements of the records involved. As with physical file locking, the six major locking call types are available.

Log Physical Record (BCh) (Handle)

This call is supported in NetWare version 4.6, in Advanced NetWare versions 1.0, 1.02, 2.0, and 2.1, and in NetWare 386 and later versions. It's the first call used with record locks. It places the location and the length of the record in a workstation log table which resides on the file server. The programmer has the option of locking the record. Again, the call is often used when placing a group of records into a log table to be locked at once with Lock Physical Record Set call. The developer must have the file handle, the record offset, and record length to make this call.

Registers in:

AH	BCh
AL	Locking Directive
BX	File Handle
CX	High Record Offset (WORD)
DX	Low Record Offset (WORD)
BP	Timeout Limit
SI	High Record Length (WORD)
DI	Low Record Length (WORD)

Registers out:

AL	Completion Code

Completion Codes:

00	Success
96h	Server Out of Memory
FEh	Timeout Failure
FFh	Failure

The Locking Directive has three possible values with this call:

00	Log record
01	Log and lock record with an exclusive lock
03	Log and lock record with a shareable, read-only lock

A shareable, read-only lock allows other stations to lock and read the record and prevents the record from being written to.

File Handle is the DOS file handle of the target file. The programmer can obtain it through the DOS Create File call or the DOS Open File call.

Record Offset is a LONG (unsigned long) value expressed in two WORDs (unsigned ints) containing the offset from the beginning of the file where the record begins. The programmer must place the more significant WORD in High Record Offset and less significant WORD in Low Record Offset.

Record Length is a LONG value expressed in two WORDs (High and Low) containing the length of the record. The programmer must place the more significant WORD in High Record Offset and less significant WORD in Low Record Offset.

The NetWare C Interface format is:

```
int LogPhysicalRecord( int fileHandle, long recordStartOffset,
    long recordLength, BYTE lockDirective, WORD timeoutLimit );
```

Log Physical Record (BFh) (FCB)

This call is supported in NetWare version 4.6, in Advanced NetWare versions 1.0, 1.02, 2.0, and 2.1, and in NetWare 386. It performs the same function as the preceding call, but uses FCBs. This function, according to Novell, is supported through NetWare 386, but will not be supported after 1990.

Registers in:

AH	BFh
AL	Locking Directive
BX	High Record Offset (WORD)
CX	Low Record Offset (WORD)
DS:DX	Address of opened File Control Block (non-extended)
BP	Timeout Limit
SI	High Record Length (WORD)
DI	Low Record Length (WORD)

Registers out:
AL Completion Code

Completion Codes:
00Success
96h Server Out of Memory
FEh Timeout Failure
FFh Failure

The NetWare C Interface format is not supported.

Lock Physical Record Set (C2h)

This call is supported in NetWare version 4.6, in Advanced NetWare versions 1.0, 1.02, 2.0, and 2.1, and in NetWare 386 and later versions. When all necessary records are logged, it is used to lock all of the records at once. It is all or nothing and fails if any of the records cannot be locked.

Registers in:
AH C2h
AL Lock Directive
BP Timeout Limit (0 = no wait, -1 = wait forever)
Registers out:
AL Completion Code

Completion Codes:
00h Success
FEh Timeout Failure
FFh Failure

The NetWare C Interface format is:

```
int LockPhysicalRecordSet( BYTE lockDirective, WORD timeoutLimit );
```

Release Physical Record (BDh) (Handle)

This call is supported in NetWare version 4.6, in Advanced NetWare versions 1.0, 1.02, 2.0, and 2.1, and in NetWare 386 and later versions. It is used when the developer wishes to unlock a specific record. The developer provides the location and length of the record and the file handle of the target file, and the network unlocks the physical record. Note that like other release calls, the record is unlocked, but it is not removed from the log table.

Registers in:
AH BDh
BX File Handle

CX High Record Offset
DX Low Record Offset
SI High Record Length
DI Low Record Length

Registers out:
AL Completion Code

Completion Codes:
00 Success
FFh No Locked Record Found

The NetWare C Interface format is:

```
int ReleasePhysicalRecord( int fileHandle,
   long recordStartOffset, long recordLength );
```

Release Physical Record (C0h) (FCB)

This call is supported in NetWare version 4.6, in Advanced NetWare versions 1.0, 1.02, 2.0, and 2.1, and in NetWare 386. It performs the same function as the preceding call, but uses FCBs. This function, according to Novell, is supported through NetWare 386, but will not be supported after 1990.

Registers in:
AH C0h
DS:DX Address of opened File Control Block (nonextended)
BX High Record Offset
CX Low Record Offset

Registers out:
AL Completion Code

Completion Codes:
00 Success
FFh Invalid record

The NetWare C Interface format is not supported.

Release Physical Record Set (C3h)

This call is supported in NetWare version 4.6, in Advanced NetWare versions 1.0, 1.02, 2.0, and 2.1, and in NetWare 386 and later versions. It unlocks all records in the log table but doesn't remove them from the table.

Registers in:
AH C3h

Registers out:
none

The NetWare C Interface format is:

```
void ReleasePhysicalRecordSet( void );
```

Clear Physical Record (BEh) (Handle)

This call is supported in NetWare version 4.6, in Advanced NetWare versions 1.0, 1.02, 2.0, and 2.1, and in NetWare 386 and later versions. It is used when the developer wishes to unlock a specific record and remove it from the log table. In this call, the developer provides the location and length of the record and the file handle of the target file, and the network unlocks the physical record and clears its entry from the log table.

Registers in:

AH	BEh
BX	File Handle
CX	High Record Offset
DX	Low Record Offset
SI	High Record Length
DI	Low Record Length

Registers out:

AL	Completion Code

Completion Codes:

00	Success
FFh	No Locked Record Found

The NetWare C Interface format is:

```
int ClearPhysicalRecord( int fileHandle, long recordStartOffset,
    long recordLength );
```

Clear Physical Record (C1h) (FCB)

This call is supported in NetWare version 4.6, in Advanced NetWare versions 1.0, 1.02, 2.0, and 2.1, and in NetWare 386. It performs the same function as the preceding call, but uses FCBs. This function, according to Novell, is supported through NetWare 386, but will not be supported after 1990.

Registers in:

AH	C1h
BX	High Record Offset
CX	Low Record Offset
DS:DX	Address of opened FCB (non-extended)

Registers out:
AL Completion Code

Completion Codes:
00 Success
FFh Invalid Record

The NetWare C Interface format is not supported.

Clear Physical Record Set (C4h)

This call is supported in NetWare version 4.6, in Advanced NetWare versions 1.0, 1.02, 2.0, and 2.1, and in NetWare 386 and later versions. It unlocks all records in the log table and removes them from the log table.

Registers in:
AH C4h

Registers out:
none

The NetWare C Interface format is:

```
void ClearPhysicalRecordSet( void );
```

Logical record locking calls

When a lock is logical rather than physical it must be respected by the user who sets the lock and by the other cooperating users reading the lock status. All those stations know where the lock is in the file but the file itself is not physically locked, so anyone can read from or write to any part of the physical file. This freedom and flexibility demand that applications using logical record locking stress cooperation, and that all users that write to the file use the same logical locking convention.

Log Logical Record (D0h)

This call is supported in NetWare versions 4.0 and 4.6, in Advanced NetWare versions 1.0, 1.02, 2.0, and 2.1, and in NetWare 386 and later versions. It places the logical record in the log table, giving the developer the choice to lock the file immediately or not. Again, the choice most often is to place a group of records into the table for later simultaneous locking with a Lock Logical Record Set. Here the developer must provide the name of the logical record and the length of the name.

Under lock mode 0, the compatibility mode, use:

Registers in:
AH D0h
DS:DX Request Packet Address

Registers out:
AL Completion Code

Completion Codes:
00h Success
FFh Failure

Under lock mode 1, the extended mode, use:

Registers in:
AH D0h
AL Locking Directive
DS:DX Request Packet Address
BP Timeout Limit

Registers out:
AL Completion Code

Completion Codes:
00 Success
FEh Timeout Failure
FFh Failure

Request Packet:
Logical Record Name Length(1-99) BYTE
Logical Record Name BYTE[*Length*]

Locking Directive here again affords three options:

00 Log record
01 Log and lock record with an exclusive lock
03 Log and lock record with a shareable, read-only lock

And the NetWare C Interface format is:

```
int LogLogicalRecord( char *logicalRecordName,
   BYTE lockDirective, WORD timeoutLimit );
```

Lock Logical Record Set (D1h)

This call is supported in NetWare versions 4.0 and 4.6, in Advanced NetWare versions 1.0, 1.02, 2.0, and 2.1, and in NetWare 386 and later versions. Again an all or nothing call, this one fails if any of the records in the set cannot be locked after the maximum timeout.

Under lock mode 0, the compatibility mode, use:

Registers in:
AH D1h
DL Mode (0 = No wait, 1 = Wait)

Registers out:
AL Completion Code

Completion Codes:
00h Success
FFh Failure

Under lock mode 1, the extended mode, use:

Registers in:
AH D1h
AL Lock Directive
BP Timeout Limit

Registers out:
AL Completion Code

Completion Codes:
00h Success
FEh Timeout Failure
FFh Failure

Locking Directive here determines what kind of lock is set. The options are:

00 Lock with an exclusive lock
01 Lock record with a shareable lock

The NetWare C Interface format is:

```
int LockLogicalRecordSet( WORD timeoutLimit );
```

Release Logical Record (D2h)

This call is supported in NetWare versions 4.0 and 4.6, in Advanced NetWare versions 1.0, 1.02, 2.0, and 2.1, and in NetWare 386 and later versions. With this call, the programmer unlocks a specific record but does not remove it from the log table.

Registers in:
AH D2h
DS:DX Request Packet Address

Registers out:
AL Completion Code

Completion Codes:
00 Success
FFh No Record Found

Request Packet:

Logical Record Name Length(1-99)	BYTE
Logical Record Name	BYTE[*Length*]

The NetWare C Interface format is:

```
int ReleaseLogicalRecord( char *logicalRecordName );
```

Release Logical Record Set (D3h)

This call is supported in NetWare versions 4.0 and 4.6, in Advanced NetWare versions 1.0, 1.02, 2.0, and 2.1, and in NetWare 386 and later versions. It unlocks all records in the log table, but doesn't remove them from the log table.

Registers in:
AH D3h

Registers out:
none

The NetWare C Interface format is:

```
void ReleaseLogicalRecordSet( void );
```

Clear Logical Record (D4h)

This call is supported in NetWare versions 4.0 and 4.6, in Advanced NetWare versions 1.0, 1.02, 2.0, and 2.1, and in NetWare 386 and later versions. It is the call to unlock a specific record and remove it from the log table.

Registers in:
AH D4h
DS:DX Request Buffer Address

Registers out:
AL Completion Code

Completion Codes:
00 Success
FFh No Record Found

Request Packet:

Logical Record Name Length(1-99)	BYTE
Logical Record Name	BYTE[*Length*]

The NetWare C Interface format is:

```
int ClearLogicalRecord( char *logicalRecordName );
```

Clear Logical Record Set (D5h)

This call is supported in NetWare versions 4.0 and 4.6, in Advanced NetWare versions 1.0, 1.02, 2.0, and 2.1, and in NetWare 386 and later versions. It unlocks and removes all records from the log table.

Registers in:
AH D5h

Registers out:
none

The NetWare C Interface format is:

```
void ClearLogicalRecordSet( void );
```

Semaphore calls

Semaphores allow more than one station simultaneous access to a locked logical record. They are useful in applications that wish to limit the number of users to a fixed amount. A programmer can Open, Examine, Wait On, Signal, and Close Semaphores.

As with logical records, programmers use ASCII strings to identify semaphores. When creating the semaphore, however, the programmer sets the maximum number of concurrent users (Semaphore Value) to, for example, 7 (for eight users 0-7).

When a workstation wishes to access the semaphore, the program uses the Open Semaphore call and checks the status of the Semaphore Value. If the value is greater than or equal to 0, the application decrements the value and calls Wait On Semaphore.

When finished with the application, the station uses Signal Semaphore which increments the Semaphore Value. If an application opens a semaphore and the Value is negative, the station may request to wait a certain period of time for the application to become available, or try again later.

Open Semaphore (C5h 00h)

This call is supported in NetWare version 4.6, in Advanced NetWare versions 1.0, 1.02, 2.0, and 2.1, and in NetWare 386 and later versions. It opens an existing semaphore, or creates one if the passed name does not exist. The Semaphore Handle is important to keep since it is used in the other semaphore calls.

Registers in:

AH	C5h
AL	00h
DS:DX	Request Buffer Address
CL	Semaphore Value (1-127)

Registers out:

AL	Completion Code
BL	Open Count
CX,DX	Semaphore Handle

Request Packet (Max - 128):

Semaphore Name Length (1-127)	BYTE
Semaphore Name	BYTE[*Length*]

Completion Codes:

00h	Successful
FEh	Invalid Semaphore Name Length
FFh	Invalid Semaphore Value

Semaphore Value must start as a positive number, the number of available openings in the semaphore. When it goes negative, the value is the number of stations in the queue waiting for semaphores to become available. The number of available slots is between -127 and 127 if Semaphore Value >= 0; if Semaphore Value < 0, it is the number of users queued up to access the semaphore.

Open Count is the number of stations that have opened the semaphore. This number is incremented when the station uses Open Semaphore and decremented when the station calls Close Semaphore.

Semaphore Handle is a two-word value returned by the call Open Semaphore; it is used in all of the subsequent semaphore calls.

The NetWare C Interface format is:

```
int Open Semaphore( char *semaphoreName, int initialValue,
   long *semaphoreHandle, WORD *openCount );
```

Examine Semaphore (C5h 01h)

This call is supported in NetWare version 4.6, in Advanced NetWare versions 1.0, 1.02, 2.0, and 2.1, and in NetWare 386 and later versions. It checks the status of the semaphore and returns the Semaphore Value and the Open Count. This call only returns values, it does not modify the Semaphore Value or the Open Count.

Registers in:

AH C5h
AL 01h
CX,DX Semaphore Handle

Registers out:

AL Completion Code
CX Semaphore Value
DL Open Count

Completion Codes:

00h Successful
FFh Invalid Semaphore Handle

The NetWare C Interface format is:

```
int ExamineSemaphore( long semaphoreHandle, int *semaphoreValue,
    WORD *openCount );
```

Wait On Semaphore (C5h 02h)

This call is supported in NetWare version 4.6, in Advanced NetWare versions 1.0, 1.02, 2.0, and 2.1, and in NetWare 386 and later versions. It is used when the developer wishes to use a semaphore after it has been opened. When Wait On Semaphore is called, the Semaphore Value is decremented. If this value is still greater than or equal to zero, the call returns successful and the resource may be used. If however, the value is less than zero after call is made, the user must wait for another user to call Signal Semaphore.

The call waits for this Signal Semaphore for the time specified in Timeout Limit. If, when the timeout expires, the Semaphore Value is zero or greater, the user may access the resource, but if it is still negative, the call will remove the user from the semaphore queue and increment the Semaphore Value back to what it was before the call. In that case, the call returns a Timeout Failure.

Registers In:

AH C5h
AL 02h
CX,DX Semaphore Handle
BP Timeout Limit

Registers Out:

AL Completion Code

Completion Codes:

00h Successful
FEh Timeout Failure
FFh Invalid Semaphore Handle

The NetWare C Interface format is:

```
int WaitOnSemaphore( long semaphoreHandle, WORD timeoutLimit );
```

Signal Semaphore (C5h 03h)

This call is supported in NetWare version 4.6, in Advanced NetWare versions 1.0, 1.02, 2.0, and 2.1, and in NetWare 386 and later versions. It is made when the user is finished with the resource being locked by a semaphore. When the semaphore is Signaled, its Semaphore Value is increased. Signaling the semaphore also allows the next station in the semaphore queue to access the semaphore.

Registers in:

AH	C5h
AL	03h
CX,DX	Semaphore Handle

Registers out:

AL	Completion Code

Completion Codes:

00h	Successful
01h	Semaphore Overflow (Value was increased over 127)
FFh	Invalid Semaphore Handle

The NetWare C Interface format is:

```
int SignalSemaphore( long semaphoreHandle );
```

Close Semaphore (C5h 04h)

This call is supported in NetWare version 4.6, in Advanced NetWare versions 1.0, 1.02, 2.0, and 2.1, and in NetWare 386 and later versions. Used to close a semaphore when the user is finished, this call decrements the Open Count for the semaphore. If the Open Count drops to zero because of this call, the semaphore is deleted.

Registers in:

AH	C5h
AL	04h
CX,DX	Semaphore Handle

Registers out:

AL	Completion Code

Completion Codes:

00h	Successful
FFh	Invalid Semaphore Handle

The NetWare C Interface format is:

```
int CloseSemaphore( long semaphoreHandle );
```

Sample code: TestLock.C

TestLock is a program that provides a front end to the record locking functions and gives developers an opportunity to break the lock-read-modify-write-unlock process into steps to see what happens at each step.

A menu is presented to the user as front end to a simple name and phone number database, displaying options, such as to read a record, write a record, lock or unlock a record, change the locking type (Exclusive/Shared), etc.

TestLock begins by calling SetLockMode() which sets the lock mode to 1. As discussed above, the lock mode should be 1, the default, for locking calls used on file servers running NetWare 4.6 and above.

The program then attempts to open the file we will use to store our test data. If the file does not exist, it is created. Next the program enters a loop, displays a menu to the user and uses a switch/case statement to act on the user's choice.

If a user chooses 1, the program requests the record number to read and the current record is read into memory. Option 2 will write the current record to disk. Option 3 allows the user to type in the current record.

Options 4 and 5 deal with the physical record locking and unlocking of the current record. The Log Physical Record call is issued, requesting a log and immediate lock of the record and the return value is described to the user. If there was an error, it is printed and the program halts. Otherwise, a message describing the success of the operation is printed and the program continues.

Option 6 allows the user to choose a new record number and option 7 toggles between exclusive and shared locking modes. Finally, option 8 allows the user to quit.

Programmers can use this code as an example of how to make some of the NetWare calls involved as well as some of the steps in the opening, locking, reading, writing, and unlocking of the files.

Ideally, a developer should have access to two stations when performing locking-related development to see the results of one station's operations on another. For instance, lock and read record 0 on one station (with a shared lock), and try to lock and read record 0 on another station. After that, switch to an exclusive lock and try the operation again.

```
/*                                                                    */
/* TestLock - Tests Locking mechanism, allows user to see locks       */
/*          interactively                                             */
/*                                                                    */
/* by Charles Rose                                                    */
/*                                                                    */

#include <stdio.h>
#include <io.h>
#include <fcntl.h>
#include <stdlib.h>
#include <dos.h>

typedef unsigned char BYTE;
typedef unsigned int WORD;

#define SHAREABLE 0x80                  /* Directory Attribute for Shareable */

/* Local prototypes                                                   */
void ShowMenu( void );
void ShowRecord( void );
void SetLockMode( void );

/* Local variables                                                    */
struct record_type {
                    char        Name[20];
                    char        Phone[10];
               } currentRecord;

long recordNumber;
int handle, done = 0, oldbp, lockType = 1;

main()
{
    char x, recordString[10];
    int result;

    /* Set our lock mode */
    SetLockMode();

    /* Attempt to open or create the file */
    if ( ( handle = _open( "testlock.dat", O_RDWR | O_BINARY ) ) == -1 )
    {
            /* If the problem was no file found */
            if ( errno == 2 )
            {
                    /* Then create the file... */
                    if ( ( handle = _creat( "testlock.dat", SHAREABLE ) )  == -1
)
                    {
                                perror( "\nCan't create TESTLOCK.DAT" );
                                exit(1);
                    }
            }
            else
            /* otherwise, there's something more serious wrong */
            {
                    perror( "\nCan't open TESTLOCK.DAT" );
                    exit(1);
            }
    }
```

```
while (!done)
{
        /* Display menu */
        ShowMenu();

        /* Get user input */
        x = getche();

        switch( x ) {

                    /* Read record */
                    case '1' :      printf( "\nEnter record number to read >" );
                       gets( recordString );
                       recordNumber = atol( recordString );
                       lseek( handle,
                       recordNumber * sizeof(currentRecord), SEEK_SET );
                       if ( read( handle, &currentRecord,
                       sizeof( currentRecord ) ) == -1 )
                       perror( "\nError reading file" );
                       break;

                     /* Write current record */
                     case '2' :      lseek( handle,
                     recordNumber * sizeof(currentRecord), SEEK_SET );
                       if ( write( handle, &currentRecord,
                       sizeof( currentRecord ) ) == -1 )
                             perror( "\nkError writing to file" );
                       break;

                     /* Display/Edit record */
                     case '3' :      printf( "\nEnter new name > " );
                        gets( currentRecord.Name );

                        printf( "\nEnter new phone > " );
                        gets( currentRecord.Phone );
                        break;

                     /* Lock record */
                     case '4' :     printf(" \nTrying to lock record %ld ... \n",
                     recordNumber );

                        result = LogPhysicalRecord( lockType, handle,
                        recordNumber * sizeof(currentRecord),

                             (long)sizeof(currentRecord), 36 );

                                      if ( result )
                                              switch ( result )
                                              {
                                                 case 0xFF :
printf(" \nError: Failure to lock record " );

                                                      break;
                                                 case 0xFE :
printf(" \nError: Timeout Failure trying to lock record " );

                                                      break;
                                                 case 0xFD :
printf(" \nError: Record is already locked by this workstation " );

                                                      break;
```

```
                        case 0x96 : printf(" \nError: Server is out of memory " );

                                    break;
                }
        else
                printf( "\nLock of current record was successful." );
                                    break;

                            /* Unlock record */
                            case '5' :          result = ClearPhysicalRecord( handle,
                            recordNumber * sizeof(currentRecord),

                                    (long)sizeof(currentRecord) );

                                    if ( result )
                                       printf( "\nNo locked record was found" );
                                    else
                          printf( "\nClear of current record lock was successful" );

                                    break;

                            /* Change current record number */
                            case '6' :          printf( "\nEnter new record number > " );
                                                 gets( recordString );
                                                 recordNumber = atol( recordString );
                                                 break;

                            /* Toggle lock type */
                            case '7' :          lockType = ( lockType == 1 ) ? 3 : 1;
                                                 break;

                            /* Quit */
                            case '8' :          done++;
                                                 break;
                }
    }

    if ( ( close( handle ) ) == -1 )
            perror( "\nCan't close TESTLOCK.DAT" );

}

void ShowMenu( void )
{
    ShowRecord();

    printf( "\n            Locking Test Menu                    \n\n" );
    printf( " 1. Read a record                               \n" );
    printf( " 2. Write current record                        \n\n" );
    printf( " 3. Change record                               \n\n" );
    printf( " 4. Lock a record                               \n" );
    printf( " 5. Unlock a record                                     \n\n" );
    printf( " 6. Change current record number                \n" );
    printf( " 7. Toggle lock type (Exclusive/Shared)         \n\n" );
    printf( " 8. Quit                                                \n\n" );
    printf( " Enter your choice > " );
}

void ShowRecord( void )
{
    printf( "\n\n***************************************************\n" );
    printf( " Current Record - %ld\n", recordNumber );
```

```
    printf( " Name: [%s]\n", currentRecord.Name );
    printf( " Phone: [%s]\n", currentRecord.Phone );
    printf( " Locking Type: %s\n",
            ( ( lockType == 1 ) ? "Exclusive" : "Shared" ) );
    printf( "***************************************************\n" );
}

int LogPhysicalRecord( BYTE Directive, WORD FileHandle, long RecordOffset,
    long RecordLength, WORD TimeoutLimit )
{
     oldbp = _BP;

    _AH = 0xBC;
    _AL = Directive;                  /* 0 Log, 1 Log & Lock */
                                   /* 3 Log/Lock shared/read only */
    _BX = FileHandle;
    _CX = 0;
    _DX = (unsigned)RecordOffset;
    _SI = 0;
    _DI = (unsigned)RecordLength;
    _BP = TimeoutLimit;

    geninterrupt( 0x21 );

    _BP = oldbp;

    return _AL;
}

int ClearPhysicalRecord( WORD FileHandle, long RecordOffset, long RecordLength )
{
    _AH = 0xBE;
    _BX = FileHandle;
    _CX = 0;                          /* In this program we KNOW that       */
    _DX = (unsigned)RecordOffset;     /* no record number will be > 65535   */
    _SI = 0;                          /* So most significant word can be 0  */
    _DI = (unsigned)RecordLength;

    geninterrupt( 0x21 );

    return _AL;
}

void SetLockMode( void )
{
    _AH = 0xC6;
    _AL = 0x01;
    geninterrupt(0x21);
 }
```

Sample code: SemaTest.C

Semaphores are often used when synchronization is needed, but not for files. The classic use of semaphores is for software metering, to check how many stations are using a particular application. Semaphores can also be used to allow only a certain number of stations in an application at once, where resources are limited or the supervisor needs to limit concurrent access because of copyright restrictions, for example.

SemaTest is a program that limits the number of people who may use it at once. When you execute SemaTest, it checks the semaphore it uses to see if there are any slots left. If not, it informs the user that all of the slots are full and exits. If there are slots free, it goes into a loop, continuously displaying the number of stations running the program and how many slots are left. When a user presses any key, the program exits, releasing the used semaphore.

The program begins by defining the maximum number of stations (INITIAL_SEMAPHORE_VALUE) that can get in at once and the timing interval (WAIT_SECONDS) to wait before checking the semaphore.

In any program that polls the network, it's not good for performance to barrage the file server with requests as often as the workstation can throw them out. Instead, a reasonable time period (like a second or two) should be used to send the semaphore requests out. Twenty stations sending as many requests as they can would slow even a fast server considerably.

It is best to send out polling requests in measured doses. The best way to handle the situation is to use a define statement, as in this program (or a command-line argument), so you can try out different values and measure the server burden vs. performance.

The program then has its local function prototypes listed as well as the global variables. *openCount* keeps track of the number of stations having the semaphore open at once; *semValue* is the current semaphore value; and *semHandle* is the handle of the semaphore returned by the file server.The main() function starts by opening the semaphore with the OpenSemaphore() function call. I didn't check the return value because the only two completion codes that indicate errors are for a bad name length or a bad initial value. Since these are fixed by the program and not by the user, they will not generate errors.

Next, WaitSemaphore() is called to get permission to use the resource. If the routine returns 0, success, the user was granted the resource; otherwise, if FEh was returned, the slots for the semaphore were all in use. If this is the case, the program reports it and quits.

Once the program is granted the semaphore, it begins a loop to examine the state of the semaphore. The program clears the screen with clrscr() and prints "Press any key to exit" on the last line of the screen using gotoxy() to move the cursor. If your compiler does not support these screen i/o routines, they may be removed or substituted with others.

Next, ExamineSemaphore() is called to get the initial values of the semValue and the *openCount*. SemaTest then enters a loop that prints the status of the semaphore at the bottom of the screen, checks the keyboard, waits, and calls ExamineSemaphore() again to get new values. WaitAWhile() uses the system timer to determine how many seconds have passed. Other means may also be appropriate for your C compiler.

This program demonstrates the ease with which semaphores may be used for monitoring network resources. One extension of the program would be to integrate it into a menu system, returning ERRORLEVEL if the program the user wished to run was already in use by the maximum number of stations. In this way, a metering system could be built for other applications that may not be network-aware (or at least semaphore-aware).

```
/*                                                                      */
/* SemaTest - Tests semaphores by showing application metering example */
/*                                                                      */
/* by Charles Rose                                                      */
/*                                                                      */

#include <stdio.h>
#include <dos.h>
#include <time.h>

/* Defines & types                                                      */
typedef unsigned char BYTE;
typedef unsigned int WORD;

#define INITIAL_SEMAPHORE_VALUE 2
#define WAIT_SECONDS 2

/* Local routines                                                       */
int OpenSemaphore( char *semName, char semValue, WORD *openCount,
    WORD *semHandle );
int ExamineSemaphore( WORD *semHandle, char *semValue, WORD *openCount );
int WaitSemaphore( WORD *semHandle, WORD timeoutLimit );
int SignalSemaphore( WORD *semHandle );
int CloseSemaphore( WORD *semHandle );
void WaitAWhile();

/* Global data                                                          */
BYTE openCount;
char semValue;
long semHandle;

int oldbp;

main()
{
    int result, done = 0;

    /* Open Semaphore                                                   */
    semValue = INITIAL_SEMAPHORE_VALUE;
                    /* Need in case we're creating the semaphore */
    OpenSemaphore( "Semaphore Test", semValue, &openCount,
            &semHandle );

    /* Wait on the Semaphore (get permission to use the resource) */
```

```
    result = WaitSemaphore( &semHandle, 0 );/* 0 = Don't wait */
    if ( result == 0xFE )
    {
            printf( "Sorry, all of the slots for this resource are
            currently in use\n" );
            exit(1);
    }

    clrscr();
    gotoxy( 24,24 );
    printf( "Press any key to exit" );

    ExamineSemaphore( &semHandle, &semValue, &openCount );
    /* Wait loop */
    while ( !done )
    {
            gotoxy( 1,23 );
            printf( "Semaphore Test -> Open at [%d] stations ***
                    Value is [%d]                        ",
                    openCount, semValue );

            if ( bioskey( 1 ) )
                    done++;

            WaitAWhile();

            gotoxy( 60,23 );
            printf( "Checking..." );

            ExamineSemaphore( &semHandle, &semValue, &openCount );
    }

    /* Signal Semaphore (that we're through with the resource) */
    SignalSemaphore( &semHandle );

    /* Close Semaphore */
    CloseSemaphore( &semHandle );
}

int OpenSemaphore( char *semName, char semValue, WORD *openCount, WORD
     *semHandle )
{
    char requestBuffer[128];
    int semLen;

    if ( ( semLen = strlen(semName) ) > 127 )
    {
            printf(" Semaphore name is greater than 127 characters. " );
            exit(1);
    }

    *requestBuffer = semLen;                          /* Offset 0: Length        */
    movmem( semName, &requestBuffer[1], semLen );        /* Offset 1: Name      */

    _AH = 0xC5;
    _AL = 0;
    _DX = (unsigned)requestBuffer;
    _CL = semValue;

    geninterrupt( 0x21 );

    if ( !_AL )
```

```
    {
            *openCount = _BL;
            *semHandle = _CX;
            *(semHandle+1) = _DX;
    }

    return _AL;
}

int ExamineSemaphore( WORD *semHandle, char *semValue, WORD *openCount )
{
    _AH = 0xC5;
    _AL = 1;
    _CX = *semHandle;
    _DX = *(semHandle+1);

    geninterrupt( 0x21 );

    if ( !_AL )
    {
            *semValue = _CX;
            *openCount = _DL;
    }

    return _AL;
}

int WaitSemaphore( WORD *semHandle, WORD timeoutLimit )
{
    oldbp = _BP;

    _AH = 0xC5;
    _AL = 2;
    _CX = *semHandle;
    _DX = *(semHandle+1);
    _BP = timeoutLimit;

    geninterrupt( 0x21 );

    _BP = oldbp;

    return _AL;
}

int SignalSemaphore( WORD *semHandle )
{
    _AH = 0xC5;
    _AL = 3;
    _CX = *semHandle;
    _DX = *(semHandle+1);

    geninterrupt( 0x21 );

    return _AL;
}

int CloseSemaphore( WORD *semHandle )
{
    _AH = 0xC5;
    _AL = 4;
    _CX = *semHandle;
    _DX = *(semHandle+1);
```

```
    geninterrupt( 0x21 );

    return _AL;
}

void WaitAWhile()
{
    time_t start, elapsed;

    time(&start);

    while ( time( &elapsed ) - start < WAIT_SECONDS );

    return;
}
```

Exercises

1. Use the TestLock program to become familiar with the locking process. Try various combinations until you become familiar with the responses from the network. You will need more than one station to test the program adequately.

2. Run the SemaTest program, compiling with different values for INITIAL_SEMAPHORE_VALUE. Also, change WAIT_SECONDS and monitor the traffic on the LAN.

3. Write a small test program that uses the Log-Lock-Release-Clear set of functions for either physical file, physical record, or logical record locking.

4. Write a test program that simulates fatal embrace and test to see if you have buffering or over-write problems.

5. Devise a system for managing writes to the end of a file (the file-extension problem).

6. Write a sample order-entry program where several people will need access to records at the same time.

3 File Services

The most basic DOS services involve files, the most common "objects" in the operating system. The NetWare shell lets the programmer use all the file services provided by the various versions of DOS. NetWare supplements these DOS calls with several of its own, however. These network-specific calls allow the developer to manipulate files at the server level and in some cases reduce traffic on the network. With the NetWare File Services API the developer can copy files, change a file's attributes and other file information, erase files, and purge or restore erased files.

- File Server File Copy
- Get or Set File Attributes
- Get Extended File Attributes
- Set Extended File Attributes
- Get File Information
- Set File Information
- File Erasing:
  - Erase Files
  - Purge Erased Files
  - Purge All Erased Files
  - Restore Erased File

File paths in NetWare

When making calls to NetWare for file services, the programmer must provide a complete file path name or a base directory handle and a file path extension. So an understanding of how NetWare path names differ from DOS path names is essential.

In a DOS environment, disk drives are the highest order storage devices; there is nothing larger than a drive. But with NetWare, the drives are dynamic; there may be several file servers, each with several volumes, each with many directories.

Within NetWare, file servers contain volumes which contain directories; drives are logically assigned to directories on the file server rather than being physically assigned to a partition of a drive, as in DOS. This logical assignment provides for a dynamic environment where file server directories can be assigned to drive letters and changed or removed as needed.

To assign a directory to a drive, the file server needs to know where to find the directory. So the DOS path name–the drive letter and directory, for instance, "C:\DOS,"–must be extended. So, for example, in NetWare the file server name "ACCOUNTING/" plus the volume name "SYS:" plus the directory name "DATA\GL" forms the complete path name "ACCOUNTING/SYS:DATA\GL".

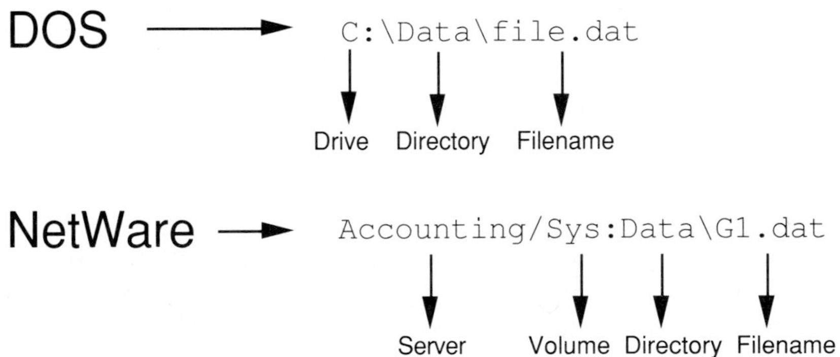

Figure 4: A comparison of NetWare and DOS full paths.

Directory handles

Some calls permit shortcuts. For each workstation, the file server maintains a table of pointers (255) that correspond to volumes or directories. These directory handles may be used with file path extensions to provide a full pathname. For example, assume that, in the file server "ACCOUNTING," directory handle 4 points to "SYS:DATA\XYZ" and the file path extension is "WP.DAT." By passing that information to the server in the appropriate bytes of a request packet, the programmer specifies the full file path "ACCOUNTING/SYS:DATA\XYZ\WP.DAT."

If a full file path is specified, the directory handle is not needed. If the server name is left out, the default server will be used. If no directory handle is needed, 0 should be passed.

File path searches

Wildcards may also be used to identify files or groups of files, and they're especially handy when searching for files. NetWare has its own system of wildcards that extends the DOS asterisk and question mark wildcards. In the following table, augmented means the high bit is set:

Wildcards under NetWare

* Asterisk	Matches any string (0-x characters)
Example:	* Anything
	. Anything with a period in it (X.Z)
? Question Mark	Matches any character
Example:	A? AB
^. Augmented Period	Matches a period or end of string
Example:	ZA^. ZA. or ZA but not ZAX
^? Aug. Question Mark	Matches no character or any single character except a period
Example:	FR^? FRX or FR but not FRXX or FR.
^* Augmented Asterisk	Matches any characters except a period
Example:	A^* ABC or A but not A.Z or A.

Search attributes

NetWare provides a way to search for hidden or system files as well as normal files. This direction is passed through the Search Attribute byte. The settings are:

0	Normal only
2	Normal and hidden
4	Normal and system
6	Normal, hidden, and system

Calls in the File Services API

The following descriptions will include which versions of NetWare support which calls. Throughout the book, we explain fields within the calls only at the first mention of each field in each chapter. Appendix B contains a comprehensive, alphabetical listing of the fields for quick reference.

File Server File Copy (F3h) (Handle)

This call is supported in Advanced NetWare versions 2.0 and 2.1, and in Netware 386 and later versions. It lets the programmer write file copy routines into applications that copy the files without having them leave the file server. This way, no data is brought to the workstation just to be sent back to the file server at a different place on the disk, so network traffic is reduced.

Registers in:

AH	F3h
ES:DI	Request Buffer

Registers out:

AL	Completion Code
CX,DX	Number of Bytes Copied

Completion Codes:

00	Success

Request Packet:

Offset	Description	Type	Order
0	Source File Handle	WORD	lo-hi
2	Destination File Handle	WORD	lo-hi
4	Source File Offset	DWORD	lo-hi
8	Destination File Offset	DWORD	lo-hi
12	Number of Bytes to Copy	DWORD	lo-hi

File Handle is the DOS file handle of a target file. The programmer can obtain it through the DOS Create File call or the DOS Open File call.

The file to be copied and its destination file or directory must both be on the same file server. The programmer must supply the file handles of the source and target files, as well as the offsets in the files where the copy should take place and the numbers of bytes to copy.

These variables afford the developer great flexibility. A portion of one file can be copied to the end of another, or one file can be completely copied to a new file (just specify 0 as the start of both and length as the entire length of the source file), or a portion of one file can be copied into a portion in the middle of another file. The possibilities are endless.

The NetWare C Interface format is:

```
int FileServerFileCopy( int sourceFileHandle,
        int destinationFileHandle, long sourceFileOffset,
        long destinationFileOffset,
        long numberOfBytesToCopy, long *numberOfBytesCopied );
```

File Server File Copy (E6h) (FCB)

This call is supported in NetWare versions 4.0 and 4.6, in Advanced NetWare versions 1.0, 1.02, 2.0, and 2.1, and in NetWare 386. It performs the same function as the last, only FCBs are used. This function, according to Novell, is supported through NetWare 386, but will not be supported after 1990.

Registers in:

AH	E6h
CX	Low order WORD Number of bytes to copy
DX	High order WORD Number of bytes to copy
DS:SI	Address of opened source FCB
ES:DI	Address of opened destination FCB

Registers out:

AL Completion Code

Completion Codes.

00 Success

The random record offset locations for both the source and destination FCBs have to be set to the starting location to be copied.

The NetWare C Interface format is not supported.

Get (43h 00h) or Set (43h 01h) File Attributes

This DOS call is supported in NetWare versions 4.0 and 4.6, in Advanced NetWare versions 1.0, 1.02, 2.0, and 2.1, and in NetWare 386 and later versions.

It is used to get or set the attributes of a file, given its name.

Registers in:

AH	43h
AL	Function (00 = Get File Attributes, 01 = Set File Attributes)
CX	Attributes (if Function is 01)
DS:DX	Pointer to ASCIIZ filename

Registers out:

With Carry flag set:

AL Completion Code

With Carry flag clear:

CX Attributes (if Function is 00)

Completion codes:

01	Invalid Function
03	Path Not Found
05	Access Denied

Attributes are attributes of a file that can be set or got with this call are:

01h	Read Only
02h	Hidden
04h	System
80h	Shareable

The default for Attributes is 00, which would mean a nonshareable, nonsystem, nonhidden, read and write file.

The NetWare C Interface format is not supported.

Get Extended File Attributes (B6h 00h)

This call is supported in NetWare SFT Level II, Advanced NetWare 2.1, and in NetWare versions 386 and later.

Registers in:

AH	B6h
AL	0
DS:DX	File Path (ASCIIZ 1-255 bytes)

Registers out:

AL	Completion Code
CL	Extended File Attributes

Completion Codes:

00	Success
FFh	File Not Found — Carry flag is set.
FEh	No Search Rights — Carry flag is set.

In DOS, File Attributes are bit fields in a byte that resides in the directory entry of each file. The DOS File Attributes are read-only, hidden, system, or archive. NetWare extends the DOS File Attributes to include four network-specific ones: the Transaction Bit, the Index Bit, and the Read and Write Audit Bits.

The Transaction Bit, bit 4 (10h), is set to work with Novell's Transaction Tracking System (TTS, see Chapter 5). If this bit is set, the TTS will track all writes to this file during a transaction. Also, if this bit is set, it cannot be deleted or renamed until the bit is cleared by the Set Extended File Attributes call.

When the Index Bit, bit 5 (20h), is set, NetWare will index the file's File Allocation Tables (FATs), which will speed file access. Novell recommends setting this bit for files that are randomly accessed and are larger than 2MB.

The Read and Write Audit Bits, bit 6 (40h) and bit 7 (80h), are not yet used.

The Get Extended File Attributes call collects the Extended File Attribute bits for a specified file. It requires search rights to the directory where the file resides.

The NetWare C Interface format is:

```
int GetExtendedFileAttributes( char *filePath,
   BYTE *extendedFileAttributes);
```

Set Extended File Attributes (B6h 01h)

This call is supported in NetWare SFT Level II, Advanced NetWare 2.1, and in NetWare versions 386 and later. It uses the information garnered from Get Extended File Attributes to modify the extended attributes of a file. Use the previous call to get the attributes of a file, modify them, then use this call to write them back. This call requires modify rights to the directory where the file resides.

Registers in:

AH	B6h
AL	1
DS:DX	File Path (ASCIIZ 1-255 bytes)
CL	Extended File Attributes

Registers out:

AL	Completion Code

Completion Codes:

00	Success
FFh	File Not Found - Carry flag is set if this code obtains
FEh	Insufficient Access Privileges

The NetWare C Interface format is:

```
int SetExtendedFileAttributes( char *filePath,
   BYTE extendedFileAttributes);
```

Get File Information (E3h 0Fh)

This call is supported in Advanced NetWare versions 1.0, 1.02, 2.0, and 2.1, and in NetWare 386 and later versions. In addition to the attributes presented above, NetWare offers a superset of the attributes in the Get File Information call. This call returns the name of the file, the DOS File Attributes, the extended attributes, the file size, creation date, last access date, last update date and time, the identification of the file's creator, and the last archive date and time.

Although much of this information is available through DOS calls, in NetWare the programmer gets it with just one call. By using wildcards, the programmer can get the information on a succession of files with that one call.

Registers in:

AH	E3h
DS:SI	Request Buffer Address
ES:DI	Reply Buffer Address

Registers out:

AL	Completion Code

Completion Codes:

00	Success
89h	No Search Privileges
FFh	No More Matching Files

Request Packet (max size = 263 bytes):

Offset	Content	Type	Order
0	Request Buffer Length - 2	WORD	lo-hi
2	0Fh	BYTE	
3	Sequence Number	WORD	hi-lo
5	Directory Handle	BYTE	
6	Search Attributes	BYTE	
7	File Path Length(1-255)	BYTE	
8	File Path	BYTE[*Length*]	

Reply Packet (max size = 97 bytes):

Offset	Content	Type	Order
0	Reply Buffer Length - 2	WORD	lo-hi
2	Sequence Number	WORD	hi-lo
4	File Name	BYTE[15]	
19	File Attributes	BYTE	
20	Extended File Attributes	BYTE	
21	File Size	LONG	hi-lo
25	Creation Date	WORD	hi-lo
27	Last Access Date	WORD	hi-lo
29	Last Update Date & Time	LONG	hi-lo
33	Owner Object ID	LONG	hi-lo
37	Last Archive Date & Time	LONG	hi-lo
41	Reserved	BYTE[56]	

Reply Buffer Length must be initialized to the length of the buffer minus two before the call is issued.

Sequence numbering begins with 0FFFFh (-1) for the first call. For subsequent calls, the programmer should insert the returned Sequence Number from the request packet's Sequence Number field.

Search Attributes is a bit field that specifies the type of file to be returned:

00 Normal Files
02 Normal and hidden files
04 Normal and system files
06 Normal, hidden and system

The *File Attributes* bit field contains information about the directory entry. A user must have modify rights to change these bits:

01h Read-Only Bit
(File may be read but not written to.)
02h Hidden Bit
(File will not be shown in directory listing.)
04h System Bit
(File will not be shown in directory listing.)
08h Execute Only Bit
(File can be executed, but not read or written to; once set, this bit cannot be cleared.)
10h Subdirectory Bit
(Entry is a subdirectory.)
20h Archive Bit
(Bit is set if file has changed since last backup.)
40h Shareable Bit
(Set if more than one user can access this file at once.)

Creation Date and *Last Access Date* are specified in two bytes. *Last Update Date* and *Time* and *Last Archive Date and Time* are in four-byte format.

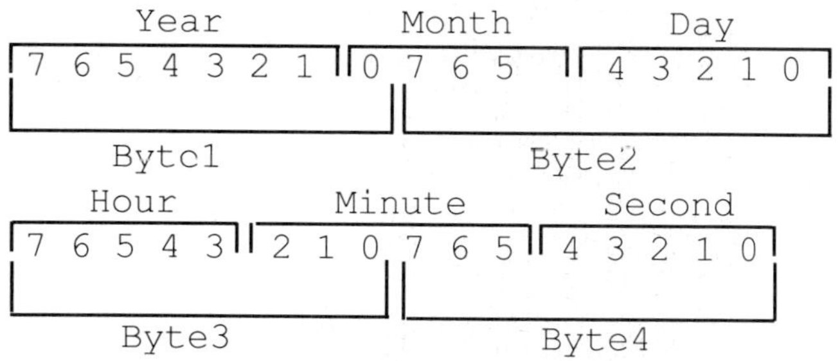

Owner Object ID is the Bindery object identification of the user that created the file.

The NetWare C Interface format is:

```
int ScanFileInformation( BYTE directoryHandle, char *filePath,
    BYTE searchAttributes, int *sequenceNumber, char *fileName,
    BYTE *fileAttributes, BYTE *extendedFileAttributes,
    long *fileSize, char *creationDate, char *lastAccessDate,
    char *lastUpdateDateAndTime, char *lastArchiveDateAndTime,
    long *fileOwnerID );
```

Set File Information (E3h 10h)

This call is supported in Advanced NetWare versions 1.0, 1.02, 2.0, and 2.1, and in NetWare 386 and later versions. It saves the information obtained with the preceding call.

Registers in:

AH	E3h
DS:SI	Request Buffer Address
ES:DI	Reply Buffer Address

Registers out:

AL	Completion Code

Completion Codes:

00	Success

Request Packet (max size = 339 bytes):

Offset	Content	Type	Order
0	Request Buffer Length - 2	WORD	lo-hi
2	10h	BYTE	
3	File Attributes	BYTE	
4	Extended File Attributes	BYTE	
5	Reserved	LONG	hi-lo
9	Creation Date	WORD	hi-lo
11	Last Access Date	WORD	hi-lo
13	Last Update Date & Time	LONG	hi-lo
17	Owner Object ID	LONG	hi-lo
21	Last Archive Date & Time	LONG	hi-lo
25	Reserved	BYTE[56]	
81	Directory Handle	BYTE	
82	Search Attributes	BYTE	
83	File Path Length (1-255)	BYTE	
84	File Path	BYTE[*Length*]	

Reply Packet (2 bytes):

0	0000	WORD	lo-hi

The NetWare C Interface format is:

```
int SetFileInformation( BYTE directoryHandle, char *filePath,
        BYTE searchAttributes, BYTE fileAttributes,
        BYTE extendedFileAttributes, char *creationDate,
        char *lastAccessDate, char *lastUpdateDateAndTime,
        char *lastArchiveDateAndTime, long fileOwnerID );
```

File deletion and recovery routines

Under DOS, when a file is "deleted" its directory entry is marked as deleted and the file no longer shows up in directory listings, but the file remains intact until someone writes another file to its space on the disk. The Norton and other utilities allow users to change these "deleted" directory entries, thus recovering "deleted" files.

The Novell environment provides a similar layer of security. As in DOS, when a file is erased from the network it is marked "deleted" and doesn't show up in the directory. With NetWare, however, the user may quickly use the "SALVAGE xyz" command to recover any files on the "xyz" volume that were erased but not purged from the volume.

The NetWare purge is automatic. If you issue a delete command, removing a set of one or more files, you put it in the position of the preceding set, and the preceding file set is consigned to oblivion. So the user must issue the SALVAGE command promptly. This rarely happens because users don't often realize they have deleted something they need immediately after they type the delete command.

NetWare 386 takes a more sensible approach to recovering deleted files. Using a different disk space recovery algorithm, it works like DOS, only better. When a user of NetWare 386 deletes a file, the file is removed from the directory, but is stored on a part of the disk that is unused. Only when the disk starts filling up to the point of overwriting the deleted-file space will it begin to overwrite the files that were deleted, using a least-recently used (LRU) algorithm. NetWare architect Drew Major jokingly called this a "poor man's version control system."

In NetWare 286 and below, the programmer may use the following calls to restore and purge files: Restore Erased File, Purge Erased Files, and Purge All Erased Files. These calls are being phased out under NetWare 386 and replaced with Purge Salvageable File and Recover Salvageable File.

Erase Files (F2h 44h)

This call is supported in Advanced NetWare version 2.1, and in NetWare 386 and later versions. It marks files for deletion.

Registers in:

AH	F2h
AL	44h
DS:SI	Request Buffer Address
ES:DI	Reply Buffer Address

Registers out:

AL	Completion Code

Completion Codes:

00	Success
98h	Volume does not exist
9Bh	Bad directory handle
9Ch	Invalid path
FFh	No files found error

Request Packet (max size = 258 bytes):

Offset	**Content**	**Type**	**Order**
0	Directory Handle	BYTE	
1	Search Attributes	BYTE	
2	File Path Length(1-255)	BYTE	
3	File Path	BYTE[*Length*]	

Reply Packet (2 bytes):

Offset	**Content**	**Type**	**Order**
0	0000	WORD	lo-hi

The NetWare C Interface format is:

```
int EraseFiles( BYTE directoryHandle, char *filePath,
   BYTE searchAttributes);
```

Restore Erased File (E2h 11h)

This call is supported in NetWare versions 4.0 and 4.6, and in Advanced NetWare versions 1.0, 1.02, 2.0, and 2.1. It is the last chance to recover a file before it is purged. The programmer specifies the directory handle, if any, to a particular directory. The programmer must pass to the server the name (terminated with a colon) of the volume where the erased file resides. If there is a file marked for deletion but not yet purged on that volume, the file will be recovered to the directory whence it was erased. If a number files have been deleted but have not yet been restored, this call must be used iteratively until the call returns No More Erased Files (FFh).

The call returns both the name of the erased file and the name of the restored file. This is a safeguard. If in the interim between erasure and restoration someone has created a file with the same name as the deleted file, the restored file will be renamed and stored with the last two characters of its file extension as 00.

Registers in:

AH	E2h
DS:SI	Request Buffer Address
ES:DI	Reply Buffer Address

Registers out:

AL	Completion Code

Completion Codes:

00	Success
98h	Volume Does Not Exist
FFh	No More Erased Files

Request Packet (max size = 21 bytes):

Offset	Content	Type	Order
0	Request Buffer Length-2	WORD	lo-hi
2	11h	BYTE	
3	Directory Handle	BYTE	
4	Volume Name Length	BYTE	
5	Volume Name	BYTE[*VOLLENGTH*]	

Reply Packet (32 bytes):

0	Reply Buffer Length-2	WORD	lo-hi
2	Erased File Name	BYTE[15]	ASCIIZ
17	Restored File Name	BYTE[15]	ASCIIZ

The NetWare C Interface format is:

```
int RestoreErasedFile( BYTE directoryHandle, char *volumeName,
    char *erasedFileName, char *restoredFileName );
```

Purge Erased Files (E2h 10h)

This call is supported in NetWare versions 4.0 and 4.6, and in Advanced NetWare versions 1.0, 1.02, 2.0, and 2.1. With it, the programmer purges all those files that have been marked for deletion by a particular workstation and frees up the space those files were occupying.

Registers in:

AH	E2h
DS:SI	Request Buffer Address
ES:DI	Reply Buffer Address

Registers out:

AL	Completion Code

Completion Codes:

00	Success

Request Packet (max size = 3 bytes):

Offset	Content	Type	Order
0	Request Buffer Length-2	WORD	lo-hi
2	10h	BYTE	

Reply Packet (2 bytes):

0	0000	WORD	lo-hi

The NetWare C Interface format is:

```
int PurgeErasedFiles( void );
```

Purge All Erased Files (E3h CEh)

This call is supported in Advanced NetWare 2.1. It purges all erased files of all workstations. To use it, the user must have console operator rights.

Registers in:

AH	E3h
DS:SI	Request Buffer Address
ES:DI	Reply Buffer Address

Registers out:

AL	Completion Code

Completion Codes:

00	Success

Request Packet (max size = 3 bytes):

Offset	Content	Type	Order
0	Request Buffer Length-2	WORD	lo-hi
2	CEh	BYTE	

Reply Packet (2 bytes):

0	0000	WORD	lo-hi

The NetWare C Interface format is:

```
int PurgeAllErasedFiles( void );
```

The following calls are provided because of their relevance to the File Services API. Although Novell has not documented FCB functions for several years, they have been supported through NetWare 386. Representatives of Novell say that support for these functions will be eliminated after the end of 1990.

Set File Attributes (E4h) (FCB)

This call is supported in NetWare versions 4.0 and 4.6, in Advanced NetWare versions 1.0, 1.02, 2.0, and 2.1, and in NetWare 386, but will not be supported after 1990. It is used to modify the attributes of a file, given its File Control Block.

Registers in:

AH	E4h
CL	File Attribute(s)
DS:DX	Address of FCB

Registers out:

AL	Completion Code

File Attributes are those set with this call. The following values are possible:

01h	Read Only
02h	Hidden
04h	System
80h	Shareable

The default for File Attributes is 00, which would mean a non-shareable, non-system, non-hidden, read and write file. The file attribute code is found at offset 24 of the FCB.

The NetWare C Interface format is not supported.

Update File Size (E5h) (FCB)

This call is supported in NetWare versions 4.0 and 4.6, in Advanced NetWare versions 1.0, 1.02, 2.0, and 2.1, and in NetWare 386, but will not be supported after 1990. It is used to update the size of a file on the network once it has been updated.

Registers in:

AH	E5h
DS:DX	Address of opened FCB

Registers out:

AL	Completion Code

This call is used when two stations are sharing a file. When one station has modified the file so that the size has changed since it was opened, the other station can use this call to update the FCB in memory to reflect the true file size. This same action can be accomplished for file handles through the DOS function call 42h, Seek to End of File.

The NetWare C Interface format is not supported.

Code sample: FileInfo.C

FileInfo uses the file services call Get File Information to report on the various attributes associated with each file. The user specifies a Volume:path combination and the program returns about a half a screen of information about each file: the name, size, attributes, creation and last access dates, and the last update and last archive dates and times.

FileInfo begins with the request/reply structures needed for the Get File Information call. Since this is the only function call in the program, I have called the structure variables request and reply and made them global. The function prototypes follow and we begin with main().

First, main() checks the command line arguments to see if a path was specified. If two arguments weren't specified (the program name, FILEINFO.EXE, and the path), the program quits and prompts the user for correct syntax.

Next the request and reply structures are initialized. The sequence number is set to -1 and the Search Attributes are set to 6 to search for all files (Hidden, System, and Normal). The rest of the program consists of cycling through a while loop, iteratively calling GetFileInfo(), and exiting if there is an error completion code. If the call is successful, the program prints the information returned and sets the sequence number to the next value.

The most difficult part about writing this program was not the call to Get File Information, but the data manipulation required to transform the reply structure fields from Novell format to something printable. There is a LongSwitch() and a WordSwitch() routine to convert hi-lo Novell format to lo-hi Intel format (for LONG and WORD values). Also, there is a ShowDate() and a ShowDateAndTime() routine to decode the 2-byte date and 2-byte time.

The functions use bit and's (&&) and right shifts (>>) to manipulate the bits in the date and time fields. Although routines like these may take time to write the first time, they may be used in all subsequent applications that need to perform their function, so the developer should keep track of them.

In this book we'll try to provide many more functions the developer can use frequently and not have to code again. The program does what it's supposed to, but it's fairly inflexible: you must supply a volume and a full pathname. In the real world, most users don't know what pathnames are, let alone volumes, so we need to make the program a bit more flexible. We will extend this example program in the next chapter, which deals with the NetWare Directory Services.

Code Sample: FileInfo.C

```
/*                                                                         */
/* FileInfo - Lists all the NetWare file onfo on selected files            */
/*                                                                         */
/* by Charles Rose                                                         */
/*                                                                         */

#include <stdio.h>
#include <dos.h>
#include <dir.h>
#include <string.h>

typedef unsigned char BYTE;
typedef unsigned int WORD;
typedef unsigned long LONG;

/* Request and Reply structures */
struct scanFileReq {
    WORD    Length;
    BYTE    Function;
    WORD    SequenceNumber;
    BYTE    DirectoryHandle;
    BYTE    SearchAttributes;
    BYTE    FilePathLength;
    BYTE    FilePath[255];
} request;

struct scanFileRep {
    WORD    Length;
    WORD    SequenceNumber;
    BYTE    FileName[14];
    BYTE    FileAttributes;
    BYTE    ExtendedFileAttributes;
    LONG    FileSize;
    WORD    CreationDate;
    WORD    LastAccessDate;
    LONG    LastUpdateDateAndTime;
    LONG    OwnerObjectID;
    LONG    LastArchiveDateAndTime;
    BYTE    Reserved[56];
} reply;

/* Local Routines                                                          */
void PrintFileInfo( void );
int GetFileInfo( struct scanFileReq *request, struct scanFileRep *reply );
void ShowDate( BYTE *date );
void ShowDateAndTime( WORD *dateAndTime );
LONG LongSwitch( BYTE *before );
WORD WordSwitch( BYTE *before );

main( int argc, char *argv[] )
{
    int result;

    if ( argc != 2 )
    {
            printf( "Usage: FILEINFO path\n" );
            exit(1);
    }
```

```
    /* Initialize Request & Reply structures */
    request.Length = sizeof( request ) - 2;
    request.Function = 0x0F;             /* Function F - Get file info        */
    request.SequenceNumber = 0xFFFF;     /* Use -1 as first sequence          */
    request.DirectoryHandle = 0;         /* No handle, use full path from user */
    request.SearchAttributes = 6;        /* Search Normal, Hidden, & System   */
    request.FilePathLength = strlen( argv[1] );
    movmem( argv[1], request.FilePath, request.FilePathLength );

    reply.Length = sizeof( reply ) - 2;

    /* Now cycle through calls to GetFileInfo until no more files are found   */
    while (1)
    {
            result = GetFileInfo( &request, &reply );
            if ( result == 0x89 )
            {
                    printf( "No Search Privileges for this path\n" );
                    exit(1);
            }

            if ( result == 0x98 )
            {
                    printf( "Volume does not exist,
                       use Volume:Directory\\Directory\\File\n" );
                    exit(1);
            }

            if ( result == 0x9C )
            {
                    printf( "Invalid path,
                       use Volume:Directory\\Directory\\File\n" );
                    exit(1);
            }

            if ( result == 0xFF )
                    exit(1);

            PrintFileInfo();

            request.SequenceNumber = reply.SequenceNumber;
    }

}

int GetFileInfo( struct scanFileReq *request, struct scanFileRep *reply )
{
    _AH = 0xE3;
    _SI = (unsigned)request;
    _DI = (unsigned)reply;
    _ES = _DS;

    geninterrupt( 0x21 );

    return _AL;
}

void PrintFileInfo( void )
{
```

```
    printf( "┌──────────────────────────────────────────┐\n" );
    printf( "│%-15s                                   │ \n", reply.FileName );
    printf( "├──────────────────────────────────────────┤\n" );
    printf( "│ File Size: %10ld│ %-20s│ %-20s│ \n", LongSwitch( &reply.FileSize ),
            ( reply.ExtendedFileAttributes & 0x10 ) ? "Transaction Bit Set" : " ",
            ( reply.ExtendedFileAttributes & 0x20 ) ? "Index Bit Set" : " " );
    printf( "├──────────────────────────────────────────┤\n" );
    printf( "│%-8s │%-8s │%-8s │%-8s │%-8s │%-8s │%-8s │\n",
            ( reply.FileAttributes & 0x01 ) ? "ReadOnly" : " ",
            ( reply.FileAttributes & 0x02 ) ? "Hidden  " : " ",
            ( reply.FileAttributes & 0x04 ) ? "System  " : " ",
            ( reply.FileAttributes & 0x08 ) ? "Execute " : " ",
            ( reply.FileAttributes & 0x10 ) ? "Subdir  " : " ",
            ( reply.FileAttributes & 0x20 ) ? "Archive " : " ",
            ( reply.FileAttributes & 0x80 ) ? "Sharable" : " " );
    printf( "├──────────────────────────────────────────┤\n" );
    printf( "│Creation    Last Access    Last Update    Last Archive       │\n" );

    printf( "│" );
    ShowDate( &reply.CreationDate );
    printf( "    " );
    ShowDate( &reply.LastAccessDate );
    printf( "      " );
    ShowDateAndTime( &reply.LastUpdateDateAndTime );
    printf( "    " );
    ShowDateAndTime( &reply.LastArchiveDateAndTime );
    printf( "    │\n" );

    printf( "└──────────────────────────────────────────┘\n" );
}

void ShowDate( BYTE *date )
{
    int year, month, day;
    WORD newDate;

    newDate = WordSwitch( date );

    if ( !newDate )
    {
        printf( "  /  /  " );
        return;
    }

    day = newDate & 0x1F;

    newDate >>= 5;
    month = newDate & 0xF;

    newDate >>= 4;
    year = ( newDate & 0x3F ) + 80;

    printf( "%02d/%02d/%02d", month, day, year );
}

void ShowDateAndTime( WORD *dateAndTime )
{
    int hours, minutes, seconds;
    WORD time;

    ShowDate( dateAndTime );
```

```
    time = WordSwitch( dateAndTime + 1 );
    if ( !time )
    {
            printf( "   :  :  " );
            return;
    }

    seconds = ( time & 0x1F ) * 2;

    time >>= 5;
    minutes = time & 0x3F;

    time >>= 6;
    hours = time & 0x1F;

    printf( " %02d:%02d:%02d", hours, minutes, seconds );
}

LONG LongSwitch( BYTE *before )
{
    BYTE after[4];

    after[0] = before[3];
    after[1] = before[2];
    after[2] = before[1];
    after[3] = before[0];

    return *( (LONG *)after );
}

WORD WordSwitch( BYTE *before )
{
    BYTE after[2];

    after[0] = before[1];
    after[1] = before[0];

    return *( (WORD *) after );
}
```

Exercises

1. Run the example program FileInfo and try various combinations of volume and pathnames. Use wildcard characters to describe different searches. Trace through the code to see how the data is coming in from the file server and how we are manipulating it for user viewing.

2. Use the example program, passing the path SYS:SYSTEM*.* — you can see the bindery files and others marked Hidden and System. This utility can be a tool to discover more about how the NetWare environment is constructed.

3. Issue an NCOPY command by hand, then code a small program to perform the same task. Time a multifile DOS copy vs. a file server copy.

4. Construct a short program, similar to the FLAG utility, that displays the extended attributes for the files specified.

5. Use the DOS ERASE command and PURGE and SALVAGE files on the DOS command line. Learn how the process of deleting and recovering works at the DOS command level before trying it at the code level.

4 Directory Services

Early LANs were only disk servers, responding to PCs' requests for track and sector coordinates on disks. At this level of operation, there could be no effective directory management or security. Because NetWare operates at the file service level, on the other hand, these services are not just available, they're of vital importance.

When files from PCs are grouped on a file server, several new issues become important: logical drive (volume) management, directory management, security, and logical drive control. The NetWare Directory Services API lets programmers deal with those issues. With Directory Services, developers can find out information about volumes, work with directory handles, map drives, perform basic directory operations (create, delete, rename, etc.) and administer directory-level security.

We will cover each of those activities, providing code examples for most, but first we need to discuss a pervasive element of Directory Services — the tables. The NetWare file server and shell maintain several: the Directory Table, the Directory Handle Table, the Drive Handle Table, the Drive Flag Table, the Drive Connection ID Table, and the Volume Table.

Directory Table

The Directory Table is maintained by the file server. It defines the directory structure for a volume and is used by all of the Directory Services calls. All the information pertinent to directories, files in the directories, and trustee assignments for directories are housed in the Directory Table in three types of entries: Directory, File and Trustee.

The Directory Entry contains the name of the directory, the directory's attributes, the Maximum Rights Mask, the directory creation date, the identification of the creator, a pointer to the parent Directory Entry and a pointer to the Trustee entry.

The File Entry contains the name of the file, the file's attributes and extended attributes, the size of the file, the creation date and creator of the file, the date the file was last accessed, the date and time the file was last updated and archived, and a pointer to the parent Directory Entry.

The Trustee Entry names up to five trustees and contains the rights masks for those trustees, a pointer to the parent Directory Entry and a pointer to the next Trustee Entry (if there are more than five trustees).

Although the Directory Table is not accessed directly, it is important to understand the structure of the table as background for the other tables and Directory Services calls.

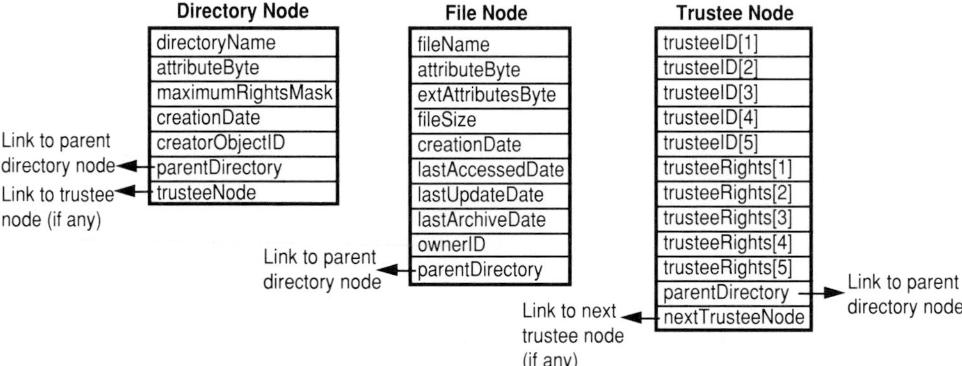

Figure 5: The Directory Table

Directory Handle Table

The file server also maintains a Directory Handle Table for each workstation logged in. This 255-entry table (1 to 255) is used when a program allocates a directory handle. When a handle is allocated, two pointers are stored in this table. One points to the volume table and corresponds to the volume for this directory handle; the other points at a directory entry in the Directory Table.

Drive Tables

The shell maintains three tables to manage its handling of logical drives. There are 32 entries in each table, corresponding to permanent drives A..Z and the six possible temporary drives: [, \,], ^, _, and ‘. The three tables are the Drive Handle Table, the Drive Flag Table, and the Drive Connection ID Table.

Drive Handle Table

The entries in this table index into to the Directory Handle Table, identifying which directory is mapped to which drive.

Drive Flag Table

An entry in this table contains a number with bits set to indicate that the drive is allocated, a local or network drive, or a permanent or temporary drive.

Drive Connection ID Table

This table indexes the Server Name Table and the Connection Information Table, showing which server each drive is mapped to. When this drive becomes the default drive, the server this entry points to becomes the default server. The Server Name Table and the Connection Information Table will be discussed in chapter nine.

Volume Table

The file server tracks all its volumes in the Volume Table. The Volume Table has a maximum of 32 entries (0 to 31) and contains the name of each volume, the maximum and currently available disk blocks, the sectors per block, the maximum and currently available directory slots, and a flag telling whether or not the volume is removable.

Volume management

Volumes are names given to partitions on physical disk drives in the NetWare 286 environment; a user may map a logical drive to a volume using the MAP command. For instance, the command "MAP F:=SYS:APPS\WP" would assign the F logical drive to the SYS: volume and the APPS\WP directory.

The first volume (volume 0) on any NetWare file server must be called SYS: and it is the volume the server boots from (if it doesn't boot from floppy). When installing NetWare, the NETGEN program names the subsequent volumes VOL1:, VOL2:, etc., although integrators may change the volume names to whatever they choose. NetWare 286 file servers may have up to 32 volumes (NetWare 386 increases this maximum exponentially).

Note that when a drive is mapped to a volume and a directory, at the shell level a directory handle is first allocated (to point to the Directory Table). Next, the directory handle is placed in the Drive Handle Table at an offset corresponding to the drive letter's number. (Drive A is 0, drive F is 5 — so in this example, the Directory Handle would be put at offset 5 in the Drive Handle Table.)

The Drive Flag Table also is updated to reflect an allocated, permanent network drive, and the Drive Connection ID table gets a pointer to the server associated with the volume.

The Directory Services API provides several capabilities: A developer may find out how much space (both in terms of bytes and directory entries) is left on a volume, and such general information as whether a volume is hashed, cached, removable, or mounted. A developer may also ask for the volume's name given its number, or for its number given its name.

Calls in the Directory Services API

The following descriptions include which versions of NetWare support which calls. Throughout the book, we explain fields within the calls only at the first mention of each field in each chapter. Appendix B contains a comprehensive, alphabetical listing of the fields for quick reference.

Get Volume Name (E2h 06h)

This call is supported in NetWare versions 4.0 and 4.6, in Advanced NetWare versions 1.0, 1.02, 2.0, and 2.1, and in NetWare 386 and later versions. It returns the volume name given the number of the volume.

Registers in:

AH	E2h
DS:SI	Request Buffer Address
ES:DI	Reply Buffer Address

Registers out:

AL	Completion Code

Completion Codes:

00	Success
98h	Volume Does Not Exist

Request Packet (4 bytes):

Offset	Description	Type	Order
0	Request Buffer Length-2	WORD	lo-hi
2	06	BYTE	
3	Volume Number	BYTE	

Reply Packet (19 bytes):

Offset	Description	Type	Order
0	Reply Buffer Length-2	WORD	lo-hi
2	Volume Name Length(1-16)	BYTE	
3	Volume Name	BYTE[16]	

Volume Number is a volume's offset into the Volume Table. This call returns the name with no colon at the end (SYS: is returned as SYS). If a removable volume is not mounted at the entry specified, the name length will be 0.

The NetWare C Interface format is:

```
int GetVolumeName( int volumeNumber, char *volumeName );
```

Get Volume Number (E2h 05h)

This call is supported in NetWare versions 4.0 and 4.6, in Advanced NetWare versions 1.0, 1.02, 2.0, and 2.1, and in NetWare 386 and later versions. It returns the number of the volume, given the name.

Registers in:

AH	E2h
DS:SI	Request Buffer Address
ES:DI	Reply Buffer Address

Registers out:

AL	Completion Code

Completion Codes:

00	Success
98h	Volume Does Not Exist

Request Packet (20 bytes):

Offset	**Description**	**Type**	**Order**
0	Request Buffer Length-2	WORD	lo-hi
2	05	BYTE	
3	Volume Name Length(1-16)	BYTE	
4	Volume Name	BYTE[16]	

Reply Packet (3 bytes):

Offset	**Description**	**Type**	**Order**
0	Reply Buffer Length-2	WORD	lo-hi
2	Volume Number	BYTE	

Volume Name must be no longer than 16 characters and must not contain spaces, asterisks, question marks, colons, backslashes or forward slashes. If a wildcard is used for the name, the first name found will be returned.

The NetWare C Interface format is:

```
int GetVolumeNumber( char *volumeName, int *volumeNumber );
```

Get Volume Info With Handle (E2h 15h)

This call is supported in NetWare versions 4.0 and 4.6, in Advanced NetWare versions 1.0, 1.02, 2.0, and 2.1, and in NetWare 386 and later versions. It returns information about a volume, given a directory handle.

Registers in:

AH	E2h
DS:SI	Request Buffer Address
ES:DI	Reply Buffer Address

Registers out:

AL	Completion Code

Completion Codes:

00	Success

Request Packet (4 bytes):

Offset	Description	Type	Order
0	Request Buffer Length-2	WORD	lo-hi
2	15h	BYTE	
3	Directory Handle	BYTE	

Reply Packet (30 bytes):

Offset	Description	Type	Order
0	Reply Buffer Length-2	WORD	lo-hi
2	Sectors Per Block	WORD	hi-lo
4	Total Blocks	WORD	hi-lo
6	Available Blocks	WORD	hi-lo
8	Total Directory Slots	WORD	hi-lo
10	Available Directory Slots	WORD	hi-lo
12	Volume Name	BYTE[16]	
28	Volume Is Removable	WORD	hi-lo

Sectors Per Block is the number of 512-byte sectors in each block of a volume.

Total Blocks is the number of blocks on a volume.

Available Blocks is the number of unused blocks on a volume.

Total Directory Slots is the maximum number of slots on a volume. These slots correspond to entries in the Directory Table (i.e., a new file will take up space and a directory slot).

Available Directory Slots is the number of slots currently unused.

Volume Is Removable is a bit field for the flag telling whether the volume can be physically removed from the file server (such as in a removable hard disk cartridge-type drive). A value indicates the volume is removable, zero indicates it is not.

The NetWare C Interface format is:

```
int GetVolumeInfoWithHandle( BYTE directoryHandle,
        char *volumeName, WORD *totalBlocks,
        WORD *sectorsPerBlock, WORD *availableBlocks,
        WORD *totalDirectorySlots,
        WORD *availableDirectorySlots,
        WORD *volumeIsRemovable );
```

Get Volume Info With Number (DAh)

This call is supported in NetWare versions 4.0 and 4.6, in Advanced NetWare versions 1.0, 1.02, 2.0, and 2.1, and in NetWare 386 and later versions. It returns information about a volume, given its number.

Registers in:

AH	DAh
DL	Volume Number
ES:DI	Reply Buffer Address

Registers out:

AL	Completion Code

Completion Codes:

00	Succcss

Reply Packet (28 bytes):

Offset	Description	Type	Order
0	Sectors Per Block	WORD	hi-lo
2	Total Blocks	WORD	hi-lo
4	Available Blocks	WORD	hi-lo
6	Total Directory Slots	WORD	hi-lo
8	Available Directory Slots	WORD	hi-lo
10	Volume Name	BYTE[16]	
26	Volume Is Removable	WORD	hi-lo

The NetWare C Interface format is:

```
int GetVolumeInfoWithNumber( BYTE volumeNumber,
        char *volumeName, WORD *totalBlocks,
        WORD *sectorsPerBlock, WORD *availableBlocks,
        WORD *totalDirectorySlots,
        WORD *availableDirectorySlots,
        WORD *volumeIsRemovable );
```

Get Volume Information (E3h E9h)

This call is supported in Advanced NetWare 2.1 and in NetWare versions 386 and later. It returns the most complete information available on a volume given its number (entry into the Volume Table).

Registers in:

AH	E3h
DS:SI	Request Buffer Address
ES:DI	Reply Buffer Address

Registers out:

AL	Completion Code

Completion Codes:

00	Success

Request Packet (4 bytes):

Offset	Description	Type	Order
0	Request Buffer Length-2	WORD	lo-hi
2	E9h	BYTE	
3	Volume Number	BYTE	

Reply Packet (40 bytes):

Offset	Description	Type	Order
0	Reply Buffer Length-2	WORD	lo-hi
2	System Elapsed Time	WORD	hi-lo
6	Volume Number	BYTE	
7	Logical Drive Number	BYTE	
8	Sectors Per Block	WORD	hi-lo
10	Starting Block	WORD	hi-lo
12	Total Blocks	WORD	hi-lo
14	Available Blocks	WORD	hi-lo
16	Total Directory Slots	WORD	hi-lo
18	Avail. Directory Slots	WORD	hi-lo
20	Actual Max Used Dir Slots	WORD	hi-lo
22	Volume Is Hashed	BYTE	
23	Volume Is Cached	BYTE	
24	Volume is Removable	BYTE	
25	Volume is Mounted	BYTE	
26	Volume Name	BYTE[16]	

System Elapsed Time is the file server's interval marker, a count of the number of ticks (18 per second) on its clock at the time of a call. This field can be used to measure time between calls.

Starting Block is the number of the first block of the volume.

Actual Maximum Used Directory Slots is the most directory slots ever used at one time on a volume.

Volume Is Hashed shows whether a volume's Directory Table is stored in file server memory, which improves performance.

Volume Is Cached shows whether a volume is cached. Caching is the process of storing the most recent reads and writes to memory so that subsequent requests may read from memory instead of the drive. It is used to improve performance on the drive.

Volume Is Removable tells whether a volume can be removed from the system.

Volume Is Mounted tells whether a volume is mounted in the file server.

The NetWare C Interface format is:

```
int GetVolumeInformation( WORD connectionID, BYTE volumeNumber,
    int structSize, VOLUME_STATS *volumeStatistics );
```

Code Sample: VolStat.C

VolStat is similar to the NetWare VolInfo program; it shows how the Get Volume Information call can be used to show volume information.

This program first defines the reply structure to be used in GetVolumeInformation(). Since it is the only structure used in the program, I defined it globally; the function prototypes are listed right after that definition.

The main() code block consists of a loop from 0 to 31 to check each volume. If GetVolumeInformation returns 98h, there are no more volumes; if 98h does not return, PrintResults() is called to print the information in Reply.

The flags Hashed, Cached, Fixed, and Mounted are displayed as being either turned on or off, and the logical drive number and the sectors per block are displayed. Next the storage space is shown, both in blocks and in megabytes (VolInfo displays kilobytes). Also, the total and remaining directory slots are shown.

```
/*                                                                    */
/* VolStat - Lists all Volume Information for each volume on the      */
/*          current server                                            */
/*                                                                    */
/* by Charles Rose                                                    */
/*                                                                    */

#include <stdio.h>
#include <dos.h>

typedef unsigned char BYTE;
typedef unsigned int WORD;
typedef unsigned long LONG;

/* Reply structure */
struct getVolInfoRep {
    WORD    Length;
    LONG    ElapsedTime;             /* Wrong in Novell Docs, it says WORD */
    BYTE    VolumeNumber;
    BYTE    LogicalDriveNumber;
    WORD    SectorsPerBlock;
    WORD    StartingBlock;
    WORD    TotalBlocks;
    WORD    AvailableBlocks;
    WORD    TotalDirSlots;
    WORD    AvailableDirSlots;
    WORD    ActualMaxUsedDirSlots;
    BYTE    IsHashed;
    BYTE    IsCached;
    BYTE    IsRemovable;
    BYTE    IsMounted;
    BYTE    VolumeName[16];
} Reply;

int GetVolumeInformation( BYTE volume );
void PrintResults( void );
```

```
WORD WordSwitch( BYTE *before );

main()
{
    int x, result;

    for ( x = 0; x < 31; x++ )
    {
            if ( ( result = GetVolumeInformation( x ) ) == 0x98 )
                    exit(1);
            else if ( result )
            {
                    printf( "Error on Volume %d, code %X\n", x, result );
                    exit(1);
            }
            PrintResults();
    }
}

int GetVolumeInformation( BYTE volume )
{
    BYTE Request[4] = { 2, 0, 0xE9, 0 };

    Request[3] = volume;
    Reply.Length = sizeof( struct getVolInfoRep ) - 2;

    _AH = 0xE3;
    _SI = (unsigned)Request;
    _DI = (unsigned)&Reply;
    _ES = _DS;

    geninterrupt( 0x21 );

    return _AL;
}

void PrintResults( void )
{
    printf( "Volume #%d [%s]\n", (WORD)Reply.VolumeNumber, Reply.VolumeName );

    if ( Reply.IsHashed ) printf( "Hashed  " ); else printf( "NOT Hashed  " );
    if ( Reply.IsCached ) printf( "Cached  " ); else printf( "NOT Cached  " );
    if ( Reply.IsRemovable ) printf( "Removable  " ); else printf( "Fixed  " );
    if ( Reply.IsMounted ) printf( "Mounted  "   ); else printf( "NOT MOUNTED  " );
    printf( "\n" );

    printf( "Logical Drive #: %d          Sectors Per Block: %d\n ",
            (WORD)Reply.LogicalDriveNumber, WordSwitch( &Reply.SectorsPerBlock ) );

    printf( "-Storage Space-\n" );
    printf( "  Total Blocks: %10d  Total Megabytes: %lu\n ",
                    WordSwitch( &Reply.TotalBlocks ),
            ( (LONG)WordSwitch( &Reply.TotalBlocks ) *
            (LONG)WordSwitch( &Reply.SectorsPerBlock ) *
            (LONG)512 ) / ((LONG)1024*(LONG)1024) );
    printf( " Blocks Left : %10d  Megabytes Left : %lu\n ",
                    WordSwitch( &Reply.AvailableBlocks ),
            ( (LONG)WordSwitch( &Reply.AvailableBlocks ) *
            (LONG)WordSwitch( &Reply.SectorsPerBlock ) *
            (LONG)512 ) / ((LONG)1024*(LONG)1024) );

    printf( "-Directories-\n" );
```

```
    printf( "  Total Slots : %10d  Slots Left     : %d\n",
                WordSwitch( &Reply.TotalDirSlots ),
            WordSwitch( &Reply.AvailableDirSlots ) );

    printf( "\n" );
}

WORD WordSwitch( BYTE *before )
{
    BYTE after[2];

    after[0] = before[1];
    after[1] = before[0];

    return *( (WORD *) after );
}
```

Directory Handles

Directory handles are used in most calls. A handle is simply the index into the Directory Handle Table, which contains a pointer to the Directory Table and a pointer to the Volume Table. So when we have a directory handle, we know it describes a volume and a directory, such as "SYS:PUBLIC".

If no directory handle is used in a call, the programmer must specify the full path name, including the volume, directory and subdirectory names, in the format VOLUME:DIRECTORY\SUBDIRECTORY\SUBDIRECTORY.

Although usually a directory name is indicated by the handle and a filename is passed as an extension, if a directory handle is used, it may specify a full path; if so, then no path need be included in the function call. If no path is needed, the length must be set to zero before making the call.

A third variation is to use a directory handle as the base of the path and send the remainder of the path as an offset. For example, if our directory handle pointed to "SYS:DATA\" and our path was "DBDATA" then the final directory would be "SYS:DATA\DBDATA".

The directory handles calls are used to find handles given drive numbers, to set handles to different directories, and to save and restore handles.

These calls directly manipulate the Directory Handle Table. We could do very much the same work by getting the address of the Directory Handle Table and manipulating it directly, but these calls were provided for convenience and Novell may change the table in the future. So not only is it more straightforward in most cases to use these calls, but also, it is more likely to assure compatibility with future versions of NetWare.

Get Directory Handle (E9h 00h)

This call is supported in NetWare versions 4.0 and 4.6, in Advanced NetWare versions 1.0, 1.02, 2.0, and 2.1, and in NetWare 386 and later versions. It returns the current directory handle for a drive. It is often used to find the directory to which a drive is mapped.

Registers in:

AH	E9h
AL	00
DX	Drive Number

Registers out:

AL	Directory Handle
AH	Status Flags

Completion Codes:
None

Drive Number corresponds to an index into the Drive Handle Table (0 to 31) for permanent drives (A..Z)(0..25) and temporary drives ([,\,],^,_,')(26..31). Example: Drive A is 0, drive F is 5, etc.

The *Directory Handle* field will be 0 if the drive number is invalid.

The *Status Flags* indicate whether the drive is not currently mapped (00h), mapped to a permanent directory handle (01h), mapped to a temporary directory handle (02h), or whether the drive is local (80h).

The NetWare C Interface format is:

```
BYTE GetDirectoryHandle( BYTE driveNumber );
```

Set Directory Handle (E2h 00h)

This call is supported in NetWare versions 4.0 and 4.6, in Advanced NetWare versions 1.0, 1.02, 2.0, and 2.1, and in NetWare 386 and later versions. It is used to change the path (volume and directory) a directory handle points to by providing another handle and/or a new path.

Registers in:

AH	E2h
DS:SI	Request Buffer Address
ES:DI	Reply Buffer Address

Registers out:

AL	Completion Code

Completion Codes:

0	Success
98h	Volume Does Not Exist
9Bh	Bad Directory Handle
9Ch	Invalid Path

Request Packet (max = 261 bytes):

Offset	Description	Type	Order
0	Request Buffer Length-2	WORD	lo-hi
2	00h	BYTE	
3	Target Directory Handle	BYTE	
4	Source Directory Handle	BYTE	
5	Source Dir Path Length	BYTE (1-255)	
6	Source Directory Path	BYTE[*LENGTH*]	

Reply Packet (2 bytes):

Offset	Description	Type	Order
0	0000	WORD	lo-hi

Directory Path can be the full path itself or an offset to the source directory handle. If no source directory handle is specified, the volume name must be specified in the format "VOLUME:DIRECTORY\SUBDIRECTORY". If a directory handle is specified, the path can be used as an offset to it. If the directory handle describes the full path, the Source Directory Path field is not necessary.

In this call, the Target Directory Handle is set to point to the volume and directory described by the Source Directory Handle and the Source Directory Path.

The NetWare C Interface format is:

```
int SetDirectoryHandle( BYTE sourceDirectoryHandle,
   char *sourceDirectoryPath, BYTE targetDirectoryHandle );
```

Save Directory Handle (E2h 17h)

This call is supported in Advanced NetWare 2.0 and 2.1, and in NetWare versions 386 and later. It saves information on a directory handle. It can be used in situations where one station needs to duplicate the directory handles of another. Novell has suggested that these two calls, Save Directory Handle and Restore Directory Handle, be used in remote job handling, such as print spooling, or for batch jobs, etc.

Registers in:

AH	E2h
DS:SI	Request Buffer Address
ES:DI	Reply Buffer Address

Registers out:

AL	Completion Code

Completion Codes:

0	Success
	Error code (positive) if unsuccessful

Request Packet (4 bytes):

Offset	Description	Type	Order
0	Request Buffer Length-2	WORD	lo-hi
2	17h	BYTE	
3	Directory Handle	BYTE	

Reply Packet (18 bytes):

Offset	Description	Type	Order
0	Reply Buffer Length - 2	WORD	lo-hi
2	Save Buffer	BYTE[16]	

Save Buffer is a 16-byte buffer that contains the information on the volume and directory pointed to by the directory handle. This buffer will be used in the next call to restore the Directory Handle.

The NetWare C Interface format is:

```
int SaveDirectoryHandle( BYTE directoryHandle, char saveBuffer[16] );
```

Restore Directory Handle (E2h 18h)

This call is supported in Advanced NetWare 2.0 and 2.1, and in NetWare versions 386 and later. It restores the directory handle saved by the preceding call.

Registers in:

AH	E2h
DS:SI	Request Buffer Address
ES:DI	Reply Buffer Address

Registers out:

AL	Completion Code

Completion Codes:

0	Success
	Error code (positive) if unsuccessful

Request Packet (19 bytes):

Offset	Description	Type	Order
0	Request Buffer Length-2	WORD	lo-hi
2	18h	BYTE	
3	Save Buffer	BYTE[16]	

Reply Packet (4 bytes):

Offset	Description	Type	Order
0	Reply Buffer Length - 2	WORD	lo-hi
2	New Directory Handle	BYTE	
3	Effective Rights Mask	BYTE	

The *Effective Rights Mask* is a byte describing the rights available for this directory. The following bits are used:

0x01	Read	- may read files
0x02	Write	- may write to files
0x04	Open	- may open files
0x08	Create	- may create files
0x10	Delete	- may delete files
0x20	Parental	- may create or delete subdirectories and trustee rights can be granted or revoked
0x40	Search	- may search directory
0x80	Modify	- may change file attributes

The NetWare C Interface format is:

```
int RestoreDirectoryHandle( char saveBuffer[16],
   BYTE *newDirectoryHandle, BYTE *effectiveRightsMask );
```

Code sample: FileInfo.C (enhanced version)

This program is identical to FileInfo in the last chapter, except it has been enhanced by calls to the Directory Services. This illustrates how different API groups can be used together to enhance the functionality of a program.

In main() after the program has checked the command line argument, it looks to see if the user has specified a volume name by checking for a colon (":") in the path (the program will not accept drive letters as a prefixes to the path). If no colon is found, the program uses getdisk() to find the current drive.

The current drive is passed to GetDirectoryHandle() which finds the directory handle and passes it to GetDirectoryPath(). Finally, GetDirectoryPath() places the current path in currentDirectory.

Next, FileInfo truncates the *currentDirectory* string after the colon, leaving only the volume name. The command line-specified directory is appended, and the volume:directory string *currentDirectory* is ready to be placed in the request structure.

```
/*                                                                            */
/* FileInfo - Lists all the NetWare file info on selected files              */
/*                                                                            */
/* by Charles Rose                                                            */
/*                                                                            */

#include <stdio.h>
#include <dos.h>
#include <dir.h>
#include <string.h>

typedef unsigned char BYTE;
typedef unsigned int WORD;
typedef unsigned long LONG;

/* Request and Reply structures */
struct scanFileReq {
        WORD    Length;
        BYTE    Function;
        WORD    SequenceNumber;
        BYTE    DirectoryHandle;
        BYTE    SearchAttributes;
        BYTE    FilePathLength;
        BYTE    FilePath[255];
} request;

struct scanFileRep {
        WORD    Length;
        WORD    SequenceNumber;
        BYTE    FileName[14];
        BYTE    FileAttributes;
        BYTE    ExtendedFileAttributes;
        LONG    FileSize;
        WORD    CreationDate;
        WORD    LastAccessDate;
        LONG    LastUpdateDateAndTime;
        LONG    OwnerObjectID;
        LONG    LastArchiveDateAndTime;
        BYTE    Reserved[56];
} reply;

/* Local Routines */
void PrintFileInfo( void );
int GetFileInfo( struct scanFileReq *request, struct scanFileRep *reply );
void ShowDate( BYTE *date );
void ShowDateAndTime( WORD *dateAndTime );
LONG LongSwitch( BYTE *before );
WORD WordSwitch( BYTE *before );
BYTE GetDirectoryHandle( WORD driveNumber );
int GetDirectoryPath( BYTE directoryHandle, char *directoryPath );

main( int argc, char *argv[] )
{
        int result;
        char currentDirectory[255], tempPath[255], volume[255];

        if ( argc != 2 )
        {
                printf( "Usage: FILEINFO path\n" );
                exit(1);
        }
```

```
        /* Use directory services to insert the volume name into the path     */
        /* if the user hasn't done it                                          */

        if ( !strstr( argv[1], ":" ) )
        {
                memset( currentDirectory, 0, 255 );
                memset( tempPath, 0, 255 );
                GetDirectoryPath( GetDirectoryHandle( getdisk() ),
                        currentDirectory );
                *( strstr( currentDirectory, ":" ) + 1 ) = NULL;
                strcat( tempPath, currentDirectory );
                strcat( tempPath, argv[1] );
        }
        else
                strcpy( tempPath, argv[1] );

        /* Initialize Request & Reply structures */
        request.Length = sizeof( request ) - 2;
        request.Function = 0x0F;          /* Function F - Get file info        */
        request.SequenceNumber = 0xFFFF;          /* Use -1 as first sequence   */
        request.DirectoryHandle = 0;      /* No handle, use full path from user */
        request.SearchAttributes = 6;     /* Search Normal, Hidden, & System    */
        request.FilePathLength = strlen( tempPath );
        movmem( tempPath, request.FilePath, request.FilePathLength );

        reply.Length = sizeof( reply ) - 2;

        /* Now cycle through calls to GetFileInfo until no more files are found*/
        while (1)
        {
                result = GetFileInfo( &request, &reply );
                if ( result == 0x89 )
                {
                        printf( "No Search Privileges for this path\n" );
                        exit(1);
                }

                if ( result == 0x98 )
                {
                        printf( "Volume does not exist, use
                                Volume:Directory\\Directory\\File\n" );
                        exit(1);
                }

                if ( result == 0x9C )
                {
                        printf( "Invalid path, use
                                Volume:Directory\\Directory\\File\n" );
                        exit(1);
                }

                if ( result == 0xFF )
                        exit(1);

                PrintFileInfo();

                request.SequenceNumber = reply.SequenceNumber;
        }


int GetFileInfo( struct scanFileReq *request, struct scanFileRep *reply )
```

```
{
        _AH = 0xE3;
        _SI = (unsigned)request;
        _DI = (unsigned)reply;
        _ES = _DS;

        geninterrupt( 0x21 );

        return _AL;
}

void PrintFileInfo( void )
{
        printf( "┌──────────────────────────────────────────────────┐\n" );
        printf( "│ %-15s                                          │  \n", reply.FileName );
        printf( "├──────────────────────────────────────────────────┤\n" );
        printf( "│File Size:  %10ld │ %-20s │ %-20s   │\n",
                    LongSwitch( &reply.FileSize ),
          ( reply.ExtendedFileAttributes & 0x10 ) ? "Transaction Bit Set" : " ",
          ( reply.ExtendedFileAttributes & 0x20 ) ? "Index Bit Set" : " " );
        printf( "├──────────────────────────────────────────────────┤\n" );
        printf( " │ %-8s  │ %-8s  │ %-8s  │%-8s  │%-8s  │%-8s  │ %-8s │\n",
                ( reply.FileAttributes & 0x01 ) ? "ReadOnly" : " ",
                ( reply.FileAttributes & 0x02 ) ? "Hidden  " : " ",
                ( reply.FileAttributes & 0x04 ) ? "System  " : " ",
                ( reply.FileAttributes & 0x08 ) ? "Execute " : " ",
                ( reply.FileAttributes & 0x10 ) ? "Subdir  " : " ",
                ( reply.FileAttributes & 0x20 ) ? "Archive " : " ",
                ( reply.FileAttributes & 0x80 ) ? "Sharable" : " " );
        printf( "├──────────────────────────────────────────────────┤ \n" );
        printf( "│ Creation  Last Access  Last Update  Last Archive    │\n" );

        printf( " │ " );
        ShowDate( &reply.CreationDate );
        printf( "      " );
        ShowDate( &reply.LastAccessDate );
        printf( "        " );
        ShowDateAndTime( &reply.LastUpdateDateAndTime );
        printf( "      " );
        ShowDateAndTime( &reply.LastArchiveDateAndTime );
        printf( "    │\n" );

        printf( "└──────────────────────────────────────────────────────────┘\n" );
}

void ShowDate( BYTE *date )
{
        int year, month, day;
        WORD newDate;

        newDate = WordSwitch( date );

        if ( !newDate )
        {
                printf( "  /  /  " );
                return;
        }

        day = newDate & 0x1F;

        newDate >>= 5;
        month = newDate & 0xF;
```

```
        newDate >>= 4;
        year = ( newDate & 0x3F ) + 80;

        printf( "%02d/%02d/%02d", month, day, year );
}

void ShowDateAndTime( WORD *dateAndTime )
{
        int hours, minutes, seconds;
        WORD time;

        ShowDate( dateAndTime );

        time = WordSwitch( dateAndTime + 1 );
        if ( !time )
        {
                printf( "   :  :  " );
                return;
        }

        seconds = ( time & 0x1F ) * 2;

        time >>= 5;
        minutes = time & 0x3F;

        time >>= 6;
        hours = time & 0x1F;

        printf( " %02d:%02d:%02d", hours, minutes, seconds );
}

LONG LongSwitch( BYTE *before )
{
        BYTE after[4];

        after[0] = before[3];
        after[1] = before[2];
        after[2] = before[1];
        after[3] = before[0];

        return *( (LONG *)after );
}

WORD WordSwitch( BYTE *before )
{
        BYTE after[2];

        after[0] = before[1];
        after[1] = before[0];

        return *( (WORD *) after );
}

BYTE GetDirectoryHandle( WORD driveNumber )
{
        _AH = 0xE9;
        _AL = 0;
        _DX = driveNumber;
        geninterrupt( 0x21 );

        return _AL;
}
```

```
int GetDirectoryPath( BYTE directoryHandle, char *directoryPath )
{
        BYTE request[4] = { 2, 0, 1, 0 }, reply[258], retval;

        request[3] = directoryHandle;
        *((WORD *)reply) = 256;

        _AH = 0xE2;
        _SI = (unsigned)request;
        _DI = (unsigned)reply;
        _ES = _DS;

        geninterrupt( 0x21 );

        if ( !( retval  = _AL ) )
                movmem( &reply[3], directoryPath, reply[2] );

        return retval;
}
```

Mapping Drives

Most NetWare users are familiar with the MAP command that allows the user to access a particular file server volume directory at a particular logical drive. Setting up the pointers so a logical drive may be used to access this full path is called "mapping a drive."

NetWare developers have three calls with which they can: allocate a permanent handle, thereby mapping a drive that will last past the duration of the current session; allocate a temporary handle, mapping a drive that will only last for the duration of the current session; or deallocate the handle, thereby deleting the map.

Drives may be mapped temporarily, i.e. for the duration of a program, or permanently, keeping the new drive map after the program ends. A special case allows for a temporary map where the directory cannot be changed.

Allocate Permanent Directory Handle (E2h 12h)

This call is supported in NetWare versions 4.0 and 4.6, in Advanced NetWare versions 1.0, 1.02, 2.0, and 2.1, and in NetWare 386 and later versions. It permanently assigns a logical drive to a network directory described by a directory handle/path combination. It first allocates a directory handle to the path specified by the Directory Handle/Directory Path combination and then assigns it to the specified drive.

Registers in:

AH	E2h
DS:SI	Request Buffer Address
ES:DI	Reply Buffer Address

Registers out:

AL	Completion Code

Completion Codes:

0	Success
98h	Volume Does Not Exist
9Ch	Invalid Path

Request Packet (max = 261 bytes):

Offset	Description	Type	Order
0	Request Buffer Length-2	WORD	lo-hi
2	12h	BYTE	
3	Directory Handle	BYTE	
4	Drive Letter (A..Z)	BYTE	
5	Directory Path Length	BYTE (0-255)	
6	Directory Path	BYTE[*LENGTH*]	

Reply Packet (4 bytes):

Offset	Description	Type	Order
0	Reply Buffer Length - 2	WORD	lo-hi
2	New Directory Handle	BYTE	
3	Effective Rights Mask	BYTE	

The NetWare C Interface format is:

```
int AllocPermanentDirectoryHandle( BYTE directoryHandle,
        char *directoryPath, char driveLetter,
        BYTE *newDirectoryHandle, BYTE *effectiveRightsMask );
```

Allocate Temporary Directory Handle (E2h 13h)

This call is supported in NetWare versions 4.0 and 4.6, in Advanced NetWare versions 1.0, 1.02, 2.0, and 2.1, and in NetWare 386 and later versions. It assigns a logical drive to a network directory, described by a directory handle-path combination, for the duration of the program or until explicitly deallocated. When the program terminates and an End of Job is generated by the shell, the handle is deallocated and the drive removed.

This call first allocates a directory handle to the path specified by the Directory Handle/Directory Path combination and then assigns it to the specified drive. (If a temporary directory name is the same as a name for which a "permanent" directory handle has already been allocated, the "permanent" directory handle will be lost.)

Registers in:

AH	E2h
DS:SI	Request Buffer Address
ES:DI	Reply Buffer Address

Registers out:

AL	Completion Code

Completion Codes:

0	Success
98h	Volume Does Not Exist
9Ch	Invalid Path

Request Packet (max = 261 bytes):

Offset	Description	Type	Order
0	Request Buffer Length-2	WORD	lo-hi
2	13h	BYTE	
3	Directory Handle	BYTE	
4	Drive Letter (A..Z)([..')	BYTE	
5	Directory Path Length	BYTE (0-255)	
6	Directory Path	BYTE[*LENGTH*]	

Reply Packet (4 bytes):

Offset	Description	Type	Order
0	Reply Buffer Length - 2	WORD	lo-hi
2	New Directory Handle	BYTE	
3	Effective Rights Mask	BYTE	

In this call, the *Drive Letter* may include the permanent drive letters A-Z and the temporary drives [,\,],^,_,'.

If no *Directory Path* is used, zero should be placed in the Directory Path Length field.

The NetWare C Interface format is:

```
int AllocTemporaryDirectoryHandle( BYTE directoryHandle,
   char *directoryPath, char driveLetter,
   BYTE *newDirectoryHandle, BYTE *effectiveRightsMask );
```

Allocate Special Directory Handle (E2h 16h)

This call is supported in NetWare versions 4.0 and 4.6, in Advanced NetWare versions 1.0, 1.02, 2.0, and 2.1, and in NetWare 386. It provides the same function as the preceding one, except the directory mapped cannot be changed. The purpose of this function is to support special internal use by the workstation shell but will not be supported after 1990.

Registers in:

AH	E2h
DS:SI	Request Buffer Address
ES:DI	Reply Buffer Address

Registers out:

AL	Completion Code

Completion Codes:

0	Success
98h	Volume Does Not Exist
9Ch	Invalid Path

Request Packet (max = 261 bytes):

Offset	Description	Type	Order
0	Request Buffer Length-2	WORD	lo-hi
2	13h	BYTE	
3	Directory Handle	BYTE	
4	Drive Letter (A..Z)([..')	BYTE	
5	Directory Path Length	BYTE (0-255)	
6	Directory Path	BYTE[*LENGTH*]	

Reply Packet (4 bytes):

Offset	Description	Type	Order
0	Reply Buffer Length - 2	WORD	lo-hi
2	New Directory Handle	BYTE	
3	Effective Rights Mask	BYTE	

In this call, the *Drive Letter* may include the permanent drive letters A..Z and the temporary drives [,\,],^,_,'.

The NetWare C Interface format is not supported.

Deallocate Directory Handle (E2h 14h)

This call is supported in NetWare versions 4.0 and 4.6, in Advanced NetWare versions 1.0, 1.02, 2.0, and 2.1, and in NetWare 386 and later versions. It deallocates either a permanent or a temporary directory handle and removes the drive map associated with it.

Registers in:

AH	E2h
DS:SI	Request Buffer Address
ES:DI	Reply Buffer Address

Registers out:

AL	Completion Code

Completion Codes:

0	Success
9Bh	Bad Directory Handle

Request Packet (4 bytes):

Offset	Description	Type	Order
0	Request Buffer Length-2	WORD	lo-hi
2	14h	BYTE	
3	Directory Handle	BYTE	

Reply Packet (2 bytes):

Offset	Description	Type	Order
0	0000	WORD	hi-lo

The NetWare C Interface format is:

```
int DeallocateDirectoryHandle( BYTE directoryHandle );
```

Code sample: MapIt.C

MapIt is designed to illustrate the process of mapping a directory to a drive and removing the mapped directory. The Novell call Allocate Permanent Directory Handle is used to map a drive and Deallocate Permanent Directory Handle is used to remove that mapping.

MapIt takes a drive letter as a command line argument and maps the SYS:PUBLIC directory to it. If a -d is specified in the command line, the mapping is removed.

The program defines a request packet globally; this will be used by both the Allocate and the Deallocate Directory Handle calls. After defining local prototypes, the main() first checks the command line for too many or too few parameters, then proceeds to look for a -d in that line. If one is found, DeallocatePermanentDirHandle() is called, passing the drive to be removed.

If no -d is found, the program proceeds to get the current directory handle and pass it to AllocatePermanentDirHandle(), mapping the drive.

```
/*                                                                        */
/* MapIt - Maps a user-specified drive to the SYS:PUBLIC directory        */
/*                                                                        */
/* by Charles Rose                                                        */
/*                                                                        */

#include <stdio.h>
#include <dos.h>

typedef unsigned char BYTE;
typedef unsigned int WORD;
typedef unsigned long LONG;

/* Reply structure */
struct allocPermDirHandleReq {
        WORD    Length;
        BYTE    Function;
        BYTE    DirHandle;
        BYTE    Drive;
        BYTE    DirPathLength;
        BYTE    DirPath[255];
} Request;

int AllocatePermanentDirHandle( char *Drive );
int DeallocatePermanentDirHandle( BYTE DirHandle );
BYTE GetDirectoryHandle( WORD driveNumber );

main( int argc, char *argv[] )
{
        int result;
        BYTE dirHandle;

        if ( ( argc < 2 ) || ( argc > 3 ) )
        {
                printf( "Usage: MAPIT drive [-d]\n" );
                printf( "Maps SYS:PUBLIC to drive specified.  Use -d to remove
                        mapping.\n" );
                exit(1);
        }

        if ( stricmp( "-d", argv[2] ) )
        {
                /* Map the drive */
                result = AllocatePermanentDirHandle( argv[1] );

                if ( result )
                {
                        printf( "Error trying to allocate directory,
                                Error #%X\n", result );
                        exit(1);
                }
                else
                        printf( "Drive %s has been mapped to SYS:PUBLIC\n",
                        argv[1] );
        }
        else
        {
                /* Remove the mapping */
                dirHandle = GetDirectoryHandle( (WORD)( toupper(*argv[1]) - 'A' ) );
```

```
                result = DeallocatePermanentDirHandle( dirHandle );
                if ( result )
                {
                        printf( "Error trying to de-allocate directory,
                                Error #%X\n", result );
                        exit(1);
                }
                else
                        printf( "Drive %s has had its drive mapping deleted.\n",
                                argv[1] );
        }
}

int AllocatePermanentDirHandle( char *Drive )
{
        BYTE Reply[4] = { 2, 0, 0, 0 };

        strcpy( Request.DirPath, "SYS:PUBLIC" );

        Request.Length = sizeof( struct allocPermDirHandleReq ) - 2;
        Request.Function = 0x12;
        Request.DirHandle = 0;
        Request.Drive = toupper( *Drive );              /* Make it uppercase */
        Request.DirPathLength = strlen( Request.DirPath );

        _AH = 0xE2;
        _SI = (unsigned)&Request;
        _DI = (unsigned)Reply;
        _ES = _DS;

        geninterrupt( 0x21 );

        return _AL;
}

int DeallocatePermanentDirHandle( BYTE dirHandle )
{
        BYTE Reply[2] = { 0, 0 };

        Request.Length = sizeof( struct allocPermDirHandleReq ) - 2;
        Request.Function = 0x14;
        Request.DirHandle = dirHandle;

        _AH = 0xE2;
        _SI = (unsigned)&Request;
        _DI = (unsigned)Reply;
        _ES = _DS;

        geninterrupt( 0x21 );

        return _AL;
}

BYTE GetDirectoryHandle( WORD driveNumber )
{
        _AH = 0xE9;
        _AL = 0;
        _DX = driveNumber;

        geninterrupt( 0x21 );

        return _AL;
}
```

Directory operations

In addition to the more advanced directory services available to developers, Novell has also provided a group of basic directory services to handle such mundane work as creating, deleting, renaming, and changing directories. These facilities are also provided to find out about and change specific directory information.

Create Directory (E2h 0Ah)

This call is supported in NetWare versions 4.0 and 4.6, in Advanced NetWare versions 1.0, 1.02, 2.0, and 2.1, and in NetWare 386 and later versions. It creates a directory on a file server, given the directory path and the maximum rights for the directory.

Registers in:

AH	E2h
DS:SI	Request Buffer Address
ES:DI	Reply Buffer Address

Registers out:

AL	Completion Code

Completion Codes:

0	Success
84h	No Create Privileges
98h	Volume Does Not Exist

Request Packet (max = 261 bytes):

Offset	**Description**	**Type**	**Order**
0	Request Buffer Length-2	WORD	lo-hi
2	0Ah	BYTE	
3	Directory Handle	BYTE	
4	Maximum Rights Mask	BYTE	
5	Directory Path Length	BYTE (0-255)	
6	Directory Path	BYTE[*LENGTH*]	

Reply Packet (2 bytes):

Offset	**Description**	**Type**	**Order**
0	0000	WORD	hi-lo

The *Maximum Rights Mask* is a byte containing bit fields specifying privileges. The bit assignments are:

0x01	Read	- may read files
0x02	Write	- may write to files
0x04	Open	- may open files
0x08	Create	- may create files
0x10	Delete	- may delete files
0x20	Parental	- may create or delete subdirectories and trustee rights can be granted or revoked
0x40	Search	- may search directory
0x80	Modify	- may change file attributes

The NetWare C Interface format is:

```
int CreateDirectory( BYTE directoryHandle, char *directoryPath,
    BYTE maximumRightsMask );
```

Delete Directory (E2h 0Bh)

This call is supported in NetWare versions 4.0 and 4.6, in Advanced NetWare versions 1.0, 1.02, 2.0, and 2.1, and in NetWare 386 and later versions. It deletes a directory on a file server, given the directory path and the maximum rights for the directory.

Registers in:

AH	E2h
DS:SI	Request Buffer Address
ES:DI	Reply Buffer Address

Registers out:

AL	Completion Code

Completion Codes:

0	Success
8Ah	No Delete Privileges
98h	Volume Does Not Exist
9Bh	Bad Directory Handle
9Ch	Invalid Path
9Fh	Directory In Use
A0h	Directory Not Empty

Request Packet (max = 261 bytes):

Offset	Description	Type	Order
0	Request Buffer Length-2	WORD	lo-hi
2	0Bh	BYTE	
3	Directory Handle	BYTE	
4	Unused	BYTE	
5	Directory Path Length	BYTE (0-255)	
6	Directory Path	BYTE[*LENGTH*]	

Reply Packet (2 bytes):

Offset	Description	Type	Order
0	0000	WORD	hi-lo

After a directory has been deleted, directory handles that point to that directory are no longer valid. Drives mapped to deleted directories must be remapped.

The NetWare C Interface format is:

```
int DeleteDirectory( BYTE directoryHandle, char *directoryPath );
```

Get Current Directory (47h)

This DOS 2.x call returns a string containing the current directory, given the drive number.

Registers in:

AH 47h
DS:SI Address of Directory String (char *)
DL Drive Number

Registers out:

AL Completion Code

Completion Codes:

0 Success

The NetWare C Interface format is:

```
int GetCurrentDirectory( BYTE driveNumber, char *directory );
```

Get Directory Path (E2h 01h)

This call is supported in NetWare versions 4.0 and 4.6, in Advanced NetWare versions 1.0, 1.02, 2.0, and 2.1, and in NetWare 386 and later versions. It returns the full directory path given a directory handle.

Registers in:

AH	E2h
DS:SI	Request Buffer Address
ES:DI	Reply Buffer Address

Registers out:

AL	Completion Code

Completion Codes:

0	Success
9Bh	Bad Directory Handle

Request Packet (4 bytes):

Offset	**Description**	**Type**	**Order**
0	Request Buffer Length-2	WORD	lo-hi
2	1	BYTE	
3	Directory Handle	BYTE	

Reply Packet (max = 258 bytes):

Offset	**Description**	**Type**	**Order**
0	Reply Buffer Length - 2	WORD	hi-lo
2	Directory Path Length	BYTE (1-255)	
3	Directory Path	BYTE[*LENGTH*]	

The NetWare C Interface format is:

```
int GetDirectoryPath( BYTE directoryHandle, char *directoryPath );
```

Rename Directory (E2h 0Fh)

This call is supported in NetWare versions 4.0 and 4.6, in Advanced NetWare versions 1.0, 1.02, 2.0, and 2.1, and in NetWare 386 and later versions. It allows the developer to change the name of a directory, given the directory handle/path specification and the new name of the directory.

Registers in:

AH	E2h
DS:SI	Request Buffer Address
ES:DI	Reply Buffer Address

Registers out:

AL	Completion Code

Completion Codes:

0	Success
8Bh	No Rename Privileges
9Bh	Bad Directory Handle
9Ch	Invalid Path
9Eh	Invalid File Name

Request Packet (max = 275 bytes):

Offset	Description	Type	Order
0	Request Buffer Length-2	WORD	lo-hi
2	0Fh	BYTE	
3	Directory Handle	BYTE	
4	Directory Path Length	BYTE (0-255)	
5	Directory Path	BYTE[*LENGTH*]	
?	New Directory Name Len	BYTE (1-14)	
?	New Directory Name	BYTE[*LENGTH*]	

Reply Packet (2 bytes):

Offset	Description	Type	Order
0	0000	WORD	hi-lo

New Directory Name here is a regular DOS file or directory name (up to an 8-character name and 3-character extension, separated by a period). The Directory Name cannot include the following characters: *, ?, :, \, /. Directory names longer than 14 characters get truncated.

The user logged in must have parental and modify rights in the directory's parent directory to issue a Rename Directory call. The standard directories (such as MAIL, SYSTEM, PUBLIC, LOGIN) cannot be renamed.

The NetWare C Interface format is:

```
int RenameDirectory( BYTE directoryHandle, char *directoryPath,
    char *newDirectoryName );
```

Scan Directory Information (E2h 02h)

This call is supported in NetWare versions 4.0 and 4.6, in Advanced NetWare versions 1.0, 1.02, 2.0, and 2.1, and in NetWare 386 and later versions. It returns information about a directory (or its subdirectories), including the creation date and time, the owner (creator) identification of the directory, and the Maximum Rights Mask.

Registers in:

AH	E2h
DS:SI	Request Buffer Address
ES:DI	Reply Buffer Address

Registers out:

AL	Completion Code

Completion Codes:

0	Success
98h	Volume Does Not Exist
9Bh	Bad Directory Handle
9Ch	Invalid Path

Request Packet (max = 262 bytes):

Offset	**Description**	**Type**	**Order**
0	Request Buffer Length-2	WORD	lo-hi
2	2	BYTE	
3	Directory Handle	BYTE	
4	Subdirectory Number	WORD	hi-lo
6	Directory Path Length	BYTE (0-255)	
7	Directory Path	BYTE[*LENGTH*]	

Reply Packet (29 bytes):

Offset	**Description**	**Type**	**Order**
0	Reply Buffer Length - 2	WORD	lo-hi
2	Subdirectory Name	BYTE[16]	
18	Creation Date And Time	BYTE[4]	
22	Owner Object ID	LONG	hi-lo
26	Maximum Rights Mask	BYTE	
27	Unused	BYTE	
28	Subdirectory Number	WORD	hi-lo

Subdirectory Number should be 0 for the first call. If the developer wishes to retrieve information about subdirectories of the target directory, the Subdirectory Number should be taken from the reply packet and placed in this field with 1 added to it. This call can be reiterated until all subdirectories have been retrieved (the completion code will be 9Ch).

Subdirectory Name is a regular DOS file/directory name (up to an eight-character name and three-character extension, separated by a period).

Creation Date and *Time* are in four-byte format.

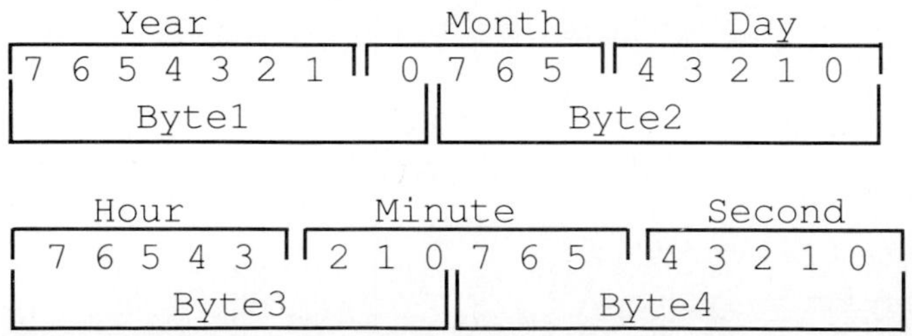

Owner Object ID is the Bindery object identification of the user that created the directory.

The NetWare C Interface format is:

```
int ScanDirectoryInformation( BYTE directoryHandle,
   char *searchDirectoryPath, int *sequenceNumber,
   char *directoryName, BYTE *creationDateAndTime,
   long *ownerObjectID, BYTE *maximumRightsMask );
```

Set Directory Information (E2h 19h)

This call is supported in Advanced NetWare versions 1.0, 1.02, 2.0, and 2.1, and in NetWare versions 386 and later. It allows the developer to change information about a directory, including the creation date and time, the owner identification, and the Maximum Rights Mask.

Registers in:

AH	E2h
DS:SI	Request Buffer Address
ES:DI	Reply Buffer Address

Registers out:

AL	Completion Code

Completion Codes:

0	Success
9Bh	Bad Directory Handle
9Ch	Invalid Path

Request Packet (max = 269 bytes):

Offset	Description	Type	Order
0	Request Buffer Length-2	WORD	lo-hi
2	19h	BYTE	
3	Directory Handle	BYTE	
4	Creation Date And Time	LONG	hi-lo
8	Owner Object ID	LONG	hi-lo
12	Maximum Rights Mask	BYTE	
13	Directory Path Length	BYTE (0-255)	
14	Directory Path	BYTE[*LENGTH*]	

Reply Packet (2 bytes):

Offset	Description	Type	Order
0	0000	WORD	lo-hi

The NetWare C Interface format is:

```
int SetDirectoryInformation( BYTE directoryHandle,
    char *directoryPath, BYTE *newCreationDateAndTime,
    long newOwnerObjectID, BYTE newMaximumRightsMask );
```

Trustees and rights management

NetWare administers its file-based security by limiting the operations that may be performed on each directory (in NetWare 286). To provide flexibility, there are two ways users are given file privileges: in a directory's Maximum Rights Mask and in a user's trustee assignments. See appendix C for differences in trustee-rights management between NetWare 286 and 386.

Maximum Rights Mask

This "mask" is a byte containing bit fields specifying privileges. The bit assignments, first explained under the Restore Directory Handle call in this chapter, are repeated here for convenience:

0x01	Read	- may read files
0x02	Write	- may write to files
0x04	Open	- may open files
0x08	Create	- may create files
0x10	Delete	- may delete files
0x20	Parental	- may create or delete subdirectories and trustee rights can be granted or revoked
0x40	Search	- may search directory
0x80	Modify	- may change file attributes

Programmers may AND the mask value with individual bit values to determine what rights are available. The Maximum Rights mask determines the absolute maximum privileges that anyone could have in this directory area. If someone had trustee rights that gave them all rights to the area, but the directory's Maximum Rights Mask was "Read, Open, and Search," then that would be all the user could do (except for the Supervisor or Supervisor equivalent users, who have all rights to everything).

Trustee Rights Mask

This mask is usually created through SYSCON, when the user identification is created. It is entered in the TRUSTEE ASSIGNMENTS section and the system manager enters the full path names (VOLUME:DIRECTORY) of the directories involved and the rights to be administered.

A user's effective rights, those that are in effect for a particular directory, are determined by ANDing the Maximum Rights Mask and the Trustee Rights Mask — only if both bits are present in a particular field is the user granted that particular right. Rights are also based on group membership and security equivalence.

Six calls manipulate trustee assignments. With them, the developer can add or delete trustees (users) to a directory, modify the Maximum Rights Mask for a directory, and retrieve trustee paths for a user or user trustee rights for a directory.

To any developer dealing with file-level security, these calls become important in determining and modifying the security levels in place for certain directories on the file server. Rather than waiting for a read or write call to bomb and acting on error codes, programmers have the opportunity to check what the user's directory rights are before any I/O call is made. This makes the application much more sensitive to network security and allows it to exploit the advantages of network-based security rather than simply being a slave to it.

Add Trustee To Directory (E2h 0Dh)

This call is supported in NetWare versions 4.0 and 4.6, in Advanced NetWare versions 1.0, 1.02, 2.0, and 2.1, and in NetWare 386 and later versions. It allows the programmer to add a trustee to a directory's trustee list, specifying the Bindery object ID of the trustee, the trustee's rights mask for the directory, and the directory handle-path specification identifying the directory.

Registers in:

AH	E2h
DS:SI	Request Buffer Address
ES:DI	Reply Buffer Address

Registers out:

AL	Completion Code

Completion Codes:

0	Success
8Ch	No Modify Privileges
FCh	No Such Bindery Object

Request Packet (max = 265 bytes):

Offset	**Description**	**Type**	**Order**
0	Request Buffer Length-2	WORD	lo-hi
2	0Dh	BYTE	
3	Directory Handle	BYTE	
4	Trustee Object ID	LONG	hi-lo
8	Trustee Rights Mask	BYTE	
9	Directory Path Length	BYTE (0-255)	
10	Directory Path	BYTE[*LENGTH*]	

Reply Packet (2 bytes):

Offset	**Description**	**Type**	**Order**
0	0000	WORD	lo-hi

Trustee Object ID is the Bindery object identification of the trustee that will be placed in the directory's trustee list with the rights specified in Trustee Rights Mask. Since this field is required, a user must be associated with a Bindery object to be added to the trustee list.

If the user specified in the Bindery object identification already has trustee rights to this directory, they will be replaced by the most current Trustee Rights Mask. A user must have parental rights to the target (or its parent) directory in order to make this call.

The NetWare C Interface format is:

```
int AddTrusteeToDirectory( BYTE directoryHandle,
        char *directoryPath, long trusteeObjectID,
        BYTE trusteeRightsMask );
```

Delete Trustee From Directory (E2h 0Eh)

This call is supported in NetWare versions 4.0 and 4.6, in Advanced NetWare versions 1.0, 1.02, 2.0, and 2.1, and in NetWare 386 and later versions. It removes a trustee from a particular directory's trustee list.

Registers in:

AH	E2h
DS:SI	Request Buffer Address
ES:DI	Reply Buffer Address

Registers out:

AL	Completion Code

Completion Codes:

0	Success
98h	Volume Does Not Exist
9Bh	Bad Directory Handle
9Ch	Invalid Path

Request Packet (max = 265 bytes):

Offset	**Description**	**Type**	**Order**
0	Request Buffer Length-2	WORD	lo-hi
2	0Eh	BYTE	
3	Directory Handle	BYTE	
4	Trustee Object ID	LONG	hi-lo
8	Unused	BYTE	
9	Directory Path Length	BYTE (0-255)	
10	Directory Path	BYTE[*LENGTH*]	

Reply Packet (2 bytes):

Offset	Description	Type	Order
0	0000	WORD	lo-hi

All of the rights granted to the user for this directory (in the previous call) are revoked by this call. A user must have parental rights to the target (or its parent) directory to make this call.

The NetWare C Interface format is:

```
int DeleteTrusteeFromDirectory( BYTE directoryHandle,
   char *directoryPath, long trusteeObjectID );
```

Get Effective Directory Rights (E2h 03H)

This call is supported in NetWare versions 4.0 and 4.6, in Advanced NetWare versions 1.0, 1.02, 2.0, and 2.1, and in NetWare 386 and later versions. It returns the user's effective rights to a specified directory.

Registers in:

AH	E2h
DS:SI	Request Buffer Address
ES:DI	Reply Buffer Address

Registers out:

AL	Completion Code

Completion Codes:

0	Success
98h	Volume Does Not Exist
9Bh	Bad Directory Handle

Request Packet (max = 260 bytes):

Offset	Description	Type	Order
0	Request Buffer Length-2	WORD	lo-hi
2	3h	BYTE	
3	Directory Handle	BYTE	
4	Directory Path Length	BYTE (0-255)	
5	Directory Path	BYTE[*LENGTH*]	

Reply Packet (3 bytes):

Offset	Description	Type	Order
0	Reply Buffer Length - 2	WORD	lo-hi
2	Effective Rights Mask	BYTE	

The NetWare C Interface format is:

```
int GetEffectiveDirectoryRights( BYTE directoryHandle,
   char *directoryPath, BYTE *effectiveRightsMask );
```

Modify Maximum Rights Mask (E2h 04h)

This call is supported in NetWare versions 4.0 and 4.6, in Advanced NetWare versions 1.0, 1.02, 2.0, and 2.1, and in NetWare 386 and later versions. It changes the maximum rights from one mask to another for a specified directory.

Registers in:

AH	E2h
DS:SI	Request Buffer Address
ES:DI	Reply Buffer Address

Registers out:

AL	Completion Code

Completion Codes:

0	Success
8Ch	No Modify Privileges
98h	Volume Does Not Exist
9Ch	Invalid Path

Request Packet (max = 262 bytes):

Offset	Description	Type	Order
0	Request Buffer Length-2	WORD	lo-hi
2	4h	BYTE	
3	Directory Handle	BYTE	
4	Grant Rights Mask	BYTE	
5	Revoke Rights Mask	BYTE	
6	Directory Path Length	BYTE (0-255)	
7	Directory Path	BYTE[*LENGTH*]	

Reply Packet (3 bytes):

Offset	Description	Type	Order
0	Reply Buffer Length - 2	WORD	lo-hi
2	Effective Rights Mask	BYTE	

Grant Rights Mask contains the rights to be granted to the directory's Maximum Rights Mask.

Revoke Rights Mask contains the rights to be removed from the directory's Maximum Rights Mask. To clear the rights and start over, the Revoke Rights Mask can be set to FFh (revoking all) and the Grant Rights Mask can be set to grant those rights desired.

The NetWare C Interface format is:

```
int ModifyMaximumRightsMask( BYTE directoryHandle,
 char *directoryPath, BYTE revokeRightsMask, BYTE grantRightsMask );
```

Scan Bindery Object Trustee Paths (E3h 47h)

This call is supported in Advanced NetWare versions 1.0, 1.02, 2.0, and 2.1, and in NetWare versions 386 and later. This call and the next deal with finding out about the trustees for a specific directory. In this call, all of the trustee rights are returned for a particular user/object ID. The next call does the opposite, returning the trustee users given a particular directory.

Registers in:

AH	E3h
DS:SI	Request Buffer Address
ES:DI	Reply Buffer Address

Registers out:

AL	Completion Code

Completion Codes:

0	Success
96h	Server Out Of Memory
F0h	Wildcard Not Allowed
F1h	Invalid Bindery Security
FCh	No Such Object
FEh	Server Bindery Locked
FFh	Bindery Failure

Request Packet (10 bytes):

Offset	**Description**	**Type**	**Order**
0	Request Buffer Length-2	WORD	lo-hi
2	47h	BYTE	
3	Volume Number	BYTE (0-31)	
4	Last Sequence Number	WORD	hi-lo
6	Object ID	LONG	hi-lo

Reply Packet (max = 265 bytes):

Offset	**Description**	**Type**	**Order**
0	Reply Buffer Length - 2	WORD	lo-hi
2	Next Sequence Number	WORD	hi-lo
4	Object ID	LONG	hi-lo
8	Trustee Access Mask	BYTE	
9	Trustee Path Length	BYTE	
10	Trustee Path	BYTE[*LENGTH*]	

Volume Number here is an index into the Volume Table (0-31).

Last Sequence Number is the field used to reiterate this call to find all the trustees for a particular user/object ID. On the first call, initialize this field to 0; for subsequent calls, place the Next Sequence Number value returned in it.

Trustee Path is the path of the directory for which the Trustee Access Mask applies to the Object identification.

To make this call, the user must be either the supervisor or supervisor equivalent, or logged in as the target object.

The NetWare C Interface format is:

```
int ScanBinderyObjectTrusteePaths( long objectID, BYTE volumeNumber,
    int *sequenceNumber, char *trusteeAccessMask, char *trusteePathName );
```

Scan Directory For Trustees (E2h 0Ch)

This call is supported in Advanced NetWare versions 1.0, 1.02, 2.0, and 2.1, and in NetWare versions 386 and later. It performs the inverse of the previous call, providing the trustees for a particular directory.

Registers in:

AH	E3h
DS:SI	Request Buffer Address
ES:DI	Reply Buffer Address

Registers out:

AL	Completion Code

Completion Codes:

0	Success
9Ch	No More Trustees

Request Packet (max = 261 bytes):

Offset	**Description**	**Type**	**Order**
0	Request Buffer Length-2	WORD	lo-hi
2	0Ch	BYTE	
3	Directory Handle	BYTE	
4	Sequence Number	BYTE	
5	Directory Path Length	BYTE (0-255)	
6	Directory Path	BYTE[*LENGTH*]	

Reply Packet (39 bytes):

Offset	Description	Type	Order
0	Reply Buffer Length - 2	WORD	lo-hi
2	Directory Name	BYTE[16]	
18	Creation Date And Time	LONG	hi-lo
22	Owner Object ID	WORD	hi-lo
26	Trustee Object ID 0	WORD	hi-lo
30	Trustee Object ID 1	WORD	hi-lo
34	Trustee Object ID 2	WORD	hi-lo
38	Trustee Object ID 3	WORD	hi-lo
42	Trustee Object ID 4	WORD	hi-lo
46	Trustee Rights Mask 0	BYTE	
47	Trustee Rights Mask 1	BYTE	
48	Trustee Rights Mask 2	BYTE	
49	Trustee Rights Mask 3	BYTE	
50	Trustee Rights Mask 4	BYTE	

Sequence Number is used to reiterate this call to find out all of the trustees for a particular directory. Although a directory may have any number of trustees, only five are stored at one time. So on the first call, initialize this field to 0. For subsequent calls, increment this value by 1 and make the call again until the completion code is 9C — No More Trustees.

Trustee Object IDs 0-4 are the Bindery object IDs for the Trustee Rights Masks (0-4). Trustee Object ID 0 corresponds to Trustee Rights Mask 0. A 0 in this field indicates there are no more trustees for this directory.

Trustee Rights Masks 0-4 contain the rights particular users may enjoy in this directory if the Maximum Rights Mask concurs.

The NetWare C Interface format is:

```
int ScanDirectoryForTrustees( BYTE directoryHandle,
    char *directoryPath, int *sequenceNumber,
    char *directoryName, BYTE *creationDateAndTime,
    long *ownerID, long *trusteeIDs, BYTE *trusteeRights );
```

Code sample: GetRites.C

Directory services provide the mechanism for directory-level security in the form of trustee rights. GetRites takes as an argument a drive letter (which points to the directory) the user wishes to get his rights to. If no drive is specified, the default drive is used. This program is in many ways, equivalent to the NetWare Rights program, and it illustrates how the rights to a directory may be retrieved.

The program begins by defining the prototypes for the local functions. Next, main() starts, clearing the directory string and checking for bad command line syntax.

The next step places the target drive in the drive variable, either by using the drive specified in the command line or, if none was specified, retrieving the current drive.

GetDirectoryHandle() is called to get the handle of the current directory which is passed to GetDirectoryPath() which returns the VOLUME:PATH combination for that directory handle. Finally, the rights are retrieved by passing the handle to GetEffectiveDirectoryRights().

Other than making the NetWare calls, the only other task was to display the rights to the user in ShowRights(). A flag variable was setup in ShowRights() corresponding to each right and a bitwise AND (&&) was used to test the mask with each bit value, setting the flag if the bit was set. These flags are printed to the screen, as in the Novell rights command "[RWOCDPSM]" and then each flag is tested again for printing full descriptions of each right that is available.

Note that in some cases such as GetDirectoryHandle() there were no request or reply packets used, so we only manipulated the register variables. Also, GetEffectiveDirectoryRights() uses a C structure for the request packet, since it is a fixed length and is more legible, but uses a 3-byte string for Reply since it is so small.

A C structure could have been used for the reply, but I chose to use the string, since I could easily initialize the length in the declaration of Reply and the declaration only took one line, whereas it would have taken several for a structure. The developer is faced with whether to use a structure or a block (or some other means) for the holding and managing packets and although several ways will work, the programmer must choose which is the best.

```
/*                                                                          */
/* GetRites - Queries the file server for the current user's effective      */
/*              rights to either the current or a specified directory       */
/*                                                                          */
/* by Charles Rose                                                          */
/*                                                                          */

#include <stdio.h>
#include <dos.h>
#include <dir.h>
#include <string.h>

typedef unsigned char BYTE;
typedef unsigned int WORD;
typedef unsigned long LONG;


BYTE GetDirectoryHandle( WORD driveNumber );
int GetEffectiveDirectoryRights( BYTE handle, char *directory, BYTE *mask );
void ShowRights( BYTE mask );
int GetDirectoryPath( BYTE directoryHandle, char *directoryPath );

main( int argc, char *argv[] )
{
        int drive, handle, mask, result;
        char directory[255];

        memset( directory, NULL, 255 );

        if ( argc > 3 )
        {
```

```
            printf( "Usage: GETRITES drive\n" );
            printf( "Shows the user's effective rights to the directory on
                    'drive'.\n" );
            exit(1);
        }

        if ( argc == 2 )
            drive = toupper( *argv[1] ) - 'A';
        else
            drive = getdisk();

        handle = GetDirectoryHandle( drive );
        result = GetDirectoryPath( handle, directory );
        if ( result )
        {
            printf( "Error in Get Directory Path, completion code = %X\n",
                    result );
            exit(1);
        }

        result = GetEffectiveDirectoryRights( handle, NULL, &mask );
        if ( result )
        {
            printf( "Error in Get Effective Directory Rights,
                    completion code = %X\n", result );
            exit(1);
        }
        else
        {
            printf( "Rights for drive %c: directory %s are:\n", 'A' + drive,
                    directory );
            ShowRights( mask );
            printf( "\n" );
        }
}

BYTE GetDirectoryHandle( WORD driveNumber )
{
        _AH = 0xE9;
        _AL = 0;
        _DX = driveNumber;

        geninterrupt( 0x21 );

        return _AL;
}

int GetEffectiveDirectoryRights( BYTE handle, char *directory, BYTE *mask )
{
        struct getRitesReq {
                WORD    Length;
                BYTE    Function;
                BYTE    DirHandle;
                BYTE    DirPathLength;
                BYTE    DirPath[255];
        } Request;

        BYTE Reply[3] = { 2, 0, 0 }, retval;

        Request.Length = sizeof( struct getRitesReq ) - 2;
```

```
        Request.Function = 3;
        Request.DirHandle = handle;
        Request.DirPathLength = strlen( directory );

        strcpy( Request.DirPath, directory );

        _AH = 0xE2;
        _SI = (unsigned)&Request;
        _DI = (unsigned)Reply;
        _ES = _DS;

        geninterrupt( 0x21 );

        retval = _AL;

        *mask = Reply[2];

        return retval;
}

void ShowRights( BYTE mask )
{
        BYTE r=0, w=0, o=0, c=0, d=0, p=0, s=0, m=0;

        printf( "  Your effective rights are: [" );
        if ( mask & 0x01 ) r++; printf( "%c", r ? 'R' : ' ' );
        if ( mask & 0x02 ) w++; printf( "%c", w ? 'W' : ' ' );
        if ( mask & 0x04 ) o++; printf( "%c", o ? 'O' : ' ' );
        if ( mask & 0x08 ) c++; printf( "%c", c ? 'C' : ' ' );
        if ( mask & 0x10 ) d++; printf( "%c", d ? 'D' : ' ' );
        if ( mask & 0x20 ) p++; printf( "%c", p ? 'P' : ' ' );
        if ( mask & 0x40 ) s++; printf( "%c", s ? 'S' : ' ' );
        if ( mask & 0x80 ) m++; printf( "%c", m ? 'M' : ' ' );
        printf( "]\n" );

        if ( r )
                printf( " You may READ from this directory.\n" );

        if ( w )
                printf( " You may WRITE to this directory.\n" );

        if ( o )
                printf( " You may OPEN files in this directory.\n" );

        if ( c )
                printf( " You may CREATE files in this directory.\n" );

        if ( d )
                printf( " You may DELETE files from this directory.\n" );

        if ( p )
        {
                printf( " You may CREATE AND DELETE SUBDIRECTORIES in this
                        directory,\n" );
                printf( "     and you may GRANT OR REVOKE TRUSTEE RIGHTS in this
                        directory.\n" );
        }

        if ( s )
                printf( " You may SEARCH this directory.\n" );
```

```
        if ( m )
                printf( " You may MODIFY FILE ATTRIBUTES in this directory. \n"
);
}

int GetDirectoryPath( BYTE directoryHandle, char *directoryPath )
{
        BYTE request[4] = { 2, 0, 1, 0 }, reply[258], retval;

        request[3] = directoryHandle;
        *((WORD *)reply) = 256;

        _AH = 0xE2;
        _SI = (unsigned)request;
        _DI = (unsigned)reply;
        _ES = _DS;

        geninterrupt( 0x21 );

        if ( !(retval = _AL) )
                movmem( &reply[3], directoryPath, reply[2] );

        return retval;
}
```

Exercises

1. Run VolStat. Note how GetVolumeInformation() is called and how the information is displayed. Examine the reply packet after being returned from the file server; notice the conversions with WordSwitch() before displaying to the screen.

2. Run FileInfo with various command-line parameters. Extend the program by distinguishing between the user specifying a drive letter and a volume name. For instance, if the user passed G:DATA*.* as the path, the program would now assume that G is a volume name. A test could be run to see if G were a valid volume and if not, treat G: as a drive.

3. Allow the user of FileInfo to input different command-line arguments, for example, /Vvolume name and /Ddriveletter to specify volumes or drives (or eventually /Sserver name).

4. Try MapIt. Use temporary drives instead of permanent ones and see the result.

5. Execute GetRites. Notice how the different request/reply packets are formed. Try different ways of representing the structures. Contrast the benefits and costs of using the structure method vs. the block method.

5 TTS

NetWare's Transaction Tracking System, or TTS, first appeared in SFT Level II NetWare; it has since been incorporated in System Fault Tolerant NetWare 286 and in NetWare 386.

With the TTS, programs can treat groups of writes as transactions, tracking exactly what was written to disk, and keeping a copy of what was originally on the disk until all of the data has been written. If for some reason the file server crashes or some other problem befalls the system, the transaction can be backed out, i.e., the old data can be written back to the disk and preserved.

The TTS is a subject, and source, of much confusion, despite its simplicity. There are only nine calls, and they involve, at the most, only a few registers and no request or reply packets. But its intimate ties to record locking can deal programmers some nasty surprises.

If, for example, an application uses semaphores for data synchronization, transactions will not be tracked correctly. Only record locks imposed with physical or logical NetWare record locking calls, or with DOS function 5Ch, Control Record Access (see Chapter 2), correctly signal NetWare when implicit transactions begin and end.

So in this chapter we'll try to help programmers avoid those pitfalls by going into some detail on the concepts behind as well as the operation of the TTS. We'll discuss transaction backouts and how the file server enables and disables the TTS. We'll also provide some installation tips, discuss the user's perspective of the TTS, and document the calls. And we'll provide a sample program to test the TTS mechanism and show the developer how to make the calls.

How does the TTS work?

A file server begins processing a transaction when a software application running on a workstation either locks a record or makes the TTS Begin Transaction call. Then the workstation writes the data to the file server. When this happens, the data that is to be written is stored in the file server's cache memory. The server then examines the target file on disk, locates the place to write, and reads the old data into cache memory, along with the name and directory of the target file and the length and offset of the target record. The target file is still unaffected at this point.

The old data (record) from the target file is next written to the Transaction Work File on the Transaction Work Volume (specified in NetGen). Finally the new data is written from cache memory to the target file. It is now that the physical record is amended.

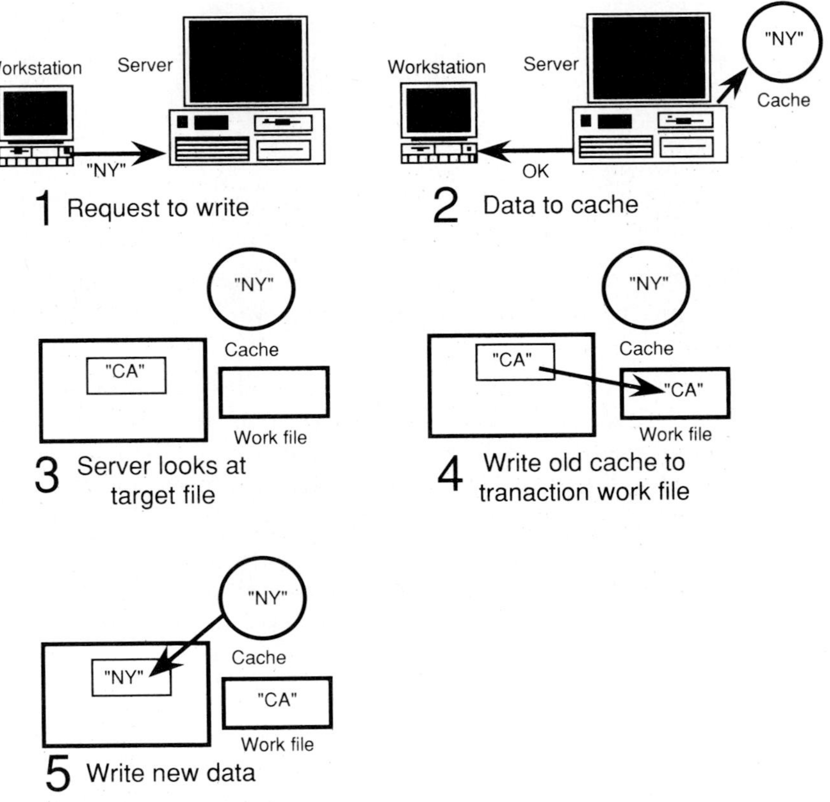

Figure 6: The five steps of the typical TTS transaction.

Record locking and implicit and explicit tracking

Transactions can be tracked two ways. Implicit transaction tracking is for programs that weren't written for the TTS, but are still supported. Explicit tracking is for developers who write directly to the TTS API. In either type, record locking and the TTS are inextricably tied together.

Implicit transaction tracking occurs when the data files of a program are flagged transactional by the user (FLAG filename /TRANSACTIONAL) and the program uses record locks (either physical or logical) to synchronize input and output. A transaction begins when a certain number of locks (user- or program-set lock threshold) is imposed; it ends when the number of concurrent locks falls below that number. Any data written to any file during this period is part of the transaction.

Because an implicit transaction is based on the first lock to be placed and the last lock to be released, programmers must be careful not to unlock a record too early. If in unlocking a record before locking another record the programmer unlocks the last locked record, the transaction ends and another begins.

This causes an undue fragmentation of transactions. Fragmentation can be avoided by keeping all locks in effect until the entire transaction is complete. That approach, however, sacrifices resolution in tracking as well as network resources, and it runs the risk of generating transactions too large to be stored on the work volume.

These risks are not run in explicit tracking. Explicit tracking allows developers to make specific calls to NetWare to begin and end transactions. Much more flexibility is given to the developer, along with the ability to abort a transaction should the program require, and to monitor the status of the transaction to make sure it was written to disk.

Explicit tracking is not without risk, however, and again it is because of the intimacy of locking and tracking. Implicitly, when a program locks, a transaction is produced. Explicitly, when a transaction is started, a lock is produced.

In either case, the TTS physically locks all records that become part of a transaction, locks all files that are written to during the transaction, and the locks stay in effect until the end of the transaction. This protects the files that are a part of the transaction but can cause problems if you need to unlock one of those records before the transaction is over.

If you do that, the file server will dutifully return a successful (00) completion code, but it will not actually unlock the file until the transaction is over, until the data has been written.

Programmers must also remain aware that when files are logically locked and become part of a transaction they are also physically locked. In explicit tracking the most common result of failure to be aware of these timing considerations is a fatal embrace.

In this embrace, two stations may have "unlocked" their records but have not ended their transactions. Each then tries to lock the file the other station thinks it has unlocked while the file server still holds the file locked. This can be avoided by always locking record sets rather than individual records, and by careful coordination among stations when single-record locks must be used.

Fatal embrace may be the most dramatic pitfall for programmers working with the TTS, but it is not the only one. To avoid the subtler ones, the programmer must understand not only why backouts occur but also how users and system managers may intervene.

Transaction backouts

Many transaction backouts arise from file server or workstation hardware or operator failures. However, software-related backouts also occur. Here are the ways a backout may be initiated.

If in five minutes a file server does not receive a packet from a workstation it "knows" is attached (is in its Connection ID table), the server sends a "watchdog" packet to the workstation. If the workstation doesn't respond, the server keeps sending watchdog packets for 15 minutes, then clears the connection if no response is given.

Backout also occurs if an application terminates and leaves records locked. This means that a backout occurs any time a transaction is interrupted, be it by the user pressing CTRL-BREAK or by the program itself terminating. If a DOWN or CLEAR STATION command is given at the file server during a transaction, a backout is performed.

If a workstation operator, during a transaction, reboots, reloads the shell and attaches to the same server, the server will perform a transaction backout. If the station attached to a different server after rebooting, the watchdog process would detect its absence and backout the transaction.

When a transaction is backed out, the user may not know exactly what data was backed out. The file server may read

```
"Transaction being backed out for station X"
```

listing the number, X, of the workstation for which the transaction was backed out. Or, if the file server went down during the transaction, when the server comes back up, it will read something similar to:

```
"Transactions need to be backed out.
Type a character to start the backout."
```

If the problem was server related, it may take several seconds once the server is brought back up to backout the transactions fully.

After a backout, the user should always check to see if the last record entered is all there. The user should be sensitive to the possibility of a partial update and make sure either the entire record is there or none of it exists. (This won't be the case for applications that perform transaction tracking correctly.)

If a station freezes, the user (or supervisor) may clear the station manually by typing "CLEAR CONNECTION" at the file server, assuring a backout without waiting 15 minutes for the watchdog.

The programmer, on the other hand, would use the TTS Transaction Status call. This call always lets the application (and the user) know whether a transaction made it onto the disk or not.

File server enabling and disabling of TTS

A file server with TTS responds to the console commands "DISABLE TRANSACTIONS" and "ENABLE TRANSACTIONS." It should be noted that even while transactions are disabled, the TTS Begin Transaction and TTS End

Transaction calls still work, marking the beginnings and ends of discrete transactions and locking the records associated with them. Also, the TTS Transaction Status still functions, returning the correct status. All that is different when transactions are disabled at the console is that they cannot be backed out in case of system failure.

Note also that whether a transaction can or cannot be backed out depends on the status of the file server when the transaction began. If transactions were enabled when that transaction began, it can be backed out even if transactions are suddenly disabled at the file server. The converse is also true: If transactions are disabled at the console when a transaction begins, then enabled while the transaction is in progress, the transaction cannot be backed out.

Install TTS carefully

Programmers will have fewer problems with TTS if they take care at installation to get the system running smoothly. Here's what to watch for. When installing NetWare with NetGen, the user may specify the volume of the transaction work files, and the number of transactions the file server should monitor at one time. The volume chosen should have sufficient space to house the transaction data. If the volume for the work files is on a different disk channel than the volume for the data files, then the data and the transaction data can be written simultaneously.

The number of transactions to be monitored can be set at anywhere from 50 to 200. The server can only monitor one transaction for each DOS task, however, and if the server receives several transaction requests at about the same time, it will queue and service them one-by-one.

Transaction length

Although a transaction can be of any length, it is important to be aware of the space limitations of the work volume. Locks should as brief as possible; so should transactions. Keep in mind that writing takes at least twice as long with TTS enabled.

Other operations can take up more transaction workspace than is obvious. For example, if a file is truncated from 20 megabytes to 5 megabytes, a 15-megabyte work file is required for the operation.

Should the file server run out of space on the work volume, the following message is generated:

```
"Transaction Tracking disabled because the volume is full."
```

If this happens, processing can continue, but transaction tracking is disabled and the same rules hold as when it is disabled manually. At this point, the supervisor should free up space on the file server. The supervisor must manually enable TTS at the file server with the "ENABLE TRANSACTIONS" command.

Disk cache buffer

System thrashing can occur if the file server has an insufficient number of cache buffers. TTS uses more buffers than are normally required, so the system should have at least 8K of disk cache buffers per station.

Flagging transactional files

Tracking will only work on those files that have had their transactional flag set. This can be set through the FLAG command, by using the /TRANSACTIONAL parameter, for example: "FLAG *.db /TRANSACTIONAL". The transactional bit (10h) can also be set programmatically, by using the Set Extended File Attributes call. A file marked transactional cannot be deleted or renamed. It must be FLAGGed back to normal and then deleted or renamed (and reFLAGGed). Programmers should beware of backup programs that restore network files without restoring their original extended attributes.

Multiple file servers

Although transactions can span multiple file servers, Novell recommends against it because servers don't synchronize the transactions. If span you must, you need to make separate calls to each server to begin and end the transaction. If one server goes down during the transaction and the other does not, the user must do all the programming to test what was finished and what was not, what gets backed out and what does not.

NetWare system files

NetWare uses transaction tracking on all writes to the Bindery and Queue Management Files.

TTS calls to a nonTTS server

NetWare will return successful completion codes for TTS calls made to a non-TTS server. This feature allows programs to be TTS-aware, and not have separate versions for TTS servers and nonTTS servers. These calls will even work in non-NetWare environments, such as exclusively MS-DOS. If the Shell is not loaded, DOS returns 0 in AL for the explicit calls, and the carry flag is not affected.

Compressing files

Novell suggests that if a file is to be compressed that it not be done as a transaction. The file to be compressed should be flagged non-transactional, compressed, and reflagged back to transactional.

Helping users along

TTS demands cooperation between programmers and users. Programmers, for example, should make users aware when they have to flag files as transactional (if this is not done programmatically). For example, since the transactional bit is part of a file's extended attributes and most backup software does not record those attributes, if the file is restored, the transactional bit will be cleared and must be reset.

TTS utilities

The system manager should also be familiar with SetTTS, a utility provided with TTS that allows the supervisor to set the workstation thresholds for applications that use implicit transaction tracking. Note though that programmers can make the same calls as SetTTS in their own programs.

Calls in the Transaction Tracking Services API

The following calls are supported in SFT Level II NetWare, System Fault Tolerant NetWare 286 and NetWare 386. Throughout the book, we explain fields within the calls only at the first mention of each field in each chapter. Appendix B contains a comprehensive, alphabetical listing of the fields for quick reference.

TTS Is Available (C7h 02h)

This call queries the default file server to see if it supports transaction tracking.

Registers in:

AH	C7h
AL	2

Registers out:

AL	Completion Code (carry flag is unaffected)

Completion Codes:

00h	Transaction Tracking Not Available
01h	Transaction Tracking Available
FDh	Transaction Tracking Disabled

The NetWare C Interface format is:

```
int TTSIsAvailable( void );
```

TTS Begin Transaction (C7h 00h)

This call begins an explicit transaction.

Registers in:

AH	C7h
AL	0

Registers out:

AL	Completion Code

Completion Codes:

Carry flag cleared:

00h	Successful

Carry flag set:

96h	Out of Dynamic Workspace
FEh	Implicit Transaction Already Active (active implicit transaction now converted to an explicit transaction)
FFh	Explicit Transaction Already Active (existing explicit transaction continues normally)

The NetWare C Interface format is:

```
int TTSBeginTransaction( void );
```

TTS End Transaction (C7h 01h)

This call ends an explicit (or implicit) transaction and returns, providing the programmer with a transaction reference number. This number can be used with TTS Transaction Status to determine the state of the transaction.

Registers in:

AH	C7h
AL	1

Registers out:

AL	Completion Code

Completion Codes:

Carry flag cleared:

00h	Successful
FDh	Transaction Tracking Disabled
FEh	Transaction Ended Records Locked

Carry flag set:

FFh	No Explicit Transaction Was Active

It is important to note that the transaction is not necessarily finished and written to disk when this call returns. For that, the programmer needs to call TTS Transaction Status to determine if the transaction was written to disk.

This call can tell the programmer if TTS was disabled during the transaction and if so, TTS Transaction Status can be used to determine the status of the write.

The NetWare C Interface format is:

```
int TTSEndTransaction( long *transactionNumber );
```

TTS Transaction Status (C7h 04h)

This call returns whether a transaction has been written to the disk. As an argument, it takes the Transaction Number returned from TTS End Transaction.

Registers in:
AH C7h
AL 4
CX, DX Transaction Number

Registers out:
AL Completion Code

Completion Codes:
Carry flag cleared:
00h Successful
FFh Transaction Not Yet Written To Disk

Note that it may take the file server five seconds or longer to actually write the transaction to the disk once the TTS End Transaction call has been made (for explicit transactions) or once the last file has been unlocked (for implicit transactions). Transactions are, however, written to disk in the order they were ended.

The NetWare C Interface format is:

```
int TTSTransactionStatus( long transactionNumber );
```

TTS Abort Transaction (C7h 03h)

This call aborts both explicit and implicit transactions.

Registers in:
AH C7h
AL 3

Registers out:
AL Completion Code

Completion Codes:
Carry flag cleared:
00h Successful

Carry flag set:
FDh Transaction Tracking Disabled (No backout performed)
FEh Transaction Ended, Records Locked
FFh No Explicit Transaction Active

When this call returns, the transaction has been backed out completely and successfully. All writes during the transaction are aborted and the backout takes the file to the state it was in before the transaction.

The NetWare C Interface format is:

```
int TTSAbortTransaction( void );
```

TTS Get Application Thresholds (C7h 05h)

This call returns the application threshold for implicit transactions.

Registers in:
AH C7h
AL 5

Registers out:
AL Completion Code
CL Logical Record Lock Threshold (0 to 255)
CH Physical Record Lock Threshold (0 to 255)

Completion Codes:
00 Successful

With this call, the number of logical or physical record locks can be gotten so that implicit locking doesn't start until the *n*th lock is placed on a file. This is useful for programs that maintain locks throughout the duration of the program, preventing all disk writes from occurring as one large transaction.

This call can be used with TTS Set Application Thresholds to save and set the threshold, and later restore it to its original value.

The NetWare C Interface format is:

```
int TTSGetApplicationThresholds( BYTE *logicalRecordLockThreshold,
   BYTE *physicalRecordLockThreshold );
```

TTS Set Application Thresholds (C7h 06h)

This call sets the application threshold for implicit transactions.

Registers in:

AH C7h
AL 6
CL Logical Record Lock Threshold (0 to 255)
CH Physical Record Lock Threshold (0 to 255)

Registers out:

AL Completion Code

Completion Codes:

00 Successful

The Threshold values contain the number of logical and physical locks that may be set before a transaction is begun.

Application thresholds differ from Workstation thresholds in that the application ones supercede workstation thresholds, and last only through the duration of the program. Workstation thresholds become the default for any application that has no application thresholds set.

The NetWare C Interface format is:

```
int TTSSetApplicationThresholds( BYTE logicalRecordLockThreshold,
   BYTE physicalRecordLockThreshold );
```

TTS Get Workstation Thresholds (C7h 07h)

This call returns the workstation threshold for implicit transactions.

Registers in:

AH C7h
AL 7

Registers out:

AL Completion Code
CL Logical Record Lock Threshold (0 to 255)
CH Physical Record Lock Threshold (0 to 255)

Completion Codes:

00 Successful

With this call, the limit of logical or physical record locks can be returned for a workstation (before transactions begin).

Workstation thresholds are permanent, staying in effect even when an application terminates. This call can be used with TTS Set Workstation Thresholds to save and set the threshold, and later restore it to its original value.

The default for the thresholds is 0, but they can be set to FFh which will turn off implicit transactions. This call may be used by applications that use explicit transactions, but make writes to files that shouldn't be implicitly tracked.

The NetWare C Interface format is:

```
int TTSGetWorkstationThresholds( BYTE *logicalRecordLockThreshold,
  BYTE *physicalRecordLockThreshold );
```

TTS Set Workstation Thresholds (C7h 08h)

This call sets the workstation threshold for implicit transactions.

Registers in:

AH	C7h
AL	8
CL	Logical Record Lock Threshold (0 to 255)
CH	Physical Record Lock Threshold (0 to 255)

Registers out:

AL	Completion Code

Completion Codes:

00	Successful

With this call, the number of logical or physical record locks can be set so that implicit locking doesn't start until the *n*th lock is placed on a file. This is useful for programs that maintain locks throughout the duration of the program, preventing all disk writes from occurring as one large transaction.

The default for the thresholds is 0, but they can be set to FFh which will turn off implicit transactions. This may be used by applications that use explicit transactions, but make writes to files that shouldn't be implicitly tracked.

This call is the programmer's equivalent of the SetTTS program, provided in NetWare.

The NetWare C Interface format is:

```
int TTSSetWorkstationThresholds( BYTE logicalRecordLockThreshold,
  BYTE physicalRecordLockThreshold );
```

Code sample: CheckTTS.C

CheckTTS was designed to test the TTS system by attempting to simulate a backed-out transaction. The program performs an explicit transaction creating two files and writing the character "1" to them. The second transaction writes a "2" to just the first file and then terminates. The Transaction Tracking System should back out the second transaction, leaving each file with a 1 in it.

The program defines its prototypes and begins by setting up the two files with a call to OpenOrCreate(), passing the name of the file to be opened or created. The routine tries to open the file or, if the file was not found, the routine attempts to create it. Note that after the file's transactional bit is set, we need to close the file and reopen it for TTS to recognize the file as being transactional.

If the file was successfully opened or created, the handle is returned to be stored in *handle1* and *handle2*. Next an explicit transaction is started and the value of 1 is written to both files. The transaction is ended and program enters a while loop, waiting for the transaction status to signal that the transaction has been written.

Next the program starts another explicit transaction and writes a 2 to the first file. It then pauses for the user to press any key. Once the user does this, he or she should TYPE the two files, CheckTTS.D1 and CheckTTS.D2 to see what the values are.

The TTS functions are fairly straightforward as they deal exclusively with registers, making them simpler to code and work with.

```
/*                                                                    */
/* CheckTTS - Tests the TTS mechanism to show how TTS works           */
/*                                                                    */
/* by Charles Rose                                                    */
/*                                                                    */

#include <stdio.h>
#include <dos.h>
#include <dir.h>
#include <string.h>
#include <fcntl.h>
#include <stdlib.h>
#include <conio.h>

#define TRANSACTIONAL 0x10
#define SHAREABLE 0x80

typedef unsigned char BYTE;
typedef unsigned int WORD;
typedef unsigned long LONG;

/* Local Prototypes */
int OpenOrCreate( char *fileName );
int GetExtFileAttributes( char *Path, BYTE *attributes );
int SetExtFileAttributes( char *Path, BYTE *attributes );
int TTSBeginTransaction( void );
int TTSEndTransaction( WORD *transactionNumber );
int TTSTransactionStatus( WORD *transactionNumber );

main()
{
    int handle1, handle2;
    LONG transactionNumber;

    clrscr();

    /* Show TTS working */

        gotoxy( 1, 20 );
        printf( "Opening files..." );
```

```
/* Attempt to open or create the files */
handle1 = OpenOrCreate( "checktts.d1" );
handle2 = OpenOrCreate( "checktts.d2" );

/* ... and write some text */
gotoxy( 1, 21 );
printf( "Writing header to files..." );

write( handle1, "This is file1, value is : :\n", 28 );
write( handle2, "This is file2, value is : :\n", 28 );

/* Start an explicit transaction */
TTSBeginTransaction();

/* Write to two files */
gotoxy( 1, 22 );
printf( "Started transaction, writing value to files..." );

lseek( handle1, (long)25, 0 );
write( handle1, "1", 1 );

lseek( handle2, (long)25, 0 );
write( handle2, "1", 1 );

/* End transaction */
TTSEndTransaction( &transactionNumber );

/* Wait on transaction status */
gotoxy( 1, 23 );
printf( "Transaction Complete.  Waiting for server to write ..."  );

while ( TTSTransactionStatus( &transactionNumber ) );

printf( "written." );

gotoxy( 1, 24 );
printf( "Press any key to continue." );
getch();

clrscr();

/* Show a backed out transaction */

/* Start an explicit transaction */
TTSBeginTransaction();

/* Write to two files */
gotoxy( 1, 21 );
printf( "Started transaction, writing value to file #1..." );

lseek( handle1, (long)25, 0 );
write( handle1, "2", 1 );

/* Now we'll quit and let the user examine the results              */
gotoxy( 1, 22 );
printf( "Only file 1 was written to.  The program will now terminate.\n" );
printf( "Press any key and TYPE CHECKTTS.D1 and CHECKTTS.D2, they should\n" );
printf( "  have the same value because the file #1 write was backed-out\n" );
getch();

close( handle1 );
```

```
        close( handle2 );
}

int OpenOrCreate( char *fileName )
{
    int handle;
    char problem[255];
    BYTE attributes;

    if ( ( handle = open( fileName, O_RDWR | O_BINARY ) ) == -1 )
    {
        /* If the problem was no file found */
        if ( errno == 2 )
        {
            /* Then create the file... */
            if ( ( handle = _creat( fileName, SHAREABLE ) ) == -1 )
            {
                sprintf( problem, "\nCan't create %s", fileName );
                perror( problem );
                exit(1);
            }
            else
            {
                /* File created, now make it transactional */
                GetExtFileAttributes( fileName, &attributes );
                attributes |= TRANSACTIONAL;
                SetExtFileAttributes( fileName, &attributes );

                close( handle );
                handle = open( fileName, O_RDWR |
                    O_BINARY );

            }
        }
        else
        /* otherwise, there's something more serious wrong */
        {
            sprintf( problem, "\nCan't open %s", fileName );
            perror( problem );
            exit(1);
        }
    }
    return handle;
}

int GetExtFileAttributes( char *Path, BYTE *attributes )
{
    _AH = 0xB6;
    _AL = 0;
    _DX = (unsigned)Path;

    geninterrupt( 0x21 );

    if ( _AL )
        return _AL;
    else
    {
        *attributes = _CL;
        return 0;
    }
}
```

```
int SetExtFileAttributes( char *Path, BYTE *attributes )
{
    _AH = 0xB6;
    _AL = 1;
    _DX = (unsigned)Path;
    _CL = *attributes;

    geninterrupt( 0x21 );

    return _AL;
}

int TTSBeginTransaction( void )
{
    _AH = 0xC7;
    _AL = 0;

    geninterrupt( 0x21 );

    return _AL;
}

int TTSEndTransaction( WORD *transactionNumber )
{
    _AH = 0xC7;
    _AL = 1;

    geninterrupt( 0x21 );

    if (_AL)
        return _AL;
    else
    {
        transactionNumber[0] = _CX;
        transactionNumber[1] = _DX;
        return 0;
    }
}

int TTSTransactionStatus( WORD *transactionNumber )
{
    _AH = 0xC7;
    _AL = 4;
    _CX = transactionNumber[0];
    _DX = transactionNumber[1];

    geninterrupt( 0x21 );

    return _AL;
}
```

Exercises

1. Run CheckTTS and test the transaction backout process. Notice the messages on the file server. Disable transaction tracking at the file server and try it again.

2. Use TTS with nonTTS-aware programs (implicit TTS). Set different thresholds with SetTTS.

3. Write a counter into CheckTTS that times how long it takes the file server to return from the TTS Transaction Status call. Write larger blocks of data and see the difference.

6 Bindery Services

Resident on each NetWare file server is the Bindery, a small database of vital information about users, groups, queues and other servers. The Bindery provides a foundation for NetWare's original naming service, and was designed to furnish a consistent interface to information on resources available on a server. The Bindery manages dynamic objects such as file servers that appear and disappear on the network, as well as more persistent objects such as users.

Novell also offers the NetWare Name Service. This more formal service extends the idea of server-specific properties to "domain-specific" properties, a domain being essentially a group of servers. For example, instead of having to define a user on each file server on an internetwork one-by-one, a supervisor would make that user part of a domain that included the necessary file servers. The Name Service uses the Bindery Services calls which we will focus on in this chapter.

Conceptually, the Bindery is a three-tiered database, composed of objects, "properties" associated with those objects, and values of those properties. These three elements provide a simple but effective mechanism for resource management. (See diagram on the next page.)

Bindery objects

The basic element in the Bindery is the object. An object is identified by its name and its type, which can be a user, a group, a file server, a print queue, or anything else a developer wishes. (Part of the beauty of the Bindery is that while NetWare uses it for its own processes, developers are free to use the Bindery for their own pursuits. Novell cautions, however, that storing too much information in the Bindery degrades performance.)

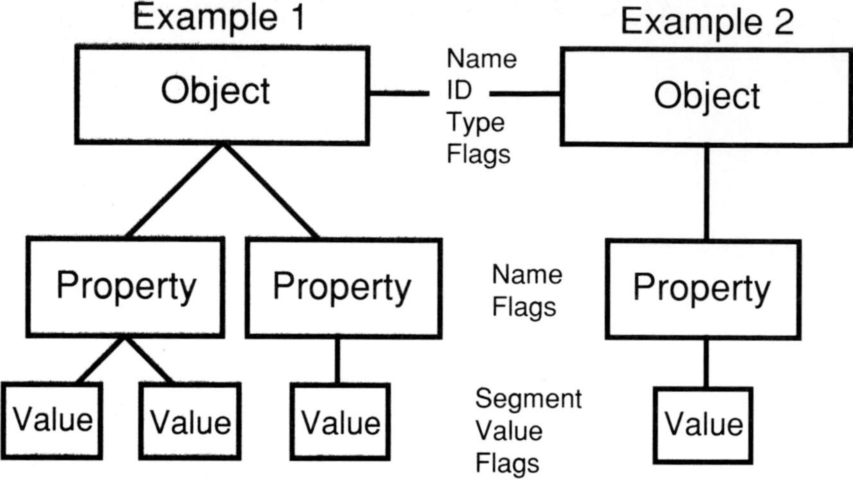

Figure 7: Objects, properties, and values in NetWare.

Properties are associated with each object. For example, information relevant to a user includes the groups the user belongs to, login information, and password. The corresponding Bindery properties are called GROUPS_I'M_IN, LOGIN_CONTROL, and PASSWORD.

Properties can be of two types: sets, which are lists of four-byte object identification numbers (such as for GROUPS_I'M_IN); or items, which contain data that is customized for the particular field (such as PASSWORD, which is a string of characters).

Each property has a value. For example, the GROUPS_I'M_IN property would contain a list of the groups the user is in and the PASSWORD property would contain the actual encrypted password of the user.

As stated before, in addition to NetWare using the Bindery, programmers may use it, but they are cautioned not to become over zealous and store too much information in the Bindery. Performance becomes an issue when too much information is stored in this usually small database because, for example, searches take longer.

Novell suggests that, when a large amount of data is to be stored for each user, the information be placed in the user's mail directory (SYS:MAIL/*objectID* where objectID is the number identifying the object, in this case the user, in the Bindery). Also, NetWare makes no attempt at synchronizing Bindery reads or writes. For synchronization with the Bindery, logical locks may be used.

Object security

The Bindery is vital to network security, much of which is administered through the security levels set up in the Bindery. For each Bindery object and property, there are certain minimum rights that other objects may have. They are shown in the accompanying table.

Bindery Access Levels

0 Anyone	Any object has access, whether or not it is logged into the file server.
1 Logged	Access is granted to any client logged into the file server.
2 Object	Access is granted to any clients logged into the file server with a this object's name, type and password.
3 Supervisor	Access is granted only to the supervisor or an object that is supervisor-equivalent. An object is supervisor-equivalent if its SECURITY_EQUALS property contains the object ID of the supervisor.
4 NetWare	Only NetWare can access an object or property with this security level.

There are two security settings for each object and property. One grants or denies read privileges (scan for and find the entity), the other controls write privileges (add or delete properties or values). The security settings are contained in a single byte, with the high-order four-bit nibble defining write privileges and the low-order nibble defining read privileges. The NetWare default is logged read, supervisor write.

Objects

Objects are the basic elements of the Bindery. A Bindery object is defined by name and type. (So you could have two objects named SERVER_1 but one object could be a file server and the other could be a print server.) There are several other fields associated with each object that define it further—the flag, identification and security fields.

Bindery object names

A Bindery object's name may be up to 48 characters long, with the the last character used as a null terminator. Until Advanced NetWare 1.0, the object names and passwords were limited to 15 characters. Under Advanced NetWare and later versions, object names may be up to 48 characters and passwords may have as much as 128. Only the printable ASCII characters 21h through 7Dh may be used. This excludes control characters, spaces, slashes, backslashes, colons, semicolons, commas, asterisks, question marks, and tildes from object names. (Asterisks and question marks are used in wildcard searches, as described below.) Because names are recorded in uppercase in the Bindery, in any search the object's name should be converted to upper case before the call is made. Note: this is done for the programmer in most NetWare C Interface calls.

Object identification numbers

When each Bindery object is created it is assigned a four-byte number that uniquely identifies it within its file server. It is important to stress that object IDs are unique only within a file server and not among multiple file servers.

Bindery object types

A two-byte value describes the purpose of every Bindery object. The value can be set to 0 if the object's type is not known, or it can be set to -1 (Wild) when scanning for an object whose type is unknown or irrelevant. The types from 1 to 0x8000 have been reserved by Novell for such common objects as users and servers.

All other numbers are available for assignment by developers, and developers should have their object types registered by Novell.

It is important to remember that object type defines the behavior as well as the purpose of an object. Developers should be careful. If, for example, a developer creates a type-9 Bindery object, an Archive Server, it must conform to the behavior and protocols of Novell's Archive Server.

Some object types currently assigned by Novell are:

Type	Value
Unknown	0h
User	1h
User Group	2h
Print Queue	3h
File Server	4h
Job Server	5h
Gateway	6h
Print Server	7h
Archive Queue	8h
Archive Server	9h
Job Queue	Ah
Administration	Bh
Remote Bridge Server	24h
Advertising Printer Server	47h
Reserved up to	8000h
Wild	FFFFh (-1)

The Bindery object flag

The one-byte object flag identifies an object as either static (0) or dynamic (1). A static object exists until it is explicitly deleted. A dynamic object is automatically deleted when the file server goes down. A user is an example of static object; an advertising file server that is frequently added to or deleted from other file-server binderies is an example of a dynamic object. (See chapter 16.)

The Bindery security flag

The one-byte security flag determines who may read from or write to an object, as discussed above.

Properties of Bindery objects

In NetWare, "properties" are data items associated with objects; these properties may or may not correspond to specific characteristics of objects. For example, NetWare-defined properties of users include GROUPS_I'M_IN, IDENTIFICATION, and SECURITY_EQUALS. These properties are a list of groups, a name as defined in SysCon, and a list of objects.

Properties themselves do not contain data. For instance, the IDENTIFICATION property does not contain the user name. Values contain the actual data associated with properties. Properties simply specify which values are associated with which objects. And like objects, properties are described in several data fields: property name, property flags and property security.

Bindery property names

A Bindery property's name may be up to 15 characters long and, as for object names, only the printable characters 21h through 7Dh may be used. This again excludes control characters, spaces, slashes, backslashes, colons, semicolons, commas, asterisks, question marks, and tildes from object names. (Asterisks and question marks are used in wildcard searches, as described below.) And again, because names are recorded in uppercase in the Bindery, in any search the object's name should be converted to upper case before the call is made.

The property security flag

Just like the corresponding object flag, this one-byte flag defines the read-write security of the property, as shown in the preceding table on Bindery security.

The Bindery property flag

Similar to the object flag, this is a one-byte flag whose bit field tells whether the property is static (0) or dynamic (1). Again, static denotes a property that must be explicitly deleted from the Bindery, dynamic a property that is automatically deleted at shutdown. (When dynamic objects are deleted their properties and values are also.) Unlike the object flag, the high nibble of this field contains another flag that specifies whether the property is an item (0) or a set (1).

As mentioned earlier, a set is a list of four-byte object IDs; an item is a custom field containing information of any structure. Whether a property is an item or set property, those defined by Novell are stored in high-low order. Brief descriptions of the Novell-defined properties follow.

ACCOUNT_BALANCE

This static property is an item, usually in monetary units, that tells the amount of credit remaining in a user's account. Read access is granted to the object (user), write access to the supervisor. This property is discussed in more detail in chapter 11.

ACCOUNT_HOLDS

This dynamic property is an item that tells whether up to 16 servers have put holds on the user's account. Access is user (object) read, supervisor write. As discussed in detail in chapter 11, a server may, before servicing a user request, put a hold on the user's account to assure that it contains sufficient funds to pay for the service.

ACCOUNT_SERVERS

This static set property is a list of all servers authorized to charge a user for services. Access to this property is logged read, supervisor write. As detailed in chapter 11, the object of this property can be a file server, a print server, a database server, a user or any other object.

ACCOUNT_LOCKOUT

This static item property of a file server tells which accounts are locked out for that file server. Default access is supervisor read and write.

BLOCKS_READ

As detailed in chapter 11, this static item property of a file server tells what the server will charge for the number of blocks read since login. Default access is logged read, supervisor write.

BLOCKS_WRITTEN

As detailed in chapter 11, this static item property of a file server tells what the server will charge for the number of blocks written since login. Default access is logged read, supervisor write.

CONNECT_TIME

As detailed in chapter 11, this static item property of a file server tells what the server will charge for connect time from login to logout. Default access is logged read, supervisor write.

DISK_STORAGE

As detailed in chapter 11, this static item property of a file server tells what the server will charge for disk storage. Default access is logged read, supervisor write.

GROUP_MEMBERS

This static set property contains the names of members of a user group. Default access is logged read and supervisor write.

GROUPS_I'M_IN

The inverse of GROUP_MEMBERS, this static set property contains a list of groups to which a user belongs. Default access is logged read, supervisor write.

IDENTIFICATION

This static item property contains the full name of an object, either a user or user group, as defined in SysCon. Up to 128 bytes (1 byte is used as terminating 0). Default access is logged read, supervisor write.

LOGIN_CONTROL

This static item property is of type user. The SysCon utility places user configuration information such as how long the password is required to be, the password expiration date, and whether unique passwords are required or not in it. Default access is object read, supervisor write.

NET_ADDRESS

This dynamic item property of file servers is used by NetWare to hold the 12-byte internetwork address of a known file server. Default access is anyone read, NetWare write. This field gets created by the Service Advertising Protocol (see chapter 16).

NODE_CONTROL

This static item property has a user as its object and is used by SysCon to list stations where that user can log in. Default access is object read, supervisor write.

OLD_PASSWORDS

This static item property has a user as its object and keeps track of up to eight of the user's previous passwords. Default access is supervisor read and write. This property exists only if a unique password is required in the LOGIN_CONTROL property.

OPERATORS

This static property of file servers contains the set of objects authorized to operate the file server console through the FConsole utility. Default access is supervisor read and write.

PASSWORD

This static item property contains the user's encrypted password and is required for login. Because access to this property is NetWare read and write privileges, it cannot be manipulated directly with the standard property calls. The Change Bindery Object Password call can be used, however, to change or add a password.

Q_DIRECTORY

This static item property has a print queue as object and contains the complete path and directory of a NetWare queue, as detailed in chapter 8. Default access is supervisor read and write.

Q_OPERATORS

This static set property has a print queue as object and lists operators authorized to manipulate queues, as detailed in chapter 8. Default access is logged read and supervisor write.

Q_SERVERS

This static set property has a print queue as object and lists servers authorized to take jobs from a queue, as detailed in chapter 8. Default access is logged read and supervisor write.

Q_USERS

This static set property has a print queue as object and lists users authorized to place jobs in a queue, as detailed in chapter 8. Default access is logged read and supervisor write.

REQUESTS_MADE

As detailed in chapter 11, this static item property of a file server tells what the server will charge for a request made of it by a programmer. Default access is logged read, supervisor write.

SECURITY_EQUALS

This static set property contains a list of the objects to which a user is equivalent in security. For instance, if a user's SECURITY_EQUALS property contains the Object ID of the Supervisor, then he has all of the access privileges the Supervisor has. Access to this property is object read and supervisor write.

USER_DEFAULTS

This static item property has a supervisor as its object and is used by SysCon to hold the value of the LOGIN_CONTROL property which will be assigned to each new user. Default access is logged read, supervisor write.

Values

Values are the actual data connected with the properties. A value is an item or a set depending on the Bindery property flag. Values can be larger than the 128-bytes of a reply packet, so packets may have to be chained together into multiple 128-byte packets.

Bindery files

The NetWare 286 Bindery is composed of two files: NET$BIND.SYS, which contains objects and properties; and NET$BVAL.SYS, which contains values.Under NetWare 386 there are three Bindery files: NET$OBJ.SYS, NET$PROP.SYS and NET$VAL.SYS. These files are marked Hidden and System and are stored in the SYS:SYSTEM directory of each file server. The server keeps them open and locked, so access for the frequent backups they require is only possible with the Close Bindery call issued by a supervisor or supervisor-equivalent. When the Bindery is closed, few network functions can be performed, so developers should back up these files as quickly as possible then promptly restore normal operation with the Open Bindery call.

Here's how to back up the Bindery:

(The following files should not be backed up: NET$SPL.QUE, NET$MSG.SYS, DIRSTAMP.SYS.)

To archive files:
1. Close the Bindery.
2. Back up the Bindery files.
3. Open the Bindery.

As files and directories are backed up, call:
4. Get File Information (chapter 3)
5. Scan Directory for Trustees (chapter 4)
6. Scan Directory Information (chapter 4)

To restore files:
1. Restore the Bindery.

Then call:
2. Set File Information (chapter 3)
3. Add Trustee To Directory (chapter 4)
4. Set Directory Information (chapter 4)

Calls in the Bindery APIs

The following descriptions will include which versions of NetWare support which calls. Throughout the book, we have tried to explain fields within the calls only at the first mention of each field in each chapter; here we have gone into some key field descriptions as necessary to our overview of the Bindery. Appendix B contains a comprehensive, alphabetical listing of the fields for quick reference.

Open Bindery (E3h 45h)

This call is supported in Advanced NetWare versions 1.0, 1.02, 2.0 and 2.1, and in NetWare 386 and later versions. It opens the Bindery. It must be called after using the Close Bindery call; no other Bindery call will work while the Bindery is closed.

Registers in:

AH	E3h
DS:SI	Request Buffer Address
ES:DI	Reply Buffer Address

Registers out:

AL	Completion Code

Completion Codes:

00	Success

Request Packet (max size = 3 bytes):

Offset	**Content**	**Type**	**Order**
0	Request Buffer Length-2	WORD	lo-hi
2	45h	BYTE	

Reply Packet (2 bytes):

Offset	**Content**	**Type**	**Order**
0	0000	WORD	lo-hi

The NetWare C Interface format is:

```
int OpenBindery( void );
```

Close Bindery (E3h 44h)

This call is supported in Advanced NetWare versions 1.0, 1.02, 2.0, and 2.1, and in NetWare 386 and later versions. It closes the Bindery. It must be called before archiving the Bindery, since the Bindery files must be closed to be backed up. Only the supervisor or a user that is supervisor equivalent can close the Bindery.

Registers in:

AH	E3h
DS:SI	Request Buffer Address
ES:DI	Reply Buffer Address

Registers out:

AL	Completion Code

Completion Codes:

00	Success

Request Packet (max size = 3 bytes):

Offset	**Content**	**Type**	**Order**
0	Request Buffer Length-2	WORD	lo-hi
2	44h	BYTE	

Reply Packet (2 bytes):

Offset	**Content**	**Type**	**Order**
0	0000	WORD	lo-hi

The NetWare C Interface format is:

```
int CloseBindery( void );
```

Create Bindery Object (E3h 32h)

This call is supported in Advanced NetWare versions 1.0, 1.02, 2.0, and 2.1, and in NetWare 386 and later versions. It creates an object in the Bindery. It requires the requesting programmer to specify the object's name, type, security and static/dynamic flag.

Registers in:

AH	E3h
DS:SI	Request Buffer Address
ES:DI	Reply Buffer Address

Registers out:

AL	Completion Code

Completion Codes:

00	Success
96h	Server Out Of Memory
EEh	Object Already Exists
EFh	Invalid Name
F1h	Invalid Bindery Security
F5h	No Object Create Privileges
FEh	Server Bindery Locked
FFh	Bindery Failure

Request Packet (max size = 56 bytes):

Offset	**Content**	**Type**	**Order**
0	Request Buffer Length-2	WORD	lo-hi
2	32h	BYTE	
3	Object Flag	BYTE	
4	Object Security	BYTE	
5	Object Type	WORD	hi-lo
6	Object Name Length	BYTE [1-48]	
7	Object Name	BYTE[*LENGTH*]	

Reply Packet (2 bytes):

Offset	**Content**	**Type**	**Order**
0	0000	WORD	lo-hi

Object Flag is one byte identifying an object as either static (0) or dynamic (1).

Object Security is a single byte, with the high-order four-bit nibble defining write privileges and the low-order nibble defining read privileges.

Hex	Access	Explanation
0	Anyone	Any object has access, whether or not it is logged into the file server.
1	Logged	Access is granted to any object logged into the file server.
2	Object	Access is granted only to objects logged into the file server with their names, types and passwords.
3	Supervisor	Access is granted only to the supervisor or an object that is supervisor-equivalent. An object is supervisor-equivalent if its SECURITY_EQUALS property contains the object ID of the supervisor.
4	NetWare	Only NetWare can access an object or property with this security level.

Thus, access 0x31 is supervisor write, logged read; access 0x33 is supervisor read and write, etc.

Object Type is a two-byte value. It can be set to 0 if the object's type is not known, or it can be set to -1 (Wild) when scanning for an object whose type is unknown or irrelevant. The types from 1 to 0x8000 are reserved and assigned by Novell; all others are available for assignment by developers, who may have their own object types registered by Novell.

The object types currently assigned by Novell are:

Type	Value
Unknown	0h
User	1h
User Group	2h
Print Queue	3h
File Server	4h
Job Server	5h
Gateway	6h
Print Server	7h
Archive Queue	8h
Archive Server	9h
Job Queue	Ah
Administration	Bh
Remote Bridge Server	24h
Advertising Printer Server	47h
Reserved up to	8000h
Wild	FFFFh (-1)

Object Name Length is the number of characters in a Bindery object's name.

Object Name is up to 48 uppercase characters long. Only printable ASCII characters 21h through 7Dh may be used; excluded are control characters, spaces, slashes, backslashes, colons, semicolons, commas, asterisks, question marks, and tildes.

The NetWare C Interface format is:

```
int CreateBinderyObject( char *objectName, WORD objectType,
    BYTE objectFlag, BYTE objectSecurity );
```

Delete Bindery Object (E3h 33h)

This call is supported in Advanced NetWare versions 1.0, 1.02, 2.0, and 2.1, and in NetWare 386 and later versions. It deletes a Bindery object and all associated properties. The object's name and type must be specified.

Registers in:

AH	E3h
DS:SI	Request Buffer Address
ES:DI	Reply Buffer Address

Registers out:

AL	Completion Code

Completion Codes:

00	Success
96h	Server Out Of Memory
EFh	Invalid Name
F0h	Wildcard Not Allowed
F4h	No Object Delete Privileges
FCh	No Such Object
FEh	Server Bindery Locked
FFh	Bindery Failure

Request Packet (max size = 54 bytes):

Offset	**Content**	**Type**	**Order**
0	Request Buffer Length-2	WORD	lo-hi
2	33h	BYTE	
3	Object Type	WORD	hi-lo
5	Object Name Length	BYTE [1-48]	
6	Object Name	BYTE[*LENGTH*]	

Reply Packet (2 bytes):

Offset	**Content**	**Type**	**Order**
0	0000	WORD	lo-hi

The NetWare C Interface format is:

```
int DeleteBinderyObject( char *objectName, WORD objectType );
```

Scan Bindery Object (E3h 37h)

This call is supported in Advanced NetWare versions 1.0, 1.02, 2.0, and 2.1, and in NetWare 386 and later versions. It scans the Bindery, returning one or more objects and complete information about each Bindery object (ID, name, type, static/dynamic flag, security flag, and a flag indicating the presence or absence of properties). Wildcard characters may be specified in the Object Name and Type fields of the request buffer to return multiple objects.

Registers in:

AH	E3h
DS:SI	Request Buffer Address
ES:DI	Reply Buffer Address

Registers out:

AL	Completion Code

Completion Codes:

00	Success
96h	Server Out Of Memory
EFh	Invalid Name
FCh	No Such Object
FEh	Server Bindery Locked
FFh	Bindery Failure

Request Packet (max size = 58 bytes):

Offset	Content	Type	Order
0	Request Buffer Length-2	WORD	lo-hi
2	37h	BYTE	
3	Last Object ID	LONG	hi-lo
7	Object Type	WORD	hi-lo
9	Object Name Length	BYTE [1-48]	
10	Object Name	BYTE[*LENGTH*]	

Reply Packet (59 bytes):

Offset	Content	Type	Order
0	Reply Buffer Length-2	WORD	lo-hi
2	Object ID	LONG	hi-lo
6	Object Type	WORD	hi-lo
8	Object Name	BYTE [48]	

56	Object Flag	BYTE
57	Object Security	BYTE
58	Object Has Properties	BYTE

The *Last Object ID* field may be used to iteratively request multiple objects. The first time this call is made, this field should contain FFFFFFFFh (-1). Subsequent calls can be made placing the reply packet's Object ID in this field. The process can be repeated until a completion code of FCh (No Such Object) is returned.

Object ID is a four-byte number assigned by the file server when an object is created; object IDs are unique only within their file servers.

Object Has Properties is a flag specifying whether or not properties exist for this object. A value in this field (TRUE) indicates the presence of properties, while no value (FALSE) indicates no properties.

To make this call, the workstation must be attached and have read access to the Bindery object(s) being scanned.

The NetWare C Interface format is:

```
int ScanBinderyObject( char *searchObjectName, WORD searchObjectType,
        long *objectID, char *objectName, WORD *objectType,
        char *objectHasProperties, char *objectFlag,
        char *objectSecurity );
```

Rename Bindery Object (E3h 34h)

This call is supported in Advanced NetWare versions 1.0, 1.02, 2.0, and 2.1, and in NetWare 386 and later versions. It allows the programmer to change the name of a Bindery object.

Registers in:

AH	E3h
DS:SI	Request Buffer Address
ES:DI	Reply Buffer Address

Registers out:

AL	Completion Code

Completion Codes:

00	Success
96h	Server Out Of Memory
EFh	Invalid Name
F0h	Wildcard Not Allowed
F3h	No Object Rename Privileges
FCh	No Such Object
FEh	Server Bindery Locked
FFh	Bindery Failure

Request Packet (max size = 105 bytes):

Offset	Content	Type	Order
0	Request Buffer Length-2	WORD	lo-hi
2	34h	BYTE	
3	Object Type	WORD	hi-lo
5	Object Name Length	BYTE [1-48]	
6	Object Name	BYTE[*LENGTH*]	
?	New Object Name Length	BYTE [1-48]	
?	New Object Name	BYTE[*LENGTH*]	

Reply Packet (2 bytes):

Offset	Content	Type	Order
0	0000	WORD	lo-hi

Object Type and *Object Name* must uniquely identify an object. No wildcards may be used for either field. To make this call, the user must have supervisor equivalency or be the supervisor.

The NetWare C Interface format is:

```
int RenameBinderyObject( char *objectName, char *newObjectName,
  WORD objectType );
```

Is Bindery Object In Set (E3h 43h)

This call is supported in Advanced NetWare versions 1.0, 1.02, 2.0, and 2.1, and in NetWare 386 and later versions. It allows the programmer to check whether a Bindery object is a member of a set property. This saves the developer from having to manually scan all of the property values.

Registers in:

AH	E3h
DS:SI	Request Buffer Address
ES:DI	Reply Buffer Address

Registers out:

AL	Completion Code

Completion Codes:

00	Success
96h	Server Out Of Memory
EAh	No Such Member
EBh	Not Group Property
F0h	Wildcard Not Allowed
F9h	No Property Read Privileges
FCh	No Such Object
FEh	Server Bindery Locked
FFh	Bindery Failure

Request Packet (max size = 122 bytes):

Offset	Content	Type	Order
0	Request Buffer Length-2	WORD	lo-hi
2	43h	BYTE	
3	Object Type	WORD	hi-lo
5	Object Name Length	BYTE [1-48]	
6	Object Name	BYTE[*LENGTH*]	
?	Property Name Length	BYTE [1-15]	
?	Property Name	BYTE[*LENGTH*]	
?	Member Type	WORD	hi-lo
?	Member Name Length	BYTE [1-48]	
?	Member Name	BYTE[*LENGTH*]	

Reply Packet (2 bytes):

Offset	Content	Type	Order
0	0000	WORD	lo-hi

Property Name is the property containing the set to be searched.

Member Name is the object to check for in the property set. In this call, the file server uses the Member's Name and Type to find the four-byte Object ID. Then, the file server searches for that ID in all of the 128-byte value segments associated with the object's property. If found, a Successful (00) completion code is returned, otherwise, No Such Member (EAh) is returned. To make this call, the user must have read rights to the object and the property.

The NetWare C Interface format is:

```
int IsBinderyObjectInSet( char *objectName, WORD objectType,
   char *propertyName, char *memberName, WORD memberType );
```

Add Bindery Object To Set (E3h 41h)

This call is supported in Advanced NetWare versions 1.0, 1.02, 2.0, and 2.1, and in NetWare 386 and later versions. It adds a Bindery object to a property set.

Registers in:

AH	E3h
DS:SI	Request Buffer Address
ES:DI	Reply Buffer Address

Registers out:

AL	Completion Code

Completion Codes:

00	Success
96h	Server Out Of Memory
E9h	Member Already Exists
EBh	Not Group Property
F0h	Wildcard Not Allowed
F8h	No Property Write Privileges
FCh	No Such Object
FEh	Server Bindery Locked
FFh	Bindery Failure

Request Packet (max size = 122 bytes):

Offset	Content	Type	Order
0	Request Buffer Length-2	WORD	lo-hi
2	41h	BYTE	
3	Object Type	WORD	hi-lo
5	Object Name Length	BYTE [1-48]	
6	Object Name	BYTE[*LENGTH*]	
?	Property Name Length	BYTE [1-15]	
?	Property Name	BYTE[*LENGTH*]	
?	Member Object Type	WORD	hi-lo
?	Member Name Length	BYTE [1-48]	
?	Member Name	BYTE[*LENGTH*]	

Reply Packet (2 bytes):

Offset	Content	Type	Order
0	0000	WORD	lo-hi

In this call, the *Member Name's Object ID* is found, then the set from the property is found. Finally, the property is added to the Property Set.

A new property segment (128 bytes) will be added if the member list fills a segment and there are no free object ID entries in that segment.

To make this call, the user must have write access to the property.

The NetWare C Interface format is:

```
int AddBinderyObjectToSet( char *objectName, WORD objectType,
   char *propertyName, char *memberName, WORD memberType );
```

Delete Bindery Object From Set (E3h 42h)

This call is supported in Advanced NetWare versions 1.0, 1.02, 2.0, and 2.1, and in NetWare 386 and later versions. It deletes a Bindery object from a property set.

Registers in:

AH	E3h
DS:SI	Request Buffer Address
ES:DI	Reply Buffer Address

Registers out:

AL	Completion Code

Completion Codes:

00	Success
96h	Server Out Of Memory
EAh	No Such Member
EBh	Not Group Property
F0h	Wildcard Not Allowed
F8h	No Property Write Privileges
FBh	No Such Property
FCh	No Such Object
FEh	Server Bindery Locked
FFh	Bindery Failure

Request Packet (max size = 122 bytes):

Offset	**Content**	**Type**	**Order**
0	Request Buffer Length-2	WORD	lo-hi
2	42h	BYTE	
3	Object Type	WORD	hi-lo
5	Object Name Length	BYTE [1-48]	
6	Object Name	BYTE[*LENGTH*]	
?	Property Name Length	BYTE [1-15]	
?	Property Name	BYTE[*LENGTH*]	
?	Member Object Type	WORD	hi-lo
?	Member Name Length	BYTE [1-48]	
?	Member Name	BYTE[*LENGTH*]	

Reply Packet (2 bytes):

Offset	**Content**	**Type**	**Order**
0	0000	WORD	lo-hi

In this call, the *Member Name's Object ID* is found, then the set is found. Finally, the Member Name's Object ID is deleted from the set. To make this call, the user must have write access to the property.

The NetWare C Interface format is:

```
int DeleteBinderyObjectFromSet( char *objectName, WORD objectType,
    char *propertyName, char *memberName, WORD memberType );
```

Get Bindery Object ID (E3h 35h)

This call is supported in Advanced NetWare versions 1.0, 1.02, 2.0, and 2.1, and in NetWare 386 and later versions. It returns the four-byte ID of an object given its name and type.

Registers in:

AH	E3h
DS:SI	Request Buffer Address
ES:DI	Reply Buffer Address

Registers out:

AL	Completion Code

Completion Codes:

00	Success
96h	Server Out Of Memory
EFh	Invalid Name
F0h	Wildcard Not Allowed
FCh	No Such Object
FEh	Server Bindery Locked
FFh	Bindery Failure

Request Packet (max size = 54 bytes):

Offset	Content	Type	Order
0	Request Buffer Length-2	WORD	lo-hi
2	35h	BYTE	
3	Object Type	WORD	hi-lo
5	Object Name Length	BYTE [1-48]	
6	Object Name	BYTE[*LENGTH*]	

Reply Packet (56 bytes):

0	Reply Buffer Length - 2	WORD	lo-hi
2	Object ID	LONG	hi-lo
6	Object Type	WORD	hi-lo
8	Object Name	BYTE[48]	

The NetWare C Interface format is:

```
int GetBinderyObjectID( char *objectName, WORD objectType,
   long *objectID );
```

Get Bindery Object Name (E3h 36h)

This call is supported in Advanced NetWare versions 1.0, 1.02, 2.0, and 2.1, and in NetWare 386 and later versions. The opposite of the preceding one, this one returns the type and name of an object, given its four-byte ID.

Registers in:

AH	E3h
DS:SI	Request Buffer Address
ES:DI	Reply Buffer Address

Registers out:

AL	Completion Code

Completion Codes:

00	Success
96h	Server Out Of Memory
FCh	No Such Object
FEh	Server Bindery Locked
FFh	Bindery Failure

Request Packet (size = 7 bytes):

Offset	Content	Type	Order
0	Request Buffer Length-2	WORD	lo-hi
2	36h	BYTE	
3	Object ID	LONG	hi-lo

Reply Packet (56 bytes):

Offset	Content	Type	Order
0	Reply Buffer Length - 2	WORD	lo-hi
2	Object ID	LONG	hi-lo
6	Object Type	WORD	hi-lo
8	Object Name	BYTE[48]	

The NetWare C Interface format is:

```
int GetBinderyObjectName( long objectID, char *objectName,
   WORD *objectType);
```

Verify Bindery Object Password (E3h 3Fh)

This call is supported in Advanced NetWare versions 1.0, 1.02, 2.0, and 2.1, and in NetWare 386 and later versions. It verifies the accuracy of a password for a Bindery object.

Registers in:

AH	E3h
DS:SI	Request Buffer Address
ES:DI	Reply Buffer Address

Registers out:

AL	Completion Code

Completion Codes:

00	Success
96h	Server Out Of Memory
F0h	Wildcard Not Allowed
FBh	No Such Property
FCh	No Such Object
FEh	Server Bindery Locked
FFh	Bindery Failure (No such object or bad password)

Request Packet (max size = 183 bytes):

Offset	Content	Type	Order
0	Request Buffer Length-2	WORD	lo-hi
2	3Fh	BYTE	
3	Object Type	WORD	hi-lo
5	Object Name Length	BYTE [1-48]	
6	Object Name	BYTE[*LENGTH*]	
?	Password Length	BYTE [1-128]	
?	Password	BYTE[*LENGTH*]	

Reply Packet (2 bytes):

Offset	Content	Type	Order
0	0000	WORD	lo-hi

The *Password* of the object to be verified must be uppercase and can be NULL if there is no password.

This call checks the password given against the password in the Bindery and returns Successful (00) if they match and Bindery Failure (FFh) if they don't.

The NetWare C Interface format is:

```
int VerifyBinderyObjectPassword( char *objectName, WORD objectType,
    char *password );
```

Change Bindery Object Security (E3h 38h)

This call is supported in Advanced NetWare versions 1.0, 1.02, 2.0, and 2.1, and in NetWare 386 and later versions. It changes the security of a Bindery object.

Registers in:

AH	E3h
DS:SI	Request Buffer Address
ES:DI	Reply Buffer Address

Registers out:

AL	Completion Code

Completion Codes:

00	Success
96h	Server Out Of Memory
F0h	Wildcard Not Allowed
F1h	Invalid Bindery Security
FCh	No Such Object
FEh	Server Bindery Locked
FFh	Bindery Failure

Request Packet (max size = 54 bytes):

Offset	**Content**	**Type**	**Order**
0	Request Buffer Length-2	WORD	lo-hi
2	38h	BYTE	
3	New Object Security	BYTE	
4	Object Type	WORD	hi-lo
6	Object Name Length	BYTE [1-48]	
7	Object Name	BYTE[*LENGTH*]	

Reply Packet (2 bytes):

Offset	**Content**	**Type**	**Order**
0	0000	WORD	lo-hi

New Object Security becomes the new security value for the Object unless NetWare read or NetWare write security has been specified, in which case security cannot be changed. To make this call, the user must be logged in as the supervisor or as an object that is supervisor-equivalent.

The NetWare C Interface format is:

```
int ChangeBinderyObjectSecurity( char *objectName, WORD objectType,
    BYTE newObjectSecurity );
```

Change Bindery Object Password (E3h 40h)

This call is supported in Advanced NetWare versions 1.0, 1.02, 2.0 and 2.1, and in NetWare 386 and later versions. It changes the password of a Bindery object.

Registers in:

AH	E3h
DS:SI	Request Buffer Address
ES:DI	Reply Buffer Address

Registers out:

AL	Completion Code

Completion Codes:

00	Success
96h	Server Out Of Memory
F0h	Wildcard Not Allowed
FBh	No Such Property
FCh	No Such Object
FEh	Server Bindery Locked
FFh	No Such Object
	No Password Associated with Object
	or Old Password Invalid

Request Packet (max size = 311 bytes):

Offset	**Content**	**Type**	**Order**
0	Request Buffer Length-2	WORD	lo-hi
2	40h	BYTE	
3	Object Type	WORD	hi-lo
5	Object Name Length	BYTE [1-48]	
6	Object Name	BYTE[*LENGTH*]	
?	Old Password Length	BYTE [0-128]	
?	Old Password	BYTE[*LENGTH*]	
?	New Password Length	BYTE [0-128]	
?	New Password	BYTE[*LENGTH*]	

Reply Packet (2 bytes)

Offset	**Content**	**Type**	**Order**
0	0000	WORD	lo-hi

If there is no PASSWORD property associated with the Bindery object, the file server will add one to the object, assigning security level 44h (NetWare read/write). The Old Password must be all upper-case and can be NULL. To log into a file server, an object must have a PASSWORD property, although it is not necessary to have a value associated with that property.

To make this call, the user must have read and write access to the Bindery object.

The NetWare C Interface format is:

```
int ChangeBinderyObjectPassword( char *objectName, WORD objectType,
    char *oldPassword, char *newPassword );
```

Create Property (E3h 39h)

This call is supported in Advanced NetWare versions 1.0, 1.02, 2.0, and 2.1, and in NetWare 386 and later versions. It creates a property to be associated with a Bindery object. Given the name and type of the object, and the property's name, flags, and security, the call adds the property to the object in the Bindery.

Registers in:

AH	E3h
DS:SI	Request Buffer Address
ES:DI	Reply Buffer Address

Registers out:

AL	Completion Code

Completion Codes:

00	Success
96h	Server Out Of Memory
EDh	Property Already Exists
EFh	Invalid Name
F0h	Wildcard Not Allowed
F1h	Invalid Bindery Security
F7h	No Property Create Privileges
FCh	No Such Object
FEh	Server Bindery Locked
FFh	Bindery Failure

Request Packet (max size = 73 bytes):

Offset	Content	Type	Order
0	Request Buffer Length-2	WORD	lo-hi
2	39h	BYTE	
3	Object Type	WORD	hi-lo
5	Object Name Length	BYTE [1-48]	
6	Object Name	BYTE[*LENGTH*]	
?	Property Flags	BYTE	
?	Property Security	BYTE	
?	Property Name Length	BYTE [1-15]	
?	Property Name	BYTE[*LENGTH*]	

Reply Packet (2 bytes):

Offset	Content	Type	Order
0	0000	WORD	lo-hi

Property Flags tell whether a property is dynamic or static and whether a property is a set or an item.

To make this call, the user must have read and write access to the Bindery object.

The NetWare C Interface format is:

```
int CreateProperty( char *objectName, WORD objectType,
   char *propertyName, BYTE propertyFlags, BYTE propertySecurity );
```

Delete Property (E3h 3Ah)

This call is supported in Advanced NetWare versions 1.0, 1.02, 2.0, and 2.1, and in NetWare 386 and later versions. It deletes a property from a particular object. Given the object name and type and the property name, the property is deleted.

Registers in:

AH	E3h
DS:SI	Request Buffer Address
ES:DI	Reply Buffer Address

Registers out:

AL	Completion Code

Completion Codes:

00	Success
96h	Server Out Of Memory
F0h	Wildcard Not Allowed
F1h	Invalid Bindery Security
F6h	No Property Delete Privileges
FBh	No Such Property
FCh	No Such Object
FEh	Server Bindery Locked
FFh	Bindery Failure

Request Packet (max size = 71 bytes):

Offset	Content	Type	Order
0	Request Buffer Length-2	WORD	lo-hi
2	3Ah	BYTE	
3	Object Type	WORD	hi-lo
5	Object Name Length	BYTE [1-48]	
6	Object Name	BYTE[*LENGTH*]	
?	Property Name Length	BYTE [1-15]	
?	Property Name	BYTE[*LENGTH*]	

Reply Packet (2 bytes):

Offset	Content	Type	Order
0	0000	WORD	lo-hi

To make this call, the user must have write access to the Bindery object and its property.

The *Object Name* and *Type* fields may not contain wildcards but the Property Name field may.

The NetWare C Interface format is:

```
int DeleteProperty( char *objectName, WORD objectType,
    char *propertyName );
```

Scan Property (E3h 3Ch)

This call is supported in Advanced NetWare versions 1.0, 1.02, 2.0, and 2.1, and in NetWare 386 and later versions. It returns all of the properties associated with a particular object.

Registers in:

AH	E3h
DS:SI	Request Buffer Address
ES:DI	Reply Buffer Address

Registers out:

AL	Completion Code

Completion Codes:

00	Success
96h	Server Out Of Memory
F1h	Invalid Bindery Security
FBh	No Such Property
FCh	No Such Object
FEh	Server Bindery Locked
FFh	Bindery Failure

Request Packet (max size = 75 bytes):

Offset	**Content**	**Type**	**Order**
0	Request Buffer Length-2	WORD	lo-hi
2	3Ch	BYTE	
3	Object Type	WORD	hi-lo
5	Object Name Length	BYTE [1-48]	
6	Object Name	BYTE[*LENGTH*]	
?	Sequence Number	LONG	hi-lo
?	Property Name Length	BYTE [1-15]	
?	Property Name	BYTE[*LENGTH*]	

Reply Packet (26 bytes):

0	Reply Buffer Length-2	WORD	lo-hi
2	Property Name	BYTE[16]	
18	Property Flags	BYTE	
19	Property Security	BYTE	
20	Sequence Number	LONG	hi-lo
24	Property Has Value	BYTE	
25	More Properties	BYTE	

Sequence Number should be FFFFFFFFh (-1) the first time the programmer makes this call. In subsequent calls, the returned Sequence Number should be placed here. The call can be reiterated this way until More Properties is set to 0 or a completion code of No Such Property (FBh) is returned.

Property Name may contain wildcards.

Property Has Value is a flag that tells (0 = False, FFh = True) whether or not this particular property contains a value. If so, the call Read Property Value can be used to extract the value.

More Properties is a flag set (FFh) if more properties exist for this object, or to zero if not.

To make this call, the user must have read access to the Bindery object and its properties.

The NetWare C Interface format is:

```
int ScanProperty( char *objectName, WORD objectType,
    char *searchPropertyName, long *sequenceNumber,
    char *propertyName, char *propertyFlags, char *propertySecurity,
    char *propertyHasValue, char *moreProperties );
```

Read Property Value (E3h 3Dh)

This call is supported in Advanced NetWare versions 1.0, 1.02, 2.0, and 2.1, and in NetWare 386 and later versions. It returns the value of a property associated with a Bindery object.

Registers in:

AH	E3h
DS:SI	Request Buffer Address
ES:DI	Reply Buffer Address

Registers out:

AL	Completion Code

Completion Codes:

00	Success
96h	Server Out Of Memory
ECh	No Such Segment
F0h	Wildcard Not Allowed

F1h	Invalid Bindery Security
FBh	No Such Property
FCh	No Such Object
FEh	Server Bindery Locked
FFh	Bindery Failure

Request Packet (max size = 72 bytes):

Offset	**Content**	**Type**	**Order**
0	Request Buffer Length-2	WORD	lo-hi
2	3Dh	BYTE	
3	Object Type	WORD	hi-lo
5	Object Name Length	BYTE [1-48]	
6	Object Name	BYTE[*LENGTH*]	
?	Segment Number	BYTE	
?	Property Name Length	BYTE [1-15]	
?	Property Name	BYTE[*LENGTH*]	

Reply Packet (132 bytes)

Offset	**Content**	**Type**	**Order**
0	Reply Buffer Length-2	WORD	lo-hi
2	Property Value	BYTE[128]	
130	More Segments	BYTE	
131	Property Flags	BYTE	

If the More Segments flag is set, the programmer should increment the Segment Number by 1 and make the call again. The call can continue to be made in this manner until More Segments is set to 0 or a completion code of No Such Segment (ECh) is returned.

More Segments is a flag set to true (FFh) if there are more 128-byte value segments for this property, to false (00) if not.

Property Flags bit is the Item/Set Flag. Return of a 1 indicates the property is a set, meaning its value is a list of four-byte object IDs. Return of a 0 indicates the property is an item, and the property segment can contain any structure.

If the property type is set then, as in an ASCIIZ string, the list is terminated with an object ID of 0. However, if an object ID has been deleted from the middle of a list, only the list for the current segment was compacted. Therefore, programmers should check the More Segments flag to make sure there are no more segments and not rely entirely on an end-of-list 0 in the Value field.

It is important to remember that the Bindery does no coordination of updates. One potential problem scenario involves one station writing a property value on one segment while another workstation reads the partially updated value. Developers may wish to use logical record locks when updating the Bindery to ensure no partial updates. Also, programmers may want to use the Get or Set Preferred File Server calls to ensure that the correct file server receives the request.

To make this call, the user must have read access to the property.

The NetWare C Interface format is:

```
int ReadPropertyValue( char *objectName, WORD objectType,
    char *propertyName, int segmentNumber, BYTE *propertyValue,
    BYTE *moreSegments, BYTE *propertyFlags );
```

Write Property Value (E3h 3Eh)

This call is supported in Advanced NetWare versions 1.0, 1.02, 2.0, and 2.1, and in NetWare 386 and later versions. It changes the value of a property associated with a Bindery object.

Registers in:

AH	E3h
DS:SI	Request Buffer Address
ES:DI	Reply Buffer Address

Registers out:

AL	Completion Code

Completion Codes:

00	Success
96h	Server Out Of Memory
E8h	Not Item Property
ECh	No Such Segment
F0h	Wildcard Not Allowed
F1h	Invalid Bindery Security
F8h	No Property Write Privileges
FBh	No Such Property
FCh	No Such Object
FEh	Server Bindery Locked
FFh	Bindery Failure

Request Packet (max size = 201 bytes):

Offset	**Content**	**Type**	**Order**
0	Request Buffer Length-2	WORD	lo-hi
2	3Eh	BYTE	
3	Object Type	WORD	hi-lo
5	Object Name Length	BYTE [1-48]	
6	Object Name	BYTE[*LENGTH*]	
?	Segment Number	BYTE	
?	Erase Remaining Segments	BYTE	
?	Property Name Length	BYTE [1-15]	
?	Property Name	BYTE[*LENGTH*]	
?	Property Value Segment	BYTE[128]	

Reply Packet (2 bytes):

Offset	Content	Type	Order
0	0000	WORD	lo-hi

Segment Number should be set to 1 the first time the programmer makes this call. If there are more segments to write, this value should be incremented by 1. Segments must be added in order; one may over-write an earlier segment, but cannot skip ahead to a later segment. That is, if the last written segment was 3, you can overwrite segment 1 but you can't skip up to and write segment 5.

Erase Remaining Segments is a flag set true (FFh) if this is the last segment for this property. If so, any later segments are erased. The flag should be set to 0 until the last segment is written.

This call should not be made to write values to properties of type set. That should be done with the call Add Bindery Object to Set. It is again important to remember that the Bindery does no coordination of updates.

To make this call, the user must have write access to the property.

The NetWare C Interface format is:

```
int WritePropertyValue( char *objectName, WORD objectType,
    char *propertyName, int segmentNumber, BYTE *propertyValue,
    BYTE moreSegments );
```

Change Property Security (E3h 3Bh)

This call is supported in Advanced NetWare versions 1.0, 1.02, 2.0, and 2.1, and in NetWare 386 and later versions. It allows the developer to change the security of a property.

Registers in:

AH	E3h
DS:SI	Request Buffer Address
ES:DI	Reply Buffer Address

Registers out:

AL	Completion Code

Completion Codes:

00	Success
96h	Server Out Of Memory
F0h	Wildcard Not Allowed
F1h	Invalid Bindery Security
FBh	No Such Property
FCh	No Such Object
FEh	Server Bindery Locked
FFh	Bindery Failure

Request Packet (max size = 72 bytes):

Offset	Content	Type	Order
0	Request Buffer Length-2	WORD	lo-hi
2	3Bh	BYTE	
3	Object Type	WORD	hi-lo
5	Object Name Length	BYTE [1-48]	
6	Object Name	BYTE[*LENGTH*]	
?	New Property Security	BYTE	
?	Property Name Length	BYTE [1-15]	
?	Property Name	BYTE[*LENGTH*]	

Reply Packet (2 bytes):

Offset	Content	Type	Order
0	0000	WORD	lo-hi

To make this call, the user must have read and write access to the Bindery object. This call cannot assign security greater than the workstation's security level for the object. No user can change NetWare's access to an object. Wildcards are not allowed in this call.

The NetWare C Interface format is:

```
int ChangePropertySecurity( char *objectName, WORD objectType,
    char *propertyName, BYTE newPropertySecurity );
```

Get Bindery Access Level (E3h 46h)

This call is supported in Advanced NetWare versions 1.0, 1.02, 2.0, and 2.1, and in NetWare 386 and later versions. It returns the user's access level to the Bindery.

Registers in:

AH	E3h
DS:SI	Request Buffer Address
ES:DI	Reply Buffer Address

Registers out:

AL	Completion Code

Completion Codes:

00	Success

Request Packet (3 bytes):

Offset	Content	Type	Order
0	Request Buffer Length-2	WORD	lo-hi
2	46h	BYTE	

Reply Packet (7 bytes):

Offset	Content	Type	Order
0	Reply Buffer Length - 2	WORD	lo-hi
2	Access level	BYTE	
3	Object ID	LONG	hi-lo

The NetWare C Interface format is:

```
int GetBinderyAccessLevel( BYTE *securityAccessLevel,
    long *objectID );
```

Code Sample: UserInfo.C

UserInfo displays information about each Bindery object of type user and the properties and property values associated with each. The user may specify no command-line arguments and all users will be displayed, or the user may specify a wildcard, such as "C*" and all users beginning with C will be shown.

UserInfo first defines the structures used in the Scan Bindery Object, Scan Property, and Read Property Value function calls and sets up local prototypes.

The main() function begins by initializing all of the Request/Reply structures to 0 and checks the command-line arguments to make sure there were not too many input. Next, the program begins to set up the *ScanBindRequest* packet, setting the *LastObjectID* to -1 and the object type to type USER. Object type user is actually 1 but because Novell wants the type in hi-lo format, we place it into *ScanBind-Request.ObjectType* as 0x0100.

Next, the program checks to see if there was a command-line argument specified. If so, it is copied into the Request structure and its length is recorded; if not, a star '*' is used (meaning, include everything) and its length of 1 is used.

The rest of main() is contained in a WHILE loop, getting the next object and its properties, and the values of the properties and reporting the results at each step. First in the loop is the call ScanBinderyObject which looks for the first object matching the given criteria. If the return code is FCh then there are no more matching objects and the program ends. If the result was nonzero, the program halts and reports the error. Otherwise, the call is successful and main() calls PrintBindery-ScanResults() which displays the name of the user, the Bindery object type, the static/dynamic flag, and the security of the user object.

Next, if there are properties (the *ScanBindReply.ObjectHasProperties* is TRUE) the *ScanPropRequest* structure is initialized. Note that since the *Object Name* in the *ScanPropRequest* field can be up to 48 characters then the next three variables could really be placed at any offset, which is why in the Novell documentation, the offset of these fields has the value "?".

I dealt with this problem by fixing the size of the *Object Name* at the maximum, 48 bytes. If this is done, then when you go to fill in the *Object Name* and *Object Name Length*, the *Object Name Length* needs to be 48. This is done using the sizeof() function to set *ScanPropRequest.ObjectNameLength* to sizeof(ScanProp-Request.ObjectName).

Once the request packet is initialized, main() enters another WHILE loop to iterate through all of the properties for this object. ScanProperty is called and if the result is FBh (No More Properties), control reverts to the outer WHILE loop and the next object is queried.

If result evaluates to TRUE the error is printed and the program exits. Otherwise, the name of the property and its static/dynamic flag as well as its item/set flag and the security are printed.

Next, the program checks *PropertyHasValue* to see if any values are present for this property. If so, the *ReadPropRequest* structure is set up and a third WHILE loop is entered to read all of the values for this property. If ReadPropertyValue() returns ECh (No More Values) then control reverts to the outer WHILE loop and goes on to the next property.

If there is an error, it is printed and the program halts. Otherwise, PrintPropertyValueReadResults() is called, printing the value of the property. If the property is IDENTIFICATION, it is considered a string and is printed as such, or if it is a set then PrintSetValues() is called to print the value of each member of the set. If the property is an item and is not IDENTIFICATION, the program returns.

PrintSetValues() iterates through each of the 32 possible values in one reply structure, using the Bindery call GetName() to get the name of the Bindery object ID passed to it. The name is then printed to the screen.

The GetType() and GetSecurity() functions are used by the printing routines to print the type and security values for the objects and properties. They each use case statements to test the values of the variables.

```
/*                                                                        */
/* UserInfo - Displays all of the bindery properties for each user        */
/*                                                                        */
/* by Charles Rose                                                        */
/*                                                                        */

#include <stdio.h>
#include <dos.h>
#include <dir.h>
#include <string.h>

#define USER 0x0100     /* Not 0x0001 because this is a hi-lo number */
#define SET  0x2

typedef unsigned char BYTE;
typedef unsigned int WORD;
typedef unsigned long LONG;

struct scanBindReq {
    WORD  Length;
    BYTE  Function;
    LONG  LastObjectID;
    WORD  ObjectType;
    BYTE  ObjectNameLength;
    BYTE  ObjectName[48];
    };
```

```
struct scanBindRep {
    WORD  Length;
    LONG  ObjectID;
    WORD  ObjectType;
    BYTE  ObjectName[48];
    BYTE  ObjectFlag;
    BYTE  ObjectSecurity;
    BYTE  ObjectHasProperties;
    };

struct scanPropReq {
    WORD  Length;
    BYTE  Function;
    WORD  ObjectType;
    BYTE  ObjectNameLength;
    BYTE  ObjectName[48];
    LONG  SequenceNumber;
    BYTE  PropertyNameLength;
    BYTE  PropertyName[16];
    };

struct scanPropRep {
    WORD  Length;
    BYTE  PropertyName[16];
    BYTE  PropertyFlags;
    BYTE  PropertySecurity;
    LONG  SequenceNumber;
    BYTE  PropertyHasValue;
    BYTE  MoreProperties;
    };

struct readPropValueReq {
    WORD  Length;
    BYTE  Function;
    WORD  ObjectType;
    BYTE  ObjectNameLength;
    BYTE  ObjectName[48];2
    BYTE  SegmentNumber;
    BYTE  PropertyNameLength;
    BYTE  PropertyName[16];
    };

struct readPropValueRep {
    WORD  Length;
    BYTE  PropertyValue[128];
    BYTE  MoreSegments;
    BYTE  PropertyFlags;
    };

int ScanBinderyObject( struct scanBindReq *Request, struct scanBindRep *Reply );
int ScanProperty( struct scanPropReq *Request, struct scanPropRep *Reply );
int ReadPropertyValue( struct readPropValueReq *Request,
   struct readPropValueRep *Reply );
void PrintBinderyScanResults( struct scanBindRep *Reply );
void PrintPropertyScanResults( struct scanPropRep *Reply );
void PrintPropertyValueReadResults( char *PropertyName,
   struct readPropValueRep *Reply );
void PrintSetValues( char *data );
int GetName( LONG objectID, char *ObjectName, WORD *type );
char *GetType( WORD ObjectType );
char *GetSecurity( BYTE Security );
```

```
/* Global Data */
char work[100];

main( int argc, char *argv[] )
{
    struct scanBindReq ScanBindRequest;
    struct scanBindRep ScanBindReply;
    struct scanPropReq ScanPropRequest;
    struct scanPropRep ScanPropReply;
    struct readPropValueReq ReadPropRequest;
    struct readPropValueRep ReadPropReply;

    int result;

    /* Initialize Request/Reply packets to 0 */
    memset( &ScanBindRequest, NULL, sizeof( ScanBindRequest ) );
    memset( &ScanBindReply, NULL, sizeof( ScanBindReply ) );
    memset( &ScanPropRequest, NULL, sizeof( ScanPropRequest ) );
    memset( &ScanPropReply, NULL, sizeof( ScanPropReply ) );
    memset( &ReadPropRequest, NULL, sizeof( ReadPropRequest ) );
    memset( &ReadPropReply, NULL, sizeof( ReadPropReply ) );

    if ( argc > 2 )
    {
      printf( "Usage: USERINFO [wildcard] - Optional wildcard for user names.\n" );
      exit(1);
    }

    ScanBindRequest.LastObjectID = 0xFFFFFFFF;
    ScanBindRequest.ObjectType = USER;

    if ( argc == 2 )
    {
       /* User specified object wildcard, so include it */
       ScanBindRequest.ObjectNameLength = strlen( argv[1] );
       strcpy( ScanBindRequest.ObjectName, strupr( argv[1] ) );
    }
    else
    {
       /* Otherwise, show info for all users */
       ScanBindRequest.ObjectNameLength = 1;
       ScanBindRequest.ObjectName[0] = '*';
    }

    while( 1 )
    {
       result = ScanBinderyObject( &ScanBindRequest, &ScanBindReply );
       if ( result == 0xFC )
          break;
       else if ( result )
       {
          printf( "Error scanning bindery object, code = %X\n",
          result );
          exit(1);
       }

       PrintBinderyScanResults( &ScanBindReply );

       if ( ScanBindReply.ObjectHasProperties )
       {
          printf( "  Properties:\n" );
```

```
  ScanPropRequest.ObjectType = ScanBindReply.ObjectType;

  /* In this implementation,
     this length must be the length of the field (48) */
  ScanPropRequest.ObjectNameLength = sizeof
  (ScanPropRequest.ObjectName );

  strcpy( ScanPropRequest.ObjectName,
     ScanBindReply.ObjectName );
  ScanPropRequest.SequenceNumber = 0xFFFFFFFF;
  ScanPropRequest.PropertyNameLength = 1;
  ScanPropRequest.PropertyName[0] = '*';

  while ( 1 )
  {
     result = ScanProperty( &ScanPropRequest,
     &ScanPropReply );
     if ( result == 0xFB )
        break;
     else if ( result )
     {
        printf( "Error scanning property, code = %X\n", result );
        exit(1);
     }

     PrintPropertyScanResults( &ScanPropReply );

     if ( ScanPropReply.PropertyHasValue )
     {
        printf( " Values:\n" );

ReadPropRequest.ObjectType = ScanBindReply.ObjectType;
ReadPropRequest.ObjectNameLength = sizeof( ReadPropRequest.ObjectName );
strcpy( ReadPropRequest.ObjectName, ScanBindReply.ObjectName );
ReadPropRequest.SegmentNumber = 1;
ReadPropRequest.PropertyNameLength = strlen( ScanPropReply.PropertyName );
movmem( ScanPropReply.PropertyName,  ReadPropRequest.PropertyName,
  ReadPropRequest.PropertyNameLength );

        while ( 1 )
        {
           result = ReadPropertyValue( &ReadPropRequest, &ReadPropReply );
           if ( result == 0xEC )
           {
              printf( "\n" );
              break;
           }
           else if ( result )
           {
              printf( "Error scanning property, code = %X\n", result );
              exit(1);
           }

           PrintPropertyValueReadResults( ScanPropReply.PropertyName,
              &ReadPropReply );

           ReadPropRequest.SegmentNumber++;
        }

     }
     ScanPropRequest.SequenceNumber = ScanPropReply.SequenceNumber;
  }
```

```
            ScanBindRequest.LastObjectID = ScanBindReply.ObjectID;
        }
    }
}

int ScanBinderyObject( struct scanBindReq *Request, struct scanBindRep *Reply )
{
    Request->Function = 0x37;
    Request->Length = sizeof( struct scanBindReq ) - 2;
    Reply->Length = sizeof( struct scanBindRep ) - 2;

    _AH = 0xE3;
    _SI = (unsigned)Request;
    _DI = (unsigned)Reply;
    _ES = _DS;

    geninterrupt( 0x21 );

    return _AL;
}

int ScanProperty( struct scanPropReq *Request, struct scanPropRep *Reply )
{
    Request->Function = 0x3C;
    Request->Length = sizeof( struct scanPropReq ) - 2;
    Reply->Length = sizeof( struct scanPropRep ) - 2;

    _AH = 0xE3;
    _SI = (unsigned)Request;
    _DI = (unsigned)Reply;
    _ES = _DS;

    geninterrupt( 0x21 );

    return _AL;
}

int ReadPropertyValue( struct readPropValueReq *Request,
   struct readPropValueRep *Reply )
{
    Request->Function = 0x3D;
    Request->Length = sizeof( struct readPropValueReq ) - 2;
    Reply->Length = sizeof( struct readPropValueRep ) - 2;

    _AH = 0xE3;
    _SI = (unsigned)Request;
    _DI = (unsigned)Reply;
    _ES = _DS;

    geninterrupt( 0x21 );

    return _AL;
}

void PrintBinderyScanResults( struct scanBindRep *Reply )
{
    printf( "\nUser :%s:\n\n", Reply->ObjectName );
    printf( "Bindery Object Type: %s\n", GetType( Reply->ObjectType ) );
    printf( "Static/Dynamic Flag: %s\n",
       Reply->ObjectFlag ? "Dynamic" : "Static" );
    printf( "Object Security  : %s\n\n", GetSecurity( Reply->ObjectSecurity ) );
}
```

```
void PrintPropertyScanResults( struct scanPropRep *Reply )
{
    printf( "    %s  - ", Reply->PropertyName );
    printf( "(%s) ", ( Reply->PropertyFlags & 1 ) ? "Dynamic" : "Static" );
    printf( "(%s) ", ( Reply->PropertyFlags & 2 ) ? "Set" : "Item" );
    printf( "(%s)\n", GetSecurity( Reply->PropertySecurity ) );
}

void PrintPropertyValueReadResults( char *PropertyName,
   struct readPropValueRep *Reply )
{
    if ( Reply->PropertyFlags & SET )
       PrintSetValues( Reply->PropertyValue ),

    if ( !strcmp( PropertyName, "IDENTIFICATION" ) )
       printf("    %s\n", Reply->PropertyValue );
}

void PrintSetValues( char *data )
{
    LONG objectID;
    WORD i, type;
    char name[48];

    for ( i = 0; i < 32; i++ )
    {
       objectID = *((LONG *)(data + (i*4)));
       if ( !objectID ) return;
       GetName( objectID, name, &type );
       printf( "      %s\n", name );
    }
}

int GetName( LONG objectID, char *ObjectName, WORD *type )
{
    BYTE Request[7] = { 5, 0, 0x36, 0, 0, 0, 0 };
    BYTE Reply[56];

    *Reply = 54;                            /* Set Length */
    *((LONG *)(Request + 3)) = objectID;    /* Place objectID in Request packet */

    _AH = 0xE3;
    _SI = (unsigned)Request;
    _DI = (unsigned)Reply;
    _ES = _DS;

    geninterrupt( 0x21 );

    if ( _AL )
       return _AL;
    else
    {
       *type = *((WORD *)(Reply + 6));  /* Return type */
       strcpy( ObjectName, &Reply[8] ); /* and Object Name */
       return 0;
    }
}

char *GetType( WORD ObjectType )
```

```
{
    switch ( ObjectType )
    {
       case 0x0000:     strcpy( work, "Unknown" );
                 break;
       case 0x0100:     strcpy( work, "User" );
                 break;
       case 0x0200:     strcpy( work, "User Group" );
                 break;
       case 0x0300:     strcpy( work, "Print Queue" );
                 break;
       case 0x0400:     strcpy( work, "File Server" );
                 break;
    }

    return work;
}

char *GetSecurity( BYTE Security )
{
    BYTE lo, hi;

    lo = Security & 0x0F;
    hi = (Security & 0xF0) >> 4;

    *work = NULL;

    switch( lo )
    {
       case 0:         strcpy( work, "Anyone Read, " );
                 break;
       case 1:         strcpy( work, "Logged Read, " );
                 break;
       case 2:         strcpy( work, "Object Read, " );
                 break;
       case 3:         strcpy( work, "Supervisor Read, " );
                 break;
       case 4:         strcpy( work, "NetWare Read, " );
                 break;
    }

    switch( hi )
    {
       case 0:         strcat( work, "Anyone Write" );
                 break;
       case 1:         strcat( work, "Logged Write" );
                 break;
       case 2:         strcat( work, "Object Write" );
                 break;
       case 3:         strcat( work, "Supervisor Write" );
                 break;
       case 4:         strcat( work, "NetWare Write" );
                 break;
    }
}
```

Exercises

1. Run UserInfo. Try it with different command-line arguments. Compare your results with those obtained in SysCon.

2. Add other criteria to UserInfo in PrintPropertyValueReadResults(). Right now it only handles sets and the IDENTIFICATION property. Add handlers for other properties, such as LOGIN_CONTROL.

3. Trace through the program. Make sure you see the hierarchy of objects, properties and values, and how the calls are constructed with them.

4. Modify UserInfo to scan for other Bindery types. Make a SvrInfo or a GroupNfo program.

5. Write a program where you create your own properties and add them to various users. You can use UserInfo to test your success.

7 Queue Services

The Queue Management System (QMS) is one of the most powerful additions to NetWare 2.1x. Whereas in NetWare 2.0a and below, the queue system was built into the server, dedicated to servicing print jobs, it has since been "generalized" and made available for programmers to use to its fullest advantage.

These services allow developers to exploit the true distributed processing potentials of NetWare 2.1x. Powerful workstations can be turned into job servers, performing tasks such as batch processing, compiling, file copying, archiving, or printing while freeing up other workstations to do other tasks. These applications allow the network to make the most of its resources.

For a queue-based application to work, there must be three entities involved: a queueing workstation that places jobs into a queue (it is this station that needs the work done), a queue maintenance facility that manages the operation of the queues (the file server performs this task but workstations may modify certain queue characteristics, such as the order of the jobs) and a queue job servicer that takes jobs out of the queue and processes them.

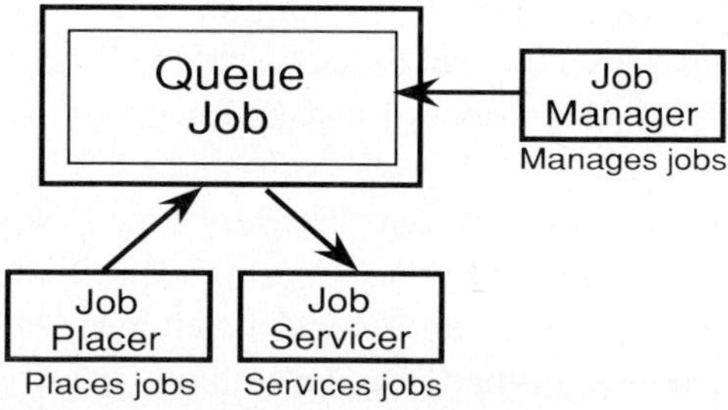

Figure 8: Three entities involved in queue management.

These entities (except for the file server) must be developed by the programmer in routines to place jobs into the queue, routines to modify the queue and routines to remove and service queue jobs.

In this chapter, we will discuss the elements of the QMS and the advantages of using it; the way the QMS interacts with the Bindery; and the Job Entry structure used by the QMS to service its jobs. The function calls will be enumerated and explained and a sample program provided.

Advantages of queue management

There are several advantages to using a queue-based solution to a distributed processing problem. Queues are ideally suited to handling large amounts of incoming data when, although processing needs be quick, instant return is not necessary. Real-time applications or applications requiring immediate attention from application servers are less suited to queue-based solutions. These types of applications are better suited to peer-to-peer strategies, which will be discussed in a later chapter.

Queues provide a measure of control not found in peer-to-peer applications. The job servicer (or another monitoring station) can sort, rearrange, prioritize, or otherwise manage queue jobs before servicing them.

Queues also give programmers a substantial flexibility. Developers have free rein to design whatever protocols they wish to service queue jobs. Each queue job has a header associated with it that contains information pertinent to the job. Although much of this information is created and maintained by the QMS, a part of this header (152 bytes called the Client Record Area) is available for the developer to use in whatever manner desired. NetWare uses this Client Record Area in its own printing routines to store information for the banner; so programmers can use it to define whatever protocols they wish to interact with queue jobs.

Further, the close relation of queues to the file server's Bindery permits development of flexible and sophisticated security systems, providing the ability not only to protect data but also to restrict users to those designated to work with the queues in prescribed manners.

Queues as Bindery objects

Because queues are Bindery objects themselves, they are subject to the read and write access restrictions the Bindery imposes. Also, queues have several Bindery properties that define who can use the queue, who can service the queue, and who can perform certain other operations. It is important to note that, while this allows the queue functions to take advantage of the power of the Bindery to provide security and management facilities, developers must be aware of Novell's standards for Bindery objects.

Chapter 6 provided a list of standard Bindery types. Novell has reserved the types through 0x8000 as predefined types. Again, because object type defines the behavior as well as the purpose of an object, developers must be careful. If, for example, a developer creates a type-9 Bindery object, an Archive Server, it must conform to the behavior and protocols of Novell's Archive Server. And the same applies to queues.

Thus, print queues should be type 3, archive queues should be type 8 and general job queues should be type 10. If you are going to create a queue that does not behave like any of the predefined types, use a type number over 0x8000. (If needed for a commercial product, Novell can permanently assign you a type number.)

Access to queue objects is anyone read, supervisor write. The read security allows anyone to scan the Bindery for queues of a particular type, while the write security protects the queue from being modified by anyone other than the supervisor or equivalent.

Each queue is defined as a Bindery object, complete with its own name, type, ID number, security levels and properties. The properties help define where a queue operates and who can use it, who can change it, and who can service it. Although other properties may be created for the developer's custom use, only the standard properties are used by the QMS to manage what directories files are placed in, or who can use, operate, or service the queues:

Q_DIRECTORY

Queues have directories wherein are stored the queue system files and the job files to be processed. The directory SYS:SYSTEM is often used, but any directory may be used for this purpose. The full directory is derived from concatenating the path specified and the queue's ID number.

For instance, if the programmer specifies SYS:SYSTEM as the directory and the object ID of the queue is "04F3A" then the directory used by the QMS will be "SYS:SYSTEM\04F3A".

The maximum number of characters possible in this property is 118 (including null terminator). This property is an item and there is only one per queue object.

Q_USERS

Q_USERS is a set property that contains a list of all of the object IDs of users and groups that can place jobs in the queue. The QMS uses this property as a part of its security mechanism to make sure only those users that are authorized can place jobs in the queue. Any user security-equivalent to any of the users or groups listed will also be able to place jobs. Also, members of groups that are in the list will have access.

According to Novell, the supervisor must be included in this property. If the supervisor would like any user to be able to write to the queue, the group EVERYONE could be added, allowing any user to place jobs in the queue. Also, if this property is removed, any logged-in object will be able to place jobs in the queue. In this way, a measure of flexibility is provided: the developer may choose to use the security facilities, or not.

Q_SERVERS

Whereas Q_USERS determines who can submit jobs to a queue, Q_SERVERS determines who can service a queue. Q_SERVERS is a set property containing the Bindery object IDs of those objects that can attach to a queue and service its jobs.

The Q_SERVERS property is read when an application uses the Attach Server To Queue call. The Q_SERVERS property is read to see if the calling object is a member of the property (or is security equivalent to a member of the property). If the calling object is not a member (or security equivalent to one), the call will fail, returning an error code.

It is common to place the object IDs of the users who are allowed to start the job-servicing application into this property. Novell suggests that in some circumstances it may be helpful to create a separate login entity (other than type USER) with the privilege of starting the job servicing application. (See chapter 6 for the Bindery calls to create the new entity and chapter 9 for the Connection/Workstation calls to log it in.)

Programmers are requested to use the conventions for queue server types in setting the type of the entity to log in. (Novell has set type 5 as a Job Server, type 7 as a Print Server, and type 9 as an Archive server. The Bindery chapter contains a complete list of Bindery object types.)

The object type can be helpful if an application needs to scan the Bindery for all servers on a network of a certain type. Alternatively, a user could specify that only a certain server could service the job being placed into the queue. Or, the user could specify that any server could service the job.

The bottom line on these options is that much flexibility has been built into the system to allow the developer creative freedom in choosing exactly how to implement the queue servicing mechanism.

Q_OPERATORS

Just like the two previous properties, Q_OPERATORS is a set property. It contains a list of the IDs of objects that can perform certain operations on the queue such as change fields in the Job Entry Structure, reorder the jobs, or change the status of a queue.

As with the Q_USERS property, user or group object IDs can be added to this property. The supervisor does not have inherent operator privileges, so its object ID should be added to this property (to enable the supervisor to perform the operations on the queue).

All these properties are created with the Create Queue function call, but only the Q_DIRECTORY property is initialized. Other properties may be modified through the Bindery Services API.

The developer should keep in mind that to create a queue and change the user list of a property, an application must be logged in as a supervisor-equivalent user.

Job Entry structure

For each job submitted to a queue, there is a corresponding Job Entry that contains information relating to the job. Some of the information for this entry is provided by the QMS while other information is provided by the application. Once submitted, the entry is not set in concrete: the user submitting the job or any user that is a member of Q_OPERATORS can modify the entry.

The following are the elements of the Job Entry:

Client Station	BYTE	
Client Task Number	BYTE	
Client ID Number	LONG	hi-lo
Target Server ID Number	LONG	hi-lo
Target Execution Time	BYTE[6]	
Job Entry Time	BYTE[6]	
Job Number	WORD	hi-lo
Job Type	WORD	hi-lo
Job Position	BYTE	
Job Control Flags	BYTE	
Job File Name	BYTE[14]	
Job File Handle	BYTE[6]	
Server Station	BYTE	
Server Task Number	BYTE	
Server ID Number	LONG	hi-lo
Text Job Description	BYTE[50]	
Client Record Area	BYTE[152]	

Client Station, provided by the QMS, is the connection number of the station that placed the job in the queue. This station has read-write access to the Job Entry's associated file.

Client Task Number, provided by the QMS, is a field containing the number of the task active on the workstation when the job was placed in the queue.

Client ID Number, provided by the QMS, returns the object ID number of the station that placed the job in the queue. The QMS uses this field to recalculate directory access rights when the job server requests the client's rights to service the client's job.

Target Server ID Number, provided by the program, is the Bindery object ID number of the queue server that can service the job. If this field is set to FFFFFFFFh, any job server can service the job. If the specified job server is not attached to the queue, QMS does not place the job in the queue.

Target Execution Time, provided by the program, is the earliest time that the job can be serviced. The format is year, month, day, hour, minute, second. If this field is set to FFFFFFFFFFFFh, the job is serviced at the first opportunity.

Job Entry Time, provided by the QMS, is when the job entered the queue, according to the system clock of the file server. The format is year, month, day, hour, minute, second (one byte each).

Job Number, provided by the QMS, returns the Job Entry number that QMS assigned to the job when it first entered the queue.

Job Type, provided by the QMS, contains a number specifying a type of job represented the Job Entry. A job server can request specific job types from a queue when making a request to service a job. This field should be set to 0 if not used, and should never be set to -1 (wildcard).

Job Position, provided by the QMS, returns the entry's position within the queue. The first entry in a queue is at position one, the second at position two, and so on. As jobs are removed or added, the position numbers of remaining jobs entries are updated to reflect their new positions in the queue.

The *Job Control Flags*, provided by the program, indicate the status of the job. Bits in the field are set as follows.

When bit 08h (the Service Auto-Start flag) is set, the job will be serviced if a job server connection is broken, even if the client has not explicitly started the job. If the bit is cleared when a server connection is broken, and the client has not yet released the job to the queue, QMS removes the job from the queue.

When bit 10h (the Service Restart flag) is set, the job remains in the queue (in its current position) after a job server has aborted the job. If this bit is cleared when a server aborts the job, QMS removes the job from the queue.

QMS sets bit 20h (the Entry Open flag) to indicate that the client has not filled the associated job file. Close File And Start Queue Job clears this bit, indicating that the job is ready for service if the User Hold flag and Operator Hold flag are clear.

When bit 40h (the User Hold flag) is set, the job continues to advance in the queue, but cannot be serviced until the client who placed the job, or the operator, clears the flag.

Bit 80h (the Operator Hold Flag) prevents the job from being serviced, as does the User Hold flag; only operators can clear or set the Operator Hold flag.

Job File Name and *Job File Handle*, provided by the QMS, specify the name and file handle of the job file created by QMS corresponding to the Job Entry. The calling station places information (commands, text, etc.) destined for the job server in this file. Job File Handle is not a standard DOS handle, but is a special NetWare handle. Programs may, with the DOS shell ID, open the device NETQ: after creating a job. Then standard DOS I/O calls may be made to write to the NETQ: device. Writing to that device will place data into the queue job file.

Server Station, provided by the QMS, contains the station number of the job server servicing the job. If no server is servicing the job, this field is undefined.

Server Task Number, provided by the QMS, contains the task number of the job server servicing the job. When no server is servicing the job, this field is undefined.

Server ID Number, provided by the QMS, contains the ID number of the job server servicing the job. When no server is servicing the job, this field is set to zero. This field should be checked to determine if a job is being serviced and, therefore, if the values in the Server Station and Server Task fields are valid.

Text Job Description can contain a null-terminated ASCII text description of the content or purpose of a job. QMS can display this text as part of the job description when users or operators examine a queue. This field can also be used to pass parameters to the job server. The client creating the queue job must supply this field.

Client Record Area contains additional information passed to the job server by the client. The information can take any format agreed upon by both the client and the job server. This field must be supplied by the client creating the queue job.

How Queues Interact with the Filing System

The QMS uses the Q_DIRECTORY property to determine where to place the files associated with the queue. Any jobs submitted to the queue are named with a "Q$" preceding the last four digits of the queue's ID number. The extension of the file is the corresponding three-digit Job Number. Therefore, for queue 0xF0315A42, job 134, the associated job file will be placed in the Q_DIRECTORY directory as the file Q$5A42.134.

Queues also keep two other files in the directory. One file, with the extension .SRV, lists the currently attached servers for the queue; the other uses the extension .SYS and contains the Job Entry records for the queue. These files, like the job files, are prefixed by a "Q$" and the last four digits of the Queue ID. They are flagged hidden when created.

As jobs are added to the queue, the .SYS file fills up (to a maximum of 250 entries) and as jobs are serviced, the records in the .SYS file are removed.

The QMS does not use the queue job file. The developer is free to put whatever information is desired into the file. The NetWare Print Services API places the data to be printed in this file, whereas a job server might use this file for instructions to be performed, etc.

Calls in the Queue Services API

All of the Queue Services API calls are supported in Advanced NetWare version 2.1, NetWare 386, and later versions. Throughout the book, we explain fields within the calls only at the first mention of each field in each chapter. Appendix B contains a comprehensive, alphabetical listing of the fields for quick reference.

Create Queue (E3h 64h)

This call creates a queue of the specified type and name in the Bindery of the file server.

Registers in:

AH	E3h
DS:SI	Request Buffer Address
ES:DI	Reply Buffer Address

Registers out:

AL	Completion Code

Completion Codes:

00	Success
96h	Server Out Of Memory
99h	Directory Full

9Bh	Bad Directory Handle
9Ch	Invalid Path
EDh	Property Already Exists
EEh	Object Already Exists
EFh	Invalid Name
F0h	Wildcard Not Allowed
F1h	Invalid Bindery Security
F5h	No Object Create Privilege
F7h	No Property Create Privilege
FCh	No Such Object
FEh	Server Bindery Locked
FFh	Bindery Failure

Request Packet (max = 174 bytes):

Offset	Content	Type	Order
0	Request Buffer Length-2	WORD	lo-hi
2	64h	BYTE	
3	Queue Type	WORD	hi-lo
4	Queue Name Length	BYTE (1-48)	
5	Queue Name	BYTE[*LENGTH*]	
?	Directory Handle	BYTE	
?	Path Name Length	BYTE (1-118)	
?	Path Name	BYTE	

Reply Packet (6 bytes):

Offset	Content	Type	Order
0	Reply Packet Length-2	WORD	lo-hi
2	Queue ID	LONG	hi-lo

Queue Type is the Bindery object type of the queue. Queue Name is 1-48 characters long including a one-byte null terminator.

Directory Handle is a number (1-255), corresponding to an index to the Directory Handle Table, which points to a volume/directory combination and describes a full path on the network.

Directory Path may be the full path itself or an offset to the source Directory Handle. If no source Directory Handle is specified, the volume name must be specified in the format "VOLUME:DIRECTORY\SUBDIRECTORY". If a Directory Handle is specified, the path can be used as an offset to it. If the Directory Handle describes the full path, the Source Directory Path field is not necessary. If the full path is specified, the Directory Handle can be set to zero.

Queue ID is the Bindery object ID for the queue that is created.

The *Directory Handle* and *Directory Path* are used to describe the subdirectory associated with the queue. An often used area is SYS:SYSTEM (set the Directory Handle to 0, path length to 10, and the path name to "SYS:SYSTEM").

This call creates a Bindery object of type Queue Type with the name Queue Name; an item property Q_DIRECTORY, with its value set to the value of the directory specified in the call; and a new subdirectory of the described directory whose name is the eight-character hex value of the Object ID of the queue. It also creates the set properties Q_SERVERS, Q_OPERATORS, and Q_USERS, but with no values.

Obviously, these objects and properties could be created with individual Bindery calls. This call is intended to be a shortcut for programmers, providing a sort of macro for creating a queue. Another advantage to this call is that if any step fails, the entire transaction is backed out and a completion code is returned describing the problem.

The calling station needs supervisor privileges in order to make this call.

The NetWare C Interface format is:

```
int CreateQueue( char *queueName, int queueType,
   char directoryHandle, char *pathName, long *queueID );
```

Destroy Queue (E3h 65h)

This call destroys the specified queue.

Registers in:

AH	E3h
DS:SI	Request Buffer Address
ES:DI	Reply Buffer Address

Registers out:

AL	Completion Code

Completion Codes:

00	Success
96h	Server Out Of Memory
9Ch	Invalid Path
D0h	Queue Error
D1h	No Queue
FFh	Hardware Failure

Request Packet (7 bytes):

Offset	Content	Type	Order
0	Request Buffer Length-2	WORD	lo-hi
2	65h	BYTE	
3	Queue ID	LONG	hi-lo

Reply Packet (2 bytes):

Offset	Content	Type	Order
0	0000	WORD	

When a queue is destroyed all active jobs are aborted. All jobs in the queue are destroyed. Files associated with the queue are deleted. The queue object and all of its properties are deleted from the Bindery. And the queue directory and all of its files and associated subdirectories are deleted.

The NetWare C Interface format is:

```
int DestroyQueue( long queueID );
```

Read Queue Current Status (E3h 76h)

This call retrieves the current status of a queue.

Registers in:

AH	E3h
DS:SI	Request Buffer Address
ES:DI	Reply Buffer Address

Registers out:

AL	Completion Code

Completion Codes:

00h	Successful
96h	Server Out of Memory
9Ch	Invalid Path
D1h	No Queue
D2h	No Q Server
D3h	No Q Rights
F1h	Invalid Bindery Security
FCh	No Such Object
FEH	Server Bindery Locked
FFh	Bindery Failure

Request Packet (7 bytes):

Offset	Content	Type	Order
0	Request Buffer Length - 2	WORD	lo-hi
2	66h	BYTE	
3	Queue ID	LONG	hi-lo

Reply Packet (max length = 135):

Offset	Content	Type	Order
0	Reply Packet Length - 2	WORD	lo-hi
2	Queue ID	LONG	hi-lo
6	Queue Status	BYTE	
7	Number of Jobs	BYTE	

8	Number of Servers	BYTE
9	Server ID List	LONG[Number of Servers] hi-lo
109	Server Stations List	BYTE[Number of Servers]
134	Max Number of Servers	BYTE

The *Queue Status* byte indicates the overall status of the queue, with bits set as follows. 01h means the operator does not want new jobs added to the queue. 02h means the operator does not want additional job servers attaching to the queue. 04h means the operator does not want job servers servicing jobs in the queue. Clearing a bit has the opposite effect.

The *Current Entries* field contains a count of the jobs currently in the queue (0-250).

The *Current Servers* field contains the number of currently attached job servers that can service the queue (0-25).

The *Server ID List* and *Server Stations* contain the Server Object IDs and station attachments of the job servers currently servicing the queue.

Maximum Number of Servers is the maximum number of connections to be returned.

Any station security equivalent to one of the objects listed in the queue's Q_USERS group property or Q_OPERATORS group property can make this call. (See also Attach Queue Server To Queue, Detach Queue Server From Queue, and Set Queue Current Status.)

The NetWare C Interface format is:

```
int ReadQueueCurrentStatus( long queueID, BYTE *queueStatus,
   BYTE *numberOfJobs, BYTE *numberOfServers, long *serverIDList,
   WORD *serverStationList, WORD maxNumberOfServers );
```

Set Queue Current Status (E3h 67h)

This call allows a queue operator to control the adding of jobs and job servers to a queue, or the preventing of current jobs from being serviced, by setting or clearing bits in the Queue Status byte.

Registers in:

AH	E3h
DS:SI	Request Buffer Address
ES:DI	Request Buffer Address

Registers out:

AL	Completion Code

Completion Codes:

00h	Success
96h	Server Out Of Memory
9Ch	Invalid Path
D0h	Q Error
D1h	No Queue
D3h	No Q Rights
FEh	Server Bindery Locked
FFh	Bindery Failure

Request Packet (8 bytes):

Offset	**Content**	**Type**	**Order**
0	Request Buffer Length-2	WORD	lo-hi
2	67h	BYTE	
3	Queue ID	LONG	hi-lo
7	Queue Status	BYTE	

Reply Packet (2 bytes):

Offset	**Content**	**Type**	**Order**
0	0000h	WORD	lo-hi

Only a station with operator privileges can make this call.
The NetWare C Interface format is:

```
int SetQueueCurrentStatus( long queueID, BYTE queueStatus );
```

Create Queue Job and File (E3h 68h)

This call enters a new job into a queue.

Registers in:

AH	E3h
DS:SI	Request Buffer Address
ES:DI	Request Buffer Address

Registers out:

AL	Completion Code

Completion Codes:

00h	Success
96h	Server Out of Memory
99h	Directory Full
9Ch	Invalid Path
D0h	Q Error

D1h	No Queue
D2h	No Q Server
D3h	No Q Rights
D4h	Q Full
DAh	Q Halted
EDh	Property Already Exists
EFh	Invalid Name
F0h	Wildcard Not Allowed
F1h	Invalid Bindery Security
F7h	No Property Create Privilege
FCh	No Such Object
FEh	Server Bindery Locked
FFh	Bindery Failure

Request Packet (263 bytes):

Offset	Content	Type	Order
0	Request Buffer Length-2	WORD	lo-hi
2	6Dh	BYTE	
3	Queue ID	LONG	hi-lo
7	Client Station	BYTE	
8	Client Task Number	BYTE	
9	Client ID Number	LONG	
13	Target Server ID Number	LONG	hi-lo
17	Target Execution Time	BYTE[6]	
23	Job Entry Time	BYTE[6]	
29	Job Number	WORD	hi-lo
31	Job Type	WORD	hi-lo
33	Job Position	BYTE	
34	Job Control Flags	BYTE	
35	Job File Name	BYTE[14]	
49	Job File Handle	BYTE[6]	
55	Server Station	BYTE	
56	Server Task Number	BYTE	
57	Server ID Number	LONG	
61	Text Job Description	BYTE[50]	
111	Client Record Area	BYTE[152]	

Reply Packet (56 bytes):

Offset	Content	Type	Order
0	Reply Packet Length-2	WORD	lo-hi
2	Client Station	BYTE	
3	Client Task Number	BYTE	
4	Client ID Number	LONG	hi-lo
8	Target Server ID Number	LONG	hi-lo
12	Target Execution Time	BYTE[6]	

Offset	Content	Type	Order
18	Job Entry Time	BYTE[6]	
24	Job Number	WORD	hi-lo
26	Job Type	WORD	hi-lo
28	Job Position	BYTE	
29	Job Control Flags	BYTE	
30	Job File Name	BYTE[14]	
44	Job File Handle	BYTE[6]	
50	Server Station	BYTE	
51	Server Task Number	BYTE	
52	Server ID Number	LONG	hi-lo

See the earlier section on Job Entry structure or Appendix B for details on request and reply parameters. Any station that is security equivalent to one of the objects listed in the target queue's Q_USER property can make this call.

The NetWare C Interface format is:

```
int CreateQueueJobAndFile( long queueID, JobStruct *job, int *fileHandle );
```

Close File and Start Queue Job (E3h 69h)

This call closes a job file and marks the job ready for service.

Registers in:

AH	E3h
DS:SI	Request Buffer Address
ES:DI	Request Buffer Address

Registers out:

AL	Completion Code

Completion Codes:

00h	Success
96h	Server Out of Memory
D0h	Q Error
D1h	No Queue
D3h	No Q Rights
D5h	No Q Job
D6h	No Job Rights
FEh	Server Bindery Locked
FFh	Bindery Failure

Request Packet (9 bytes):

Offset	Content	Type	Order
0	Request Buffer Length-2	WORD	lo-hi
2	69h	BYTE	
3	Queue ID	LONG	hi-lo
7	Job Number	WORD	hi-lo

Reply Packet (2 bytes)

Offset	Content	Type	Order
0	0000h	WORD	lo-hi

Only the station that created the job can make this call.
The NetWare C Interface format is:

```
int CloseFileAndStartQueueJob( long queueID, WORD jobNumber,
   int fileHandle );
```

Remove Job From Queue (E3h 6Ah)

This call removes a job from a queue, and closes the associated file. If the specified job is being serviced, Remove Job From Queue aborts the service. Any further IO requests made by the job server to the job file associated with the job will return an Illegal File Handle error.

Registers in:

AH	E3h
DS:SI	Request Buffer Address
ES:DI	Request Buffer Address

Registers out:

AL	Completion Code

Completion Codes:

00h	Success
96h	Server Out of Memory
D0h	Q Error
D1h	No Queue
D3h	No Q Rights
D5h	No Q Job
D6h	No Job Rights
FEh	Server Bindery Locked
FFh	Bindery Failure

Request Packet (9 bytes):

Offset	Content	Type	Order
0	Request Buffer Length-2	WORD	lo-hi
2	6Ah	BYTE	
3	Queue ID	LONG	hi-lo
7	Job Number	WORD	hi-lo

Reply Packet (2 bytes):

Offset	Content	Type	Order
0	0000h	WORD	lo-hi

Only the user who created the job, or an operator, can make this call. The NetWare C Interface format is:

```
int RemoveJobFromQueue( long queueID, WORD jobNumber );
```

Get Queue Job List (E3h 6Bh)

This call lists all jobs contained in a specified queue.

Registers in:

AH	E3h
DS:SI	Request Buffer Address
ES:DI	Reply Buffer Address

Registers out:

AL	Completion Code

Completion Codes:

00h	Success
96h	Server Out of Memory
9Ch	Invalid Path
D0h	Q Error
D1h	No Queue
D2h	No Q Server
D3h	No Q Rights
FCh	No Such Object
FEh	Server Bindery Locked
FFh	Bindery Failure

Request Packet (7 bytes):

Offset	Content	Type	Order
0	Request Buffer Length-2	WORD	lo-hi
2	6Bh	BYTE	
3	Queue ID	LONG	hi-lo

Reply Packet (max 506 bytes):

Offset	Content	Type	Order
0	Reply Packet Length-2	WORD	lo-hi
2	Job Count (1 to 250)	WORD	hi-lo
4	Job Number List	WORD[Job Count]	hi-lo

Job Count returns the number of job entries currently in the queue.

Job Numbers returns an array containing the Job Entry numbers that QMS assigned to the jobs when they entered the queue, listed according to their positions in the queue.

If a call to read information about a job in the queue fails with a No Queue Job error, the calling station can assume that the job has been completed or that it has been deleted from the queue.

Any station that is security equivalent to an object listed in the queue's Q_USERS group property or Q_OPERATORS group property can make this call.

The NetWare C Interface format is:

```
int GetQueueJobList( long QueueID, WORD *jobCount,
   WORD *jobNumberList, WORD maxJobNumbers );
```

Read Queue Job Entry (E3h 6Ch)

This call retrieves information about a specified job in a queue.

Registers in:

AH	E3h
DS:SI	Request Buffer Address
ES:DI	Reply Buffer Address

Registers out:

AL	Completion Code

Completion codes:

00h	Success
96h	Server Out of Memory
D0h	Q Error
D1h	No Queue
D2h	No Q Server
D3h	No Q Rights
D5h	No Q job
FCh	No such Object
FEh	Server Bindery Locked
FFh	Bindery Failure

Request Packet (9 bytes):

Offset	Content	Type	Order
0	Request Buffer Length-2	WORD	lo-hi
2	6Ch	BYTE	
3	Queue ID	LONG	hi-lo
7	Job Number	WORD	hi-lo

Reply Packet (258 bytes):

Offset	Content	Type	Order
0	Reply Packet Length-2	WORD	lo-hi
2	Client Station	BYTE	
3	Client Task Number	BYTE	
4	Client ID Number	LONG	hi-lo
8	Target Server ID Number	LONG	hi-lo
12	Target Execution Time	BYTE[6]	
18	Job Entry Time	BYTE[6]	
24	Job Number	WORD	hi-lo
26	Job Type	WORD	hi-lo
28	Job Position	BYTE	
29	Job Control Flags	BYTE	
30	Job File Name	BYTE[14]	
44	Job File Handle	BYTE[6]	
50	Server Station	BYTE	
51	Server Task Number	BYTE	
52	Server ID Number	LONG	hi-lo
56	Text Job Description	BYTE[50]	
106	Client Record Area	BYTE[152]	

Any station that is security equivalent to an object listed in the queue's Q_USERS group property, Q_OPERATORS group property, or Q_SERVERS group property can make this call.

The NetWare C Interface format is:

```
int ReadQueueJobEntry( long queueID, WORD jobNumber,
   JobStruct *job );
```

Change Queue Job Entry (E3h 6Dh)

This call is used to change information in a job's entry record.

Registers in:

AH	E3h
DS:SI	Request Buffer Address
ES:DI	Reply Buffer Address

Registers out:

AL	Completion Code

Completion Codes:

00h	Success
96h	Server Out of Memory
D0H	Queue Error
D1h	No Queue
D5h	No Queue Job
D7h	Queue Servicing
FEh	Server Bindery Locked
FFh	Bindery Failure

Request Packet (263 bytes):

Offset	**Content**	**Type**	**Order**
0	Request Buffer Length-2	WORD	lo-hi
2	6Dh	BYTE	
3	Queue ID	LONG	hi-lo
7	Client Station	BYTE	
8	Client Task Number	BYTE	
9	Client ID Number	LONG	
13	Target Server ID Number	LONG	hi-lo
17	Target Execution Time	BYTE[6]	
23	Job Entry Time	BYTE[6]	
29	Job Number	WORD	hi-lo
31	Job Type	WORD	hi-lo
33	Job Position	BYTE	
34	Job Control Flags	BYTE	
35	Job File Name	BYTE[14]	
49	Job File Handle	BYTE[6]	
55	Server Station	BYTE	
56	Server Task Number	BYTE	
57	Server ID Number	LONG	
61	Text Job Description	BYTE[50]	
111	Client Record Area	BYTE[152]	

Reply Packet (2 bytes):

Offset	**Content**	**Type**	**Order**
0	0000h	WORD	lo-hi

This call can be used in conjunction with the Read Queue Job Entry call to change a portion of the job's entry record. However, if the target entry is already being serviced, Change Queue Job Entry returns a Q_SERVICING error and makes no changes to the job's entry record.

The following fields can be modified: Target Server ID, Target Execution, Job Type, Job Control Flags, Text Job Description, and Client Record Area.

This call can be made by the user who originally created the job or by an operator.

The NetWare C Interface format is:

```
int ChangeQueueJobEntry( long queueID, JobStruct *job );
```

Change Queue Job Position (E3h 6Eh)

This call changes a job's position in a queue.

Registers in:

AH	E3h
DS:SI	Request Buffer Address
ES:DI	Reply Buffer Address

Registers out:

AL	Completion Code

Completion Codes:

00h	Successful
96h	Server Out Of Memory
D0h	Queue Error
D1h	No Queue
D5h	No Queue Job
D6h	No Job Rights
FEh	Server Bindery Locked
FFh	Bindery Failure

Request Packet (10 bytes):

Offset	Content	Type	Order
0	Request Buffer Length-2	WORD	lo-hi
2	6Eh	BYTE	
3	Queue ID	LONG	hi-lo
7	Job Number	WORD	hi-lo
9	New Position	BYTE	

Reply Packet (2 bytes):

Offset	Content	Type	Order
0	0000h	WORD	lo-hi

Job Number is the Job Entry number assigned by QMS to the job when it is entered the queue, specifying the job to be repositioned.

The *New Position* value can be from 1 to 250. Position 1 is the first position and position 250 is the last position in a full queue. If an operator specifies a position number higher than the position number of the job currently at the end of the queue, the job is placed at the end of the queue. When a job is moved, the Job Position fields of all job entries in the queue are updated to reflect the new positions.

When an operator changes the position of a job being serviced, the service is not affected; service continues until the job is finished or aborted. Similarly, if an operator moves a job not being serviced ahead of one that is being serviced, the job being serviced is completed before the new job is serviced. Only an operator can make this call.

The NetWare C Interface format is:

```
int ChangeQueueJobPosition( long queueID, WORD jobNumber, BYTE
    newPosition );
```

Attach Queue Server To Queue (E3h 6Fh)

This call allows a job server to attach itself to a specified queue.

Registers in:

AH	E3h
DS:SI	Request Buffer Address
ES:DI	Reply Buffer Address

Registers out:

AL	Completion Code

Completion Codes:

00h	Successful
96h	Server Out Of Memory
9Ch	Invalid Path
D0h	Queue Error
D1h	No Queue
D3h	No Queue Rights
DAh	Queue Halted
DBh	Max Queue Servers
FEh	Server Bindery Locked
FFh	Bindery Failure
	No Such Property
	No Such Member

Request Packet (7 bytes):

Offset	**Content**	**Type**	**Order**
0	Request Buffer Length-2	WORD	lo-hi
2	6Fh	BYTE	
3	Queue ID	LONG	hi-lo

Reply Packet (2 bytes):

Offset	Content	Type	Order
0	0000h	WORD	lo-hi

A job server must attach itself to a queue before it can service jobs from the queue. A queue can have as many as 25 job servers attached to it at a time. If 25 job servers are already attached to the target queue, Attach Queue Server to Queue returns a Max Queue Servers error. Stations making this call must be security equivalent to one of the objects listed in the queue's Q_SERVERS property.

The NetWare C Interface format is:

```
int AttachQueueServerToQueue( long queueID );
```

Detach Queue Server From Queue (E3h 70h)

This call removes the calling job server from the specified queue's list of active job servers.

Registers in:

AH	E3h
DS:SI	Request Buffer Address
ES:DI	Reply Buffer Address

Registers out:

AL	Completion Code

Completion Codes

00h	Successful
96h	Server Out Of Memory
9Ch	Invalid Path
D0h	Q Error
D1h	No Queue
D2h	No Q Server
FEh	Server Bindery Locked
FFh	Bindery Failure

Request Packet (7 bytes)

Offset	Content	Type	Order
0	Request Buffer Length-2	WORD	lo-hi
2	70h	BYTE	hi-lo
3	Queue ID	LONG	hi-lo

Reply Packet (2 bytes)

Offset	Content	Type	Order
0	0000	WORD	lo-hi

If the station making this call is servicing a job, the job's service is automatically aborted.

The NetWare C Interface format is:

```
int DetachQueueServerFromQueue( long queueID );
```

Service Queue Job and Open File (E3h 71h)

This call allows a job server to select a new job for servicing.

Registers in:

AH	E3h
DS:SI	Request Buffer Address
ES:DI	Reply Buffer Address

Registers out:

AL	Completion Code

Completion Codes

00h	Successful
96h	Server Out of Memory
9Ch	Invalid Path
D0h	Q Error
D1h	No Queue
D3h	No Q Rights
D5h	No Q Job
D9h	Stn Not Server
DAh	Q Halted
FEh	Server Bindery Locked
FFh	Bindery Failure

Request Packet (9 bytes)

Offset	Content	Type	Order
0	Request Packet Length-2	WORD	lo-hi
2	71h	BYTE	
3	Queue ID	LONG	hi-lo
7	Target Job Type	WORD	hi-lo

Reply Packet (56 bytes)

Offset	Content	Type	Order
0	Reply Packet Length -2	WORD	lo-hi
2	Client Station	BYTE	
3	Client Task Number	BYTE	
4	Client ID Number	LONG	hi-lo
8	Target Server ID Number	LONG	hi-lo

Offset	Content	Type	Order
12	Target Execution Time	BYTE[6]	
18	Job Entry Time	BYTE[6]	
24	Job Number	WORD	hi-lo
26	Job Type	WORD	hi-lo
28	Job Position	BYTE	
29	Job Control Flags	BYTE	
30	Job File Name	BYTE[14]	
44	Job File Handle	BYTE[6]	
50	Server Station	BYTE	
51	Server Task Number	BYTE	
52	Server ID Number	LONG	hi-lo

Target Job Type contains a number specifying the job types (as indicated by the Job Type field in the Job Entry header) that the station will accept for service. If this field is set to FFFFh, the job server will accept any job type in the queue.

Use the call Read Queue Job Entry to obtain the Text Job description and Client Record Area for this job. The specified queue is searched from front to back for a job that meets the following criteria.

The *Target Server ID Number* field must either be FFFFFFFFh or must match the ID number of the calling job server.

The *Target Execution Time* field must either be FFFFFFFFFFFFh or must specify a time earlier than the time indicated on the current system clock.

The *Job Type* field must match the job server's target server type, or Target Job Type must be FFFFh.

In the *Job Control Flags* field, Operator Hold, User Hold, and Entry Open must all be set to zero.

The *Server ID Number* field must be zero, indicating that the job is not currently being serviced by some other job server.

If a job meets all of the above criteria, the job is marked for servicing by the calling station as follows.

The job server's station number, task number, and object ID are entered into the job's Server Station, Server Task, and Server ID Number fields respectively.

The associated job file is opened for read/write access by the job server.

The updated Job Entry record is delivered to the calling job server for service. The job server can access the job file associated with the job it is servicing by opening the device NETQ. When the device is opened, the DOS file handle is connected to the returned NetWare file handle, and the job server can then read from or write to the file using the DOS file handle.

This call can only be used by a station that has previously attached itself to the specified queue as a server. The station must also be security equivalent to an object listed in the queue's Q_USERS group property, Q_OPERATORS group property, or Q_SERVERS group property to make this call.

The NetWare C Interface format is:

```
int ServiceQueueJobAndOpenFile( long queueID, WORD targetJobType,
    JobStruct *job, int *fileHandle );
```

Finish Servicing Queue Job and File (E3h 72h)

This call allows a job server to signal QMS that it has finished servicing a job.

Registers in:

AH	E3h
DS:SI	Request Packet Address
ES:DI	Reply Buffer Address

Registers out:

AL	Completion Code

Completion Codes:

00h	Successful
96h	Server Out Of Memory
D0h	Q Error
D1h	No Queue
D6h	No Job Rights

Request Packet (13 bytes):

Offset	**Content**	**Type**	**Order**
0	Request Buffer Length -2	WORD	lo-hi
2	72h	BYTE	
3	Queue ID	LONG	hi-lo
7	Job Number	WORD	hi-lo
9	Charge	LONG	hi-lo

Reply Packet (2 bytes):

Offset	**Content**	**Type**	**Order**
0	000h	WORD	lo-hi

This call removes the Job Entry, closes and deletes the associated job file, and (if the job server has changed to the client's directory access rights) restores the calling job server's directory access rights to their original (login) value.

The *Charge accounting information* field is not used in the current QMS, but is provided to allow job servers to charge their customers and to log accounting information in future NetWare releases.

Only a job server that has previously obtained a job for service can make this call.

The NetWare C Interface format is:

```
int FinishServicingQueueJobAndFile( long queueID, WORD jobNumber,
    long charge, int fileHandle );
```

Abort Servicing Queue Job and File (E3h 73h)

This call allows a job server to inform the QMS that it cannot finish servicing a job it previously accepted for servicing.

Registers in:

AH	E3h
DS:SI	Request Packet Address
ES:DI	Reply Buffer Address

Registers out:

AL	Completion Code

Completion Codes:

00h	Successful
96h	Server Out Of Memory
D0h	Q Error
D1h	No Queue
D6h	No Job Rights
D9h	Stn Not Server

Request Packet (9 bytes):

Offset	Content	Type	Order
0	Request Packet Length-2	WORD	lo-hi
2	73h	BYTE	
3	Queue ID	LONG	hi-lo
7	Job Number	WORD	hi-lo

Reply Packet (2 bytes):

Offset	Content	Type	Order
0	0000h	WORD	lo-hi

This call closes a job file and, if the job server has changed the client's directory-access rights, resets the access rights to their original (login) values. When a job is aborted, the QMS checks the Job Entry's Service Restart flag to determine whether the job can be restarted automatically. If the Job Entry's Service Restart flag is set, QMS clears the Job Entry's Server Station, Server Task, and Server ID Number fields and leaves the entry in its current position in the queue.

For example, if a job is at the beginning of the queue when obtained for service by a job server, it remains at the beginning of the queue after being aborted. An aborted job could, therefore, be next in line for service. For this reason, a job server should not abort a job because of an error in the job's format or in its requests; the server should use Finish Servicing Queue Job And File to remove the job from the queue.

If the value of the Service Restart flag in an aborted Job Entry is zero, QMS removes the entry from the queue and deletes the job's associated file.

A job server should abort a job only if some temporary internal problem prevents it from completing the job. For example, a print server might abort a job due to a paper jam in the printer. After the paper jam is fixed, the print server could service the same job successfully.

Also, if the Job Entry has invalid parameters or some other problem, it would be continually requeued as the next available job. As a result, the job server would be in an endless loop of obtaining and rejecting the same job.

Only a job server that has previously obtained a job for servicing can make this call.

The NetWare C Interface format is:

```
int AbortServicingQueueJobAndFile( long queueID, WORD jobNumber,
   int fileHandle );
```

Change To Client Rights (E3h 74h)

This call allows a job server to assume the login identity (and therefore, the privileges) of the client that placed the job being serviced in the queue.

Registers in:

AH	E3h
DS:SI	Request Packet Address
ES:DI	Reply Buffer Address

Registers out:

AL	Completion Code

Request Packet (9 bytes):

Offset	**Content**	**Type**	**Order**
O	Request Packet Length-2	WORD	lo-hi
2	74h	BYTE	
3	Queue Object ID	LONG	hi-lo
7	Job Number	WORD	hi-lo

Reply Packet (2 bytes):

Offset	**Content**	**Type**	**Order**
0	0000h	WORD	lo-hi

Completion Codes:

00h	Successful
96h	Server Out Of Memory
D0h	Q Error
D1h	No Queue
D6h	No Job Rights
D9h	Stn Not Server

A job being serviced may require that the job server access directories and files using the access rights of the client that placed the job into the queue. Change To Client Rights enables a job server to temporarily assume the login ID and security equivalence list of the client that created the job being serviced.

This call does not change any of the job server's path mappings (directory handles) on the file server. However, all access rights to those directories are recalculated to conform with the client's rights. This recalculation is based on the client's object ID placed in the Job Entry record at the time the Job Entry was placed in the queue. Therefore, only directories or the file server where the queue exists can be accessed.

Any files opened before this call is made continue to be accessible with the job server's rights; any files opened after this call is made are accessible only with the client's rights. The job server creates any path mappings it requires to carry out the client's requests after this call is made.

The Restore Queue Server Rights call reverses the effects of this call. In addition, the job server's rights are automatically reset if the job server calls Finish Servicing Queue Job And File or Abort Servicing Queue Job And File.

Only a job server that has previously obtained a job for service can make this call.

The NetWare C Interface format is:

```
int ChangeToClientRights( long queueID, WORD jobNumber );
```

Restore Queue Server Rights (E3h 75h)

This call restores a job server's own identity/privileges after it has assumed its client's login identity/privileges.

Registers in:

AH	E3h
DS:SI	Request Packet Address
ES:DI	Reply Buffer Address

Registers out:

AL	Completion Code

Completion Codes:

00h	Successful
96h	Server Out Of Memory
9Ch	Invalid Path
D0h	Q Error
D1h	No Queue
D3h	No Q Rights
D5h	No Q Job
D9h	Stn Not Server
DAh	Q Halted
FEh	Server Bindery Locked
FFh	Bindery Failure

Request Packet (3 bytes):

Offset	Content	Type	Order
0	Request Packet Length-2	WORD	lo-hi
2	75h	BYTE	

Reply Packet (2 bytes):

Offset	Content	Type	Order
0	000h	WORD	lo-hi

This call restores the job server's login user ID and associated security equivalence list to the server's own values after it has assumed its client's login identity.

This call does not change any job server path mappings (directory handles) on the file server. However, all access rights to those directories are recalculated to conform with the job server's rights. If the job server changes some of its path mappings in order to service the job, the job server must restore its own directory handles.

Any files opened before this call is made continue to be accessible with the rights of the client.

Any files opened after this call is made are accessible to any station with the rights of the job server.

Only a job server that has previously changed its identity using the Change To Client Rights call can make this call.

The NetWare C Interface format is:

```
int RestoreQueueServerRights( void );
```

Read Queue Server Current Status (E3h 76h)

This call reads the current status of a job queue server.

Registers in:

AH	E3h
DS:SI	Request Packet Address
ES:DI	Reply Buffer Address

Registers out:

AL	Completion Code

Completion Codes:

00h	Successful
96h	Server Out Of Memory
9Ch	Invalid Path
D1h	No Queue
D2h	No Q Server
D3h	No Q Rights
F1h	Invalid Bindery Security
FCh	No Such Object
FEh	Server Bindery Locked
FFh	Bindery Failure

Request Packet (11 bytes):

Offset	Content	Type	Order
0	Request Packet Length -2	WORD	lo-hi
2	Queue ID	LONG	hi-lo
6	Server ID Number	LONG	hi-lo
10	Server Station	BYTE	

Reply Packet (66 bytes):

Offset	Content	Type	Order
0	Reply Packet Length-2	WORD	lo-hi
2	Server Status Record	BYTE [64]	

Read Queue Server Current Status returns the Server Status Record of a job server attached to the queue identified by the Queue ID field.

Server Status Record is the 64-byte field associated with the specified job server. QMS does not interpret the contents of this record; the information in the record can be anything of use to job servers and queue users. The first four bytes of this record should contain an estimated price for the given job server to complete an average job.

Any station that is security equivalent to one of the objects listed in the queue's Q_USERS group property or Q_OPERATORS group property can make this call. The job server whose status record is desired must be attached to the queue at the time this request is made.

The NetWare C Interface format is:

```
int ReadQueueServerCurrentStatus( long queueID, long serverID,
   char serverStation, char *serverStatusRecord );
```

Set Queue Server Current Status (E3h 77h)

This call updates the QMS's copy of a job server's status record.

Registers in:

AH	E3h
DS:SI	Request Packet Address
ES:DI	Reply Buffer Address

Registers out:

AL	Completion Code

Completion Codes:

00h	Successful
96h	Server Out Of Memory
9Ch	Invalid Path
D0h	Q Error
D1h	No Queue
FEh	Server Bindery Locked
FFh	Bindery Failure

Request Packet (71 bytes):

Offset	**Content**	**Type**	**Order**
0	Request Packet Length-2	WORD	lo-hi
2	77h	BYTE	
3	Queue ID	LONG	hi-lo
7	Server Status Record	BYTE [64]	

Reply Packet (2 bytes)

Offset	**Content**	**Type**	**Order**
0	0000h	WORD	lo-hi

Server Status Record is the 64-byte field associated with the specified job server. QMS does not interpret the contents of this record; the information in the record can be anything of use to job servers and queue users. The first 4 bytes of this record should contain an estimated price for the given job server to complete an average job.

Only a job server that has previously attached to the specified queue can make this call.

The NetWare C Interface format is:

```
int SetQueueServerCurrentStatus( long queueID,
   BYTE *serverStatusRecord );
```

Get Queue Job's File Size (E3h 78h)

This call returns the size of an associated file.

Registers in:

AH	E3h
DS:SI	Request Packet Address
ES:DI	Reply Buffer Address

Registers out:

AL	Completion Code

Completion Codes:

00h	Successful

Request Packet (9 bytes):

Offset	Content	Type	Order
0	Request Packet Length-2	WORD	lo-hi
2	78h	BYTE	
3	Queue ID	LONG	hi-lo
7	Job Number	WORD	hi-lo

Reply Packet (12 bytes):

Offset	Content	Type	Order
0	Reply Packet Length-2	WORD	lo-hi
2	Queue Object ID	LONG	hi-lo
6	Job Number	WORD	hi-lo
0	File Size	LONG	hi-lo

Job Number is the Job Entry number that QMS assigned to the job when it first entered the queue; here it specifies which job's associated file size is to be returned.

File Size returns the size of the file associated with the specified job. If the Job Entry is still open (not committed by the creating application: the Entry Open flag is set) or in service, the entry size returned by this call probably does not accurately reflect the final file size.

Any station that is security equivalent to an object listed in the queue's Q_USERS group property, Q_OPERATORS group property, or Q_SERVERS can make this call.

The NetWare C Interface format is:

```
int GetQueueJobsFileSize( long queueID, int jobNumber,
   long fileSize );
```

Code example: PLACEJOB.C and SVCJOB.C

Queue Services are a powerful set of tools for creating server-assisted applications. The QMS is perfect for situations where computing resources are available on the network and stations need those resources; the QMS routines put together stations that can process with those that need processing, all in an organized manner.

For our example, we create two programs that do just that: One program queues up requests for a service and the other services those requests. Although this example doesn't do anything application-specific, it shows how one might use the QMS API calls in such a scenario.

Two programs are necessary for our example: PlaceJob and SvcJob. PlaceJob finds our queue in the Bindery, or creates it if it does not exist, and adds the "job" to the queue.

SvcJob monitors the queue for new jobs, displaying all relevant information on the screen. If no jobs are in the queue, it polls the queue for a time interval set at the beginning of the program, looking for new jobs.

We begin our explanation with PlaceJob, describe SvcJob, and end by discussing how to use the two together.

PlaceJob begins by defining our Queue Type, 8100h, which is defined to the QUEUE_TYPE constant as 0x0081 because of the hi-lo conversion. Also defined are the Bindery user type and the name of our queue, "Q_DEMO."

Next we define the structures used in our Bindery calls and in the QMS Create Queue call. We define our local prototypes and begin with the main() function.

The main() function's first step is to look for our Q_DEMO queue, in case it already exists. We clear the *ScanBindRequest* and *ScanBindReply* structures and set them up to make the Bindery call Scan Bindery Object. We use our Queue Type and Queue Name. If the call returns an FCh error code, it was not found, so the pro-gram calls MakeQueue() to create the queue, passing back the Queue ID.

If the queue was found in the Bindery, we set the *QueueID* variable and print out that it was found. Since it was already found, we can skip step two.

In step two in the code we add the current logged in user (you should be logged in as Supervisor to test this program) to the Q_USERS and Q_SERVERS properties of our Q_DEMO queue object. We use the Bindery Add Bindery Object To Set call.

Next, in step three we actually place the job in the queue with the QMS Create Queue Job and File call. When doing this we pass the ID of the queue and a test word from the command-line to serve as our Client Record Area.

This call returns the job number which we print to the screen and pass back to the QMS in the Close File and Start Queue Job routine. Calling this routine closes the queue file and sends it to the file server to be placed in the queue for servicing.

With this step done, the program terminates. Note the different ways we constructed the API calls. In ScanBinderyObject(), we used a structure, so all we had to do was pass the address of the request and reply structure. This makes it easy on the ScanBinderyObject() function but requires more setup beforehand. The function MakeQueue() used byte blocks and employed casting to set the WORD starting at offset 3 to the QUEUE_TYPE. The line is:

```
*( (WORD *) ( Request + 3 ) ) = QUEUE_TYPE
```

What's happening is we're casting the address pointed to at *Request + 3* to a WORD pointer, dereferencing it, and setting it to QUEUE_TYPE. This is the method employed most in Novell's C Interface Library. There are advantages and disadvantages to both the structure and block style, as we have mentioned before. If you program your own routines, you have the freedom of choosing from these two or any other method you like. These are presented as possibilities.

SvcJob starts much like PlaceJob, with defines, structure definitions and local prototypes. The main() function begins with trying to locate our queue created in PlaceJob and getting its object ID. This is done with a scan of the Bindery identical to our scan at the start of PlaceJob: we're looking for queue Q_DEMO of type 8100h. If not found, the program exits.

Once the queue has been found and the QueueID variable has been set, we pass it to the AttachQueueServerToQueue() function which will attach us, the queue server, to the queue. To reiterate, for the purposes of this test, you should run these two programs as the Supervisor. One of the exercises will be to impose security restrictions on the process.

Once attached, the program enters a while loop, calling ServiceQueueJobAndOpenFile() to see if there are any jobs. If D5h is returned, the queue is empty and this message is displayed on the screen. If it is empty, the CheckKB() function is called, which checks the time and waits for TIME_INTERVAL seconds. We need some sort of interval so we don't flood the network with requests.

If no jobs are entered into the queue and the user doesn't press the keyboard, the program stays in a "watchful" state, waiting for jobs to be placed in the queue. This gives the feel of a dedicated processor. Designers may want to create a situation where several machines are dedicated to serving a queue, or nondedicated, servicing the queue in the background.

Once a queue job is detected, the program makes the Read Queue Job Entry call, passing the job number received in the ServiceQueueJobAndOpenFile() call. The ReadQueueJobEntry() function also prints the reply structure of the call to the screen, showing the programmer exactly what was returned. If you put a command-line argument in PlaceJob, the Client Record Area field should contain what you wrote.

Once the user presses a key, the program calls DestroyQueue() and exits.

In the ServiceQueueJobAndOpenFile() function, when interrupt 21h finishes, it places the completion code in the AL register. We set the result variable to the value of AL while testing whether it contains a value with the following statement:

```
if ( result = _AL )
     return _AL;
  else...
```

Although some compilers (like Turbo C) will say this may be a mistake, it is not, since we're setting *result* to the value of _AL and testing *result*. If _AL is logically true, we return, otherwise, we've set *result* in the process which we'll return in the else statement that follows. The point is we need to save AL in *result* at the if statement, or save it before in another variable, because by the time the code gets to the else statement, _AL will have already been changed several times.

To assemble a test scenario for these two programs, you can use one workstation, but the most dramatic results are shown with two. Login to both workstations as the Supervisor and run PlaceJob on the first, passing a command-line argument like "Testing...."

Next execute SvcJob on the second workstation. It will see the job already in the queue and show it to you. You should see the "Testing...." message in the Client Record Area (or whatever you typed). Hit the space bar to clear the screen and wait for another job.

Now on the first station you can run PlaceJob several times to heap some jobs onto the queue. SvcJob should detect them and take them off for you to "service" one by one.

When you're done, press any key on the second workstation to end SvcJob and delete the test queue.

```
/*                                                                              */
/* PlaceJob -   Places a job in the queue, SvcJob will service it             */
/*                                                                              */
/* by Charles Rose                                                              */
/*                                                                              */

#include <stdio.h>
#include <dos.h>
#include <dir.h>
#include <string.h>

typedef unsigned char BYTE;
typedef unsigned int WORD;
typedef unsigned long LONG;

#define QUEUE_TYPE 0x0081                /* Our Queue Type is 8100h */
#define USER 0x0100
#define QUEUE_NAME "Q_DEMO"

/* Global Types */
struct scanBindReq {
        WORD    Length;
        BYTE    Function;
        LONG    LastObjectID;
        WORD    ObjectType;
        BYTE    ObjectNameLength;
        BYTE    ObjectName[48];
        };
```

```
struct scanBindRep {
        WORD    Length;
        LONG    ObjectID;
        WORD    ObjectType;
        BYTE    ObjectName[48];
        BYTE    ObjectFlag;
        BYTE    ObjectSecurity;
        BYTE    ObjectHasProperties;
        };

struct createQueueReq {
        WORD    Length;
        BYTE    Function;
        WORD    QueueType;
        BYTE    QueueNameLength;
        BYTE    QueueName[48];
        BYTE    DirectoryHandle;
        BYTE    PathNameLength;
        BYTE    PathName[118];
};

struct createQueueRep {
        WORD    Length;
        LONG    QueueID;
};

/* Local Prototypes */
int ScanBinderyObject( struct scanBindReq *Request, struct scanBindRep *Reply );
void MakeQueue( LONG *QueueID );
int CreateQueue( BYTE *Request, BYTE *Reply );
int AddBinderyObjectToSet( char *ObjectName, WORD ObjectType,
   char *PropertyName, WORD MemberType, char *MemberName );
int CreateQueueJobAndFile( LONG QueueID, char *ClientArea, WORD *jobNumber );
int CloseFileAndStartQueueJob( LONG QueueID, WORD jobNumber );
void Error( char *description, int code );
LONG LongSwap( LONG num );
int IntSwap( int num );

main( int argc, char *argv[] )
{
        struct scanBindReq ScanBindRequest;
        struct scanBindRep ScanBindReply;
        int result, created = 0;
        WORD jobNumber;
        LONG QueueID;

        /* ——————————————————————————————— */
        /*  Step 1:  Locate Queue and get it's object ID or create it*/
        /* ——————————————————————————————— */

        printf( "\nLooking for Queue..." );

        /* Initialize Request/Reply packets to 0 */
        memset( &ScanBindRequest, NULL, sizeof( struct scanBindReq ) );
        memset( &ScanBindReply, NULL, sizeof( struct scanBindRep ) );

        /* Setup for call to scan bindery for our queue */
        ScanBindRequest.LastObjectID = 0xFFFFFFFFL;
        ScanBindRequest.ObjectType = QUEUE_TYPE;
        strcpy( ScanBindRequest.ObjectName, QUEUE_NAME );
        ScanBindRequest.ObjectNameLength = strlen( ScanBindRequest.ObjectName );
```

```
        result = ScanBinderyObject( &ScanBindRequest, &ScanBindReply );
        if ( result == 0xFC )
        {
                printf( "Queue not found, creating queue...\n" );
                MakeQueue( &QueueID );
                created++;
        }
        else if ( result )
                Error( "Error scanning for queue", result );
        else
        {
                QueueID = ScanBindReply.ObjectID;
                printf( "Queue found, ID = %lX\n", LongSwap( QueueID ) );
        }

        /* ────────────────────────────── */
        /*  Step 2: Add the current logged in user (Supervisor) to the   */
        /*           Q_USERS and Q_SERVERS properties in the bindery     */
        /* ────────────────────────────── */

        if ( created )
        {
                printf( "Now adding user SUPERVISOR to Q_USERS and
                        Q_SERVERS...\n" );

                result = AddBinderyObjectToSet( QUEUE_NAME, QUEUE_TYPE,
                "Q_USERS", USER, "SUPERVISOR" );
                if ( result && ( result != 0xE9 ) )
                        Error( "Error adding value to Q_USERS property", result );

                result = AddBinderyObjectToSet( QUEUE_NAME, QUEUE_TYPE,
                "Q_SERVERS", USER, "SUPERVISOR" );
                if ( result && ( result != 0xE9 ) )
                        Error( "Error adding value to Q_SERVERS property",
                        result );
        }

        /* ────────────────────────────── */
        /*  Step 3: Place job into queue with CreateQueueJobAndFile and */
        /*           close the file with CloseFileAndStartQueueJob */
        /* ────────────────────────────── */

        printf( "Creating Queue Job...\n" );

        result = CreateQueueJobAndFile( QueueID, argv[1], &jobNumber );
        if ( result )
                Error( "Error creating queue job and file", result );
        else
  printf( "Queue job and file have been successfully created.  Job number is %d.\n",
                        IntSwap( jobNumber ) );

        result = CloseFileAndStartQueueJob( QueueID, jobNumber );
        if ( result )
                Error( "Error closing queue job and file", result );
        else
                printf( "Job has been successfully sent to the queue.\n" );
}

int ScanBinderyObject( struct scanBindReq *Request, struct scanBindRep *Reply )
{
        Request->Function = 0x37;
```

```
        Request->Length = sizeof( struct scanBindReq ) - 2;
        Reply->Length = sizeof( struct scanBindRep ) - 2;

        _AH = 0xE3;
        _SI = (unsigned)Request;
        _DI = (unsigned)Reply;
        _ES = _DS;

        geninterrupt( 0x21 );

        return _AL;
}

void MakeQueue( LONG *QueueID )
{
        BYTE Request[173], Reply[6];
        int result;
        WORD queueNameLen;

        *( (WORD *) ( Request + 3 ) ) = QUEUE_TYPE;       /* Queue Type */
        strcpy( Request + 6, QUEUE_NAME );                /* Queue Name */
        queueNameLen = strlen( Request + 6 );
        Request[5] = queueNameLen;                        /* Queue Name Length */
        Request[6 + queueNameLen] = 0;                    /* Directory Handle */
        strcpy( Request + 6 + queueNameLen + 2 , "SYS:SYSTEM" );
        Request[6 + queueNameLen + 1] = strlen( Request + 6 + queueNameLen + 2);

        result = CreateQueue( &Request, &Reply );
        if ( result )
        {
                printf( "Error creating Queue, code = %X\n", result );
                exit( 1 );
        }
        *QueueID = *( (LONG *) ( Reply + 2 ) );
}

int CreateQueue( BYTE *Request, BYTE *Reply )
{
        *( (WORD *) Request ) = sizeof( struct createQueueReq );
        Request[2] = 0x64;

        *( (WORD *) Reply ) = 4;

        _AH = 0xE3;
        _SI = (unsigned)Request;
        _DI = (unsigned)Reply;
        _ES = _DS;

        geninterrupt( 0x21 );

        return _AL;
}

int AddBinderyObjectToSet( char *ObjectName, WORD ObjectType,
    char *PropertyName, WORD MemberType, char *MemberName )
{
        BYTE Request[119];
        int Reply = 0;

        memset( Request, NULL, 119 );

        Request[0] = sizeof( Request );
```

```
        Request[2] = 0x41;
        *( (WORD *) (Request + 3) ) = ObjectType;
        Request[5] = 48;
        strcpy( Request + 6, ObjectName );
        Request[54] = 15;
        strcpy( Request + 55, PropertyName );
        *( (WORD *) (Request + 70 ) ) = MemberType;
        Request[72] = 48;
        strcpy( Request + 73, MemberName );

        _AH = 0xE3;
        _SI = (unsigned)Request;
        _DI = (unsigned)&Reply;
        _ES = _DS;

        geninterrupt( 0x21 );

        return _AL;
}

int CreateQueueJobAndFile( LONG QueueID, char *ClientArea, WORD *jobNumber )
{
        int result;


        struct createQueueJobReq {
                WORD    Length;
                BYTE    Function;
                LONG    QueueID;
                BYTE    ClientStation;
                BYTE    ClientTaskNumber;
                LONG    ClientIDNumber;
                LONG    TargetServerIDNumber;
                BYTE    TargetExecutionTime[6];
                BYTE    JobEntryTime[6];
                WORD    JobNumber;
                WORD    JobType;
                BYTE    JobPosition;
                BYTE    JobControlFlags;
                BYTE    JobFileName[14];
                BYTE    JobFileHandle[6];
                BYTE    ServerStation;
                BYTE    ServerTaskNumber;
                LONG    ServerIDNumber;
                BYTE    TextJobDescription[50];
                BYTE    ClientRecordArea[152];
                } Request;

        struct createQueueJobRep {
                WORD    Length;
                BYTE    ClientStation;
                BYTE    ClientTaskNumber;
                LONG    ClientIDNumber;
                LONG    TargetServerIDNumber;
                BYTE    TargetExecutionTime[6];
                BYTE    JobEntryTime[6];
                WORD    JobNumber;
                WORD    JobType;
                BYTE    JobPosition;
                BYTE    JobControlFlags;
                BYTE    JobFileName[14];
                BYTE    JobFileHandle[6];
```

```
                BYTE    ServerStation;
                BYTE    ServerTaskNumber;
                LONG    ServerIDNumber;
                } Reply;

        /* Initialize Request/Reply packets to 0 */
        memset( &Request, NULL, sizeof( Request ) );
        memset( &Reply, NULL, sizeof( Reply ) );

        Request.Length = sizeof( Request ) - 2;
       Request.Function = 0x68; /* Monumental confusion, Novell manual says 6D */
        Request.QueueID = QueueID;
        Request.TargetServerIDNumber = 0xFFFFFFFF;
        memset( Request.TargetExecutionTime, 0xFF, 6 );
        strcpy( Request.ClientRecordArea, ClientArea );

        Reply.Length = sizeof( Reply ) - 2;

        _AH = 0xE3;
        _SI = (unsigned)&Request;
        _DI = (unsigned)&Reply;
        _ES = _DS;

        geninterrupt( 0x21 );

        result = _AL;
        *jobNumber = Reply.JobNumber;

        return result;
}

int CloseFileAndStartQueueJob( LONG QueueID, WORD jobNumber )
{
        BYTE Request[9] = { 9, 0, 0x69, 0, 0, 0, 0, 0, 0 };
        WORD Reply = 0;

        *( (LONG *) ( Request + 3 ) ) = QueueID;
        *( (WORD *) ( Request + 7 ) ) = jobNumber;

        _AH = 0xE3;
        _SI = (unsigned)Request;
        _DI = (unsigned)&Reply;
        _ES = _DS;

        geninterrupt( 0x21 );

        return _AL;
}

void Error( char *description, int code )
{
        printf( "%s. Completion Code = %X\n", description, code );
        exit(1);
}

LONG LongSwap( LONG num )
{
        LONG temp;

        temp = ( num & 0xFF000000 ) >> 24;
```

```
        temp += ( num & 0xFF0000 ) >> 8;
        temp += ( num & 0xFF00 ) << 8;
        temp += ( num & 0xFF ) << 24;

        return temp;
}

int IntSwap( int num )
{
        int temp;

        temp = ( num & 0xFF00 ) >> 8;
        temp += ( num & 0xFF ) << 8;

        return temp;
}
```

Code Sample: Svcjob.C

```
/*                                                                      */
/* ServiceJob - Services a job in the queue created with PlaceJob       */
/*                                                                      */
/* by Charles Rose                                                      */
/*                                                                      */

#include <stdio.h>
#include <dos.h>
#include <dir.h>
#include <string.h>
#include <conio.h>
#include <time.h>
#include <bios.h>

typedef unsigned char BYTE;
typedef unsigned int WORD;
typedef unsigned long LONG;

#define QUEUE_TYPE 0x0081              /* Our Queue Type is 8100h */
#define USER 0x0100
#define QUEUE_NAME "Q_DEMO"
#define TIME_INTERVAL 3                /* 3 seconds */

struct scanBindReq {
        WORD    Length;
        BYTE    Function;
        LONG    LastObjectID;
        WORD    ObjectType;
        BYTE    ObjectNameLength;
        BYTE    ObjectName[48];
        };

struct scanBindRep {
        WORD    Length;
        LONG    ObjectID;
        WORD    ObjectType;
        BYTE    ObjectName[48];
```

```
        BYTE    ObjectFlag;
        BYTE    ObjectSecurity;
        BYTE    ObjectHasProperties;
        };

int ScanBinderyObject( struct scanBindReq *Request, struct scanBindRep *Reply );
int AttachQueueServerToQueue( LONG QueueID );
int ServiceQueueJobAndOpenFile( LONG QueueID, WORD *JobNumber );
int ReadQueueJobEntry( LONG QueueID, WORD JobNumber );
int FinishServicingQueueJobAndFile( LONG QueueID, WORD JobNumber );
void Error( char *description, int code );
LONG LongSwap( LONG num );
int IntSwap( int num );
void DestroyQueue( LONG QueueID );
int CheckKB( void );

main()
{
        struct scanBindReq ScanBindRequest;
        struct scanBindRep ScanBindReply;
        int result, done = 0;
        WORD jobNumber;
        LONG QueueID;

        /* ———————————————————————————————— */
        /*  Step 1:  Locate Queue and get it's object ID         */
        /* ———————————————————————————————— */

        clrscr();
        printf( "Looking for queue in the bindery...\n" );

        /* Initialize Request/Reply packets to 0 */
        memset( &ScanBindRequest, NULL, sizeof( ScanBindRequest ) );
        memset( &ScanBindReply, NULL, sizeof( ScanBindReply ) );

        /* Setup for call to scan bindery for our queue */
        ScanBindRequest.LastObjectID = 0xFFFFFFFF;
        ScanBindRequest.ObjectType = QUEUE_TYPE;
        strcpy( ScanBindRequest.ObjectName, QUEUE_NAME );
        ScanBindRequest.ObjectNameLength = strlen( ScanBindRequest.ObjectName );

        result = ScanBinderyObject( &ScanBindRequest, &ScanBindReply );
        if ( result == 0xFC )
                Error( "Queue not found", result );
        else
        if ( result )
                Error( "Error scanning bindery object", result );
        else
                QueueID = ScanBindReply.ObjectID;

        /* ———————————————————————————————— */
        /*  Step 2: Need to Attach the Queue Server To the Queue */
        /* ———————————————————————————————— */

        printf( "Queue found, attaching to queue...\n" );

        result = AttachQueueServerToQueue( QueueID );
        if ( result )
                Error( "Error attaching to Queue, code = %X\n", result );
```

```
/* ------------------------------------------ */
/*  Step 3: Loop to service jobs                          */
/* ------------------------------------------ */

printf( "Attached to queue, querying for jobs.\n" );
printf( "____________________________________________________________\n" );

while ( 1 )
{
        gotoxy( 40, 3 );
        printf( "Checking..." );

        /* Check to see if anything is in the queue; get next job */
        result = ServiceQueueJobAndOpenFile( QueueID, &jobNumber );
        if ( result == 0xD5 )
        {
                gotoxy( 5, 7 );
                printf( "The queue is empty." );

                /* See if user wants to quit */
                done = CheckKB();

                if ( done )
                        break;
                else
                        continue;
        }
        else
        if ( result )
                Error( "Error Servicing the Queue", result );

        /* ------------------------------------------ */
        /*  Step 4: Read the Queue Job Entry that was returned  */
        /*          and release the job to the QMS to be removed */
        /* ------------------------------------------ */

        gotoxy( 5, 7 );
        clreol();
        printf( "Now servicing job %d\n", IntSwap( jobNumber ) );

        result = ReadQueueJobEntry( QueueID, jobNumber );
        if ( result )
                Error( "Error reading the Queue job entry", result );

        result = FinishServicingQueueJobAndFile( QueueID, jobNumber );
        if ( result )
             Error( "Error finishing servicing the queue job", result );


        gotoxy( 10, 22 );
        printf( "When finished with job, press any key to continue...");
        bioskey( 0 );
        gotoxy( 10, 22 );
        clreol();
}

/* ------------------------------------------ */
/*  Step 5: This program is done, so let's remove the queue       */
/*          from the bindery and quit              */
/* ------------------------------------------ */

DestroyQueue( QueueID );
```

```
}

int ScanBinderyObject( struct scanBindReq *Request, struct scanBindRep *Reply )
{
        Request->Function = 0x37;
        Request->Length = sizeof( struct scanBindReq ) - 2;
        Reply->Length = sizeof( struct scanBindRep ) - 2;

        _AH = 0xE3;
        _SI = (unsigned)Request;
        _DI = (unsigned)Reply;
        _ES = _DS;

        geninterrupt( 0x21 );

        return _AL;
}

int AttachQueueServerToQueue( LONG QueueID )
{
        char Request[7] = { 7, 0, 0x6F, 0, 0, 0, 0 };
        int Reply = 0;

        *( (LONG *) (Request + 3) ) = QueueID;

        _AH = 0xE3;
        _SI = (unsigned)Request;
        _DI = (unsigned)&Reply;
        _ES = _DS;

        geninterrupt( 0x21 );

        return _AL;
}

int ServiceQueueJobAndOpenFile( LONG QueueID, WORD *JobNumber )
{

        struct svcQueueReq {
                WORD    Length;
                BYTE    Function;
                LONG    QueueID;
                WORD    JobType;
                } Request;

        struct svcQueueRep {
                WORD    Length;
                BYTE    ClientStation;
                BYTE    ClientTaskNumber;
                LONG    ClientIDNumber;
                LONG    TargetServerIDNumber;
                BYTE    TargetExecutionTime[6];
                BYTE    JobEntryTime[6];
                WORD    JobNumber;
                WORD    JobType;
                BYTE    JobPosition;
                BYTE    JobControlFlags;
                BYTE    JobFileName[14];
                BYTE    JobFileHandle[6];
```

```
		BYTE	ServerStation;
		BYTE	ServerTaskNumber;
		LONG	ServerIDNumber;
		} Reply;

	int result;

	Request.Length = sizeof( struct svcQueueReq );
	Request.Function = 0x71;
	Request.QueueID = QueueID;
	Request.JobType = 0;

	Reply.Length = sizeof( struct svcQueueRep );

	_AH = 0xE3;
	_SI = (unsigned)&Request;
	_DI = (unsigned)&Reply;
	_ES = _DS;

	geninterrupt( 0x21 );

	if ( result = _AL )
		return _AL;
	else
	{
		*JobNumber = Reply.JobNumber;
		return result;
	}
}

int ReadQueueJobEntry( LONG QueueID, WORD JobNumber )
{
	struct readQueueReq {
		WORD	Length;
		BYTE	Function;
		LONG	QueueID;
		WORD	JobNumber;
		} Request;

	struct readQueueRep {
		WORD	Length;
		BYTE	ClientStation;
		BYTE	ClientTaskNumber;
		LONG	ClientIDNumber;
		LONG	TargetServerIDNumber;
		BYTE	TargetExecutionTime[6];
		BYTE	JobEntryTime[6];
		WORD	JobNumber;
		WORD	JobType;
		BYTE	JobPosition;
		BYTE	JobControlFlags;
		BYTE	JobFileName[14];
		BYTE	JobFileHandle[6];
		BYTE	ServerStation;
		BYTE	ServerTaskNumber;
		LONG	ServerIDNumber;
		BYTE	TextJobDescription[50];
		BYTE	ClientRecordArea[152];
		} Reply;

	int result;
```

such as LPT1, LPT2, LPT3 or PRN. Captures may be in effect for several LPTs simultaneously since each has its own set of print flags.

When the first character is sent to be printed, the network creates a capture file to hold the data before it is printed, and assigns a queue to the job, depending on how queues are mapped to the printers at the server level (for NetWare, queues were hard-wired to the printers; Advanced NetWare provides more flexibility, but usually printer 0 is mapped to PRINTQ_0).

At this point, all of the information sent to the printer is redirected to the queue, which places it in the capture file. As soon as there is data in that capture file, the application may flush, cancel, or end the capture.

Flushing a capture entails closing the capture file and releasing its contents to the Queue Management System (QMS) for servicing by the printer, while opening a new capture file and continuing the capture.

Ending a capture is the natural way to terminate the capture process. The capture file is closed and sent to the printer, but the capturing process is turned off. Any subsequent printing would go only to the local LPT device.

Cancelling a capture, like ending a capture, terminates the capturing process, but does not send any data in the capture file to the printer.

One useful option for programmers is to let this process stop at the capture file, sending no data to the printer. The program may use the Specify Capture File call to direct printing to a file for later manipulation or printing. Ending or cancelling a capture to a permanent file does not delete the file, it only closes it.

There are two sets of capture calls, one for the default LPT device and one for specified LPT devices. Each set contains a start, flush, cancel and end capture call as well as get and set capture flags calls.

The NetWare capture flags

NetWare maintains tables of information about the capture process in each workstation's shell. Three tables are maintained, one for each LPT device, so there could be a different configuration for each printing target, and those targets could print simultaneously.

The Capture Flags Table consists of 63 bytes of information about the capture process, including the text on the banner, the form number, the number of copies, and several other flags. As a maximum, although all can be read, only 42 of the 63 bytes can be modified, and there is no minimum, so a programmer could specify a two-byte packet just to change the first two flags.

The Status flag

The Status flag is used internally by the shell and should always be set to 0. It indicates whether capture is enabled (0) or disabled (any other value) for the default LPT device.

The Print Flags byte

The Print Flag byte contains four bit fields that control different aspects of the print job. The default value for this field is 0x80. Possible values are:

0x04	Print job is released to be printed if the capture is interrupted by a breach of connection with the file server.
0x08	Automatic form feed is suppressed after the document is printed.
0x40	Tabs are converted to spaces (and other control characters are con verted). Tab size is specified in the next field.
0x80	Banners are printed before documents.

The Tab Size flag

The Tab Size flag holds a number from 1 to 18 that determines how many spaces each tab contains. The default is 8. Tabs conversion is based on the Print Flags field.

The Server Printer flag

The Server Printer flag holds the number of the printer (0-4) to which the print job will be sent. (Under NetWare 2.0a, the network printer meant the network printer. With NetWare 2.1x, the network printer is the spooler setup at the file server. Spoolers send their data to queues which printers service.) The default setting is 0.

The Number of Copies flag

The Number of Copies flag is set at a number from 0 to 255. The default is 1; 0 means don't print anything (on a printer; zero may be used to print to a file).

The Form Type flag

The Form Type flag tells which of 256 (0-255) forms to use. The default form is 0. If the type of form is different from the one in the printer, the server, which tracks which forms are mounted in which printers, will stop printing and wait for a "MOUNT FORM x" instruction.

Developers should take heed: Any programs using forms should alert users and supervisors as to how to change forms. Much confusion has resulted from users believing their printers or servers were damaged when their servers were simply waiting for forms.

The Banner Text flag

The Banner Text flag contains the text of the bottom half of the banner. This is an uppercase, 13-character ASCIIZ string. The default is the name of the file to be printed. (If this call returns all nulls, that is what will be printed.)

The Local LPT Device flag

The Local LPT Device flag specifies which LPT device is the default. 0 = LPT1, 1 = LPT2, 2 = LPT3.

The Flush Capture Timeout Count flag

The Flush Capture Timeout Count flag (value 0-65535) resets every time interrupt 17h is called; if the flag reaches zero before another interrupt 17h is called, the buffer is flushed, so the program should set this flag to the number of clock ticks desired between flushes. The value is checked every tick. When the timeout expires, the buffer is flushed: The capture file is closed, the queue job entry is released for printing, and a new capture is started for the workstation. If an application prints more data before the first timeout expires, the timeout is reset and starts from its original value.

The Flush Capture On Device Close flag

The Flush Capture On Device Close flag tells whether (any value) or not (0) to flush the capture file when an application ends the capture by closing the LPT. The default is false (0).

The Maximum Lines flag

The Maximum Lines flag tells the maximum lines per page, up to 65535; default is 66.

The Maximum Characters flag

The Maximum Characters flag specifies the maximum characters per line, up to 65535; default is 132.

The Form Name flag

The Form Name flag contains the name of the form to be mounted in the file server. This field is only for reference. It is not used by the server, which uses only the Form Number field in determining the form to use.

The LPT Capture flag

The LPT Capture flag indicates whether (any value) or not (0) capture of a specified LPT is currently taking place.

The File Capture flag

The File Capture flag is set when a capture filename has been specified. Data to be printed is then sent to the file, rather than being queued for printing. (The Specify Capture File call uses this flag.)

The Timing Out flag

The Timing Out flag is set to FFh when the Flush Capture Timeout is decrementing, to 0 when no timeout count is under way.

The Printer Setup Buffer Address flag

The Printer Setup Buffer Address flag contains a long pointer to a buffer that contains a printer setup string that is written to the printer (or capture file). The size of the buffer is specified in the SHELL.CFG file and stored in the first word of the buffer. This buffer can be filled by the programmer.

The Printer Reset Buffer Address flag

The Printer Reset Buffer Address flag contains a long pointer to a buffer containing the printer reset string. The size of the buffer is specified in the SHELL.CFG file.

The Connection ID Queue Print Job flag

The Connection ID Queue Print Job flag contains a value (1 - 8) indicating the position in the workstation's Connection ID Table of the server receiving the print job.

The Capture In Progress flag

The Capture In Progress flag is set when the first character is sent to the specified LPT device. At this point, the print queue job entry is created and is given a job number. All characters printed to the specified LPT device are captured and sent to the capture file for this queue job. The flag is cleared when the capture is ended, cancelled, or flushed. Once the capture is complete, the job may be printed.

The Print Queue flag

The Print Queue flag is set when the print queue job entry is placed in the print queue. When the capture is ended or cancelled, this flag is cleared.

The Print Job Valid flag

The Print Job Valid flag is set while the capture file is open to receive captured characters. When the capture process is ended, cancelled, or flushed, the flag is cleared.

The Print Queue ID flag

The Print Queue ID flag contains the Bindery object ID (four bytes) of the print queue on the target server. This field is only valid when the Print Queue flag is set.

The Print Job Number flag

The Print Job Number flag contains a number (1-999) that the Queue Management Service (QMS) assigns to print queue job entries. Console operators may use this job number to change the position, cancel, or manipulate the contents of the print queue job entry through the QMS API.

Queue management and the Print Services API

NetWare 2.1x uses the Queue Management System (QMS) to handle all printing requests. The Print Services API simply provides a convenient mechanism for capturing data and printing it to the file server, although the QMS could be manipulated directly. This section will show the interaction between the Print Services API and the QMS.

Tables and the Queue Management System

The workstation shell maintains several tables for use with the Print Services API. In addition to the capture flags already discussed, these tables hold print and queue information.

The NetWare queue is a group of jobs waiting to be serviced; it is also an object in the NetWare file server's Bindery. To add a job to a queue, you need a file and a file header. The file contains the information to be processed. In Print Services, the queue file holds captured data. The file header contains information on what the job is, when it can be started, which server should process it, etc.

The first 104 bytes of any file header are boilerplate, the same for any kind of queue operation. The last 152 bytes, comprising the Client Record Area, vary with the type of job to be performed.

QMS Queue File Header

Offset	Field	Type
0	Client Station	BYTE
1	Client Task Number	BYTE
2	Client ID Number	LONG
6	Target Server ID Number	LONG
10	Target Execution Time	BYTE[6]
16	Job Entry Time	BYTE[6]
22	Job Number	WORD
24	Job Type	WORD
26	Job Position	BYTE

27	Job Control Flags	BYTE
28	Job File Name	BYTE[14]
42	Job File Handle	BYTE[6]
48	Server Station	BYTE
49	Server Task Number	BYTE
50	Server ID Number	LONG
54	Text Job Description	BYTE[50]
104	Client Record Area	BYTE[152]

The Client Record Area is a 152-byte custom area that each application fills in according to its own specification. The Print Services' specification for the Client Record Area is:

Offset	**Field**	**Type**
0	Client Record Area Ver.	BYTE
1	Tab Size	WORD
3	Number of Copies	WORD
5	Control Flags	WORD
7	Maximum Lines	WORD
9	Maximum Characters	WORD
11	Form Name (ASCIIZ)	BYTE[16]
27	Reserved	BYTE[6]
33	Banner Name	BYTE[14]
47	File Name on Banner	BYTE[13]
60	File Name in Header	BYTE[14]
74	Directory Path	BYTE[80]

The Client Record area is created by the Print Services and is used primarily in specifying banner information.

The flexibility of NetWare is apparent in the developer's ability to use the printing services to move printed data to a queue and write a custom print service to print the data elsewhere. A developer could create a custom print service that serviced jobs from a particular queue, sending them to another station for printing, archiving them on some slow, but large backup device, or faxing them through a shared fax board to some other destination.

On the other hand, the developer could use the QMS to service print jobs and could replace the Print Services API with his or her own routines, placing jobs to be printed directly into queues. However, the following calls often provide the more elegant approach to simple print jobs.

Calls in the Print Services API

The following descriptions will include which versions of NetWare support which calls. Throughout the book, we explain fields within the calls only at the first mention of each field in each chapter. Appendix B contains a comprehensive, alphabetical listing of the fields for quick reference.

Start LPT Capture (DFh 00h)

This call is supported in NetWare versions 4.0 and 4.6, in Advanced NetWare versions 1.0, 1.02, 2.0 and 2.1, and in NetWare 386 and later versions. It initiates the capture process of the default LPT device.

Registers in:
AH DFh
DL 00h

Registers out:
AL Completion Code

Completion Codes
00 Successful

This call redirects to a network printer any data that applications send to their default LPT device. The network printer and other specifics such as the number of copies, time between flushes, etc. are managed by the Get and Set Default Capture Flags calls.

Current Default Capture Flags are used automatically when this call is made. The file server waits for the first character to be printed before creating a queue file and adding the job entry to the print queue. This call sets the LPT Capture flag and clears the Capture In Progress flag. (Both flags are in the table manipulated by Get/Set Default Capture Flags calls).

The NetWare C Interface format is:

```
int StartLPTCapture( void );
```

Flush LPT Capture (DFh 03h)

This call is supported in Advanced NetWare versions 2.0 and 2.1, and in NetWare 386 and later versions. It closes the capture file associated with the default LPT device.

Registers In:
AH DFh
DL 03h

Registers Out:
AL Completion Code

Completion Codes
00h Successful

If printing has occurred, this call closes the capture file associated with the default LPT. If capturing to a network printer, the job is released for printing. If capturing to a file, the file is closed.

This call maintains the connection to the print queue and continues redirection of data to the file server for printing. When the next character after the Flush is printed, a new capture file is created.

The Capture In Progress flag and the Print Job Valid Flag are cleared by this call; the LPT Capture Flag and Print Queue Flag stay set.

The NetWare C Interface format is:

```
int FlushLPTCapture( void );
```

Cancel LPT Capture (DFh 02h)

This call is supported in NetWare versions 4.0 and 4.6, in Advanced NetWare versions 1.0, 1.02, 2.0 and 2.1, and in NetWare 386 and later versions. It cancels a capture. It terminates the capturing process, but does not send any data in the capture file to the printer.

Registers In:
AH DFh
DL 02h

Registers Out:
AL Completion Code

Completion Codes
00h Successful

This call effectively closes up shop on the capture process: The capture is ended (print reverts back to the local PC); the print queue job entry is removed; and the capture file is deleted. The LPT Capture Print Queue and Print Job Valid flags are cleared.

If the workstation was capturing to a permanent file the call closes the file but does not delete it.

The NetWare C Interface format is:

```
int CancelLPTCapture( void );
```

End LPT Capture (DFh 01h)

This call is supported in NetWare versions 4.0 and 4.6, in Advanced NetWare versions 1.0, 1.02, 2.0 and 2.1, and in NetWare 386 and later versions. It ends the capture of the default LPT device.

Registers In:
AH DFh
DL 01h

Registers Out:
AL Completion Code

Completion Codes
00h Successful

Like the preceding call, this call ends the capturing process; unlike that call, it does release the captured data to the printer. This call is the normal way to terminate the capturing process if the data that has been captured should be printed.

After this call is made, the workstation no longer captures data to the network (printing reverts to the local workstation). The capture file is closed and the queue job entry is released to be printed. If the workstation was capturing to a file, the file is closed. If nothing was printed during the capture, the workstation merely reverts back to local printing.

This call clears the LPT capture flag, the Print Queue flag and the Print Job Valid flag.

The NetWare C Interface format is:

```
int EndLPTCapture( void );
```

Spool Data to a Capture File (E0h 00h)

This call is supported in NetWare versions 4.0 and 4.6, in Advanced NetWare versions 1.0, 1.02, 2.0 and 2.1, and in NetWare 386. It adds data to a capture file and has been replaced by higher-level functions such as Start LPT Capture, but is shown here for completeness.

Registers In:

AH	E0h
DS:SI	Request Buffer
ES:DI	Reply Buffer

Registers Out:

AL	Completion Code

Completion Codes

00h	Successful

Request Packet (max 259 bytes):

Offset	Content	Type	Order
0	Request Buffer Length-2	WORD	lo-hi
2	00h	BYTE	
3	Data to Send	BYTE (1-256)	

Reply Packet (2 bytes):

Offset	Content	Type	Order
0	0000	WORD	lo-hi

If no capture file is currently open, the file server will create one in the SYS:SYSTEM directory, naming it SPLpp$ss.xxx (where pp is the printer number, ss is the station number and xxx is the incrementing number indicating the number of catch files the network has made for this station.) Workstations may use the Specify Capture File call to explicitly create a capture file.

The NetWare C Interface format is not supported.

Close and Queue Capture File (E0h 01h)

This call is supported in NetWare versions 4.0 and 4.6, in Advanced NetWare versions 1.0, 1.02, 2.0 and 2.1, and in NetWare 386. It closes the station's current capture file and queues it for printing. This function has been replaced by higher-level functions such as End LPT Capture, but is shown here for completeness.

Registers In:

AH	E0h
DS:SI	Request Buffer
ES:DI	Reply Buffer

Registers Out:

AL	Completion Code

Completion Codes

00h	Successful

Request Packet (4 bytes):

Offset	**Content**	**Type**	**Order**
0	Request Buffer Length-2	WORD	lo-hi
2	01h	BYTE	
3	Abort Flag	BYTE	

Reply Packet (2 bytes):

Offset	**Content**	**Type**	**Order**
0	0000	WORD	lo-hi

Abort Flag, if nonzero, will delete the capture file rather than queueing it for printing. If no capture file is open, this call will be ignored.

The NetWare C Interface format is not supported.

Get Default Capture Flags (B8h 00h)

This call is supported in Advanced NetWare versions 2.0 and 2.1, and in NetWare 386 and later versions. It returns the print job flags for the default LPT.

Registers In:

AH	B8h
AL	00h
CX	Reply Buffer Length (1-63)
ES:BX	Reply Buffer

Registers Out:

AL	Completion Code

Completion Codes

00h	Successful

Reply Packet (63 bytes)

Offset	Content	Type	Order	
0	Status	BYTE		
1	Flags	BYTE		
2	Tab Size	BYTE (1-18)		
3	Server Printer	BYTE (0-4)		
4	Number of Copies	BYTE (0-255)		
5	Form Type	BYTE (0-255)		
6	Reserved	BYTE		
7	Banner Text (ASCIIZ)	BYTE[13]		
20	Reserved	BYTE		
21	Local LPT Device	BYTE		
22	Flush Capture Timeout	WORD	hi-lo	
24	Flush Capture On Device Close	BYTE		

/* All fields below this are Adv. NetWare 2.1 and above compatible only. */

Offset	Content	Type	Order	
25	Max Lines	WORD	hi-lo	
27	Max Chars	WORD	hi-lo	
29	Form Name (ASCIIZ)	BYTE[13]		
42	LPT Capture Flag	BYTE		
43	File Capture Flag	BYTE		
44	Timing Out Flag	BYTE		
45	Printer Setup Buffer Address	LONG	hi-lo	/*Different*/
49	Printer Reset Buffer Address	LONG	hi-lo	""
53	Connection ID Queue Print Job	BYTE		
54	Capture In Progress	BYTE		
55	Print Queue Flag	BYTE		
56	Print Job Valid	BYTE		
57	Print Queue ID	LONG	hi-lo	
61	Print Job Number	WORD	hi-lo	(1-999)

Although the reply packet has a length of 63, the developer can setup a reply packet of any size between 1 and 63 and the call will return only the information that can fit in the packet.

Status is always set to 0.

Print Flags is a byte containing 4 bit fields with the following values:

0x04	Print job is released to be printed if the capture is interrupted by a breach of connection with the file server.
0x08	Automatic form feed is suppressed after the document is printed.
0x40	Tabs will be converted to spaces (and other control characters will be converted). Tab size is specified in the next field.
0x80	Banners will be printed before documents.

Tab Size is a value between 1 and 18 that determines the number of spaces to convert a tab into. The default is 8. Tabs are converted based on the Print Flags - Tabs field.

Server Printer is the number of the printer (0-4) to which the print job will be sent. (Under NetWare 2.0a, the network printer meant the network printer. With NetWare 2.1x, the network printer is the spooler setup at the file server. Spoolers send their data to queues which printers service.)

Number of Copies to print can be from 1 to 255. The default is 1; 0 means don't print anything.

Form Type is the number (0-255) of the form to be used. If it differs from the one in the printer, the server stops printing and waits for a "MOUNT FORM x" instruction. The default form is 0.

Banner Text specifies the bottom half of the banner. This is an uppercase, 13-character ASCIIZ string. The default is the name of the file to be printed (if this call returns all nulls, this is what will be printed).

Local LPT Device specifies which LPT is the default: 0 = LPT1, 1 = LPT2, 2= LPT3.

Flush Capture Timeout Count is the value (0-65535) from which countdown begins when an application prints any data. When the timeout expires, the capture is flushed and a new capture is started for the workstation. If an application prints more data before the first timeout expires, the timeout is reset to its original value.

Flush Capture On Device Close is a flag (with zero False, any other value True) indicating whether or not to flush the capture file when the application sends an End Capture call. The default is False.

Max Lines is a number from 0 to 65535; default is 66 lines. Max Chars is a number from 0 to 65535; default is 132 characters.

Form Name is for reference only; the Form Number field alone determines the form to use.

LPT Capture Flag indicates whether or not capturing of the default LPT data is currently taking place.

The *File Capture Flag* is set when a capture filename has been specified with the Specify Capture Call.

The *Timing Out Flag* is set when the Flush Capture Timeout is decrementing (and not set when it isn't).

The *Printer Setup Buffer Address* field contains a pointer to a buffer that contains a printer setup string that is written to the printer (or capture file). The size of the buffer is specified in the SHELL.CFG file. The buffer size is stored in the first word of the buffer.

The *Printer Reset Buffer Address* field is identical to the preceding field except the data is sent after the printed data rather than before it.

Connection ID Queue Print Job is a value (1-8) indicating the position in the workstation's Connection ID Table of the server receiving the print job.

The *Capture In Progress* flag is set when the first character is sent to the default LPT. At this point, the print queue job entry is created and is given a job number. All characters printed to the default LPT are then captured and sent to the capture file for this queue job. The flag is cleared when the capture is ended, cancelled, or flushed.

The *Print Queue* flag is set when the print queue job entry is placed in the print queue. When the capture is ended or cancelled, this flag is cleared.

The *Print Job Valid* flag is set when the capture file is open to receive characters. When the capture is ended, canceled, or flushed, the flag is cleared.

Print Queue ID is the Bindery object ID (4 bytes) of the print queue on the target server. This field is only valid when the Print Queue flag is set.

Print Job Number, a value from 1 to 999, is assigned by the Queue Management Service (QMS) to the print queue job entries. Console operators may use this job number to change the position, cancel, or manipulate the contents of the print queue job entry through the QMS API.

The NetWare C Interface format is:

```
int GetDefaultCaptureFlags( CAPTURE_FLAGS *captureFlags );
```

Set Default Capture Flags (B8h 01h)

This call is supported in Advanced NetWare versions 2.0 and 2.1, and in NetWare 386 and later versions. It sets the print job flags for the default LPT.

Registers In:

AH	B8h
AL	01h
CX	Request Buffer Length (1-63)
ES:BX	Request Buffer

Registers Out:

AL	Completion Code

Completion Codes

00h	Successful

Reply Packet (53 bytes):

Offset	Content	Type	Order
0	Status	BYTE	
1	Flags	BYTE	
2	Tab Size	BYTE (1-18)	
3	Server Printer	BYTE (0-4)	
4	Number of Copies	BYTE (0-255)	
5	Form Type	BYTE (0-255)	
6	Reserved	BYTE	
7	Banner Text (ASCIIZ)	BYTE[13]	
20	Reserved	BYTE	
21	Local LPT Device	BYTE	
22	Flush Capture Timeout	WORD	hi-lo
24	Flush Capture On Device Close	BYTE	

/* All fields below this are Adv. NetWare 2.1 and above compatible only.*/

25	Max Lines	WORD	hi-lo
27	Max Chars	WORD	hi-lo
29	Form Name (ASCIIZ)	BYTE[13]	
42	LPT Capture Flag	BYTE	
43	File Capture Flag	BYTE	
44	Timing Out Flag	BYTE	
45	Printer Setup Buffer Address	LONG	hi-lo /*Different*/
49	Printer Reset Buffer Address	LONG	hi-lo ""

Only the default printing flags for the requesting workstation are affected by this call. To change a workstation's default capture flags, the developer should make a call to Get Default Capture Flags, change any fields, and make this call. Although the reply packet has a length of 63, the developer can set up a request packet of any size between and 1 and 63 and the call will return only the information that can fit in the packet.

The NetWare C Interface format is:

```
int SetDefaultCaptureFlags( SET_CAPTURE_FLAGS *captureFlags );
```

Set Spool Flags (E0h 02h)

This call is supported in NetWare versions 4.0 and 4.6, in Advanced NetWare versions 1.0, 1.02, 2.0 and 2.1, and in NetWare 386. It sets the flags the spooler will use. This function has been replaced by higher-level functions such as the Set Default Capture Flags call, but is shown here for completeness.

Registers In:

AH	E0h
DS:SI	Request Buffer
ES:DI	Reply Buffer

Registers Out:

AL	Completion Code

Completion Codes

00h	Successful

Request Packet (23 bytes):

Offset	Content	Type	Order
0	Request Buffer Length-2	WORD	lo-hi
2	02h	BYTE	
3	Print Flags	BYTE	
4	Tab Size	BYTE (1-20)	
5	Target Printer	BYTE (1-5)	
6	Copies	BYTE (0-255)	
7	Form Type	BYTE (0-255)	
8	Reserved	BYTE	
9	Banner	BYTE[13]	
22	Terminator (00h)	BYTE	

Reply Packet (2 bytes):

Offset	Content	Type	Order
0	0000	WORD	lo-hi

Print Flags

0x08	Suppress automatic form feed at end of print job
0x20	Delete spool file after printing
0x40	Enable tab expansion
0x80	Print banner page

The NetWare C Interface format is not supported.

Start Specific LPT Capture (DFh 04h)

This call is supported in Advanced NetWare version 2.1, and in NetWare 386 and later versions. It initiates the capture process of the specified LPT.

Registers In:

AH	DFh
DL	04h
DH	LPT Device (0 = LPT1, 1 = LPT2, 2 = LPT3)

Registers out:

AL	Completion Code

Completion Codes

00	Successful

This call redirects to a network printer any data that applications send to the specified LPT. The network printer and other specifics such as the number of copies, time between flushes, etc. are managed by the Get and Set Specific Capture Flags calls.

Current Specific Capture Flags will be used automatically when this call is made. The file server waits for the first character to be printed before creating a queue file and adding the job entry to the print queue.

This call also sets the LPT Capture flag and clears the Capture In Progress flag.

The NetWare C Interface format is:

```
int StartSpecificLPTCapture( BYTE LPTDevice );
```

Flush Specific LPT Capture (DFh 07h)

This call is supported in Advanced NetWare version 2.1, and in NetWare 386 and later versions. It closes the capture file associated with the specified LPT.

Registers In:

AH	DFh
DL	07h
DH	LPT Device (0 = LPT1, 1 = LPT2, 2 = LPT3)

Registers Out:

AL	Completion Code

Completion Codes
00h Successful

If printing has occurred, this call closes the capture file associated with the specified LPT. If capture is to a network printer, the job is released for printing; if to a file, the file is closed.

This call maintains the connection to the print queue and continues redirecting printed data to the file server for printing. When the next character after the Flush is printed, a new capture file is created. The Capture In Progress flag and the Print Job Valid Flag are cleared. The LPT Capture Flag and Print Queue Flag stay set.

The NetWare C Interface format is:

```
int FlushSpecificLPTCapture( BYTE LPTDevice );
```

Cancel Specific LPT Capture (DFh 06h)

This call is supported in Advanced NetWare version 2.1, and in NetWare 386 and later versions. It cancels the capture to the specified LPT.

Registers In:
AH DFh
DL 06h
DH LPT Device (0 = LPT1, 1 = LPT2, 2 = LPT3)

Registers Out:
AL Completion Code

Completion Codes
00h Successful

This call effectively closes up shop on the capture process: Capture ends (print reverts back to the local PC); the print queue job entry is removed; and the capture file is deleted. The LPT Capture Print Queue and Print Job Valid flags are cleared.

If the workstation was capturing to a permanent file the call closes the file, but does not delete it. This must be done by the developer.

The NetWare C Interface format is:

```
int CancelSpecificLPTCapture( BYTE LPTDevice );
```

End Specific LPT Capture (DFh 05h)

This call is supported in Advanced NetWare version 2.1, and in NetWare 386 and later versions. It ends the capture of the specified LPT.

Registers In:

AH	DFh
DL	05h
DH	LPT Device (0 = LPT1, 1 = LPT2, 2 = LPT3)

Registers Out:

AL	Completion Code

Completion Codes

00h	Successful

Like the preceding call, this ends the capturing process, although it does release the captured data to be printed. This call is the normal way to terminate the capturing process if the data that has been captured should be printed.

After this call is made, the workstation no longer captures data to the network (printing reverts to the local workstation). The capture file is closed and the queue job entry is released to be printed. If the workstation was capturing to a file, the file is closed. If nothing was printed during the capture, the workstation merely reverts back to local printing.

This call clears the LPT capture flag, the Print Queue flag and the Print Job Valid flag.

The NetWare C Interface format is:

```
int EndSpecificLPTCapture( BYTE LPTDevice );
```

Get Specific Capture Flags (B8h 02h)

This call is supported in Advanced NetWare version 2.1, and in NetWare 386 and later versions. It gets the print job flags for the specified LPT device.

Registers In:

AH	B8h
AL	02h
CX	Reply Buffer Length (1..63)
ES:BX	Reply Buffer
DH	LPT Device (0 = LPT1, 1 = LPT2, 2 = LPT3)

Registers Out:
AL Completion Code

Completion Codes
00h Successful

Reply Packet (63 bytes)

Offset	Content	Type	Order
0	Status	BYTE	
1	Flags	BYTE	
2	Tab Size	BYTE (1-18)	
3	Server Printer	BYTE (0-4)	
4	Number of Copies	BYTE (0-255)	
5	Form Type	BYTE (0-255)	
6	Reserved	BYTE	
7	Banner Text (ASCIIZ)	BYTE[13]	
20	Reserved	BYTE	
21	Local LPT Device	BYTE	
22	Flush Capture Timeout	WORD	hi-lo
24	Flush Capture On Device Close	BYTE	
25	Max Lines	WORD	hi-lo
27	Max Chars	WORD	hi-lo
29	Form Name (ASCIIZ)	BYTE[13]	
42	LPT Capture Flag	BYTE	
43	File Capture Flag	BYTE	
44	Timing Out Flag	BYTE	
45	Printer Setup Buffer Address	LONG	hi-lo /*Different*/
49	Printer Reset Buffer Address	LONG	hi-lo ""
53	Connection ID Queue Print Job	BYTE	
54	Capture In Progress	BYTE	
55	Print Queue Flag	BYTE	
56	Print Job Valid	BYTE	
57	Print Queue ID	LONG	hi-lo
61	Print Job Number	WORD	hi-lo (1-999)

The NetWare C Interface format is:

```
int GetSpecificCaptureFlags( BYTE localLPTDevice,
   CAPTURE_FLAGS *captureFlags );
```

Set Specific Capture Flags (B8h 03h)

Supported in Advanced NetWare version 2.1, and in NetWare 386 and later versions, this call sets the print job flags for the specified LPT.

Registers In:

AH	B8h
AL	03h
CX	Request Buffer Length (1-63)
ES:BX	Request Buffer
DH	LPT Device (0 = LPT1, 1 = LPT2, 2 = LPT3)

Registers Out:

AL	Completion Code

Completion Codes

00h	Successful

Request Packet (53 bytes):

Offset	**Content**	**Type**	**Order**	
0	Status	BYTE		
1	Flags	BYTE		
2	Tab Size	BYTE (1-18)		
3	Server Printer	BYTE (0-4)		
4	Number of Copies	BYTE (0-255)		
5	Form Type	BYTE (0-255)		
6	Reserved	BYTE		
7	Banner Text (ASCIIZ)	BYTE[13]		
20	Reserved	BYTE		
21	Local LPT Device	BYTE		
22	Flush Capture Timeout	WORD	hi-lo	
24	Flush Capture On Device Close	BYTE		
25	Max Lines	WORD	hi-lo	
27	Max Chars	WORD	hi-lo	
29	Form Name (ASCIIZ)	BYTE[13]		
42	LPT Capture Flag	BYTE		
43	File Capture Flag	BYTE		
44	Timing Out Flag	BYTE		
45	Printer Setup Buffer Address	LONG	hi-lo	/*Different*/
49	Printer Reset Buffer Address	LONG	hi-lo	""

Only the specific printing flags for the requesting workstation are affected by this call. To change a workstation's specific capture flags, the developer should make a call to Get Specific Capture Flags, change any fields, and make this call.

The NetWare C Interface format is:

```
int SetSpecificCaptureFlags( BYTE LPTDevice,
   SET_CAPTURE_FLAGS *setCaptureFlags );
```

Get LPT Capture Status (F0h 03h)

Supported in Advanced NetWare versions 1.0, 1.02, 2.0 and 2.1, and in NetWare 386 and later versions, this call returns whether the default capture is active.

Registers In:

AH	F0h
AL	03h

Registers Out:

AH	Completion Code
AL	Connection ID (1-8)

Completion Codes

00h	Successful
FFh	Capture Is Active

When the default LPT is being captured, this call returns FFh and the Connection ID of the server queueing the job. When a capture is not active, the completion code is 0 and the Connection ID is not defined. The Connection ID is an index into the workstation's Connection ID table and indicates a specific server that is receiving the captured information.

The NetWare C Interface format is:

```
int GetLPTCaptureStatus( WORD *serverNumber );
```

Get Default Local Printer (B8h 04h)

This call is supported in Advanced NetWare version 2.1, and in NetWare 386 and later versions. It returns the number of the default LPT.

Registers In:

AH	B8h
AL	04h

Registers Out:
DH   Default LPT Device (0 = LPT1, 1 = LPT2, 2 = LPT3)

The NetWare C Interface format is:

```
int GetDefaultLocalPrinter( void );
```

Set Default Local Printer (B8h 05h)

This call is supported in Advanced NetWare version 2.1, and in NetWare 386 and later versions. It sets the LPT to be used as the default.

Registers In:
AH   B8h
AL   05h
DH   LPT Device (0 = LPT1, 1 = LPT2, 2 = LPT3)

Registers Out:
AL   Completion Code

Completion Codes:
00   Successful

Once this call is made, the default LPT will not change until it is modified through this call or specified in the default capture flags, or until the workstation is rebooted.

The NetWare C Interface format is:

```
int SetDefaultLocalPrinter( BYTE LPTDevice );
```

Get Printer Status (E0h 06h)

This call is supported in NetWare versions 4.0 and 4.6, in Advanced NetWare versions 1.0, 1.02, 2.0 and 2.1, and in NetWare 386 and later versions. It returns the status of a specified file server printer.

Registers In:
AH   E0h
DS:SI   Request Packet Address
ES:DI   Reply Packet Address

Registers Out:

AL	Completion Code

Completion Codes:

00	Successful
FFh	No Such Printer

Request Packet (4 bytes):

Offset	Content	Type	Order
0	Request Buffer Length-2	WORD	lo-hi
2	06h	BYTE	
3	Printer Number	BYTE (0-4)	

Reply Packet (6 bytes):

0	Reply Buffer Length - 2	WORD	lo-hi
2	Printer Halted	BYTE	
3	Printer Offline	BYTE	
4	Form Type	BYTE (0-255)	
5	Target Printer Number	BYTE (0-4)	

Printer Number, the number of the printer for which the call is requesting information, is the same as the Target Printer number if the server isn't rerouting the printers. If it is, this number indicates the routed printer number.

Printer Halted is a flag that, if set, indicates that the printer has been stopped from the server console. A PRINTER x START will restart the printer, if it was stopped with a PRINTER x STOP call (these are for NetWare 2.1, for versions below, use STOP PRINTER x and START PRINTER x).

Printer Offline is a flag that indicates whether the specified printer is on-line or off-line. If set, this flag indicates the printer is off-line due to a printer malfunction (out of paper, jam, no power, etc.). If a printer is offline, the server will not change the state of that printer until there is a job placed in an empty queue.

The NetWare C Interface format is:

```
int GetPrinterStatus( int printerNumber, BYTE *printerHalted,
   BYTE *printerOffLine, int *formType, int *targetPrinter );
```

Get Banner User Name (B8h 08h)

This call is supported in Advanced NetWare version 2.1, and in NetWare 386 and later versions. It returns the name of the user that is printed on the banner page.

Registers In:

AH	B8h
AL	08h
ES:BX	Reply Packet Address

Registers Out:

AL	Completion Code

Completion Codes

0	Successful

Reply Packet (12 bytes)

Offset	**Content**	**Type**	**Order**
0	Banner User Name	BYTE[12]	

If a user name has not been set through the Set Banner User Name, then the user name of the currently logged user will be returned.

The NetWare C Interface format is:

```
int GetBannerUserName( char *userName );
```

Set Banner User Name (B8h 09h)

This call is supported in Advanced NetWare version 2.1, and in NetWare 386 and later versions. It sets the name of the user that is printed on the banner page.

Registers In:

AH	B8h
AL	09h
ES:BX	Request Packet Address

Registers Out:

AL	Completion Code

Completion Codes

0	Successful

Request Packet (12 bytes)

Offset	**Content**	**Type**	**Order**
0	Banner User Name	BYTE[12]	

The *Banner User Name* is the name printed on the banners that are included with print jobs. An application cannot have different banner names for different LPTs. If no name is specified, the current (when the capture was in progress) user's name is used.

The NetWare C Interface format is:

```
int SetBannerUserName( char *userName );
```

Set Capture Print Job (B8h 07h)

This call is supported in Advanced NetWare version 2.1, and in NetWare 386 and later versions. It assigns a print queue job number to a specified LPT device.

Registers In:

AH	B8h
AL	07h
DH	LPT Device (0 = LPT1, 1 = LPT2, 2 = LPT3)
BX	Job Number
SI,DI,CX	NetWare File Handle

Registers Out:

AL	Completion Code

Completion Codes

00	Successful
FFh	Print Job Already Queued

After this call is made, the next capture of the specified LPT will be queued, using the NetWare File Handle (6 bytes) as the handle of the capture file and using the Job Number as the number of the job in the queue. First, call Create Queue Job and File; the Job Number and Handle to be used in this call will be returned. This call simply sets the shell's local flags. The NetWare file handle is obtained from the job structure; it's the Job File Handle element.

The NetWare C Interface format is:

```
int SetCapturePrintJob( BYTE LPTDevice, WORD jobNumber,
   BYTE *jobFileHandle );
```

Set Capture Print Queue (B8h 06h)

This call is supported in Advanced NetWare version 2.1, and in NetWare 386 and later versions. It sets the print queue (Queue ID) for the next capture of the specified LPT.

Registers In:

AH	B8h
AL	06h
DH	LPT Device (0 = LPT1, 1 = LPT2, 2 = LPT3)
BX,CX	Queue ID

Registers Out:

AL	Completion Code

Completion Codes

00	Successful
FFh	Print Job Already Set

When this call is made, the next capture of the specified LPT is queued to the queue specified in Queue ID. The Queue ID is the Bindery object ID of the target print queue. The Bindery object ID is a four-byte value, so the first word should be placed in BX and the second in CX.

The NetWare C Interface format is:

```
int SetCapturePrintQueue( BYTE LPTDevice,
   BYTE serverNumberConnectionID, long QueueID );
```

Specify Capture File (E0h 09h)

This call is supported in NetWare versions 4.0 and 4.6, in Advanced NetWare versions 1.0, 1.02, 2.0 and 2.1, and in NetWare 386 and later versions. It creates the specified capture file for the next print capture.

Registers In:

AH	E0h
AL	09h
DS:SI	Request Packet Address
ES:DI	Reply Packet Address

Registers Out:

AL	Completion Code

Completion Codes

00	Successful
9Ch	Invalid Path

Request Packet (max = 260 bytes):

Offset	**Content**	**Type**	**Order**
0	Request Buffer Length-2	WORD	lo-hi
2	09h	BYTE	
3	Directory Handle	BYTE	
4	File Path Length	BYTE (1-255)	
5	File Path	BYTE[*LENGTH*]	

Reply Packet (2 bytes):

Offset	**Content**	**Type**
0	0000	WORD

Directory Handle is a number (1-255) that corresponds to an index to the Directory Handle Table, which in turn points to a volume-directory combination and describes a full path on the network.

File Path is the path of the file to receive captured data. It can be the full path itself or an offset to the source directory handle. If no source directory handle is specified, the volume name must be specified in the format "VOLUME:DIRECTORY\SUBDIRECTORY". If a directory handle is specified, the path can be used as an offset to it. If the directory handle describes the full path, the File Path field is not necessary.

This call allows an application to send captured data to a permanent file rather than to a print queue. After capturing the file, the programmer may choose to print the file using a Queue Services function call. The workstation making this call must have read, write, and create rights to the directory where the capture file will be created.

The steps suggested for this application are: make a call to Specify Capture File; start the capturing with Start LPT Capture; send data to the captured LPT; and end, cancel, or flush the data to the file.

An application may reopen the file to capture more data, but be aware that reopening the file moves the file pointer to the beginning of the file, so data overwrite may occur. Also remember that if a capture is cancelled, the File Capture flag is cleared, but the capture file is not deleted, it is only closed.

The NetWare C Interface format is:

```
int SpecifyCaptureFile( BYTE driveHandle, char *filePath );
```

Spool Existing File (E0h 03h)

This call is supported in NetWare versions 4.0 and 4.6, in Advanced NetWare versions 1.0, 1.02, 2.0 and 2.1, and in NetWare 386. It queues an existing file for printing. This function has been replaced by higher-level functions, but is shown here for completeness. The user must have file open and read privileges to the file in order to make this call.

Registers In:

AH	E0h
DS:SI	Request Buffer
ES:DI	Reply Buffer

Registers Out:

AL	Completion Code

Completion Codes

00h	Successful

Request Packet (max 261 bytes):

Offset	**Content**	**Type**	**Order**
0	Request Buffer Length-2	WORD	lo-hi
2	03h	BYTE	
3	Directory Handle	BYTE	
4	File Path Length	BYTE (0-255)	
5	File Path	BYTE[*LENGTH*]	

Reply Packet(2 bytes):

Offset	**Content**	**Type**	**Order**
0	0000	WORD	lo-hi

The NetWare C Interface format is not supported.

Get Spool Queue Entry (E0h 04h)

This call is supported in NetWare versions 4.0 and 4.6, in Advanced NetWare versions 1.0, 1.02, 2.0 and 2.1, and in NetWare 386. It can be used in succession to scan the print queue for a given job. This function has been replaced by higher-level functions such as the Queue Management System calls, but is shown here for completeness.

Registers In:

AH	E0h
DS:SI	Request Buffer
ES:DI	Reply Buffer

Registers Out:

AL	Completion Code

Completion Codes

00h	Successful

Request Packet (5 bytes):

Offset	Content	Type	Order
0	Request Buffer Length-2	WORD	lo-hi
2	04h	BYTE	
3	Printer Number	BYTE	
4	Job Number	BYTE	

Reply Packet (83 bytes):

Offset	Content	Type	Order
0	Reply Packet Length - 2	WORD	lo-hi
2	Job Number	BYTE	
3	Filler	BYTE[2]	
5	File Name	BYTE[14]	
19	Print Volume	BYTE	
20	Print Flags	BYTE	
21	Tab Size	BYTE	
22	Printer	BYTE	
23	Copies	BYTE	
24	Form Type	BYTE	

25	Station	BYTE	
26	Spool Time	BYTE[6]	
32	User Name	BYTE[15]	
47	Banner Name	BYTE[14]	
61	Path Name	BYTE[18]	
79	User ID	LONG	hi-lo /* only on NetWare 2.0 and above */

Job Number should be set to 0 when the call is first made and can be filled with the Job Number returned in the reply packet to iteratively scan through the queue entries.

Print Volume is the number of the volume where the file is stored.

Print Flags are the 4.0-style print flags — Print Banner, Expand Tabs, and Delete File after printing. See Set Spool Flags call.

Spool Time is the time the job was spooled to the print queue.

User Name is the name of the user who placed the job in the queue.

Path Name is the first 18 bytes of the path specification where the file resides.

User ID is the Bindery object ID of the user who placed the job in the queue.

The NetWare C Interface format is not supported.

Remove Entry from Spool Queue (E0h 05h)

This call is supported in NetWare versions 4.0 and 4.6, in Advanced NetWare versions 1.0, 1.02, 2.0 and 2.1, and in NetWare 386. It removes one or more jobs from the queue. This function has been replaced by higher-level functions such as the QMS calls, but is shown here for completeness.

Registers In:

AH	E0h
DS:SI	Request Buffer
ES:DI	Reply Buffer

Registers Out:

AL	Completion Code

Completion Codes

00h	Successful

Request Packet (min 5 bytes):

Offset	**Content**	**Type**	**Order**
0	Request Buffer Length-2	WORD	lo-hi
2	05h	BYTE	
3	Printer Number	BYTE	
4	Job Number	BYTE (1-99)	

Reply Packet (2 bytes):

Offset	**Content**	**Type**	**Order**
0	0000	WORD	lo-hi

The *Job Number* field contains the job number(s) to be removed from the queue. The job numbers can be determined from the previous call, Get Spool Queue Entry. If the requesting station's user ID is the same as the one that placed the job in the queue, the job is removed. If the IDs are different, the file server checks the rights of the requesting user to the indicated file. If the requesting user has the right to delete the queued file, the job is removed, otherwise the request is denied.

The NetWare C Interface format is not supported.

Code Sample: PrtTest.C

PrtTest is a program that presents the user with the options for manipulating the capture status of a program. The user may start, end, cancel, or flush a captured job. Also, the user may send data to the printer and display the current capture flags.

These options would most likely be incorporated into an application and performed automatically for the user, but shown in this way, it can give the developer a sense of both how the function calls can be made and how the function calls work.

PrtTest begins by defining the captureFlags, a large structure that houses all of the fields in the capture flags packet. Also, the program defines the local function prototypes.

Next, main() calls ShowMenu() to display the menu of choices to the user, and the next line solicits a response. Finally, a switch statement is used to handle each menu option.

StartLPTCapture(), FlushLPTCapture(), EndLPTCapture(), and CancelLPTCapture() all perform their respective NetWare printing services function calls.

Option 5 allows the user to send text to the printer by first using gets() to place an ASCII string into text. Next, fprintf is used to send the actual output to the printer (LPT1).

Option 6 calls ShowFlags() which displays the elements of the captureFlags structure after calling GetDefaultCaptureFlags(). This section has been left intentionally blank for the reader to fill in.

Option 7 terminates the while loop and exits.

Although not an elaborate program, PrtTest demonstrates the use of the print services calls that allow developers to access network printers from their applications. Too many applications today force the user to issue capture statements before run-ning programs. With just a few extra lines, these applications can become "NetWare-aware."

```
/*                                                                              */
/* PrtTest      - Tests the capture/print mechanism                             */
/*                                                                              */
/* by Charles Rose                                                              */
/*                                                                              */

#include <stdio.h>
#include <dos.h>
#include <dir.h>
#include <string.h>

typedef unsigned char BYTE;
typedef unsigned int WORD;
typedef unsigned long LONG;

struct captureFlags {
        BYTE    Status;
        BYTE    Flags;
        BYTE    TabSize;
        BYTE    ServerPrinter;
        BYTE    Copies;
        BYTE    FormType;
        BYTE    Reserved1;
        BYTE    BannerText[13];
        BYTE    Reserved2;
        BYTE    LocalLPTDevice;
        WORD    FlushTimeout;
        BYTE    FlushCaptureOnDeviceClose;
        WORD    MaxLines;
        WORD    MaxChars;
        BYTE    FormName[13];
        BYTE    LPTCaptureFlag;
        BYTE    FileCaptureFlag;
        BYTE    TimingOutFlag;
        LONG    PrinterSetupBuffer;
        LONG    PrinterResetBuffer;
        BYTE    ConnectionIDQueuePrintJob;
```

```
        BYTE    CaptureInProgress;
        BYTE    PrintQueueFlag;
        BYTE    PrintJobValid;
        LONG    PrintQueueID;
        WORD    PrintJobNumber;
};

int StartLPTCapture( void );
int GetDefaultLocalPrinter( void );
int FlushLPTCapture( void );
int EndLPTCapture( void );
int CancelLPTCapture( void );
int GetDefaultCaptureFlags( struct captureFlags *Reply );
void ShowMenu( void );
void ShowFlags( void );

main()
{
        int x, done = 0;
        char text[255];

        while (!done)
        {
                /* Display menu */
                ShowMenu();

                /* Get user input */
                x = getche();

                switch( x ) {

                                case '1' :      StartLPTCapture();
                                                break;

                                case '2' :      FlushLPTCapture();
                                                break;

                                case '3' :      EndLPTCapture();
                                                break;

                                case '4' :      CancelLPTCapture();
                                                break;

                                case '5' :      printf( "\nEnter text to print >" );
                                                gets( text );
                                                fprintf( stdprn, "%s\n", text );
                                                break;

                                case '6' :      ShowFlags();
                                                break;

                                /* Quit */
                                case '7' :      done++;
                                                break;
```

```
int StartLPTCapture( void )
{
        _AH = 0xDF;
        _DL = 0;

        geninterrupt( 0x21 );

        return _AL;
}

int GetDefaultLocalPrinter( void )
{
        _AH = 0xB8;
        _AL = 4;

        geninterrupt( 0x21 );

        return _DH;
}

int FlushLPTCapture( void )
{
        _AH = 0xDF;
        _DL = 3;

        geninterrupt( 0x21 );

        return _AL;
}

int EndLPTCapture( void )
{
        _AH = 0xDF;
        _DL = 1;

        geninterrupt( 0x21 );

        return _AL;
}

int CancelLPTCapture( void )
{
        _AH = 0xDF;
        _DL = 2;

        geninterrupt( 0x21 );

        return _AL;
}

int GetDefaultCaptureFlags( struct captureFlags *Reply )
{
        _AH = 0xB8;
        _AL = 0;
        _CX = sizeof( struct captureFlags );
        _BX = (WORD)Reply;
        _ES = _DS;
```

```
        geninterrupt( 0x21 );

        return _AL;
}

void ShowMenu( void )
{
        printf( "\n            Printing Test Menu                \n\n" );
        printf( " 1. Start LPT Capture                         \n" );
        printf( " 2. Flush LPT Capture                         \n" );
        printf( " 3. End LPT Capture                           \n" );
        printf( " 4. Cancel LPT Capture                        \n\n" );
        printf( " 5. Send data to printer                      \n\n" );
        printf( " 6. Show Flags                                \n\n" );
        printf( " 7. Quit                                      \n\n" );
        printf( " Enter your choice > " );
}

void ShowFlags( void )
{
        struct captureFlags Reply;

        GetDefaultCaptureFlags( &Reply );
}
```

Exercises

1. Run PrtTest. Start capturing, send some data and end the capture. Did it print? Experiment with the flush and cancel options.

2. Write the ShowFlags() routine. Be wary of data conversions that may need to be done, such as converting hi-lo WORDs to lo-hi format.

3. Change the options to use the "specific" LPT calls. If you have an LPT2 or LPT3 port, capture to these.

9 Connection/Workstation Services APIs

The Connection and Workstation Services APIs are used to manage the most vital link in the NetWare environment, the link between workstation and file server. The Connection Services allow an object to establish a connection with a file server and log in and out of it. The Workstation Services manage and report information regarding the workstation shell, the software that lies between DOS and the network, facilitating DOS compatibility and network functionality.

Connection Services

A connection is a formal establishment of communication between a workstation and a file server. With NetWare 286, each file server can support up to 100 connections (numbered 1 to 100), and each workstation can support up to eight connections to different servers. This means a server can have up to 100 users logged in at once and a user may be logged in to (attached to) up to eight servers at once. NetWare 386 supports up to 250 concurrent users.

It is important to remember that NetWare 2.1 generalizes the concept of logged in users to logged in objects. NetWare versions through Advanced NetWare 1.02 allowed only users to log in, but later (Advanced NetWare 2.0 and 2.1, NetWare 286 and later) versions allow an object of any type to log into a file server. This feature gives great flexibility to developers of LAN applications and of such resources as print and archive servers.

There is a formal process for logging in to a file server, whether as a user or another Bindery object type (print server, job server, etc.).These steps are:

1: The workstation obtains the name and address of the file server it wishes to log in to. This may be done in various ways, for example, scan the Bindery of the nearest server for names and addresses of servers on an internetwork (a network of multiple servers) by scanning for objects of type file server. Once a server object is returned, read the value of the NET_ADDRESS property to obtain the network address.

2: Once the name and address are obtained, the address of the shell's Connection ID and Server Name tables are found and the Connection ID table is searched for an open slot. If an open slot is found, it is marked used (FFh) and the order number is placed in the table (if there are already three servers in the table, numbered 1-3, then the order number would be 4). The internetwork address found in step 1 is placed in the table and the server name is placed in the shell's Server Name Table.

3: Attach To File Server is called, passing the number of the slot that was used in step 2.

4: If Attach To File Server was successful (returning 0), the network addresses must be sorted before logging into the new file server. The order numbers must reflect the order of the network addresses. Only the order number field should be changed. Lower network addresses should have lower order numbers.

5: Set Preferred File server is called to set the new server as preferred so that the next call will apply to the new server. Login To File Server may now be called, passing the name and password of the object to be logged in.

6: If Login To File Server succeeds, then the user is logged into the target server and drives may be mapped with the Allocate Permanent (or Temporary) Directory Handle, or other operations can be performed.

A station wishing to log out from a file server can do so in one of two ways. It can issue the Logout call which logs the station out of all file servers, detaches the workstation from all servers except the default server, and maps a drive to the default server's SYS:LOGIN directory. Or it may issue the Logout From File Server call which effects a logout from only one file server. In this case, after receiving the server Connection ID (index to the Connection ID table), the shell logs the workstation out of the server but does not detach from it. The shell also removes all drives mapped to the target server and maps one drive to the SYS:LOGIN directory on that server.

Connection Services include several other calls, including calls to obtain the physical node address of the requesting station or any other workstation (provided their connection numbers are known), or to find which stations (file server connections) a particular Bindery object is logged into or which connection number is used for the current workstation (on its default server), among others.

Workstation Services

Workstation Services give the developer much flexibility in working with the shell. Much of the information managed by Workstation Services resides in the shell itself. Among other things, the default, preferred, and primary file servers may be set with the workstation services.

Many of the calls used by these services operate on tables, such as the Connection ID table, the File Server Name table, and the Drive handle, flag and connection tables. In addition, functions such as shell version identification, End of Job handling, and error handling can be manipulated through these calls.

Preferred, default and primary servers

NetWare uses the terms default, preferred, and primary to prioritize servers a user is logged in to. The question they deal with is essentially, "Which server gets the information I'm sending now?"

The preferred server bears the highest priority for shell requests. A preferred server must be explicitly appointed by the workstation with the Workstation Services call Set Preferred Connection ID. Once appointed, that server receives all requests until the preferred server is changed.

If there is no preferred server, the default server is mapped with the default drive. For example, if the default drive is drive F: and drive F: is mapped to FS1 and there is no preferred server defined, then file server FS1 is the default server.

If the current drive is a local drive, the primary server is used. The primary server is the lowest connection priority of the three servers and is usually the server the shell first attached to when it was started. The primary server is used only if the default drive is set to a local drive and there is no preferred file server.

Workstation Services tables

Tables are an important part of Workstation Services. For openers, the Connection ID table is used to manage connections with file servers. And entries in the server name table correspond to the entries in the Connection ID table, showing the name of each file server attached.

Connection ID Table

Offset	Field	Type	Order
0	In Use Flag	BYTE	
1	Order Number	BYTE	
2	Network Number	BYTE[4]	hi-lo
6	Node Address	BYTE[6]	hi-lo
12	Socket Number	BYTE[2]	hi-lo
14	Receive Timeout	BYTE[2]	hi-lo
16	Routing Node	BYTE[6]	hi-lo

22	Packet Sequence	BYTE	
23	Connection Number	BYTE	
24	Connection Status	BYTE	
25	Maximum Timeout	BYTE[2]	hi-lo
27	Padding/Reserved	BYTE[5]	

The *In Use Flag* displays the state of whatever activity the shell is performing. Possible values for this field are:

0xE0	AES Temporary Indicator
0xF8	Critical Holding (IPX in critical process)
0xFA	Processing
0xFB	Holding (in processing after an event occurred)
0xFC	AES Waiting
0xFD	Waiting
0xFE	Receiving
0xFF	Sending

The *In Use Flag* is set to 0xFF from 0 when a server is being attached.

Order Number is a field that shows the order of the server's network/node address relative to the others in the table. An order of 1 indicates the server has the lowest network/node address, 2 indicates the next lowest, etc.

Network Number is the server's four-byte network address, Node Address the server's six-byte node address.

Socket Number is the number of the socket on which the server will receive requests.

Receive Timeout is the number of clock ticks the workstation will wait for a response from the file server before timing out. This field is used in the shell's retry-management scheme; it changes to adapt to differing traffic levels on the network.

Routing Node is the address of the preferred bridge to route through if the connection is not direct (on the same network).

Packet Sequence Number contains the sequence ID number for the current request sent to the file server. The shell uses this number to make sure that a sequenced exchange of packets occurs with the file server.

Connection Number is assigned by the file server to this workstation.

Connection Status contains 0xFF when the connection is active, zero when it is not.

Maximum Timeout, the maximum number of clock ticks the Receive Timeout is allowed to reach, is set by the shell when it attaches to the file server.

Retries and timeouts

The NetWare shell follows the IPX (Internetwork Packet Exchange) protocol to minimize overhead and maximize speed. This protocol provides no verification of data or packet sequencing. Because IPX does not guarantee packet delivery, the shell must perform some packet monitoring.

To that end, the shell employs "implied acknowledgment," reckoning that if a file server is responding to a function call then it must have received the request in the first place. The file server has until the Receive Timeout to reply to the response.

The scenario for interacting with the file server is: The shell sends a request to the file server and starts a timer. If the timeout expires waiting for the server to respond, the shell increases the Receive Timeout and reissues the request. If the timeout expires without a response from the server, the shell will retry a fixed number of times. The default retry count is 20, but the SHELL.CFG file may be changed with the line "IPX RETRY COUNT = number" to set a new retry count.

If the file server needs more time to respond to a request, it will inform the shell. The shell responds by increasing the timeout value. This way, the Receive Timeout is changed to reflect fluctuations in network traffic and processing loads.

The Maximum Timeout field in the Connection ID table shows the maximum value the Receive Timeout is allowed to reach.

If a connection has failed, the shell will make an effort to re-establish the connection. The shell will search for routing information from the internetwork's bridges and file servers and will determine if an alternate route is available to the failed connection. If these efforts prove unsuccessful, the shell will abort the connection.

The shell stamps each packet with the Connection Number and the current Packet Sequence Number from the Connection ID table. The file server stamps its responses with the same values. If the reply packet from the server is not correct, the shell knows a sequence error has occurred. This way, the server monitors the sequence of packets without the overhead of such protocols as SPX (Sequenced Packet Exchange).

File Server Name Table

This table contains eight file server names of 32 bytes each that correspond to the entries in the Connection ID table.

Drive tables

The drive tables show which drives are network and which are local, and to which server and directory each drive points. (For example, drive F: may be a network drive that points to file server FS1 directory SYS:PUBLIC.) Each table contains 32 entries, one for each drive letter and one for the temporary drives: [, \,], ^, _, and ‘.

The Drive Flag Table

This table tracks each of the workstation drives and shows whether the drive is mapped to a permanent network drive, a temporary network drive, or a local drive, or not mapped at all. In addition, the table shows whether the original drive was once a local drive (in the instance of C: being mapped as a network drive).

Value	Description
0	Drive is not mapped
01h	Drive is a permanent network drive
02h	Drive is a temporary network drive
80h	Drive is mapped to a local drive
81h	Drive is a local drive allocated as a permanent network drive
82h	Drive is a local drive allocated as a temporary network drive

The call Get Drive Flag may be used to get the address of this table.

The Drive Connection ID Table

This table shows which server a particular drive is mapped to. Each entry contains a server connection number, an index into the Connection ID table. The call Get Drive Connection ID may be used to find the address of this table.

Drive Handle Table

This table holds the file server directory handles to which each drive is mapped. Local and unmapped drives do not have entries. The Drive Handle is an index to the file server's Directory Handle Table, which is a list maintained for each workstation and containing pointers to volume:directory combinations. (See chapter 4, Directory Services, for a more thorough discussion of directory handles.)

Error modes

The NetWare shell handles DOS error messages the same way DOS does: The AL register returns the error code and the DOS call Get Extended Error Information can be used to get more detail. Critical errors (Interrupt 24h) in DOS are those that provoke the "Abort, Retry, Ignore" message; trying to access a floppy drive with the door open is an example of such an error.

The NetWare shell has three different ways of handling the critical error modes:

0: Default mode follows the DOS format, allowing the user to choose the appropriate action ("Abort, Retry, Ignore/Fail").

1: No critical error/NetWare code, where the shell doesn't call the Int 24h critical error handler and returns in AL the NetWare code for file I/O functions.

2: No critical error/DOS code, where the shell doesn't call the Int 24h handler but tries to map the NetWare error code to an appropriate DOS code, returning the DOS error code.

In addition to using modes 1 and 2 to avoid the critical error handler, developers can patch the Interrupt 24h vector to define their own critical error handlers. For example, with a custom critical error handler installed, if an application's attempt to write to a network drive were foiled by a hardware failure (such as an open cable), the programmer's custom handler could set a flag stating that the write operation had failed; upon detecting that failure, the application could write to the local C: drive instead, to preserve the data.

The following are two examples of how the different error modes would respond in different situations.

Noncritical file I/O

An application attempts to open a file without having open privileges:

Mode 0: No error message. Return DOS error 2 in AL.
Mode 1: Return extended error 130 in AL.
Mode 2: Return DOS error 2 in AL (since file I/O was noncritical).

Critical file I/O

An application attempts to open a file using a handle whose file is already open. (If the open attempt were to use extended open modes NetWare would return DOS error 5: Access denied.)

Mode 0: Network error: file in use during OPEN. The shell would invoke INT 24h and print the above message on the workstation's screen along with: File = <*filename*> Abort, Retry, Ignore?
Mode 1: Returns an extended error 128 in AL
Mode 2: Returns an extended error 128 in AL

The error mode is automatically set back to 0 when an End of Job (EOJ) occurs (such as when an application is exited). Also, child processes inherit the error mode from their parents, but parent processes are not changed by the error mode of their children being changed.

The End of Job (EOJ) command

The shell clears several flags and internal registers when an application terminates. When an application exits to DOS, an End of Job (EOJ) command is sent to the file server to perform End of Job processing. All locked files and records are unlocked and cleared and all open network and local files are closed. Also, the error mode and lock modes are reset and all network resources, such as semaphores, queueing services, etc., are released.

An End of Job signal may be generated in one of three ways: by terminating an application, by returning control to COMMAND.COM, or by explicitly generating one through the End Of Job function call. The EOJ call when COMMAND.COM is loaded is provided for those applications that terminate abnormally. This feature can be turned off with the Set End Of Job Status function call.

Other workstation calls

There are other calls available in the Workstation Services that allow an application to find out the number of local drives and get the current version of the shell software.

Calls in the Connection/Workstation APIs

The following descriptions will include which versions of NetWare support which calls. Throughout the book, we explain fields within the calls only at the first mention of each field in each chapter. Appendix B contains a comprehensive, alphabetical listing of the fields for quick reference.

Attach To File Server (F1h 00h)

This call is supported in Advanced NetWare versions 1.0, 1.02, 2.0 and 2.1, and in NetWare 386 and later versions. It attaches the requesting workstation to the specified file server.

Registers in:

AH	F1h
AL	00h
DL	Server Connection ID (1 to 8)

Registers out:

AL	Completion Code

Completion codes:

00h	Successful
F8h	Already Attached To Server
F9h	No Free Connection Slots at Server
FAh	No More Server Slots
FCh	Unknown File Server
FEh	Server Bindery Locked
FFh	No Response From Server (Server Address Illegal)

To make this call, the requesting workstation should already be attached to at least one file server on the internetwork. The workstation will search the Bindery of that file server for the internetwork address of the requested file server

Also, the workstation will create a *Server Connection ID* for the new attachment by placing the new server's internetwork address in the shell's Connection ID Table and the server name in the Server Name Table.

It gets a connection number (1 to 100) for the workstation in the File Server Connection Table of the newly attached file server.

Once this call has returned 00h, confirming a successful attachment, the Connection ID Table is ready, and the object can log in and map drives to the new file server.

A workstation can be attached to a maximum of eight file servers.

The NetWare C Interface format is:

```
int AttachToFileServer( char *serverName, WORD *connectionID );
```

Detach From File Server (F1h 01h)

This call is supported in Advanced NetWare versions 1.0, 1.02, 2.0 and 2.1, and in NetWare 386 and later versions. It attaches the requesting workstation to the specified file server.

Registers in:

AH	F1h
AL	01h
DL	Server Connection ID (1 to 8)

Registers out:

AL	Completion Code

Completion codes:

00h	Successful
FFh	Connection Does Not Exist

Programmers should distinguish between detaching from a file server and logging out of one. Detaching relinquishes the file server connection number the workstation was using and breaks the connection. To send any more requests to that file server, a new attachment must be created. Logging out, however, does not relinquish the connection number; it retains it for continued use.

When this call is made, the shell removes all drives mapped to the detached file server.

The NetWare C Interface format is:

```
int DetachFromFileServer( WORD connectionID );
```

Enter Login Area (E3h 0Ah)

This call is supported in NetWare versions 4.0 and 4.6, in Advanced NetWare versions 1.0, 1.02, 2.0 and 2.1, and in NetWare 386 and later versions. It changes the login directory for the requesting workstation.

Registers in:

AH	E3h
DS:SI	Address of Request Buffer
ES:DI	Address of Reply Buffer

Completion codes:

00h	Successful

Request Buffer (maximum buffer length = 260 bytes):

Offset	Content	Type	Order
0	Request Buffer Length-2	WORD	lo-hi
2	0Ah	BYTE	
3	Number of Local Drives	BYTE	
4	Subdirectory Name Length	BYTE (0-255)	
5	Subdirectory Name	BYTE[*LENGTH*]	

Reply Buffer (2 bytes):

Offset	Content	Type	Order
0	0000h	WORD	lo-hi

This call is not often used in application programs; it is used the enable boot ROMs to access machine-specific information when initializing a workstation. It directs the network to a subdirectory under SYS:LOGIN where the Login utility can be loaded by the requesting workstation.

The *Number of Local Drives* is used to determine the workstation drive ID to assign to the server's SYS volume.

The *Login Subdirectory Name* is an ASCII string containing the name of the subdirectory below SYS:LOGIN where the file LOGIN.EXE can be executed. For example, if the Login utility is to be executed from the SYS:LOGIN/IBM/V3.3 directory the login Subdirectory Name should contain IBM/V3.3.

If the login subdirectory name length is 0, the SYS:LOGIN is assumed. If the workstation boots from the network without local disks, a copy of the appropriate operating system must be in the specified directory along with the LOGIN utility. The ROM must be intelligent enough to open and read the operating system file.

The NetWare C Interface format is:

```
int EnterLoginArea( char *loginSubdirectoryName,
    int numberOfLocalDrives );
```

Login To File Server (E3h 14h)

This call is supported in Advanced NetWare versions 1.0, 1.02, 2.0 and 2.1, and in NetWare 386 and later versions. It logs a Bindery object in to the default file server.

Registers in:

AH	E3h
DS:SI	Address of Request Buffer
ES:DI	Address of Reply Buffer

Registers out:

AL	Completion Code

Completion codes:

00h	Successful

Request Packet (maximum buffer length = 181 bytes):

Offset	Content	Type	Order
0	Request Buffer Length-2	WORD	lo-hi
2	14h	BYTE	
3	Object Type	WORD	hi-lo
5	Object Name Length (1 to 47)	BYTE	
6	Object Name	BYTE[*LENGTH*]	
?	Object Password Length	BYTE (0-127)	
?	Object Password	BYTE[*LENGTH*]	

Reply Buffer (2 bytes):

Offset	Content	Type	Order
0	0000h	WORD	lo-hi

This call logs a Bindery object in to a server by passing the object type, object name, and object password. When a Bindery object logs in to a file server from a workstation, the file server places the Bindery object's ID number in the file server's Password Table in the same position that the attached workstation occupies in the File Server Connection Table. For example, if the workstation occupies position 97 in the File Server Connection Table, then the Bindery object's ID number is placed in the 97th position in the Password Table. Therefore, if a Bindery object logs in to a specific server from three workstations, its Bindery object ID number is placed in the Password Table three times, in the positions reserved for each workstation.

The NetWare C Interface format is:

```
int LoginToFileServer( char *objectName, WORD objectType );
```

Logout (D7h)

This call is supported in NetWare versions 4.0 and 4.6, in Advanced NetWare versions 1.0, 1.02, 2.0 and 2.1, and in NetWare 386 and later versions. It logs the user out of the default file server.

Registers in:

AH	D7h

Completion codes:
None

This call closes all open files belonging to the object, logs the object out from all file servers, detaches the workstation from all file servers except the default file server, and maps a drive to the default file server's SYS:LOGIN directory.

After a Logout has been executed, all of the tables allocated for the user at the file server are cleared. However, the workstation remains attached and retains its position in the File Server Connection Table. Also, this call can be considered an effective End of Job.

The NetWare C Interface format is:

```
void Logout( void );
```

Logout From File Server (F1h 02h)

This call is supported in Advanced NetWare versions 1.0, 1.02, 2.0 and 2.1, and in NetWare 386 and later versions. It logs an object out of a specified file server but does not detach the workstation from the server.

Registers in:

AH	F1h
AL	02h
DL	Server Connection ID (1 to 8)

The *Server Connection ID* is the position that the server occupies in the workstation shell's Connection ID Table.

Logging out from a file server is not the same as detaching from a file server. Logging out from a file server does not relinquish the connection number, but retains the connection for continued service. Detaching from a file server relinquishes the connection number that the workstation was using and breaks the connection. Before the workstation can send further requests to that file server, a new attachment must be created.

The shell automatically removes all drives mapped to the specified file server and maps one drive to the SYS:LOGIN directory on that file server.

The NetWare C Interface format is:

```
int LogoutFromFileServer( WORD connectionID );
```

Get Connection Information (E3h 16h)

This call is supported in Advanced NetWare versions 1.0, 1.02, 2.0 and 2.1, and in NetWare 386 and later versions. It returns information about the object logged in at the specified connection number.

Registers in:

AH	E3h
DS:SI	Address of Request Buffer
ES:DI	Address of Reply Buffer

Registers out:

AL	Completion Code

Completion codes:

00h	Successful

Request Buffer (4 bytes)

Offset	Content	Type	Order
0	Request Buffer Length-2	WORD	lo-hi
2	16h	BYTE	
3	Logical Connection Number	BYTE (1-100) for NetWare 286	

Reply Buffer (63 bytes)

Offset	Content	Type	Order
0	Reply Buffer Length-2	WORD	lo-hi
2	Object ID	LONG	hi-lo
6	Object Type	WORD	hi-lo
8	Object Name	BYTE[48]	
56	Login Time	BYTE[7]	

The *Logical Connection Number* is the position of the attached workstation in the File Server Connection Table.

If an *Object ID* is returned 0, there is no object logged into that connection number.

The *Login Time* format is as follows:

Byte	Content	
0	Year	(0 to 99, where a value of 80 = 1980, 81 = 1981, etc.; however, if the value is less than 80, the year is considered to be in the twenty-first century.)
1	Month	(1 to 12)
2	Day	(1 to 31)
3	Hour	(0 to 23)
4	Minute	(0 to 59)
5	Second	(0 to 59)
6	Day	(0 to 6, where a value of 0 = Sunday, 1 = Monday, etc.)

The NetWare C Interface format is:

```
int GetConnectionInformation( WORD connectionNumber,
    char *objectName, WORD *objectType, long *objectID,
    BYTE *loginTime );
```

Get Connection Number (DCh)

This call is supported in NetWare versions 4.0 and 4.6, in Advanced NetWare versions 1.0, 1.02, 2.0 and 2.1, and in NetWare 386 and later versions. It returns the connection number of the user logged in at the station making the call.

Registers in:

AH	DCh

Registers out:

AL	Logical Connection Number (1 to 100)
CH	Second digit of Logical Connection Number
CL	First digit of Logical Connection Number

The NetWare C Interface format is:

```
WORD GetConnectionNumber( void );
```

Get Object Connection Numbers (E3h 15h)

This call is supported in Advanced NetWare versions 1.0, 1.02, 2.0 and 2.1, and in NetWare 386 and later versions. It returns a list of connection numbers where a Bindery object is logged into the default file server.

Registers in:

AH	E3h
DS:SI	Address of Request Buffer
ES:DI	Address of Reply Buffer

Registers out:

AL	Completion Code

Completion codes:

00h	Successful

Request Buffer (maximum buffer length = 53 bytes):

Offset	**Content**	**Type**	**Order**
0	Request Buffer Length-2	WORD	lo-hi
2	15h	BYTE	
3	Object Type	WORD	hi-lo
5	Object Name Length (1 to 47)	BYTE	
6	Object Name	BYTE[*LENGTH*]	

Reply Buffer (maximum buffer length = 103 bytes):

Offset	**Content**	**Type**	**Order**
0	Reply Buffer Length-2	WORD	lo-hi
2	Number Of Connections	BYTE	
3	Logical Connection List	BYTE[*COUNT*](1-100) for 286	

The *Number Of Connections* is the length of the logical connection list which is 0 to 100 bytes long.

The NetWare C Interface format is:

```
int GetObjectConnectionNumbers( char *objectName, WORD objectType,
        WORD *numberOfConnections, WORD *connectionList,
        WORD maxConnections );
```

Get Internet Address (E3h 13h)

This call is supported in Advanced NetWare versions 1.0, 1.02, 2.0 and 2.1, and in NetWare 386 and later versions. It returns a connection's internetwork address.

Registers in:

AH	E3h
DS:SI	Address of Request Buffer
ES:DI	Address of Reply Buffer

Registers out:

AL	Completion Code

Completion code:

00h	Successful

Request Buffer (4 bytes)

Offset	**Content**	**Type**	**Order**
0	Request Buffer Length-2	WORD	lo-hi
2	13h	BYTE	
3	Logical Connection Number	BYTE	

Reply Buffer (14 bytes)

Offset	**Content**	**Type**	**Order**
0	Reply Buffer Length-2	WORD	lo-hi
2	Network Number	BYTE[4]	
6	Physical Node Address	BYTE[6]	
12	Socket Number	BYTE[2]	

Network Number identifies the file server to which the workstation is physically attached.

Physical Node Address is the address of the workstation's LAN board.

Socket Number identifies the socket that the shell uses to communicate with the file server. This socket must not be used by other applications. Applications that require peer-to-peer communications need to use unique sockets for their communications and would normally use one of the dynamic sockets (4000h-7FFFh). See the IPX-SPX chapter for further details.

The NetWare C Interface format is:

```
int GetInternetAddress( WORD connectionNumber,
    char *networkNumber, char *physicalNodeAddress,
    int *socketNumber );
```

Get Station Address (EEh)

This call is supported in NetWare versions 4.6, in Advanced NetWare versions 1.0, 1.02, 2.0 and 2.1, and in NetWare 386 and later versions. It returns the physical node address of the requesting workstation.

Registers in:

AH	EEh

Registers out:

CX, BX, AX	Physical Node Address

Completion codes:
None

This call returns the station's 6-byte physical node address.

The NetWare C Interface format is:

```
void GetStationAddress( BYTE *physicalNodeAddress );
```

Get Connection ID (EFh 03h)

This call is supported in Advanced NetWare versions 1.0, 1.02, 2.0 and 2.1, and in NetWare 386 and later versions. It returns a pointer to the shell's Connection ID Table.

Registers in:

AH	EFh
AL	03h

Registers out:

ES:SI	Pointer to Shell's Connection ID Table

Each workstation shell has a Connection ID Table and a File Server Name Table. The Connection ID Table consists of up to eight entries (1 to 8) that are each 32 bytes in length. Each of the eight entries in the Connection ID Table contains the following information:

Slot in Use (0=empty, FF=used)	BYTE
Server Order Number (1 to 8)	BYTE
Server's Network Number	BYTE[4]
Physical Node Address	BYTE[6]
Socket Number	BYTE[2]
Receive Timeout	BYTE[2]
Router's physical node address	BYTE[6]
Packet Sequence Number	BYTE
Connection Number (FFh = no connection)	BYTE
Connection Status (0 = connection functioning)	BYTE
Maximum Timeout	BYTE[2]
Filler	BYTE[5]

Slot in Use indicates whether a slot in the Connection ID Table is in use.

Server Order Number indicates the order number (1 through 8) assigned to the corresponding server. The lowest order number indicates the server with the lowest network/node address. The second lowest number indicates the second lowest address, etc.

The rest of the Connection ID Table is manipulated by the shell.The Receive Timeout indicates how long the shell should wait before resending an unanswered request. It is adjusted dynamically and will not exceed Maximum Timeout. The shell uses the Packet Sequence Number as a packet ID to ensure that the last reply received was in answer to the last request.

The NetWare C Interface format is:

```
int GetConnectionID( char *fileServerName, WORD *connectionID );
```

Get Default Connection ID (F0h 02h)

This call is supported in Advanced NetWare versions 1.0, 1.02, 2.0 and 2.1, and in NetWare 386 and later versions. It returns the Connection ID of the file server to which request packets are being sent.

Registers in:

AH	F0h
AL	02h

Registers out:

AL	Connection ID of file server to which packets are sent (1 to 8)

The NetWare C Interface format is:

```
WORD GetDefaultConnectionID( void );
```

Get Preferred Connection ID (F0h 01h)

This call is supported in Advanced NetWare versions 1.0, 1.02, 2.0 and 2.1, and in NetWare 386 and later versions. It returns the Connection ID of the preferred file server.

Registers in:

AH	F0h
AL	01h

Registers out:

AL	Connection ID of the preferred file server (1 to 8) or a 0 if the preferred file server is not set

The *preferred Connection ID* is reset to 0 (unspecified) by the shell when an End of Job is done for a terminating process, or the End of Job is made.

The NetWare C Interface format is:

```
WORD GetPreferredConnectionID( void );
```

Set Preferred Connection ID (F0h 00h)

This call is supported in Advanced NetWare versions 1.0, 1.02, 2.0 and 2.1, and in NetWare 386 and later versions. It sets the preferred file server.

Registers in:

AH	F0h
AL	00h
DL	Connection ID of the preferred file server (1 to 8), or 0 (if the preferred server is not set)

The preferred server is the default server to which request packets are sent.

The NetWare C Interface format is:

```
void SetPreferredConnectionID( BYTE connectionID );
```

Get Primary Connection ID (F0h 05h)

This call is supported in Advanced NetWare versions 2.0 and 2.1, and in NetWare 386 and later versions. It returns the Connection ID of the primary file server.

Registers in:

AH F0h
AL 05h

Registers out:

AL Connection ID of the primary file server (1 to 8, or 0 if the primary File Server is not set)

The NetWare C Interface format is:

```
WORD GetPrimaryConnectionID( void );
```

Set Primary Connection ID (F0h 04h)

This call is supported in Advanced NetWare versions 1.0, 1.02, 2.0 and 2.1, and in NetWare 386 and later versions. It sets the primary file server.

Registers in:

AH F0h
AL 04h
DL Connection ID of the primary file server (1 to 8), or 0 (if the primary file server is not set)

The NetWare C Interface format is:

```
void SetPrimaryConnectionID( int primaryConnectionID );
```

Get Drive Handle Table (EFh 00h)

This call is supported in Advanced NetWare versions 1.0, 1.02, 2.0 and 2.1, and in NetWare 386 and later versions. It returns a pointer to the shell's Drive Handle Table.

Registers in:

AH EFh
AL 00h

Registers out:

ES:SI Pointer to Shell's Drive Handle Table

The Drive Handle Table contains 32 entries of one byte each. If a drive has been assigned a directory handle on the file server, the directory handle's number appears in this table at the corresponding drive letter position.

The NetWare C Interface format is not supported.

Get Drive Flag Table (EFh 01h)

This call is supported in Advanced NetWare versions 1.0, 1.02, 2.0 and 2.1, and in NetWare 386 and later versions. It returns a pointer to the shell's Drive Flag Table.

Registers in:

AH	EFh
AL	01h

Registers out:

ES:SI	Pointer to Shell's Drive Flag Table

The Drive Flag Table contains 32 entries of one byte each. Each entry indicates a drive's status (permanent, temporary, local, unassigned).

The NetWare C Interface format is not supported.

Get Drive Connection ID Table (EFh 02h)

This call is supported in Advanced NetWare versions 1.0, 1.02, 2.0 and 2.1, and in NetWare 386 and later versions. It returns a pointer to the shell's Drive Connection ID Table.

Registers in:

AH	EFh
AL	02h

Registers out:

ES:SI	Pointer to Shell's Drive Connection ID Table

The Drive Connection ID Table contains 32 entries of one byte each. Each entry contains the Connection ID (1 to 8) of the server that is associated with that drive. A value of 0 indicates that the drive is not mapped to a file server (local drive or drive not used).

The NetWare C Interface format is not supported.

Get File Server Name Table (EFh 04h)

This call is supported in NetWare versions 4.0 and 4.6, in Advanced NetWare versions 1.0, 1.02, 2.0 and 2.1, and in NetWare 386 and later versions. It returns a pointer to the shell's File Server Name Table.

Registers in:

AH	EFh
AL	04h

Registers out:

ES:SI	Pointer to Shell's Server Name Table

The File Server Name Table consists of eight entries (1 to 8) that are each 48 bytes in length. Each entry in the File Server Name Table can contain a null-terminated server name.

The NetWare C Interface format is:

```
void GetFileServerName( WORD connectionID, char *fileServerName );
```

(this call returns the file server name at the offset connectionID)

Get Shell Version Information (EAh 01h)

This call is supported in NetWare versions 4.6, in Advanced NetWare versions 1.0, 1.02, 2.0 and 2.1, and in NetWare 386 and later versions. It returns information about a workstation's environment.

Registers in:

AH	EAh
AL	01h
BX	00h
ES:DI	Reply Buffer Address

Registers out:

AH	Workstation Operating System(0=DOS)
AL	Customization Code
BH	Major NetWare Shell Version
BL	Minor NetWare Shell Version
CL	Shell Revision Number (1=A,2=B,etc.)

Completion codes:
None

Reply Packet

Offset	Content	Type
0	Operating System Type	BYTE
?	Operating System Version	BYTE
?	Hardware Type	BYTE
?	Short Hardware Type	BYTE

This call allows an application to determine what hardware and operating system the shell supports. It returns information about shell version and customization. It does not query the workstation or hardware to verify what type it is. The reply packet contains the following four null-terminated ASCIIZ strings: Operating System (e.g., MS DOS); Operating System Version (e.g., v3.30); Hardware Type at the workstation (e.g., IBM-PC); and Short Hardware Type contains the type of hardware without specifying the model (e.g., IBM).

The following table gives the values of Hardware Type and Short Hardware Type that can be returned by v2.12 of the shell, for example.

Computer	Customization Code	Hardware type	Short Hardware Type
IBM Compatible	0	"IBM_PC"	"IBM"
Victor 9000	1	"VICTOR_9000"	"VIC9"
TI Professional	2	"TIPROFESSIONAL"	"TIPR"
DEC Rainbow	3	"DEC_RAINBOW"	"DECR"
NEC	4	"NEC_APC3"	"APC3"

The NetWare C Interface format is:

```
int GetShellVersionInformation( BYTE *majorVersion,
    BYTE *minorVersion, BYTE *revisionLevel );
```

Set NetWare Error Mode (DDh)

This call is supported in Advanced NetWare versions 2.0 and 2.1, and in NetWare 386 and later versions. It sets the network error handling mode for the requesting workstation.

Registers in:

AH	DDh	
DL	Error Mode:	00h
		01h
		02h

Registers out:

AL Previous Error Mode

This call sets a mode that determines how the shell responds to DOS emulation call errors. It has no effect on NetWare specific calls. DOS differentiates between normal errors and critical errors. Normal errors are listed in the DOS Technical

Reference manual. Critical errors are typically nonrecoverable errors detected by DOS which then invoke the INT 24h Critical Error Handler. Whether an error code or INT 24h is invoked is determined by the specific error. The shell has three error modes: 0, 1, and 2.

Mode 0 is the default mode and follows the common response format used by DOS (i.e., "Abort, Retry, Fail").

When the error mode is set to 1, the shell does not invoke the INT 24h handler. It returns the NetWare error code for all file I/O calls in AL.

When the error mode is set to 2, the shell attempts to map the NetWare error code to a DOS error code and return it.

Both error modes 1 and 2 will cause the shell to return error codes instead of invoking INT 24h on some, but not all, network errors.

For an application that uses the DOS functions calls (beginning with DOS v3.0), the shell returns the standard DOS extended error codes. An application is free to install its own INT 24h Critical Error Handler.

NOTES:

If an application running DOS 3.1 or above uses network-aware calls (extended open), it does not matter what the NetWare Error Mode is set to. The shell returns the same errors that DOS would in the same situation. For example, if an application attempts to open a locked file, the shell will return in DOS Error 5, Access Denied.

It is also important to emphasize that all NetWare errors that go to the user screen go through INT 24h and, therefore, can be trapped and acted upon under program control using a critical error handler.

The following are two examples of how modes 0, 1, and 2 handle errors:

Example 1: Noncritical file I/O: Application attempts to open a file without having open privileges.

Mode 0: No error message. Returns a DOS error 02 in AL.
Mode 1: Returns an extended error 130 in AL.
Mode 2: Returns a DOS error 02 in AL (because file I/O was noncritical).

Example 2: NetWare critical file I/O: Application attempts to open (file handle) a file that is already open. (If the open attempt uses extended modes, NetWare returns in DOS Error 5, Access Denied.)

Mode 0: Network error: file in use during OPEN. The shell invokes INT 24h and the following message appears on the screen:
File = <filename>~ Abort, Retry, Ignore?
Mode 1: Returns an extended error 128 in AL.
Mode 2: Returns an extended error 128 in AL.

The error mode is automatically reset to mode 0 whenever an End of Job occurs. A child process inherits the error mode set by its parent. However, if a child process sets the error mode, the error mode is not inherited by the parent. When control returns from the parent to DOS, the error mode is reset to the default mode of 0.

The NetWare C Interface format is:

```
int SetNetWareErrorMode( BYTE errorMode );
```

End Of Job (D6h)

This call is supported in NetWare versions 4.0 and 4.6, in Advanced NetWare versions 1.0, 1.02, 2.0 and 2.1, and in NetWare 386 and later versions. The shell issues this call when an application exits to automatically reset the workstation environment.

Registers in:

AH	D6h
BX	Job Flag
	00h (current process only)
	FFFFh (all processes on workstation)

This call causes an End Of Job (EOJ) command to be sent to the file server and causes the shell to reset all internal tables for that application. The EOJ at the file server releases all resources (open files, file and record locks, logical locks, semaphores, etc.) allocated on the file server to the current task.

The shell will automatically generate the same EOJ action when an application terminates (i.e. DOS calls 00h and 4Ch). When the shell detects control returned to the root COMMAND.COM (the first one started by DOS), the shell will send an EOJ command to the server that releases all resources allocated to all tasks on the workstation.

The NetWare C Interface format is:

```
void EndOfJob( void );
```

Set End Of Job Status (BBh)

This call is supported in NetWare version 4.6, in Advanced NetWare versions 1.0, 1.02, 2.0 and 2.1, and in NetWare 386 and later versions. It enables or disables the End of Job generated automatically by the shell when control returns to the root COMMAND.COM.

Registers in:

AH	BBh
AL	End Of Job Flag (0 = Disabled, 1 = Enabled)

Registers out:
AL Previous End Of Job Flag (0 = Disabled, 1 = Enabled)

Whenever a call is made to DOS 19h the NetWare shell will try to detect if the root COMMAND.COM is making the call. COMMAND.COM always calls DOS 19h when it regains control. When the shell detects control has returned to the root COMMAND.COM (the first one started by DOS), the shell by default assumes all processes and applications have terminated. The shell sends an End Of Job (EOJ) command to the server that will release all file server resources allocated to the workstation (open files, physical and logical locks, semaphores, etc.).

The Set End Of Job call allows an application to enable or disable the generation of the EOJ command when control returns to the root COMMAND.COM.

The NetWare C Interface format is:

```
BYTE SetEndOfJobStatus( BYTE endOfJobFlag );
```

Get Number Of Local Drives (DBh)

This call is supported in NetWare versions 4.0 and 4.6, in Advanced NetWare versions 1.0, 1.02, 2.0 and 2.1, and in NetWare 386 and later versions. It returns the number of local drives on the requesting workstation.

Registers in:
AL DBh

Registers out:
AL Number of Local Drives

The shell uses this call upon initialization to determine the number of local drives. This call allows developers to determine at which drive letter to begin mapping network drives.

The NetWare C Interface format is:

```
int GetNumberOfLocalDrives( void );
```

Login (E3h 00h)

This call is supported in NetWare versions 4.0 and 4.6, in Advanced NetWare versions 1.0, 1.02, 2.0 and 2.1, and in NetWare 386. It logs an object of type user into the file server and has been replaced by higher-level functions such as Login To File Server, but is shown here for completeness.

Registers in:

AH	E3h
DS:SI	Address of Request buffer
ES:DI	Address of Reply buffer

Registers out:

AL	Completion Code

Completion codes:

00h	Successful

Request Packet (maximum buffer length = 179 bytes):

Offset	Content	Type	Order
0	Request Buffer Length-2	WORD	lo-hi
2	00h	BYTE	
3	User Name Length	BYTE (1-47)	
4	User Name	BYTE[*LENGTH*]	
?	User Password Length	BYTE (0-127)	
?	User Password	BYTE[*LENGTH*]	

Reply Buffer (2 bytes):

Offset	Content	Type	Order
0	0000h	WORD	lo-hi

The NetWare C Interface format is not supported.

Change Password (E3h 01h)

This call is supported in NetWare versions 4.0 and 4.6, in Advanced NetWare versions 1.0, 1.02, 2.0 and 2.1, and in NetWare 386. It changes the password of a user and has been replaced by higher-level Bindery Services API calls such as Change Bindery Object Password, but is shown here for completeness.

Registers in:

AH	E3h
DS:SI	Address of Request buffer
ES:DI	Address of Reply buffer

Registers out:

AL	Completion Code

Completion codes:

00h	Successful

Request Packet (maximum buffer length = 307 bytes):

Offset	Content	Type	Order
0	Request Buffer Length-2	WORD	lo-hi
2	01h	BYTE	
3	User Name Length (1 to 47)	BYTE	
4	User Name	BYTE[*LENGTH*]	
?	User Password Length	BYTE (0-127)	
?	User Password	BYTE[*LENGTH*]	
?	User New Password Length	BYTE (0-127)	
?	User New Password	BYTE[*LENGTH*]	

Reply Buffer (2 bytes):

Offset	Content	Type	Order
0	0000h	WORD	lo-hi

The NetWare C Interface format is not supported.

Map User to Station Set (E3h 02h)

This call is supported in NetWare versions 4.0 and 4.6, in Advanced NetWare versions 1.0, 1.02, 2.0 and 2.1, and in NetWare 386. It returns the stations where a user is logged in and has been replaced by higher-level calls such as the Get Object Connection Numbers call but is shown here for completeness.

Registers in:

AH	E3h
DS:SI	Address of Request buffer
ES:DI	Address of Reply buffer

Registers out:

AL	Completion Code

Completion codes:

00h	Successful

Request Packet (maximum buffer length = 51 bytes):

Offset	Content	Type	Order
0	Request Buffer Length-2	WORD	lo-hi
2	02h	BYTE	
3	User Name Length (1 to 47)	BYTE	
4	User Name	BYTE[*LENGTH*]	

Reply Buffer (2 bytes):

Offset	Content	Type	Order
0	Reply Buffer Length-2	WORD	lo-hi
2	Station List Length	BYTE	
3	Station List	BYTE[*LENGTH*]	

The NetWare C Interface format is not supported.

Map Object To Number (E3h 03h)

This call is supported in NetWare versions 4.0 and 4.6, in Advanced NetWare versions 1.0, 1.02, 2.0 and 2.1, and in NetWare 386. It returns the object ID for the named object and has been replaced by higher-level Bindery Services API calls such as the Get Object Number call but is shown here for completeness.

Registers in:

AH	E3h
DS:SI	Address of Request buffer
ES:DI	Address of Reply buffer

Registers out:

AL	Completion Code

Completion codes:

00h	Successful

Request Packet (maximum buffer length = 51 bytes):

Offset	Content	Type	Order
0	Request Buffer Length-2	WORD	lo-hi
2	03h	BYTE	
3	User Name Length (1 to 47)	BYTE	
4	User Name	BYTE[*LENGTH*]	

Reply Buffer (6 bytes):

Offset	Content	Type	Order
0	Reply Buffer Length-2	WORD	lo-hi
2	Object ID	LONG	hi-lo

The NetWare C Interface format is not supported.

Map Number To Object (E3h 04h)

This call is supported in NetWare versions 4.0 and 4.6, in Advanced NetWare versions 1.0, 1.02, 2.0 and 2.1, and in NetWare 386. The reverse of the last call, it returns the name of a user given the object ID and has been replaced by higher-level

Bindery Services API calls such as the Get Bindery Object Name call but is shown here for completeness.

Registers in:

AH	E3h
DS:SI	Address of Request buffer
ES:DI	Address of Reply buffer

Registers out:

AL	Completion Code

Completion codes:

00h	Successful

Request Packet (7 bytes):

Offset	**Content**	**Type**	**Order**
0	Request Buffer Length-2	WORD	lo-hi
2	04h	BYTE	
3	User ID	LONG	hi-lo

Reply Buffer (52 bytes):

Offset	**Content**	**Type**	**Order**
0	Reply Buffer Length-2	WORD	lo-hi
2	User Name	BYTE[16]	
18	Full Name	BYTE[30]	
48	User ID	LONG	

The NetWare C Interface format is not supported.

Get Station's Logged Information (E3h 05h)

This call is supported in NetWare versions 4.0 and 4.6, in Advanced NetWare versions 1.0, 1.02, 2.0 and 2.1, and in NetWare 386. It returns the log record for a user, given the logical connection number, and has been replaced by higher-level calls such as Get Connection Information call but is shown here for completeness.

Registers in:

AH	E3h
DS:SI	Address of Request buffer
ES:DI	Address of Reply buffer

Registers out:

AL	Completion Code

Completion codes:

00h	Successful

Request Packet (maximum buffer length = 51 bytes):

Offset	**Content**	**Type**	**Order**
0	Request Buffer Length-2	WORD	lo-hi
2	05h	BYTE	
3	Connection Number	BYTE	

Reply Buffer (max = 288 bytes):

Offset	**Content**	**Type**	**Order**
0	Reply Buffer Length-2	WORD	lo-hi
2	User Name	BYTE[16]	
18	Log Time	BYTE[7]	
25	Reserved	BYTE[9]	
34	Full Name	BYTE[30]	
64	User ID	LONG	
68	User Groups	LONG[32]	hi-lo
196	Home Directory	BYTE[64]	

The NetWare C Interface format is not supported.

Map Number To Group Name (E3h 08h)

This call is supported in NetWare versions 4.0 and 4.6, in Advanced NetWare versions 1.0, 1.02, 2.0 and 2.1, and in NetWare 386. It returns the group name given its object ID and has been replaced by higher-level Bindery Services API calls such as the Get Bindery Object Name call but is shown here for completeness.

Registers in:

AH	E3h
DS:SI	Address of Request buffer
ES:DI	Address of Reply buffer

Registers out:

AL	Completion Code

Completion codes:

00h	Successful

Request Packet (7 bytes):

Offset	**Content**	**Type**	**Order**
0	Request Buffer Length-2	WORD	lo-hi
2	08h	BYTE	
3	Group ID	LONG	hi-lo

Reply Buffer (8 bytes):

Offset	Content	Type	Order
0	Reply Buffer Length-2	WORD	lo-hi
2	Group ID	LONG	hi-lo
6	Group Name Length	BYTE	
7	Group Name	BYTE [1-47]	

The NetWare C Interface format is not supported.

Get Member Set M of Group G (E3h 09h)

This call is supported in NetWare versions 4.0 and 4.6, in Advanced NetWare versions 1.0, 1.02, 2.0 and 2.1, and in NetWare 386. It returns the members of a group and has been replaced by higher-level Bindery Services API calls such as the Scan Bindery Object and Read Property Value but is shown here for completeness.

Registers in:

AH	E3h
DS:SI	Address of Request buffer
ES:DI	Address of Reply buffer

Registers out:

AL	Completion Code

Completion codes:

00h	Successful

Request Packet (9 bytes):

Offset	Content	Type	Order
0	Request Buffer Length-2	WORD	lo-hi
2	09h	BYTE	
3	Group ID	LONG	hi-lo
7	Member Set	WORD	

Reply Buffer (202 bytes):

Offset	Content	Type	Order
0	Reply Buffer Length-2	WORD	lo-hi
2	Group Members	LONG[50]	hi-lo

Group Members are the object IDs of the users that belong to that group. They are returned 50 at a time. The Member Set variable should be set to 1 for the first call and should be incremented by 1 for additional calls.

The NetWare C Interface format is not supported.

Code Sample: TestLog.C

TestLog was designed to show the process an application would go through using the Connection and Workstation Services to attach and log into a file server. This program shows the user the File Server Name table and the Connection ID table and how they change at each step along the way. It takes one command line argument, the name of the target server.

At the beginning of TestLog, I setup up the structures I will use for the ReadPropertyValue() and GetConnectionID() calls. Then I list the function prototypes for the local functions and begin main().

First, TestLog checks to see if there was one command line argument. If not, the program ends with a reprimand.

If so, we setup the *ReadPropRequest* and *ReadPropReply* structures for a call to Read a Property Value in the Bindery. The purpose of this call is to look for the value of the NET_ADDRESS property for the file server. (Each file server has temporary Bindery objects with the names and address of every other file server on the internetwork. This lets servers "advertise" their services to each other.)

After the ReadPropRequest structure fields are filled in, ReadPropertyValue is called and the return code is checked. If the call was successful, the program prints out the value of NET_ADDRESS.

Next we need to get the address of the Connection ID table and the Server Name Table. GetConnectionID() retrieves the Connection ID table for us and GetFileServerName() returns the Server Name Table. After getting the address of each of these tables, TestLog calls a function to print the contents of those tables to the screen to show the user what they look like.

After pausing for the user to view the displayed tables, the next step the program needs to perform is to set up a new entry in the Connection ID Table.

The program now uses a FOR loop to iterate through the eight entries in the Connection ID table, looking for a free entry that we can use (a free entry will have its In Use flag set to 0).

At this point we want to check to see if we're already attached to one of these servers. Supposedly, if you place the address of a server in the table that's already in the table (i.e. you try to attach to a server you're already attached to) the function call Attach To File Server should give you an error code on return. I found that it would give you a successful code on return, then freeze.

One important point about working at lower levels of network programming, such as manipulating connections: be careful. The old cliche about saving early and often applies here. It is easy to get a small detail wrong while adding/removing connections and somehow impact your own connection, severing you from the server and freezing your workstation. As long as you save with some frequency, especially before executing any code, you should be fine.

If TestLog detects that we're already attached (if the NET_ADDRESS value is identical to one of the Network, Node, and Socket combinations in the Connection ID Table) it will print an error message to that effect and exit. Also, if all eight slots are in use, it will print an error message and exit.

Next, we assign a pointer to the Server Name Table based on our index. Also, we set the variable *freeslot* to *i*, the index number of our new connection.

Now that we have a free slot to work with, we need to fill the Connection ID Table entry with the relevant information and call Attach To Server. We set the *In Use* field to 0xFF, indicating that it is used; set the Server Order number to the next sequential number after the last entry; set the network address to the value in NET_ADDRESS; and set the server name in the Server Name Table to *argv[1]*, the command-line argument stating the name of the target server.

When all of the fields are filled, we display them on the screen and pause. Next AttachToFileServer() is called and we use a switch statement to act on the return code. If the attach returns anything but a successful code, we print it to the screen and exit, otherwise, we display the Connection ID table after the attach, showing the fields filled in by the shell. Next, we sort the server addresses into the correct order.

The final step is to request the user name and password from the user and pass them to the LoginToFileServer() function call. Then we print the results of the call to the screen. Now that we have logged into the new server, we can go through the process of mapping drives and using the new file server.

At this point, some Novell commands can be run to verify that you are logged in. SList may be used to verify attachment to the target server and UserList can be used to show the connection number assigned by the target server.

This kind of program can be used by any developer needing to attach to, or log a user into or out of, a file server without involving the user. Also, applications that wish to present their services to the network may need to attach and later log in to a server (not necessarily as a user, perhaps as a job server, archive server, etc.) and can use this format.

```
/*                                                                          */
/* TestLog - Tests the server login/logout mechanism using connection API   */
/*                                                                          */
/*                                                                          */
/* by Charles Rose                                                          */
/*                                                                          */

#include <stdio.h>
#include <dos.h>
#include <dir.h>
#include <string.h>

typedef unsigned char BYTE;
typedef unsigned int WORD;
typedef unsigned long LONG;

#define USER 0x0100
#define FILE_SERVER 0x0400

struct readPropValueReq {
        WORD    Length;
        BYTE    Function;
        WORD    ObjectType;
        BYTE    ObjectNameLength;
        BYTE    ObjectName[48];
        BYTE    SegmentNumber;
```

```
        BYTE    PropertyNameLength;
        BYTE    PropertyName[16];
        };

struct readPropValueRep {
        WORD    Length;
        BYTE    PropertyValue[128];
        BYTE    MoreSegments;
        BYTE    PropertyFlags;
        };

struct connectionIDTableType {
        BYTE    SlotInUse;
        BYTE    ServerOrder;
        BYTE    Network[4];
        BYTE    Node[6];
        BYTE    Socket[2];
        BYTE    ReceiveTimeout[2];
        BYTE    RouterNode[6];
        BYTE    PacketSequence;
        BYTE    ConnectionNumber;
        BYTE    ConnectionStatus;
        BYTE    MaxTimeout[2];
        BYTE    Reserved[5];
        };

int ReadPropertyValue( struct readPropValueReq *Request,
   struct readPropValueRep *Reply );
BYTE far *GetConnectionID( void );
BYTE far *GetFileServerName( void );
void ShowConnectionTable( struct connectionIDTableType far *Table );
void ShowNameTable( BYTE far *serverNameTable );
void PrintNum( BYTE *num, int count );
void FarPrintNum( BYTE far *num, int count );
int AttachToFileServer( BYTE freeSlot );
int LoginToFileServer( WORD type, char *name, char *password );
BYTE GetPreferredConnectionID( void );
void SetPreferredConnectionID( BYTE newConn );
int sort_func( const void *a, const void *b );

main( int argc, char *argv[] )
{
        struct readPropValueReq ReadPropRequest;
        struct readPropValueRep ReadPropReply;

        struct connectionIDTableType far *connectionIDTable, far *tablePtr;
        BYTE far *serverNameTable, far *serverTablePtr, far *iNetAddr;

        /* We will use this table to sort our 12-byte network addresses      */
        /* the 13th byte we'll use for the original order number             */
        BYTE newTable[8][13];

        int result, i, j, freeSlot = 0;
        BYTE oldConnID;

        char loginName[48], password[128];

        if ( argc != 2 )
        {
                printf( "Usage: TESTLOG fileServerName\n" );
                exit( 1 );
        }
```

```
/*   First get Network Address for server specified */

memset( &ReadPropRequest, NULL, sizeof( ReadPropRequest ) );
memset( &ReadPropReply, NULL, sizeof( ReadPropReply ) );

ReadPropRequest.ObjectType = FILE_SERVER;
strcpy( ReadPropRequest.ObjectName, strupr( argv[1] ) );
ReadPropRequest.ObjectNameLength = sizeof( ReadPropRequest.ObjectName );
ReadPropRequest.SegmentNumber = 1;
strcpy( ReadPropRequest.PropertyName, "NET_ADDRESS" );
ReadPropRequest.PropertyNameLength = 11;

result = ReadPropertyValue( &ReadPropRequest, &ReadPropReply );
if ( result )
{
        printf( "Error reading property value of NET_ADDRESS on %s,
           code = %X\n", argv[1], result );
        exit( 1 );
}
else
{
        printf( "Server %s found. Address = ", argv[1] );
        PrintNum( ReadPropReply.PropertyValue, 4 );
        printf( ":" );
        PrintNum( ReadPropReply.PropertyValue + 4, 6 );
        printf( ":" );
        PrintNum( ReadPropReply.PropertyValue + 10, 2 );
        printf( "\n" );
}

printf( "WORKSTATION TABLES UPON ENTRY TO PROGRAM:\n" );

/* Get Connection ID table */
connectionIDTable = GetConnectionID();
ShowConnectionTable( connectionIDTable );

/* Get Server Name Table */
serverNameTable = GetFileServerName();
ShowNameTable( serverNameTable );

/*                                              */
/* Attempt to connect to specified file server  */
/*                                              */
printf("Press any key to setup registers for attach to %s...", argv[1] );
getch();

/* Setup first available free slot in Connection ID table and check   */
/* to see if we're already connected to target server                 */
tablePtr = connectionIDTable;
for ( i = 0; i < 8; i++, tablePtr++ )
{
        iNetAddr = tablePtr->Network;
        for ( j = 0; j < 12; j++ )
                if ( iNetAddr[j] != ReadPropReply.PropertyValue[j] )
                        break;
        if ( j == 12 )
        {
                printf( "\nCannot attach, already connected to %s.\n",
                   argv[1] );
                exit(1);
        }
```

```
        /* If we have not already got the number of a free slot       */
        /* then check the SlotInUse field to see if it is in use      */
        /* or not. If so, make that our slot.                         */
        if ( !freeSlot )
                if ( !tablePtr->SlotInUse )
                        freeSlot = i;

}

if ( !freeSlot )
{
        printf( "\nAll 8 server slots are in use, cannot attach.\n" );
        exit(1);
}

serverTablePtr = serverNameTable + ( freeSlot * 48 );

/* Now that we have a free slot, mark it used and set the preliminary
        order */
tablePtr = connectionIDTable + freeSlot;
tablePtr->SlotInUse = 0xFF;
tablePtr->ServerOrder = freeSlot + 1;

/* and copy in the internet address of our target server */
iNetAddr = tablePtr->Network;
for ( i = 0; i < 12; i++ )
        iNetAddr[i] = ReadPropReply.PropertyValue[i];

/* and copy the server name into the server name table */
i = 0;
do
        serverTablePtr[i] = argv[1][i];
while ( argv[1][i++] );

/* and show the tables again... */
printf( "\nWORKSTATION TABLES JUST BEFORE ATTACH CALL:\n" );
ShowConnectionTable( connectionIDTable );
ShowNameTable( serverNameTable );

printf("Press any key to attempt to attach to %s...\n", argv[1] );
getch();

/* Now try to attach to the new server */
result = AttachToFileServer( freeSlot + 1 );
switch ( result )
{
    case 0x00:  printf( "Successfully attached to file server %s\n",
                argv[1] );
        break;

    case 0xF8:  printf( "Already attached to server %s\n", argv[1] );
        exit(1);

    case 0xF9:  printf( "Server has no more free connection slots\n" );
        exit(1);

    case 0xFA:  printf( "No more server slots available\n" );
        exit(1);
```

```
    case 0xFC:  printf( "File Server unknown\n" );
        exit(1);

    case 0xFE:  printf( "Server bindery locked\n" );
        exit(1);

    case 0xFF:  printf( "No response from server (illegal server address)\n" );
        exit(1);

    default:    printf( "Error attaching to server, code = %X", result );
        exit(1);

}

printf("WORKSTATION TABLES AFTER ATTACH CALL:\n" );
ShowConnectionTable( connectionIDTable );
ShowNameTable( serverNameTable );

printf("Press any key to attempt to login to %s...", argv[1] );
getch();

/* Before we log in, we must sort the addresses                       */
/* Because of far pointers, we must use our own copy routine          */

/* Place the addresses in newTable, use last byte to hold original order */
tablePtr = connectionIDTable;
for ( i = 0; i < 8; i++, tablePtr++ )
{
        /* Copy connectionID table to newTable. If the slot is not in   */
        /* use, set to all 0xFF's so they will float to bottom in sort */
        for ( j = 0; j < 12; j++ )
        {
                if ( !tablePtr->SlotInUse )
                        newTable[i][j] = 0xFF;
                else
                        newTable[i][j] = tablePtr->Network[j];
        }
        newTable[i][j] = i;
}

/* Use Turbo C's builting quicksort routine to sort the table         */
/* any other sort routine could be substituted                        */
qsort( newTable, 8, 13, sort_func );

/* now go put the new orders in */
for ( i = 0; i < 8; i++ )
{
        tablePtr = connectionIDTable + newTable[i][12];
        /* Only put an order back in if the slot is in use */
        if ( tablePtr->SlotInUse )
                tablePtr->ServerOrder = i + 1;
}

/* Set the connection ID of our new attachment as our preferred       */
/* server so that is the server that will receive the Login request   */

/* get old conn id, if any                                            */
oldConnID = GetPreferredConnectionID();

/* set our new one                                                    */
SetPreferredConnectionID( freeSlot + 1 );
```

```
        printf( "\n\nEnter name to log in as: " );
        gets( loginName );
        printf( "\nEnter password: " );
        gets( password );

        result = LoginToFileServer( USER, loginName, password );
        if ( result )
        {
                printf( "Error logging in to file server %s, code = %x\n",
                        argv[1], result );
                exit(1);
        }

        /* Set preferred server back to what it was, if any                */
        SetPreferredConnectionID( oldConnID );

        printf( "Successfully logged in to file server %s\n", argv[1] );

}

int ReadPropertyValue( struct readPropValueReq *Request,
   struct readPropValueRep *Reply )
{
        Request->Function = 0x3D;
        Request->Length = sizeof( struct readPropValueReq ) - 2;
        Reply->Length = sizeof( struct readPropValueRep ) - 2;

        _SI = (unsigned)Request;
        _DI = (unsigned)Reply;
        _ES = _DS;
        _AH = 0xE3;

        geninterrupt( 0x21 );

        return _AL;
}

BYTE far *GetConnectionID( void )
{
        _AH = 0xEF;
        _AL = 3;

        geninterrupt( 0x21 );

        return MK_FP( _ES, _SI );
}

BYTE far *GetFileServerName( void )
{
        _AH = 0xEF;
        _AL = 4;

        geninterrupt( 0x21 );

        return MK_FP( _ES, _SI );
}

void ShowConnectionTable( struct connectionIDTableType far *Table )
{
        int i;
        struct connectionIDTableType far *T = Table;
```

```
        printf( "\n                          Workstation Connection ID Table\n" );
        printf( "InUse Order Net  Node  Socket TimeOut Router Seq Conn Status\n" );
        for ( i = 0; i < 8; i++, T++ )
        {
            printf( "%02X    %02X    ", T->SlotInUse, T->ServerOrder );
            FarPrintNum( T->Network, 4 ); printf( " " );
            FarPrintNum( T->Node, 6 ); printf( " " );
            FarPrintNum( T->Socket, 2 ); printf( "    " );
            FarPrintNum( T->ReceiveTimeout, 2 ); printf( "     " );
            FarPrintNum( T->RouterNode, 6 ); printf( " " );
            printf( "%02X  %02X   %02X\n", T->PacketSequence, T->ConnectionNumber,
                        T->ConnectionStatus );
        }
}

void ShowNameTable( BYTE far *serverNameTable )
{
        int i;
        BYTE far *name = serverNameTable;

        printf( "\n     Workstation File Server Name Table\n" );
        printf( "Slot    Server Name\n" );
        for ( i = 0; i < 8; i++, name += 48 )
                printf( "%1d:             %Fs\n", i, name );
}

void PrintNum( BYTE *num, int count )
{
        int i;

        for ( i = 0; i < count; i++ )
                printf( "%02X", num[i] );
}

void FarPrintNum( BYTE far *num, int count )
{
        int i;

        for ( i = 0; i < count; i++ )
                printf( "%02X", num[i] );
}

int AttachToFileServer( BYTE freeSlot )
{
        _AH = 0xF1;
        _AL = 0;
        _DL = freeSlot;

        geninterrupt( 0x21 );

        return _AL;
}

int LoginToFileServer( WORD type, char *name, char *password )
{
        BYTE Request[183];
        int Reply = 0;

        Request[2] = 0x14;
        *( (WORD *) (Request + 3) ) = type;
        Request[5] = strlen( name );
        strcpy( Request + 6, strupr(name) );
        Request[ 6 + Request[5] ] = strlen( password );
```

```
        strcpy( Request + 6 + Request[5] + 1, strupr(password ) );
        Request[0] = 5 + strlen( password ) + strlen( name );

        _SI = (unsigned)Request;
        _DI = (unsigned)&Reply;
        _ES = _DS;
        _AH = 0xE3;

        geninterrupt( 0x21 );

        return _AL;
}

BYTE GetPreferredConnectionID( void )
{
        _AH = 0xF0;
        _AL = 1;

        geninterrupt( 0x21 );

        return _AL;
}

void SetPreferredConnectionID( BYTE newConn )
{
        _AH = 0xF0;
        _AL = 0;
        _DL = newConn;

        geninterrupt( 0x21 );

        return _AL;
}

int sort_func( const void *a, const void *b )
{
        int i;

        for ( i = 0; i < 13; i++ )
        {
                if ( *( (BYTE*) a) < *( (BYTE*) b) ) return -1;
                if ( *( (BYTE*) a) > *( (BYTE*) b) ) return 1;
                ( (BYTE*) a)++;
                ( (BYTE*) b)++;
        }
        return 0;
}
```

Exercises

1. Run TestLog. You will need two file servers to test the program. When the shell is loaded, it attaches to a file server and the program will only work when attaching to a server other than one already connected to.

2. When running TestLog, examine the Connection ID table to see how it is constructed. Understand the function of the fields in the table.

3. Write a program that gets and sets the Default, Preferred, and Primary file server. How do the three differ? How do the differences appear in the DOS environment?

4. Get the Drive Handle, Drive Flag and drive Connection ID tables through their appropriate calls. What do they tell you about the drive mappings and how can you apply these tables to your applications?

5. Use the Get Object Connection Numbers call in conjunction with Bindery calls to scan for a user and find at what stations that user is logged in.

6. Use the Set NetWare Error mode call. How does this affect the operation of normal DOS programs? Experiment.

7. A multiserver environment is one that provides a multitude of resources. Use the Connection Services, starting with TestLog as a guide, to attach to, log in, and log out of file servers on an internetwork. Occasionally, programs will need to attach, log in, and log out of a file server to take advantage of some service, without the user knowing. Once learned, these services can be valuable. For instance, to print to a distant server, both the Workstation Services calls that manipulate Default/Preferred/Primary servers as well as the Connection Services calls that attach, log in and log out of file servers will be needed. Construct a program to print to a distant server.

10 Message Services

Message Services are designed to provide a high-level interface to allow programmers to send messages to other stations or to the console. Messages are of two types. Broadcast messages, such as those used in the NetWare SEND command, may be emulated; or pipes may be used to provide a six-message queue at each station for heavier communications loads.

Developers should remember that Message Services are a high-level implementation of station-to-station communication and do involve the file server for processing so they are not completely peer-to-peer (i.e. they do not go straight from one station to the other). This API should be used when simple, nonreal-time communication is needed.

It should be noted that Novell has said that the Message Services calls will not be supported in NetWare 386 by the end of 1990 because the communications functionality provided by the Message Services can be achieved through the IPX-SPX communication calls (chapter 14).

Broadcast messages

Programmers know broadcast messages as those produced by the NetWare SEND command. They can be up to 55 bytes long. They show up on line 25 of the target workstations in inverse video. When one appears, the station sounds a beep and waits for the user to press CTRL-ENTER to clear the message. This API allows the programmer to simulate this process if an application needs to send messages to any user or the console of the file server.

Broadcast message modes

Each workstation reserves a 55-byte buffer for broadcast messages. Because there is only one such buffer, if a workstation receives more than one message only the most recent will appear. A file server also stores a buffer, so at any given time two messages could be in the pipeline, one at the workstation and one at the file server. Programmers needing to send more messages must use message pipes.

A broadcast message can be sent by a file server or a workstation to either a workstation or a file server console. The file server informs the workstation when a message arrives and the shell retrieves and displays the message, depending on the mode set by the workstation. Only a message from the file server itself can overwrite a message stored in a file server's buffer.

There are four modes that the developer may set (using the Get Broadcast Mode and Set Broadcast Mode calls) to determine how messages are handled by the workstation:

Mode 0: (Default Mode) The server stores both the user and server messages intended for a workstation. The shell displays each message on the screen.

Mode 1: The server stores server messages but discards user messages. The shell displays each server message on the screen.

Mode 2: The server stores server messages but discards user messages. The shell does not automatically display each server message. Applications needing to access the server messages must poll for and retrieve the most recently stored message by calling the Get Broadcast Message function.

Mode 3: The server stores both user and server messages but doesn't automatically display either. An application can poll for them using Get Broadcast Message.

Broadcast Inform

Incoming broadcast messages can be harmful or even fatal in some environments. This is especially true with Microsoft Windows and some other graphical user interfaces. In this case, programs must intercept messages by using Broadcast Inform.

To intercept incoming messages, takeover the DOS multiplex interrupt (2Fh) and look for the AX register to contain 7A85h. When this is the case, the CX register will contain the connection ID of the server with the message waiting. If the program wants to handle the message, it should set CX to 0, which informs the shell that another process has handled the message. The program should then chain to the next 2Fh address.

To retrieve the message: get and save the connection ID of the current server, set the preferred server to the connection ID from the paragraph above, make a call to Get Broadcast Message and restore the original server.

Using broadcast messages

The following calls are used in conjunction with broadcast messages:

Send Broadcast Messages — sends a broadcast message through the file server to any number of workstations.
Get Broadcast Message — retrieves a broadcast message (may be used for polling).
Broadcast to Console — sends a message to the file server console.

Message pipes

Pipes are more functional than broadcast messages, providing 126-byte messages and a six-byte queue, but they require more work on the part of the programmer.

A developer wishing to use pipes must use the Open Message Pipe function to open one at each station that will be communicating. Once the pipes are open, the Send Personal Message call can be used to send messages through the pipe and Get Personal Message can be used to poll for and retrieve messages from the workstation's queue.

Pipes should be closed (using the Close Message Pipe call) when the communication session is terminated. If the pipe were not closed, messages would pile up in the queue and the sending stations would not know the messages weren't being monitored.

Pipes enable each workstation to hold six 126-byte messages in a queue. The messages placed in the queue can only be removed in FIFO (first in, first out) order. The file server manages message delivery. The status of each pipe can be monitored with the Check Pipe Status function.

Calls in the Message Services API

These calls are supported in NetWare versions 4.0 and 4.6, in Advanced NetWare versions 1.0, 1.02, 2.0 and 2.1, and in NetWare 386, but will not be supported in 386 versions dated after 1990. Throughout the book, we explain fields within the calls only at the first mention of each field in each chapter. Appendix B contains a comprehensive, alphabetical listing of the fields for quick reference.

Get Broadcast Mode (DEh 04h)

This call returns the message mode of the requesting workstation.

Registers in:
AH DEh
DL 04h

Registers out:
AL Message Mode

Completion codes:
None

File servers reserve one 55-byte message buffer in memory for each attached workstation. Messages bound for the workstation are kept in this buffer. The file server might initiate these messages, or they might originate from other workstations.

Usually, the file server informs the workstation that a message has arrived, and the workstation retrieves and displays the message. Only messages originating from the file server can overwrite messages already stored in the message buffer.

A Message Mode can be set for each workstation to indicate whether attached file servers store or reject messages sent to the workstation. The mode also indicates whether workstations should be notified of messages (by sounding a beep on the speaker and displaying the message in inverse on the 25th line of the workstation's screen).

The following message modes are defined:

00h Attached servers store both user and server messages intended for the workstation. The shell automatically retrieves and displays each message.

01h The server stores server messages but discards user messages intended for this station. The shell automatically retrieves and displays each console message.

02h The server stores server messages but discards user messages intended for this station. The shell ignores the file server's notification that a message exists in the message buffer. Applications can poll for and retrieve the most recently stored message by calling Get Broadcast Message.

03h The server stores both user and server messages intended for this station. The shell ignores the fileserver's notification that a message exists in the message buffer. Applications can poll for and retrieve the most recently stored message by calling Get Broadcast Message.

The default message mode is 00h.

The NetWare C Interface format is:

```
BYTE GetBroadcastMode( void );
```

Set Broadcast Mode (DEh)

This call sets the message mode of the requesting workstation.

Registers in:

AH	DEh
DL	Target Message Mode

Registers out:

AL	Message Mode

Completion codes:
None

The Target Message Mode field specifies the new message mode. The Message Mode field returns and confirms the new message mode.

The NetWare C Interface format is:

```
void SetBroadcastMode( BYTE broadcastMode );
```

Send Broadcast Message (E1h 00h)

This call sends a broadcast message to the specified logical connection(s) on the default file server.

Registers in:

AH	E1h
DS:SI	Request Buffer Address
ES:DI	Reply Buffer Address

Registers out:

AL	Completion Code

Completion codes:

00h	Successful
FEh	I/O Failure; Lack Of Dynamic Workspace

Request Buffer (maximum buffer length = 160 bytes):

Offset	**Content**	**Type**	**Order**
0	Request Buffer Length - 2	WORD	lo-hi
2	00h	BYTE	
3	Connection Count (1 to 100)	BYTE	
4	Connection List	BYTE[*COUNT*]	
?	Message Length (1 to 55)	BYTE	
?	Message	BYTE[*LENGTH*]	

Reply Buffer (maximum buffer length = 103 bytes):

Offset	**Content**	**Type**	**Order**
0	Reply Buffer Length - 2	WORD	lo-hi
2	Connection Count(1 to 100)	BYTE	
3	Result List	BYTE[*COUNT*]	

The *Connection Count* field specifies the number of stations (1 to 100) to which the message is sent.

The *Connection List* field specifies the connection number of each station to which the message is sent. Each byte in the connection list field has a corresponding byte in the Result List field below.

The *Result List* field returns a result code for each connection number contained in the Connection List field. The following result codes are defined:

00h	Successful	The server stored the message in the target connection's message buffer. (It is the target connection's responsibility to retrieve and display the message.)
FCh	Rejected	The target connection's message buffer is already holding a message.
FDh	Invalid Connection Number	The specified connection number is unknown.
FFh	Blocked	The target connection's message mode is set to block messages, or the target connection is not is use.

The NetWare C Interface format is:

```
int SendBroadcastMessage( char *message, WORD *connectionList,
      BYTE *resultList, WORD connectionCount );
```

Get Broadcast Message (E1h 01h)

An application can use this call to poll for and return a broadcast message from the default file server.

Registers in:

AH	E1h
DS:SI	Request Buffer Address
ES:DI	Reply Buffer Address

Registers out:

AL	Completion Code

Completion codes:

00h	Successful
FCh	Message Queue Full
FEh	I/O Failure; Lack Of Dynamic Workspace

Request Buffer (3 bytes):

Offset	Content	Type	Order
0	Request Buffer Length - 2	WORD	lo-hi
2	01h	BYTE	

Reply Buffer (maximum buffer length = 58 bytes):

Offset	Content	Type	Order
0	Reply Buffer Length - 2	WORD	lo-hi
2	Message Length (0 to 55)	BYTE	
3	Message	BYTE[*LENGTH*]	

When the workstation's message mode is set to two or three, thus ignoring notifications, an application can use this call to poll for and get new messages.

The NetWare C Interface format is:

```
int GetBroadcastMessage( char *messageBuffer );
```

Broadcast To Console (E1h 09h)

This call broadcasts a message to the default file server's system console.

Registers in:

AH	E1h
DS:SI	Request Buffer Address
ES:DI	Reply Buffer Address

Registers out:

AL	Completion Code

Completion codes:

00h	Successful
FCh	Message Queue Full
FEh	I/O Failure; Lack Of Dynamic Workspace

Request Buffer (maximum buffer length = 64 bytes):

Offset	Content	Type	Order
0	Request Buffer Length - 2	WORD	lo-hi
2	09h	BYTE	
3	Message Length (1 to 60)	BYTE	
4	Message	BYTE[*LENGTH*]	

Reply Buffer (maximum buffer length = 2 bytes):

Offset	Content	Type
0	0000	WORD

Message contains the message to be sent. It can be from 1 to 60 bytes long and cannot contain ASCII characters less than 20h or greater than 7Eh. When the message is received, the file server will display a colon (:) followed by the message. New messages overwrite old ones.

The NetWare C Interface format is:

```
int BroadcastToConsole( char *message );
```

Send Personal Message (E1h 04h)

This call sends a pipe message to the specified logical connection(s) on the default file server.

Registers in:

AH	E1h
DS:SI	Request Buffer Address
ES:DI	Reply Buffer Address

Registers out:

AL	Completion Code

Completion codes:

00h	Successful
FEh	I/O Failure; Lack Of Dynamic Workspace

Request Buffer (maximum buffer length = 231 bytes):

Offset	Content	Type	Order
0	Request Buffer Length - 2	WORD	lo-hi
2	04h	BYTE	
3	Connection Count (1 to 100)	BYTE	
4	Connection List	BYTE[*COUNT*]	
?	Message Length (1 to 126)	BYTE	
?	Message	BYTE[*LENGTH*]	

Reply Buffer (maximum buffer length = 103 bytes):

Offset	Content	Type	Order
0	Reply Buffer Length - 2	WORD	lo-hi
2	Connection Count (1 to 100)	BYTE	
3	Result List	BYTE[*COUNT*]	

Before an application can make this call to send a pipe message, both the sending workstation and the receiving workstation must call Open Message Pipe to establish a complete message pipe. Send Personal Message instructs the default file server to place a message in the pipe message queue of each client in the connection list.

Messages can be no more than 126 bytes; longer ones are truncated. Also, a workstation can have no more than six messages pending in its pipe message queue at once. If six are waiting, others will be rejected.

The *Connection Count* and *Connection List* specify how many and which stations the message will be sent to.

The NetWare C Interface format is:

```
int SendPersonalMessage( char *message, WORD *connectionList,
   BYTE *resultList, WORD connectionCount );
```

Get Personal Message (E1h 05h)

This call retrieves the oldest message from the requesting workstation's pipe queue on the default file server.

Registers in:

AH	E1h
DS:SI	Request Buffer Address
ES:DI	Reply Buffer Address

Registers out:

AL	Completion Code

Completion codes:

00h	Successful
FEh	I/O Failure; Lack Of Dynamic Workspace

Request Buffer (3 bytes):

Offset	Content	Type	Order
0	Request Buffer Length - 2	WORD	lo-hi
2	05h	BYTE	

Reply Buffer (maximum buffer length = 130 bytes):

Offset	Content	Type	Order
0	Reply Buffer Length - 2	WORD	lo-hi
2	Source Connection	BYTE	
3	Message Length (0 to 126)	BYTE	
4	Message	BYTE[*LENGTH*]	

This call may be used to poll for and return the next message in the workstation's pipe queue (on the default server).

The *Source Connection* field returns the connection number of the sending station.

The NetWare C Interface format is:

```
int GetPersonalMessage( char *messageBuffer, WORD *sourceConnection );
```

Log Network Message (E3h 0Dh)

This call logs a message in the default file server's NET$LOG.MSG file.

Registers in:

AH	E3h
DS:SI	Request Buffer Address
ES:DI	Reply Buffer Address

Completion codes:

00h	Successful

Request Buffer (maximum buffer length = 84 bytes):

Offset	Content	Type	Order
0	Request Buffer Length - 2	WORD	lo-hi
2	0Dh	BYTE	
3	Message Length (0 to 80)	BYTE	
4	Message	BYTE[*LENGTH*]	

Reply Buffer (2 bytes):

Offset	Content	Type	Order
0	0000h	WORD	lo-hi

This call appends the message to the NET$LOG.MSG file in the SYS:SYSTEM directory of the default file server. The message is prefaced with the current date and time, as well as the logical connection number of the station making the call. The resulting format is:

```
Month/Day/Year Hours:Minutes STN Station: Message
```

(where Station is the logical connection number of the requesting station and Message is the message sent)

An example log entry might be:

```
01/08/88 06:54 STN 34: Database record 12 modified
```

Novell intended this call for use by utilities or other programs that need to log usage information for accounting purposes.

The NetWare C Interface format is:

```
int LogNetworkMessage( char *message );
```

Open Message Pipe (E1h 06h)

This call creates the requesting workstation's side of one or more message pipes offered to one or more logical connections on the default file server.

Registers in:

AH	E1h
DS:SI	Request Buffer Address
ES:DI	Reply Buffer Address

Registers out:

AL	Completion Code

Completion codes:

00h	Successful
FEh	I/O Failure; Lack Of Dynamic Workspace

Request Buffer (maximum buffer length = 104 bytes):

Offset	**Content**	**Type**	**Order**
0	Request Buffer Length - 2	WORD	lo-hi
2	06h	BYTE	
3	Connection Count(1 to 100)	BYTE	
4	Connection List	BYTE[*COUNT*]	

Reply Buffer (maximum buffer length = 103 bytes):

Offset	**Content**	**Type**	**Order**
0	Reply Buffer Length - 2	WORD	lo-hi
2	Connection Count(1 to 100)	BYTE	
3	Result list	BYTE[*COUNT*]	

This call must be made by both stations before they can exchange pipe messages.

The NetWare C Interface format is:

```
int OpenMessagePipe( WORD *connectionList, BYTE *resultList,
  WORD connectionCount );
```

Close Message Pipe (E1h 07h)

This call closes the requesting workstation's end of one or more message pipes offered to one or more logical connections on the default file server.

Registers in:

AH	E1h
DS:SI	Request Buffer Address
ES:DI	Reply Buffer Address

Registers out:

AL	Completion Code

Completion codes:

00h	Successful
FCh	Message Queue Full
FEh	I/O Failure; Lack Of Dynamic Workspace

Request Buffer (maximum buffer length = 104 bytes):

Offset	Content	Type	Order
0	Request Buffer Length - 2	WORD	lo-hi
2	07h	BYTE	
3	Connection Count(1 to 100)	BYTE	
4	Connection List	BYTE[*COUNT*]	

Reply Buffer (maximum buffer length = 103 bytes):

Offset	Content	Type	Order
0	Reply Buffer Length - 2	WORD	lo-hi
2	Connection Count (1 to 100)	BYTE	
3	Result List	BYTE[*COUNT*]	

This call closes the pipe and discards all waiting messages.

The NetWare C Interface format is:

```
int CloseMessagePipe( WORD *connectionList, BYTE *resultList,
      WORD connectionCount );
```

Check Pipe Status (E1h 08h)

This call allows a client to monitor the status of one or more of its message pipes.

Registers in:

AH	E1h
DS:SI	Request Buffer Address
ES:DI	Reply Buffer Address

Registers out:

AL	Completion Code

Completion codes:

00h	Successful

Request Buffer (maximum buffer length = 104 bytes):

Offset	Content	Type	Order
0	Request Buffer Length - 2	WORD	lo-hi
2	08h	BYTE	
3	Connection Count(1 to 100)	BYTE	
4	Connection List	BYTE[*COUNT*]	

Reply Buffer (maximum buffer length = 103 bytes):

0	Reply Buffer Length - 2	WORD	lo-hi
2	Connection Count(1 to 100)	BYTE	
3	Pipe Status List	BYTE[*COUNT*]	

The *Pipe Status List* field returns a pipe status code for each connection number contained in the Connection List field. The following pipe status codes are defined:

00h	Open. The message pipe is complete at both ends.
FEh	Incomplete. The target connection's half of the message pipe does not exist.
FFh	Closed. The calling client's half of the message pipe does not exist, or the connection number is not in use or is invalid.

The NetWare C Interface format is:

```
int CheckPipeStatus( WORD *connectionList, BYTE *resultList,
  WORD connectionCount );
```

Disable Station Broadcasts (E1h 02h)

This call allows a station to refuse broadcast messages.

Registers in:

AH	E1h
DS:SI	Request Buffer Address
ES:DI	Reply Buffer Address

Registers out:

AL	Completion Code

Completion codes:

00h	Successful

Request Buffer (3 bytes):

Offset	Content	Type	Order
0	Request Buffer Length - 2	WORD	lo-hi
2	2	BYTE	

Reply Buffer

Offset	Content	Type	Order
0	0000	WORD	

Set Broadcast Mode can perform the same action as this call.
The NetWare C Interface format is not supported.

Enable Station Broadcasts (E1h 03h)

This call allows a station to accept broadcast messages.

Registers in:

AH	E1h
DS:SI	Request Buffer Address
ES:DI	Reply Buffer Address

Registers out:

AL	Completion Code

Completion codes:

00h	Successful

Request Buffer (3 bytes):

Offset	Content	Type	Order
0	Request Buffer Length - 2	WORD	lo-hi
2	3	BYTE	

Reply Buffer

Offset	Content	Type	Order
0	0000	WORD	

Set Broadcast Mode can perform the same action as this call. It also reverses the action of the previous call.

The NetWare C Interface format is not supported.

Code Summary: PipeChat.C

PipeChat uses the Message Services and demonstrates their use in a chat program where two users can talk to each other simultaneously. Message Services represent the highest level of station-to-station communication available under NetWare. Later, we will show how IPX-SPX can be used for high-performance, true peer-to-peer applications and we will demonstrate with a chat program written using IPX.

PipeChat allows two users to talk to each other. User A contacts user B by typing "PIPECHAT B". PipeChat sends a message to B that A wants to talk. In response, B types "PIPECHAT A" and a two-way chat session is begun. When one user presses the ESC key, the session is ended.

The program begins by defining the PipeFunction types and the Get Object Connection request and reply packets. Instead of having three different functions, Open, Close, and Check Pipe, I consolidated them into one call and passed the only element of the call that changed, the Function number.

After the local prototypes are defined, PipeChat begins execution at main() by checking the command line argument for a user to chat with. If no user is found, an error message is printed and execution halts.

The first task is to invite the target user to chat. This is accomplished by making a call to GetObjectConnectionNumbers() which will return the connections a particular object (in this case an object of type user with the name specified on the command line) is logged in to. If the user is not logged in or if the user is logged in to more than one station, the program will say so and exit. A possible enhancement to the program would be to handle multiple sessions, i.e. conferencing.

What we needed to invite the target user to chat was his connection number so we record it in the connection variable and call SendBroadcastMessage() to send the invitation. The target user will receive the message at the bottom of the screen (just like in a SEND command). After the call, we check the status variable to see if the message was sent and received successfully.

If the message was received all right, we open a pipe with the PipeFunction() (OPEN_PIPE) function and wait for the target user to respond by opening their side of the pipe. To wait, we enter a while loop to check the status of the keyboard (for the user to abort by pressing any key) and we check the status of the pipe (by calling PipeFunction() (CHECK_PIPE)). If they have opened the pipe, the variable status will be set.

If the user did reply by typing "PIPECHAT x" where x is who we are logged in as then we should receive the pipe message. Next the program enters its main loop, having established the chat session between the two stations.

The *message* variable is cleared and GetPersonalMessage() is called to check the pipe for any incoming messages to us. If there was a message, it is printed. If the message indicates the other user quit (by pressing the ESC key) we need to do likewise and the Quit() function is called, closing the pipe and exiting the program. Next, the *message* variable is set back to nulls.

The program then checks our side of the session, checking the status of the keyboard. If a key was pressed, PipeChat places it in the first element of *message* and checks to see if it was the ESC key. If it was, we send a quit message to the other side and call Quit().

If we hit any other key, it is printed to the screen with printf() and gets() is called to get the rest of the screen. For performance reasons, as well as for aesthetics, I chose to send commands line-by-line instead of character-by-character.

There would be tremendous overhead in sending a message packet for each character typed. This could (with several chatters going) cause a loss of network performance from all of the traffic introduced as well as a performance loss at the server from all of the requests it would have to service. The line-by-line method works well here because it doesn't overwrite one user's text with the other's.

The program loops, printing whatever is received, and when it notices the user has pressed a key, it waits for the user to enter a full line and hit the return key. The current user's messages are prefaced with two dashes (—) and the other user's messages are prefaced with a colon (:) so everyone knows who has said what.

Our other chat program, IPXChat, explained in the IPX-SPX chapter, will show how a faster, albeit more complex character-by-character chat can be built using IPX.

```
/*                                                                              */
/* PipeChat - Allows two stations to chat using NetWare pipes                   */
/*                                                                              */
/* by Charles Rose                                                              */
/*                                                                              */

#include <stdio.h>
#include <dos.h>
#include <dir.h>
#include <string.h>

#define USER 0x0100
#define ESC 0x1b

#define OPEN_PIPE 0x06
#define CLOSE_PIPE 0x07
#define CHECK_PIPE 0x08

typedef unsigned char BYTE;
typedef unsigned int WORD;
typedef unsigned long LONG;

struct getObjConnReq {
     WORD Length;
     BYTE Function;
     WORD ObjectType;
     BYTE ObjectNameLength;
     BYTE ObjectName[48];
};

struct getObjConnRep {
     WORD       Length;
     BYTE NumberOfConnections;
     BYTE Connections[100];
};
```

```
int SendBroadcastMessage( BYTE *Connections, BYTE *Result,
        BYTE NumberOfConnections, BYTE *Message );
int GetObjectConnectionNumbers( struct getObjConnReq *Request,
        struct getObjConnRep *Reply );
int PipeFunction( BYTE Function, BYTE *Connections, BYTE *Result,
        BYTE NumberOfConnections );
void Quit( BYTE *connection );
int GetPersonalMessage( BYTE *Message );
int SendPersonalMessage( BYTE *Connections, BYTE *Result,
        BYTE NumberOfConnections, BYTE *Message );

main( int argc, char *argv[] )
{
     int i, result,
     struct getObjConnReq Request;
     struct getObjConnRep Reply;
     BYTE connection, status, message[126];

     if ( argc != 2 )
     {
          printf( "Usage: PIPECHAT username\n" );
          exit(1);
     }

     /* Find out the connection number of the target user                    */

     Request.ObjectType = USER;
     Request.ObjectNameLength = strlen( argv[1] );
     strcpy( Request.ObjectName, strupr( argv[1] ) );

     GetObjectConnectionNumbers( &Request, &Reply );

     if ( !Reply.NumberOfConnections )
     {
          printf( "User %s is not logged in.\n", argv[1] );
          exit(1);
     }

     if ( Reply.NumberOfConnections > 1 )
     {
          printf( "User %s is logged in at %d stations.\nPipeChat can only talk
                      to one at a time.\n", argv[1], Reply.NumberOfConnections );
          exit(1);
     }

     connection = Reply.Connections[0];

     /* Send a message to target user inviting him to chat                    */

     result = SendBroadcastMessage( &connection, &status, 1,
               "Invitation to chat from SUPERVISOR" );
     if ( result )
     {
        printf( "Error sending broadcast message, code = %X\n", result );
        exit(1);
     }

     switch(status)
     {
        case 0x00:      printf( "Message sent successfully.\n" );
                        break;
```

```
   case 0xFC: printf( "Message was rejected (target message buffer full).\n" );
           exit(1);
   case 0xFD:      printf( "Message not sent - Invalid Connection Number\n" );
                   exit(1);
   case 0xFF:      printf( "Message was blocked (target station ran CASTOFF
                           or was not in use).\n" );
                   exit(1);
}

/* Open Pipe and wait for other station to open pipe as well */
result = PipeFunction( OPEN_PIPE, &connection, &status, 1 );
if ( result )
{
   printf( "Error opening pipe, code = %X\n", result );
   exit(1);
}

printf( "Waiting for other user to respond.  Press any key to abort...\n" );
while ( status )
{
   if ( bioskey(1) )
           Quit( &connection );

   result = PipeFunction( CHECK_PIPE, &connection, &status, 1 );
   if ( result )
   {
           printf( "Error checking pipe, code = %X\n", result );
           exit(1);
   }
}

/* Enter main loop: check keyboard to send and check pipe to print      */
/*  and exit if the user hits ESC                                        */

while( 1 )
{
           memset( message, 0, 126 );

           result = GetPersonalMessage( message );
           if ( result )
           {
                   printf( "Error getting personal message, code = %X\n",
                   result );
                   exit(1);
           }
           if ( *message )
                   printf( ":> %s\n", message );

           if ( !strcmp( message, "**Other user quit**" ) )
                   Quit( &connection );

           memset( message, 0, 126 );

           if ( bioskey(1) )
           {
                   *message = bioskey(0);

                   if ( message[0] == ESC )
                   {
                           strcpy( message, "**Other user quit**" );
                           SendPersonalMessage( &connection, &status, 1,
                           message );
```

```
                                        if ( result )
                                        {
                                                printf( "Error sending personal message,
                                                        code = %X\n", result );
                                                exit(1);
                                        }
                                        Quit( &connection );
                                }

                                printf( "-%c", *message );
                                gets( &message[1] );
                                SendPersonalMessage( &connection, &status, 1, message );
                                if ( result )
                                {
                                        printf( "Error sending personal message, code =
                                                %X\n", result );
                                        exit(1);
                                }
                        }

        }

}

int GetObjectConnectionNumbers( struct getObjConnReq *Request,
        struct getObjConnRep *Reply )
{
        Request->Length = sizeof( struct getObjConnReq );
        Reply->Length = sizeof( struct getObjConnRep );

        Request->Function = 0x15;

        _AH = 0xE3;
        _SI = (WORD)Request;
        _DI = (WORD)Reply;
        _ES = _DS;

        geninterrupt( 0x21 );

        return _AL;
}

int SendBroadcastMessage( BYTE *Connections, BYTE *Result,
        BYTE NumberOfConnections, BYTE *Message )
{
        BYTE Request[160], Reply[103];
        int i;

        memset( Request, 0, 160 );
        memset( Reply, 0, 103 );

        Request[0] = 160;
        Request[2] = 0;
        Request[3] = NumberOfConnections;
        for ( i = 0; i < NumberOfConnections; i++ )
                Request[4+i] = Connections[i];
        Request[4+i] = strlen( Message );
        strcpy( Request+4+i+1, Message );

        Reply[0] = 103;

        _AH = 0xE1;
```

```
        _SI = (unsigned)Request;
        _DI = (unsigned)Reply;
        _ES = _DS;

        geninterrupt( 0x21 );

        if ( _AL )
                return _AL;

        for ( i = 0; i < NumberOfConnections; i++ )
                Result[i] = Reply[3+i];

        return 0;
}

int PipeFunction( BYTE Function, BYTE *Connections, BYTE *Result,
        BYTE NumberOfConnections )
{
        struct {
                WORD    Length;
                BYTE    Function;
                BYTE    NumberOfConnections;
                BYTE    Connections[100];
        } Request;

        struct {
                WORD    Length;
                BYTE    NumberOfConnections;
                BYTE    Result[100];
        } Reply;

        int i;

        Request.Length = sizeof( Request );
        Request.Function = Function;
        Request.NumberOfConnections = NumberOfConnections;
        for ( i = 0; i < NumberOfConnections; i++ )
                Request.Connections[i] = Connections[i];

        Reply.Length = sizeof( Reply );

        _AH = 0xE1;
        _SI = (unsigned)&Request;
        _DI = (unsigned)&Reply;
        _ES = _DS;

        geninterrupt( 0x21 );

        if ( _AL )
                return _AL;

        for ( i = 0; i < NumberOfConnections; i++ )
                Result[i] = Reply.Result[i];

        return 0;
}

void Quit( BYTE *connection )
{
        BYTE status;

        printf("—Quitting...\n" );
```

```
        PipeFunction( CLOSE_PIPE, connection, &status, 1 );
        exit(1);
}

int GetPersonalMessage( BYTE *Message )
{
        int i;

        struct {
                WORD Length;
                BYTE Function;
        } Request;

        struct {
                WORD Length;
                BYTE SourceConnection;
                BYTE MessageLength;
                BYTE Message[126];
        } Reply;

        memset( &Reply, 0, sizeof( Reply ) );

        Request.Length = sizeof( Request );
        Request.Function = 5;

        Reply.Length = sizeof( Reply );

        _AH = 0xE1;
        _SI = (unsigned)&Request;
        _DI = (unsigned)&Reply;
        _ES = _DS;

        geninterrupt( 0x21 );

        if ( _AL )
                return _AL;

        for ( i = 0; i < Reply.MessageLength; i++ )
                Message[i] = Reply.Message[i];
        Message[i] = NULL;

        return 0;
}

int SendPersonalMessage( BYTE *Connections, BYTE *Result,
        BYTE NumberOfConnections, BYTE *Message )
{
        BYTE Request[231], Reply[103];
        int i;

        memset( Request, 0, 231 );
        memset( Reply, 0, 103 );

        Request[0] = 231;
        Request[2] = 4;
        Request[3] = NumberOfConnections;
        for ( i = 0; i < NumberOfConnections; i++ )
                Request[4+i] = Connections[i];
        Request[4+i] = strlen( Message );
        strcpy( Request+4+i+1, Message );

        Reply[0] = 103;
```

```
    _AH = 0xE1;
    _SI = (unsigned)Request;
    _DI = (unsigned)Reply;
    _ES = _DS;

    geninterrupt( 0x21 );

    if ( _AL )
            return _AL;

    for ( i = 0; i < NumberOfConnections; i++ )
            Result[i] = Reply[3+i];


    return 0;
}
```

Exercises

1. Run PipeChat. How would you improve it? What other API groups would enrich the functionality of the program (other than IPX-SPX calls)?

2. Write an application that uses the Log Network Message command to record useful information. Find another way of implementing the same task without use of this call.

11 Accounting Services

Accounting Services were added to the NetWare APIs with NetWare 2.1. They allow applications to charge for network resources based on such network parameters as time logged in, disk space used, and number of pages printed, or based on such application-defined parameters as the number of reports generated and the number of searches performed.

Although there are only four calls in this API group, they provide a powerful capability for tracking system use. Three Bindery properties are used to determine who can impose charges, what a user's account balance is, and what holds have been placed on a user's account. Other Bindery properties set rates for network resources. And an audit file maintained by the system is also available for the programmer to use. These powerful tools lend themselves to a number of uses.

System resource management

Accounting Services may be used by network administrators to manage and control use of network resources. For example, the manager may wish to track or control the number of disk blocks used by different users. The system administrator may vary charges for different resources, making those that are the most popular "expensive" so that they may be shared more effectively.

Tracking usage by user

These services may be used to maintain an accounting of who is using what, how much, and for how long. A detailed report may be generated by the NetWare PAudit utility, or the developer may construct a different one to suit individual needs.

Time/billing for clients

Law practices or others who need to track system time or other resource use could use Accounting Services with a billing system to track resources spent while working on a particular client's case.

Shared billing

One classic use of Accounting Services is in a multicompany environment or in environments where the cost of the LAN is shared by different entities. Accounting Services can be used to track who is using more of the network, and to what extent.

Installing Accounting Services

Before delving into the programmer's use of Accounting Services, the developer should understand how to install Accounting Services and how to change charge rates.

To install this module, the developer should log in to the file server as the supervisor (or a supervisor-equivalent user), run SysCon and choose the "Accounting" option from the menu. If accounting is not installed, the system will ask whether installation is desired. Choose "Yes" to install Accounting and go to the next menu.

The Accounting Menu shows the Accounting Servers and the rates for the various elements of the network that may be charged for: Blocks Read, Blocks Written, Connect Time, Disk Storage, and Service Requests. For each element the user may specify a charge rate during a particular time for a unit of service.

For instance, under Blocks Read the rate set is for the number of blocks read in a half hour, the standard unit of charge time. As many as 20 different rates may be charged for different times of day and different days of the week. The default for each category is "No Charge" so, until charge rates are added, the file server does not charge users for anything; it does, however, note login and logout times.

SysCon and Accounting Services

When charge rates are set for different services, they are stored in tables accessed by SysCon; a record of each charge is kept in the NET$ACCT.DAT file stored in the SYS:SYSTEM directory. The PAudit utility, also in SYS:SYSTEM, reads the NET$ACCT.DAT file and decodes it to show what was charged to whom for what service, and when.

It is through this mechanism that a file server may charge for services on the LAN. The Accounting Services API was designed to allow applications and custom servers to charge for services in the same way.

Bindery Properties

When installation is complete, the developer must begin to manage the API's Bindery properties. Three Bindery properties are used by the Accounting Services API to store who can make charges to users, what the balance is for each user, and what are the holds placed on each user. These are the ACCOUNT_SERVERS, ACCOUNT_BALANCE, and ACCOUNT_HOLDS properties.

ACCOUNT_SERVERS

This property is created by SysCon when the supervisor chooses to "Install Accounting." The property, when created, is attached to the file server object (object of the same name as the file server of type FILE_SERVER, 4) on the default server. This property contains the Bindery IDs of the objects that are allowed to make charges to users. If a user, supervisor, or value-added server is to impose charges, its Bindery object ID must be in the file server's ACCOUNT_SERVERS property in the Bindery. (Security equivalence applies here, so if an object is security-equivalent to an object in this property, it too can impose charges.)

Access to this set property is supervisor read and write. If a file server does not have this property, the developer should assume that accounting has been disabled for that server.

ACCOUNT_BALANCE

This property is also created by SysCon when Accounting is installed. Each user object is then given this property and new users, when created through SysCon, also are given this property.

This property stores the object's Account Balance and minimum Balance. If an object does not have this property, a server may deny it services.

The structure of the property is:

Offset	Field	Type	Order
0	Balance	LONG	hi-lo
4	Credit Limit	LONG	hi-lo
8	Reserved	BYTE[120]	

Balance contains the account balance for the object. The balance may be positive or negative.

Credit Limit is the minimum balance. As charges are made, the Balance drops. Services that would cause the Balance to drop below this number should be denied. The developer has the option of setting this positive so that some funds are always kept in the account, or allowing this to be negative, letting the user "charge" for services.

The *Reserved* field is for NetWare internal information.

Balances in NetWare are usually in units of money, such as cents. It is important for all applications using the Accounting Services API to be consistent in their treatment of account units.

It is recommended that servers use the Credit Limit field in this property and refuse services to users whose balances have dropped below their credit limits. Services can, however, be performed and charged to users who have a negative Balance (since this uses a signed long). If the programmer wishes to set no Credit Limit, this field should be set to 80000000h (the lowest negative number for a signed long) which would indicate no minimum balance.

ACCOUNT_HOLDS

Generally, before an object is charged for services, a hold is placed against the account for the amount that will be charged. If the hold succeeds, the account has sufficient funds to cover the charge and the resource can be used. Once the actual charge is made, the hold can be removed.

If a hold would cause an account's Balance to fall below the Credit Limit, or if 16 servers already have holds on the account, the hold request fails.

Placing holds on accounts before charging is not required, it is merely provided as a convenience. Another possibility that exists for developers is to check the actual account balance (by reading the value of the ACCOUNT_BALANCE property) before supplying a service. Then, if the balance is below the minimum, the service may be refused.

When a server is disconnected, all of its holds are cleared. The holding server can also clear the hold explicitly. If a server submits more than one hold for a particular object, they accumulate into one larger hold.

This item property is dynamic. Access is object read and supervisor write. The structure of the ACCOUNT_HOLDS property is:

Offset	**Field**	**Type**	**Order**
0	Server 1 Object ID	LONG	hi-lo
4	Server 1 Amount	LONG signed	hi-lo
.			
.			
.			
120	Server 16 Object ID	LONG	hi-lo
124	Server 16 Amount	LONG signed	hi-lo

Object ID is a field containing the object ID of the server placing the hold. If this field is zero, the hold slot is not in use regardless of the contents of the amount field, which contains the amount of the hold.

The audit file: NET$ACCT.DAT

The audit file contains the records of charges written by a file server or by an application using the Accounting Services API. There are two different kinds of records in the file, Charges and Notes.

A Charge record contains information used in submitting a charge to an account (with the Submit Account Charge call) and affects the account balance. A Note (sent with the Submit Account Note call) has no effect on the account balance; it is used only for informing, as in recording the login and logout times for users.

NET$ACCT.DAT is stored in SYS:SYSTEM. Except for being shareable, the file has normal attributes and contains binary information. The PAudit utility takes the information in the Charge and Note structures and prints the contents of the file to the screen.

Charge record structure

Offset	Field	Type	Order
0	Length	WORD	lo-hi
2	Server ID	LONG	hi-lo
6	Time Stamp	BYTE[6]	
12	Record Type	BYTE	
13	Completion Code	BYTE	
14	Service Type	WORD	hi-lo
16	Client ID	LONG	hi-lo
20	Amount	LONG	hi-lo
24	Comment Type	WORD	hi-lo
26	Comment	BYTE[?] - *length dependent on Comment Type*	

Note record structure

Offset	Field	Type	Order
0	Length	WORD	lo-hi
2	Server ID	LONG	hi-lo
6	Time Stamp	BYTE[6]	
12	Record Type	BYTE	
13	Reserved	BYTE	
14	Service Type	WORD	hi-lo
16	Client ID	LONG	hi-lo
20	Comment Type	WORD	hi-lo
22	Comment	BYTE[?] - *length dependent on Comment Type*	

The *Reserved* field is for Novell's use.

Length is the length of the structure minus 2 (its own length, a WORD).

Server ID is the Bindery object ID of the server submitting the charge.

Time Stamp holds the date and time the server submitted the charge. The format is year (where year = current year - 1900), month, day, hour, month, second, where each is a byte-sized integer.

Record Type is 1 for a Charge, 2 for a Note.

Completion Code contains the completion code of the Submit Account Charge call. If the completion code is SUCCESSFUL (0) or CREDIT_EXCEEDED (C2h) the Account Balance is affected.

Service Type signals the specific type of service for which the charge is being made. Novell recommends that external servers use their own standard object types; a file server, for example, should set this field to 0004h. (See chapter 6 for a list of standard object types.) If no appropriate object type exists, it is recommended that the developer contact Novell to get one.

Client ID is the Bindery object ID of the client being charged for the service.

Amount if positive is a charge, if negative a credit.

Comment Type is one of six that are defined by Novell or created by developers, as explained below. This field determines the type of charge and the next field, Comment, actually contains the information relating to the charge.

Comment is an entry that the server makes in the audit record in the SYS:SYSTEM\NET$ACCT.DAT file. It is a "canned" printf() statement associated with a charge or a note. For instance, Comment Type 2 is for charges for disk storage. The associated comment string is: "%lu disk blocks stored for %lu half hours". Comment Type would point to this string and the two long unsigned integers would be stored in the next field.

Types of comments

Comment types are used by Novell to describe the types of charges being made and to provide an efficient method of storage of the accounting data and what it means. Rather than storing the string "10 disk blocks stored for 2 half hours" to the NET$ACCT.DAT file, Accounting Services merely stores the 10, the 2, and a type indicator specifying that the 10 and the 2 are used in the disk block message.

Since there is a file containing the accounting information (including the hypothetical 10 and 2) there is a corresponding file containing the string "%lu disk blocks stored for %lu half hours" and 5 others that pertain to other types of charges. These are stored in the NET$REC.DAT file.

Developers wishing to create their own types (format strings) may do so, but Novell asks that it be allowed to approve the types, reserve them for developers' exclusive use, and publish the types so others don't use different strings for those type numbers.

However, developers wishing to try out different types may use those over 8000h since Novell has set them aside for experimental usage.

What follows is a listing of the six preset Comment Types, followed by the actual structure of the NET$ACCT.DAT file.

Comment Type 1: connect time charge note

This type is recorded by the file server and contains the number of minutes a station was connected to the server, the number of packets that were sent to the server, and the numbers of bytes written to and read from the file server. This type and the next are the only two types the server will make relating to an account charge. The other four types relate to Notes the file server will make regarding login, logout, intruder lockout, and a server time change.

Offset	Field	Type
0	Connect Time	LONG
4	Request Count	LONG
8	Bytes Read Hi	WORD
10	Bytes Read 2	WORD
12	Bytes Read Lo	WORD

14	Bytes Written Hi	WORD
16	Bytes Written 2	WORD
18	Bytes Written Lo	WORD

The format string is: "Connected %lu minutes: %lu requests; %04x%04x%04xh bytes read; %04x%04x%04xh bytes written."

Comment Type 2: disk storage charge note

This type, recorded by the file server, contains the number of blocks owned by an account at the time of the charge and the number of half hours charged.

Offset	Field	Type
0	Blocks Owned	LONG
4	Number of half hours	LONG

The format string is: "%lu disk blocks stored for %lu half hours."

Comment Type 3: login note

This type of comment is recorded by the file server whenever an object successfully logs in. The structure contains the physical address of the station logging in.

Offset	Field	Type
0	Net	LONG
4	Node(high)	LONG
8	Node(low)	WORD

The Node is a six-byte field. The format string is: "Login from address %lx:%lx%lx."

Comment Type 4: logout note

This is the counterpart to the login note and is recorded by the file server when an object logs out. The structure also contains the physical address of the station logging out.

Offset	Field	Type
0	Net	LONG
4	Node(high)	LONG
8	Node(low)	WORD

The format string is: "Logout from address %lx:%lx%lx."

Comment Type 5: account locked note

This comment is recorded by the file server whenever an account is locked because of too many incorrect login attempts (an intruder lockout). The Client field in the Note Record contains the object ID of the object being locked out. The structure of this comment field contains the address where the lockout took place.

Offset	Field	Type
0	Net	LONG
4	Node(high)	LONG
8	Node(low)	WORD

The format string is: "Account intruder lockout caused by address %lx:%lx%lx."

Comment Type 6: server time modified note

This comment is recorded by the file server whenever the server time is changed by a user. The Time Stamp field in the Note Record contains the current time before the change was made and the Client ID contains the object ID of the object that changed the time. This structure contains the new date and time.

Offset	Field	Type
0	Year since 1900	BYTE
1	Month	BYTE
2	Day	BYTE
3	Hour	BYTE
4	Minute	BYTE
5	Second	BYTE

The format string is: "System time changed to 19%02d-%02d-%02d %d:%02d:%02d."

Comment record definitions

The format strings for comments are stored in the NET$REC.DAT file in the SYS:SYSTEM directory. The file is flagged Shareable Read-Only. The file holds binary records containing format strings associated with various comment types that are used in the Charge and Note records that the API programmer or the file server can make.

Developers may use this file to print out the current accounting data in NET$ACCT.DAT and NET$REC.DAT by using the following procedure:

1. Read the next record from NET$ACCT.DAT.
2. Use the Comment Type field as an index to read NET$REC.DAT.
3. Display to screen, using NET$REC.DAT format string in a printf() statement, passing the individual fields in the Comment field of NET$ACCT.DAT.
4. Go to step 1.

Also, the NET$REC.DAT field may be supplemented with custom Comment Types. Novell recommends using types over 8000h for experimental purposes, but registering types below 8000h with Novell. The structure of the NET$REC.DAT file is:

Offset	Field	Type
0	Length	WORD
2	Comment Type	WORD
4	Field Count	BYTE
5	Data Type	BYTE[?]
.		
.		
.		
?	Format Length	BYTE
/	Format String	char[?]

Here *Length* contains the length of the record not including the Length field itself. The formula for the length is Field Count + Format Length + 4.

Field Count contains the number of fields in this type of record.

Data Type contains the data types of the record. Data types larger than a LONG should be described as series of BYTE, WORD, and LONG fields. Valid types are:

Value	Type
1 (BYTE)	An 8-bit value
2 (WORD)	A 16-bit value, hi-lo order
3 (LONG)	A 32-bit value, hi-lo order
4 (TEXT)	A length byte followed by a string of printable characters

Format Length contains the length of the format control string used to print the comment records associated with the Charge or Note Record. It contains printf()-style format expressions. The program that displays the string converts numeric fields to low-high order before running the display routine, for example, "Physical Address: %lx:%lx%x". The fields in that record are LONG, LONG and WORD. A C program might print the record with:

```
printf( formatString, LongSwap( field1 ), LongSwap( field2 ),
        IntSwap( field3 ) );
```

LongSwap() and IntSwap() in this example convert hi-lo to lo-hi format.

File server charges

File servers may make charges to accounts based on five parameters: connection time, blocks read, blocks written, disk storage, and requests made. The rates for these services may be set through SysCon, but they are saved in Bindery properties under the file server object. These rate properties may be queried or modified by the supervisor. The amount of the charges may be changed every half hour for each day of the week.

The first four properties--CONNECT_TIME, REQUESTS_MADE, BLOCKS_READ and BLOCKS_WRITTEN--have identical structures. The last property, DISK_STORAGE, has a unique structure.

CONNECT_TIME

This property determines the amount the file server will charge for connect time, measured from login to logout. The account is checked each half hour to see if the object still has sufficient funds to cover the charges being made. If the Account Balance falls below the Credit Limit, the user is disconnected after being given 5-minute and 1-minute warnings.

REQUESTS_MADE

This property determines the amount the file server will charge for individual requests made to the file server. After logging out, the user is charged for the total number of requests made to the file server since logging in. Like the CONNECT_TIME property, the Account Balance is checked every half hour for sufficient funds. Objects with Balances below the minimum are logged out following 5-minute and 1-minute warnings.

BLOCKS_READ and BLOCKS_WRITTEN

These two properties determine the rates for reading or writing a block of data (4096 bytes). After logging out, the user is charged for the total number of blocks read and written. Like the other properties, the Account Balance is checked every half hour for sufficient funds. Objects with Balances below the minimum are logged out following 5-minute and 1-minute warnings.

DISK_STORAGE

This property determines the amount the file server will charge for disk storage. To compute the charge: Total disk storage for each user is calculated; total disk storage is multiplied by the number of half hours since the last disk storage charge was made; and the result is multiplied by the current charge rate.

Unlike the other charges, the list of times and the charge rates in this property includes a specific time a charge is imposed as well as a specific rate for the charge.

Structures of the properties

CONNECT_TIME, REQUESTS_MADE, BLOCKS_READ, and BLOCKS_WRITTEN have the following structure.

Offset	Field	Type	Order
0	Time of Next Charge	LONG	hi-lo
4	Current Charge Rate Multiplier	WORD	hi-lo
6	Current Charge Rate Divisor	WORD	hi-lo

8	Days Charge Occurs Mask 1	BYTE	
9	Time Charge Occurs 1	BYTE	
10	Charge Rate Multiplier 1	WORD	hi-lo
12	Charge Rate Divisor 1	WORD	hi-lo
.			
.			
.			
122	Days Charge Occurs Mask 20	BYTE	
123	Time Charge Occurs 20	BYTE	
124	Charge Rate Multiplier 20	WORD	hi-lo
126	Charge Rate Divisor 20	WORD	hi-lo

Time of Next Charge contains the time of the next charge, measured in minutes since January 1, 1985.

Current Charge Rate Multiplier and Divisor fields contain the Current Charge Rate Multiplier and Divisor. The charge is computed as follows: The unit of service (connect time, requests made, blocks read or written) is multiplied by the Current Charge Rate Multiplier; the resulting value is divided by the Current Charge Rate Divisor to give the charge made against the user's account.

Days Charge Occurs Mask is a field that contains a bit mask that specifies the days of the week for which the charge rate applies. If the bit corresponding to the day of the week is set (bit 0 = Sunday, bit 6 = Saturday) the charge is made during that day at the half hour specified in Time Charge Occurs. If this field is 0, no charges are made.

The *Time Charge Occurs* field contains the half hour (12am = 0, 11:30pm = 47) during which the specified charge rate takes effect. These changes in the charge rate are listed in this property structure according to increasing half hours.

Charge Rate Multiplier and Divisor fields contain the charge rate that takes effect at the specified time.

The DISK_STORAGE property structure is:

Offset	**Field**	**Type**	**Order**
0	Time of Next Charge	LONG	hi-lo
4	Time of Previous Charge	LONG	hi-lo
8	Days Charge Occurs Mask 1	BYTE	
9	Time Charge Occurs 1	BYTE	
10	Charge Rate Multiplier 1	WORD	hi-lo
12	Charge Rate Divisor 1	WORD	hi-lo
.			
.			
.			
122	Days Charge Occurs Mask 20	BYTE	
123	Time Charge Occurs 20	BYTE	
124	Charge Rate Multiplier 20	WORD	hi-lo
126	Charge Rate Divisor 20	WORD	hi-lo

Time of Previous Charge contains the time of the previous charge, measured in minutes since January 1, 1985.

The *Charge Rate Multiplier and Divisor* fields contain the charge rate used to calculate the disk storage charge at the specified half hour on the specified days. The charge is computed as follows: The current disk storage for each user is calculated in 4K blocks; current disk storage is multiplied by the number of half hours since the last disk storage charge was made; and the result is multiplied by the charge rate multiplier and divided by the charge rate divisor to produce the final disk storage charge.

Calls in the Accounting Services API

All of the Accounting Services API calls are supported in Advanced NetWare version 2.1, NetWare 386, and later versions.

Throughout the book, we explain fields within the calls only at the first mention of each field in each chapter. Appendix B contains a comprehensive, alphabetical listing of the fields for quick reference.

Get Account Status (E3h 96h)

This function returns the account status of a Bindery object.

Registers in:

AH	E3h
DS:SI	Request Buffer Address
ES:DI	Reply Buffer Address

Registers out:

AL	Completion Code

Completion codes:

00h	Successful
C0h	No Account Privileges
C1h	No Account Balance

Request Buffer (maximum buffer length = 54 bytes):

Offset	Content	Type	Order
0	Request Buffer Length-2	WORD	lo-hi
2	96h	BYTE	
3	Bindery Object Type	WORD	hi-lo
5	Object Name Length (1 to 48)	BYTE	
6	Bindery Object Name	BYTE[*LENGTH*]	

Reply Buffer (258 bytes):

Offset	Content	Type	Order
0	Reply Buffer Length-2	WORD	lo-hi
2	Account Balance	LONG	hi-lo
6	Credit Limit	LONG	hi-lo
10	Reserved[120]	BYTE	
130	Server1 (ObjectID)	LONG	hi-lo
134	Server1 (Amount)	LONG	hi-lo
.			
.			
.			
248	Server 16 (Object ID)	LONG	hi-lo
252	Server 16 (Amount)	LONG	hi-lo

The function returns the object's Account Balance and Credit Limit. It also returns a list of the servers that have issued Submit Account Hold calls against the object, and the amount that each account server has reserved.

The NetWare C Interface format is:

```
int GetAccountStatus( WORD BinderyObjectType, char *BinderyObjectName,
  long *balance, long *limit, long *holds );
```

Submit Account Hold (E3h 98h)

This function reserves a certain amount of an object's Account Balance pending a Submit Account Charge call.

Registers in:

AH	E3h
DS:SI	Request Buffer Address
ES:DI	Reply Buffer Address

Registers out:

AL	Completion Code

Completion codes:

00h	Successful
C0h	No Account Privileges
C1h	No Account Balance
C2h	Account Credit Limit Exceeded
C3h	Account Too Many Holds

Request Buffer (maximum buffer length = 58 bytes):

Offset	Content	Type	Order
0	Request Buffer Length-2	WORD	lo-hi
2	98h	BYTE	
3	Reserve Amount	LONG	hi-lo
7	Bindery Object Type	WORD	hi-lo
9	Object Name Length (1 to 48)	BYTE	
10	Bindery Object Name	BYTE[*LENGTH*]	

Reply Buffer (2 bytes):

Offset	Content	Type	Order
0	0000h	WORD	lo-hi

This function reserves a specified amount of an object's Account Balance before the object receives a service on the network and a charge for the service.

The *Reserve Amount* is the amount that the account server expects to charge for the service it is about to provide to the object. No more than 16 different servers can reserve amounts of an object's Account Balance at one time. The server combines multiple holds from the same server.

The NetWare C Interface format is:

```
int SubmitAccountHold( WORD BinderyObjectType,
   char *BinderyObjectName, long reserveAmount );
```

Submit Account Charge (E3h 97h)

This function updates the account of a Bindery object.

Registers in:

AH	E3h
DS:SI	Request Buffer Address
ES:DI	Reply Buffer Address

Registers out:

AL	Completion Code

Completion codes:

00h	Successful
C0h	No Account Privileges
C1h	No Account Balance
C2h	Credit Limit Exceeded

Request Buffer (maximum buffer length = 322):

Offset	Content	Type	Order
0	Request Buffer Length-2	WORD	lo-hi
2	97h	BYTE	
3	Service Type	WORD	hi-lo

5	Charge Amount	LONG	hi-lo
9	Cancel Hold Amount	LONG	hi-lo
13	Bindery Object Type	WORD	hi-lo
15	Comment Type	WORD	hi-lo
17	Object Name Length (1 to 48)	BYTE	
18	Bindery Object Name	BYTE[*LENGTH*]	
?	Comment Length (0 to 255)	BYTE	
?	Comment	BYTE[*LENGTH*]	

Reply Buffer (2 bytes)

Offset	**Content**	**Type**	**Order**
0	0000h	WORD	lo-hi

This call allows a server to submit a charge to a client account. The charge is subtracted from the client object's Account Balance, and an audit record is generated.

Cancel Hold Amount should be the same as the amount specified in the corresponding Submit Account Hold call. If no Submit Account Hold call was made prior to providing the service, the hold amount should be zero. A hold cancel amount of zero has no effect on other outstanding holds by the server.

Charge Amount is the amount the server charges for the service it provides.

The *Bindery Object Type* identifies the type of Bindery object whose account is to be updated. The object type WILD (FFFFh) cannot be used with this function.

The NetWare C Interface format is:

```
int SubmitAccountCharge( WORD BinderyObjectType,
   char *BinderyObjectName, WORD serviceType, long chargeAmount,
   long cancelHoldAmount, WORD commentType, char *comment );
```

Submit Account Note (E3h 99h)

This function adds a note about an object's account into an audit file on the file server.

Registers in:

AH	E3h
DS:SI	Request Buffer Address
ES:DI	Reply Buffer Address

Registers out:

AL	Completion Code

Completion codes:

00h	Successful
C0h	No Account Privileges

Request Buffer (maximum buffer length = 314):

Offset	Content	Type	Order
0	Request Buffer Length	WORD	lo-hi
2	99h	BYTE	
3	Service Type	WORD	hi-lo
5	Bindery Object Type	WORD	hi-lo
7	Comment Type	WORD	hi-lo
9	Object Name Length	BYTE	
10	Bindery Object Name (1 to 48)	BYTE[*LENGTH*]	
?	Comment Length (0 to 255)	BYTE	
?	Comment	BYTE[*LENGTH*]	

Reply Buffer (2 bytes)

Offset	Content	Type	Order
0	0000h	WORD	lo-hi

This function adds a note about an accounting transaction to an audit record. The audit record is placed in a file called NET$ACCT.DAT located in the SYS:SYSTEM directory.

The NetWare C Interface format is:

```
int SubmitAccountNote( WORD BinderyObjectType,
   char *BinderyObjectName, WORD serviceType, WORD commentType,
   char *comment );
```

Code Sample: TestAcct.C

TestAcct shows how the Accounting Services may be used to set up initial Account Balances and make charges to accounts. The program uses the Bindery and Accounting Services to first set a user's (here the supervisor's) Balance to $50.00 and the Credit Limit to -$10.00. This means that there is initially $50.00 in the account to spend and the minimum balance of the account is -$10.00 which gives the user a line of "credit" if the Balance drops below $0.00.

The program first declares the structures that will be used: the request and reply packets for Get Account Status, and the Submit Account Charge packet. The function prototypes follow, just before the main() function begins. The code itself takes the form of several steps that set up the account and make a charge for the current user. The program was written for the supervisor to be logged in since it will be making the charge to itself.

The steps taken by TestAcct are:

1. Add the current logged-in user (supervisor) to the ACCOUNT_SERVERS property in the Bindery. This is done so that the supervisor can make charges. When accounting is installed, only the server it was installed on can make charges to users on that server. If an object will be making charges, its ID must be placed in this set

property. The Add Bindery Object To Set call (a Bindery Services call) is used to add the supervisor's object ID to the ACCOUNT_SERVERS property.

2. Set the current Balance and Credit Limit for the current user. We accomplish this by first reading the property, using the Read Property Value call. Next the Balance (the first four bytes) and the Credit Limit (the next four bytes) are set to their respective values. Finally, the Balance is written back using the Write Property Value call. This read-modify-write cycle can be used if the Balance or Credit Limit needs to be modified (such as in a 10% reduction). We use the cycle in this instance because it preserves any information that may be needed by NetWare in the rest of the 128-byte value.

3. Check the account status of the current user. The Status Request packet is set up with the supervisor's Object Type and Name and Get Account Status is called.

4. Submit an account charge to the current user. The Charge Request structure is filled in with information about the amount of the charge, who's making the charge (supervisor) and the type of charge. In this case, we're simulating a charge for disk storage.

5. Check the account status again to make sure the charge was imposed. This is the same as step 3.

```
/*                                                                     */
/* TestAcct - Tests the Accounting Services API by sending charges     */
/*              for the supervisor to the file server                  */
/*                                                                     */
/* by Charles Rose                                                     */
/*                                                                     */

#include <stdio.h>
#include <dos.h>
#include <dir.h>
#include <string.h>

#define USER 0x0100
#define FILE_SERVER 0x0400

typedef unsigned char BYTE;
typedef unsigned int WORD;
typedef unsigned long LONG;

struct getAcctStatusReq {
    WORD     Length;
    BYTE     Function;
    WORD     ObjectType;
    BYTE     ObjectNameLength;
    BYTE     ObjectName[48];
};

struct hold {
    LONG     ObjectID;
    long     Amount;
```

```
};

struct getAcctStatusRep {
    WORD            Length;
    long            AcctBalance;
    long            CreditLimit;
    BYTE            Reserved[120];
    struct hold     Holds[16];
};

struct submitChargeReq {
    WORD     Length;
    BYTE     Function;
    WORD     ServiceType;
    long     ChargeAmount;
    long     CancelHoldAmount;
    WORD     ObjectType;
    WORD     CommentType;
    BYTE     ObjectNameLength;
    BYTE     ObjectName[48];
    BYTE     CommentLength;
    BYTE     Comment[254];
};

long LongSwap( long num );
int GetAccountStatus( struct getAcctStatusReq *Request,
   struct getAcctStatusRep *Reply );
int SubmitAccountCharge( struct submitChargeReq *Request );
int AddBinderyObjectToSet( char *ObjectName, WORD ObjectType,
   char *PropertyName, WORD MemberType, char *MemberName );
void Error( char *description, int code );
int ReadPropertyValue( char *objectName, WORD objectType, char *propertyName,
   char *propValue );
int WritePropertyValue( char *objectName, WORD objectType, char *propertyName,
   char *propValue );

main()
{
    int result;
    struct getAcctStatusReq StatusRequest;
    struct getAcctStatusRep StatusReply;
    struct submitChargeReq ChargeRequest;
    char propValue[128];

    /* Initialize Request/Reply packets to 0                                */
    memset( &StatusRequest, NULL, sizeof( struct getAcctStatusReq ) );
    memset( &StatusReply, NULL, sizeof( struct getAcctStatusRep ) );
    memset( &ChargeRequest, NULL, sizeof( struct submitChargeReq ) );

    /* ------------------------------                                       */
    /*  Step 1: Add the current logged in user (Supervisor) to the          */
    /*          ACCOUNT_SERVERS property in the bindery                     */
    /* ------------------------------                                       */

    printf( "Now adding user SUPERVISOR to ACCOUNT_SERVERS property...\n" );

    result = AddBinderyObjectToSet( "ROSEWARE", FILE_SERVER, "ACCOUNT_SERVERS",
                USER, "SUPERVISOR" );

    if ( result && ( result != 0xE9 ) )
         Error( "Error adding value to ACCOUNT_SERVERS property", result );
```

```
/* ——————————————————————————                              */
/*  Step 2: Set the current balance and the credit limit for */
/*          the current user (Supervisor)                   */
/* ——————————————————————————                              */

printf( "Now setting balance to $50 and credit limit to $-10...\n" );

result = ReadPropertyValue( "SUPERVISOR", USER, "ACCOUNT_BALANCE", propValue );
if ( result && ( result != 0xE9 ) )
        Error( "Error adding value to ACCOUNT_SERVERS property", result );

*( (long *) propValue ) = LongSwap( (long)5000 );
/* Set balance to $50                                       */
*( (long *) propValue + 1 ) = LongSwap( (long)-1000 );
/* Set credit limit to -$10                                 */

result = WritePropertyValue( "SUPERVISOR", USER, "ACCOUNT_BALANCE", propValue );
if ( result && ( result != 0xE9 ) )
        Error( "Error adding value to ACCOUNT_SERVERS property", result );

/* ——————————————————————————                              */
/*  Step 3: Check the account status of the current user    */
/*          (Supervisor)                                    */
/* ——————————————————————————                              */
StatusRequest.ObjectType = USER;
StatusRequest.ObjectNameLength = strlen( "SUPERVISOR" );
strcpy( StatusRequest.ObjectName, "SUPERVISOR" );

result = GetAccountStatus( &StatusRequest, &StatusReply );
if ( result == 0xC0 )
        Error( "No Account Privileges", result);

if ( result == 0xC1 )
        Error( "No Account Balance", result );

printf( "Your Account Balance is $%.2f  Credit Limit is $%.2f\n",
        ((float)(LongSwap( StatusReply.AcctBalance )) / (float)100),
        ((float)(LongSwap( StatusReply.CreditLimit )) / (float)100) );

/* ——————————————————————————                              */
/*  Step 4: Submit an account charge to the current user    */
/*          (Supervisor)                                    */
/* ——————————————————————————                              */
ChargeRequest.ServiceType = FILE_SERVER;
ChargeRequest.ChargeAmount = LongSwap( 500 );      /* Charge $5.00 */
ChargeRequest.CancelHoldAmount = 0;
ChargeRequest.ObjectNameLength = 48;
strcpy( ChargeRequest.ObjectName, "SUPERVISOR" );
ChargeRequest.ObjectType = USER;
ChargeRequest.CommentType = 0x0200;
/* Type 2: Disk storage                                     */
ChargeRequest.CommentLength = 8;
*( (long *) ChargeRequest.Comment ) = LongSwap( 100  );
/* Charge for 100 disk blocks                               */
*( (long *) ChargeRequest.Comment + 1 ) = LongSwap( 2 );
/* stored for 2 half-hour periods                           */

result = SubmitAccountCharge( &ChargeRequest );
if ( result == 0xC0 )
        Error( "No Account Privileges", result );
```

```
    if ( result == 0xC1 )
            Error( "No Account Balance", result );

    if ( result == 0xC2 )
            Error( "Credit Limit Exceeded", result );

    printf( "Successful charge sent.\n" );

    /* ----------------------------------                                   */
    /*  Step 5: Check the account status of the current user              */
    /*          (Supervisor)                                                */
    /* ----------------------------------                                   */
    result = GetAccountStatus( &StatusRequest, &StatusReply );
    if ( result == 0xC0 )
            Error( "No Account Privileges", result);

    if ( result == 0xC1 )
            Error( "No Account Balance", result );

    printf( "Your Account Balance is $%.2f  Credit Limit is $%.2f\n",
            ((float)(LongSwap( StatusReply.AcctBalance )) / (float)100),
            ((float)(LongSwap( StatusReply.CreditLimit )) / (float)100) );
}

long LongSwap( long num )
{
    long temp;

    temp = ( num & 0xFF000000 ) >> 24;
    temp += ( num & 0xFF0000 ) >> 8;
    temp += ( num & 0xFF00 ) << 8;
    temp += ( num & 0xFF ) << 24;

    return temp;
}

int GetAccountStatus( struct getAcctStatusReq *Request,
    struct getAcctStatusRep *Reply )
{
    Request->Length = sizeof( struct getAcctStatusReq ) - 2;
    Request->Function = 0x96;
    Reply->Length = sizeof( struct getAcctStatusRep ) - 2;

    _AH = 0xE3;
    _SI = (unsigned)Request;
    _DI = (unsigned)Reply;
    _ES = _DS;

    geninterrupt( 0x21 );

    return _AL;
}

int SubmitAccountCharge( struct submitChargeReq *Request )
{
    int Reply = 0;

    Request->Length = sizeof( struct submitChargeReq ) - 2;
    Request->Function = 0x97;

    _AH = 0xE3;
```

```
    _SI = (unsigned)Request;
    _DI = (unsigned)&Reply;
    _ES = _DS;

    geninterrupt( 0x21 );

    return _AL;
}

int AddBinderyObjectToSet( char *ObjectName, WORD ObjectType,
    char *PropertyName, WORD MemberType, char *MemberName )
{
    BYTE Request[119];
    int Reply = 0;

    memset( Request, NULL, 119 );

    Request[0] = sizeof( Request );
    Request[2] = 0x41;
    *( (WORD *) (Request + 3) ) = ObjectType;
    Request[5] = 48;
    strcpy( Request + 6, ObjectName );
    Request[54] = 15;
    strcpy( Request + 55, PropertyName );
    *( (WORD *) (Request + 70 ) ) = MemberType;
    Request[72] = 48;
    strcpy( Request + 73, MemberName );

    _AH = 0xE3;
    _SI = (unsigned)Request;
    _DI = (unsigned)&Reply;
    _ES = _DS;

    geninterrupt( 0x21 );

    return _AL;
}

void Error( char *description, int code )
{
    printf( "%s. Completion Code = %X\n", description, code );
    exit(1);
}

int ReadPropertyValue( char *objectName, WORD objectType, char *propertyName,
   char *propValue )
{
    struct {
            WORD Length;
            BYTE Function;
            WORD ObjectType;
            BYTE ObjectNameLength;
            BYTE ObjectName[48];
            BYTE SegmentNumber;
            BYTE PropertyNameLength;
            BYTE PropertyName[16];
    } Request;

    struct {
            WORD Length;
            BYTE PropValue[128];
            BYTE MoreSegments;
            BYTE PropertyFlags;
    } Reply;
```

```
    memset( &Request, 0, sizeof( Request ) );
    memset( &Reply, 0, sizeof( Reply ) );

    Request.Length = sizeof( Request ) - 2;
    Request.Function = 0x3D;
    Request.ObjectType = objectType;
    Request.ObjectNameLength = 48;
    strcpy( Request.ObjectName, objectName );
    Request.SegmentNumber = 1;
    Request.PropertyNameLength = 16;
    strcpy( Request.PropertyName, propertyName );

    Reply.Length = sizeof( Reply ) - 2;

    _AH = 0xE3;
    _SI = (unsigned)&Request;
    _DI = (unsigned)&Reply;
    _ES = _DS;

    geninterrupt( 0x21 );

    if ( _AL )
            return _AL;

    memcpy( propValue, Reply.PropValue, 128 );

    return 0;
}

int WritePropertyValue( char *objectName, WORD objectType, char *propertyName,
    char *propValue )
{
    struct {
            WORD Length;
            BYTE Function;
            WORD ObjectType;
            BYTE ObjectNameLength;
            BYTE ObjectName[48];
            BYTE SegmentNumber;
            BYTE EraseRemaining;
            BYTE PropertyNameLength;
            BYTE PropertyName[16];
            BYTE PropertyValue[128];
    } Request;

    int Reply = 0;

    memset( &Request, 0, sizeof( Request ) );

    Request.Length = sizeof( Request ) - 2;
    Request.Function = 0x3E;
    Request.ObjectType = objectType;
    Request.ObjectNameLength = 48;
    strcpy( Request.ObjectName, objectName );
    Request.SegmentNumber = 1;
    Request.EraseRemaining = 0;
    Request.PropertyNameLength = 16;
    strcpy( Request.PropertyName, propertyName );
    memcpy( Request.PropertyValue, propValue, 128 );
```

```
    _AH = 0xE3;
    _SI = (unsigned)&Request;
    _DI = (unsigned)&Reply;
    _ES = _DS;

    geninterrupt( 0x21 );

    return _AL;
}
```

Exercises

1. Run the above program. Experiment with different Comment Types, Credit Limits, and other fields.

2. Run the Novell PAudit and Atotal utilities while logged in as the supervisor in the SYS:SYSTEM directory.

3. One of the issues facing users of the accounting services is how to manage the NET$ACCT.DAT file in SYS:SYSTEM. It accumulates all of the accounting data ad nauseum. Devise a way of archiving old data so the file does not grow to immense proportions.

4. Write a program using the accounting services; submit a hold on a user's account, allow the user to perform certain actions and charge for them, and submit notes to the NET$ACCT.DAT file as a test. Figure how an application could take the best advantage of this network resource.

12 AppleTalk Filing Protocol

One of the additions of NetWare 2.15 was compatibility with the Apple Macintosh computer. Novell NetWare file servers running NetWare 2.15 and later can now have Macs running as workstations on the network. The Macs can log in to file servers as well as write and read files; in other words, Macs now have available the same network resources as do IBM PC-compatible workstations.

The AppleTalk Filing Protocol (AFP) governs how the Macintosh computer stores files. For networks to support the Mac, a file server (or bridge) must be running the appropriate Novell Macintosh VAPs (value-added processes). These VAPs act as converters between NetWare and AFP. Since AFP files and DOS files have different formats, the directory structure has been expanded to include both. The VAP acts as a Service Protocol Gateway, saving Mac files so that DOS computers can read them and giving the Mac access to DOS files.

The AFP Services allow the developer to manipulate files created in the AFP environment — to open, create, delete, rename or get information about those files. AFP Services are probably most helpful for those with applications that must manipulate large quantities of files and need to be AFP-aware so no information is lost. (Using normal DOS calls to copy an AFP file would result in data loss.)

Is AFP supported?

Since AFP was brought to the programming arena fairly recently, prudent developers should check whether AFP is supported on their workstations. Support for AFP is tested for in two ways: checking the workstation and checking the file server. First, the version of the shell is checked using the Workstation Services call Get Shell Version Information. This call returns the version of the shell which should be at least version 2.15.

Next, the server is checked by executing an AFP call to see if it will be successful. In the following code, we use AFP Get Entry ID From Path Name which returns an AFP handle, given a path. We pass "SYS:" and check the completion code for success (0). If the call was successful and the shell version is 2.15 or later, then AFP is supported in this workstation/server environment.

```
int AFPSupported( void )
{
   BYTE major, minor, rev;
   int result;
   long AFPEntryID;

   GetShellVersionInformation( &major, &minor, &rev );

   result = AFPGetEntryIDFromPathName( 0, "SYS:", &AFPEntryID );

   /* If AFPGetEntryIDFromPathName() call worked, and the    */
   /* shell is version 2.15 or higher, then return TRUE (1) */
   if ( !result && ( major > 2 || ( ( major == 2 ) && ( minor >= 15 ) ) ) )
    return 1;
   else
        return 0;
}
```

Data forks and resource forks

Data forks are slots in the directory table where NetWare stores information about the data portion of a file. DOS files have only data forks. AFP files also require resource forks which store information about the icons, executable code, and other resources peculiar to the Mac. Resource forks can be thought of as a "shadow directory," to the regular DOS directory.

Data forks can be managed by DOS and resource forks are created and managed by AFP. It is when Macs try to read DOS files and DOS computers try to read AFP files that more steps are needed.

When a Macintosh asks for a DOS file, it assigns a default icon to that file denoting that the file was created in DOS.

The Mac VAP in the file server automatically creates a resource fork for each DOS file that is opened on a Mac. This resource fork is set to null. Macs recognize this as a DOS file and use a standard icon to represent it in the "folder" or Apple file directory. Without the resource fork, even a null one, the Mac would not place the file in the folder.

So there is no work that must be done by the developer to make Macs aware of DOS files, because that is done automatically by the VAP. However, manipulation of existing files requires AFP calls; using DOS calls loses the resource forks associated with the files. For instance, copying file A to drive B and back using DOS calls would not copy the resource fork along with the data. AFP calls must be used to preserve the Apple-specific information.

AFP paths

The Apple computers provide more flexibility than DOS computers when it comes to naming files. Files may have up to 31 characters in their names and these may include any keyboard character except the colon ":". Macintosh file paths use the first character to represent the length of the path and use nulls instead of backslashes "\" to separate directories and file names.

The following are a normal DOS path string and an AFP path string:

```
DOS          SYS:DATA\COMMON\TEST.WP
AFP          #SYS:DATA0COMMON0TEST.WP
```

Here the pound sign # represents the length of the string (23).

Novell suggests that, if the command line is to specify an AFP path string, each element of the command line be iteratively added to the AFP path since the path is retrieved argv[1], argv[2], etc. The following code fragment shows how this may be accomplished:

```
strcpy( AFPPathString + 1, argv[1] );
for ( j = 2; j < argc; j++ )
{
     strcat( AFPPathString+1, "\0" );
     strcat( AFPPathString+1, argv[j] );
}
AFPPathString[0] = strlen( AFPPathString+1 );
```

The long and short of filenames

DOS uses what we will call a short name (eight characters, a dot and an optional three-character extension) for filenames. AFP uses 1-31 character names that may use any character except the colon ":". Thus some conversion is needed to transform an Apple filename to a DOS filename. The following illustrates the process of name conversion:

Apple "long" filename: TEST OF ACCOUNTING DATA
DOS "short" filename: TESTOFAC

The spaces are removed, eight characters are added and no extension is made. If there is a period in the first nine characters of the name, the first eight characters are placed before a period and the first three are added after the period, excluding other periods. The following example shows this rule:

Apple "long" filename: TEST.OF.ACCOUNTING.DATA
DOS "short" filename: TEST.OF

If there are two files with the same DOS "short" name for a file, the file server will create the next file with a number as the last character. For example:

Apple "long" filename: TEST OF ACCOUNTING DATA
Apple "long" filename: TEST OF ACCOUNTING STUFF

The first file would be named TESTOFAC and the second would be named TESTOFA1. If the second file were to be copied to a different directory or to a floppy, the 1 would be removed and the name would be restored to TESTOFAC since no conflict would occur; however the resource fork would not be transferred to the floppy.

AFP calls require long names for AFP Directory Path strings. AFP long names must be used with AFP Entry ID's only, just as DOS short names should be used exclusively with DOS or NetWare file handles. The only exception to this is when you need to specify a long name for a file that was created in DOS. In this case the short filename is identical to the long name.

Macintosh Finder information

The Finder (and System) are the equivalent of DOS on the Mac, providing not only management of the filing system, but also a graphical user interface, among other features. Files are represented by icons on the "desktop" and directories are shown as folders. To be represented on the desktop, directories and files on the file servers must have associated Finder information.

AFP directory entries

The AFP Directory Entry call should be used when opening AFP files to determine whether AFP-specific information is available for the target entity. If it does have AFP characteristics, then these AFP calls should be used to access it.

The AFP Rename call is useful for moving and renaming directory entries. One powerful operation inherent in this call is that it allows a DOS program to move large directory tree structures with one call, a feature that is quite simple in the Macintosh graphical environment. When a program specifies in a destination path a parent directory different from the one in the source path, the source directory and all of its files and subdirectories will be immediately moved.

Calls in the AFP Services API

All of the AFP Services API calls are supported in Advanced NetWare version 2.1, NetWare 386, and later versions.

Throughout the book, we explain fields within the calls only at the first mention of each field in each chapter. Appendix B contains a comprehensive, alphabetical listing of the fields for quick reference.

AFP Create Directory (F2h 01h)

This call creates a directory with an AFP directory name.

Registers in:

AL	23h
DS:SI	Request Buffer Address
CX	Request Buffer Length

ES:DI	Reply Buffer Address
DX	Reply Buffer Length
AH	F2h

Registers out:

AL	Completion Code

Completion codes:

0h	Successful
9Ch	Invalid Path

Request Buffer (maximum buffer length = 297 bytes):

Offset	**Content**	**Type**	**Order**
0	Request Buffer Length	WORD	lo-hi
2	01h	BYTE	
3	Volume Number	BYTE	
4	AFP Entry ID	LONG	hi-lo
8	Reserved	BYTE	
9	Finder Information	BYTE[32]	
41	AFP Directory Path Length	BYTE (0-255)	
42	AFP Directory Path	BYTE[*LENGTH*]	

Reply Buffer (4 bytes):

Offset	**Content**	**Type**	**Order**
0	New AFP Entry ID	LONG	hi-lo

A four-byte *AFP Entry ID* is the Apple equivalent of a NetWare directory handle, with one exception: A NetWare directory handle points to a file server volume or directory and an AFP entry ID points to a file server volume, directory, or file.

Finder Information should be initialized to all zeros.

AFP Directory Path specifies at least the target AFP directory name, and optionally the names of one or more parent directories. The field is 1 to 255 bytes long.

New AFP Entry ID is an AFP entry ID that points to the newly created AFP directory.

The NetWare C Interface format is:

```
int AFPCreateDirectory( WORD connectionID, int volumeNum,
   long AFPEntryID, BYTE *finderInfo, char *AFPPathString,
   long *newAFPEntryID );
```

AFP Create File (F2h 02h)

This call creates a file with an AFP file name.

Registers in:

AL	23h
DS:SI	Request Buffer Address
CX	Request Buffer Length
ES:DI	Reply Buffer Address
DX	Reply Buffer Length
AH	F2h

Registers out:

AL	Completion Code

Completion codes:

00h	Successful
9Ch	Invalid Path

Request Buffer (maximum buffer length = 297 bytes):

Offset	Content	Type	Order
0	Request Buffer Length - 2	WORD	lo-hi
2	02h	BYTE	
3	Volume Number	BYTE	
4	AFP Entry ID	LONG	hi-lo
8	Delete Existing File	BYTE	
9	Finder Information	BYTE[32]	
41	AFP File Path Length	BYTE (0-255)	
42	AFP File Path	BYTE[*LENGTH*]	

Reply Buffer (4 bytes):

Offset	Content	Type	Order
0	New AFP Entry ID	LONG	hi-lo

The resulting file is not opened. The call creates a normal read-write file with system and hidden bits cleared.

Delete Existing File indicates whether the call deletes the specified file (00h = do not delete; 01h = delete).

The NetWare C Interface format is:

```
int AFPCreateFile( WORD connectionID, int volumeNum, long AFPEntryID,
  BYTE deleteExistingFile, BYTE *finderInfo, char *AFPPathString,
  long *newAFPEntryID );
```

AFP Delete (F2h 03h)

This call deletes the specified file or directory.

Registers in:

AL	23h
DS:SI	Request Buffer Address
CX	Request Buffer Length
AH	F2h

Registers out:

AL	Completion Code

Request Buffer (maximum buffer length = 260 bytes):

Offset	Content	Type	Order
0	Request Buffer Length -2	WORD	lo-hi
2	03h	BYTE	
3	Volume Number	BYTE	
4	AFP Entry ID	LONG	
8	AFP Directory/File Path Length	BYTE	(0..255)
9	AFP Directory/File Path	BYTE[*LENGTH*]	

Reply Buffer

none

Completion codes:

00h	Successful
9Ch	Invalid Path

The NetWare C Interface format is:

```
int AFPDelete( WORD connectionID, int volumeNum, long AFPEntryID,
   char *AFPPathString );
```

AFP Get Entry ID From Name (F2h 04h)

This call returns the AFP entry ID for the specified AFP file or directory.

Registers in:

AL	23h
DS:SI	Request Buffer Address
CX	Request Buffer Length
ES:DI	Reply Buffer Address
DX	Reply Buffer Length
AH	F2h

Registers out:

AL	Completion Code

Completion codes:

00h	Successful
9Ch	Invalid Path

Request Buffer (maximum buffer length = 264 bytes):

Offset	Content	Type	Order
0	Request Buffer Length - 2	WORD	lo-hi
2	04h	BYTE	
3	Volume Number	BYTE	
4	AFP Entry ID	LONG	hi-lo
8	AFP Directory/File Path Length	BYTE (0-255)	
9	AFP Directory/File Path	BYTE[*LENGTH*]	

Reply Buffer (4 bytes)

Offset	Content	Type	Order
0	New AFP Entry ID	LONG	hi-lo

The NetWare C Interface format is:

```
int AFPGetEntryIDFromName( WORD connectionID, int volumeNum,
   long AFPEntryID, char *AFPPathString, long *newAFPEntryID );
```

AFP Get Entry ID From NetWare Handle (F2h 06h)

This call returns an AFP Entry ID for the specified file.

Registers in:

AL	23h
DS:SI	Request Buffer Address
CX	Request Buffer Length
ES:DI	Reply Buffer Address
DX	Reply Buffer Length
AH	F2h

Registers out:

AL	Completion Code

Completion codes:

00h	Successful

Request Buffer (maximum buffer length = 9 bytes):

Offset	Content	Type	Order
0	Request Buffer Length - 2	WORD	lo-hi
2	06h	BYTE	
3	NetWare File Handle	BYTE[6]	

Reply Buffer (6 bytes):

Offset	Content	Type	Order
0	Volume Number	BYTE	
1	AFP Entry ID	LONG	hi-lo
5	Fork Indicator	BYTE	

The *NetWare File Handle* field specifies a six-byte NetWare file handle.

Fork Indicator tells whether the returned AFP Entry ID points to a data fork (0) or to a resource fork (1).

The NetWare C Interface format is:

```
int AFPGetEntryIDFromNetWareHandle( int NetWareHandle, int volumeNum,
  long *AFPEntryID, BYTE *forkIndicator );
```

AFP Get Entry ID From Path Name (F2h 0Ch)

This call maps an AFP Entry ID to a NetWare directory or file path.

Registers in:

AL	23h
DS:SI	Request Buffer Address
CX	Request Buffer Length
ES:DI	Reply Buffer Address
DX	Reply Buffer Length
AH	F2h

Registers out:

AL	Completion Code

Completion codes:

00h	Successful
9Ch	Invalid_Path

Request Buffer (maximum buffer length = 261 bytes):

Offset	Content	Type	Order
0	Request Buffer Length - 2	WORD	lo-hi
2	0Ch	BYTE	
3	NetWare Directory Handle	BYTE	
4	NetWare Directory/File Path Length	BYTE (0-255)	
5	NetWare Directory/File Path	BYTE[*LENGTH*]	

Reply Buffer (4 bytes):

Offset	Content	Type	Order
0	AFP Entry ID	LONG	hi-lo

The NetWare C Interface format is:

```
int AFPGetEntryIDFromPathName( WORD connectionID,
   BYTE directoryHandle, char *pathName, long *AFPEntryID );
```

AFP Get File Information (F2h 05h)

This call returns information about the AFP side of the specified file or directory.

Registers in:

AL	23h
DS:SI	Request Buffer Address
CX	Request Buffer Length
ES:DI	Reply Buffer Address
DX	Reply Buffer Length
AH	F2h

Registers out:

AL	Completion Code

Completion codes:

00h	Successful
9Ch	Invalid Path

Request Buffer (maximum buffer length = 266 bytes):

Offset	Content	Type	Order
0	Request Buffer Length - 2	WORD	lo-hi
2	05h	BYTE	
3	Volume Number	BYTE	
4	AFP Entry ID	LONG	hi-lo
8	Request Bit Map	WORD	hi-lo
10	AFP Directory/File Path Length	BYTE (0-255)	
11	AFP Directory/File Path	BYTE[*LENGTH*]	

Reply Buffer (116 bytes):

Offset	Content	Type	Order
0	AFP Entry ID	LONG	hi-lo
4	AFP Parent Entry ID	LONG	hi-lo
8	Attributes	WORD	hi-lo
10	Data Fork Length	LONG	hi-lo

14	Resource Fork Length	LONG	hi-lo
18	Number of Offspring	WORD	hi-lo
20	Creation Date	WORD	hi-lo
22	Access Date	WORD	hi-lo
24	Modify Date	WORD	hi-lo
26	Modify Time	WORD	hi-lo
28	Backup Date	WORD	hi-lo
30	Backup Time	WORD	hi-lo
32	Finder Information	BYTE[32]	
64	Long Directory/File Name	BYTE[32]	
96	Owner Object ID	LONG	hi-lo
100	Short Directory/File Name	BYTE[12]	
112	Access Rights	WORD	

The *Request Bit Map* field specifies which information is returned by this call. The bits are defined as follows:

High Byte

0x01	Return AFP Entry ID
0x02	Return Data Fork Length
0x04	Return Resource Fork Length
0x08	Return Number Of Offspring
0x10	Return Owner Object ID
0x20	Return Short Name

Low Byte

0x01	Return Attributes
0x02	Return AFP Parent Entry ID
0x04	Return Creation Date
0x08	Return Access Date
0x10	Return Modify Date/Time
0x20	Return Backup Date/Time
0x40	Return Finder Information
0x80	Return Long Name

AFP Parent Entry ID is the AFP entry ID for the parent directory of the target file or directory.

The *Attributes* field returns the attributes of the directory or file. The bit definitions are as follows:

High Byte

0x01	Read-Only Bit
0x02	Hidden Bit
0x04	System Bit
0x08	Execute-Only Bit
0x10	Subdirectory Bit
0x20	Archive Bit
0x40	Undefined
0x80	Shareable File Bit

Low Byte

0x01	Search Mode Bit
0x02	Search Mode Bit
0x04	Search Mode Bit
0x08	Undefined
0x10	Transaction Bit
0x20	Index Bit
0x40	Read Audit Bit (Unused)
0x80	Write Audit Bit (Unused)

Data Fork Size is the data size of the target AFP file. If the AFP Directory/File Path specifies an AFP directory, the Data Fork Size field returns a zero.

Resource Fork Size returns the size of the target AFP file's resource portion. If the AFP Directory/File Path specifies an AFP directory, the Resource Fork Size field returns a zero.

The *Number Of Offspring* field returns the number of files and subdirectories contained within the specified directory. If the AFP Directory/File Path specifies an AFP file, the Number Of Offspring field returns a zero.

Access Date field returns the last accessed date of the target AFP file. If the AFP Directory/File Path specifies an AFP directory, the Creation Date field returns a zero.

Modify Date and *Modify Time* fields return the last modified date and time of the target AFP file. If the AFP Directory/File Path specifies an AFP directory, these fields return zeros.

Backup Date and *Backup Time* fields return the last backup date and time of the specified directory or file.

Finder Information returns the 32-byte Finder Information structure associated with each AFP directory or file.

Long Directory/File Name returns the AFP directory or file name of the specified directory or file. An AFP directory or file name must be 32 characters long.

Owner Object ID field returns the four-byte bindery object ID of the entity that created or last modified the file.

Short Directory/File Name field returns the NetWare directory or file name of the specified directory or file. A NetWare directory or filename can be 13 characters long including an 8-character name, a period, and a 3-character extension.

Access Rights field returns a one-word bit mask of the calling station's privileges for accessing the specified file or directory. The Access Privileges field contains the following bits:

High Byte

0x01	Read
0x02	Write
0x04	Open
0x08	Create
0x10	Delete

0x20	Parental
0x40	Search
0x80	Modify

The NetWare C Interface format is:

```
int AFPGetFileInformation( WORD connectionID, int volumeNum,
   long AFPEntryID, WORD requestBitMap, char *AFPPathString,
   WORD strucSize, AFPFileInfo *AFPFileInfo );
```

AFP Rename (F2h 07h)

This call moves and/or renames a file or directory.

Registers in:

AL	23h
DS:SI	Request Buffer Address
CX	Request Buffer Length
ES:DI	Reply Buffer Address
DX	Reply Buffer Length
AH	F2h

Registers out:

AL	Completion Code

Completion codes:

00h	Successful
9Ch	Invalid Path

Request Buffer (maximum buffer length = 524 bytes):

Offset	**Content**	**Type**	**Order**
0	Request Buffer Length-2	WORD	lo-hi
2	07h	BYTE	
3	Volume Number	BYTE	
4	Source AFP Entry ID	LONG	hi-lo
8	Destination AFP Entry ID	LONG	hi-lo
12	Source AFP Directory/File Path Length	BYTE (0-255)	
13	Source AFP Directory/File Path	BYTE[*LENGTH*]	
?	Destination AFP Directory/File Path Length	BYTE (0-255)	
?	Destination AFP Directory/ File Path	BYTE[*LENGTH*]	

Reply Buffer (2 bytes):

Offset	Content	Type	Order
0	0000h	WORD	lo-hi

To move a directory or file without renaming it, pass a value of zero in the Destination AFP Directory/ File Path Length field.

To rename a directory or file without moving it,pass the same value in both the Source AFP Entry ID and Destination AFP Entry ID fields. Also, pass the old directory or file name in the Source AFP Directory/File Path field, and the new name in the Destination AFP Directory/File Path field.

To move and rename a directory or file: specify the new directory or file name as the last item in the Destination AFP Directory/File Path field.

The NetWare C Interface format is:

```
int AFPRename( WORD connectionID, int volumeNum,
    long AFPSourceEntryID, long AFPDestEntryID, char *AFPSourcePath,
    char *AFPDestPath );
```

AFP Open File Fork (F2h 08h)

This call opens an AFP file fork (data fork or resource fork) from a DOS environment.

Registers in:

AL	23h
DS:SI	Request Buffer Address
CX	Request Buffer Length
ES:DI	Reply Buffer Address
DX	Reply Buffer Length
AH	F2h

Registers out:

AL	Completion Code

Completion codes:

00h	Successful
9Ch	Invalid_Path

Request Buffer (maximum buffer length = 266 bytes):

Offset	Content	Type	Order
0	Request Buffer Length -2	WORD	lo-hi
2	08h	BYTE	
3	Volume Number	BYTE	
4	AFP Entry ID	LONG	hi-lo
8	Fork Indicator	BYTE	
9	Access Mode	BYTE	
10	AFP File Path Length	BYTE (0-255)	
11	AFP File Path	BYTE[*LENGTH*]	

Reply Buffer (14 bytes):

Offset	Content	Type	Order
0	AFP Entry ID	LONG	hi-lo
4	Fork Length	LONG	hi-lo
8	NetWare File Handle	BYTE[6]	

If this call specifies a nonexistent resource fork, the call automatically creates and opens a resource fork.

Access Mode defines how the call opens the target file. The following bits are defined:

0x01	Read Access
0x02	Write Access
0x04	Deny Read Access to Others
0x08	Deny Write Access to Others

The *NetWare File Handle* field returns a six byte NetWare file handle. The following call converts a six byte file handle into a one byte DOS file handle.

The NetWare C Interface format is:

```
int AFPOpenFileFork( WORD connectionID, int volumeNum,
   long AFPEntryID, BYTE forkIndicator, BYTE accessMode,
   char *AFPPathString, long *fileID, long *forkLength,
   BYTE *NetWareHandle, int *fileHandle );
```

Convert Novell Handle To DOS (B4h)

Registers in:

AH	B4h
DS:SI	Request Buffer Address
ES:DI	Reply Buffer Address

Registers out:

Carry flag set:

AX	Completion code (if no DOS file handle exists)

Carry flag clear:

AL	DOS File Handle

Request Buffer (12 bytes):

Offset	Content	Type	Order
0	Connection ID	BYTE	
1	Access Mode	BYTE	
2	NetWare File Handle	BYTE[6]	
8	Fork Size	LONG	hi-lo

Reply Buffer (2 bytes):

Offset	Content	Type	Order
0	0000	WORD	lo-hi

The NetWare C Interface format is:

```
int _ConvertHandle( WORD connectionID, BYTE accessMode,
   BYTE netwareHandle[6], LONG forkLength, int *DOSHandle );
```

AFP Scan File Information (F2h 0Ah)

An application should execute this call iteratively to return information about each entry (subdirectory and file) contained in the specified directory.

Registers in:

AL	23h
DS:SI	Request Buffer Address
CX	Request Buffer Length
ES:DI	Reply Buffer Address
DX	Reply Buffer Length
AH	F2h

Registers out:

AL	Completion Code

Completion codes:

00h	Successful
9Ch	Invalid_Path

Request Buffer (maximum buffer length = 274 bytes):

Offset	Content	Type	Order
0	Request Buffer Length - 2	WORD	lo-hi
2	0Ah	BYTE	
3	Volume Number	BYTE	
4	AFP Entry ID	LONG	hi-lo
8	AFP Last Seen ID	LONG	hi-lo
12	Desired Response Count (1 to 4)	WORD	hi-lo
14	Search Bit Map	WORD	hi-lo
16	Request Bit Map	WORD	hi-lo
18	AFP Directory/File Path Length	BYTE (0-255)	
19	AFP Directory/File Path	BYTE[*LENGTH*]	

Reply Buffer (118 bytes):

Offset	Content	Type	Order
0	Responses Found	WORD	hi-lo
2	AFP Entry	LONG	hi-lo
6	AFP Parent Entry ID	LONG	hi-lo
10	Attributes	WORD	hi-lo
12	Data Fork Length	LONG	hi-lo
16	Resource Fork Length	LONG	hi-lo
20	Number Of Offspring	WORD	hi-lo
22	Creation Date	WORD	hi-lo
24	Access Date	WORD	hi-lo
26	Modify Date	WORD	hi-lo
28	Modify Time	WORD	hi-lo
30	Backup Date	WORD	hi-lo
32	Backup Time	WORD	hi-lo
34	Finder Information	BYTE[32]	
66	Long Directory/File Name	BYTE[32]	
98	Owner Object ID	LONG	hi-lo
102	Short Directory/File Name	BYTE[14]	
116	Access Rights	WORD	

For the first call, an application must pass -1 in the Request Buffer's AFP Last Seen ID field. Thereafter, it should receive the contents of the AFP Entry ID in the reply packet.

Desired Response Count specifies the number of subdirectories or files (1 to 4) for which the calls returns reply buffers.

The *Search Bit Map* field determines what kinds of subdirectories and/or files to search for. The following bits are defined:

Low Byte	
0x01	Hidden files and Directories
0x02	System files and Directories
0x04	Subdirectories
0x08	Files

Responses Found indicates how many sets of information (1 to 4) the call is returning.

The NetWare C Interface format is:

```
int AFPScanFileInformation( WORD connectionID, int volumeNum,
   long AFPEntryID, long *AFPLastSeenID, WORD searchBitMap,
   WORD requestBitMap, char *AFPPathString, WORD strucSize,
   AFPFileInfo *AFPScanFileInfo );
```

AFP Set File Information (F2h 09h)

This call sets information pertaining to the specified AFP file or directory.

Registers in:

AL	23h
DS:SI	Request Buffer Address
CX	Request Buffer Length
ES:DI	Reply Buffer Address
DX	Reply Buffer Length
AH	F2h

Registers out:

AL	Completion Code

Completion codes:

00h	Successful
9Ch	Invalid Path

Request Buffer (maximum buffer length = 312 bytes):

Offset	**Content**	**Type**	**Order**
0	Request Buffer Length - 2	WORD	lo-hi
2	09h	BYTE	
3	Volume Number	BYTE	
4	AFP Entry ID	LONG	hi-lo
8	Request Bit Map	WORD	hi-lo
10	Attributes	WORD	hi-lo
12	Creation Date	WORD	hi-lo
14	Access Date	WORD	hi-lo
16	Modify Date	WORD	hi-lo
18	Modify Time	WORD	hi-lo
20	Backup Date	WORD	hi-lo
22	Backup Time	WORD	hi-lo
24	Finder Information	BYTE[32]	
56	AFP Directory/File Path Length	BYTE (0-255)	
57	AFP Directory/File Path	BYTE[*LENGTH*]	

Reply Buffer (2 bytes)

Offset	**Content**	**Type**	**Order**
0	0000h	WORD	lo-hi

The NetWare C Interface format is:

```
int AFPSetFileInformation( WORD connectionID, int volumeNum,
   long AFPEntryID, WORD requestBitMap, char *AFPPathString,
   WORD strucSize, AFPSETINFO *AFPSetInfo );
```

AFP Alloc Temporary Directory Handle (F2h 0Bh)

This call maps a NetWare directory handle to an AFP directory.

Registers in:

AL	23h
DS:SI	Request Buffer Address
CX	Request Buffer Length
ES:DI	Reply Buffer Address
DX	Reply Buffer Length
AH	F2h

Registers out:

AL	Completion Code

Completion codes:

00h	Successful
9Ch	Invalid Path

Request Buffer (maximum buffer length = 264 bytes)

Offset	Content	Type	Order
0	Request Buffer Length-2	WORD	lo-hi
2	0Bh	BYTE	
3	Volume Number	BYTE	
4	AFP Entry ID	LONG	hi-lo
8	AFP Directory Path Length	BYTE (0-255)	
9	AFP Directory Path	BYTE[*LENGTH*]	

Reply Buffer (2 bytes)

Offset	Content	Type	Order
0	NetWare Directory Handle	BYTE	
1	Access Rights	BYTE	

The *Access Rights* field returns the user's effective rights for the workstation where the application resides.

The NetWare C Interface format is:

```
int AFPAllocTemporaryDirHandle( WORD connectionID, int volumeNum,
    long AFPEntryID, char *AFPPathString, BYTE *NetWareDirectoryHandle,
    BYTE *accessRights );
```

Code Sample: FileInfo.C

For our code example, I'll go back to the FileInfo program that we started in File Services and extended with Directory Services. In this section, we will improve FileInfo to be AFP-aware and show the AFP information, if any, on the files we've selected.

This program shows how AFP may be used to enhance existing programs by making them AFP-aware. Although there will be programs written specifically to work only with AFP, since it is a relatively new addition to NetWare, developers will most likely be interested in adding this capability to applications that manipulate files (delete, copy, rename, etc.) or applications that wish to change the Finder or other information contained in the files' resource forks.

For this example, FileInfo has been enhanced in two ways: First, it checks to see if AFP is supported on the file server; second, when the information on a file is printed out, if AFP is supported, the AFP information is retrieved (using the AFP Get File Information call) and included with the DOS information about the file.

We discussed earlier how the AFPSupported() call is configured. Here, an AFP call is tested and the version of the shell is checked. To print the AFP information on each file, the program first checks the flag we set after checking if AFP was supported, *AFPAvail*. If *AFPAvail* tests TRUE (1) we begin setting up the *getFileInfoRequest* structure. The *RequestBitMap* field is set to FFFFh, indicating we wish all information to be returned, and the *VolumeNumber* field is set with a call to GetVolumeNumber().

The final task is getting the *AFPEntryID* for the file. We concatenate the path from the file request structure with the file name returned in the file reply structure, passing the result to AFPGetEntryIDFromPathName() which returns the AFP-EntryID. Since the EntryID is based on the complete pathname, we don't use the AFP File Path, so the length for this is set to zero.

The final step is to call AFPGetFileInformation() and print the results with PrintAFPFileInfo(). After printing the results to the screen, the loop continues with the next file.

```
/*                                                                    */
/* FileInfo - Lists all the NetWare file info on selected files       */
/*         now AFP-aware                                              */
/*                                                                    */
/* by Charles Rose                                                    */
/*                                                                    */

#include <stdio.h>
#include <dos.h>
#include <dir.h>
#include <string.h>

typedef unsigned char BYTE;
typedef unsigned int WORD;
typedef unsigned long LONG;

/* Request and Reply structures                                       */
struct scanFileReq {
    WORD    Length;
    BYTE    Function;
    WORD    SequenceNumber;
    BYTE    DirectoryHandle;
    BYTE    SearchAttributes;
    BYTE    FilePathLength;
    BYTE    FilePath[255];
} scanFileRequest;

struct scanFileRep {
    WORD    Length;
    WORD    SequenceNumber;
    BYTE    FileName[14];
    BYTE    FileAttributes;
    BYTE    ExtendedFileAttributes;
    LONG    FileSize;
    WORD    CreationDate;
    WORD    LastAccessDate;
    LONG    LastUpdateDateAndTime;
    LONG    OwnerObjectID;
    LONG    LastArchiveDateAndTime;
    BYTE    Reserved[56];
} scanFileReply;

struct getFileInfoReq {
    WORD    Length;
    BYTE    Function;
    BYTE    VolumeNumber;
    LONG    AFPEntryID;
    WORD    RequestBitMap;
    BYTE    AFPDirFilePathLength;
    BYTE    AFPDirFilePath[255];
} getFileInfoRequest;

struct getFileInfoRep {
    LONG    AFPEntryID;
    LONG    AFPParentEntryID;
    WORD    Attributes;
    LONG    DataForkLength;
    LONG    ResourceForkLength;
    WORD    NumberOfOffspring;
    WORD    CreationDate;
    WORD    AccessDate;
    WORD    ModifyDate;
```

```
    WORD     BackupDate;
    BYTE     FinderInfo[36];
    BYTE     LongDirFileName[32];
    LONG     OwnerObjectID;
    BYTE     ShortDirFileName[12];
    WORD     AccessRights;
} getFileInfoReply;

/* Local Routines                                                              */
void PrintFileInfo( void );
int GetFileInfo( struct scanFileReq *request, struct scanFileRep *reply );
void ShowDate( BYTE *date );
void ShowDateAndTime( WORD *dateAndTime );
LONG LongSwitch( BYTE *before );
WORD WordSwitch( BYTE *before );
BYTE GetDirectoryHandle( WORD driveNumber );
int GetDirectoryPath( BYTE directoryHandle, char *directoryPath );

int AFPSupported( void );
int AFPGetEntryIDFromPathName( BYTE handle, BYTE *path, long *AFPEntryID );
void GetShellVersionInformation( BYTE *major, BYTE *minor, BYTE *rev );
int GetVolumeNumber( BYTE *volumeName, BYTE *volumeNumber );
int AFPGetFileInformation( struct getFileInfoReq *request,
   struct getFileInfoRep *reply );
void PrintAFPFileInfo( void );

int AFPAvail = 0;

main( int argc, char *argv[] )
{
    /* Pass a filename, such as "SYS:PUBLIC\*.*"                               */

    int result, i, offset;
    char currentDirectory[255], tempPath[255], volume[255];

    if ( AFPSupported() )
    {
    printf( "AppleTalk Filing Protocol (AFP) is supported on this file server.\n" );
            AFPAvail++;
    }

    if ( argc != 2 )
    {
            printf( "Usage: FILEINFO path\n" );
            exit(1);
    }

    /* Use directory services to insert the volume name into the path          */
    /* if the user hasn't done it                                              */

    if ( !strstr( argv[1], ":" ) )
    {
            memset( currentDirectory, 0, 255 );
            memset( tempPath, 0, 255 );
            GetDirectoryPath( GetDirectoryHandle( getdisk() ), currentDirectory );
            *( strstr( currentDirectory, ":" ) + 1 ) = NULL;
            strcat( tempPath, currentDirectory );
            strcat( tempPath, argv[1] );
    }
    else
            strcpy( tempPath, argv[1] );
```

```
/* Initialize Request & Reply structures                                  */
scanFileRequest.Length = sizeof( scanFileRequest ) - 2;
scanFileRequest.Function = 0x0F;     /* Function F - Get file info         */
scanFileRequest.SequenceNumber = 0xFFFF;    /* Use -1 as first sequence   */
scanFileRequest.DirectoryHandle = 0;
        /* No handle, use full path from use                              */
scanFileRequest.SearchAttributes = 6;
        /* Search Normal, Hidden, & System                                */
scanFileRequest.FilePathLength = strlen( tempPath );
movmem( tempPath, scanFileRequest.FilePath, scanFileRequest.FilePathLength );

scanFileReply.Length = sizeof( scanFileReply ) - 2;

/* Now cycle through calls to GetFileInfo until no more files are found   */
while (1)
{
        result = GetFileInfo( &scanFileRequest, &scanFileReply );
        if ( result == 0x89 )
        {
                printf( "No Search Privileges for this path\n" );
                exit(1),
        }

        if ( result == 0x98 )
        {
     printf( "Volume does not exist, use Volume:Directory\\Directory\\File\n" );
                exit(1);
        }

        if ( result == 0x9C )
        {
             printf( "Invalid path, use Volume:Directory\\Directory\\File\n" );
                exit(1);
        }

        if ( result == 0xFF )
                exit(1);

        PrintFileInfo();

        scanFileRequest.SequenceNumber = scanFileReply.SequenceNumber;

        if ( AFPAvail )
        {

                getFileInfoRequest.RequestBitMap = 0xFFFF;/* Get all info */

                strcpy( volume, scanFileRequest.FilePath );
                *( strstr( volume, ":" ) + 1 ) = NULL;
                GetVolumeNumber( volume, &getFileInfoRequest.VolumeNumber );

                /* Get File Entry ID                                      */
                strcpy( currentDirectory, scanFileRequest.FilePath );
                *( strrchr( currentDirectory, '\\' ) + 1 ) = NULL;
                strcat( currentDirectory, scanFileReply.FileName );
                result = AFPGetEntryIDFromPathName( 0, currentDirectory,
                    &getFileInfoRequest.AFPEntryID );

                /* Get File Path & its size                               */
                getFileInfoRequest.AFPDirFilePathLength = 0;
```

```
                    result = AFPGetFileInformation( &getFileInfoRequest,
                        &getFileInfoReply );
                    if ( result )
                    {
                printf( "Error in AFPGetFileInformation, code = %X\n", result );
                        exit(1);
                    }

                    PrintAFPFileInfo();

            }

    }

}

int GetFileInfo( struct scanFileReq *request, struct scanFileRep *reply )
{
    _AH = 0xE3;
    _SI = (unsigned)request;
    _DI = (unsigned)reply;
    _ES = _DS;

    geninterrupt( 0x21 );

    return _AL;
}

void PrintFileInfo( void )
{
    printf( "┌──────────────────────────────────┐\n" );
    printf( "│  %-15s                           │\n", scanFileReply.FileName );
    printf( "├──────────────────────────────────┤\n" );
    printf( " │ File Size: %10ld  │ %-20s  │ %-20s       │  \n",
        LongSwitch( &scanFileReply.FileSize ),
  ( scanFileReply.ExtendedFileAttributes & 0x10 ) ? "Transaction Bit Set" : " ",
    ( scanFileReply.ExtendedFileAttributes & 0x20 ) ? "Index Bit Set" : " " );
    printf( " ┌──────────────────────────────────┐ \n" );
    printf( " │%-8s │ %-8s │ %-8s │ %-8s │ %-8s │ %-8s │ %-8s │\n",
            ( scanFileReply.FileAttributes & 0x01 ) ? "ReadOnly" : " ",
            ( scanFileReply.FileAttributes & 0x02 ) ? "Hidden  " : " ",
            ( scanFileReply.FileAttributes & 0x04 ) ? "System  " : " ",
            ( scanFileReply.FileAttributes & 0x08 ) ? "Execute " : " ",
            ( scanFileReply.FileAttributes & 0x10 ) ? "Subdir  " : " ",
            ( scanFileReply.FileAttributes & 0x20 ) ? "Archive " : " ",
            ( scanFileReply.FileAttributes & 0x80 ) ? "Sharable" : " " );
    printf( " ├──────────────────────────────────┤ \n" );
    printf( " │Creation    Last Access    Last Update    Last Archive    │\n" );

    printf( " │ " );
    ShowDate( &scanFileReply.CreationDate );
    printf( "      " );
    ShowDate( &scanFileReply.LastAccessDate );
    printf( "        " );
    ShowDateAndTime( &scanFileReply.LastUpdateDateAndTime );
    printf( "      " );
    ShowDateAndTime( &scanFileReply.LastArchiveDateAndTime );
    printf( "      │ \n" );

    printf( "└──────────────────────────────────┘n" );
}
```

```
void ShowDate( BYTE *date )
{
     int year, month, day;
     WORD newDate;

     newDate = WordSwitch( date );

     if ( !newDate )
     {
             printf( "  /  /  " );
             return;
     }

     day = newDate & 0x1F;

     newDate >>= 5;
     month = newDate & 0xF;

     newDate >>= 4;
     year = ( newDate & 0x3F ) + 80;

     printf( "%02d/%02d/%02d", month, day, year );
}

void ShowDateAndTime( WORD *dateAndTime )
{
     int hours, minutes, seconds;
     WORD time;

     ShowDate( dateAndTime );

     time = WordSwitch( dateAndTime + 1 );
     if ( !time )
     {
             printf( "   :  :  " );
             return;
     }

     seconds = ( time & 0x1F ) * 2;

     time >>= 5;
     minutes = time & 0x3F;

     time >>= 6;
     hours = time & 0x1F;

     printf( " %02d:%02d:%02d", hours, minutes, seconds );
}

LONG LongSwitch( BYTE *before )
{
     BYTE after[4];

     after[0] = before[3];
     after[1] = before[2];
     after[2] = before[1];
     after[3] = before[0];

     return *( (LONG *)after );
}
```

```
WORD WordSwitch( BYTE *before )
{
    BYTE after[2];

    after[0] = before[1];
    after[1] = before[0];

    return *( (WORD *) after );
}

BYTE GetDirectoryHandle( WORD driveNumber )
{
    _AH = 0xE9;
    _AL = 0;
    _DX = driveNumber;

    geninterrupt( 0x21 );

    return _AL;
}

int GetDirectoryPath( BYTE directoryHandle, char *directoryPath )
{
    BYTE request[4] = { 2, 0, 1, 0 }, reply[258], retval;

    request[3] = directoryHandle;
    *((WORD *)reply) = 256;

    _AH = 0xE2;
    _SI = (unsigned)request;
    _DI = (unsigned)reply;
    _ES = _DS;

    geninterrupt( 0x21 );

    if ( !( retval = _AL ) )
            movmem( &reply[3], directoryPath, reply[2] );

    return retval;
}

int AFPSupported( void )
{
    BYTE major, minor, rev;
    int result;
    long AFPEntryID;

    GetShellVersionInformation( &major, &minor, &rev );

    result = AFPGetEntryIDFromPathName( 0, "SYS:", &AFPEntryID );

    /* If AFPGetEntryIDFromPathName() call worked, and the                 */
    /*  shell is version 2.15 or higher, then return TRUE (1)              */
    if ( !result && ( major > 2 || ( ( major == 2 ) && ( minor >= 15 ) ) ) )
            return 1;
    else
            return 0;
}
```

```
int AFPGetEntryIDFromPathName( BYTE handle, BYTE *path, long *AFPEntryID )
{
    BYTE Request[260];
    LONG Reply;
    WORD Length;

    Request[2] = 0xC;
    Request[3] = handle;
    Request[4] = strlen( path );
    strcpy( Request + 5, path );
    Length = 3 + Request[4];
    *( (WORD *) Request ) = WordSwitch( &Length );

    _SI = (unsigned)Request;
    _CX = 5 + Request[4];
    _DI = (unsigned)&Reply;
    _DX = 4;
    _ES = _DS;
    _AL = 0x23;
    _AH = 0xF2;

    geninterrupt( 0x21 );

    if ( _AL )
            return _AL;

    *AFPEntryID = Reply;
    return 0;

}

void GetShellVersionInformation( BYTE *major, BYTE *minor, BYTE *rev )
{
    BYTE Reply[40], maj, min, r;

    _AH = 0xEA;
    _AL = 1;
    _BX = 0;
    _DI = (unsigned)Reply;
    _ES = _DS;

    geninterrupt( 0x21 );

    /* Need this step because assigning *major = _BH clobbers other regs      */
    maj = _BH;
    min = _BL;
    r = _CL;

    *major = maj;
    *minor = min;
    *rev = r;
}

int GetVolumeNumber( BYTE *volumeName, BYTE *volumeNumber )
{
    BYTE Request[20], Reply[3] = { 3, 0, 0 };

    Request[2] = 5;
    Request[3] = strlen( volumeName );
    strcpy( Request + 4, volumeName );
    *( (WORD *) Request ) = 2 + Request[3];
```

```
    _AH = 0xE2;
    _SI = (unsigned)Request;
    _DI = (unsigned)Reply;
    _ES = _DS;

    geninterrupt( 0x21 );

    if ( _AL )
            return _AL;

    *volumeNumber = Reply[2];
    return 0;
}

int AFPGetFileInformation( struct getFileInfoReq *request,
   struct getFileInfoRep *reply )
{
    request->Length = 9 + request->AFPDirFilePathLength;
    request->Function = 0x5;

    _AH = 0xF2;
    _AL = 0x23;
    _SI = (unsigned)request;
    _CX = request->Length + 2;
    _DI = (unsigned)reply;
    _DX = sizeof( struct getFileInfoRep );
    _ES = _DS;

    geninterrupt( 0x21 );

    return _AL;
}

void PrintAFPFileInfo( void )
{
    printf("AFP File Information:\n" );
    printf(" AFPEntryID: %08lXh \n",
      LongSwitch( &getFileInfoReply.AFPEntryID ) );
    printf(" AFPParentEntryID: %08lXh \n",
      LongSwitch( &getFileInfoReply.AFPParentEntryID ) );
    printf(" Attributes: %X \n", WordSwitch( &getFileInfoReply.Attributes ) );
    printf(" Data Fork Length: %ld \n",
      LongSwitch( &getFileInfoReply.DataForkLength ) );
    printf(" Resource Fork Length: %ld \n",
      LongSwitch( &getFileInfoReply.ResourceForkLength ) );
    printf(" Number of Offspring: %d \n",
      WordSwitch( &getFileInfoReply.NumberOfOffspring ) );
    printf(" Creation Date: "); ShowDate( &getFileInfoReply.CreationDate );
printf( "\n" );
    printf(" Access Date: "); ShowDate( &getFileInfoReply.AccessDate );
printf( "\n" );
    printf(" Modify Date: "); ShowDate( &getFileInfoReply.ModifyDate );
printf( "\n" );
    printf(" Backup Date: "); ShowDate( &getFileInfoReply.BackupDate );
printf( "\n" );
    printf(" Long Directory File Name: %s\n",
      getFileInfoReply.LongDirFileName );
    printf(" Owner Object ID: %08lXh\n",
      LongSwitch( &getFileInfoReply.OwnerObjectID ) );
    printf(" Short Directory File Name: %s\n",
      getFileInfoReply.ShortDirFileName );
    printf(" Access Rights: %X \n", WordSwitch( &getFileInfoReply.AccessRights ) );
}
```

Exercises

1. Run FileInfo. Examine the AFP side of the files.

2. Create files with a Macintosh computer on the network and view their directory information with FileInfo.

3. Practice AFP file manipulation with the directory & file creation, deletion, and rename routines. Familiarize yourself with the three Get Entry ID calls.

4. Construct an application that is "AFP-aware," testing for the presence of AFP and, if present, using the AFP calls for the file manipulation. What kinds of Mac/PC applications can be created to take advantage of these calls?

5. Use the AFP Rename call to move files and directory structures. This could be accomplished in a character, or graphical user interface (GUI) environment (see chapter 18).

13 File Server Services

The File Server Environment Services API is where programs monitor and manage file servers. There are 35 calls in this API; they allow programmers to get such information about a connection as its open files, semaphores, and disk caching, channeling, and utilization statistics, and much more. One can get or set file server time, enable and disable login and TTS, or even shut the server down.

The information and action available through this API will be familiar to programmers already well-versed in the NetWare FConsole utility. The calls are fairly straightforward and require little explanation. Most return "sensitive" information, such as the file server statistics, so callers need console operator or supervisor access.

Calls in the File Server Environment Services API

All of the File Server Environment Services API calls are supported in Advanced NetWare version 2.1, except for the Get Disk Utilization and the Get File Server Information calls which have been supported since Advanced NetWare 1.0. The Get File Server Date and Time call has been supported since NetWare 4.0.

Throughout the book, we explain fields within the calls only at the first mention of each field in each chapter. Appendix B contains a comprehensive, alphabetical listing of the fields for quick reference.

Check Console Privileges (E3h C8h)

This call determines whether the logged object is a console operator.

Registers in:

AH	E3h
DS:SI	Request Buffer Address
ES:DI	Reply Buffer Address

Registers out:

AL	Completion Code

Completion codes:

00h	Successful
C6h	No Console Rights

Request Buffer (3 bytes):

Offset	**Content**	**Type**	**Order**
0	Request Buffer Length - 2	WORD	lo-hi
2	C8h	BYTE	

Reply Buffer (2 bytes):

Offset	**Content**	**Type**	**Order**
0	0000h	WORD	lo-hi

To be an operator, a Bindery object must have its ID placed in the value set of the OPERATOR property which is associated with a file server object (the name of the object is the name of the file server). This call is a quick way to see if a user or another Bindery object is an operator.

The NetWare C Interface format is:

```
int CheckConsolePrivileges( void );
```

Get File Server Login Status (E3h CDh)

This call returns the file server's login status.

Registers in:

AH	E3h
DS:SI	Request Buffer Address
ES:DI	Reply Buffer Address

Registers out:

AL	Completion Code

Completion code:

00h	Successful
C6h	No Console Rights

Request Buffer (3 bytes):

Offset	Content	Type	Order
0	Reply Buffer Length - 2	WORD	lo-hi
2	CDh	BYTE	

Reply Buffer (3 bytes):

Offset	Content	Type	Order
0	Reply Buffer Length - 2	WORD	lo-hi
2	Login Enabled Flag	BYTE	

The Login Enabled Flag indicates whether login is enabled (1) or disabled (0). The caller must have operator rights.

The NetWare C Interface format is:

```
int GetFileServerLoginStatus( int *loginEnabledFlag );
```

Disable File Server Login (E3h CBh)

This call disables all logins to a file server.

Registers in:

AH	E3h
DS:SI	Request Buffer Address
ES:DI	Reply Buffer Address

Registers out:

AL	Completion Code

Request Buffer (3 bytes):

Offset	Content	Type	Order
0	Request Buffer Length -2	WORD	lo-hi
2	CBh	BYTE	

Reply Buffer (2 bytes):

Offset	Content	Type	Order
0	0000h	WORD	lo-hi

Completion codes:

00h	Successful
C6h	No Console Rights

This call is often used when preparing to bring down the file server. Typing "Disable Login" at the file server console has the same effect. The caller must have operator rights.

The NetWare C Interface format is:

```
int DisableFileServerLogin( void );
```

Enable File Server Login (E3h CCh)

This call enables logins to the default file server.

Registers in:

AH	E3h
DS:SI	Request Buffer Address
ES:DI	Reply Buffer Address

Registers out:

AL	Completion Code

Completion code:

00h	Successful
C6h	No Console Rights

Request Buffer (3 bytes):

Offset	**Content**	**Type**	**Order**
0	Request Buffer Length - 2	WORD	lo-hi
2	CCh	BYTE	

Reply Buffer (2 bytes):

Offset	**Content**	**Type**	**Order**
0	0000h	WORD	lo-hi

This call reverses the action of the preceding call, allowing users to log in again. This can also be accomplished by typing "Enable Login" at the file server console.

The NetWare C Interface format is:

```
int EnableFileServerLogin( void );
```

Down File Server (E3h D3h)

This call brings the file server down.

Registers in:

AH	E3h
DS:SI	Request Buffer Address
ES:DI	Reply Buffer Address

Registers out:

AL	Completion Code

Completion code:

00h	Successful
C6h	No Console Rights
FFh	Open Files

Request Buffer (4 bytes):

Offset	**Content**	**Type**	**Order**
0	Request Buffer Length -2	WORD	lo-hi
2	D3h	BYTE	
3	Force Flag	BYTE	

Reply Buffer (2 bytes):

Offset	**Content**	**Type**	**Order**
0	0000h	WORD	lo-hi

Force Flag indicates whether the file server should force itself down even when files are open. Placing 00 in this field will cause the call to abort if files are open; 1 will down the server. The caller must have supervisor rights.

The NetWare C Interface format is:

```
int DownFileServer( int forceFlag );
```

Disable Transaction Tracking (E3h CFh)

This call disables transaction tracking on the default file server.

Registers in:

AH	E3h
DS:SI	Request Buffer Address
ES:DI	Reply Buffer Address

Registers out:

AL	Completion Code

Completion code:

00h	Successful
C6h	No Console Rights

Request Buffer (3 bytes):

Offset	**Content**	**Type**	**Order**
0	Request Buffer Length - 2	WORD	lo-hi
2	CFh	BYTE	

Reply Buffer (2 bytes):

Offset	Content	Type	Order
0	0000h	WORD	lo-hi

This call is usually made to disable transaction tracking temporarily. The caller must have operator rights.

The NetWare C Interface format is:

```
int DisableTransactionTracking( void );
```

Enable Transaction Tracking (E3h D0h)

This call enables transaction tracking on the default file server.

Registers in:

AH	E3h
DS:SI	Request Buffer Address
ES:DI	Reply Buffer Address

Registers out:

AL	Completion Code

Completion code:

00h	Successful
C6h	No Console Rights

Request Buffer (3 bytes):

Offset	Content	Type	Order
0	Request Buffer Length - 2	WORD	lo-hi
2	D0h	BYTE	

Reply Buffer (2 bytes):

Offset	Content	Type	Order
0	0000h	WORD	lo-hi

This call enables transaction tracking after it has been disabled, either explicitly by the preceding call or automatically by the file server because the TTS volume was full. The caller must have operator rights.

The NetWare C Interface format is:

```
int EnableTransactionTracking( void );
```

TTS Get Statistics (E3h D5h)

This call returns statistics from the default file server's Transaction Tracking System.

Registers in:

AH	E3h
DS:SI	Request Buffer Address
ES:DI	Reply Buffer Address

Registers out:

AL	Completion Code

Completion code:

00h	Successful
C6h	No Console Rights

Request Buffer (3 bytes):

Offset	Content	Type	Order
0	Request Buffer Length - 2	WORD	lo-hi
2	D5h	BYTE	

Reply Buffer (maximum buffer length = 446 bytes):

Offset	Content	Type	Order
0	Reply Buffer Length - 2	WORD	lo-hi
2	System Elapsed Time	LONG	hi-lo
6	Transaction Tracking Supported	BYTE	
7	Transaction Tracking Enabled	BYTE	
8	Transaction Volume Number	WORD	hi-lo
10	Configured Max Simultaneous Transactions	WORD	hi-lo
12	Actual Max Simultaneous Transactions	WORD	hi-lo
14	Current Transaction Count	WORD	hi-lo
16	Total Transactions	LONG	hi-lo
20	Total Write Transactions Performed	LONG	hi-lo
24	Total Transactions Backed Out	LONG	hi-lo
28	Total Unfilled Backout Requests	WORD	hi-lo
30	Transaction Disk Space	WORD	hi-lo
32	Transaction FAT Allocations	LONG	hi-lo
36	Transaction File Size Changes	LONG	hi-lo
40	Transaction Files Truncated	LONG	hi-lo
44	Records	BYTE	

Active Transaction (repeated Records times)

?	Logical Connection Number	BYTE
?	Task Number	BYTE

System Elapsed Time is the time elapsed since the server was brought up, in ticks each approximately 1/18th of a second.

Transaction Tracking Supported tells whether the server supports TTS. If this field is zero, the server does not support TTS and the rest of the fields are undefined.

Transaction Volume Number identifies the volume used for the transaction work file.

Configured Maximum Simultaneous Transactions is the most transactions the server can track simultaneously. It is set with the Install/NetGen utility.

Actual Maximum Simultaneous Transactions is the highest number of transactions that have occurred simultaneously since the server was brought up.

Current Transaction Count is the number of transactions in progress.

Total Transactions Performed is the number of transactions performed by the server since it was brought up.

Total Write Transactions Performed is the number of transactions that required the file server to track file changes. If a workstation requests a transaction but does not actually modify (write) a file during the transaction, the transaction tracking software ignores the transaction.

Total Transactions Backed Out is the number of transactions backed out since the file server was brought up. Backouts occur upon workstation requests or if a workstation fails during a transaction. The value in this field includes backout

Total Unfilled Backout Requests is the number of backouts that failed because transaction tracking was disabled.

Transaction Disk Space is the number of disk blocks being used by the transaction tracking software (1 block = 4,096 bytes).

Transaction FAT (File Allocation Table) *Allocations* is the number of blocks that have been allocated for FATs of files being tracked since the server was brought up.

Transaction File Size Changes is the number of times files being tracked changed their sizes within transactions since the server was brought up.

Transaction Files Truncated is the number of times files being tracked have been truncated within transactions since the server was brought up.

Records is the number of transactions to be performed.

Logical Connection Number identifies the logical connection involved in a transaction.

Task Number is which task within a logical connection is involved in a transaction.

The caller must have operator rights.

The NetWare C Interface format is:

```
int TTSGetStats( WORD connectionID, int structSize,
   TTS_STATS *TTSStats );
```

Get Bindery Object Disk Space Left (E3h E6h)

This call returns a Bindery object's remaining disk space.

Registers in:

AH	E3h
DS:SI	Request Buffer Address
ES:DI	Reply Buffer Address

Registers out:

AL	Completion Code

Completion code:

00h	Successful
C6h	No Console Rights

Request Buffer (7 bytes):

Offset	Content	Type	Order
0	Request Buffer Length - 2	WORD	lo-hi
2	E6h	BYTE	
3	Object ID	LONG	hi-lo

Reply Buffer (15 bytes):

Offset	Content	Type	Order
0	Reply Buffer Length - 2	WORD	lo-hi
2	System Elapsed Time	LONG	hi-lo
6	Object ID	LONG	hi-lo
10	Unused Disk Blocks	LONG	hi-lo
14	Restrictions Enforced	BYTE	

This call allows the requesting workstation to get remaining disk space for its own logged Bindery object.

Unused Disk Blocks is the number of remaining blocks the Bindery object can allocate.

Restrictions Enforced tells whether limits are placed upon use of disk resources (00h = enforced, FFh = not enforced) when the network was installed.

The NetWare C Interface format is:

```
int BinderyObjectDiskSpaceLeft( WORD connectionID, long binderyObjectID,
 long *systemElapsedTime, long *unusedDiskBlocks,
 int *restrictionEnforced );
```

Clear Connection Number (E3h D2h)

This call clears a logical connection from the file server.

Registers in:

AH	E3h
DS:SI	Request Buffer Address
ES:DI	Reply Buffer Address

Registers out:

AL	Completion Code

Completion code:

00h	Successful
C6h	No Console Rights

Request Buffer (4 bytes):

Offset	**Content**	**Type**	**Order**
0	Request Buffer Length - 2	WORD	lo-hi
2	D2h	BYTE	
3	Connection Number	BYTE	

Reply Buffer (2 bytes)

Offset	**Content**	**Type**	**Order**
0	0000h	WORD	lo-hi

This call closes a connection's open files and releases its file locks. On a TTS file server this call causes a connection's transactions to be aborted. The caller must have supervisor rights.

The NetWare C Interface format is:

```
int ClearConnectionNumber( WORD connectionNumber );
```

Get Connection's Open Files (E3h (DBh)

This call returns information about the files a connection has open.

Registers in:

AH	E3h
DS:SI	Request Buffer Address
ES:DI	Reply Buffer Address

Registers out:

AL	Completion Code

Completion code:

00h	Successful
C6h	No Console Rights

Request Buffer (7 bytes):

Offset	Content	Type	Order
0	Request Buffer Length - 2	WORD	lo-hi
2	DBh	BYTE	
3	Logical Connection Number	WORD	hi-lo
5	Last Record Seen	WORD	hi-lo

Reply Buffer (maximum buffer = 512 bytes):

Offset	Content	Type	Order
0	Reply Buffer Length - 2	WORD	lo-hi
2	Next Request Record	WORD	hi-lo
4	Records	BYTE	

File Information (repeated Records times):

?	Task Number	BYTE	
?	Lock Flag	BYTE	
?	Access Flag	BYTE	
?	Lock Type	BYTE	
?	Volume Number (0 to 31)	BYTE	
?	Directory Entry	WORD	hi-lo
?	File Name (ASCIIZ string)	BYTE[14]	

Last Record Seen contains the Next Request Record field returned in the last reply packet returned. On the first call, it should be set to zero. If the value returned in the Next Request Record field is zero, there is no more information to come from the file server.

Task Number is the task number within the workstation that has the file open.

Lock Flag contains bit flags indicating the file's lock information, as shown below.

0x01	Locked
0x02	Open Shareable
0x04	Logged
0x04	Open Normal
0x40	TTS Holding Lock
0x80	Transaction Flag Set on this File

Access Flag contains bit flags indicating the connection's access rights for the file, as shown below.

0x01	Open For Read by this Station
0x02	Open For Write by this Station
0x04	Deny Read Requests from Other Stations
0x08	Deny Write Requests from Other Stations
0x10	File Detached
0x20	TTS Holding Detach
0x40	TTS Holding Open

Lock Type contains a flag indicating the type of lock, if any, on the file, as shown below.

00h	Not Locked
FEh	Locked by a File Lock
FFh	Locked by Begin Share File Set

Directory Entry is an offset into the file server's Directory Entry Table for the volume. To access the file this Directory Entry identifies, use the Get Path From Directory Entry call.

The caller must have operator rights.

The NetWare C Interface format is:

```
int GetConnectionsOpenFiles( WORD connectionID, WORD connectionNumber,
int *lastRecord, int *lastTask, int structSize, CON_OPEN_FILES *open-
Files );
```

Get Connection's Semaphores (E3h E1h)

This call returns information about a connection's open semaphores.

Registers in:

AH	E3h
DS:SI	Request Buffer Address
ES:DI	Reply Buffer Address

Registers out:

AL	Completion Code

Completion code:

00h	Successful
C6h	No Console Rights

Request Buffer (7 bytes):

Offset	Content	Type	Order
0	Request Buffer Length - 2	WORD	lo-hi
2	E1h	BYTE	
3	Logical Connection Number	WORD	hi-lo
5	Last Record Seen	WORD	hi-lo

Reply Buffer (maximum buffer length = 512 bytes):

Offset	Content	Type	Order
0	Reply Buffer Length - 2	WORD	lo-hi
2	Next Request Record	WORD	hi-lo
4	Records	BYTE	

File Information (repeated Records times):

?	Open Count	WORD
?	Semaphore Value (-127 to 128)	SIGNED BYTE
?	Task Number	BYTE
?	Lock Type	BYTE
?	Semaphore Name Length (1 to 127)	BYTE
?	Semaphore Name	BYTE[*LENGTH*]
?	File Name	BYTE[14]

Open Count is the number of logical connections that have this semaphore open.

Semaphore Value is the current value of the semaphore (-127 to 128).

The caller must have operator rights.

The NetWare C Interface format is:

```
int GetConnectionsSemaphores( WORD connectionID, WORD connectionNumber,
  int *lastRecord, int lastTask, int structSize,
  CONN_SEMAPHORE *connectionSemaphores );
```

Get Connection's Task Information (E3h DAh)

This call returns information on a logical connection's active tasks.

Registers in:

AH	E3h
DS:SI	Request Buffer Address
ES:DI	Reply Buffer Address

Registers out:

AL	Completion Code

Completion code:

00h	Successful
C6h	No Console Rights

Request Buffer (5 bytes):

Offset	**Content**	**Type**	**Order**
0	Request Buffer Length - 2	WORD	lo-hi
2	DAh	BYTE	
3	Logical Connection Number	WORD	hi-lo

Reply Buffer (maximum buffer length = 512 bytes):

Offset	**Content**	**Type**	**Order**
0	Reply Buffer Length - 2	WORD	lo-hi
2	Connection's Lock Status	BYTE	
3	Status Information	structure	
?	Records	BYTE	

Active task Information (repeated Records times):

?	Task Number(1 to 225)	BYTE
?	Task State	BYTE

Connection's Lock Status is:

0 = Normal (connection free to run)
1 = Connection waiting on physical record lock
2 = Connection waiting on file lock
3 = Connection waiting on logical record lock
4 = Connection waiting on a semaphore

Status Information contains information about the lock state of the connection. If the connection is waiting on a lock request, the Status Information field contains information about the resource the connection is waiting for. Therefore, the Status Information structure varies depending on which lock status is returned.

If lock status = 0, the Status Information field receives no information.

If lock status = 1, the Status Information field receives information on the physical record lock.

Offset	**Content**	**Type**
?	Waiting task number	BYTE
?	Begin address	LONG
?	End address	LONG
?	Volume number	BYTE

?	Directory Entry	WORD
?	File name (ASCIIZ string)	BYTE[14]

If lock status = 2, the Status Information field receives information on the file lock.

Offset	Content	Type
?	Waiting task number	BYTE
?	Volume number	BYTE
?	Directory Entry	WORD
?	File name (ASCIIZ string)	BYTE[14]

If lock status = 3, the Status Information field receives information on the logical record lock.

Offset	Content	Type
?	Waiting task number	BYTE
?	Record name length	BYTE
?	Record name (ASCIIZ string)	BYTE[*LENGTH*]

If lock status = 4, the Status Information field receives information on the semaphore lock.

Offset	Content	Type
?	Waiting task number	BYTE
?	Semaphore name length	BYTE
?	Semaphore name (ASCIIZ string)	BYTE[*LENGTH*]

Task State is the state of the task for which information is to be returned:

01h = TTS Explicit transaction in progress
02h = TTS Implicit transaction in progress
04h = Shared file set lock in progress

The caller must have operator rights.
The NetWare C Interface format is:

```
int GetConnectionsTaskInformation( WORD connectionID,
   WORD connectionNumber, int *taskPointer, int structSize,
   CONN_TASK_INFO *connectionTaskInfo );
```

Get Connection's Usage Statistics (E3h E5h)

This call returns a logical connection's usage statistics.

Registers in:

AH	E3h
DS:SI	Request Buffer Address
ES:DI	Reply Buffer Address

Registers out:

AL	Completion Code

Completion code:

00h	Successful
C6h	No Console Rights

Request Buffer (5 bytes):

Offset	**Content**	**Type**	**Order**
0	Request Buffer Length - 2	WORD	lo-hi
2	E5h	BYTE	
3	Logical Connection Number	WORD	

Reply Buffer (22 bytes):

Offset	**Content**	**Type**	**Order**
0	Reply Buffer Length - 2	WORD	lo-hi
2	System Elapsed Time	LONG	hi-lo
6	Bytes Read	BYTE[6]	
12	Bytes Written	BYTE[6]	
18	Total Request Packets	LONG	hi-lo

This call returns statistics about the operation of a logical connection.

Bytes Read and *Bytes Written* indicate the number of bytes the logical connection has read or written since the workstation logged in.

Total Request Packets is the number of request packets the logical connection has sent to the server since the workstation attached.

The caller must have operator rights.

The NetWare C Interface format is:

```
int GetConnectionsUsageStats( WORD connectionID, WORD connectionNumber,
   int structSize, CONN_USAGE *connectionUsage );
```

Get Connections Using a File (E3h DCh)

This call returns all logical connections using a file.

Registers in:

AH	E3h
DS:SI	Request Buffer Address
ES:DI	Reply Buffer Address

Registers out:

AL	Completion Code

Completion code:

00h	Successful
C6h	No Console Rights

Request Buffer (maximum buffer length = 262):

Offset	Content	Type	Order
0	Request Buffer Length - 2	WORD	lo-hi
2	DCh	BYTE	
3	Last Record	WORD	hi-lo
5	Directory Handle	BYTE	
6	File Path Length (1 to 255)	BYTE	
7	File Path (ASCIIZ string)	BYTE[*LENGTH*]	

Reply Buffer (maximum buffer = 512 bytes):

Offset	Content	Type	Order
0	Reply Buffer Length - 2	WORD	lo-hi
2	Use Count	WORD	hi-lo
4	Open Count	WORD	hi-lo
6	Open For Read Count	WORD	hi-lo
8	Open For Write Count	WORD	hi-lo
10	Deny Read Count	WORD	hi-lo
12	Deny Write Count	WORD	hi-lo
14	Next Request Record	WORD	hi-lo
16	Locked	BYTE	
17	Records	BYTE	

File Usage Information (repeated Records times):

?	Logical Connection Number	WORD	hi-lo
?	Task Number	BYTE	
?	Lock Flag byte	BYTE	
?	Access Flag	BYTE	
?	Lock Type	BYTE	

Use Count is the number of tasks that have opened or logged the file.

Deny Read Count and *Deny Write* are the numbers of logical connections that have denied other stations read or write privileges to the file.

Locked is whether the file is locked exclusively (0 = not locked exclusively).

Operator rights required.

The NetWare C Interface format is:

```
int GetConnectionsUsingAFile( WORD connectionID, int *lastRecord,
   int *taskID, BYTE directoryHandle, char *filePath, int structSize,
   CONN_USING_FILE *fileUse );
```

Get Disk Cache Statistics (E3h D6h)

This call returns statistics about the default file server's cache.

Registers in:

AH	E3h
DS:SI	Request Buffer Address
ES:DI	Reply Buffer Address

Registers out:

AL	Completion Code

Completion code:

00h	Successful
C6h	No Console Rights

Request Buffer (3 bytes):

Offset	Content	Type	Order
0	Reply Buffer Length - 2	WORD	lo-hi
2	D6h	BYTE	

Reply Buffer (80 bytes):

Offset	Content	Type	Order
0	Reply Buffer Length - 2	WORD	lo-hi
2	System Elapsed Time	LONG	hi-lo
6	Cache Buffer Count	WORD	hi-lo
8	Cache Buffer Size	WORD	hi-lo
10	Dirty Cache Buffers	WORD	hi-lo
12	Cache Read Requests	LONG	hi-lo
16	Cache Write Requests	LONG	hi-lo
20	Cache Hits	LONG	hi-lo
24	Cache Misses	LONG	hi-lo
28	Physical Read Requests	LONG	hi-lo
32	Physical Write Requests	LONG	hi-lo

36	Physical Read Errors	WORD	hi-lo
38	Physical Write Errors	WORD	hi-lo
40	Cache Get Requests	LONG	hi-lo
44	Cache Full Write Requests	LONG	hi-lo
48	Cache Partial Write Requests	LONG	hi-lo
52	Background Dirty Writes	LONG	hi-lo
56	Background Aged Writes	LONG	hi-lo
60	Total Cache Writes	LONG	hi-lo
64	Cache Allocations	LONG	hi-lo
68	Thrashing Count	WORD	hi-lo
70	LRU Block Was Dirty	WORD	hi-lo
72	Read Beyond Write	WORD	hi-lo
74	Fragmented Write Occurred	WORD	hi-lo
76	Cache Hit On Unavailable Block	WORD	hi-lo
78	Cache Block Scrapped	WORD	hi-lo

Cache Buffer Count is the number of cache buffers in the server.

Cache Buffer Size is the number of bytes in a cache buffer.

Dirty Cache Buffers is the number of cache buffers containing data that has not been written to disk.

Cache Read Requests and *Cache Write Requests* indicate the number of times the cache software was asked to read or write data.

Cache Hits is the number of times cache requests were serviced from existing cache blocks.

Cache Misses is the number of times cache requests could not be serviced from existing cache blocks.

Physical Read Requests is the number of times the cache software issued a physical read request to a disk driver. A physical read request reads in as much data as the cache block holds.

Physical Write Requests is the number of times the cache software issued a physical write request to a disk driver.

Physical Read Errors and *Physical Write Errors* are the number of times the cache software received an error from the disk driver on a disk read or write request.

Cache Get Requests is the number of times the cache software was asked to read information from the disk.

Cache Full Write Requests is the number of times the cache software was instructed to write information that exactly filled one or more sectors.

Cache Partial Write Requests is the number of times the cache software was instructed to write information that did not exactly fill a sector.

Background Dirty Writes is the number of times a cache block that was written to disk was completely filled with information, i. e., the whole cache block was written.

Background Aged Writes is the number of times the background disk write process wrote a partially filled cache block to disk, or how many times the cache block was written to disk because the block had not been accessed for a significant period of time.

Total Cache Writes is the total number of cache buffers written to disk.

Cache Allocations is the number of times a cache block was allocated for use.

Thrashing Count is the number of times a cache block was not available when a cache block allocation was requested.

LRU Block Was Dirty is the number of times the Least-Recently-Used cache block allocation algorithm reclaimed a dirty cache block.

Read Beyond Write is the number of times a file read request was made when file write requests had not yet filled the cache block.

Fragmented Write Occurred is the number of times a dirty cache block contained noncontiguous sectors of information to be written, and the skipped sectors were not preread from the disk. (Multiple disk writes were issued to write out the cache buffer.)

Cache Hit On Unavailable Block is the number of times a cache request could be serviced from an available cache block, but the cache buffer could not be used because it was in the process of being written to or read from disk.

Cache Block Scrapped contains the number of times a cache block is scrapped due to the following scenario: A process was put to sleep because it needed a cache block and the Least-Recently-Used block had to be written to disk before it could be reused. When the process awoke after the block had been written and freed, the process checked and discovered that while it was asleep another process had come in, allocated a different block, and read into it the information that the sleeping process was seeking. In this case, the newly awakened process must free the cache block, and use the block that already contains the sought information.

The number returned in *Cache Get Requests* includes Cache Read Requests, and Cache Write Requests that do not fill a complete sector and therefore require a preread to service.

The caller must have console operator rights.

The NetWare C Interface format is:

```
int GetDiskCacheStats( WORD connectionID, int structSize,
   DISK_CACHE_STATS *cacheStats );
```

Get Disk Channel Statistics (E3h D9h)

This call returns statistics about the default file server's disk channels.

Registers in:

AH	E3h
DS:SI	Request Buffer Address
ES:DI	Reply Buffer Address

Registers out:

AL	Completion Code

Completion code:

00h	Successful
C6h	No Console Rights

Request Buffer (4 bytes):

Offset	Content	Type	Order
0	Request Buffer Length - 2	WORD	lo-hi
2	D9h	BYTE	
3	Channel Number	BYTE	

Reply Buffer (170):

Offset	Content	Type	Order
0	Reply Buffer Length - 2	WORD	lo-hi
2	System Elapsed Time	LONG	hi-lo
6	Channel State	WORD	hi-lo
8	Channel Synchronization State	WORD	hi-lo
10	Driver Type	BYTE	
11	Driver Major Version	BYTE	
12	Driver Minor Version	BYTE	
13	Driver Description (ASCIIZ)	BYTE[65]	
78	First IO Address Used	WORD	hi-lo
80	First IO Address Length	WORD	hi-lo
82	Second IO Address Length	WORD	hi-lo
84	Second IO Address Length	WORD	hi-lo
86	First Shared Memory Address	BYTE[3]	
89	First Shared Memory Address Length	BYTE[2]	
91	Second Shared Memory Address	BYTE[3]	
94	Second Shared Memory Address Length	BYTE[2]	
96	First Interrupt Number In Use	BYTE	
97	First Interrupt Number Used	BYTE	
98	Second Interrupt Number In Use	BYTE	
99	Second Interrupt Number Used	BYTE	
100	First DMA Channel Used	BYTE	
101	First DMA Channel Used	BYTE	
102	Second DMA Channel Used	BYTE	
103	Second DMA Channel Used	BYTE	
104	Flag Bits	BYTE	
105	Reserved	BYTE	
106	Configuration Description	BYTE[80]	

This call can be used iteratively to get updated information.

Channel Number is the number of the disk channel to be queried.

Channel State is the state of the disk channel:

00h	Channel running
01h	Channel being stopped
02h	Channel stopped
03h	Channel nonfunctional

Channel Synchronization State is the control state of the disk channel. In nondedicated versions of NetWare, the disk channel may be used by more than one piece of software, and control of the channel must be synchronized. This field can have the following values:

0	Channel is not being used.
2	NetWare is using the channel; no one else requests it.
4	NetWare is using the channel; someone else requests it.
6	Someone else is using the channel; NetWare does not need it.
8	Someone else is using the channel; NetWare needs it.
10	Someone else has released the channel; NetWare should use it.

If the first WORD of the IO addresses used is nonzero, the Channel Synchronization State field contains the beginning IO address of the range, and the second WORD contains the range length. If the third WORD is nonzero, the Channel Synchronization State field contains the beginning IO address of the second range, and the fourth WORD contains the range length.

If the first WORD of shared memory addresses is nonzero, the Channel Synchronization State field contains the beginning address of the shared memory range. The addresses are returned as segments, with the offset 0. The second WORD contains the number of bytes in the shared memory address range. If the third WORD is nonzero, the Channel Synchronization State field contains the beginning of the second shared memory range address, and the fourth WORD contains the length in bytes of the second shared memory range.

If the first byte of interrupt numbers is nonzero, the second byte contains the interrupt number used. If the third byte is nonzero, the fourth byte contains the number of the second interrupt used.

If the first byte of DMA channels is nonzero, the second byte contains the number of the DMA channel used. If the third byte is nonzero, the fourth byte contains the number of the second DMA channel used.

Driver Type contains a number indicating the type of disk driver software installed on the disk channel.

First IO Address Used and *Second IO Address Used* contain the addresses the disk driver uses to control the disk channel.

First IO Address Used Length and *Second IO Address Used Length* contain the lengths of the IO addresses used.

First Shared Memory Address and *Second Shared Memory Address* are fields that the disk driver uses to control the specified disk channel.

First Shared Memory Address Length and *Second Shared Memory Address Length* contain the length of the shared memory addresses.

First Interrupt Numbers Used In Use Flag and *Second Interrupt Numbers Used In Use Flag* are flag fields for the Interrupt Numbers Used fields explained below.

First Interrupt Numbers Used and *Second Interrupt Numbers Used* contain the interrupt numbers the disk driver uses to communicate with the disk channel.

First DMA Channels Used In Use Flag and *Second DMA Channels Used In Use Flag* are flag fields for the DMA Channels Used fields explained below.

First DMA Channels Used and *Second DMA Channels Used* list the DMA controllers the disk driver uses to control the disk channel.

Configuration Description contains an ASCIIZ string indicating the channel's current I/O driver configuration.

The caller must have operator rights.

The NetWare C Interface format is:

```
int GetDiskChannelStats( WORD connectionID, int channelNumber,
   int structSize, DISK_CHANNEL_STATS *channelStats );
```

Get Disk Utilization (E3h 0Eh)

This call returns the disk usage of a Bindery object on a volume.

Registers in:

AH	E3h
DS:SI	Request Buffer Address
ES:DI	Reply Buffer Address

Registers out:

AL	Completion Code

Completion code:

00h	Successful
98h	Volume Does Not Exist
F2h	No Object Read Privileges

Request Buffer (8 bytes):

Offset	**Content**	**Type**	**Order**
0	Request Buffer Length - 2	WORD	lo-hi
2	0Eh	BYTE	
3	Volume Number (0 to 31)	BYTE	
4	Object ID	LONG	hi-lo

Reply Buffer (13 bytes):

Offset	Content	Type	Order
0	Reply Buffer Length - 2	WORD	lo-hi
2	Volume Number (0 to 31)	BYTE	
3	Object ID	LONG	hi-lo
7	Used Directories	WORD	hi-lo
9	Used Files	WORD	hi-lo
11	Used Blocks	WORD	hi-lo

Used Directories are the number of directories owned by the Bindery object.

Used Files are the number of files created by the Bindery object.

To determine the number of bytes a Bindery object is using on a volume, use the following equation:

Bytes used = used blocks * sectors/block * bytes/sector

Current network implementations allocate eight 512-byte sectors per block (4KB per block).

This call requires read privileges at the Bindery object level.

The NetWare C Interface format is:

```
int GetDiskUtilization( long objectID, char volumeNumber,
   WORD *usedDirectories, WORD *usedFiles, WORD *usedBlocks );
```

Get Drive Mapping Table (E3h D7h)

This call returns the drive mapping table from the default file server.

Registers in:

AH	E3h
DS:SI	Request Buffer Address
ES:DI	Reply Buffer Address

Registers out:

AL	Completion Code

Completion code:

00h	Successful
C6h	No Console Rights

Request Buffer (3 bytes):

Offset	Content	Type	Order
0	Reply Buffer Length - 2	WORD	lo-hi
2	D7h	BYTE	

Reply Buffer (238 bytes):

Offset	Content	Type	Order
0	Reply Buffer Length - 2	WORD	lo-hi
2	System Elapsed Time	LONG	hi-lo
6	SFT Level	BYTE	
7	Logical Drive Count	BYTE	
8	Physical Drive Count	BYTE	
9	Disk Channel Table	BYTE[5]	
14	Pending IO Commands	WORD	hi-lo
16	Mapping Table	BYTE[32]	
48	Drive Mirror Table	BYTE[32]	
80	Dead Mirror Table	BYTE[32]	
112	Remirrored Drive	BYTE	
113	Reserved	BYTE	
114	Remirrored Block	LONG	hi-lo
118	SFT Error Table	WORD[60]	hi-lo

SFT Level is the SFT level offered by the file server. SFT Level I offers hot disk error fix. SFT Level II offers disk mirroring and transaction tracking. SFT Level III offers physical file server mirroring.

Logical Drive Count is the number of logical drives attached to the server. If the file server supports SFT Level II or above and disks are mirrored, the logical drive count will be lower than the actual number of physical disk subsystems attached to the file server. A set of mirrored disks is considered to be one logical drive.

Physical Drive Count is the number of physical disk units attached to the server.

Disk Channel Table is a five-byte table that tells which disk channels exist on the server and what their drive types are. (Each channel is one byte.) A nonzero value in the disk channel table means that the corresponding disk channel exists in the file server (1 = XT drive type, 2 = AT drive type, 3 = SCSI drive type, 4 = disk coprocessor drive type, 50 to 255 = value-added disk drive types).

Pending IO Commands is the number of outstanding disk controller commands.

Drive Mapping Table is a 32-byte table containing the primary physical drive that each logical drive is mapped to (FFh = no such logical drive exists on the server).

Driver Mirror Table is a 32-byte table containing the secondary physical drive that each logical drive is mapped to (FFh = no such logical drive exists on the server).

Dead Mirror Table is a 32-byte table containing the secondary physical drive that each logical drive was last mapped to (FFh = logical drive was never mirrored). The Dead Mirror Table is used in conjunction with the Drive Mirror Table. If the Drive Mirror Table indicates that a drive is not currently mirrored, this table can be used to determine the drive that previously mirrored the logical drive. This table is used to remirror a logical drive after a mirror failure.

Remirrored Drive is the physical drive number of the disk currently being remirrored (FFh = no disk being remirrored).

Remirrored Block contains the block number that is currently being remirrored.

SFT Error Table is a 60-byte table containing SFT internal error counters.

The caller must have operator rights.

The NetWare C Interface format is:

```
int GetDriveMappingTable( WORD connectionID, int structSize,
   DRIVE_MAP_TABLE *driveMappingTable );
```

Get File Server Date And Time (E7h)

This call returns the date and time from the file server.

Registers in:

AH	E3h
DS:DX	Reply Buffer Address

Registers out:
None

Completion codes:
None

Reply Buffer (7 bytes):

Offset	**Content**	**Type**
0	Year (0 to 99)	BYTE
1	Month (1 to 12)	BYTE
2	Day (1 to 31)	BYTE
3	Hour (0 to 23)	BYTE
4	Minute (0 to 59)	BYTE
5	Second (0 to 59)	BYTE
6	Day Of Week (0 to 6) (0=Sunday)	BYTE

Year field is added to 1900 for the correct date. Values less than 80 are considered to be in the twenty-first century (05 would be 2005).

The NetWare C Interface format is:

```
int GetFileServerDateAndTime( BYTE *dateAndTime );
```

Set File Server Date And Time (E3h CAh)

This call sets the date and time on the file server.

Registers in:

AH	E3h
DS:SI	Request Buffer Address
ES:DI	Reply Buffer Address

Registers out:

AL	Completion Code

Completion codes:

00h	Successful
C6h	No Console Operator

Request Buffer (9 bytes):

Offset	Content	Type	Order
0	Request Buffer Length - 2	WORD	lo-hi
2	CAh	BYTE	
3	Year(0 to 99)	BYTE	
4	Month (1 to 12)	BYTE	
5	Day (1 to 31)	BYTE	
6	Hour (0 to 23)	BYTE	
7	Minute (0 to 59)	BYTE	
8	Second (0 to 59)	BYTE	

Reply Buffer:

Offset	Content	Type	Order
0	0000h	WORD	lo-hi

If an invalid value is specified (e.g., 250 for the month), an error is not returned, and the file server is set to an undefined, but valid, date and time.

The caller must have operator rights.

The NetWare C Interface format is:

```
int SetFileServerDateAndTime( WORD year, WORD month, WORD day,
   WORD hour, WORD minute, WORD second );
```

Get File Server Description Strings (E3h C9h)

This call returns the name of the company that distributed this copy of NetWare.

Registers in:

AH	E3h
DS:SI	Request Buffer Address
ES:DI	Reply Buffer Address

Registers out:

AL	Completion Code

Completion code:

00h	Successful

Request Buffer (3 bytes):

Offset	**Content**	**Type**	**Order**
0	Request Buffer Length - 2	WORD	lo-hi
2	C9h	BYTE	

Reply Buffer (514 bytes):

Offset	**Content**	**Type**	**Order**
0	Reply Buffer Length - 2	WORD	lo-hi
2	Description Strings	BYTE[512]	

The Description Strings field contains the following four ASCIIZ strings:

Company Name:	Name of the company that distributed this copy of NetWare
Revision:	NetWare version and revision
Revision Date:	Revision date in the form of mm/dd/yy
Copyright Notice:	Copyright notice

This call requires only attachment to the file server.
The NetWare C Interface format is:

```
int GetFileServerDescriptionStrings( char *companyName, char *revision,
   char *revisionDate, copyrightNotice );
```

Get File Server Information (E3h 11h)

This call returns information about the default file server.

Registers in:

AH	E3h
DS:SI	Request Buffer Address
ES:DI	Reply Buffer Address

Registers out:

AL	Completion Code

Completion code:
00h Successful

Request Buffer (3 bytes):

Offset	Content	Type	Order
0	Request Buffer Length - 2	WORD	lo-hi
2	11h	BYTE	

Reply Buffer (130 bytes):

Offset	Content	Type	Order
0	Reply Buffer Length - 2	WORD	lo-hi
2	Server Name	BYTE[48]	
50	NetWare Version (1 to 255)	BYTE	
51	NetWare Subversion (0 to 99)	BYTE	
52	Connections Supported	WORD	hi-lo
54	Connections In Use	WORD	hi-lo
56	Max Connected Volumes	WORD	hi-lo
58	OS Revision Number	BYTE	
59	SFT Level	BYTE	
60	TTS Level	BYTE	
61	Peak Connections Used	WORD	hi-lo
63	Accounting Version	BYTE	
64	VAP Version	BYTE	
65	Queuing Version	BYTE	
66	Print Server Version	BYTE	
67	Virtual Console Version	BYTE	
68	Security Restrictions Level	BYTE	
69	Internetwork Bridge Version	BYTE	
70	Reserved	BYTE[60]	

NetWare Version (1 to 255) is the version of NetWare running on the default server (2 = Advanced NetWare 2.x).

The NetWare C Interface format is:

```
int GetServerInformation( int structSize, FILE_SERV_INFO *serverInfo );
```

Get File Server LAN IO Statistics (E3h E7h)

This call returns statistical information about packets being received and sent by the default file server.

Registers in:
AH E3h
DS:SI Request Buffer Address
ES:DI Reply Buffer Address

Registers out:

AL	Completion Code

Completion code:

00h	Successful
C6h	No Console Rights

Request Buffer (3 bytes):

Offset	**Content**	**Type**	**Order**
0	Request Buffer Length - 2	WORD	lo-hi
2	E7h	BYTE	

Reply Buffer (68 bytes):

Offset	**Content**	**Type**	**Order**
0	Reply Buffer Length - 2	WORD	lo-hi
2	System Elapsed Time	LONG	hi-lo
6	Configured Max Routing Buffers	WORD	hi-lo
8	Actual Max Used Routing Buffers	WORD	hi-lo
10	Currently Used Routing Buffers	WORD	hi-lo
12	Total File Service Packets	LONG	hi-lo
16	File Service Packet Buffered	LONG	hi-lo
18	Invalid Connection Packets	WORD	hi-lo
20	Bad Logical Connection Number Packets	WORD	hi-lo
22	Packets Received During Processing	WORD	hi-lo
24	Reprocessed Requests	WORD	hi-lo
26	Bad Sequence Number Packets	WORD	hi-lo
28	Duplicate Replies Sent	WORD	hi-lo
30	Acknowledgements Sent	WORD	hi-lo
32	Packets With Bad Request Type	WORD	hi-lo
34	Attach During Processing	WORD	hi-lo
36	Attach While Processing Attach	WORD	hi-lo
38	Forced Detach Requests	WORD	hi-lo
40	Detach For Bad Connection Number	WORD	hi-lo
42	Detach During Processing	WORD	hi-lo
44	Replies Cancelled	WORD	hi-lo
46	Packets Discarded By Hop Count	WORD	hi-lo

48	Packets Discarded Unknown Net	WORD	hi-lo
50	Incoming Packet Discarded No DGroup Buffer	WORD	hi-lo
52	Outgoing Packet Discarded No Buffer	WORD	hi-lo
54	IPX Not MY Network	WORD	hi-lo
56	NetBIOS Broadcast Was Propagated	LONG	hi-lo
60	Total Other Packets	LONG	hi-lo
64	Total Routed Packets	LONG	hi-lo

Actual Maximum Used Routing Buffers is the maximum number of routing buffers that have been in use simultaneously since the server was brought up.

Currently Used Routing Buffers is the number of routing buffers that are being used by the server.

Total File Service Packets is the number of request packets serviced by the file server.

File Service Packets Buffered is the number of times file service request packets were stored in routing buffers.

Invalid Connection Packets is the count of all request packets with invalid logical connection numbers. A connection packet is invalid if it contains a logical connection number that has not been allocated or a source address that does not match the address the file server has assigned to the logical connection.

Bad Logical Connection Number Packets is the count of all request packets with invalid logical connection numbers, which are those numbers not supported by the file server (such as 573).

Packets Received During Processing is the number of times a new request was received while the previous request was still being processed. Packets are most likely to be received during processing if a workstation generated a duplicate request while the response to its first was en route.

Reprocessed Requests is the count of requests that were reprocessed by the server.

Bad Sequence Number Packets is a count of request packets the server received from a connection where the sequence number in the packet did not match the current sequence number or the next sequence number. (Packets with bad sequence numbers are discarded.)

Duplicate Replies Sent is a count of request packets for which the server had to send duplicate replies. Duplicate replies are only sent for requests the server cannot process.

Acknowledgements Sent is a count of acknowledgements sent by the server. An acknowledgement is sent when a workstation repeats a request that is being serviced.

Packets With Bad Request Type is a count of request packets containing invalid request types.

Attach During Processing is the number of requests to establish connections from workstations for which the server is currently processing a request. In this case, the server discards the response to the request that was being processed and re-establishes a connection with the workstation.

Attach While Processing Attach is the number of times a request to establish a connection from a workstation was received when the server was already processing a request to establish a connection with that workstation. The second request is ignored.

Forged Detach Requests is a count of requests to terminate connections where the source addresses does not match the addresses the server has assigned to the connections. The detach requests are ignored.

Detach For Bad Connection Number is a count of requests to terminate a connection where the connection number is not supported by the server.

Detach During Processing is the number of requests to terminate a connection from a workstation that were received while previous requests were still being processed for that connection.

Replies Cancelled is the number of replies that were canceled because the connection was reallocated while the request was being processed.

Packets Discarded By Hop Count is the number of packets that were discarded because they had passed through more than 16 bridges without reaching their destinations.

Packets Discarded Unknown Net is the number of packets that were discarded because their destination networks were unknown to the server.

Incoming Packet Discarded No DGroup Buffer is the number of incoming packets that were received in a routing buffer that needed to be transferred to a DGroup buffer so the socket dispatcher could transfer the packet to the correct socket. If no buffers are available, the packet is lost.

Outgoing Packet Discarded No Buffer is the number of packets the server attempted to send which were lost because no routing buffers were available.

IPX Not My Network is a count of packets received that were destined for the B, C, or D side drivers.

NetBIOS Broadcast Was Propagated is a count of NetBIOS packets propagated through this network.

Total Other Packets is a count of all packets received that are not requests for file services.

Total Routed Packets is a count of all packets routed by the server.

The caller must have operator rights.

The NetWare C Interface format is:

```
int GetFileServerLANIOStats( WORD connectionID, int structSize,
   SERVER_LAN_IO *serverLANIOStats );
```

Get File Server Misc Information (E3h E8h)

This call returns miscellaneous information about the file server.

Registers in:

AH	E3h
DS:SI	Request Buffer Address
ES:DI	Reply Buffer Address

Registers out:

AL	Completion Code

Completion code:

00h	Successful
C6h	No Console Rights

Request Buffer (3 bytes):

Offset	Content	Type	Order
0	Request Buffer Length - 2	WORD	lo-hi
2	E8h	BYTE	

Reply Buffer (maximum buffer length = 58 bytes):

Offset	Content	Type	Order
0	Reply Buffer Length - 2	WORD	lo-hi
2	System Elapsed Time	LONG	hi-lo
6	Processor Type	BYTE	
7	Reserved	BYTE	
8	Number Of Service Processes	BYTE	
9	Server Utilization Percentage	BYTE	
10	Configured Max Bindery Objects	WORD	hi-lo
12	Actual Max Bindery Objects	WORD	hi-lo
14	Current Used Bindery Objects	WORD	hi-lo
16	Total Server Memory	WORD	hi-lo
18	Wasted Server Memory	WORD	hi-lo
20	Records	WORD	hi-lo

Dynamic memory information (repeated Records times):

?	Total Dynamic Space	LONG	hi-lo
?	Max Used Dynamic Space	LONG	hi-lo
?	Current Used Dynamic Space	LONG	hi-lo

Processor Type contains the number which is the processor type:

0 = Motorola 68000
1 = Intel 8086, 8088 or V20
2 = 80286 (or higher, i.e. 80386)

Number Of Service Processes is the number of service processes in the serverl; a service process handles incoming service requests.

Server Utilization Percentage is the current server utilization percentage (0 to 100), updated once a second.

Configured Maximum Bindery Objects is the maximum number of Bindery objects that the file server will track (0 = unlimited).

Actual Maximum Bindery Objects is the maximum number of Bindery objects that have been used concurrently since the file server came up. This field is only meaningful if the preceding field is set.

Current Used Bindery Objects is the number of Bindery objects currently in use on the server.

Total Server Memory is the total amount of memory the server has installed (1KB units).

Wasted Server Memory is the amount of memory in the server that is not being used (1KB units). Wasted Server Memory will normally be 0. If this field is nonzero, the file server has more memory installed than can be used. Usually all extra memory is used for cache blocks.

Records is the number of dynamic areas used by the server (1 to 3).

Total Dynamic Space is the amount of memory in the dynamic memory area.

Maximum Used Dynamic Space is the maximum amount of memory in the dynamic memory area that has been in use since the server was brought up.

Current Used Dynamic Space is the amount of memory in the dynamic memory area that is currently in use.

The caller must have operator rights.

The NetWare C Interface format is:

```
int GetFileServerMiscInformation( WORD connectionID, int structSize,
   SERVER_MISC_INFO *miscInformation );
```

Get File System Statistics (E3h D4h)

This call returns statistics about a server's file system.

Registers in:

AH	E3h
DS:SI	Request Buffer Address
ES:DI	Reply Buffer Address

Registers out:

AL	Completion Code

Completion code:

00h	Successful
C6h	No Console Rights

Request Buffer (3 bytes):

Offset	Content	Type	Order
0	Request Buffer Length - 2	WORD	lo-hi
2	D4h	BYTE	

Reply Buffer (42 bytes):

Offset	Content	Type	Order
0	Reply Buffer Length - 2	WORD	lo-hi
2	System Elapsed Time	LONG	hi-lo
6	Configured Max Open Files	WORD	hi-lo
8	Actual Max Open Files	WORD	hi-lo
10	Current Open Files	WORD	hi-lo
12	Total Files Opened	LONG	hi-lo
16	Total Read Requests	LONG	hi-lo
20	Total Write Requests	LONG	hi-lo
24	Current Changed FATS	WORD	hi-lo
26	Total Changed FATS	LONG	hi-lo
28	FAT Write errors	LONG	hi-lo
30	Fatal FAT Write Errors	WORD	hi-lo
32	FAT Scan Errors	WORD	hi-lo
34	Actual Max Indexed Files	WORD	hi-lo
36	Active Indexed File	WORD	hi-lo
38	Attached Indexed Files	WORD	hi-lo
40	Available Indexed Files	WORD	hi-lo

Configured Maximum Open Files contains the number of files the server can open simultaneously. It is selected at installation and can be changed with the NetGen utility.

Actual Maximum Open Files contains the number of files open simultaneously since the server was brought up.

Current Open Files contains the number of files the server has open, including files opened by workstations and any internal files, such as the Bindery, that the file server has opened.

Total Files Opened contains the number of files the server has opened since the server was brought up. If this number reaches FFFFFFFFh, it wraps back to zero.

Total Read Requests contains the number of file read requests the server has received since it was brought up.

Total Write Requests contains the number of write requests the server has received since it was brought up.

Current Changed FATS contains the number of current FAT sectors the file system has modified. FAT sectors are modified when files are extended or truncated.

Total Changed FATS contains the number of FAT sectors the file system has modified since it was brought up.

FAT Write Errors contains the number of disk write errors that have occurred when writing FAT sectors to the disk. All FAT sectors are kept in duplicate on the disk, ensuring that a single disk failure will not result in loss of the FAT tables. If a FAT sector is lost, the mirrored copy is used automatically. When a disk write error occurs in both the original and mirrored copies of a FAT sector, a total error occurs.

Fatal FAT Write Errors contains the number of disk write errors that occurred in both the original and mirrored copies of a FAT sector. Fatal FAT Write Errors occur because the file system cannot recover the information required to determine where on a volume a given file resides. However, since a copy of the FAT table is kept in memory, the file server continues to call. The SYS$LOG.ERR file contains the name of the affected volume. It is recommended that all files be backed up on the affected volume before the file server is taken down.

FAT Scan Errors contains the number of times an internally inconsistent state existed in the file system.

Actual Maximum Indexed Files contains the number of indexed files the server has had active simultaneously since it was brought up.

Active Indexed Files contains the count of files that are currently active, open, and indexed.

Attached Indexed Files contains the count of indexed files ready for indexing but not ready for use. The attached index files are not currently open, but they have indexes built in memory. These indexes are reused if the attached file is reopened, or they are rebuilt for other files if needed.

Available Indexed Files contains the count of file indexes that are available for use.

The total number of indexed files that a file server will support simultaneously is a configurable parameter that can be set using the NetGen utility.

The caller must have operator rights.

The NetWare C Interface format is:

```
int GetFileSystemStats( WORD connectionID, int structSize,
   FILE_SYS_STATS *fileSysStats );
```

Get LAN Driver's Configuration Information (E3h E3h)

This call returns configuration information for the LAN drivers installed at the file server.

Registers in:

AH	E3h
DS:SI	Request Buffer Address
ES:DI	Reply Buffer Address

Registers out:

AL	Completion Code

Completion code:

00h	Successful
C6h	No Console Rights

Request Buffer (4 bytes):

Offset	Content	Type	Order
0	Request Buffer Length -2	WORD	lo-hi
2	E3h	BYTE	
3	LAN Board (0 to 3)	BYTE	

Reply Buffer (174 bytes):

Offset	Content	Type	Order
0	Reply Buffer Length - 2	WORD	lo-hi
2	Network Address	BYTE[4]	
6	Host Address	BYTE[6]	
12	LAN Driver Installed	BYTE	
13	Option Number	BYTE	
14	Configuration Text	BYTE[160]	

LAN Board is a number indicating the LAN board for which configuration information is requested (0 to 3).

Host Address is the six-byte node/host address number of the LAN board the driver is controlling.

LAN Driver Installed indicates whether a driver is installed in the specified LAN board. If the LAN Driver Installed field is zero, all fields returned are undefined.

Option Number contains the option that was selected when the driver was configured. The selected option number specifies the hardware setup the driver uses when running the LAN board.

Configuration Text contains two ASCIIZ strings. The first string contains the hardware type of the LAN board the driver is controlling (e.g., "NetWare Ethernet NP600"). The second string contains the hardware settings that are used to control the LAN board (e.g., "IRQ = 9, IO Address = 300h, DMA = 7").

The caller must have operator rights.

The NetWare C Interface format is:

```
int GetLANDriverConfigInfo( connectionID, BYTE LANBoardNumber,
    int structSize, LAN_CONFIG *LANConfiguration );
```

Get Logical Record Information (E3h E0h)

This call returns information about a logical record.

Registers in:

AH	E3h
DS:SI	Request Buffer Address
ES:DI	Reply Buffer Address

Registers out:

AL	Completion Code

Completion code:

00h	Successful
C6h	No Console Rights

Request Buffer (maximum buffer length = 105):

Offset	Content	Type	Order
0	Request Buffer Length - 2	WORD	lo-hi
2	E0h	BYTE	
3	Last Record Seen	WORD	hi-lo
5	Logical Record Name Length (1 to 99)	BYTE	
6	Logical Record Name	BYTE[*LENGTH*]	

Reply Buffer (maximum buffer = 514 bytes):

Offset	Content	Type	Order
0	Reply Buffer Length - 2	WORD	lo-hi
2	Use Count	WORD	hi-lo
4	Shareable Lock Count	WORD	hi-lo
6	Next Request Record	WORD	hi-lo
8	Locked	BYTE	
9	Records	BYTE	

Task information (repeated Records times):

?	Logical Connection Number	WORD	hi-lo
?	Task Number	BYTE	
?	Lock Status	BYTE	

Last Record Seen indicates the last record seen. On the first call, it must be set to zero; on subsequent calls it should receive the value in the Next Request Record field until it returns zero.

Use Count is the number of logical connections that have the logical record logged.

Shareable Lock Count is the number of logical connections that have a shareable lock.

Lock Status contains the bit flags indicating the file's lock status, as shown below.

0x01	Locked Exclusive
0x02	Locked Shareable
0x04	Logged
0x40	Lock is held by TTS

The caller must have operator rights.
The NetWare C Interface format is:

```
int GetLogicalRecordInformation( WORD connectionID, int *lastRecord,
    int *lastTask, char *logicalRecordName, int structSize,
    LOGICAL_REC_INFO *logicalRecInfo );
```

Get Logical Records By Connection (E3h DFh)

This call returns the logical record that a logical connection has logged with the default file server.

Registers in:

AH	E3h
DS:SI	Request Buffer Address
ES:DI	Reply Buffer Address

Registers out:

AL	Completion Code

Completion code:

00h	Successful
C6h	No Console Rights

Request Buffer (7 bytes):

Offset	**Content**	**Type**	**Order**
0	Request Buffer Length - 2	WORD	lo-hi
2	DFh	BYTE	
3	Logical Connection Number	WORD	hi-lo
5	Last Record Seen	WORD	hi-lo

Reply Buffer (maximum buffer = 512 bytes):

Offset	**Content**	**Type**	**Order**
0	Reply Buffer Length - 2	WORD	lo-hi
2	Next Request Record	WORD	hi-lo
4	Records	BYTE	

Logical Lock Information (repeated Records times):

?	Task Number	BYTE
?	Lock Status	BYTE
?	Logical Lock Name Length	BYTE
?	Logical Lock Name	BYTE[*LENGTH*]

The caller must have operator rights.

The NetWare C Interface format is:

```
int GetLogicalRecordLocksByConnection( WORD connectionID,
   WORD connectionNumber, int *lastRecord, int *lastTask,
   int structSize, LOGICAL_RECORD *logicalRecord );
```

Get Path From Directory Entry (E2h 1Ah)

This call accesses a file path listed in a server's Directory Entry Table.

Registers in:

AH	E2h
DS:SI	Request Buffer Address
ES:DI	Reply Buffer Address

Registers out:

AL	Completion Code

Completion code:

00h	Successful

Request Buffer (6 bytes):

Offset	**Content**	**Type**	**Order**
0	Request Buffer Length - 2	WORD	lo-hi
2	1Ah	BYTE	
3	Volume Number	BYTE	
4	Directory Entry	WORD	hi-lo

Reply Buffer (maximum buffer = 258 bytes):

Offset	**Content**	**Type**	**Order**
0	Reply Buffer Length - 2	WORD	lo-hi
2	Path	BYTE[256]	

This call is used in conjunction with the Get Connection's Open Files call, which returns the Directory Entry (and a 14-byte filename). Use this call to get a full (up to 256-byte) pathname.

The NetWare C Interface format is:

```
int GetFilePathFromDirectoryEntry( WORD connectionID, BYTE volumeNumber,
   WORD directoryEntry, char *path );
```

Get Physical Disk Statistics (E3h D8h)

This call returns information about a physical disk.

Registers in:

AH	E3h
DS:SI	Request Buffer Address
ES:DI	Reply Buffer Address

Registers out:

AL	Completion Code

Completion code:

00h	Successful
C6h	No Console Rights

Request Buffer (4 bytes):

Offset	**Content**	**Type**	**Order**
0	Request Buffer Length -2	WORD	lo-hi
2	D8h	BYTE	
3	Physical Disk Number	BYTE	

Reply Buffer (95 bytes):

Offset	**Content**	**Type**	**Order**
0	Reply Buffer Length - 2	WORD	lo-hi
2	System Elapsed Time	LONG	hi-lo
6	Physical Disk Channel	BYTE	
7	Drive Removable Flag	BYTE	
8	Physical Drive Type	BYTE	
9	Controller Drive Number	BYTE	
10	Controller Number	BYTE	
11	Controller Type	BYTE	
12	Drive Size	LONG	hi-lo
16	Drive Cylinders	WORD	hi-lo
18	Drive Heads	BYTE	
19	Sectors Per Track	BYTE	
20	Drive Definition String	BYTE[64]	
84	IO Error Count	WORD	
86	Hot Fix Table Start	LONG	hi-lo
90	Hot Fix Table Size	WORD	hi-lo
92	Hot Fix Blocks Available	WORD	hi-lo
94	Hot Fix Disabled	BYTE	

Physical Disk Channel is the disk channel to which the disk unit is attached.

Drive Removable Flag indicates whether a disk is removable (0 = nonremovable).

Physical Drive Type is the type of drive (1 = XT, 2 = AT, 3 = SCSI, 4 = disk coprocessor, 5 = PS/2 MFM Controller, 6 = PS/2 ESDI Controller, 7 = Convergent Technology SBIC, 50 to 255 = value-added disk drive).

Controller Drive Number is the drive number of the disk unit relative to the controller number.

Controller Number contains the address on the physical disk channel of the controller that controls the disk.

Controller Type contains the number identifying the type (make and model) of the disk controller.

Drive Size is the size of the physical drive in blocks (1 block = 4,096 bytes). The drive size does not include the portion of the disk reserved for Hot Fix redirection in the event of media errors.

Drive Cylinders is the number of physical cylinders on the drive.

Drive Heads is the number of disk heads on the drive.

Sectors Per Track is the number of sectors on each disk track (1 sector = 512 bytes).

Drive Definition String contains the make and model of the drive (ASCIIZ string).

IO Error Count is the number of times I/O errors have occurred on the disk since the server was brought up.

Hot Fix Table Start indicates the first block of the disk Hot Fix Redirection Table. This field is only meaningful with SFT NetWare Level 1 or above. The redirection table is used to replace bad disk blocks with usable blocks in the event Hot Fix Table Size is the total number of redirection blocks set aside on the disk for Hot Fix redirection. Some or all of these blocks may be in use. This field is only meaningful with SFT NetWare Level I or above. To determine the number of redirection blocks still available for future use, see the Hot Fix Blocks Available field.

Hot Fix Blocks Available is the number of redirection blocks that are still available. This field is only meaningful with SFT NetWare Level I or above.

Hot Fix Disabled indicates whether Hot Fix is enabled or disabled (0 = enabled). This field is only meaningful with SFT NetWare Level I or above.

Operator rights are required.

The NetWare C Interface format is:

```
int GetPhysicalDiskStatistics( WORD connectionID,
   BYTE physicalDiskNumber, int structSize,
   PHYS_DISK_STATS *physicalDiskStats, char *driveDefinition );
```

Get Physical Record Locks By Connection And File (E3h DDh)

This call returns a logical connection's physical record locks within a file.

Registers in:

AH	E3h
DS:SI	Request Buffer Address
ES:DI	Reply Buffer Address

Registers out:

AL	Completion Code

Completion code:

00h	Successful
C6h	No Console Rights
FFh	File Not Open

Request Buffer (24 bytes):

Offset	Content	Type	Order
0	Request Buffer Length -2	WORD	lo-hi
2	DDh	BYTE	
3	Logical Connection Number	WORD	hi-lo
5	Last Record Seen	WORD	hi-lo
7	Volume Number (0 to 31)	BYTE	
8	Directory Handle	WORD	hi-lo
10	File Path (ASCIIZ String)	BYTE[14]	

Reply Buffer (maximum buffer = 512 bytes):

Offset	Content	Type	Order
0	Reply Buffer Length -2	WORD	lo-hi
2	Next Request Record	WORD	hi-lo
4	Physical Record Lock Count	BYTE	
5	Records	BYTE	

Physical record lock information (repeated Records times):

?	Task Number	BYTE	
?	Lock Status	BYTE	
?	Record Start	LONG	hi-lo
?	Record End	LONG	hi-lo

Physical Record Lock Count is a count of the number of physical record locks. *Record Start* and *Record End* indicate byte offsets within the file.
The NetWare C Interface format is:

```
int GetPhysRecLockByConnectAndFile( WORD connectionID,
    WORD connectionNumber, BYTE volumeNumber, WORD directoryHandle,
    char *filePath, int *lastRecord, int *lastTask, int structSize,
    SHORT_PHYS_REC_LOCK *recordLock );
```

Get Physical Record Locks By File (E3h DEh)

This call returns physical records that are locked in a file.

Registers in:

AH	E3h
DS:SI	Request Buffer Address
ES:DI	Reply Buffer Address

Registers out:

AL	Completion Code

Completion code:

00h	Successful
C6h	No Console Rights
FFh	File Not Open

Request Buffer (maximum buffer = 262 bytes):

Offset	**Content**	**Type**	**Order**
0	Request Buffer Length - 2	WORD	lo-hi
2	DEh	BYTE	
3	Last Record Seen	WORD	hi-lo
5	Directory Handle	BYTE	
6	File Path Length (1 to 255)	BYTE	
7	File Path (ASCIIZ String)	BYTE[*LENGTH*]	

Reply Buffer (maximum buffer = 512 bytes):

Offset	**Content**	**Type**	**Order**
0	Reply Buffer Length - 2	WORD	lo-hi
2	Next Request Record	WORD	hi-lo
4	Physical Record Lock Count	BYTE	
5	Records	BYTE	

Physical Record Lock (repeated Records times):

?	Logged Count	WORD	hi-lo
?	Shareable Lock Count	WORD	hi-lo
?	Record Start	LONG	hi-lo
?	Record End	LONG	hi-lo
?	Logical Connection Number	WORD	hi-lo
?	Task Number	BYTE	
?	Lock Type	BYTE	

The caller must have console rights.
The NetWare C Interface format is:

```
int  GetPhysicalRecordLocksByFile( WORD connectionID,
   WORD directoryHandle, char *filePath, int *lastRecord, int *lastTask,
   int structSize, PHYS_REC_LOCK *recordLock );
```

Get Semaphore Information (E3h E2h)

This call returns information about a single semaphore.

Registers in:

AH	E3h
DS:SI	Request Buffer Address
ES:DI	Reply Buffer Address

Registers out:

AL	Completion Code

Completion code:

00h	Successful
C6h	No Console Rights

Request Buffer (maximum buffer length = 133 bytes):

Offset	Content	Type	Order
0	Request Buffer Length - 2	WORD	lo-hi
2	E2h	BYTE	
3	Last Record Seen	WORD	hi-lo
5	Semaphore Name Length (1 to 127)	BYTE	
6	Semaphore Name	BYTE[*LENGTH*]	

Reply Buffer (maximum buffer length = 512 bytes):

Offset	Content	Type	Order
0	Reply Buffer Length - 2	WORD	lo-hi
2	Next Request Record	WORD	hi-lo
4	Open Count	WORD	hi-lo
6	Semaphore Value (-127 to 128)	SIGNED BYTE	
7	Records	BYTE	

Semaphore information (repeated Records times):

?	Logical Connection Number	WORD	hi-lo
?	Task Number	BYTE	

This call should be used iteratively when a logical connection has more semaphores than can be placed in the reply buffer.

The caller must have operator rights.

The NetWare C Interface format is:

```
int GetSemaphoreInformation( char *semaphoreName, int *lastRecord,
    int *lastTask, int *openCount, char *semaphoreValue,
    WORD *connectionNumber, TYPE *taskNumber );
```

Send Console Broadcast (E3h D1h)

This call sends a message to a list of logical connections.

Registers in:

AH	E3h
DS:SI	Request Buffer Address
ES:DI	Reply Buffer Address

Registers out:

AL	Completion Code

Completion code:

00h	Successful
C6h	No Console Rights

Request Buffer (maximum buffer length = 164 bytes):

Offset	Content	Type	Order
0	Request Buffer Length - 2	WORD	lo-hi
2	D1h	BYTE	
3	Connection Count (1 max)	BYTE	
4	Connection List	BYTE[*COUNT*]	
?	Message Length (1)	BYTE	
?	Message	BYTE[*LENGTH*]	

Reply Buffer (2 bytes):

Offset	Content	Type
0	0000	WORD

Connection Count contains the number of logical connections to receive the message (0 = broadcast to all workstations).

The caller must have operator rights.

The NetWare C Interface format is:

```
int SendConsoleBroadcast( char *message, WORD connectionCount,
    WORD *connectionList );
```

Code Sample: LogLock.C

LogLock uses the Disable File Server and Enable File Server Login calls to switch the status of the Login Enabled flag. These functions are useful when trying to get all users off the network before bringing down the file server; it prevents them from logging back on.

The program defines its global routines and the main() function calls the LoginEnabled() function to check the status of the file server login flag. If login was enabled, the function returns one, otherwise zero is returned to main().

If login was enabled, ChangeLoginStatus() is called, passing the DISABLE flag, otherwise, ENABLE is passed. Since the Disable File Server Login and the Enable File Server Login are identical except for their function codes (CCh vs CBh); ChangeLoginStatus() uses the enable flag to decide which to use. This saves us from needing two different functions.

LogLock.C

```
/*                                                                  */
/* LogLock - Toggle the Allow File Server Login status flag         */
/*                                                                  */
/* by Charles Rose                                                  */
/*                                                                  */

#include <stdio.h>
#include <dos.h>

#define DISABLE 0
#define ENABLE  1

int LoginEnabled( void );
void ChangeLoginStatus( int enable );

void main()
{
        if ( LoginEnabled() )
        {
                ChangeLoginStatus( DISABLE );
                printf("Server Login Disabled\n");
        }
        else
        {
                ChangeLoginStatus( ENABLE );
                printf("Server Login Enabled\n");
        }
}

int LoginEnabled()
{
```

```
        struct
        {
                int     length;
                char    function;
        } request;

        struct
        {
                int     length;
                char    enabledFlag;
        } reply;

        union REGS inregs, outregs;

        request.length = 1;
        request.function = 0xCD;
        reply.length = 1;

        inregs.h.ah = 0xE3;
        inregs.x.si = &request;
        inregs.x.di = &reply;
        intdos( &inregs, &outregs );

        if ( !outregs.h.al )
                return reply.enabledFlag;
        else
        {
                printf("No Console Rights, Cannot Run LogLock\n");
                exit(1);
        }
}

void ChangeLoginStatus( int enable )
{
        struct
        {
                int     length;
                char    function;
        } request;

        struct
        {
                int     length;
        } reply;

        union REGS inregs, outregs;

        request.length = 1;
        reply.length = 0;

        if ( enable )
                request.function = 0xCC;
        else
                request.function = 0xCB;

        inregs.h.ah = 0xE3;
        inregs.x.si = &request;
        inregs.x.di = &reply;
        intdos( &inregs, &outregs );
```

```
                if ( outregs.h.al )
                {
                        printf("No Console Rights, Cannot Run LogLock\n");
                        exit(1);
                }
        }
```

Code Sample: DrvrInfo.C

DrvrInfo shows the information returned from the Get LAN Driver Configuration Information call. The program makes the call four times, once for each possible LAN board in the system.

GetLANDriversConfigInfo() makes the API call and ShowInfo() prints the info to the screen. Note that we need to check the LANDriverInstalled flag to see if the rest of the fields are valid. Often the calls in the File Server Environment Services will return with a successful (00) completion codes, but the programs still must check critical fields, such as LAN Driver Info (and applicable fields in other calls) to make sure the other fields contain valid data.

```
/*                                                                    */
/* DrvrInfo - Shows the info from the Get LAN Driver Config Info call */
/*                                                                    */
/* by Charles Rose                                                    */
/*                                                                    */

#include <stdio.h>
#include <dos.h>
#include <dir.h>
#include <string.h>

typedef unsigned char BYTE;
typedef unsigned int WORD;
typedef unsigned long LONG;

struct getInfoReply {
        WORD    Length;
        BYTE    NetworkAddress[4];
        BYTE    HostAddress[6];
        BYTE    LANDriverInstalled;
        BYTE    OptionNumber;
        BYTE    ConfigurationText[160];
} Reply;

int GetLANDriversConfigInfo( BYTE board, struct getInfoReply *Reply );
void ShowInfo( struct getInfoReply Info );

main()
{
        int i, result;

        for ( i = 0; i < 4; i++ )
        {
                printf("Info for LAN Board %c:\n\n", 'A' + i );
                result = GetLANDriversConfigInfo( i, &Reply );
                if ( result )
                {
```

```
                        printf( "Must have Console Operator rights to run DrvrInfo.\n" );
                        exit( 1 );
                }

                ShowInfo( Reply );
        }
}

int GetLANDriversConfigInfo( BYTE board, struct getInfoReply *Reply )
{
        BYTE Request[4] = { 2, 0, 0xE3, 0 };

        Request[3] = board;
        Reply->Length = sizeof( struct getInfoReply );

        _AH = 0xE3;
        _SI = (unsigned)Request;
        _DI = (unsigned)Reply;
        _ES = _DS;

        geninterrupt( 0x21 );

        return _AL;
}

void ShowInfo( struct getInfoReply Info )
{
        if ( !Info.LANDriverInstalled )
        {
                printf( " No Driver installed for this board.\n\n" );
                return;
        }

        printf( "Network Address      = [%02X%02X%02X%02X:%02X%02X%02X%02X%02X%02X]\n",
                Info.NetworkAddress[0],  Info.NetworkAddress[1],
                Info.NetworkAddress[2],  Info.NetworkAddress[3],
                Info.HostAddress[0], Info.HostAddress[1], Info.HostAddress[2],
                Info.HostAddress[3], Info.HostAddress[4], Info.HostAddress[5] );
        printf( "Option Number        = %d\n", Info.OptionNumber );
        printf( "Configuration Text   :\n%s\n\n", Info.ConfigurationText );
}
```

Exercises

1. Run LogLock. Test it with another station by trying to log in after it was run.

2. Run DrvrInfo. Choose another statistics call and write your own program. Call the routine every second to update the data, giving it a "live" feel.

3. Make performance tests of the system by using the Interval Marker field in many of the calls. Using a statistics call, like Get Disk Cache Statistics, Get Disk Channel Statistics, Get Connections Usage Statistics, etc., perform a server-intensive action such as making multiple calls or writing data, and make the statistics call again. Measure the differences. These calls can be used to monitor how certain activities affect network performance.

4. Incorporate some of the calls in this API into an application so the app becomes more "network-sensitive," changing its performance characteristics as the network load increases. For instance, the application could monitor the File Server Utilization field in the Get File Server Misc Information call; the application could perform more actions when the utilization went down, cut back when they went up. Obviously this would have to be for non-time-sensitive processing, but these calls can be used to make an application, or a user, more aware of the operating environment of the network.

14 IPX/SPX

Communication Services are provided under the Internetwork Packet Exchange (IPX) protocol and the Sequenced Packet Exchange (SPX) protocol, variations on the Xerox Network Systems Internet Transport protocol and two of the most powerful facilities available to the NetWare developer.

The APIs for these protocols allow developers to build true "peer-to-peer" communications into their programs. Peer-to-peer means workstations can talk to each other as peers, i.e. they need not go through a file server but may send packets directly. This enhances performance, reduces server overhead and increases flexibility.

Performance is enhanced by eliminating the middleman; stations don't need to be logged in to a file server to communicate. In fact, there doesn't even need to be a server present for two stations to communicate directly as long as the cabling system is functional and the workstation shell's IPX.COM file is loaded.

Server overhead is reduced when traffic bypasses the server, freeing up server time to devote to other tasks. The only time a server is involved in station-to-station communication is when it acts as a router. For example, if one station were to send a packet to another station on a different network, the packet would have to go through one or more file servers.

Flexibility is increased with IPX/SPX because the developer can determine exactly how workstations will communicate. This permits development of such value-added servers as databases, archive servers, or custom print servers.

Communication Services may be one of the more difficult APIs to learn, but once familiar to the developer it can prove an invaluable tool. We will begin by discussing IPX and SPX packet structures and continue with Event Control Block (ECB) structures and other concepts that relate to IPX/SPX programming. We will end with an example that uses IPX/SPX in a true peer-to-peer chat utility.

The Internetwork Packet Exchange protocol

The Internetwork Packet Exchange protocol resides on Layer 3 of the OSI model. IPX is a connectionless, or datagram, protocol. There is no need to establish a formal connection between the target and sending workstation before data can be sent. To send an IPX packet, the station simply addresses it and transmits; there is no guarantee that the packet will be delivered. (In datagram transmission, each packet is an individual entity, not part of a sequence.)

IPX is the faster of the two protocols, but because delivery is not guaranteed, it may not fulfill data verification needs. SPX is connection-oriented and will perform transport-layer verification not only of the delivery but also of the sequence of the packets as well. We will discuss SPX in the next section.

A programmer may build some verification into IPX. For example, as mentioned in chapter nine, in what Novell calls "implied verification," file servers use IPX for request and reply packets and if a server responds to a request, it is implied that it received the request. If, on the other hand, a station times out waiting for a response, it can be assumed the server never received the request.

IPX gives bridges and file servers more flexibility in routing packets because there are no predetermined delivery routes for delivery. Also, there is no program overhead in setting up the receiver and the sender simultaneously since there is no predetermined connection to set up. Unfortunately, the sender receives no verification that the packet was delivered. However, packets may be sent to multiple destinations by duplicating the packets and changing their destination addresses.

IPX packet structure

An IPX packet consists of a 30-byte header and a data portion that can be from 0 to 546 bytes. Thus minimum IPX packet length is 30 bytes (header plus a data portion of length 0) and the maximum is 576 bytes. To send a packet, the programmer must first fill in the necessary fields in the header.

IPX Packet Header

Offset	Content	Type
0	Checksum	WORD
2	Length	WORD
4	Transport Control	BYTE
5	Packet Type	BYTE
6	Destination Network	BYTE[4]
10	Destination Node	BYTE[6]
16	Destination Socket	BYTE[2]
18	Source Network	BYTE[4]
22	Source Node	BYTE[6]
28	Source Socket	BYTE[2]
30	Data	BYTE[0 to 546]

To send a packet, *Packet Type* and the *Destination address* fields (Network, Node, and Socket) must be initialized by the programmer.

All fields, except Data and those with only one byte, are high-low.

The *Checksum* field was used for compatibility with the original Xerox packet header. Now it is always set to 0xFFFF by IPX; LAN cards do hardware checksums on the entire IPX packet frame, so this field is unnecessary.

The *Length* field contains the length of the complete IPX packet (header length (30) + data). This field is set by IPX.

Transport Control is used by internetwork bridges; IPX sets this field to zero before transmission.

Packet Type indicates the type of service offered or required by the packet. Xerox has defined the following values:

0	Unknown Packet Type
1	Routing Information Packet
2	Echo Packet
3	Error Packet
4	Packet Exchange Packet
5	Sequenced Packet Protocol Packet
16-31	Experimental Protocols
17	NetWare Core Protocol

IPX users should set the Packet Type to 0 or 4, SPX users set it to 5.

Destination Network contains the number of the network on which the Destination Node resides. NetWare network numbers are four-byte values given to servers on the same network segment. When this field is set to 0, NetWare assumes the Destination Node is on the same physical network as the source node, i.e., the packet is not sent through an internetwork bridge.

Destination Node is a six-byte field that specifies the physical address of the Destination Node. The number of bytes depends on the LAN hardware used. Ethernet cards use all six, Omninet cards just one. If an address occupies fewer than six bytes, they should comprise the least significant portion of the field and the remainder should be padded with zeros. A node address of FFh FFh FFh FFh FFh FFh (all six set to FFh) sets IPX to broadcast mode, sending the packet to all nodes on the Destination Network.

Destination Socket is the socket address of the packet's destination process. Sockets route packets to different processes within each node. Xerox has reserved the following Socket Numbers:

1	Routing Information Packet
2	Echo Protocol Packet
3	Error Handler Packet
20h-3Fh	Experimental
1h-BB8h	Registered with Xerox
BB9h-	Dynamically assignable

Xerox has assigned Novell the following sockets for NetWare:

451h	File Service Packet
452h	Service Advertising Packet
453h	Routing Information Packet
455h	NetBIOS Packet
456h	Diagnostic Packet

Thus, file servers requests go to socket 0451h.

Novell administers a list of sockets; programmers writing for NetWare can have Novell assign them permanent Socket Numbers for their programs. Dynamic Socket Numbers (those randomly assigned by the shell) begin at 4000h. Socket numbers assigned by Novell begin at 8000h. Socket numbers above 8000h should be avoided unless they have been registered with Novell.

Source Network is the network number of the station sending the IPX packet. NetWare network numbers are four-byte values given to servers on the same network segment. IPX sets this field to the network number of the station making the request; if zero, the physical network is unknown.

Source Node is set by IPX to the physical address of the source node.

Source Socket, set by IPX, is the socket address of the process sending a packet, and is the socket specified in the ECB. Processes communicating peer-to-peer need not send and receive on the same Socket Number. In client-server environ-ments, the server node usually listens on a specific socket for incoming requests. In that case, the server should respond to the source socket. For example, all NetWare file servers have the same socket address, but requests to them may come from any Socket Numbers. Like destination sockets, these may be static or dynamic. Source Socket Numbers follow the same conventions as destination Socket Numbers.

The Sequenced Packet Exchange protocol

SPX provides a higher level of peer-to-peer communication, furnishing OSI transport-layer support. This enables SPX to guarantee delivery of sequenced packets, and to provide error detection and correction (with their concomitant — duplicate packet suppression). SPX, unlike IPX, is a "connection-oriented" protocol and a physical connection must be established between two workstations before communication can occur.

The price of these benefits is, of course, performance. The programmer must weigh the benefits of SPX against the higher performance of IPX. Guaranteed delivery, for example, increases overhead; in essence, two or more packets are sent for every single packet of useful information. Also, broadcast is not allowed; if it were, a connection would first have to be established with each receiver and no messages can be sent if a receiver is unavailable.

SPX packet structure

An SPX packet is identical to an IPX packet but has 12 more bytes in its header; and though the header has grown from 30 to 42 bytes, the maximum is still 576 bytes, so the data portion has shrunk to a maximum of 534 bytes. Except for Packet Type, which is always set to 5 by SPX, and Destination Node, which may not contain broadcast (six bytes of FFh) in SPX, the fields common to IPX and SPX are the same in each protocol's headers.

SPX Packet Header

Offset	Content	Type
0	Checksum	WORD
2	Length	WORD
4	Transport Control	BYTE
5	Packet Type	BYTE
6	Destination Network	BYTE[4]
10	Destination Node	BYTE[6]
16	Destination Socket	BYTE[2]
18	Source Network	BYTE[4]
22	Source Node	BYTE[6]
28	Source Socket	BYTE[2]
30	Connection Control	BYTE
31	Data Stream Type	BYTE
32	Source Connect ID	WORD
34	Dest Connection ID	WORD
36	Sequence Number	WORD
38	Acknowledge Number	WORD
40	Allocation Number	WORD
42	Data	BYTE[0 to 534]

Again, all fields (with more than one byte) are high-low.

Connection Control contains four single-bit flags used by SPX to control the bidirectional flow of data across a connection:

1-8 (Undefined) These bits are undefined in the Xerox Sequenced Packet protocol, and NetWare's SPX dutifully ignores them.

10h (End-Of-Message) A client sets this flag to signal to its partner an end of connection. SPX ignores it, passing it on unaltered.

20h (Attention) A client sets this flag if a packet is an attention packet. This feature has not been implemented, so SPX ignores this bit, too.

40h (Acknowledgment Required) SPX sets this bit if an acknowledgment packet is needed. Because SPX handles acknowledgment requests and responses, clients need not be concerned with it.

80h (System Packet) SPX sets this bit if the packet is a system packet. Such packets are not delivered to clients.

Applications should never use or modify undefined, acknowledgment, or system bits reserved by SPX for its own use.

Datastream Type is a one-byte flag that indicates the type of data found in the packet. Possible values and definitions for the field are:

0-FDh (Client Defined) This field is defined by the application and ignored by SPX.

FEh (End-of-Connection) SPX generates this packet when a client calls for termination of an active connection; it is the last message delivered on the connection.

FFh (End-of-Connection acknowledgment) SPX generates this system packet; it is not delivered to the connected clients.

Source Connection ID is a number assigned by SPX at the packet's source.

Destination Connection ID is a number assigned by SPX at the packet's destination. Because any connections active at the same time on a machine may use the same socket, this field is used to demultiplex incoming packets from different connections arriving on the same socket.

Sequence Number holds a count of packets exchanged in one direction on the connection. Each partner keeps its own count. The number wraps to 0 after FFFFh. SPX manages this field; applications need not be concerned with it.

Acknowledge Number is the Sequence Number of the next packet SPX expects to receive. Any packet with a Sequence Number less than this number is in order and need not be retransmitted. SPX manages this field; clients needn't worry about it.

Allocation Number is the number of listen buffers outstanding in one direction on the connection. SPX may only send packets until the Sequence Number equals the remote Allocation Number. Again, SPX manages this field; clients need not be concerned with it.

Event control blocks (ECBs)

Two structures are needed to send or receive packets under IPX or SPX — the IPX/SPX header and an event control block. An ECB is a structure that literally controls the "event," whether a send or a receive. There is no structural difference between a Send ECB and a Receive ECB, only a difference in content; a Send ECB needs a destination address in its Immediate Address field and a Receive ECB does not.

ECB Structure

Offset	Content	Type	Order
0	Link Address	LONG	offset-segment
4	ESR Address	LONG	offset-segment
8	In Use Flag	BYTE	
9	Completion Code	BYTE	

10	Socket Number	WORD	hi-lo
12	IPX Workspace	LONG	
16	Driver Workspace	BYTE[12]	
28	Immediate Address	BYTE[6]	hi-lo
34	Fragment Count	WORD	lo-hi
36	Fragment Address1	LONG	offset-segment
40	Fragment Size1	WORD	
42	Fragment Address2	LONG	offset-segment
46	Fragment Size2	WORD	

To send a packet the following fields must be initialized by the programmer: ESR Address, Socket Number, Immediate Address and at least one Fragment.

To receive a packet, the following fields must be initialized by the programmer: ESR Address, Socket Number and at least one Fragment.

Multiple fragment fields are provided as a convenience to the programmer.

Link Address is a field maintained by IPX while the ECB is in use and is available to the application when the ECB is not in use. If they use it at all, applications generally use it as a link field for listing free ECBs.

ESR Address, if it is used at all, contains the address of an application-defined event service routine (ESR) IPX can call when it's done sending or receiving. IPX maintains the In Use Flag and Completion Code field, so this field need not be used; a program can simply check the status of the outstanding IPX requests (ECBs) at appropriate intervals. If the ESR is not used, this field should be a null pointer (four bytes or zero).

The *In Use Flag* is reset to zero when IPX is done with an ECB. When the ECB is in use, possible values are:

FBh	A send or receive has occurred, but the ECB is in a holding queue waiting to be processed.
FDh	An event is scheduled and IPX awaits expiration of its time interval.
FEh	IPX is listening on a socket for incoming packets.
FFh	The ECB is in use for sending a packet.
FAh	The ECB is being processed by IPX.
F8h	A send was attempted while IPX was busy, so the send packet and ECB have been queued for later processing.

Completion Code is set by IPX to show the final status of an ECB; the field is not valid until IPX resets the in use flag to zero. Any of the following codes may be returned for a Send ECB:

00	(Successful) The packet was sent.
FCh	(Canceled) The send was canceled.
FDh	(Malformed) The packet is malformed. Total packet length is less than 30 bytes (IPX) or 42 bytes (SPX); or the length of the packet is greater than 576 bytes; or the first fragment is too small for a header; or the Fragment Count is zero.
FEh	(Undelivered) The packet cannot be delivered. There was no listener ready to receive the packet.
FFh	(Hardware/Network Failure) The network can't send the packet because of a hardware or network failure.

When an ECB is submitted to IPX to *listen for incoming packets*, any of the following Completion Codes may be reported.

00	(Successful) A packet has been received successfully.
FCh	(Canceled) The listen request has been canceled.
FDh	(Overflow) A packet overflow has occurred. A packet has been received, but the Fragment Count in the ECB is zero, or the available space (from the Fragment Descriptor list) is inadequate.
FFh	(Closed) The socket is closed.

When an ECB is submitted to *schedule a timer event*, the following Completion Codes may be reported.

00	(Successful) The timer event expired as indicated.
FCh	(Canceled) The timer event was canceled.

When an ECB is resubmitted to IPX for *canceling*, the following Completion Codes may be reported:

00	(Successful) The event was canceled.
F9h	(Cancel failure) The event should not be canceled.

Socket Number holds the number of the socket associated with an ECB. For a Send ECB, it's the Socket Number from which the packet is sent; for a Receive ECB, it's the Socket Number on which the packet is received.

IPX Workspace is a four-byte field reserved for IPX. It does not need to be initialized and must not be changed while IPX is using the ECB. While IPX is not using the ECB, an application may use this field.

Driver Workspace is a 12-byte field reserved for the network driver. Again, it need not be initialized, and it must not be changed while IPX is using the ECB. It can be used by applications any other time.

Immediate Address is a six-byte field containing the address of the node to which the packet is sent or from which it arrived, or the address of an internetwork bridge on the local network if the packet is not sent to or from a local network node. In IPX, an application must initialize this field before an ECB is sent. In SPX, the field is filled during creation of a connection for ECBs.

Fragment Count is the number of buffers from which a packet is formed for sending or into which it is split when received; it must be greater than zero.

Fragment Descriptor contains the address and size of the buffer to or from which a packet is sent or received. Every IPX ECB must have at least one Fragment Descriptor; each may have an arbitrary number of additional descriptors; these descriptors comprise a Fragment Descriptor list. This mechanism provides an easy way of filling in variables straight from the IPX Listen For Packet call.

Packets can be sent from or received with a single buffer by setting the fragment count to one and describing a single buffer of adequate size. The first entry in a descriptor list must be at least 30 bytes long for IPX and 42 bytes long for SPX and must hold the complete IPX or SPX packet header.

Fragment Descriptor List

Offset	Content	Type	Order
0	Address	LONG	offset-segment
4	Size	WORD	hi-lo

Asynchronous event scheduler (AES)

The asynchronous event scheduler (AES) is a timer within IPX that allows events to be executed at particular times. AES routines can help ease the programming burden of sending packets at regular intervals. For example, AES is very helpful when working with the Service Advertising Protocol (see chapter 16). There, packets identifying the server must be broadcast periodically. AES can be used to schedule those transmissions; once transmissions are scheduled, AES will continue to send packets whenever and wherever specified.

Another example of AES use is NetWare's watchdog process. If a server receives no packet from any server in its connection table for more than five minutes, it sends a watchdog packet to that station. If that station does not respond, the server sends a packet every minute for 15 minutes, then if there is still no response, the server logs out the station and resets the connection.

The IPX Schedule IPX Event call is used to start the AES and IPXCancelEvent is used to stop the scheduled AES event.

Event service routines

An event service routine (ESR) is a programmer's routine that is called after a particular event occurs. Here an event can be the completion of a send request or a listen, the recurrence of an IPX event that rescheduled itself (AES) or a special-purpose, application-defined event. As an ECB contains a field that points to an

ESR; when called, the ESR gets a pointer back to its ECB. The two are closely bound.

ESRs are called by ECBs at the conclusion of events, when the following conditions apply: The ECB's In Use Flag has been reset to zero; the Completion Code has been set; the ECB contains all appropriate information on the event; and the ECB has been removed from any IPX or AES internal lists.

An ESR is an interrupt service routine called with processor interrupts disabled. It should be designed carefully and should be treated like any other interrupt service routine: it should execute as few instructions as possible and do nothing that can be handled just as well in the body of an application.

Multiple ECBs should be allocated for applications that expect to receive several packets at one time. If this is not done, packets can be lost because not enough receive packets will be listening. One popular way of handling multiple ECBs is by creating a queue to service the ECBs and using ESRs to notify the queue that certain ECBs have been received.

Event service routine interface

When ESRs are invoked:

AL	Contains the identity of the calling process: 00h if AES called the ESR FFh if IPX called the ESR
ES:SI	Contains a pointer to the associated ECB

Before calling an event service routine, the shell pushes all flags and registers except SS and SP on the stack. Programmers should allocate their own stack. The ESR is responsible for saving SS and SP so it can return properly after execution. The shell also disables interrupts before calling the ESR.

When the shell calls the ESR, it sets the In Use Flag of the ECB to 0, records all appropriate information pertaining to the event in the ECB, and removes the ECB from any IPX or AES internal lists. The ESR is then free to manipulate the ECB.

When the ESR first starts, the program must initialize the DS register so application variables can be referenced.

Note: an ESR returns with no values or flags and with interrupts disabled, and it must return through a RETF (a far return) since it was entered through a far call.

Although a programmer is free to enable interrupts in an ESR, they should be disabled again before exiting. Developers should be aware that if interrupts are enabled, the ESR should be designed to be re-entrant since it may be called again while interrupts are enabled. Also, it should not take much time, whatever it has to do. Extensive processing in an interrupt service routine can be dangerous; send or receive events could be postponed indefinitely, even if interrupts have been re-enabled.

ESRs called by IPX or AES

These rules apply to ESRs called by IPX or the AES:

An ESR called by IPX may call any IPX (or AES) function except Close Socket.

An ESR called by IPX may reschedule itself for execution later by invoking IPX Schedule IPX Event with a pointer to its associated ECB and then executing a RETF instruction. The ESR will be called again when the event occurs. If an ESR were called by the AES, the IPX Schedule Special Event call could be used instead.

As explained above, ESRs called by IPX should do minimal processing. ESRs called by the AES, however, can execute for extended periods of time if they enable interrupts (for example to execute a popup utility). Although the integrity of AES will not suffer, there is one side effect: other scheduled ESRs during that same clock tick will be delayed until the next system clock tick.

Calls in the Communications Services API

The IPX calls (calls 00h through 0Bh) are supported in Advanced NetWare 1.02, 2.0 and 2.1, and in NetWare 386 and later versions. SPX calls (calls 10h through 17h) are supported in Advanced NetWare 2.1, and in NetWare 386 and later versions. Throughout the book, we explain fields within the calls only at the first mention of each field in each chapter. Appendix B contains a comprehensive, alphabetical listing of the fields for quick reference.

Novell suggests using interrupt 2Fh, the multiplex interrupt, to find the address of the interrupt service routine for INT 7Ah. Previously, the standard way of making IPX calls was to use INT 7Ah, but for the future, Novell recommends getting the address using 2Fh and jumping to it. The following assembly fragment illustrates this point:

```
data            segment
enterIPX        dd ?
data            ends

code   segment
   .
   .
   .
mov             AX,7A00H
int             2FH
cmp             AL,OFFH
jne             NO IPX
mov             ENTERIPX,DI
mov             AX,ES
mov             ENTERIPX + 2,AX
```

If loaded, IPX will set AL to FFh and return the far call address (of 7Ah in this case) in ES:DI. If IPX has not been loaded, AL will still be 0. Access to IPX can then be accomplished through a "CALL enterIPX" statement. The NetWare C Interface accomplishes this through the following function:

```
BYTE IPXInitialize( void );
```

IPX Open Socket (00h)

This call opens an IPX socket.

Registers in:

BX	00h
AL	Socket Longevity Flag
DX	Requested Socket Number (hi-lo)

Registers out:

AL	Completion Code
DX	Assigned Socket Number

Completion Codes:

00h	Successful
FFh	Socket Already Open
FEh	Socket Table Is Full

An application must use this call to open a socket before sending or receiving a packet on the socket.

The *Socket Longevity Flag* specifies how long the socket should remain open. Setting this field to 00h specifies that the socket will remain open until closed with the IPX Close Socket call or until the application is terminated. A value of FFh indicates that the socket will remain open until it is explicitly closed with IPX Close Socket. TSR applications (programs that terminate and stay resident) should use FFh to leave the socket open; most others should set this field to 0 to make sure the socket is closed when the application terminates.

The *Requested Socket Number* is the socket to open. If you pass 0000h in this field, IPX will assign you a socket dynamically.

By default, a workstation can have up to 20 open sockets at one time, but through the shell configuration file SHELL.CFG, this value can be increased to 150.

The NetWare C Interface format is:

```
int IPXOpenSocket( BYTE *socketNumber, BYTE socketType );
```

IPX Close Socket (01h)

This call closes an IPX socket.

Registers in:

BX	01h
DX	Socket Number (hi-lo)

Registers out:
Nothing

Completion Codes:
None

The *Socket Number* specifies the socket to be closed.

When the socket is closed, IPX cancels any outstanding events defined by the ECBs associated with the socket (such as listen events). Also, IPX returns FCh as the Completion Code in the ECB, indicating they were canceled. And last, IPX sets each ECB In Use field to 00 (available) and no ESRs are called.

TSRs should close sockets before terminating.

This call must not be called from within an event service routine.

The NetWare C Interface format is:

```
void IPXCloseSocket( WORD socketNumber );
```

IPX Get Local Target (02h)

This call returns the six-byte node address of the local target.

Registers in:

BX	02h
ES:SI	Request Buffer Address
ES:DI	Reply Buffer Address

Registers out:

AL	Completion Code
CX	Transport Time

Completion Codes:

00h	Successful
FAh	No Path to Destination Node Found

Request Buffer (12 bytes):

Offset	**Content**	**Type**	**Order**
0	Destination Network	BYTE[4]	hi-lo
4	Destination Node	BYTE[6]	hi-lo
10	Destination Socket	BYTE[2]	hi-lo

Reply Buffer (6 bytes):

Offset	**Content**	**Type**
0	Local Target	BYTE[6]

The programmer sends a full network address to the file server composed of the Destination Network, Node, and Socket. The server returns the address of the closest router (local bridge) and the estimated amount of time to deliver the packet to the destination.

Transport Time is an estimate of the time (in clock ticks of approximately 1/18 of a second) required to deliver a 576-byte to the destination.

This call should be used to get the Immediate Address for an ECB. Before calling Send Packet, an application should make this call and copy the Local Target value into the Immediate Address field of the ECB to be sent. However, if the application is responding to a recently sent packet, the listen ECB will contain the Immediate Address to send back to.

You can make this call from within an IPX event service routine, an AES Event Service Routine, or directly from an application (but cannot be called from any other interrupt service routine.)

The NetWare C Interface format is:

```
int GetLocalTarget( BYTE *networkAddress, BYTE *immediateAddress,
   int transportTime );
```

IPX Send Packet (03h)

This call initiates the sending of an IPX packet.

Registers in:
BX 03h
ES:SI ECB Address

Registers out:
Nothing

Completion Codes:
None

This call passes an ECB to IPX to send an IPX packet. The call the returns immediately while IPX attempts to send the packet.

To make this call, the application must initialize the ECB's ESR Address field, Socket Number field, Immediate Address field, Fragment Count field, and Fragment Descriptor fields. The application must also initialize the IPX packet header's Packet Type field, Destination Network field, Destination Node field, and Destination Socket field.

ECB Address points to an IPX Event Control Block.

Initially, IPX will set the ECB's In Use field to FFh to indicate that the ECB is sending a packet. IPX will also initialize the IPX packet header's Checksum field, Length field, Transport Control field, Source Network field, Source Node field, and Source Socket field.

After making this call, the programmer should call IPX Relinquish Control iteratively to wait for the packet to be sent (see example source code at end of chapter). After the packet has been sent, the programmer should check the Completion Code field of the ECB.

After sending the packet, the ECB's In Use field will be set to 0 (available) and the send ESR will be called, if any.

Possible ECB Completion Code values include the following:

00h	Successful (sent, not necessarily received).
FCh	The application canceled the send request.
FDh	The packet was malformed. (The packet size was less than 30 bytes or greater than 576 bytes, the first fragment was smaller than 30 bytes, or the value in the ECB's Fragment Count field was 00h.)
FEh	The packet was undeliverable.
FFh	IPX was unable to send the packet due to hardware or network failure.

Since this is a datagram protocol, the 00h Completion Code indicates that the packet was sent successfully but does not guarantee that the packet was received successfully by the destination node. Possible reasons for nondelivery include: The transmission media may lose or garble the packet, or the destination socket may not be open or listening. IPX does not inform the sending node if these problems occur. Guaranteed delivery is accomplished through the SPX calls.

The *FEh Completion Code* indicates that the packet is undeliverable. The ECB returns this Completion Code for one of three reasons: IPX could not find a bridge with a path to the destination network; the target node address did not exist; or the destination socket was not open or did not have any listening ECBs.

A station can send IPX packets to any station on the network including itself.

The NetWare C Interface format is:

```
void IPXSendPacket( ECB *eventControlBlock );
```

IPX Listen For Packet (04h)

This call prepares IPX to receive an IPX packet.

Registers in:

BX	04h
ES:SI	ECB Address

Registers out:

AL	Completion Code

Completion Codes:

FFh	Listening Socket Does Not Exist

This call passes an ECB to IPX to start listening for an IPX packet. The call then returns immediately while IPX attempts listens for a packet.

Before making this call, the programmer must open the socket and initialize the ECB's ESR Address field, Socket Number field, Fragment Count field, and Fragment Descriptor fields.

When this call is made, IPX sets the ECB's In Use field to FEh indicating that the ECB is waiting to receive a packet IPX also adds the ECB to a buffer pool of ECBs all listening for IPX packets on the same socket. IPX sets no limit on the number of ECBs that can be listening concurrently on a socket.

There are two ways to be notified of incoming packets: through polling or through interrupts. ESRs can be used for the interrupt method. To poll, continually check the value of the ECB's In Use field. If it drops to 0, a packet has been received. Check the Completion Code field to make sure it was received correctly.

When a packet is received, IPX places the packet in a listening ECB (they are not filled up in any order), it sets the Completion Code, and places the node address in the ECB's Immediate Address field. So, when returning the packet, the Immediate Address field is already set. Finally, IPX sets the ECB's In Use field to 0, available, and calls the ESR, if any.

Possible ECB Completion Code values include the following:

00h IPX successfully received the packet.

FCh The application canceled the receive request.

FDh IPX received the packet, but the value in the ECB's Fragment Count field is 00h, or the buffer space referenced by the ECB's Fragment Descriptor fields is too small to accommodate the packet.

FFh The socket defined by the ECB is not open.

The NetWare C Interface format is:

```
void IPXListenForPacket( ECB *eventControlBlock );
```

IPX Schedule IPX Event (05h)

This call schedules an IPX event.

Registers in:
BX 05h
AX Delay Time
ES:SI ECB Address

Registers out:
Nothing

Completion Codes:
None

This call delays an ECB for the number of ticks (1/18th of a second) given in Delay Time.

Before making this call, the programmer must initialize the ECB's ESR Address field and Socket Number field. When this call is first made, IPX sets the ECB's In Use field to FDh to indicate that the asynchronous event scheduler is counting down the delay time. On the last clock tick, IPX initiates the event, sets the ECB's In Use field to 00h, and calls the event service routine.

Any application or an ESR can invoke this call, although an application should never use this call to pass the address of an ECB currently being used by IPX.

The NetWare C Interface format is:

```
void IPXScheduleIPXEvent( WORD timeUnits, ECB *eventControlBlock );
```

IPX Cancel Event (06h)

This call cancels an event defined by an ECB.

Registers in:

BX	06h
ES:SI	ECB Address

Registers out:

AL	Completion Code

Completion Codes:

00h	Successful
F9h	ECB Cannot Be Canceled
FFh	ECB Not In Use

The events defined in an ECB canceled by this call include a send, listen, schedule, reschedule, or special-purpose event.

When this call is made, IPX sets the ECB's In Use flag to a nonzero value, indicating that the ECB is unavailable to other applications. After attempting to cancel the event defined by the ECB, IPX sets the ECB's Completion Code field to an appropriate value. It also sets the ECB's In Use field to 00h (Available For Use). IPX does not call an ESR.

Possible ECB Completion Code values include the following:

FCh	Event canceled

This call cannot cancel packets that have already been sent.

The NetWare C Interface format is:

```
int IPXCancelEvent( ECB *eventControlBlock );
```

IPX Get Interval Marker (08h)

This call gets a time marker from IPX.

Registers in:
BX 08h

Registers out:
AX Interval Marker

Completion Codes:
None

Interval Marker is a value between 0 and 65,535 (0000h and FFFFh), representing one clock tick (1/18th of a second).

An application can use this call to test the amount of time between events. Call this function once, perform the event, call again, and subtract the first from the second.

The NetWare C Interface format is:

```
unsigned IPXGetIntervalMarker( void );
```

IPX Get Internetwork Address (09h)

This call returns the network and node address of the requesting workstation.

Registers in:
BX 09h

Registers out:
ES:SI Reply Buffer Address

Completion Codes:
None

Reply Buffer (10 bytes):

Offset	**Content**	**Type**	**Order**
0	Network Address	BYTE[4]	hi-lo
4	Node Address	BYTE[6]	hi-lo

This call can be used by applications that need to inform other stations of their full network address. The two-byte socket must be appended to the end to form a full 12-byte network address. Because there can be multiple open sockets at one workstation, make sure to use the right one.

The NetWare C Interface format is:

```
void GetInternetworkAddress( BYTE *network Address );
```

IPX Relinquish Control (0Ah)

This call relinquishes control of a workstation's CPU.

Registers in:
BX 0Ah

Registers out:
None

Completion Codes:
None

When this call is made, the application temporarily relinquishes control of the processing time so that other processes in the workstation can be run. This call is most important when running on a server or a bridge since it improves efficiency.

Also, this call informs the communications driver that the CPU is temporarily free. This can be important if the driver is not interrupt driven. On a normal workstation, this call invokes a polling procedure provided by the network driver. This represents the only opportunity the driver has to use the CPU to send and receive packets.

The NetWare C Interface format is:

```
void IPXRelinquishControl( void );
```

IPX Disconnect From Target (0Bh)

This call is used to inform the specified listening socket that the application does not intend to send any more packets.

Registers in:
BX 0BH
ES:SI Request Buffer Address

Registers out:
Nothing

Completion Codes:
None

Request Buffer (12 bytes):

Offset	Content	Type	Order
0	Destination Network	BYTE[4]	hi-lo
4	Destination Node	BYTE[6]	hi-lo
10	Destination Socket	BYTE[2]	hi-lo

This call is a courtesy to network communications drivers that operate strictly on a point-to-point basis at the physical transport level. Once informed, a driver on a destination node can dismantle any virtual connection with the local node.

An application should never call this call from within an ESR.

The NetWare C Interface format is:

```
void IPXDisconnectFromTarget( BYTE *networkAddress );
```

SPX Initialize (10h)

This call determines whether SPX is installed on the node where the application is running.

Registers in:

BX	10h
AL	00h

Registers out:

AL	SPX Installation Flag
BH	SPX Major Revision Number
BL	SPX Minor Revision Number
CX	Maximum SPX Connections Supported
DX	Available SPX Connection Count

Completion Codes:
None

The *SPX Installation Flag* indicates whether SPX is installed (00h = not installed; FFh = installed).

The *SPX Major Revision Number* and the *SPX Minor Revision Number* indicate which SPX revision is installed. For example, revision 1.0 returns 1 in the first field and 0 in the second.

Maximum SPX Connections Supported is the maximum number of SPX connections set up in the SHELL.CFG file.

Available SPX Connection Count is how many SPX connections are available to the application.

The NetWare C Interface format is:

```
BYTE SPXInitialize( BYTE *majorRevisionNumber,
    BYTE *minorRevisionNumber, WORD *maxConnections,
    WORD *availableConnections );
```

SPX Establish Connection (11h)

This call attempts to establish a connection with a listening socket.

Registers in:

BX	11h
AL	Retry Count
AH	SPX Watchdog Flag
ES:SI	ECB Address

Registers out:

AL	Completion Code
DX	Connection ID

Completion Codes:

00h	SPX Attempting To Contact Destination Socket
EFh	Local Connection Table Full
FDh	Fragment Count Not 1; Buffer Size Not 42
FFh	Send Socket Not Open

When this call is made, the programmer passes a Retry Count, SPX Watchdog Flag, and ECB Address to SPX for the purpose of establishing an SPX connection. The call then returns control to the calling application while attempting to establish the connection.

Before making this call, the application must initialize an ECB's ESR Address field, Socket Number field, Fragment Count field, and Fragment Descriptor field. The Fragment Count field should be initialized to 01h. The Fragment Descriptor field must point to a 42-byte buffer containing the header of an SPX packet. Also, the application must initialize the SPX header's Destination Network field, Destination Node field, and Destination Socket field. None of these fields can be set to -1 (broadcast).

And finally, the application must create at least two listen ECBs, and pass them to SPX with SPX Listen For Sequenced Packet. Once SPX sends the Establish Connection packet mentioned above, SPX will use one of the listen ECBs to receive a confirmation packet from the destination socket.

When making this call, SPX tries to establish the connection in two steps. First, SPX creates a local connection half and verifies that the local connection half is fully functional. Second, SPX sends an Establish Connection packet through the local connection half to a specified (listening) destination socket in hopes of establishing a connection. To receive the Establish Connection packet, the destination socket have listening ECB's waiting that were posted with the SPX Listen For Connection call.

For the first step, SPX requires that the Retry Count, SPX Watchdog Flag, and ECB Address fields be set to the appropriate values.

The *Retry Count* specifies how many times SPX will resend unacknowledged packets before concluding that the destination node is not functioning properly. This field should be set 00h, instructing SPX to use its own internal retry count. A value of 1 through 255 (inclusive) indicates that SPX should resend packets the specified number of times.

The SPX watchdog process monitors an SPX connection, ensuring that the connection is functioning properly when traffic is not passing through the connection. If the watchdog process determines that an SPX connection has failed, the watchdog process signals the application by recording a value of EDh (failed connection) in the Completion Code field of any listening ECB. The watchdog process also records the failed connection ID number in the same ECB's IPX Workspace field, and calls the ECB's event service routine.

The application should initialize the SPX Watchdog Flag field to 01h thereby enabling the watchdog feature. A value of 00h disables the feature.

Once SPX creates and verifies the local connection half, the call returns a Completion Code. SPX also records this Completion Code in the Completion Code field of the sending ECB. If the call returns anything but 00h (successful), the attempt to establish a connection stops at this point.

If the call returns a Completion Code of 00h (successful), the call also returns a Connection ID. Although no connection is established yet with a destination socket, this Connection ID does occupy one entry in the node's SPX Connection Table. SPX then sends an Establish Connection packet to the destination node.

After sending the Establish Connection packet to the destination node (and resending it a specified number of times, if necessary), SPX sets the send ECB's Completion Code field to an appropriate value. SPX also sets the ECB's In Use field to 00h (available).

Possible ECB Completion Code values include the following:

EDh	SPX No Answer From Target (Either a hardware failure has occurred, or the application has used SPXAbortConnection.)
EFh	SPX connection Table Full (No further connections may be initiated until an active connection is terminated. The SPX Connection Table has room for 100 entries.)
FCh	SPX Socket Closed (The connection socket was closed before the command was completed, and the ECB's event service routine was not called.)
FDh	SPX Malformed Packet (The fragment count was not 1 or the buffer size was not 42.)
FFh	SPX Socket Not Opened

A workstation's SPX Connection Table is limited to a configurable number of connections. However, every entry in the SPX Connection Table does not necessarily represent an SPX connection. The following ECBs occupy each entry in the node's SPX Connection Table: ECBs participating in a connection, ECBs attempting to establish a connection, and ECBs attempting to listen for a connection.

Programmers should use SPX Abort Connection (not IPX Cancel Event) to cancel SPX Establish Connection.

Both sides of an SPX connection can reside in one workstation.

The NetWare C Interface format is:

```
int SPXEstablishConnection( BYTE retryCount, BYTE watchDog,
   WORD *connectionID, ECB *eventControlBlock );
```

SPX Listen For Connection (12h)

This call attempts to receive an Establish Connection packet.

Registers in:

BX	12h
AL	Retry Count
AH	SPX Watchdog Flag
ES:SI	ECB Address

Registers out:
Nothing

Completion Codes:
None

This call passes a Retry Count, SPX Watchdog Flag, and ECB Address to SPX for the purpose of listening for and receiving an Establish Connection packet. Once made, the call returns and SPX starts listening for an Establish Connection packet.

Before making this call, an application must initialize the ESR Address field and the Socket Number field of the ECB it will use, then create at least two listen ECBs, and pass them to SPX with SPX Listen For Sequenced Packet.

SPX Establish Connection and *SPX Listen For Connection* work together to establish a connection between sockets on a network.

SPX uses two steps to try to establish a connection. First, SPX creates a local connection half and verifies that it is fully functional. Second, after an Establish Connection packet is received, the function attempts to create a local connection. If successful, a confirmation packet is sent to the source node, and both sides are ready to either send or receive data on the connection. To summarize, the call listens for an Establish Connection packet sent by a source node using SPX Establish Connection, receives the packet, and sends a confirmation packet back to the source node.

To complete the first step that creates a local connection half, SPX requires that the Retry Count, SPX Watchdog Flag, and ECB Address fields be set to the appropriate value.

The SPX Watchdog flag monitors an SPX connection, ensuring that the connection is functioning properly when traffic is not passing through the connection. If the watchdog process determines that an SPX connection has failed, the watchdog process signals the application by recording a value of EDh (Failed Connection) in the Completion Code field of any listening ECB. The watchdog process also records the failed Connection ID number in the same ECB's IPX Workspace field and calls the ECB's ESR.

The application should initialize the SPX Watchdog Flag field to 01h, which enables the feature (0 disables it).

If SPX cannot create the local connection half because the socket is not open or the node's Connection Table is full, SPX writes one of the following Completion Codes in the ECB's Completion Code field and sets the In Use field to 00h (available).

EFh The local connection table is full.

FFh The receive socket is not open.

If SPX does not encounter problems, the ECB is ready to receive an Establish Connection packet.

If the application cancels the Establish Connection attempt at any time, SPX records a value of FCh (Request canceled) in the ECB's Completion Code field.

ECBs that attempt to establish connections and ECBs that participate in conversations each occupy one entry in the node's SPX Connection Table.

Programmers may use IPX Cancel Event to cancel SPX Listen For Connection.

The NetWare C Interface format is:

```
void SPXListenForConnection( BYTE retryCount, BYTE watchDog,
  ECB *eventControlBlock );
```

SPX Terminate Connection (13h)

This call terminates an SPX connection.

Registers in:

BX	13h
DX	Connection ID
ES:SI	ECB Address

Registers out:
Nothing

Completion Codes:
None

This call is made by passing a Connection ID and the address of an ECB to SPX which returns immediately to the calling program while attempting to break the connection.

Before making this call, the application must initialize the ECB's ESR Address field, Fragment Count field, and Fragment Descriptor field. The application must set the Fragment Count field to 1. The Fragment Descriptor field must point to an SPX packet.

When executing this call, SPX records a value of FEh (Terminate Connection) in the Datastream Type field of the SPX header referenced in the ECB. SPX then delivers the packet to the partner node, returns the appropriate Completion Code in the ECB's Completion Code field, and places 00h (Available For Use) in the ECB's In Use field. Finally, SPX calls the event service routine referenced by the ECB's ESR Address field (if applicable).

Possible ECB Completion Code values include the following:

00h Connection was terminated successfully.

FDh Packet was malformed. The fragment count was not 1, or the buffer size was not 42. In this case, the connection is aborted. (See the SPX Abort Connection call for a description of aborting connections.)

EEh The Connection ID Number contained in DX did not match a valid connection. No connection was terminated.

EDh The connection terminated abnormally. The remote connection partner failed to acknowledge the Terminate Connection request within an appropriate amount of time.
The connection is terminated on the local side, but SPX cannot guarantee that the connection partner saw the Terminate Connection. (This error is also returned if the network hardware fails or the packet cannot be delivered to the specified destination.)

ECh The connection was terminated by the remote partner without acknowledging this Terminate Connection packet.
The connection is closed, but SPX cannot guarantee the connection partner saw this Terminate Connection command.

Once SPX terminates a connection, the slot the Connection ID number occupied in the Connection Table becomes available.

An application should use SPX Abort Connection (not IPX Cancel Event) to cancel SPX Terminate Connection.

The NetWare C Interface format is:

```
int SPXTerminateConnection( WORD connectionIDNumber,
   ECB *eventControlBlock );
```

SPX Abort Connection (14h)

This call aborts an SPX connection.

Registers in:

BX	14h
DX	Connection ID

Registers out:
Nothing

Completion Codes:
None

Once this call is made, it returns immediately while SPX aborts only the side of the connection that made this call (unilateral abort).

SPX makes no attempt to inform the other side of the connection. The partner will discover the connection is no longer valid when it attempts to send a packet on the connection or when its watchdog makes a check after the inactivity timer expires.

Any SPX Establish Connection, SPX Terminate Connection, or SPX Send Sequenced Packet commands that are outstanding on the connection are aborted. The Completion Codes in the ECBs of such commands are set to EDh, indicating an abnormal connection termination.

The programmer should be aware that the event service routines of the affected ECBs are called (unless the ESR Address field is null). If any of the affected ECBs are in a state that does not allow them to be canceled (as when the network interface card is in the middle of sending the packet), the ECBs will be canceled at the earliest possible time. In this case, the Completion Code of the ECB is still set to EDh, and the ESR is called if it exists.

This call is included to allow a one side of a connection to unilaterally dismantle the connection if some fatal condition is detected. Under normal conditions, the SPX Terminate Connection call should be used to ensure that both connection partners abort the connection in a controlled fashion.

The NetWare C Interface format is:

```
void SPXAbortConnection( WORD connectionIDNumber );
```

SPX Get Connection Status (15h)

This call returns the status of an SPX connection

Registers in:

BX	15h
DX	Connection ID
ES:SI	Address of Reply Buffer

Registers out:
AL Completion Code

Completion Codes:
00h Connection Is Active
EEh No Such Connection

Reply Buffer (46 bytes):

Offset	Content	Type	Order
0	Connection State	BYTE	hi-lo
1	Watchdog Is On	BYTE	hi-lo
2	Local Connection ID	WORD	hi-lo
4	Remote Connection ID	WORD	hi-lo
6	Sequence Number	WORD	hi-lo
8	Local Acknowledge Number	WORD	hi-lo
10	Local Allocation Number	WORD	hi-lo
12	Remote Acknowledge Number	WORD	hi-lo
14	Remote Allocation Number	WORD	hi-lo
16	Local Socket	BYTE[2]	hi-lo
18	Immediate Address	BYTE[6]	hi-lo
24	Remote Network	BYTE[4]	hi-lo
36	Retransmission Count	WORD	hi-lo
38	Estimated Roundtrip Delay	WORD	hi-lo
40	Retransmitted Packets	WORD	hi-lo
42	Suppressed Packets	WORD	hi-lo

This call allows one to check on the current status of an SPX connection. If the specified connection does not currently exist, then the Completion Code (EEh) will be returned.

In the explanation that follows, local workstation refers to the workstation where the calling application is running and the local SPX resides. The local SPX may have several SPX connections open. This call returns information about only one of those connections. Remote workstation, however, refers to the workstation at the far end of the specified connection. The remote SPX is running on the remote workstation.

The *Connection State* field indicates the current state of the specified connection. Four possible states are defined:

01h *Waiting*. SPX is listening (SPX Listen For Connection) on the connection, waiting to receive an Establish Connection packet.

02h *Starting*. SPX is attempting to create (SPX EstablishConnection) a full connection with a remote workstation by sending Establish Connection packets on its half of the connection.

03h *Established*. SPX has established a connection with a remote workstation, and the connection is open for two-way packet transmission.

04h *Terminating*. The remote SPX has terminated the connection (SPX Terminate Connection). However, the local SPX has not yet terminated its half of the connection.

Watchdog Is On indicates whether the watchdog process is monitoring the local SPX proceedings. If set, the second bit in this field (0x02) indicates the presence of watchdog monitoring. The other seven bits of this field are for internal use.

Local Connection ID is the number of the specified SPX connection from the local workstation's point of view. The Local Connection ID is the same number the application loaded into register DX before making this call.

Remote Connection ID is the number of the specified SPX connection from the remote workstation's point of view.

The *Sequence Number* indicates the next packet the local SPX will send to the remote workstation. SPX assigns a Sequence Number (0000h to FFFFh) to each packet that it sends to the remote workstation. This ensures sequenced transmission at the local end and sequenced reception at the remote end. When the Sequence Number reaches FFFFh, it wraps to 0000h. This field is not valid if the connection state is waiting.

Local Allocation Number is the number of outstanding packet receive buffers (posted listens) available for a given SPX connection. The remote SPX is allowed to send packets with Sequence Numbers up to and including, but not exceeding, the Local Allocation Number. Meanwhile, the local SPX increments the Local Allocation Number as the local workstation generates listen ECBs. In this way, the local SPX regulates the number of packets that the remote SPX sends, and avoids being inundated with packets it is not ready to receive. When this number reaches FFFFh, it wraps back to 0h. This field is not valid if the connection state is waiting. This number is based on the number of listen ECBs outstanding.

Remote Acknowledge Number is the Sequence Number of the next packet that the remote SPX expects to receive from the local SPX. When this Sequence Number reaches FFFFh, it wraps to 0000h. This field is not valid if the connection state is waiting.

The local SPX is allowed to send packets with Sequence Numbers up to and including, but not exceeding, the Remote Allocation Number. Meanwhile, the remote SPX increments the Remote Allocation Number as the remote workstation generates listen ECBs. In this way, the remote SPX regulates the number of packets that the local SPX sends, and avoids being inundated with packets it is not ready to receive. When this number reaches FFFFh, it wraps back to 0000h. This field is not valid if the connection state is waiting. This number is based on the number of listen ECBs outstanding.

Local Socket is the Socket Number the local SPX is using to send and receive packets.

The *Immediate Address* field returns the node address of the bridge (on the local network) that routes the packets to and from the remote workstation. If the local and remote workstations reside on the same local network, the Immediate Address is the node address of the remote workstation. (In this case, a bridge is unnecessary.) This field is not valid if the connection state is waiting.

Remote Network returns the network number of the network on which the remote workstation resides.

Remote Node returns the node address of the destination node. This field is not valid if the connection state is waiting.

Remote Socket is the number of the socket that the remote SPX is using to send and receive packets. This field is not valid if the connection state is waiting.

Retransmission Count is the number of times (since SPX was loaded) that SPX attempts to retransmit an unacknowledged packet before it determines that the remote SPX has become inoperable or unreachable.

After sending a packet to the remote SPX, the local SPX waits for an acknowledgment before retransmitting the packet. The Estimated Roundtrip Delay field indicates in clock ticks the time that the local SPX waits. (Eighteen clock ticks equal approximately 1 second.) Because the local SPX observes fluctuations in throughput times and adjusts accordingly, the Estimated Roundtrip Delay value may change from time to time. This field is not valid if the connection state is waiting.

Retransmitted Packets is the number of times (since SPX was loaded) that the local SPX has had to retransmit a packet on this connection before receiving the expected acknowledgment. When this value reaches FFFFh, it wraps to 0000h. This field is valid only if the connection state is established or terminating.

Suppressed Packets is the number of times (since SPX was loaded) that the local SPX has received and discarded a packet because the packet was a duplicate of a previously received packet or because the packet was out-of-bounds for the current receive window. When this value reaches FFFFh, it wraps to 0000h. This field is valid only if the connection state is established or terminating.

The NetWare C Interface format is:

```
int SPXGetConnectionStatus( WORD connectionIDNumber,
    CONNECTION_INFO_STRUCT *connectionInfo );
```

SPX Send Sequenced Packet (16h)

This call sends an SPX packet.

Registers in:

BX	16h
DX	Connection ID
ES:SI	ECB Address

Registers out:
Nothing

Completion Codes:
None

When made, this call returns immediately while SPX attempts to send the SPX packet.

Before this call, the application must initialize the ECB's ESR Address field, Fragment Count field, and Fragment Descriptor fields. The fragment buffer referenced by the first Fragment Buffer field must contain at least a 42-byte SPX packet header. The application must also initialize the SPX packet header's End of Message bit in both the Connection Control field and the Datastream Type field.

Once made, SPX sets the ECB's In Use field to a nonzero value indicating that the ECB is sending a packet. SPX also queues the ECB/packet combination for transmission.

When SPX completes its attempt to send the packet, SPX records a Completion Code in the ECB's Completion Code field, sets the In Use field to 00h (available), and calls the event service routine, if any.

Possible ECB Completion Code values include the following:

00h	The packet was successfully sent and received in order by the connection partner. An acknowledgement from the partner was returned.
ECh	The remote partner terminated the connection without acknowledging this packet. SPX cannot guarantee that the remote partner received this packet before the connection was destroyed.
EDh	The connection ended abnormally. One of the two partners used the Abort Connection call to abort the connection, or the connection partner failed to acknowledge receipt of this packet. This error is also reported if the network hardware fails or the packet cannot be delivered to the specified destination.
EEh	The DX register does not contain the Connection ID of an established connection.
FCh	The connection's socket was closed. In this case, the event service routine is not called.
FDh	The packet was malformed. The Fragment Count is zero, the first fragment is less than 42 bytes long, or the entire packet is greater than 576 bytes long. This error causes the connection to be aborted.

The programmer should note that SPX queues and sends ECBs in the order that it receives them. Also, sockets used by SPX connections cannot be used to send or receive IPX packets. And finally, when an application or some other agent closes an SPX socket, SPX terminates all connections associated with the socket.

An application can establish a connection between two sockets residing in the same node.

An application should use SPX Abort Connection (not IPX Cancel Event) to cancel an SPX Send Sequenced Packet event.

The NetWare C Interface format is:

```
void SPX SendSequencedPacket( WORD connectionIDNumber,
   ECB *eventControlBlock );
```

SPX Listen For Sequenced Packet (17h)

This call receives an SPX sequenced packet.

Registers in:
BX 17h
ES:SI ECB Address

Registers out:
Nothing

Completion Codes:
None

When made, this call returns immediately while SPX begins listening for an incoming SPX packet.

Before making this call, the application must initialize the ECB's ESR Address field, Socket Number field, Fragment Count field, and Fragment Descriptor field. The fragment buffer referenced by the first Fragment Buffer field must be at least 42 bytes long (to receive the incoming SPX packet header).

Initially, SPX sets the ECB's In Use field to a nonzero value, indicating that the ECB is waiting to receive a packet. SPX also adds the ECB to a buffer pool of ECBs that are listening for sequenced packets on the same socket. When an incoming SPX packet arrives, SPX uses one of the listening ECBs to receive the packet. SPX records an appropriate value in the ECB's Completion Code field, sets the ECB's In Use field to 00h (Available For Use), and calls the event service routine referenced by the ECB's ESR Address field (if applicable).

Possible ECB Completion Codes include:

00h A packet was received successfully on an active connection.

FFh The socket at which the ECB was to listen is not opened, the Fragment Count field is zero, or the first fragment of the ECB's Fragment Descriptor List is less than 42 bytes long.

FDh A packet overflow occurred. A sequenced packet was received, but the available space defined by the ECB's Fragment Descriptor List was not large enough to contain the entire packet.

FCh The listen request was canceled by a Close Socket or Cancel Event call. In this case, the event service routine is not called.

EDh The SPX watchdog determined that a connection failed and aborted the connection. The Connection ID Number of the terminated connection is in the first word (first two bytes) of the ECB's IPX Workspace field.

The NetWare C Interface format is:

```
void SPXListenForSequencedPacket( ECB *eventControlBlock );
```

Code Sample: IPXChat.C

IPXChat is a peer-to-peer chat utility that allows two stations to communicate using IPX. The performance of this program should be compared to the PipeChat.C program we developed for the Message Services API (chapter 10). With PipeChat, the messages are gathered and sent line-by-line whereas with IPXChat, messages are sent by character.

With PipeChat, the user specifies at the command line whether the station will be listening for a request or sending a request. The command line switch "/r" sets up IPXChat to receive packets. First, the program opens an IPX socket to receive requests to chat, then it posts a listen ECB and enters a loop, waiting for a keystroke from the user to abort the process and polling the ECB to see if any requests have come in.

The send-a-request "/s" option requires the name of the user to send the request to following the switch (so "/s SUPERVISOR" would request to send to the supervisor). The send part of the program finds out the connection number and the address of the target user, and sends a request packet. The listening user is asked if he would like to chat, and, if he would, another socket is opened by both stations and they enter a mutual chat mode.

The main chat mode is essentially a loop that checks the keyboard for characters to send (to the screen as well as to the other station) and for characters received by the other station. If either party presses the ESC key, the other is notified, and the chat session is terminated.

We begin IPXChat with a list of include statements, gathering our standard and application-specific header files into the program. The two application-specific headers, "ipx.h" and "ncp.h" are included to provide IPX/SPX routines and Connection Services routines respectively.

We declare external and local prototypes, including the external assembly routines SendESRHandler() and ListenESRHandler(). These are our event service routines and will be called at the completion of a send or receive.

Several variables are next on our list to declare, including *InitBuffer*, which will be used to store the name of the requesting workstation when sending an invitation to the target workstation to chat. Also, *InitialECB* and *InitialIPXHeader* are declared, which are our initial ECB and initial IPX headers.

Main() begins by checking the number of arguments. If an incorrect number was entered, the user is informed of the correct syntax and the program exits. If the user entered a "/r" the MainListen() routine is called and if a "/s" was entered, MainSend() is called; otherwise, it is assumed some other bad syntax was entered and the user is informed of the correct syntax and the program exits.

MainListen()'s job is to open the invitation socket INVITE_SOCKET, post a listen request, and either respond to incoming chat requests or to abort the process at the appropriate keystroke. First, the *InitialECB* and *InitialIPXHeader* are initialized with SetupRcvPacket().This routine initializes all necessary fields, setting the ESR to the right address (in this case, NULL, since we will poll the ECB), setting the *InUseFlag* to 0, the *ECBSocket* to the correct number and the *Fragment Count* to 2.

We set the *Fragment Count* to 2 because the first fragment will contain the IPX Header and the second fragment will contain our actual data. Fragments can be used to elegantly let IPX handle placing incoming data where it should be.The *Fragment Addresses* and sizes are sent and control returns to MainListen().

MainListen() next opens the socket INVITE_SOCKET. We place the value in the target socket and pass the address of *target socket*; the IPXOpenSocket call needs the address of the variable containing the Socket Number rather than the Socket Number itself. After making sure the open worked, we post *InitialECB* as a listening ECB. We will only post one ECB since we're only expecting one other station to request a chat with us. A program expecting more simultaneous requests should post more ECBs.

Next, MainListen() enters a WHILE loop, checking the keyboard for any key hit and the *InUseFlag* of InitialECB. The *InUseFlag* will remain 0xFE while the ECB is listening, but will return to 0 once a packet is received. If a packet is received, the Completion Code is checked, and if okay (0) the user is asked if he wishes to chat with the calling party. If they do, the source address is copied into the target address and the *InitialECB* and *InitialIPXHeader* is setup to send a packet back.

IPXSendPacket() sends the reply about chatting and the program enters Chat() mode, ready to chat with the user. On the sending side, if the user has specified the "/s" command-line switch, and passed the name of the target user to chat with, then our program calls MainSend() to contact the target user and establish a communication session.

MainSend() begins by getting the connection number of the sending station. Next, it enters a loop to check each of the connections on the LAN, comparing the target user's name with the name of the user at that connection. Once the names match, the target user's connection is recorded in the *targetConn* variable. Also, the name of the sending station is stored in *InitBuffer* at offset 1; *InitBuffer* will be sent to the target workstation and contains the source user's name to be used in the following message: "Do you want to chat with x?" where x is the name in *InitBuffer*.

The Get Internet Address routine is called to determine the 12-byte address (four-byte network, six-byte node, two-byte socket) of the target connection. The socket that we will be using to request chatting is opened (INVITE_SOCKET) and the *InitialECB* and *InitialIPXHeader* are set up for sending. Next the request packet is sent and the program enters a timing loop to wait a predetermined number of seconds for the other user to respond. If the routine times out, it can be assumed that the target user was not at the workstation or ignored the request, or that the target workstation had a hardware failure.

If the target user says he does not wish to chat, MainSend() exits to DOS. If the target user wishes to chat, MainSend() transfers control to Chat() to execute the main chatting code.

Chat uses a different socket for chatting than it does for the chat invitation process. This shows how different Socket Numbers might be used for different purposes. Due to space limitations, this program does not include complete code. The program could be extended to post listen ECBs even after a chat session was established; an ESR could be setup to indicate to the requesting workstation that the current party is engaged in a chat session and cannot "talk" right now. One add-on feature might be for the target workstation to take a message for the busy user so he can return the call.

Chat() begins by opening the CHAT_SOCKET and posting a listen ECB with IPXListenForPacket(). Next, the program enters a while loop checking the keyboard for new characters to send and checking the *NewPacket* flag for new characters that have arrived. Characters typed are placed on the screen, put into *InitBuffer* and sent. Characters received are printed to the screen and IPXListenForPacket() is called again to post the ECB back to a listen state. If the ESC key is pressed by the local station, a cancel message is sent to the remote station (and vice-versa). The socket is closed and the program terminates.

Here are a few important notes about IPXChat for the developer to consider:

- The ESR used in this program, ListenESR(), simply sets the *NewPacket* flag and returns. The program checks the *NewPacket* flag to see if new packets have arrived. This is roughly equivalent to polling (the program could just check the *InUseFlag* of RcvECB). The ESR could be much more elaborate, feeding the received packets into a queue that would be serviced by another process.
- In any case, remember not to make the ESR too elaborate, as interrupts are disabled when the ESR is called and processing should be as brief as possible (or interrupts could be enabled, but the routine must be re-entrant if this is done).
- Remember to post listening ECBs back into the field after they have received packets. Once an ECB has received a packet, it won't receive any more until another Listen request is made on it. Also, allocate several ECBs if more than one station will be responding or if the amount of packets sent will be relatively high. IPXChat allocates only one packet because it is assumed the keyboard will slow down any would-be packet blasters.
- Remember that the Socket Number is stored in high-low format, therefore Socket Number 0x1234 is actually socket 0x3412.

In a later chapter, we will use the C-Worthy user interface to create a lucid front-end to our peer-to-peer chat program.

```
/*                                                                      */
/* IPXChat - A true peer-to-peer chat utility                           */
/*                                                                      */
/*                                                                      */
/* by Charles Rose                                                      */
/*                                                                      */

typedef unsigned char BYTE;
typedef unsigned int WORD;
typedef unsigned long LONG;

#include <stdio.h>
#include <conio.h>
#include <string.h>
#include <mem.h>
#include <dos.h>
#include <time.h>

#include "ipx.h"
#include "ncp.h"

#define WAITMAX 10

#define ESC       27
#define BS 8
#define CR 13

/* Foreign & domestic prototypes */

extern void SendESRHandler();
extern void ListenESRHandler();
void SendESR();
void ListenESR();

void Problem();
void SetupInitialPacket();

void MainSend( char *targetUser );
void MainListen();
void PlaceChar( char Char );

void RePostListenRequest();

/* Global data definitions */

int  NewPacket;
BYTE InitBuffer[49];

ECB InitialECB;
IPXPacket InitialIPXHeader;     /* Initial ECB/IPX for requesting chat */

BYTE    targetNetwork[4] = { 0, 0, 0, 0 };
BYTE    targetNode[6] = { 0xFF, 0xFF, 0xFF, 0xFF, 0xFF, 0xFF };

main( int argc, char *argv[] )
{
        if ( ( argc > 3 ) || ( argc < 2 ) )
        {
```

```
printf( "Usage: IPXCHAT /s username  - to send a chat request to username or \n" );
        printf( "                /r    - to wait to receive a chat request\n" );
                exit( 1 );
        }

        if ( !stricmp( argv[1], "/r" ) )
        {
                MainListen();
                exit(1);
        }

        if ( !stricmp( argv[1], "/s" ) )
        {
                MainSend( argv[2] );
                exit(1);
        }

        printf( "Invalid command-line parameter\n" );
printf( "Usage: IPXCHAT /s username  - to send a chat request to username or \n" );
        printf( "                /r     - to wait to receive a chat request\n" );
}

void Chat()
{

        ECB SendECB;
        IPXPacket SendIPXHeader;        /* Send ECB/IPX for outgoing packets */
        ECB RcvECB;
        IPXPacket RcvIPXHeader;         /* Rcv ECB/IPX for incoming packets */

        int Finished;                   /* If set, then communication is over */
        int FromHim;                    /* If set, the other guy terminated */

        BYTE SendBuffer;
        BYTE RcvBuffer;

        WORD                    targetSocket;

        char                    probdesc[80];
        int                     status, i;

        /* Setup Send & Receive structures */
        SetupSendPacket( &SendECB, &SendIPXHeader, targetNetwork,
                targetNode, CHAT_SOCKET, &SendBuffer, sizeof( SendBuffer ), 0 );

        SetupRcvPacket( &RcvECB, &RcvIPXHeader, CHAT_SOCKET,
                &RcvBuffer, sizeof( RcvBuffer ), ListenESRHandler );

        targetSocket = CHAT_SOCKET;

        status = IPXOpenSocket( ( BYTE * ) &targetSocket, TEMPORARY_SOCKET );
        if ( status != OKAY )
        {
                printf( " Can't open socket\n" );
                return;
        }

        printf( "Chat session established:\n\n\n\n" );

        IPXListenForPacket( &RcvECB );
```

```
NewPacket = 0;
SendBuffer = RcvBuffer = 0;
FromHim = Finished = 0;

while ( !(Finished) )
{
        if ( bioskey(1) )
        {

                SendBuffer = bioskey(0);

                if ( SendBuffer == ESC ) Finished++;
                else
                {
                        PlaceChar( SendBuffer );
                        IPXSendPacket( &SendECB );
                        while ( SendECB.InUseFlag != OKAY )
                                IPXRelinquishControl();

                        if ( SendECB.CompletionCode != OKAY )
                        {
                                sprintf( probdesc, " Bad code,
                                status = %x ", SendECB.CompletionCode);
                                Problem( probdesc );
                                goto Ending;
                }
                }

}

        if ( NewPacket )
        {
                NewPacket = 0;

if ( RcvECB.CompletionCode != OKAY )
                {
                        sprintf( probdesc, " Bad rcv, status = %x ",
                           RcvECB.CompletionCode);
                        Problem( probdesc );
                        goto Ending;
                }

                if ( RcvBuffer == 0xFF )
                {
   printf( "\n\n-= Other user requested quit. Chat session over =-\n" );
                        Finished++;
                        FromHim++;
                }
                else
                {
                        PlaceChar( RcvBuffer );
                        IPXListenForPacket( &RcvECB );
                }
        }
}

/* If we shut down, let him know */
if ( !FromHim )
{
        SendBuffer = 0xFF;
        IPXSendPacket( &SendECB );
```

```
                while ( SendECB.InUseFlag != OKAY )
                        IPXRelinquishControl();

                if ( SendECB.CompletionCode != OKAY )
                {
  sprintf( probdesc, " Send error in Send ECB when shutting down, status = %x ",
        SendECB.CompletionCode );
                        Problem( probdesc );
                        return;
                }

  printf( "\n\n-= Chat session cancelled.  Other user has been notified =-\n" );
        }


Ending:

        IPXCloseSocket( CHAT_SOCKET );
}

void SendESR( ECBptr )
ECB *ECBptr;
{
}

void ListenESR( ECBptr )
ECB *ECBptr;
{
        NewPacket++;
}

void Problem( char *prob )
{
        printf("%s\n", prob);
        exit(1);
}


void MainSend( char *targetUser )
{
        int                     status, numrecs, x, ourstn = 0;
        WORD                    select;
        char                    probdesc[80], reqtext[80];
        time_t                  wait_secs, start_secs;

        BYTE                    name[48], socket[2];
        WORD                    type;

        WORD                    targetSocket = INVITE_SOCKET;
        BYTE                    targetConn;
        IPXAddress              IPXaddr;

        ourstn = NCPGetOurStnNum();

        targetConn = 0;
        for ( x = 0; x < 100 ; x++ )
        {
                status = NCPGetConnInfo( x, &type, name );

                if ( (!status) && ( type == 0x100 ) )
                {
```

```
                if ( !stricmp( name, targetUser ) )
                {
                        targetConn = x;
                        break;
                }

                if ( x == ourstn )
                        strcpy( &InitBuffer[1], name );

        }
}

if ( !targetConn )
{
        printf( " Target user %s not logged in.\n", targetUser );
        return;
}

/* Setup request window & get user to talk to */

/* Here's where you get the address & put it in targetNode */
NCPGetInterNetAddr( targetConn, targetNetwork,
        targetNode, socket );

/* Set InitBuffer[0] request class to 0 ( Chat request ) */
InitBuffer[0] = 0;

/* Open Socket */
status = IPXOpenSocket( ( BYTE * ) &targetSocket, TEMPORARY_SOCKET );

/* Now setup send packet */

SetupSendPacket( &InitialECB, &InitialIPXHeader, targetNetwork,
   targetNode, INVITE_SOCKET, InitBuffer, sizeof( InitBuffer ), 0 );

/* Send Initial Packet */

IPXSendPacket( &InitialECB );
while ( InitialECB.InUseFlag != OKAY )
        IPXRelinquishControl();

if ( InitialECB.CompletionCode != OKAY )
{
        printf( " Send error in Initial ECB, status = %x ",
         InitialECB.CompletionCode );
        return;
}

/* Setup again and listen for response */

SetupRcvPacket( &InitialECB, &InitialIPXHeader, INVITE_SOCKET,
        InitBuffer, sizeof( InitBuffer ), 0 );

IPXListenForPacket( &InitialECB );

wait_secs = time( &start_secs );
printf(" Waiting for user response...\n " );
while ( ( InitialECB.InUseFlag != OKAY ) &&
         ( ( wait_secs - start_secs ) < WAITMAX ) )
{
        IPXRelinquishControl();
        time( &wait_secs );
```

```
        }

        if (  ( wait_secs - start_secs ) >= WAITMAX )
        {
                printf( " User did not respond \n");
                return;
        }

        if ( InitialECB.CompletionCode != OKAY )
        {
                printf( " Bad reception, status = %x\n ",
                        InitialECB.CompletionCode );
                return;
        }

        if ( !(InitBuffer[0]) )
        {
                printf( " User did not wish to communicate\n " );
                return;
        }

        movmem( InitialECB.ImmediateAddress, IPXaddr.Node, 6 );
        movmem( targetNetwork, IPXaddr.Network, 4 );

        Chat();
}

void MainListen()
{
        WORD    targetSocket = INVITE_SOCKET;
        int     status;
        char    prob[80];

        SetupRcvPacket( &InitialECB, &InitialIPXHeader, INVITE_SOCKET,
                InitBuffer, sizeof( InitBuffer ), 0 );

        status = IPXOpenSocket( ( BYTE * ) &targetSocket, TEMPORARY_SOCKET );

        if ( status != OKAY )
        {
                sprintf( prob, "Error # %X opening socket", status );
                Problem( prob );
        }

        IPXListenForPacket( &InitialECB );

        printf( "Now waiting for chat request...\n" );
        printf( "Press any key to exit.\n" );

        while ( 1 )
        {
                if ( bioskey( 1 ) )
                {
                        bioskey(0);
                        IPXCancelEvent( &InitialECB );
                        IPXCloseSocket( INVITE_SOCKET );
                        exit(1);
                }

                if ( !InitialECB.InUseFlag )
                {
                        if ( !InitialECB.CompletionCode )
```

```
                    {

                while ( ( InitBuffer[0] != 'Y' ) && ( InitBuffer[0] != 'N' ) )
                            {
            printf( "Do you wish to chat with %s? (Y/N)\n", &InitBuffer[1] );
                                    strupr( gets( InitBuffer ) );
                            }

                            if ( InitBuffer[0] == 'Y' )
                                    InitBuffer[0] = 1;
                            else
                                    InitBuffer[0] = 0;

        /* Place the immediate address returned into our new target node */
                            movmem( InitialIPXHeader.Source.Node,
                              targetNode, 6 );
                            movmem( InitialIPXHeader.Source.Network,
                              targetNetwork, 4 );

                            /* Setup to send the reply */
                            SetupSendPacket( &InitialECB, &InitialIPXHeader,
                              targetNetwork, targetNode, INVITE_SOCKET,
                              InitBuffer, sizeof( InitBuffer ), 0 );

            /* Send the reply about whether we want to chat or not */
                            IPXSendPacket( &InitialECB );
                            while ( InitialECB.InUseFlag != OKAY )
                                    IPXRelinquishControl();

                            if ( InitialECB.CompletionCode != OKAY )
                            {
                        printf( " Send error in Intial ECB, status = %x ",
                                            InitialECB.CompletionCode );
                                    RePostListenRequest();
                                    return;
                            }

                            if ( !InitBuffer[0] )
                            {
                                    RePostListenRequest();
                                    return;
                            }

                            Chat();
                            exit(1);
                    }
            }
        }
}

void RePostListenRequest()
{
        /* Setup for another round */

        IPXCancelEvent( &InitialECB );

        SetupRcvPacket( &InitialECB, &InitialIPXHeader, INVITE_SOCKET,
                InitBuffer, sizeof( InitBuffer ), 0 );
        IPXListenForPacket( &InitialECB );
```

```
}

void PlaceChar( char Char )
{
        if ( Char == CR )
                printf( "\n" );
        else
                printf( "%c", Char );
}
```

Exercises

1. Run IPXChat using two workstations. Examine what must be done to set up an ECB for sending or receiving. Familiarize yourself with all the calls made.

2. Write SPXChat, a program functionally equivalent to IPXChat, except use SPX routines.

3. Write a station-to-station performance testing program. Pass packets back and forth and use Get Interval Marker to time them. Use SPX. What performance differences do you see?

4. Extend IPXChat (or SPXChat) to allow a party of workstations to chat at once, similar to a CB simulator.

5. Write an application using IPX or SPX to allow workstations to share information directly.

6. Write an IPX or SPX application that allows two stations to chat; you may use IPXChat as an example, but don't use any Novell API calls. Instead, allow the user to pass the network address in the command line. Get these with the "USERLIST /A" command. Log out of the file server. You can still chat station to station even if not logged into a file server, even if there are no file servers. Why is this?

15 Diagnostic Services

Diagnostic Services open for the developer a wide array of perspectives on the configuration and health of a network. This API provides a wealth of IPX/SPX-based diagnostic capabilities, including finding all nodes on the internetwork; performing point-to-point tests; gathering statistics about certain components and component drivers; displaying network element-specific tables; building maps of the internetwork; and learning the configurations of certain nodes.

The ability to identify all nodes is a critical component of Diagnostic Services. To do so, the NetWare v2.1 shell monitors socket 456h for Configuration Request packets. Any station that boots DOS and loads the v2.1 shell listens to socket 456h, even if the station has not logged in to a file server, and even if there are no active file servers. So each user can use IPX's broadcast function to gather responses from every node with a 2.1 shell loaded on the network. SPX calls can then be used to establish connections and to query for component statistics and tables, and for driver configurations.

Another key element of Diagnostic Services is the ability to perform point-to-point tests. These tests can measure the speed and integrity of packet transmission or reception between two nodes. This lets programmers gather a number of useful statistics, such as the numbers of good and bad packets received and the times required to send the packets. And developers can build internetwork maps by finding the times of transmission between nodes.

Other statistics are available for bridge and shell components and component drivers, showing the relative health of each. Each report contains more than 20 different fields of information pertaining to the bridge or shell. Similar information is available on Value-Added Processes (or VAPs) running in bridges. Also available through Diagnostic Services are shell Server Name and Connection ID Tables, and bridge routing tables.

Configuration packets

The first step in any use of the Diagnostic Services is to send Configuration packets to all relevant nodes. To send to an individual station, its 12-byte address (four-byte Network Address, six-byte Node Address, and two-byte Socket Number) must be placed in the IPX header. Node Address must also be placed in the Immediate Address field of the ECB (with the IPX Get Local Target call).

In this case, we want to contact all stations, so the Destination Network Address begins with a value of zero, denoting the current network. The Node address is six bytes of FFh, meaning send to all stations. And the Socket Number for the Configuration Socket is 456h.

The request packet structure is quite simple: The Exclusion Count, a byte containing the number of Exclusion Addresses, is followed by an array of the actual six-byte Exclusion Addresses.

The request packet structure is quite simple: a byte containing the number of Exclusion Addresses followed by an array of the actual six-byte Exclusion Addresses. The Configuration Request and Configuration Reply structures are defined as follows:

```
typedef struct IPXConfigRequestStructure
{
     IPXPacket       IPX;
     BYTE            ExclusionCount;
     BYTE            ExclusionAddress[MAX_NODES][6];
} IPXConfigRequest;

typedef struct IPXConfigReplyStructure
{
     IPXPacket       IPX;
     BYTE            MajorVersion;
     BYTE            MinorVersion;
     WORD            SPXDiagnosticSocket;
     BYTE            ComponentCount;
     BYTE            ComponentType[MAX_COMPONENTS];
} IPXConfigReply;
```

The *Component Type* fields list the software components that reside at the responding node. Each node on a NetWare network includes one or more of the following Software Components:

0	IPX/SPX
1	Bridge Driver
2	Shell Driver
3	Shell
4	VAP Shell
5	External Bridge
6	Internal Bridge
7	Nondedicated File Server
8	Star 68000 (IPX only)

For example, a workstation includes the following:

0	IPX/SPX
2	Shell Driver
3	Shell

An external bridge is made up of the following software components:

0	IPX/SPX
1	Bridge Driver
5	External Bridge
4	VAP Shell (optional)

A dedicated file server is made up of the following software:

0	IPX/SPX
1	Bridge Driver
6	Internal Bridge
4	VAP Shell (optional)

When the initial IPX packet is sent, a program must wait a reasonable amount of time for other stations to reply. (Nodes can take up to a half a second to respond. So in our NodeList program at the end of the chapter, we wait a full second after each query just to make sure all nodes have responded.)

Those nodes that successfully respond have their Node Addresses placed in the Configuration Request Packet. The Exclusion Count is then increased and the call is sent again to gather up any stations not responding to the previous call. Usually a program needs to make several requests to contact all stations.

The exclusion mechanism does not work on bridges, because bridges respond to every configuration request. Therefore, programs must include code to assure that configuration requests are not re-sent to bridges that have already responded.

The reply that comes from each station contains the Major and Minor version numbers of its shell or bridge driver, the SPX Socket Number for corresponding about Diagnostic Services, and a list of Components present in the station: IPX/SPX, shell driver, bridge driver, and so on. Socket Number and the offset of the target in the Component list are used to establish an SPX connection with the node.

Steps in querying shell and bridge components

Programs must follow several discrete steps in getting the list of nodes and their configurations. The steps are:

1. Open socket for sending.
2. Post Listen ECBs for Configuration Reply packets.
3. Send Configuration Request packet.
4. Place responding Node Addresses in Exclusion Table.

5. Go to step 3 MAX_RETRIES times to ensure all nodes have responded.
6. Iterate through list of nodes performing the following:
   a. Establish SPX connection with target node.
   b. Query driver for configuration.
   c. Print results.
   d. Terminate SPX connection.

Here's how to make them using NodeList.C, our sample program for this chapter.

First, we must open a socket and post a sufficient number of IPX Listen ECBs to handle the returns. Next, we prepare a Configuration Request packet with no Exclusions and broadcast it on socket 456h. We add responding nodes to the Exclusion table and rebroadcast the request several (MAX_RETRIES) times to assure that NodeList gathers all nodes.

When a complete node list is built, with each node's component table and Session Socket number, we can query each individual node. For each node, we first inspect the component list for a shell or bridge driver, noting its position in the component list; we also note the SPX Session Socket number.

Next, we post SPX Listen packets for the shell or bridge's reply. Then, establish an SPX connection with the node. Finally, we send a Query Shell Driver packet or an SPX Query Bridge Driver packet to the node. When the information is returned, we print it to the screen, terminate the SPX connection, and query the next station.

Calls in the Diagnostic Services API

All of the Diagnostic Services API calls are supported in Advanced NetWare version 2.1. Although NetWare 386 does not support the Diagnostic Services for bridges or file servers, it does so for workstations. Novell does plan to support the Diagnostic API on bridges and file servers, however, in its Network Management module.

Throughout the book, we explain fields within the calls only at the first mention of each field in each chapter. Appendix B contains a comprehensive, alphabetical listing of the fields for quick reference.

Note about the NetWare C Interface calls: To use the C Interface calls in this chapter, the developer must call BeginDiagnostics() and when finished call EndDiagnostics(). See Novell's NetWare C Interface documentation for further details.

```
int BeginDiagnostics( BeginDiagnosticStruct *destination,
   WORD connectionID );

int EndDiagnostics( WORD connectionID );
```

IPX/SPX component calls

Return IPX/SPX Version (00h)

This call returns the IPX and SPX version numbers of a network station.

Request Packet (44 bytes):

Offset	Content	Type
0	SPX Packet Header	BYTE[42]
42	Component Position	BYTE
43	00h	BYTE

Reply Packet (51 bytes):

Offset	Content	Type	Order
0	SPX Packet Header	BYTE[42]	
42	Completion Code	BYTE	
43	Interval Marker	LONG	lo-hi
47	IPX Major Version	BYTE	
48	IPX Minor Version	BYTE	
49	SPX Major Version	BYTE	
50	SPX Minor Version	BYTE	

This call returns the IPX and SPX version numbers of the network station to which the diagnostic application sends the request packet. This call does not return the version number of the target node's shell or operating system.

SPX Packet Header is a 42-byte field containing information specific to SPX. See Chapter 14 for a full discussion of IPX and SPX.

Component Position is the position of the target component within the IPX Configuration Response Packet (00h = first position, 01h = second position, etc.).

Completion Code returns one of the following values:

00h	Successful
FFh	Invalid Request

Interval Marker returns a value between 0h and FFFFFFFFh, indicating the time on the internal clock of the computer where the application is running. Each clock tick equals approximately 1/18 of a second.

The *IPX and SPX Major and Minor Version* fields indicate the IPX and SPX versions installed on the responding node. Version 1.0 would mean a major version number of one and a minor version number of zero.

The NetWare C Interface format is:

```
int GetIPXSPXVersion( WORD connectionID, BYTE connectionNumber,
   AllResponseData *response, IPXSPXVersion *responseData );
```

Return IPX Statistics (01h)

This call returns IPX performance statistics for a network station.

Request Packet (44 bytes):

Offset	Content	Type
0	SPX Packet Header	BYTE[42]
42	Component Position	BYTE
43	01h	BYTE

Reply Packet (81 bytes):

Offset	Content	Type	Order
0	SPX Packet Header	BYTE[42]	
42	Completion Code	BYTE	
43	Interval Marker	LONG	lo-hi
47	Send Packet	LONG	lo-hi
51	Malformed ECBs	WORD	lo-hi
53	Inbound Packets	LONG	lo-hi
57	Lost Packets	LONG	lo-hi
61	AES Events	LONG	lo-hi
65	Postponed AES Events	WORD	lo-hi
67	Max Possible Sockets	WORD	lo-hi
69	Max Open Sockets	WORD	lo-hi
71	Open Socket Failures	WORD	lo-hi
73	Listen ECBs	LONG	lo-hi
77	Cannot Cancel ECBs	WORD	lo-hi
79	Cannot Find Route	WORD	lo-hi

This call returns IPX performance statistics for the network station to which the diagnostic application sends the request packet.

Send Packet is the number of times (since IPX was loaded) that applications have called IPX to send a packet.

Malformed ECBs is the number of times (since IPX was loaded) that applications have passed malformed ECBs to IPX. An ECB is considered malformed if the value in its Fragment Count field is 0, or if the value in its first Fragment Descriptor field's Size field is less than 30 bytes.

Inbound Packet is the number of times (since IPX was loaded) that the node's driver has given an incoming packet to IPX.

Lost Packets is the number of times (since IPX was loaded) that IPX has been unable to supply a receive ECB for an incoming packet.

AES Events is the number of times (since IPX was loaded) that IPX has used the AES to schedule an event.

Postponed AES Events is the number of times (since IPX was loaded) that IPX has been unable to service an AES event on time. For example, IPX cannot send an outgoing packet to a driver that is busy with another packet.

Maximum Possible Sockets is the maximum number of open sockets possible on the target node. (This value is configurable.)

Maximum Open Sockets is the maximum number of sockets that have been open simultaneously since IPX was loaded.

Open Socket Failures is the number of times (since IPX was loaded) that applications have unsuccessfully called the IPX Open Socket call. IPX cannot open a socket if the socket table is full or if the socket is already open.

Listen ECBs is the number of times (since IPX was loaded) that applications have given IPX a listen ECB.

Cannot Cancel ECBs is the number of times (since IPX was loaded) that IPX has been unable to cancel an ECB. For example, IPX cannot cancel an ECB if the driver and the ECB have entered a critical section just prior to sending a packet. In this case, the cancellation is too late.

Cannot Find Route is the number of times (since IPX was loaded) that IPX has been unable to find a route to a requested network address.

The NetWare C Interface format is:

```
int GetIPXStatistics( WORD connectionID, BYTE connectionNumber,
   ALLResponseData *response, IPXStatisticsStruct *responseData );
```

Return SPX Statistics (02h)

This call returns SPX performance statistics for a network station.

Request Packet (44 bytes):

Offset	Content	Type
0	SPX Packet Header	BYTE[42]
42	Component Position	BYTE
43	02h	BYTE

Reply Packet (91 bytes):

Offset	Content	Type	Order
0	SPX Packet Header	BYTE[42]	
42	Completion Code	BYTE	
43	Interval Marker	LONG	lo-hi
47	Max Possible Connections	WORD	lo-hi
49	Max Open Connections	WORD	lo-hi
51	Establish Connection Requests	WORD	lo-hi
53	Establish Connection Failures	WORD	lo-hi
55	Listen For Connection Requests	WORD	lo-hi
57	Listen For Connection Failures	WORD	lo-hi
59	Send Packet Requests	LONG	lo-hi
63	No Listen Failures	LONG	lo-hi
67	Bad Send Requests	WORD	lo-hi
69	Send Failures	WORD	lo-hi

71	Abort Connections	WORD	lo-hi
73	Listen Packet Requests	LONG	lo-hi
77	Malformed Listen ECBs	WORD	lo-hi
79	Incoming Packets	LONG	lo-hi
83	Bad Incoming Packets	WORD	lo-hi
85	Duplicate Packets	WORD	lo-hi
87	No Listen ECBs	WORD	lo-hi
89	Watchdog-Destroyed Connections	WORD	lo-hi

This call returns SPX performance statistics for the network station to which the diagnostic application sends the request packet.

Maximum Possible Connections is the maximum number of SPX connections possible on the target node. (This value is configurable.)

Maximum Open Connections is the maximum number of SPX connections that have been open simultaneously since IPX was loaded.

Establish Connection Requests is the number of times (since SPX was loaded) that applications have issued calls to SPX Establish Connection.

Establish Connection Failures is the number of times (since SPX was loaded) that calls to SPX Establish Connection have failed because the SPX Packet Header was too small, the SPX Connection Table was full, or no router was found to the target network.

Listen For Connection Requests is the number of times (since SPX was loaded) that applications have issued calls to SPX Listen For Connection.

Listen For Connection Failures is the number of times (since SPX was loaded) that calls to SPX Listen For Connection have failed because the SPX Connection Table was full.

Send Packet Requests is the number of times (since SPX was loaded) that applications have issued calls to SPX Send Sequenced Packet.

No Listen Failures is the number of times (since SPX was loaded) that SPX has failed to send a packet because the target station had not allocated a receive buffer.

Bad Send Requests is the number of times (since SPX was loaded) that applications have incorrectly called SPX Send Sequenced Packet by passing an invalid connection ID, or by passing the address of an ECB that indicates a packet header size of less than 42 bytes.

Send Failures is the number of times (since SPX was loaded) that SPX has been unable to send a packet across an SPX connection and receive acknowledgment. In such a case, SPX aborts the connection and informs the calling application.

Abort Connections is the number of times (since SPX was loaded) that applications have called SPX Abort Connection .

Listen Packet Requests is the number of times (since SPX was loaded) that applications have given listen ECBs to SPX.

Malformed Listen ECBs is the number of times (since SPX was loaded) that applications have given malformed ECBs to SPX. An ECB is malformed if the value in its Fragment Count field is 0, if the value in its first Fragment Descriptor field's Size field is less than 42, or if the listen socket is not open.

Incoming Packets is the number of times (since SPX was loaded) that the node's driver has given an incoming packet to SPX.

Bad Incoming Packets is the number of times (since SPX was loaded) that SPX has received and discarded a packet because the connection ID in the packet was wrong.

Duplicate Packets is the number of times (since SPX was loaded) that SPX has discarded inbound packets because they were duplicates of previously received packets.

No Listen ECBs is the number of times (since SPX was loaded) that SPX was forced to discard an inbound SPX Establish Connection packet because SPX lacked a corresponding SPX Listen For Connection ECB.

Watchdog-Destroyed Connections is the number of times (since SPX was loaded) that the watchdog process destroyed a connection because the connection was no longer valid.

The NetWare C Interface format is:

```
int GetSPXStatistics( WORD connectionID, BYTE connectionNumber,
   AllResponseData *response, SPXStatisticsStruct *responseData );
```

Start Sending Packets (03h)

This call initiates and controls a point-to-point diagnostic test.

Request Packet (70 bytes):

Offset	Content	Type	Order
0	SPX Packet Header	BYTE[42]	
42	Component Position	BYTE	
43	03h	BYTE	
44	Destination Network	BYTE[4]	
48	Destination Node	BYTE[6]	
54	Destination Socket	BYTE[2]	
56	Immediate Address	BYTE[6]	
62	Number of Packets	WORD	lo-hi
64	Send Interval	BYTE	
65	Packets Per Send Interval	BYTE	
66	Packet Size	WORD	lo-hi
68	Change Size	WORD	lo-hi

Reply Packet (49 bytes):

Offset	Content	Type	Order
0	SPX Packet Header	BYTE[42]	
42	Completion Code	BYTE	
43	Interval Marker	LONG	lo-hi
47	Transmit Errors	WORD	lo-hi

This call initiates and controls a point-to-point diagnostic test between the workstation to which the diagnostic application sends the request packet and any network node. The target node acts as the sending node. Before making this call, the application must send a Start Counting Packets request to another network node. After the test is completed, the application must call Return Received Packet Count.

Destination Network specifies the network address of the target node.

Destination Node specifies the LAN board number of the target node.

Destination Socket specifies the socket number of the target node. The application must obtain this number from the response packet of the Start Counting Packets call.

Immediate Address specifies the node address of the first bridge a packet encounters as it travels from the source node to the socket node. If the application sets this field to FFFFFFFFFFFFh (-1), IPX chooses a bridge.

Number of Packets is the total number of packets to be sent to the destination node during the diagnostic test.

Send Interval indicates how often the source node should send a specified number of packets to the destination node. The Send Interval is measured in units of 1/18 of a second.

Packets Per Send Interval is how many packets the source node should send to the destination node as each send interval expires. (For example, if the send interval is 3 and the Packets Per Send Interval is 5, the source node sends 5 packets every 3/18 of a second.)

Packet Size is the size of the first packet to be sent. The size must be between 30 and 512 bytes inclusive. If the packet size shrinks below 30 bytes or grows beyond 512, IPX automatically adjusts the size to a valid value.

Change Size specifies a value to increase or decrease the size of the next packet. This feature allows the packet size to vary during the diagnostic test.

Transmit Errors is the number of errors that occur during transmission of the diagnostic packets.

The NetWare C Interface format is:

```
int StartSendingPktsTimed( WORD connectionID, BYTE connectionNumber,
  SendPacketsRequestStrruct *requestData, AllResponseData *response,
  SendPacketsResponseStruct *responseData );
```

Abort Sending Packets (04h)

This call instructs the sending node in a diagnostic point-to-point test to stop sending packets.

Request Packet (44 bytes):

Offset	Content	Type
0	SPX Packet Header	BYTE[42]
42	Component Position	BYTE
43	04h	BYTE

Reply Packet:
None

The NetWare C Interface format is:

```
void AbortSendingPackets( WORD connectionID, BYTE componentNumber );
```

Start Counting Packets (05h)

This call prepares a node to participate as the destination node of a point-to-point diagnostic test.

Request Packet (44 bytes):

Offset	Content	Type
0	SPX Packet Header	BYTE[42]
42	Component Position	BYTE
43	05h	BYTE

Reply Packet (49 bytes):

Offset	Content	Type	Order
0	SPX Packet Header	BYTE[42]	
42	Completion Code	BYTE	
43	Interval Marker	LONG	lo-hi
47	Destination Socket	BYTE[2]	

This call sends a request packet that resets the counter used to track the number of point-to-point packets received by the destination node. The call also returns the socket number that the application must use in the request packet of the Start Sending Packets call.

The *Destination Socket* field returns the socket number that the application must use in the request packet of the Start Sending Packets call.

The NetWare C Interface format is:

```
int StartCountingPackets( WORD connectionID, BYTE connectionNumber,
    AllResponseData *response,
    StartCountingPacketsStruct *responseData );
```

Return Received Packet Count (06h)

This call returns information about the destination node upon completion of a point-to-point diagnostic test.

Request Packet (44 bytes):

Offset	Content	Type
0	SPX Packet Header	BYTE[42]
42	Component Position	BYTE
43	06h	BYTE

Reply Packet (49 bytes):

Offset	Content	Type	Order
0	SPX Packet Header	BYTE[42]	
42	Completion Code	BYTE	
43	Interval Marker	LONG	lo-hi
47	Reserved	BYTE[4]	

This call sends a request packet to the destination node upon completion of a point-to-point diagnostic test. The call returns the number of packets received by the destination node during the test.

Packets Received is the number of point-to-point test packets that actually arrived at the destination node during the diagnostic test.

The NetWare C Interface format is:

```
int ReturnReceivedPacketCount( WORD connectionID,
   BYTE connectionNumber, AllResponseData *response,
   ReturnReceivedPacketStruct *responseData );
```

Driver component calls

Return Shell Driver Configuration (00h)

This call returns the current configuration of the specified shell driver.

Request Packet (44 bytes):

Offset	Content	Type
0	SPX Packet Header	BYTE[42]
42	Component Position	BYTE
43	00h	BYTE

Reply Packet (269 bytes):

Offset	Content	Type	Order
0	SPX Packet Header	BYTE[42]	
42	Completion Code	BYTE	
43	Interval Marker	LONG	lo-hi
47	Reserved	BYTE[4]	
51	Node Address	BYTE[6]	
57	Reserved	BYTE	
58	Node Address Type	BYTE	
59	Maximum Data Size	WORD	lo-hi
61	Reserved	BYTE	
63	LAN Hardware ID	BYTE	
64	Transport Time	WORD	lo-hi
66	Reserved	BYTE[9]	
75	Ethernet Type	BYTE[2]	

77	Major Version	BYTE	
78	Minor Version	BYTE	
79	Misc Flags	BYTE	
80	Selected Configuration	BYTE	
81	LAN Description	BYTE[80]	
161	I/O Address 1	WORD	lo-hi
163	Decode Range 1	WORD	lo-hi
165	I/O Address 2	WORD	lo-hi
167	Decode Range 2	WORD	lo-hi
169	Memory Address 1	BYTE[3]	
172	Decode Range 1	WORD	lo-hi
174	Memory Address 2	BYTE[3]	
177	Decode Range 2	WORD	lo-hi
179	Interrupt Is Used 1	BYTE	
180	Interrupt Line 1	BYTE	
181	Interrupt Is Used 2	BYTE	
182	Interrupt Line 2	BYTE	
183	DMA Is Used l	BYTE	
184	DMA Line 1	BYTE	
185	DMA Is Used 2	BYTE	
186	DMA Line 2	BYTE	
187	Microchannel Flags	BYTE	
188	Reserved	BYTE	
189	Text Description	BYTE[80]	

This call returns the current configuration of the shell driver in the workstation to which the diagnostic application sends the request packet.

The *Reserved* field is not applicable to shell drivers. For bridge drivers, this field returns a network address.

The *Node Address* field returns the six-byte node address of the LAN board installed in the workstation. The node address uniquely identifies the driver and board on the network. If the node address is less than six bytes long (for example, 24E0h), the address appears as follows: 00 00 00 00 24 E0

The next Reserved field is not applicable to shell drivers. For bridge drivers, this field returns the LAN mode status.

The *Node Address Type* indicates who (the driver, the developer, or a configuration utility) records the node address in the driver to match the node address setting of the LAN board; how the node address is recorded in the driver; and when the node address is recorded in the driver.

The following values are defined:

00h The driver dynamically reads and records the node address by calling Driver Initialize.

01h The developer hard codes the node address in the driver code Master Configuration Table.

02h A configuration utility assigns the node address.

The *Maximum Data Size* is the maximum size of a packet's data portion for the target driver. The data portion's maximum size is always 64 bytes less than the packet size advertised with the LAN board. (The packet header and control information require 64 bytes.) The following table shows the maximum size of data portion for four packets:

Largest Transmittable Packet	Maximum Data Size
576 bytes	512 bytes
1,088 bytes	1,024 bytes
2,112 bytes	2,048 bytes
4,160 bytes	4,096 bytes

The *Reserved* field contains address information pertinent only to the driver.

The LAN Hardware ID, hard-coded into the Master Configuration Table, uniquely identifies the LAN hardware. The OEM/Driver Support Group Manager at Novell assigns this ID.

The *Transport Time* field returns a value indicating the speed of the LAN associated with the target driver and board. Speed is measured by the amount of time it takes a 576-bye packet to travel from one node on the LAN to another node. Time is measured in units of 1/18 of a second and rounded to the next highest 1/18.

The *Reserved* field is reserved for future use.

The *Ethernet Type* field is significant only for Ethernet drivers using the Ethernet protocol (not the IEEE 802.3 protocol). Xerox assigned a value of 8137h to Novell where 81 is the high-order byte and 37 is the low-order byte. Only drivers with identical Ethernet Types can communicate.

The *Major Version* and *Minor Version* fields identify the major and minor versions of the driver release. These fields do not identify the installed NetWare version. Therefore, in a station running NetWare v2.1, the driver version may be v1.0, where 1 represents the major version and 0 represents the minor version.

The *Miscellaneous Flags* field is a one-byte field with the following bits defined:

For bits 0-7:

bit 4:

off(0)	NonEthernet or nonconfigurable board drive
on(1)	Configurable Ethernet board driver

bit 0:

off	IEEE 802.3 protocol
on	Ethernet protocol

bit 2:

off	Driver can run in protected mode
on	Driver runs only in real mode on 286-based machines

The *Selected Configuration* field returns a value indicating which hardware configuration in the Hardware Configuration Table the driver is using. This value ranges from 0 to n - 1, where n is the maximum number of configurations supported by the driver.

The *LAN Description* field returns a null-terminated text string of not more than 69 bytes. The text string lists the LAN hardware supported by the driver. The following is a short example:

```
LAN Description db 'NetWare RX-NET', 0
```

Each *I/O Address* is the address of a block of I/O addresses to be decoded by the LAN board. Zeros returned in the second I/O Address field indicate that the driver is not using the field.

Each *Decode Range* field following an I/O Address is the number of ports to be decoded. Typically this value is 8, 16, or 32.

Each *Memory Address* field identifies the address of a block of memory address space to be decoded by the LAN board. The block is divided into one or more six-byte paragraphs. This is a three-byte address field. The first byte is the high-order byte. The remaining WORD makes up the low-order portion of the address. Zeros returned in the second Memory Address field indicate that the driver is not using the field.

Each *Decode Range* field following a Memory Address is the number of paragraphs in the block.

Each *Interrupt Is Used* indicates whether the value in the following Interrupt Line field is valid. The following values can appear in an Interrupt Is Used field:

00h	No Interrupt line defined
FFh	Interrupt line defined for exclusive use
FEh	Interrupt line defined for a particular LAN board, but can be shared by others of the same type

Each *Interrupt Line* field returns the value of the interrupt used by the LAN board. Zeros returned in the second Interrupt Line field indicate that the LAN board does not use the field.

Each *DMA Is Used* tells whether the value in the following DMA Line field is valid. The following values can appear in a DMA Is Used field:

00h	No DMA line defined
FFh	DMA line defined for exclusive use
FEh	DMA line defined for a particular LAN board, but can be shared by others of the same type

Each *DMA Line* field returns the value of the DMA line used by the LAN board. Zeros returned in the second DMA Line field indicate that the LAN board does not use the field.

The *Microchannel Flags* describe microchannel support for the configurations. The following bits are defined:

for bits 0-7:

bit 0:

on (1)	The configuration does not use micro channel.
off(0)	The configuration uses micro channel but cannot be combined with other configurations that do not use micro channel.

bit 1:

on	This configuration uses micro channel and can be combined with other configurations regardless of whether they use micro channel.

The *Text Description* field returns a null-terminated text string not more than 69 bytes. The text string summarizes the configuration information contained in the preceding fields. The following is a short example of how a text description might appear in a driver code:

```
db        "I/O Base=2E0h,RAM as D000:0 for 800h bytes, IRQ 2,
           no DMA",0
```

The NetWare C Interface format is:

```
int GetShellDriverConfiguration( WORD connectionID,
   BYTE connectionNumber, AllResponseData *response,
   DriverConfigurationStruct *responseData );
```

Return Shell Driver Diagnostic Statistics (01h)

This call returns the entire Driver Diagnostic Table of the specified shell driver.

Request Packet (44 bytes):

Offset	Content	Type
0	SPX Packet Header	BYTE[42]
42	Component Position	BYTE
43	01h	BYTE

Reply Packet (maximum packet size = 576 bytes):

Offset	Content	Type	Order
0	SPX Packet Header	BYTE[42]	
42	Completion Code	BYTE	
43	Interval Marker	LONG	lo-hi
47	Reserved	BYTE[2]	
49	Statistics Version	BYTE[2]	
51	Total Tx Packet Count	LONG	lo-hi

55	Total Rx Packet Count	LONG	lo-hi
59	No ECB Available Count	WORD	lo-hi
61	Packet Tx Too Big Count	WORD	lo-hi
63	Packet Tx Too Small Count	WORD	lo-hi
65	Packet Rx Overflow Count	WORD	lo-hi
67	Packet Rx Too Big Count	WORD	lo-hi
69	Packet Rx Too Small Count	WORD	lo-hi
71	Packet Tx Misc Error Count	WORD	lo-hi
73	Packet Rx Misc Error Count	WORD	lo-hi
75	Retry Tx Count	WORD	lo-hi
77	Checksum Error Count	WORD	lo-hi
79	Hardware Rx Mismatch Count	WORD	lo-hi
81	Number of Custom Variables	WORD	lo-hi
83	Custom Variable 0	WORD	lo-hi
.			
.			
.			
?	Text 0	BYTE[?]	
.			
.			
.			
?	Text Delimiter (0000h)	BYTE[2]	

This call returns the entire Driver Diagnostic Table of the shell driver in the workstation to which the diagnostic application sends the request packet. The table consists of a set of generic counters followed by a list of driver-dependent custom variables. Generic counters not meaningful for a particular driver are set to -1.

The *Statistics Version* field returns a major and minor version number that a developer assigns and updates each time the developer modifies the Driver Diagnostic Table.

The *Total Tx Packet Count* specifies the number of packets the driver has successfully transmitted since the last reset or initialization.

The *Total Rx Packet Count* specifics the number of packets the driver has successfully received and passed into the system since the last reset or initialization.

The *No ECB Available Count* specifies the number of packets the driver has received (since the last reset or initialization) for which there was no listening ECB.

The *Packet Tx Too Big Count* specifies the number of times (since the last reset or initialization) that applications have asked the driver to send a packet that has over the maximum legal size.

The *Packet Tx Too Small Count* specifies the number of times (since the last reset or initialization) that applications have asked the driver to send a packet that has under the minimum legal size.

The *Packet Rx Overflow Count* specifies the number of times (since the last reset or initialization) that the driver has received a packet larger than the buffer space allocated for the packet.

The *Packet Rx Too Big Count* specifies the number of times (since the last reset or initialization) that the driver has received a packet that has over the maximum legal size.

The *Packet Rx Too Small Count* specifies the number of times (since the last reset or initialization) that the driver has received a packet that has under the minimum legal size.

The *Packet Tx Misc Error Count* specifies the number of miscellaneous errors that have prevented the driver from transmitting a packet (since the last reset or initialization).

The *Packet Rx Misc Error Count* specifies the number of miscellaneous errors that have prevented the driver from receiving a packet (since the last reset or initialization).

The *Retry Tx Count* specifies the number of times (since the last reset or initialization) that the driver resent a packet. For example, when the driver detects a collision, the driver resends a packet.

The *Checksum Error Count* specified the number of checksum errors that have occurred while receiving packets (since the last reset or initialization).

The *Hardware Rx Mismatch Count* specifies the number of times (since the last reset or initialization) that the hardware has received more or fewer bytes than expected.

The *Number of Custom Variables* field specifies the number of Custom Variables that will follow.

Each *Custom Variable* is a WORD-length field that specifies information pertinent to the particular driver. These fields are optional.

The *Text* field is a null-terminated string that describes the corresponding Custom Variable field and each Text field.

The *Text Delimiter* is the end of the Text fields.

The NetWare C Interface format is:

```
int GetShellDriverStatistics( WORD connectionID,
  BYTE connectionNumber, AllResponseData *response,
  DriverStatisticsStruct *responseData );
```

Return Bridge Driver Status (00h)

This call returns the status of all LAN boards installed in a bridge.

Request Packet (44 bytes):

Offset	**Content**	**Type**
0	SPX Packet Header	BYTE[42]
42	Component Position	BYTE
43	00h	BYTE

Reply Packet (51 bytes):

Offset	Content	Type	Order
0	SPX Packet Header	BYTE[42]	
42	Completion Code	BYTE	
43	Interval Marker	LONG	lo-hi
47	LAN Board 0 Status	BYTE	
48	LAN Board 1 Status	BYTE	
49	LAN Board 2 Status	BYTE	
50	LAN Board 3 Status	BYTE	

This call returns the status of all LAN boards installed in the bridge to which the diagnostic application sends the request packet.

Each *LAN Board Status* field returns one of the following values to indicate the status of the corresponding LAN board:

00h	The board is alive and running.
01h	The board does not exist.
02h	The board is dead.

The NetWare C Interface format is:

```
int GetBridgeDriverStatus( WORD connectionID, BYTE connectionNumber,
  AllResponseData *response, DriverStatisticsStruct *responseData );
```

Return Bridge Driver Configuration (01h)

This call returns the current configuration of the specified bridge driver.

Request Packet (45 bytes):

Offset	Content	Type	Order
0	SPX Packet Header	BYTE[42]	
42	Component Position	BYTE	
43	01h	BYTE	
44	Bridge Driver	BYTE	

Reply Packet (269 bytes):

Offset	Content	Type	Order
0	SPX Packet Header	BYTE	
42	Completion Code	BYTE	
43	Interval Marker	LONG	lo-hi
47	Network Address	BYTE[4]	
51	Node Address	BYTE[6]	
57	LAN Mode	BYTE	
58	Node Address Type	BYTE	
59	Maximum Data Size	WORD	lo-hi

61	Reserved	BYTE[2]	
63	LAN Hardware ID	BYTE	
64	Transport Time	WORD	lo-hi
66	Reserved	BYTE[9]	
75	Ethernet Type	BYTE[2]	
77	Major Version	BYTE	
78	Minor Version	BYTE	
79	Misc Flags	BYTE	
80	Selected Configuration	BYTE	
81	LAN Description	BYTE[80]	
161	I/O Address 1	WORD	lo-hi
163	Decode Range 1	WORD	lo-hi
165	I/O Address 2	WORD	lo-hi
167	Decode Range 2	WORD	lo-hi
169	Memory Address 1	BYTE[3]	
172	Decode Range 1	WORD	lo-hi
174	Memory Address 2	BYTE[3]	
177	Decode Range 2	WORD	lo-hi
179	Interrupt Is Used 1	BYTE	
180	Interrupt Line 1	BYTE	
181	Interrupt Is Used 2	BYTE	
182	Interrupt Line 2	BYTE	
183	DMA Is Used 1	BYTE	
184	DMA Line 1	BYTE	
185	DMA Is Used 2	BYTE	
186	DMA Line 2	BYTE	
187	Microchannel Flags	BYTE	
188	Reserved	BYTE	
189	Text Description	BYTE[80]	

This call returns the current configuration of the specified bridge driver (0,1, 2, or 3) in the bridge to which the diagnostic application sends the request packet. The call returns an error if the specified bridge driver does not exist.

Bridge Driver specifies the target bridge driver (0,1, 2,or 3) within the target node. The target bridge driver corresponds to the target LAN board (0, 1, 2,or 3).

The Completion Code field returns one of the following values:

00h	Successful
01h	Invalid Board Number
FFh	Invalid Request

Network Address returns the four-byte network address of the LAN on which the driver communicates.

The *LAN Mode* is a one-byte field with the following bits defined:

bits 0-7

bit 0:

off(0)	Place-holding dummy driver
on (1)	Real driver

bit 1:

off	Not 100% guaranteed driver
on	100% guaranteed driver

bit 7:

off	Driver does not use DMA
on	Driver uses DMA; no receive block straddles 64k physical address boundary

Each *DMA Is Used* tells whether the value in the following DMA Line field is valid. The following values can appear in a DMA Is Used field:

00h	No DMA line defined
FFh	DMA line defined for exclusive use
FEh	DMA line defined for a particular LAN board, but may be shared by others of the same type

The NetWare C Interface format is:

```
int GetBridgeDriverConfiguration( WORD connectionID,
    BYTE connectionNumber, BYTE LANBoardNumber,
    AllResponseData *response,
    DriverConfigurationStruct *responseData );
```

Return Bridge Driver Diagnostic Statistics (02h)

This call returns the entire Driver Diagnostic Table of the specified bridge driver.

Request Packet (45 bytes):

Offset	Content	Type
0	SPX Packet Header	BYTE[42]
42	Component Position	BYTE
43	02h	BYTE
44	Bridge Driver	BYTE

Reply Packet (maximum packet size = 576 bytes):

Offset	Content	Type	Order
0	SPX Packet Header	BYTE[42]	
42	Completion Code	BYTE	
43	Interval Marker	LONG	lo-hi
47	Reserved	BYTE[2]	
49	Statistics Version	BYTE[2]	
51	Total TX Packet Count	LONG	lo-hi
55	Total RX Packet Count	LONG	lo-hi
59	No ECB Available Count	WORD	lo-hi
61	Packet TX Too Small Count	WORD	lo-hi
63	Packet TX Too Small Count	WORD	lo-hi
65	Packet RX Overflow Count	WORD	lo-hi
67	Packet RX Too Big Count	WORD	lo-hi
69	Packet RX Too Small Count	WORD	lo-hi
71	Packet TX Misc Error Count	WORD	lo-hi
73	Packet RX Misc Error Count	WORD	lo-hi
75	Retry TX Count	WORD	lo-hi
77	Checksum Error Count	WORD	lo-hi
79	Hardware RX Mismatch Count	WORD	lo-hi
81	Number of Custom Variables	WORD	lo-hi
83	Custom Variable 0	WORD	lo-hi
.			
.			
.			
?	Text 0	BYTE[?]	
.			
.			
.			
?	Text Delimiter(0000h)	BYTE[2]	

The Completion Code field returns one of the following values:

00h	Successful
01h	Invalid Board Number
FFh	Invalid Request

The NetWare C Interface format is:

```
int GetBridgeDriverStatus( WORD connectionID, BYTE connectionNumber,
  AllResponseData *response,
  BridgeDriverStatusStruct *responseData );
```

Shell component calls

Return OS Version (00h)

This call returns the OS version of the target workstation.

Request Packet (44 bytes):

Offset	Content	Type
0	SPX Packet Header	BYTE[42]
42	Component Position	BYTE
43	00h	BYTE

Reply Packet (maximum packet size = 88 bytes):

Offset	Content	Type	Order
0	SPX Packet Header	BYTE[42]	
42	Completion Code	BYTE	
43	Interval Marker	LONG	lo-hi
47	Machine ID	BYTE	
48	OS Text	ASCIIZ	
??	OS Version Text	ASCIIZ	
??	Hardware Type Text	ASCIIZ	

(The combined size the of the last four fields of this structure must not exceed 41 bytes.)

This call returns information about the network station to which the diagnostic application sends the request packet.

Completion Code returns one of the following values:

00h	Successful
FFh	Invalid Request

Machine ID returns a value of 00h if the target machine is an IBM PC computer or compatible.

OS Text identifies the operating system (e.g., DOS).

The *OS Version Text* identifies the operating system version (e.g., v3.1).

Hardware Type Text identifies the target machine (e.g., IBMPC, SAMSUNG 286A).

The NetWare C Interface format is:

```
int GetOSVersionInfo( WORD connectionID, BYTE connectionNumber,
   AllResponseData *response, OSVersionStruct *responseData );
```

Return Shell Address (01h)

This call returns a workstation's 12-byte IPX internetwork address.

Request Packet (44 bytes):

Offset	Content	Type	Order
0	SPX Packet Header	BYTE[42]	
42	Component Position	BYTE	
43	01h	BYTE	

Reply Packet (59 bytes):

Offset	Content	Type	Order
0	SPX Packet Header	BYTE[42]	
42	Completion Code	BYTE	
43	Interval Marker	LONG	lo-hi
47	Local Network	bytes [4]	
51	Local Node	bytes [6]	
57	Local Socket	bytes [2]	

A diagnostic application sends this request packet to a workstation. The call returns the 12-byte IPX internetwork address the workstation's shell uses to receive packets from file servers.

Completion Code returns one of the following values:

00h	Successful
FFh	Invalid Request

The NetWare C Interface format is:

```
int GetShellAddress( WORD connectionID, BYTE connectionNumber,
   AllResponseData *response, ShellStatisticsStruct *responseData );
```

Return Shell Statistics (02h)

This call returns the counters kept by the specified workstation's shell.

Request Packet (44 bytes):

Offset	Content	Type
0	SPX Packet Header	BYTE[42]
42	Component Position	BYTE
43	02h	BYTE

Reply Packet (85 bytes):

Offset	**Content**	**Type**	**Order**
0	SPX Packet Header	BYTE[42]	
42	Completion Code	BYTE	
43	Interval Marker	LONG	lo-hi
47	Shell Requests Count	LONG	lo-hi
51	Operator Aborts Count	WORD	lo-hi
53	Operator Retries Count	WORD	lo-hi
55	Timeouts Count	WORD	lo-hi
57	Write Error Count	WORD	lo-hi
59	Invalid Reply Header Count	WORD	lo-hi
61	Invalid Slot Count	WORD	lo-hi
63	Invalid Sequence Number Count	WORD	lo-hi
65	Error Receiving Count	WORD	lo-hi
67	No Router Found Count	WORD	lo-hi
69	Being Processed Count	WORD	lo-hi
71	Unknown Error Count	WORD	lo-hi
73	Invalid Server Slot Count	WORD	lo-hi
75	Network Gone Count	WORD	lo-hi
77	Reserved	WORD	lo-hi
79	Allocate Cannot Find Route	WORD	lo-hi
81	Allocate No Slots Available	WORD	lo-hi
83	Allocate Server Is Down	WORD	lo-hi

The counters returned track the number and type of requests made by the shell to file servers since the shell was activated, as well as the errors that were handled.

The Completion Code field returns one of the following values:

00h	Successful
FFh	Invalid Request

Shell Requests Count is the number of times (since the shell was activated) that the shell has made requests to a file server.

Operator Aborts Count is the number of times (since the shell was activated) that the user has aborted the shell-server connection by entering "A" in reply to a "Network Error" message.

Number of Operator Retries is the number of times (since the shell was activated) that the user has instructed the shell to retry an operation.

Timeouts Count is the number of times (since the shell was activated) that the shell has sent a request to a server and then timed out without receiving a reply. (Normally, the shell sends another request packet.)

Write Error Count is the number of times (since the shell was activated) that the driver has been unable to send a request to a file server (after repeated retries). In this case, the shell displays the message "Error writing to network" on the workstation screen. The shell does not increment this counter if, after repeated retries, the driver is able to send the request.

Invalid Reply Header Count is the number of times (since the shell was activated) that the shell has received a reply packet header whose Checksum field was -1 or whose Packet Type field indicated that the packet was not a file server reply.

Invalid Slot Count indicates the number of times (since the shell was activated) that the shell has received a file server reply packet specifying an incorrect connection ID.

Invalid Sequence Number Count indicates the number of times (since the shell was activated) that the shell has received a file server reply packet specifying an incorrect sequence number. This usually indicates that the reply was unnecessary.

Error Receiving Count is the number of times (since the shell was activated) that IPX has indicated an error even though a packet was received on the socket. This usually indicates an "Overrun" error.

No Router Found Count is the number of times (since the shell was activated) that the shell has tried and failed to find a route to a destination node. The shell attempts to reroute a packet when a connection seems to fail and the user requests a "Retry."

Being Processed Count is the number of times (since the shell was activated) that the shell has received a "being processed" reply from a file server. A file server sends this reply to a shell when the server, while processing the shell's request, receives duplicate requests from the shell for the same service.

Unknown Error Count is the number of times (since the shell was activated) that the shell has received a packet containing an undefined error value.

Connection/Address Mismatch Count is the number of times (since the shell was activated) that the shell has received an error code from a server indicating that the connection number in one of the shell's request packets did not match the shell's connection number/network address relationship recorded in the server's tables. This usually occurs when the server goes down or when the console operator issues a "clear station" command at the server.

Network Gone Count indicates the number of times (since the shell was activated) that the shell has received a packet from a file server indicating the target network has gone away. Only a 68000 file server can generate this kind of packet.

Allocate Cannot Find Route is the number of times (since the shell was activated) that the shell, asked by an application to establish a connection with a file server, could not find a route to the destination network.

Allocate No Slots Available is the number of times (since the shell was activated) that the shell, asked by an application to establish a connection with a file server, could not because the file server's connection table was full.

Allocate Server Is Down is the number of times (since the shell was activated) that the shell, asked by an application to establish a connection with a file server, could not establish the connection because the target file server was down.

The NetWare C Interface format is:

```
int GetShellStatistics( WORD connectionID, BYTE connectionNumber,
   AllResponseData *response, ShellVersionStruct *responseData );
```

Return Connection ID Table (03h)

This call returns the Connection ID Table of the specified workstation.

Request Packet (44 bytes):

Offset	Content	Type
0	SPX Packet Header	BYTE[42]
42	Component Position	BYTE
43	03h	BYTE

Reply Packet (303 bytes):

Offset	Content	Type	Order
0	SPX Packet Header	BYTE[42]	
42	Completion Code	BYTE	
43	Interval Marker	LONG	lo-hi
47	Server Used 0	BYTE	
48	Order Number 0	BYTE	
49	Server Network 0	BYTE[4]	lo-hi
53	Server Node 0	BYTE[6]	
59	Server Socket 0	BYTE[2]	
61	Receive Timeout 0	WORD	lo-hi
63	Immediate Node 0	BYTE[6]	
69	Sequence Number 0	BYTE	
70	Connection Number 0	BYTE	
71	Connection OK 0	BYTE	
72	Maximum Timeout 0	WORD	lo-hi
74	Reserved 0	BYTE[5]	
.			
.			
.			

(The entire response packet is 303 bytes long consisting of the following: (47)bytes of overhead + [8 * 32 bytes of server information].)

This call returns the complete Connection ID Table of the workstation to which the diagnostic application sends the request packet. The workstation's Connection ID Table consists of eight 32-byte entries. Each entry identifies one file server. Entry 0 in the workstation's Connection ID Table corresponds to Server Name 0 in the workstation's Server Name Table. See chapter 9 for more information about connections and the Connection ID Table.

Completion Code returns one of the following values:

00h	Successful
FFh	Invalid Request

Each Server Used tells whether the corresponding 32-byte server entry is in use. A value of zero means the slot is empty, whereas FFh means the entry is in use.

Each Order Number is the order number (1 through 8) assigned to the corresponding server. The lowest order number indicates the server with the lowest 10-byte network/node address, assuming the first byte is the most significant. The second lowest order number indicates the second lowest address, etc.

Each Received Timeout returns a value indicating the estimated round-trip time required for the target workstation to send a request packet to the file server and receive acknowledgment.

Each Immediate Node is the node address of the routing bridge the workstation uses to send packets to the file server.

Each Sequence Number returns the sequence number of the last packet the target workstation sent to the file server. Each time the workstation sends a packet to the file server, the workstation increases this counter.

Each Connection Number is the connection number the workstation is using to communicate with the file server.

Each Connection OK returns a value of 00h if the connection between the workstation and the server is bad.

Each Maximum Timeout returns a value indicating the estimated maximum round-trip time required for the target workstation to send a request packet to the file server and receive a reply packet.

The NetWare C Interface format is:

```
int GetServerAddressTable( WORD connectionID, BYTE connectionNumber,
AllResponseData *response, ServerAddressTableStruct *responseData );
```

Return Server Name Table (04h)

This call returns the entire Server Name Table of the specified workstation.

Request Packet (44 bytes):

Offset	Content	Type	Order
0	SPX Packet Header	BYTE[42]	
42	Component Position	BYTE	
43	04h	BYTE	

Reply Packet (431 bytes):

Offset	Content	Type	Order
0	SPX Packet Header	BYTE[42]	
42	Completion Code	BYTE	
43	Interval Marker	LONG	lo-hi
47	Server Name 0	BYTE[48]	
95	Server Name 1	BYTE[48]	
43	Server Name 2	BYTE[48]	
191	Server Name 3	BYTE[48]	
239	Server Name 4	BYTE[48]	
287	Server Name 5	BYTE[48]	
335	Server Name 6	BYTE[48]	
383	Server Name 7	BYTE[48]	

Server Name 0 in the table corresponds to entry 0 in the workstation's Connection ID Table.

The NetWare C Interface format is:

```
int GetServerNameTable( WORD connectionID, BYTE connectionNumber,
   AllResponseData *response, ServerNameTableStruct *responseData );
```

Return Primary Server Number (05h)

When an application sends this request to a workstation, the call returns a number (1 through 8) indicating the physical position of the primary server's address and name in the workstation's Connection ID Table and Server Name Table respectively.

Request Packet (44 bytes):

Offset	Content	Type
0	SPX Packet Header	BYTE[42]
42	Component Position	BYTE
43	05h	BYTE

Reply Packet (48 bytes):

Offset	Content	Type	Order
0	SPX Packet Header	BYTE[42]	
42	Completion Code	BYTE	
43	Interval Marker	LONG	lo-hi
47	Server Position Number	BYTE	

Completion Code returns one of the following values:

00h	Successful
FFh	Invalid Request

Server Position Number indicates the physical position of the primary server in the workstation's Connection ID Table and Server Name Table. The Server Position Number is not the server's Order Number returned by Return Connection ID Table.

The NetWare C Interface format is:

```
int GetPrimaryServerNumber( WORD connectionID,
   BYTE connectionNumber, AllResponseData *response,
   PrimaryServerStruct *responseData );
```

Return Shell Version (06h)

This call returns the version number of the specified workstation's shell.

Request Packet (44 bytes):

Offset	Content	Type
0	SPX Packet Header	BYTE[42]
42	Component Position	BYTE
43	06h	BYTE

Reply Packet (49 bytes):

Offset	Content	Type	Order
0	SPX Packet Header	BYTE[42]	
42	Completion Code	BYTE	
43	Interval Marker	LONG	lo-hi
47	Major Version	BYTE	
48	Minor Version	BYTE	

Completion Code returns one of the following values:

00h	Successful
FFh	Invalid Request

The NetWare C Interface format is:

```
int GetShellVersionInfo( WORD connectionID, BYTE connectionNumber,
    AllResponseData *response, ShellVersionStruct *responseData );
```

Shell VAP component calls

Return VAP Shell Address (01h)

This call returns a workstation's 12-byte IPX internetwork address.

Request Packet (44 bytes):

Offset	Content	Type
0	SPX Packet Header	BYTE[42]
42	Component Position	BYTE
43	01h	BYTE

Reply Packet (59 bytes):

Offset	Content	Type	Order
0	SPX Packet Header	BYTE[42]	
42	Completion Code	BYTE	
43	Interval Marker	LONG	lo-hi

47	Local Network	bytes [4]
51	Local Node	bytes [6]
57	Local Socket	bytes [2]

A diagnostic application sends this request packet to a workstation. The call returns the 12-byte IPX internetwork address the workstation's VAP shell uses to receive packets from file servers.

Completion Code returns one of the following values:

00h	Successful
FFh	Invalid Request

The NetWare C Interface format is:

```
int GetShellAddress( WORD connectionID, BYTE connectionNumber,
  AllResponseData *response, ShellStatisticsStruct *responseData );
```

Return VAP Shell Statistics (02h)

This call returns the counters kept by the specified workstation's VAP shell.

Request Packet (44 bytes):

Offset	**Content**	**Type**
0	SPX Packet Header	BYTE[42]
42	Component Position	BYTE
43	02h	BYTE

Reply Packet (85 bytes):

Offset	**Content**	**Type**	**Order**
0	SPX Packet Header	BYTE[42]	
42	Completion Code	BYTE	
43	Interval Marker	LONG	lo-hi
47	VAP Shell Requests Count	LONG	lo-hi
51	Operator Aborts Count	WORD	lo-hi
53	Operator Retries Count	WORD	lo-hi
55	Timeouts Count	WORD	lo-hi
57	Write Error Count	WORD	lo-hi
59	Invalid Reply Header Count	WORD	lo-hi
61	Invalid Slot Count	WORD	lo-hi
63	Invalid Sequence Number Count	WORD	lo-hi
65	Error Receiving Count	WORD	lo-hi
67	No Router Found Count	WORD	lo-hi
69	Being Processed Count	WORD	lo-hi
71	Unknown Error Count	WORD	lo-hi
73	Invalid Server Slot Count	WORD	lo-hi

75	Network Gone Count	WORD	lo-hi
77	Reserved	WORD	lo-hi
79	Allocate Cannot Find Route	WORD	lo-hi
81	Allocate No Slots Available	WORD	lo-hi
83	Allocate Server Is Down	WORD	lo-hi

The counters returned track the number and type of requests made by the VAP shell to file servers since the VAP shell was activated, as well as the errors that were handled.

Completion Code returns one of the following values:

00h	Successful
FFh	Invalid Request

VAP Shell Requests Count is the number of times (since the VAP shell was activated) that the VAP shell has made requests to a file server.

The NetWare C Interface format is:

```
int GetShellStatistics( WORD connectionID, BYTE connectionNumber,
   AllResponseData *response, ShellVersionStruct *responseData );
```

Return VAP Shell Version (06h)

This call returns the version number of the specified workstation's VAP shell.

Request Packet (44 bytes):

Offset	Content	Type
0	SPX Packet Header	BYTE[42]
42	Component Position	BYTE
43	06h	BYTE

Reply Packet (49 bytes):

Offset	Content	Type	Order
0	SPX Packet Header	BYTE[42]	
42	Completion Code	BYTE	
43	Interval Marker	LONG	lo-hi
47	Major Version	BYTE	
48	Minor Version	BYTE	

Completion Code returns one of the following values:

00h	Successful
FFh	Invalid Request

The NetWare C Interface format is:

```
int GetShellVersionInfo( WORD connectionID, BYTE connectionNumber,
   AllResponseData *response, ShellVersionStruct *responseData );
```

Bridge component calls

Return Bridge Statistics (00h)

This call returns statistics pertaining to the specified bridge.

Request Packet (44 bytes):

Offset	Content	Type
0	SPX Packet Header	BYTE[42]
42	Component Position	BYTE
43	00h	BYTE

Reply Packet (69 bytes):

Offset	Content	Type	Order
0	SPX Packet Header	BYTE[42]	
42	Completion Code	BYTE	
43	Interval Marker	LONG	lo-hi
47	Too Many Hops Count	WORD	lo-hi
49	Unknown Network Count	WORD	lo-hi
51	No Space For Service Count	WORD	lo-hi
53	No Receive Buffers Count	WORD	lo-hi
55	Reserved	WORD	lo-hi
57	NetBIOS Propagate Count	LONG	lo-hi
61	Total Packets Serviced	LONG	lo-hi
65	Total Packets Routed	LONG	lo-hi

Completion Code returns one of the following values:

00h	Successful
FFh	Invalid Request

Too Many Hops Count is the number of times (since the bridge was initialized) that the bridge has received packets on their fifteenth hop across an internetwork bridge. These packets are discarded.

Unknown Network Count is the number of times (since the bridge was initialized) that the bridge has received packets bound for an unknown network. These packets are discarded.

No Space For Service Count is the number of times (since the bridge was initialized) that the bridge has received internetwork packets that it could not accommodate because the router did not have enough space in its DGroup area to copy the packets. These packets are lost.

No Receive Buffers Count is the number of times (since the bridge was initialized) that the bridge could not receive inbound packets because of inadequate buffer space. These packets are lost.

NetBIOS Propagate Count is the number of times the bridge has received NETBIOS broadcasts since it was initialized.

Total Packets Serviced is the total number of packets that the bridge has serviced since the bridge was initialized.

Total Packets Routed is the total number of packets that the router actually routed.

The NetWare C Interface format is:

```
int GetBridgeStatistics( WORD connectionID, BYTE connectionNumber,
  AllResponseData *response, BridgeStatisticsStruct *responseData );
```

Return Local Tables (01h)

This call returns the node address of each LAN board installed in the specified bridge.

Request Packet (44 bytes):

Offset	Content	Type
0	SPX Packet Header	BYTE[42]
42	Component Position	BYTE
43	01h	BYTE

Reply Packet (239 bytes):

Offset	Content	Type	Order
0	SPX Packet Header	BYTE[42]	
42	Completion Code	BYTE	
43	Interval Marker	LONG	lo-hi
47	Network Number 0	BYTE[4]	
.			
.			
.			
111	Node Addresses 0	BYTE[8]	
.			
.			
.			

(The total length of the reply packet is 239 bytes. The packet includes 16 Network Number fields and 16 Node Address fields.)

This call returns the node address of each LAN board installed in the bridge to which the diagnostic application sends the request packet. The call also returns the network number that corresponds to each LAN board. In the case of remote LAN-to-LAN networks, the call also returns the node addresses of all virtual boards and their corresponding network numbers.

Completion Code returns one of the following values:

00h	Successful
FFh	Invalid Request

Each Network Number is the network defined for each LAN board. Normally, a bridge connects from one to four networks. However, in the case of remote LAN-to-LAN networks involving virtual LAN boards with their associated network numbers, a bridge can connect up to 16 networks.

Each Node Address identifies a LAN board installed in the bridge. In the case of LAN-to-LAN networks, the node address also identifies virtual LAN boards. Although this field is eight bytes long, a node address is only six bytes long.

The NetWare C Interface format is:

```
int GetLocalTables( WORD connectionID, BYTE connectionNumber,
   AllResponseData *response, LocalTablesStruct *responseData );
```

Return All Known Networks (02h)

This call returns the network address of each network known to the specified bridge.

Request Packet (46 bytes):

Offset	Content	Type	Order
0	SPX Packet Header	BYTE[42]	
42	Component Position	BYTE	
43	02h	BYTE	
44	Next Set Starting Point	WORD	lo-hi

Reply Packet (53 bytes):

Offset	Content	Type	Order
0	SPX Packet Header	BYTE[42]	
42	Completion Code	BYTE	
43	Interval Marker	LONG	lo-hi
47	Number of Network Addresses	WORD	lo-hi
49	Network Address 0	BYTE[4]	

This call returns the network address of each network known to the bridge to which the diagnostic application sends the request packet. One call to this call can return a maximum of 128 network addresses. An application can repeat this call to return sets of known network addresses.

Next Set Starting Point should be set to 0 for the first call to this call. If the call returns a full set of 128 network addresses in reply to the first call, the application should set this field to 128 for the second call, 256 for the third call, and so on until the call returns only a partial set of network addresses. The partial set of network addresses indicates the end of the known network address list.

Completion Code returns one of the following values:

00h	Successful
FFh	Invalid Request

Network Addresses is how many Network Addresses (0 to 128) the call is returning in the current set.

Each Network Address field returns one four-byte network address.

The NetWare C Interface format is:

```
int GetAllKnownNetworks( WORD connectionID, BYTE connectionNumber,
  AllResponseData *response, AllKnownNetworksStruct *responseData );
```

Return Specific Network Information (03h)

This call returns information concerning routing times and routes between the specified bridge and a specified (destination) network.

Request Packet (48 bytes):

Offset	Content	Type
0	SPX Packet Header	BYTE[42]
42	Component Position	BYTE
43	03h	BYTE
44	Specific Network Address	BYTE[4]

Reply Packet (75 bytes):

Offset	Content	Type	Order
0	SPX Packet Header	BYTE[42]	
42	Completion Code	BYTE	
43	Interval Marker	LONG	lo-hi
47	Network Address	BYTE[4]	
51	Route Hops	BYTE	
52	Reserved	BYTE[7]	
59	Route Time	WORD	lo-hi
61	Number of Known Routes	WORD	lo-hi
63	Router 0 Node Address	BYTE[6]	
69	Router 0 Next Board Position	BYTE	
70	Reserved 0	BYTE[2]	
72	Route 0 Hops	BYTE	
73	Route 0 Time	WORD	lo-hi
.			
.			
.			

This call returns information on routing times and routes between the bridge to which the diagnostic application sends the request packet and one destination network one or more hops away from the bridge. If only one route exists between the bridge and the destination network, the call returns the node address of the first interim bridge a packet meets en route from the source bridge to the destination network.

The call also returns the routing time and number of hops pertaining to that route. If more than one route exists, the call returns the node addresses of all interim bridges one hop away from the source bridge and the routing times and number of hops associated with all routes. The most efficient route appears at the top of the list in the reply packet. The field explanations that follow refer to these interim bridges (one hop away from the source bridge) as Router 0, Router 1, etc.

Specific Network Address identifies the destination network.

Completion Code returns one of the following values:

00h	Successful
FFh	Network in question does not exist

Network Address returns the network address of the destination network. This is the same address that the application passes in the request packet's Specific Network Address field.

Route Hops returns the number of hops (between the source bridge and the destination network) of the most efficient route. The value in this field and the value returned in the Route 0 Hops field are the same.

Route Time returns the route time (between the source bridge and the destination network) of the most efficient route. The value in this field and the value returned in the Route 0 Time field are the same.

Number of Known Routes is the number of routes between the source bridge and the destination network. If only one route exists, this field returns a value of 0001h.

Router 0 Node Address is the node address of the LAN board inside Router 0 that receives packets from the source bridge.

Router 0 Next Board Position indicates the position of the LAN board (inside Router 0) that receives packets from the LAN board mentioned in the preceding field. A value of 00h indicates LAN A; a value of 01h indicates LAN B, etc.

Route 0 Hops returns the number of hops a packet makes traveling between the source bridge and the destination network on route 0.

Route 0 Time field returns the time it takes a packet to travel between the source bridge and the destination network on route 0.

If more routers exist, information pertaining to these routers appears next on the list.

The NetWare C Interface format is:

```
int GetSpecificNetworkInfo( WORD connectionID,
    BYTE connectionNumber, AllResponseData *response,
    SpecificServerInfoStruct *responseData );
```

Return All Known Servers (04h)

This call returns the server type and name of each server known to the specified bridge.

Request Packet (46 bytes):

Offset	Content	Type	Order
0	SPX Packet Header	BYTE[42]	
42	Component Position	BYTE	
43	04h	BYTE	
44	Next Set Starting Point	WORD	lo-hi

Reply Packet (99 bytes):

Offset	Content	Type	Order
0	SPX Packet Header	BYTE[42]	
42	Completion Code	BYTE	
43	Interval Marker	LONG	lo-hi
47	Number of Servers	WORD	lo-hi
49	Server Type 0	WORD	lo-hi
51	Server Name 0	BYTE[48]	

This call returns the server type and name of each server known to the bridge to which the diagnostic application sends the request packet. One call can return a maximum of 10 server types and names. An application can repeat this call to return several sets of known server types and names.

Next Set Starting Point should be set to 0 for the first call to this call. If the call returns a full set of 10 server types and names in reply to the first call, the application should set this field to 10 for the second call, 20 for the third call, and so on until the call returns only a partial set of server types and names. The partial set of server types and names indicates the end of the list.

Completion Code returns one of the following values:

00h	Successful
FFh	Invalid Request

Number of Servers is how many server types and name combinations the call is returning in the current set. The maximum value this field returns is 10.

Each Server Type returns the object type of the server whose name appears in the following field. A file server's object type is 0004h. A print server's object type is 0003h. Other well-known object types appear in the introductory section to Bindery Services.

The NetWare C Interface format is:

```
int GetAllKnownServers( WORD connectionID, BYTE connectionNumber,
    WORD numberServersToSkip, AllResponseData *response,
    AllKnownServersStruct *responseData );
```

Return Specific Server Information (05h)

This call returns information concerning routing times and routes between the specified bridge and the specified (destination) server.

Request Packet (94 bytes):

Offset	Content	Type	Order
0	SPX Packet Header	BYTE[42]	
42	Component Position	BYTE	
43	05h	BYTE	
44	Server Type	WORD	lo-hi
46	Server Name	BYTE[48]	

Reply Packet (115 bytes):

Offset	Content	Type	Order
0	SPX Packet Header	BYTE[42]	
42	Completion Code	BYTE	
43	Interval Marker	LONG	lo-hi
47	Server Type	WORD	lo-hi
49	Server Name	BYTE[48]	
97	Server Address	WORD [6]	lo-hi
109	Route Hops	WORD	lo-hi
111	Reserved	BYTE[2]	
113	Number of Known Routes	WORD	lo-hi
115	Router 0 Node Address	WORD [3]	lo-hi
121	Route 0 Hops	BYTE	
122	Reserved 0	BYTE[2]	

.
.
.

This call returns information concerning routing times and routes between the bridge to which the diagnostic application sends the request packet and one destination server one or more hops away from the bridge. If only one route exists between the bridge and the destination server, the call returns the node address of the first interim bridge a packet meets en route from the source bridge to the destination server.

The call also returns the routing time and number of hops pertaining to that route. If more than one route exists, the call returns the node addresses of all interim bridges one hop away from the source bridge and the routing times and number of hops associated with all routes. The most efficient route appears at the top of the list in the reply packet. The field explanations that follow refer to these interim bridges (one hop away from the source bridge) as Router 0, Router 1, etc.

Completion Code returns one of the following values:

00h	Successful
FFh	Invalid Request

Server Address is the destination server's 12-byte internetwork address.

Route Hops returns the number of hops (between the source bridge and the destination server) of the most efficient route. The value in this field and the value returned in the Route 0 Hops field are the same.

Router 0 Node Address is the node address of the LAN board inside Router 0 that receives packets from the source bridge.

Route 0 Hops returns the number of hops a packet makes traveling between the source bridge and the destination server on route 0.

The NetWare C Interface format is:

```
int GetSpecificServerInfo( WORD connectionID, BYTE connectionNumber,
AllResponseData *response, SpecificServerInfoStruct *responseData );
```

Code Sample: NodeList.Prj, NodeList.C, IPX.H, IPXLibr.Asm

Nodelist broadcasts Configuration packets to each node and displays the Shell or Bridge Driver Configuration of each.

NodeList begins in main() by opening a socket for sending the IPX Configuration Request packets. Next main() calls IPXOpenSocket(), passing the socket number and the type of socket, temporary. A temporary socket is one that lasts only through the duration of the program.

There must be a pool of listening ECBs and Configuration Reply structures waiting for a response from the masses before any Configuration Request can be generated. To this end, the next step in the program is to set up *RcvECB* (an array of listening ECBs) and *HoldReply* (an array of Configuration Request structures).

SetupECB() initializes the relevant fields in the ECB. Whenever the program posts an ECB for the purposes of listening, IPX requires that the program initialize several fields. SetupECB() was created to take care of those fields, so all that needs to be passed is the address of the ECB, the address of the IPX Header/Fragment, and the size of the IPX Header/Fragment. SetupECB() initializes all necessary fields.

For instance, SetupECB() sets the *ESRAddress* field to NULL since there will be no Event Service Routine, and zeroes the *InUseField*. Further, SetupECB() sets the *ECBSocket* field to the socket we opened for sending, and sets the *FragmentCount* to one, since we are combining the IPX header and reply packet in one structure, *HoldReply*. Finally, SetupECB() sets *FragmentDescriptor* to the address and size of *HoldReply*.

After the *RcvECB* array elements are initialized, main() calls IPXListenForPacket(), posting the ECBs to a listen state. They are ready to receive data.

The next task is to initialize and send the first Configuration Request packet (NodeList sends several to reach all nodes). The program initializes *SendECB* with SetupECB(), which initializes fields relevant to sending in *HoldRequest*, the Configuration Request structure.

Next, main() sets the IPX address for the request packet to broadcast mode by placing FFh in *SendECB*'s *Immediate Address* field and in *HoldRequest*'s IPX Destination Node field. main() sets the *IPX Destination Network* to zero and sets the *IPX Destination Socket* to 456h in *HoldRequest*.

One important note here concerns how we store the socket in IPX calls. Since the socket is a two-byte number represented in high-low format, and Intel stores integers in low-high format, we must store the number in a C integer as 0x5604; 0x5604 in low-high format translates to 0x0456 in high-low.

IPXSendPacket() sends the packet and the program delays a full second, providing ample time for a response from the nodes on the network. The IPXGetIntervalMarker() call accomplishes this delay, returning a WORD value containing the number of clock ticks since the last call. When these ticks (18 a second) reach 18, the program continues. If this delay is not present, stations do not have ample time to respond which results in a report of only a few or no nodes.

Next, the program enters a loop where it first checks all the RcvECBs to see what has come back and adds those nodes to the Exclusion List, followed by resending the Configuration Request packet. The program loops several (MAX_RETRIES) times to ensure all stations have responded.

A counter loops through the entire *RcvECB* array, checking the *InUseFlag* and Completion Code values. The IPX drivers present in the shell set the *InUseFlag* to FEh when listening and to zero when a packet is received. The IPX drivers set the Completion Code to zero if a packet was received successfully. Currently, the program does not add nodes to the Exclusion list if the drivers return a bad completion code, assuming that a retry will clear the error. One extension of the program might allow the program to recognize possible bad Completion Codes and respond based on their values.

When the program identifies an *RcvECB* element as containing a valid node response, its IPX Source Address is copied into the Exclusion Address table in *HoldRequest* and the program increments the Exclusion Count. If the responding node is a bridge, however, the program does not add its address to the Exclusion table, since bridges do not read the Exclusion table. The fact that the responding node is a bridge is gleaned from its component list. If one of the components is a bridge driver, then the node is either an internal or an external bridge (a shell driver indicates a workstation).

The program then sends the Configuration Request packet again with IPXSendPacket(). main() delays using IPXGetIntervalMarker(), and repeats the process to ensure all nodes have responded.

Now that we have a list of all nodes in the *RcvECB* array, we can traverse the array, querying each node for configuration information.

Another loop iterates through the *RcvECB* array, checking for valid *CompletionCode* fields. Bridge nodes are tracked in an array of node addresses, *BridgeExclude*, to ensure we haven't reported on a bridge twice. This is necessary because bridges ignore exclusion lists, a fact not documented in the Novell System Calls manuals.

If the ECB is still listening, has an error in the Completion Code field, or is a node we have already reported on, the loop continues on the next *RcvECB* element.

For each valid element, main() begins the report by printing the software version numbers (Major Version and Minor Version) and the components are listed, while the program checks for a Shell Driver or a Bridge Driver.

If main() finds one of these drivers it calls PrintDriverInfo(), passing the Session Socket, the position of the driver in the Component List, and the address of the node (found in the IPX portion of HoldReply).

PrintDriverInfo() is responsible for making an SPX connection with the node sent to it in Address, using the SessionSocket and *ShellComponentPosition* passed by main(), and querying the shell or driver of the target, printing to the screen the results it finds.

This routine first closes the original socket we used for IPX and opens another for our SPX use. This is necessary because IPX and SPX traffic should not reside on the same socket.

The driver must have ECBs listening when the other drivers reply, so the next step PrintDriverInfo() takes is to post listening ECBs for the drivers' response. The routine initializes the Driver Configuration Reply packet array, InfoReply, with SetupECB(), and posts the ECBs as SPX listening packets with SPXListenForSequencedPacket().

Once the routine posts the reply ECBs, it must establish an SPX connection with the target node, followed by sending it the Driver Configuration Request packet.

NodeList has set aside a special ECB/SPX header pair specifically for establishing the SPX connection. PrintDriverInfo() sends *EstECBReq* and *EstSPXReq* to SetupECB() first, then sets their target node and network address. Then the routine sets the socket using the Session Socket passed to PrintDriverInfo(). Finally, PrintDriverInfo() calls SPXEstablishConnection() to establish the actual SPX connection.

Once the connection is made, the routine initializes the Shell Configuration Request packet, *InfoRequest*, and its corresponding ECB, *InfoRequestECB*, with SetupECB(). Then, PrintDriverInfo() records the component position and uses an if-then statement to determine how to proceed further: If the driver is a shell, only one request will be made. But if the driver is a bridge, it could have as many as four boards in the bridge, and we want the configuration of each.

For a shell, the routine sets InfoRequest's Request Number to zero, signifying the component being queried is a shell. The PrintDriverInfo() then calls QueryDriver(), which simply sends the *InfoRequest* packet to the target node. QueryDriver() scans the *InfoReply* ECB array until the station receives a packet (the InUseFlag is zero), noting the position in the array.

Finally, the routine prints the type of board and its configuration to the screen, showing the 80-byte strings of the *LANDescription* and *TextDescription* fields in InfoReply. The other bytes in the 269-byte packet contain the numeric values of the board type, settings, and other information. They could be used by developers in other applications so they wouldn't need to translate the descriptive strings.

If the target node is a bridge, QueryDriver() is called four times, with the number of the board in the bridge stored in *InfoRequest*'s *BridgeDriver* field. If there is a LAN board there, QueryDriver() prints the configuration, if not, the routine sets the CompletionCode and returns to PrintDriverInfo() without printing anything.

Another possible extension by developers would be for the program to trap all possible Completion Codes, handling them based on their value.

Finally, PrintDriverInfo() terminates the connection with a call to SPXTerminateConnection() and returns control to main() where the next node will be selected to query. When the node list has been exhausted, the program completes and exits.

NodeList.C

```
/*                                                                    */
/*      ConfTest -  Test the Configuration Request/Reply mechanism    */
/*                                                                    */
/*                                                                    */

#include <stdio.h>
#include <dos.h>

#include "ipx.h"

#define IPX_QUERY_SOCKET 0x5604
#define MAX_RETRIES 5
#define ADDED 0x55
#define BRIDGE_DRIVER 1
#define SHELL_DRIVER 2
#define FIRST_SOCKET 0x8080
#define SECOND_SOCKET 0x8181

/* Local Prototypes */
void PrintDriverInfo( BYTE DriverType, WORD SessionSocket,
                BYTE ShellComponentPosition, IPXAddress *Address );
void printAddress(BYTE byte[], int count);
void SetupECB( ECB *ECBptr, WORD *FragAddress, WORD Size );
void QueryDriver( WORD connectionID );
int InBridgeList( BYTE Node[6] );
void IPXGetProcAddress(void (*proc)(),WORD *addressField);
void IPXGetDataAddress(WORD *data,WORD *addressField);

IPXConfigRequest HoldRequest;          /* Request for Configuration Packets */
IPXConfigReply   HoldReply[MAX_NODES];
ECB              SendECB;
ECB              RcvECB[MAX_NODES];

SPXHeader        EstSPXReq;            /* Establish connection w/ target */
ECB              EstECBReq;

SPXInfoRequest   InfoRequest;      /* Make request of Shell/Bridge for Config */
ECB              InfoRequestECB;

SPXDriverReply   InfoReply[10];        /* Receive response from Shell/Bridge */
ECB              InfoReplyECB[10];

BYTE             targetNetwork[4] = { 0, 0, 0, 0 };
BYTE             targetNode[6] = { 0xFF, 0xFF, 0xFF, 0xFF, 0xFF, 0xFF };
WORD             targetSocket, socket;

BYTE             BridgeExclude[MAX_NODES][6];
int              ExcludeCount = 0;
```

```
WORD            ticks;

void main()
{
        int             retcode, i, z, retries, isbridge;
        IPXConfigReply  *reply;
        BYTE            ShellComponentPosition;
        WORD            SessionSocket, querySocket = IPX_QUERY_SOCKET;

        /* Print opening banner */
        printf("NODELIST - Lists all nodes and their configurations.\n");

        /* Make sure IPX is active and ok */
        if ( !IPXInitialize() )
        {
                printf("IPX must be loaded for this program to run.\n");
                exit(1);
        }

        /* Begin by opening a socket to send from */
        socket = FIRST_SOCKET;
        retcode = IPXOpenSocket( (BYTE*) &socket, 0 );
        if ( retcode )
        {
                printf("Error opening socket %X.  Error = %X.\n",
                        socket, retcode );
                exit(1);
        }

        /* Setup array of listening ECBs */
        for ( i = 0; i < MAX_NODES; i++ )
        {
                SetupECB( &RcvECB[i], &HoldReply[i], sizeof( IPXConfigReply ) );
                IPXListenForPacket( &RcvECB[i] );
        }

        /* Send IPX Configuration Request */
        SetupECB( &SendECB, &HoldRequest, sizeof( IPXConfigRequest ) );
        HoldRequest.IPX.PacketType = 0;
        HoldRequest.ExclusionCount = 0;

        /* Setup for broadcast mode: Place 0's in Network Address and         */
        /* 0xFF's in Node Address                                             */
        movmem( targetNode, SendECB.ImmediateAddress, 6);
        movmem( targetNetwork, HoldRequest.IPX.Destination.Network, 4);
        movmem( targetNode, HoldRequest.IPX.Destination.Node, 6);

        /* Set to broadcast on the query Socket (456h) */
        movmem( &querySocket, HoldRequest.IPX.Destination.Socket, 2);

        IPXSendPacket( &SendECB );
        while ( SendECB.InUseFlag )
                IPXRelinquishControl();

        if ( SendECB.CompletionCode )
        {
                printf( " Bad IPXSend, return = %x ", SendECB.CompletionCode );
                exit(1);
        }
```

```
/* Wait a second between each retry (give it a chance to respond) */
ticks = IPXGetIntervalMarker();
printf("Broadcasting Configuration Request...\n");
while ( ( IPXGetIntervalMarker() - ticks ) < 18 )
        ;

/* Check list of ECBs and re-send MAX_RETRIES times to be sure        */
/* all stations have responded                                        */
retries = 0;
while ( retries < MAX_RETRIES )
{
        for ( i = 0; i < MAX_NODES; i++ )
        {
           /* If this Receive ECB has received a good packet and      */
           /* we haven't already added it to our exclude lists,       */
               if ( !RcvECB[i].InUseFlag && !RcvECB[i].CompletionCode &&
                        RcvECB[i].CompletionCode != ADDED )
                {
                        /* Mark it as added */
                        RcvECB[i].CompletionCode = ADDED;

                /* Add it to the Exclusion Table if it's not a bridge */
                        /* Clear bridge flag */
                        isbridge = 0;

    /* Check component list to see if there's a BRIDGE_DRIVER present */
                      for ( z = 0; z < HoldReply[i].ComponentCount; z++ )
                    if ( HoldReply[i].ComponentType[z] == BRIDGE_DRIVER )
                                        isbridge++;

        /* If no BRIDGE_DRIVER was found, add to the exclusion table */
                              /* and update the number of exclusions  */
                        if ( !isbridge )
                                movmem( HoldReply[i].IPX.Source.Node,
        HoldRequest.ExclusionAddress[HoldRequest.ExclusionCount++], 6 );
                }
        }

        /* Re-send the configuration request */
        IPXSendPacket( &SendECB );
        while ( SendECB.InUseFlag != OKAY )
                IPXRelinquishControl();

        if ( SendECB.CompletionCode != OKAY )
        {
                printf( " Bad IPX Send, status = %x ",
                   SendECB.CompletionCode);
                exit(1);
        }

   /* Wait a second between each retry (give it a chance to respond) */
        ticks = IPXGetIntervalMarker();
        printf("Broadcasting Configuration Request...\n");
        while ( ( IPXGetIntervalMarker() - ticks ) < 18 )
                ;

        retries++;
}

/* Now iterate through list, contacting each node and producing       */
/* a report of each bridge and shell driver and their configuration   */
```

```
/* First, show bridges                                              */

printf( "=——————————————————————=\n");
printf( "=——————————————————————=\n");
printf( "              File Servers/Bridges\n");

for ( i = 0; i < MAX_NODES; i++ )
{
        /* If this ECB has not received anything, or if it received a */
        /* bad packet, move on to the next              */
        if ( RcvECB[i].CompletionCode != ADDED )
                continue;

      reply = (IPXConfigReply*) RcvECB[i].FragmentDescriptor.Address[0];

        SessionSocket = reply->SPXDiagnosticSocket;

        for ( z = 0; z < reply->ComponentCount ; z++ )
        {
                /* Ignore the shell drivers this go around           */
                if ( reply->ComponentType[z] == SHELL_DRIVER )
                        continue;

                if ( reply->ComponentType[z] == BRIDGE_DRIVER )
                {
                        /* We know this node is a bridge, let's make */
                        /* sure we haven't contacted it before       */
                    if ( !InBridgeList( HoldReply[i].IPX.Source.Node ) )
                        {
                                /* Add to Bridge List */
                                movmem( HoldReply[i].IPX.Source.Node,
                                     BridgeExclude[ExcludeCount++], 6 );

                                /* print banner */
                                printf( "=——————————————————=\n");
                                printf( "Report for Node Address: ");
                        printAddress( HoldReply[i].IPX.Source.Node, 6 );
                                printf( "\n" );


                                /* Print info on our Bridge */
                                PrintDriverInfo( BRIDGE_DRIVER,
                           SessionSocket, z, &HoldReply[i].IPX.Source );
                        }
                }
        }
}

/* Now show workstations/shells                                     */

printf( "=——————————————————————=\n");
printf( "                 Workstations\n");

for ( i = 0; i < MAX_NODES; i++ )
{
        /* If this ECB has not received anything, or if it received a */
        /* bad packet, move on to the next                            */
        if ( RcvECB[i].CompletionCode != ADDED )
                continue;
```

```
            reply = (IPXConfigReply*) RcvECB[i].FragmentDescriptor.Address[0];

            SessionSocket = reply->SPXDiagnosticSocket;

            for ( z = 0; z < reply->ComponentCount ; z++ )
            {
                    /* Show the shell drivers this go around */
                    if ( reply->ComponentType[z] == SHELL_DRIVER )
                    {
                            /* print banner */
                            printf( "=————————————————————=\n");
                            printf( "Report for Node Address: ");
                            printAddress( HoldReply[i].IPX.Source.Node, 6 );
                            printf( "\n" );

                            PrintDriverInfo( SHELL_DRIVER, SessionSocket, z,
                                    &HoldReply[i].IPX.Source );
                    }


                    /* Skip the bridges this time */
                    if ( reply->ComponentType[z] == BRIDGE_DRIVER )
                            continue;

            }

        }

        printf( "=————————————————————=\n");
        printf( "=————————————————————=\n");

        IPXCloseSocket( socket );
}


void PrintDriverInfo( BYTE DriverType, WORD SessionSocket,
   BYTE ShellComponentPosition, IPXAddress *Address )
{
        int     retcode, i, driver;
        WORD    connectionID;

        /* This section, given a Session Socket, Component Position          */
        /* and an IPXAddress structure,                                      */
        /* the routine should print the LAN Card type and configuration      */
        /* info from the shells                                              */

        /* Close old socket, open a new one */
        IPXCloseSocket( socket );
        socket = SECOND_SOCKET;
        retcode = IPXOpenSocket( (BYTE*) &socket, 0 );
        if ( retcode )
        {
                printf("Error opening socket.\n");
                exit(1);
        }

        /* Now, setup SPX connection.  First, post listens                   */
        /* You need a few here; tried w/ one and didn't work always          */
        for ( i = 0; i < 10; i++ )
        {
                SetupECB( &InfoReplyECB[i], &InfoReply[i],
                   sizeof( SPXDriverReply ) );
```

```
        SPXListenForSequencedPacket( &InfoReplyECB[i] );
}

/* Setup for Send SPX Connection Request */

/* Initialize the ECB */
SetupECB( &EstECBReq, &EstSPXReq, sizeof( SPXHeader ) );
EstSPXReq.PacketType = 5; /* SPX Packet */

/* Set Establish destination equal to config destination */
movmem( Address, &EstSPXReq.Destination, 10 );

/* Now set socket to that obtained from Configuration Request */
movmem( &SessionSocket, EstSPXReq.Destination.Socket, 2);

/* Make the connection (set retry to default (0) and set watchdog (1) */
retcode = SPXEstablishConnection( 0, 1, &connectionID, &EstECBReq );
if ( retcode )
{
        printf("Can't Establish Connection, ret = %X\n", retcode );
        exit(1);
}

while ( EstECBReq.InUseFlag && !(kbhit()) );

if ( EstECBReq.CompletionCode )
{
        printf("Can't Establish Connection, Completion Code = %X\n",
                EstECBReq.CompletionCode );
        exit(1);
}

/* Connection has been established, now query shell */
SetupECB( &InfoRequestECB, &InfoRequest, sizeof( SPXInfoRequest ) );
InfoRequest.SPX.PacketType = 5; /* SPX Packet */

InfoRequest.ComponentPosition = ShellComponentPosition;

if ( DriverType == SHELL_DRIVER )
{
        InfoRequest.RequestNumber = 0;
           /* Get Shell Driver Configuration */
        QueryDriver( connectionID );
}
else
if ( DriverType == BRIDGE_DRIVER )
{
        InfoRequest.RequestNumber = 1;
           /* Get Bridge Driver Configuration */

        for ( driver = 0; driver < 4; driver++ )
        {
                InfoRequest.BridgeDriver = driver;
                printf("LAN %c:\n", 'A' + driver );
                QueryDriver( connectionID );
        }
}

SPXTerminateConnection( connectionID, &EstECBReq );

while ( EstECBReq.InUseFlag && !kbhit() )
        ;
```

```
}

void QueryDriver( WORD connectionID )
{
        int response, i;

        /* Send the Shell Driver query */
        SPXSendSequencedPacket( connectionID, &InfoRequestECB );

        /* Now Check for a response, wait until there is one        */
        /* Scan InfoReply's for !InUseFlag, key can be hit to abort */
        response = 0;
        while ( !response && !kbhit() )
        {
                for ( i=0; i < 10; i++ )
                {
                        if ( !InfoReplyECB[i].InUseFlag )
                                response = i+1;
                }
        }
        if ( kbhit() )
        {
                getch();
                printf("Key was hit while waiting for shell to respond");
                exit(1);
        }

        /* If there is a bad response (such as when there are no more LAN      */
        /* boards), then return                                                */
        if ( InfoReply[response-1].CompletionCode )
                return;

        /* Print configuration information */
        printf("LAN Type is :\n");
        printf("%s\n", InfoReply[response-1].LANDescription );

        printf("\nLAN Setup is :\n");
        printf("%s\n", InfoReply[response-1].TextDescription );

        /* Finally, terminate the connection with this node */
        SPXListenForSequencedPacket( &InfoReplyECB[response-1] );
}

void printAddress(BYTE byte[], int count)
{
        int i;

        for (i=0; i<count; i++)
                printf("%02X", byte[i]);
}

void SetupECB( ECB *ECBptr, WORD *FragAddress, WORD Size )
{
        /* Initialize the fields necessary for all of our ECB's */

        ECBptr->ESRAddress = NULL;
        ECBptr->InUseFlag = 0;
        ECBptr->ECBSocket = socket;
        ECBptr->FragmentCount = 1;
```

```
        IPXGetDataAddress( (WORD *)FragAddress,
                           (WORD *)&ECBptr->FragmentDescriptor.Address );
        ECBptr->FragmentDescriptor.Size = Size;
}

int InBridgeList( BYTE Node[6] )
{
        int i, z, same;

        for ( i = 0; i < ExcludeCount; i++ )
        {
                same = 1;
                for ( z = 0; z < 6; z++ )
                        if ( Node[z] != BridgeExclude[i][z] )
                        {
                                same = 0;
                                break;
                        }
                if ( same )
                        return (1);
        }

        return (0);
}

void  IPXGetProcAddress(proc,addressField)
void (*proc)();
WORD addressField[2];
{
        struct SREGS segregs;

        segread(&segregs);
        segregs.es = segregs.ds;

        addressField[0] = (WORD) proc;
        addressField[1] = (WORD) segregs.cs;
}

void  IPXGetDataAddress(data,addressField)
WORD *data;
WORD addressField[2];
{
        struct SREGS segregs;

        segread(&segregs);
        segregs.es = segregs.ds;

        addressField[0] = (WORD) data;
        addressField[1] = (WORD) segregs.ds;
}
```

IPX.H

```
/*                                                                              */
/*      IPX.H -  Header file with structure definitions for IPX/SPX            */
/*                                                                              */

#define MAX_NODES 10

#define TEMPORARY_SOCKET (BYTE)0
#define PERMANENT_SOCKET (BYTE)0xFF
#define OKAY 0

typedef unsigned char BYTE;
typedef unsigned int WORD;
typedef unsigned long LONG;

typedef struct
{
        BYTE    Network[4];     /* high-low */
        BYTE    Node[6];        /* high-low */
        BYTE    Socket[2];      /* high-low */
} IPXAddress;

typedef struct IPXPacketStructure
{
        WORD                    PacketCheckSum;                 /* high-low */
        WORD                    PacketLength;                   /* high-low */
        BYTE                    PacketTransportControl;
        BYTE                    PacketType;
        IPXAddress              Destination;
        IPXAddress              Source;
} IPXPacket;

typedef struct IPXConfigRequestStructure
{
        IPXPacket               IPX;
        BYTE                    ExclusionCount;
        BYTE                    ExclusionAddress[MAX_NODES][6];
} IPXConfigRequest;

typedef struct IPXConfigReplyStructure
{
        IPXPacket               IPX;
        BYTE                    MajorVersion;
        BYTE                    MinorVersion;
        WORD                    SPXDiagnosticSocket;
        BYTE                    ComponentCount;
        BYTE                    ComponentType[100];
} IPXConfigReply;

struct  ECBFragment
{
        WORD            Address[2];                     /* offset-segment */
        WORD            Size;                           /* low-high */
};

typedef struct ECBStructure
{
        WORD                    Link[2];                /* offset-segment */
        BYTE                    far *ESRAddress;        /* offset-segment */
        BYTE                    InUseFlag;
```

```
        BYTE                    CompletionCode;
        WORD                    ECBSocket;              /* high-low */
        BYTE                    IPXWorkspace[4];        /* N/A */
        BYTE                    DriverWorkspace[12];    /* N/A */
        BYTE                    ImmediateAddress[6];    /* high-low */
        WORD                    FragmentCount;          /* low-high */
        struct ECBFragment      FragmentDescriptor;
} ECB;

typedef struct SPXPacketStructure
{
        WORD                    PacketCheckSum;                 /* high-low */
        WORD                    PacketLength;                   /* high-low */
        BYTE                    PacketTransportControl;
        BYTE                    PacketType;
        IPXAddress              Destination;
        IPXAddress              Source;
        BYTE                    ConnectionControl;
        BYTE                    DataStreamType;
        WORD                    SourceConnectionID;             /* high-low */
        WORD                    DestinationConnectionID;        /* high-low */
        WORD                    SequenceNumber;                 /* high-low */
        WORD                    AcknowledgeNumber;              /* high-low */
        WORD                    AllocationNumber;               /* high-low */
} SPXHeader;

typedef struct SPXShellReplyStructure
{
        SPXHeader               SPX;
        BYTE                    CompletionCode;
        LONG                    IntervalMarker;                 /* low-high */
        BYTE                    Reserved[4];
        BYTE                    NodeAddress[6];
        BYTE                    Reserved2;
        BYTE                    NodeAddressType;
        WORD                    MaxDataSize;                    /* low-high */
        BYTE                    Reserved3[2];
        BYTE                    LANHardwareID;
        WORD                    TransportTime;                  /* low-high */
        BYTE                    Reserved4[9];
        BYTE                    EthernetType[2];
        BYTE                    MajorVersion;
        BYTE                    MinorVersion;
        BYTE                    MiscFlags;
        BYTE                    SelectedConfiguration;
        BYTE                    LANDescription[80];
        WORD                    IOAddress1;                     /* low-high */
        WORD                    DecodeRange1a;                  /* low-high */
        WORD                    IOAddress2;                     /* low-high */
        WORD                    DecodeRange2a;                  /* low-high */
        BYTE                    MemoryAddress1[3];
        WORD                    DecodeRange1b;                  /* low-high */
        BYTE                    MemoryAddress2[3];
        WORD                    DecodeRange2b;                  /* low-high */
        BYTE                    InterruptIsUsed1;
        BYTE                    InterruptLine1;
        BYTE                    InterruptIsUsed2;
        BYTE                    InterruptLine2;
        BYTE                    DMAIsUsed1;
        BYTE                    DMALine1;
        BYTE                    DMAIsUsed2;
        BYTE                    DMALine2;
```

```
        BYTE                    MicroChannelFlags;
        BYTE                    Reserved5;
        BYTE                    TextDescription[80];
} SPXDriverReply;

typedef struct SPXInfoRequestStructure
{
        SPXHeader               SPX;
        BYTE                    ComponentPosition;
        BYTE                    RequestNumber;
        BYTE                    BridgeDriver;
} SPXInfoRequest;

/* IPX/SPX Assembly Library prototypes */
extern int IPXInitialize( void );
extern int IPXOpenSocket(BYTE *socketNumber, BYTE socketType);
extern void IPXCloseSocket(WORD socketNumber);
extern int IPXGetLocalTarget(BYTE *networkAddress,BYTE *immediateAddress,
   WORD *transportTime);
extern void IPXSendPacket(ECB *eventControlBlock);
extern int IPXListenForPacket(ECB *eventControlBlock);
extern void IPXRelinquishControl(void);
extern unsigned int IPXGetIntervalMarker(void);
extern int SPXEstablishConnection( BYTE RetryCount, BYTE Watchdog,
   WORD *connectionID, ECB *ECBptr );
extern void SPXListenForSequencedPacket( ECB *ECBptr );
extern void SPXSendSequencedPacket( WORD ConnectionID, ECB *ECBptr );
extern void SPXTerminateConnection( WORD ConnectionID, ECB *ECBptr );
```

IPXLibr.Asm

```
;
; IPXLIB.ASM    -  Library of ASM routines for IPX/SPX
;
        .MODEL SMALL

        .DATA
        ;Address of IPX
        IPXAddress dw 2 dup(0)

        .CODE

        PUBLIC _IPXInitialize
        PUBLIC _IPXOpenSocket
        PUBLIC _IPXCloseSocket
        PUBLIC _IPXGetLocalTarget
        PUBLIC _IPXSendPacket
        PUBLIC _IPXListenForPacket
        PUBLIC _IPXRelinquishControl
        PUBLIC _IPXGetIntervalMarker
        PUBLIC _SPXEstablishConnection
        PUBLIC _SPXListenForSequencedPacket
        PUBLIC _SPXSendSequencedPacket
        PUBLIC _SPXTerminateConnection


; int IPXInitialize( void );
;  Initializes IPX/SPX mechanism, returns TRUE if IPX is installed,
;  FALSE (0) if not installed.
;
```

```
_IPXInitialize  proc near
        mov      ax, 7A00h                      ; Looking for address of 7Ah
        int      2Fh                            ; Call Multiplex interrupt
        mov      IPXAddress, di                 ; Store address
        mov      IPXAddress + 2, es
        and      ax, 00FFh                      ; Mask off AH to return status in
AL
        ret
_IPXInitialize  endp

; int IPXOpenSocket(BYTE *socketNumber, BYTE socketType);
;  Opens socket socketNumber as socketType (either Temporary or Permanent)
;  Returns 0 on success.
;
_IPXOpenSocket  proc near
        push     bp                         ; Establish standard parameter frame
        mov      bp, sp

        mov      bx, [bp + 4]             ; Place socketNumber in high-low order
        mov      dl, byte ptr [bx]
        mov      dh, byte ptr [bx + 1]
        mov      al, [bp + 6]                   ; AL gets socketType
        mov      bx, 0
        call dword ptr DGROUP:IPXAddress        ; Make far call to IPXAddress

        pop      bp                             ; Restore stack frame & return
        and      ax, 00FFh
        ret
_IPXOpenSocket  endp

; void IPXCloseSocket(WORD socketNumber);
;  Close socket socketNumber.
;
_IPXCloseSocket proc near
        push     bp
        mov      bp, sp

        mov      bx, [bp + 4]
        mov      dx, bx
        mov      bx, 1
        call dword ptr DGROUP:IPXAddress

        pop      bp
        ret
_IPXCloseSocket endp

; int IPXGetLocalTarget(BYTE *networkAddress,BYTE *immediateAddress,
  WORD *transportTime);
;  A 10-byte networkAddress is passed to IPX, which returns the immediteAddress
;  to be placed in the ECB and transportTime, an estimate (in clock ticks) of the
;  time to send the packet from the source to the destination node.
;  Returns 0 on success.
;
_IPXGetLocalTarget      proc near
        push     bp
        mov      bp, sp

        push     si
        mov      bx, [bp + 4]
        mov      si, bx
        mov      bx, [bp + 6]
        mov      di, bx
```

```
        mov     bx, 2
        call dword ptr DGROUP:IPXAddress

        mov     bp, sp                          ; restore BP (IPX kills it)
        add     bp, 2                              ; account for SI push
        mov     bx, [bp + 8]                       ; get address of
        mov     [bx], cx                           ; place CX at *

        pop     si
        pop     bp
        and     ax, 00FFh
        ret
_IPXGetLocalTarget      endp

; void IPXSendPacket(ECB *eventControlBlock);
;  Sends an IPX packet.
;
_IPXSendPacket  proc near
        push    bp
        mov     bp, sp
        push    si

        mov     ax, DGROUP
        mov     es, ax
        mov     bx, [bp + 4]
        mov     si, bx
        mov     bx, 3

        call dword ptr DGROUP:IPXAddress

        push    ds
        pop     es
        pop     si
        pop     bp
        ret
_IPXSendPacket  endp

; int IPXListenForPacket(ECB *eventControlBlock);
;  Listens for an IPX packet using the passed Event Control Block.
;  Returns 0 if able to post the listen request.
;
_IPXListenForPacket     proc near
        push    bp
        mov     bp, sp
        push    si

        mov     ax, DGROUP
        mov     es, ax
        mov     bx, [bp + 4]
        mov     si, bx
        mov     bx, 4

        call dword ptr DGROUP:IPXAddress

        push    ds
        pop     es
        pop     si
        pop     bp
        and     ax, 00FFh
        ret
_IPXListenForPacket     endp
```

```
; void IPXRelinquishControl(void);
;  Relinquishes control to IPX for other processing.
;
_IPXRelinquishControl   proc near
        mov     bx, 0Ah
        call dword ptr DGROUP:IPXAddress
        ret
_IPXRelinquishControl   endp

; unsigned int IPXGetIntervalMarker(void);
;  Gets a timer tick marker from IPX.
;
_IPXGetIntervalMarker   proc near
        mov     bx, 8
        call dword ptr DGROUP:IPXAddress
        ret
_IPXGetIntervalMarker   endp

; int SPXEstablishConnection( BYTE RetryCount, BYTE Watchdog,
   WORD *connectionID, ECB *ECBptr );
;  Makes an SPX connection with the target listening node.
;  Returns 0 if able to attempt connection.
;
_SPXEstablishConnection proc near
        push    bp
        mov     bp, sp
        push    si

        mov     ax, DGROUP
        mov     es, ax

        mov     bx, [bp + 4]
        mov     al, bl
        mov     bx, [bp + 6]
        mov     ah, bl
        mov     bx, [bp + 10]
        mov     si, bx
        mov     bx, 11h

        call dword ptr DGROUP:IPXAddress

        mov     bp, sp                            ; restore BP (IPX kills it)
        add     bp, 2                                ; account for SI push
        mov     bx, [bp + 8]                         ; get address of
        mov     [bx], dx                             ; place DX at *

        push    ds
        pop     es
        pop     si
        pop     bp
        and     ax, 00FFh
        ret
_SPXEstablishConnection endp

; void SPXListenForSequencedPacket( ECB *ECBptr );
;  Posts a listening ECB to receive an SPX packet.
;
_SPXListenForSequencedPacket    proc near
        push    bp
        mov     bp, sp
        push    si
```

```
        mov     ax, DGROUP
        mov     es, ax
        mov     bx, [bp + 4]
        mov     si, bx
        mov     bx, 17h

        call dword ptr DGROUP:IPXAddress

        push    ds
        pop     es
        pop     si
        pop     bp
        ret
_SPXListenForSequencedPacket    endp

; void SPXSendSequencedPacket( WORD ConnectionID, ECB *ECBptr );
;  Sends an SPX packet.
;
_SPXSendSequencedPacket proc near
        push    bp
        mov     bp, sp
        push    si

        mov     ax, DGROUP
        mov     es, ax
        mov     bx, [bp + 4]
        mov     dx, bx
        mov     bx, [bp + 6]
        mov     si, bx
        mov     bx, 16h

        call dword ptr DGROUP:IPXAddress

        push    ds
        pop     es
        pop     si
        pop     bp
        ret
_SPXSendSequencedPacket endp

; void SPXTerminateConnection( WORD ConnectionID, ECB *ECBptr );
;  Terminates an SPX connection.
;
_SPXTerminateConnection proc near
        push    bp
        mov     bp, sp
        push    si

        mov     ax, DGROUP
        mov     es, ax
        mov     bx, [bp + 4]
        mov     dx, bx
        mov     bx, [bp + 6]
        mov     si, bx
        mov     bx, 13h

        call dword ptr DGROUP:IPXAddress

        push    ds
        pop     es
```

```
        pop     si
        pop     bp
        ret
_SPXTerminateConnection endp

        END
```

NodeList.Prj

```
nodelist ( ipx.h )
ipxlibr.obj
```

Exercises

1. Run NodeList. Examine the code thoroughly. Familiarize yourself with the mechanism that takes place in making the calls.

2. Add to NodeList the ability to query the statistics or the status of the shell or driver.

3. When listing the station information, use Bindery API calls to scan the server Bindery to determine the user and connection associated with each node address, so instead of giving information on node xyz, you display it about John, who's logged into connection 5, and has node address xyz.

4. Write-in more code to handle different completion codes and error values.

5. Use the bridge component calls to query file servers and bridges for their internal tables.

6. Use the IPX/SPX calls to develop a point-to-point test.

7. Write a program to use the calls (and the timing differences between stations) to assemble a map of the LAN.

8. Extend NodeList to query other networks. Currently, only the local network is queried.

16 Service Advertising Protocol

The Service Advertising Protocol (SAP) allows third-party, value-added servers to advertise their services on the network. It defines exactly how the servers may advertise and how they should respond to requests about them. With it, the concept of the server has been broadened from just the file server to include job servers, archive servers, print servers — and any others that developers can create.

SAP is used only in identifying the servers that a workstation or client might wish to attach to and use; it is up to the developer to design a formal attach/login protocol for the actual interaction between client and server.

The Service Advertising Protocol is much like Diagnostic Services. Under SAP, servers listen for service inquiries and periodically broadcast their identities to other servers.

Types of servers

Every server is assigned a server type number corresponding to the type of service it provides. Novell recommends that developers contact them for assignments of unique server types. The following list shows the predefined, or "well-known" server types (well-known are from 0 to 8000h):

Wild	FFFFh	Archive Server	0009h
Unknown	0000h	Remote Bridge Server	0024h
Print Server	0003h	Advertising Print Server	0047h
File Server	0004h	Reserved up to	8000h
Job Server	0005h		

Server names

The name of a server must be unique within its particular type. Most often, it is assigned by the network administrator when the server is installed. This is true of file servers as well as third-party servers.

One useful convention widely followed by developers today is to assign default names but allow the network administrator or the program to change those names.

Server socket numbers

Each server must have a socket number that it uses to send to or receive requests from the clients. This number may be assigned dynamically by IPX to be in the range of 4000h to 7FFFh or the number could be static and assigned by Novell starting at 8000h.

It is important to distinguish the socket used for communication between client and server and the socket used to query the server. Service queries, responses and advertising are all the traffic on socket 452h. Servers must listen to this socket to respond to queries and they must use it periodically to broadcast packets advertising their services.

Servers must open and use other sockets for client-server communication, such as job service. This socket may be opened dynamically, or a developer may use one of the static numbers or a number assigned by Novell (see chapter 14).

Servers must open socket 452h upon initialization. If an attempt to do so fails because the socket is already open, another process (possibly a nondedicated file server or bridge) in the node has opened the socket and is using it. In this case, the second server should not monitor the socket.

If IPX has already opened the maximum number of sockets, the programmer's server code should terminate with an appropriate message.

Identity broadcasts

A value-added server must broadcast its identity on socket 452h upon initialization and every 60 seconds thereafter. This identity information is sent to all file servers & networks on the internet by the servers or bridges on the same network as the value-added server. The broadcast informs other servers of the name and type of the broadcasting server and lets them know it is still active. All file servers monitor this socket, adding new value-added servers to their Binderies as those servers are initialized. If a server is not heard from after several minutes, it is assumed to have gone down and is removed from all Binderies.

In broadcast, a value of 2 is entered in a server identification packet's Response Type field. A value of FFh FFh FFh FFh FFh FFh is placed in the Destination Node field, and a value of 0452 in the Destination Socket field, of the IPX header packet.

Finding value-added services

Because all servers monitor the SAP socket, the simplest way for a client to find a service is by scanning the Bindery. The scan can be by name or type; once found, the value-added server can be contacted using the information in its Bindery

NET_ADDRESS property, which contains its network, node and socket addresses. (Access to this dynamic item property is anyone read, NetWare write.)

An alternative is to identify services on the network by broadcasting a service query packet. Before sending this packet, the prospective client should post several ECBs — prepared to receive service identification packets of up to 544 bytes — on its temporary socket.

The programmer may choose either method.

Service query packet

Offset	Content	Type	Order
0	IPX Header	BYTE[30]	
30	Query Type	WORD	hi-lo
32	Server Type	WORD	hi-lo

Query Type is set to 1 for a "general service" query or a 3 for a "nearest server" query.

Server Type indicates the type of server that should respond to this query. FFFFh is wild and causes all server types to respond. The wildcard is good only for general service queries.

A general service query fetches responses from all servers of the specified type (whether they are file servers or value-added servers running on file servers or bridges). So, for example, to find all servers of all types, a developer would enter the value 1 in the Query Type field and the value FFFFh (wild) in the Server Type field. (A developer can write a process to a specific type of server (file server, print server, etc.) by changing the value in the Server Type field.) Also, value-added servers will respond only if they are programmed to do so; NetWare internal and external bridges will respond with lists of known servers of the type specified.

To find the nearest (first to respond) server or the nearest server of a specific type, a developer would enter the value 3 in the Query Type field and the desired value in the Server Type field.

Server identification packets

When a value-added server receives a 34-bit query packet, it must check the Query Type and Server Type fields. If a server is the right type, it adjusts the Response Type field of its service identification packet to conform to the client's Query Type and transmits the ID packet.

A single server's identification packet is 96 bytes long. However, file servers and bridges can identify as many as eight servers in a single packet; each additional server adds 64 bytes of data to the packet, so a service ID packet has a maximum length of 544 bytes.

Offset	Content	Type	Order
0	IPX Header	BYTE[30]	
30	Response Type	WORD	hi-lo
32	Server Type	WORD	hi-lo
34	Server Name	BYTE[48]	hi-lo
82	Network	BYTE[4]	hi-lo
86	Node	BYTE[6]	hi-lo
92	Socket	WORD	hi-lo
94	Intermediate Networks	WORD	hi-lo

Response Type is set to 2 for general service or to 4 for nearest service when the server responds to the query packet. It is also set to 2 for initialization and periodic broadcasts.

Server Type is the value assigned by Novell for the service class. The server ensures that the value in this field matches the value in the query packet's Server Type field.

Server Name is a 48-byte null-terminated string that is the server's unique name within the internetwork. Any character between 21h (!) and 7Fh (DEL) may be used, except the following:

/ (slash)
\ (backslash)
: (colon)
; (semicolon)
, (comma)
* (asterisk)
? (question mark)
+ (plus)
- (minus)

The *Network* field is the network address of the LAN on which the value-added server resides. This value can be obtained by calling IPX Get Internetwork Address (see chapter 14).

Node is the node on which the value-added server resides. This value can also be obtained by calling IPX Get Internetwork Address.

Socket is the socket number on which the value-added server accepts queries (not 452h).

Intermediate Networks shows the number of hops the server ID packet is required to make traveling from the value-added server to the querying process. Initially, the field is set to 1; each time the packet passes through an intermediate network, the field is incremented. When this field is set to 0x10, the ID packet is a server shutdown packet and recipient file servers and bridges respond by purging the server from their Binderies.

Server shutdown packets

It is not mandatory that servers broadcast shutdown packets. However, it can free up space on bridge and server tables valuable seconds before silence prompts a purge, and Novell suggests using them as a matter of "courtesy to the network."

Code Sample: SAPTest.C

SAPTest was developed to show how the Service Advertising Protocol can be used to advertise a server. In this case, we will be advertising as a file server (Bindery object type 4) so we will show up on an SLIST report. The user passes the name of the server as the first command-line argument.

SAPTest first defines the *SAPData* structure which is the Server Identification Packet structure and will be used to identify our server in a global broadcast. The prototypes follow, including the global variables.

The main() routine is fairly simple: After the command-line syntax is checked, the advertising packet is started and a while loop checks for a key to be hit. When a key is hit, advertising stops and the program terminates.

The real work is done in the StartAdvertising() and StopAdvertising() functions. StartAdvertising() opens the SAP_SOCKET 452h and sets up an IPX header, an ECB, and our *SAPData* structure for periodic broadcasts. We need a far pointer in the *ESRAddress* field of *SendECB* so we cast the address of WaitESRHandler() to a far pointer.

When IPXSendPacket() completes, WaitESRHandler(), our assembly routine, is immediately called. It then loads DS, pushes the address of the ECB on the stack, and calls WaitESR().

WaitESR() switches the ESR address to AdvertiseESRHandler() and schedules an event to occur in 60 seconds. (We must broadcast this advertising packet every 60 seconds.) When the time expires, AdvertiseESRHandler() is called, which calls AdvertiseESR().

AdvertiseESR() sets the ESR address back to WaitESRHandler() and sends out the actual advertising packet. Once the packet is sent, WaitESRHandler() and then WaitESR() are called and the process continues.

This cycling is provided by the Asynchronous Event Scheduler, which calls the ESR specified in the ECB every 60 seconds. This "background timer" can be used for many possible applications.

When the user presses a key in the main() program loop and the program must terminate the advertising cycle, StopAdvertising() is called, which cancels the IPX event. Then a shutdown packet is sent, notifying other servers that this server has gone down and can be removed from their internal lists. No ESRs are used in this function.

SAPTest is a fully-functional service advertising application. All it does is advertise, but developers could use it as a starting point for creating their own custom application servers. Developers should be cautioned that when using an advertising application such as SAPTest on an internetwork, portions of the internetwork may

```
void AdvertiseESR( ECB *myECB )
{
        counter2++;
        myECB->ESRAddress = (void far *)WaitESRHandler;
        IPXSendPacket( myECB );
}

int StopAdvertising( char *name )
{

        IPXCancelEvent( &SendECB );
        while ( SendECB.InUseFlag )
                ;

        if ( SendECB.CompletionCode != 0xFC )
                return SendECB.CompletionCode;

        /* Setup SAP Data structure for shutting down */
        SAPData.ResponseType = 0x0200;  /* 2 - Type for periodic broadcast */
        SAPData.ServerType = FILE_SERVER;
        strcpy( SAPData.ServerName, strupr( name ) );
        IPXGetInternetworkAddress( SAPData.Network );
        SAPData.Socket = 0x1111;
        SAPData.IntermediateNetworks = 0x1000;
                /* 16 - Type for "down" broadcast */

        SetupSendPacket( &SendECB, &SendIPXHeader, targetNetwork,
                targetNode, SAP_SOCKET, &SAPData, sizeof( SAPData ) );

        SendECB.ESRAddress = (void far *)NULL;

        /* Send Shutdown Packet */

        IPXSendPacket( &SendECB );
        while ( SendECB.InUseFlag != OKAY )
                IPXRelinquishControl();

}
```

Exercises

1. Run SAPTest above. Did your server show up on SLIST? Did it go away after you ended SAPTest?

2. What were the counters? What does this say about the frequency with which the ESRs were called?

3. Design a protocol for communication between an application server and client workstations. Use the SAP as the means of advertising the server. Could this be done without the SAP routines?

17 Value Added Processes

The VAP Services API is perhaps the most powerful — and most elusive — element of the NetWare programming environment. Since its introduction in NetWare 2.1, the API has mystified developers; it has seemed almost unapproachably complex, possibly because of a lack of clear documentation and sufficient code examples.

It may also be because a VAP is a server-based process, i.e., the process runs in the server rather than on a client workstation. And, unlike the other API groups we've covered, this group of calls also runs on the server. So care must be taken to assure peaceful coexistence with NetWare in an environment where performance of an entire server can be seriously impaired by just one slow or inefficient VAP.

On the other hand, the profit realized on care invested in development of quick, efficient VAPs can be enormous. VAPs can, among other things, use the resources of file servers and bridges; run in both the real or protected modes of the 286 or 386 processor; receive input from the console keyboard and send output to the screen; schedule and spawn processes; afford the option of having programs reside in dedicated or nondedicated file servers; log in to file servers (if the VAP knows an object name and its password and the object has sufficient rights); make most NetWare API system calls, including those for IPX-SPX; and allocate and use file server memory (though only upon installation).

We'll begin with those design issues that must be considered before coding can begin. Next we'll address such VAP operating environment rules as those for memory allocation, process loading and error handling. Then we'll cover the issues surrounding protected-mode and real-mode programming. We'll discuss the components of the VAP: the header, the handlers, and the application code. We'll provide debugging information and the function call reference, then conclude with an illustration of VAP programming.

Design issues in the server environment

Among the key considerations in the earliest stages of development are process management and how VAPs work in the server environment. These include performance issues, perhaps the most critical element of VAP design, and questions of distribution, of deciding what will run best on a server and what will run best on the client workstations.

NetWare processes

Not all VAPs should run on the file server. NetWare's core process-management routines (the "kernel") set each process in a true multitasking environment, i.e. each process is treated independently. However, to enhance performance, NetWare was designed not to be preemptive, i.e. processes are not interrupted by other processes. A process is preempted only by a hardware interrupt (in which case, after the interrupt is serviced, processing picks up where it left off).

So absent hardware interrupts, a VAP will run until it relinquishes control to the next process. This polite, "good guy" environment, as Novell calls it, improves performance by removing the overhead of preemptive processing, but places a demand on NetWare developers to streamline processes. The same demand is made of NetWare developers who run VAPs as server processes.

A VAP may have several processes running concurrently and may "spawn" or create other processes that run as children of the parent.

When a file server is ready to run a VAP, it places it in a run queue. Only when the queue reaches the VAP is it executed. Each process running in a file server has a priority level. A higher priority process is placed in the run queue ahead of lower priority processes. Processes of equal priority are executed first-come, first-served. VAPs are assigned the lowest priority level to ensure that they will run only after critical system processes have run.

After the VAP executes, it remains idle until it needs to run again, at which time the file server schedules the process back into the queue. VAPs themselves determine when they will run again, be it as soon as possible, never, or in a specified amount of time. The next section explains the options open to the developer.

The developer should consider early on just what network resources the VAP must access. This will determine whether the VAP must log in to the file server and what API groups will be needed. Developers must weigh the advantages of centralizing the VAP in the file server versus the possible performance penalty; if a VAP is too resource intensive, the penalty might be too high.

Where processing should take place also should get early consideration. The NetWare environment presents many options for processing: A process may run entirely within the file server. A process may run entirely within a workstation. Or a process may work between file server and workstation in a client-server fashion, communicating using IPX-SPX. Novell suggests distributing work to idle CPUs on the network, but warns of the extra traffic this would place on the LAN.

Also, the programmer should consider early whether the process can be performed under NetWare's protected mode. We'll cover protected and real mode operation in detail later in this chapter. For now, the developer should note that, because the server environment is not preemptive, real-time VAPs may not be feasible; in such an environment, a VAP cannot know exactly when it will get processor time again.

In the following sections, we'll explain the issues concerning how to start or stop processes, and how to create or delete them.

Waking and sleeping processes

In the jargon of NetWare, placing a process in a run queue is called waking the process; removing it from the queue is called putting it to sleep. Processes may only put themselves to sleep, i.e. one process may not impose that condition on another, though it may wake the other.

In developing a VAP, Novell suggests, the programmer should write one main process that will receive control after initialization. (All processes are initialized when the file server is brought up.) The process may do any number of setup tasks, such as posting listen packets or spawning additional processes. After setting up, but before going to sleep, the program should place its process ID in a global variable, where other processes and handlers can use it to wake the sleeper.

A process may put itself to sleep forever or for a specified time, or it may place itself at the end of the run queue. The Sleep Process call evokes option one; a process that makes this call will remain dormant until an operator or another processes wakes it. (Remember to save the process ID or no one will be able to wake it.) A VAP put to sleep with this call can be awakened by another VAP, the Console Handler or Down Handler, an IPX Event Service Routine, or an Interrupt Service Routine.

The Delay Process call allows a VAP to put itself to sleep for a specific amount of time. When the time expires, NetWare puts the process back into the run queue. Novell suggests that any process so awakened check a flag or variable to determine whether it should become active or put itself to sleep again.

The Change Process call allows a process to put itself at the end of a run queue. This is an efficient method of scheduling, allowing a process to remain in the run queue indefinitely, and to get going again as soon as possible.

Creating and deleting processes

The Create Process and Spawn Process calls are used to create new processes. Each call forms a new process that is placed at the end of the run queue. Create Process affords the option of having the process connect to the file server; Spawn Process inherits the Connection Request Flag of its parent and receives a connection only if its parent has one. Neither of these calls should be made after initialization is complete (i.e. after Initialization Complete has been called).

The Kill Process call is used to terminate a process created with either of those two calls but must come from the process itself. A process can only terminate itself, not other processes.

Memory allocation in value-added processing

VAPs run in the extended memory of the file server, an area that is normally used for disk caching. Each VAP must allocate memory when its server is booted; this includes memory for stacks, data, and global variables. Once memory is allocated, the VAP must call Initialization Complete, signaling NetWare that the next process can be loaded.

Programmers must avoid memory-related C calls such as malloc() or calloc() when using VAPs. These calls allocate memory dynamically. If a VAP tries to allocate memory after Initialization Complete is called, it will evoke a General Protection Interrupt (GPI) error, freezing the file server.

(GPI errors signal violations of the protection of the 286/386 chip; although it is beyond the scope of this discussion to explain the workings of the 286/386 protected mode, VAP developers should familiarize themselves with this subject. There are many good third-party references on the subject as well as Intel's own programmer's documentation.)

Memory used by a VAP is memory that would otherwise have gone to the disk cache, so significant memory use by a VAP may impair file server performance.

Developers must name their executable files with appropriate extensions and place them in the SYS:SYSTEM directory (on a file server; it should be placed on the current drive on a bridge). VAPs may have numerical extensions, such as .VP0, .VP1, .VP2, etc. or the generic extension VAP. Those with numbers are loaded first.

Initializing the stack

If left to its own devices, NetWare gives the stack of each process just 100 bytes of memory. Developers must allocate more if needed. Novell suggests initializing the stack to an arbitrary, easily recognizable value to facilitate debugging.

Logging in to a file server

VAPs are considered logical workstations and must attach to the file server with the Attach To File Server call before logging in. (Use VAP Get File Server Name from this API to get the name of the file server the VAP is running on.) After attaching, the VAP can log in like any other workstation by issuing the Log In to File Server call. Novell suggests that a VAP log in as user GUEST since that account is automatically created when a server is installed.

Error handling in the VAP environment

Error handling in the VAP environment is somewhat different than in the workstation. VAPs can display error messages and optionally solicit a response from the user at the console. On file servers, VAP-generated errors are recorded in the SYSLOG.ERR file.

Also, VAPs may trap the Critical Error Handler (Interrupt 24h) to handle critical errors (those that produce the "Abort, Retry, or Ignore" message) using the Set External Process Error call.

Console control

The console is the main output device and screen of the VAP. The console may be used to send messages to the network administrator, display status information, query the user about the configuration, or show error messages. Also, the program may check whether the "monitor" display is up and see if another VAP has control of the console. The Console Control Services portion of VAP Services is explained in detail in the call reference section.

Protected mode operation

The NetWare 286 file server software can be configured to run in the protected mode of the 286/386 processor or real mode (8088 mode); NetWare bridges may also run in protected mode or real mode. Because a network administrator may want a VAP to run in either mode, Novell recommends that VAPs be developed to accommodate either.

According to Novell, NetWare's underlying design philosophy is that if a VAP follows the rules of protected mode programming, NetWare will try to ensure that it runs well in real mode. Therefore, programmers should be most concerned with the restrictions imposed by protected mode, where segment addresses are not handled directly, but are manipulated through a global descriptor table (GDT) which uses pointers. An attempt to manipulate segments directly rather than using the VAP Services calls might well result in a General Protection Interrupt (GPI) error, causing the file server to crash.

Also, developers must also know the restrictions on memory manipulation that could cause a GPI error. Performing segment arithmetic will cause a GPI, as will any violation of segment attributes or mismanagement of segment values. These precautions are common to any multitasking operating system that uses the protected mode features of the 286/386, such as OS/2. Consult 286/386 protected mode programming documentation for further information.

Compilers

Developers writing in a high-level language such as C should be wary of library routines that use interrupts. For example, all of the printf family of calls, including sprintf, use interrupt 21h. So calling sprintf in a VAP would violate protected-mode conventions and could bring the server down.

Also, developers should be careful of stack-checking services that some compilers provide. This function should be disabled if possible. If not, Novell suggests using a routine to replace the stack checker.

Microsoft C Replacement Stack Checking Routine

```
__CHKSTK proc near
    pop  cx         ; get return offset
    sub  sp, ax     ; allocate stack space
    jmp  cx         ; return to cx
__CHKSTK endp
```

Segment attributes in the protected mode

In protected mode, segments of memory are given attributes indicating whether they may be written to or read as well as which processes may access them. At startup, VAP segments can only be read or executed. The VAP must change its attribute to read/write before writing to a segment. The VAP calls Change Segment to Data and Declare Segment As Data to manipulate segment attributes.

Segment definitions

As with the segment attributes, developers should use only the VAP Services calls to work with segments; the VAP should not try to access memory not set up for that purpose in the global descriptor table or GPI errors may result. Also, VAPs must not load real-mode segments into segment registers for the same reason. Only segment descriptors can be loaded in protected mode.

VAPs requiring pointers to a segment should use the Segment To Pointer call which safely returns a far pointer to a segment. Absolute addresses may be obtained with the Calculate Absolute Address call.

Operating in real mode

Because of the use of protected mode, interrupts are handled differently in VAPs than in DOS-based processes. Interrupts, rather than being issued, are jumped to with a far call. This changes the environment where the NetWare API calls are made. See the VAP at the end of this chapter for a working example of how this is done.

DOS calls from VAPs

Because Interrupt 21h is used so frequently by DOS programmers, the VAP environment supports Interrupt 21h services in two ways. First, during initialization, all DOS calls are supported through the Shell Pass Through Enable call.

After initialization however, a VAP may on use a limited number of Interrupt 21h calls. To use one of those calls, the VAP loads the registers as for an Interrupt 21h call. Then, instead of an INT 21H instruction, the program should make a call like

```
CALL DWORD PTR CS:NETWARE_SHELL_SERVICES
```

to jump to the Interrupt 21h address (which is stored in the NETWARE_SHELL_SERVICES portion of the VAP Header).

The following calls can be made from an operating VAP in this fashion:

DOS function calls available during normal operation

Set Disk Transfer Address	1Ah
Get Disk Free Space	36h
Create Subdirectory	39h

Remove Subdirectory	3Ah
Change Current Directory	3Bh
Create File	3Ch
Open a File or Device	3Dh
Close a Handle	3Eh
Write to a File or Device	40h
Delete a File	41h
Move Read/Write Pointer	42h
Change File Mode	43h
Get Current Directory	47h
Find First Matching File	4Eh
Find Next Matching File	4Fh
Rename a File	56h
Get a File's Date and Time	57h
Create Unique File	5Ah
Create New File	5Bh

Other Int 21h functions can be accessed before the VAP is fully loaded by using the Shell Pass Through Enable call. These functions can be performed until the Initialization Complete call is made.

Components of the VAP

The VAP Header is the cornerstone of the VAP, providing information both for the file server and for the VAP itself. Novell suggests separating the VAP Header and initialization source code from the remainder of the code.

The header is critical. Without a header, no file server will run the VAP. The header contains common variables and entry points for processes that NetWare will call. Also contained in the header are pointers to services that NetWare will fill in upon initialization; these addresses will be used by the VAP when it requires the use of those services.

VAP Header Structure

Offset	Field	Bytes
0	Signature - "NWProc"	6
6	NetWare Shell Services	4
10	Process Control Services	4
14	Console Control Services	4
18	IPX-SPX Services	4
22	VAP Console Handler	4
26	VAP Down Handler	4
30	VAP Console or Down Data Segment	2
32	VAP Connection Request Flag	2
34	VAP Name String	64

98	VAP Console Keyword Count	2
100	VAP Console Keyword 0	16
116	VAP Console Keyword 1	16
132	VAP Console Keyword 2	16
.		
.		
.		
?	VAP Sign-on Message	500

Signature holds a string — NWProc — which identifies all VAPs; NetWare will not load the VAP unless it finds this string in the header.

NetWare Shell Services holds a NetWare-supplied long address pointer to Shell Services.

Process Control Services holds a NetWare-supplied long address pointer to Process Control Services.

Console Control Services holds a NetWare-supplied long address pointer to Console Control Services.

IPX SPX Services contains a NetWare-supplied long address pointer to IPX and SPX Services.

VAP Console Handler is a VAP-supplied address, a far pointer to the code that manages the VAP's interaction with the system console.

VAP Down Handler is a VAP-supplied far pointer to the code that manages a VAP's response to a file server or bridge shutdown. VAP Down Handler code is used to give the VAP a chance to clean up, close any files, log out, etc. before the file server or bridge goes down.

VAP Console or *Down Data Segment* contains the data segment used by the VAP Console Handler and the Down Handler. The VAP can put the data segment into this field directly, or indirectly by using Process Control Services.

VAP Connection Request Flag indicates whether the VAP needs connect to a file server. The VAP sets this field to 0 to prompt NetWare to provide a default connection; the default is the first file server that responds, most often the file server the VAP is running on. If this field holds a nonzero value, no connection is made. Spawned processes inherit this flag, so if the field is nonzero, spawned processes won't make connections either.

VAP Name String is a null-padded and -terminated ASCII string containing the name of the VAP that NetWare uses when displaying the VAP's services. The string must be 64 characters long, padding included.

VAP Console Keyword Count contains the number of keywords the console will recognize and how many keyword fields follow this field.

VAP Console Keyword defines a keyword, which is a console command to the VAP. It must be an all uppercase, null-terminated ASCII string, null-padded to 16 bytes. A VAP can define as many as 65,536 keywords. NetWare numbers them in order beginning with 0. If two VAPs define the same keyword, the first one loaded defines the keyword. Novell suggests using a common letter or name to prefix the keywords for a VAP. Novell will reserve VAP keywords for developers.

VAP Sign On Message is a null-terminated ASCII string displayed when the VAP has loaded.

Starting VAPs written in C

Although we're programming NetWare in C, we must use some assembly language during initialization. We combine this assembly language startup code with the VAP Header in a file separate from the main code. This is why VAPs written in high-level languages such as C, with header files containing assembly code, often follow their headers with startup procedures. This procedure is needed to establish data segment addressability and to call a procedure that contains the main process.

We'll use the following startup procedure before we call our main() C routine when we incorporate it into our sample VAP.

```
VAPStart  proc      near
    mov   ax, DGroup                          ; Change data segment to
    mov   di, 1                               ; read-write
    call  dword ptr cs:ProcessControlServices
    cli                                       ; Disable interrupts
    mov   ax, DGroup                          ; Load segs with DGroup
    mov   ds, ax                              ;  (small model)
    mov   es, ax
    mov   ss, ax
    mov   ax, OFFSET DGroup:MainStackEnd      ; Setup stack
    mov   sp, ax
    sti                                       ; Enable interrupts
    mov   ax, PGroup                          ; Setup console data seg
    mov   _MyHeaderSegment, ax
    call  _MAIN                               ; Call our main()
VAPStart  endp
```

This procedure first changes the attribute for its data segment to read/write. Then it clears interrupts and moves DGroup into the segment registers. Next, it sets up the stack and enables interrupts. The routine loads the segment of the header into _MyHeaderSegment. This will be used by the Console Handler. Finally, main() is called in the C code. Developers should be aware that with code models other than small, the data segments will have to be initialized properly. This startup procedure may be all a VAP needs to do to get going.

VAP handlers

A handler is a routine in the VAP that is called by NetWare. There are two: the Console Handler and the Down Handler. Each VAP must have one of each, even if they do nothing, that is, just issue a return(0) statement.

The Console Handler is used by NetWare to allow the VAP to handle processing when one of the VAP keywords (console commands defined in the header) is entered at the console. Only keywords belonging to that VAP may be handled. The Console Handler should act on the keyword and return control to NetWare.

The Down Handler is called by NetWare when the DOWN command is entered at the system console (or a DOWN command is issued in FConsole). The purpose of this handler is to allow the developer to do any "cleanup" before the system shuts down. This could include writing changes to disk, closing files, etc. The Down Handler itself should not perform these tasks directly, but should call a process that does.

Debugging VAPs

VAPs are perhaps the most difficult NetWare applications to debug. No one has yet developed a straightforward way to trace execution of a VAP inside a file server. And any fatal error will bring the file server down and terminate all workstation connections.

So Novell recommends, as a first cut, using console functions to display the program status at intervals throughout the VAP. Also, breakpoints (Interrupt 3) can be inserted into the VAP to be used with real-mode debuggers (such as PFixPlus, CodeView, PeriScope, Turbo Debugger, etc.) on a bridge. Novell recommends debugging VAPs initially on a bridge where, if the VAP fails and freezes the machine, the entire LAN does not go down.

Once breakpoints are placed in the VAP, the debugger may be executed (as in PFIXPLUS BRIDGE), passing BRIDGE.EXE as the argument. Start execution and let the bridge come up and load the VAP; it will stop where the first breakpoint is encountered.

This scenario will only work for real-mode execution on a bridge. Some problems may not show up on a VAP until protected mode is running (as will be the case on a file server).

Calls in the VAP Services API

All of the VAP Services API calls are supported in Advanced NetWare version 2.1.

Throughout the book, we explain fields within the calls only at the first mention of each field in each chapter. Appendix B contains a comprehensive, alphabetical listing of the fields for quick reference.

The programmer should remember that the calls that follow are not accessed through the normal INT 21h mechanism. For each function group, such as the Process Control calls, the registers (and possibly stack) should be set up as described and the program should perform a far call to the address of the group specified in the VAP Header. For a complete example of this process, see the code at the end of the chapter.

Process Control Services

Allocate Segment (00h)

This call enables a VAP to allocate system memory.

Registers in:

AX	Segment Size
DI	00h

Registers out:

AX	Segment Value

Segment Size is specified in 16-byte paragraphs.

Segment Value is either a real-mode segment or a protected-mode descriptor (Read-Write Data), depending on the mode at the time. If zero, no memory was available.

This call can be made only during VAP initialization (before calling Initialization Complete).

The NetWare C Interface format is:

```
int AllocateSegment( int segmentSize );
```

Calculate Absolute Address (11h)

This call calculates an absolute memory address from a protected or real mode segment-offset pair.

Registers in:

AX	Offset
BX	Segment
DI	11h

Registers out:

AX	Low Order Word
BL	High Order Byte

Segment and *Offset* are the segment and offset of the address from which the absolute address is to be calculated.

Low Order Word and *High Order Byte* are the three bytes that comprise the absolute address.

This call operates in either mode. In real mode, the calculation is simply: (segment * 16) + offset.

In protected mode, the call obtains the segment's physical address from the Segment Descriptor table and performs the appropriate calculation before returning the absolute address.

The NetWare C Interface format is:

```
long CalculateAbsoluteAddress( WORD segment, WORD offset );
```

Change Process (09h)

This call puts the calling process at the end of the priority level in the internal active queue and reschedules the highest priority task for execution.

Registers in:

DI	09h

If this process is the highest priority, it will be rescheduled immediately.

The NetWare C Interface format is:

```
void ChangeProcess( void );
```

Change Segment To Code (02h)

This call changes a segment type to Execute-Read Code segment.

Registers in:

AX	Segment Value
DI	02h

Segment Value is the real-mode segment value or protected-mode segment descriptor for the segment that is to be flagged as an Execute-Read Code segment.

This call allows a VAP to load or copy executable code by flagging an existing descriptor as an Execute-Read Code segment. Any attempt to write to an Execute-Read Code segment in protected mode results in a general protection interrupt.

The NetWare C Interface format is not supported.

Change Segment To Data (01h)

This call changes a segment type to Read-Write Data segment.

Registers in:

AX	Segment Value
DI	01h

When a VAP is loaded, its declared segments are added to the descriptor tables with type Execute-Read Code segment. For protected-mode compatibility, all data segments within the VAP must be declared as type Read-Write Data segments.

The NetWare C Interface format is:

```
int ChangeSegmentToData( WORD segment );
```

Create Process (18h)

This call creates a new process that runs in the NetWare internal multitasking environment.

Registers in:

AX	Connection Flag
BX	Code Segment
CX	Instruction Pointer

DX Data Segment
DI 18h

Registers out:
AX Process ID

Connection Flag determines whether the created process is to be connected with a file server. If zero, then the created process receives a default connection with a file server; if nonzero, then no connection is established. Create Process is preferred to Spawn Process, since Create Process affords the option of allowing child processes to connect to a file server regardless of whether the parent process is connected.

Code Segment and *Data Segment* are the code and data segments of the new process.

Instruction Pointer is the created process's instruction pointer.

VAP Header is a pointer to the VAP header.

Process ID receives the process ID of the created process.

When the child process begins executing, BX contains the process ID of the child process, DS points to the child process's data segment, and BP:0h points to the VAP header. SS:SP points to a 100-byte stack allocated for the created process. If necessary, the created process can call Allocate Segment during its initialization to allocate a larger stack.

Although process rescheduling can occur while Create Process is executing, the calling process retains control after this call. The created process is placed at the end of the active process queue, and begins execution after it moves to the start of the queue.

The NetWare C Interface format is:

```
int CreateProcess( WORD connectionFlag, void (*)()codePtr, WORD dataSegment,
   WORD header );
```

Declare Extended Segment (04h)

This call allows the VAP to declare memory as extended memory.

Registers in:
AX Low Order Word
BL High Order Byte
DI 04h

Registers out:
AX Segment Value

Low Order Word and *High Order Byte* are the three bytes that contain the absolute address to be declared as a segment. If the absolute address is greater than or equal to 1MB when running in real mode, this call will terminate abnormally.

Segment Value returns a real-mode segment value or protected-mode segment descriptor for the segment corresponding to the absolute address passed in Low Order Word and High Order Byte.

This call extends the Declare Segment As Data call. Although Declare Extended Segment executes correctly in either real or protected mode, it is possible to declare extended segments at addresses at or above 1MB only in protected mode. In real mode, Declare Extended Segment simply declares a segment, given an absolute address.

The NetWare C Interface format is:

```
int DeclareExtendedSegment( WORD low, BYTE high );
```

Declare Segment As Data (03h)

This call declares a memory segment as type Read-Write Data segment.

Registers in:

AX	Paragraph
DI	03h

Registers out:

AX	Segment Value

Paragraph contains the real-mode paragraph value of the memory address.

Segment Value returns either a real-mode segment value or a protected-mode segment descriptor, depending upon the processor mode in use.

Declare Segment As Data is provided for use with VAPs that read or write data on adapters having on-board RAMs or ROMs.

The NetWare C Interface format is:

```
int DeclareSegmentAsData( WORD paragraph );
```

Delay Process (0Ah)

This call enables the calling process to postpone its execution for a specified amount of time.

Registers in:

DX	Delay
DI	0Ah

Delay specifies the length of the delay interval in 1/18-second ticks.

This call removes the current process from the active queue. The process is returned to the active queue when the specified time elapses.

The NetWare C Interface format is:

```
void DelayProcess( WORD delay );
```

Do Console Error (13h)

This call displays critical error messages on the system console.

Registers in:
DS:SI Error Message
DI 13h

Error Message is a pointer to a null-terminated error message. The message cannot exceed 80 characters in length.

This call can be made from the VAP console handler or the VAP itself.

If the VAP is running on a real-mode bridge, Do Console Error sounds the bell on the system console. If the VAP is running on a server, Do Console Error enters the error message in the SYSLOG.ERR file. This call should not be used in time-critical sections of code since making this call could result in the process being rescheduled.

The NetWare C Interface format is:

```
void DoConsoleError( char *message );
```

Get Interrupt Vector (0Fh)

This call returns the Interrupt Service Routine (ISR) segment and offset of the specified interrupt.

Registers in:
AL Interrupt Vector
DI 0Fh

Registers out:
CX ISR Segment
DX ISR Offset

Interrupt Vector contains the interrupt vector number (0 to 255).

ISR Segment and *ISR Offset* are the segment and offset of the specified interrupt. ISR Segment is either a real-mode segment value or a protected-mode segment descriptor, depending upon the processor mode in use.

This call can be useful to VAPs that share interrupt vectors with other processes and applications.

The NetWare C Interface format is:

```
void GetInterruptVector( BYTE vectorNum, WORD *ISRsegment,
   WORD *ISRoffset );
```

Get Process ID (0Bh)

This call returns the process ID of the calling process.

Registers in:
DI 0Bh

Registers out:
AX Process ID

Process ID is the ID of the calling process. Making this call does not cause the calling process to be rescheduled.

The NetWare C Interface format is:

```
WORD GetProcessID( void );
```

Get VAP Header (17h)

This call enables a VAP to get information about other VAPs loaded in the system.

Registers in:
AX VAP Number
DI 17h

Registers out:
AX VAP Header Segment

NetWare numbers VAPs consecutively, starting with zero. Since there can be up to 10 VAPs installed on a system, VAP numbers range from 0 to 9.

This call returns the real-mode segment value or protected-mode segment descriptor for the specified VAP in VAP Header Segment. If VAP Header Segment is set to 00h, neither the specified VAP nor any higher-numbered VAP exists.

The NetWare C Interface format is:

```
int GetVAPHeader( int VAPnumber );
```

Initialization Complete (07h)

This call informs NetWare that a VAP process is finished allocating memory and spawning processes.

Registers in:
DI 07h

Initialization Complete must be called by each VAP process (main and spawned) after it finishes allocating memory and spawning child processes. NetWare does not resume execution until each process in a VAP has called this service. After this call, a VAP must not allocate memory or spawn another process. If the VAP has enabled shell pass-through mode so that it can access DOS functions during initialization, it should also disable it before calling Initialization Complete.

After this service is called, NetWare regains control of the file server or bridge. Control is not returned to the VAP calling process until the NetWare environment is ready and has placed the process in a run queue.

The NetWare C Interface format is:

```
void InitializationComplete( void );
```

Kill Process (08h)

This call terminates the calling process and causes the highest priority process in the active queue to be scheduled for execution.

Registers in:
DI 08h

Initialization Complete must be called before making this call; the call cannot be made in a Down Handler.

The NetWare C Interface format is:

```
void KillProcess( void );
```

Set External Process Error (12h)

This call allows a VAP to install an error routine to handle communication errors (i.e., "Abort, Retry, Ignore" messages).

Registers in:

CX	Error Handler Segment
DX	Error Handler Offset
BX	Data Segment
DI	12h

Error Handler Segment and *Error Handler Offset* are the segment and offset of the error handler to be installed by Set External Process Error.

Data Segment specifies the data segment to be used by the error handler.

When the error handler is called, it has the following environment:

AX has error code:
0 Reset error count
1 Write error
2 Read timeout error
3 Router not found error
4 Unknown communication error
5 Server invalid slot error
6 Network is gone error
7 Bad local address error

DX has the data segment that was specified in the Data Segment field during installation of the error handler.

The error handler can cause the VAP to retry the failed operation by setting the processor's Z flag and returning. Leaving the Z flag unset and returning causes the VAP to continue execution with the error condition in force.

Each time an operation occurs that could possibly return a communication error, the error handler is called with a reset error count (0) error code. This tells the handler to set its error counters to zero—an operation is going to occur for the first time. Then if an error occurs, the handler increments its counters. This enables the error handler to determine the number of attempted retries.

Since the error handler routine is called with a far call, it must return with a far return.

The NetWare C Interface format is:

```
int SetExternalProcessError( void (*)()codePtr, WORD dataSegment );
```

Set Hardware Interrupt Vector (0Eh)

This call installs hardware-triggered interrupt service routines (ISRs).

Registers in:

AL	Hardware Interrupt Number
SI	ISR Segment
BX	ISR Offset
DI	0Eh

Registers out:

AL	E0I Flag

Hardware Interrupt Number can range from 0 to 15, and specifies which hardware interrupt is to be installed.

ISR Segment and *ISR Offset* are the segment and offset of the hardware interrupt service routine that Set Hardware Interrupt Vector is to install.

This call installs the ISR at the correct interrupt vector (whether IBM XT, AT, or compatible) and sets the appropriate mask register bits.

The call returns the end-of-interrupt flag in EOI Flag. A nonzero EOI flag means the interrupt procedure needs to issue an extra EOI to the AT interrupt controller.

Note: Hardware interrupt 2 is remapped to interrupt 9 on the AT. VAPs that use IRQ2 and run on both the IBM XT and AT should check the EOI flag when using this service.

The NetWare C Interface format is:

```
BYTE SetHardwareInterruptVector( BYTE interruptNumber, WORD *ISRseg,
   WORD *ISRoffset );
```

Set Interrupt Vector (10h)

A VAP uses this call in conjunction with Get Interrupt Vector to install a specified software interrupt vector.

Registers in:

AL	Interrupt Vector Number
CX	ISR Segment
DX	ISR Offset
DI	10h

The NetWare C Interface format is:

```
void SetInterruptVector( BYTE vectorNumber, WORD ISRseg, WORD ISRoffset );
```

Shell Pass Through Enable (06h)

This call allows VAPs running on bridges to access DOS functions during initialization that would normally be unavailable during VAP operation.

Registers in:

AL	Enable Flag
DI	06h

Enable Flag is set to 00h to disable pass-through mode, and to nonzero to enable pass-through mode.

The NetWare C Interface format is:

```
void ShellPassThroughEnable( BYTE enable );
```

Sleep Process (0Ch)

This call removes the current process from the active queue.

Registers in:

DI	0Ch

The calling process is not returned to the active queue until another processor interrupt service routine passes the process ID of the sleeping process to Wake Up Process.

The NetWare C Interface format is:

```
void SleepProcess( void );
```

Spawn Process (05h)

This call creates a new process.

Registers in:

BX	Code Segment
CX	Instruction Pointer
DX	Data Segment
BP:0	VAP Header
DI05h	

Registers out:

AX	Process ID

This call can be made only during a VAP's initialization.

The calling process retains control after this call. The spawned process begins execution after it moves to the start of the active process queue.

When the child process's code is entered (i.e., when the child process begins executing), AX contains the process ID of the child process, DS points to DX (the Data Segment), and BP:0 points to the VAP header. SS:SP points to a 100-byte stack allocated for the spawned process.

The NetWare C Interface format is:

```
int SpawnProcess( void (*)()childCodePtr, WORD childDataSegment,
   WORD header );
```

VAP Attach To File Server (15h)

This call enables a VAP to attach to any file server, specified by name, on an internetwork.

Registers in:

DS:SI	Server Name
DI	15h

Registers out:

AL	Completion Code
DL	Server Number

Completion Codes:

00h	Successful
01h	Already Attached to File Server
03h	No Attachment Slot Available
04h	File Server Name Too Long

Server Name is a pointer to the name of the file server to which a connection is to be made.

Server Number contains the number of the file server to which the connection was made.

Process scheduling can occur while this call is executing.

Note: This call should be used instead of the Attach to File Server call.

The NetWare C Interface format is:

```
int VAPAttachToFileServer( char serverName, int *connectionID );
```

VAP Get Connection ID (16h)

This call returns the file server number for a specified file server name.

Registers in:

DS:SI	Server Name
DI	16h

Registers out:

AL	Completion Code
DL	Connection ID

Completion Codes:

00h	Already Attached to Server
nonzero	Not Attached to Server

Connection ID receives the connection ID of the specified file server.

The file server number is used when making certain extended NetWare calls. Since this call returns a file server number only for attached file servers, the completion code should be checked to make sure the Connection ID field is valid.

The NetWare C Interface format is:

```
itn VAPGetConnectionID( char *serverName, int *connectionID );
```

VAP Get File Server Name (14h)

This call returns the name of the file server that the VAP is running on.

Registers in:

ES:SI	Buffer
DI	14h

Registers out:

AL	Completion Code

Completion Codes:

00h	VAP Resides With a File Server
01h	VAP Resides With a Bridge

Buffer is a pointer to a 48-byte buffer that will receive the file server name if the VAP is on a file server.

The NetWare C Interface format is:

```
int VAPGetFileServerName( char *serverName );
```

Wake Up Process (0Dh)

This call is used by a VAP or a VAP interrupt service routine to wake up a sleeping VAP.

Registers in:

BX	Process ID
DI	0Dh

Process ID is the process ID of the sleeping process that is to be reawakened.

The calling process or ISR does not relinquish control during this call.

The NetWare C Interface format is:

```
void WakeUpProcess( WORD processID );
```

Console Control Services

Clear Screen (00h)

Clear Screen turns off MONITOR (if it is running on the system console), sets the screen mode to zero, and clears the system monitor screen.

Registers in:

DI	00h

Clear Screen can be called from the console handler or from within the VAP.

The NetWare C Interface format is:

```
void ClearScreen( void );
```

Console Display (05h)

This call queues a message for display on the system console.

Registers in:
DS:SI Message
DI 05h

Message is a pointer to a null-terminated message, which can be up to 80 characters long.

Queuing the message assures that the calling process retains CPU control (unlike Console Message, which might allow the operating system to reschedule processes).

The NetWare C Interface format is:

```
void ConsoleDisplay( char *message );
```

Console Error (04h)

This call displays critical error messages on the system console.

Registers in:
DS:SI Message
DI 04h

If the VAP is running on a real-mode bridge, Console Error sounds the bell. On a server, the error is placed in the SYSLOG.ERR file.

This call is equivalent to Do Console Error found under Process Control Services.

The NetWare C Interface format is:

```
void ConsoleError( char *message );
```

Console Message (03h)

This call is used to display messages on the system console.

Registers in:
DS:SI Message
DI 03h

This call may result in process rescheduling.

The NetWare C Interface format is:

```
void ConsoleMessage( char *message );
```

Console Query (06h)

This call displays a prompt on the system console and obtains a YES or NO response.

Registers in:

DS:SI	Prompt
DI	06h

Registers out:

AX	Completion Code

Completion Codes:

00h	NO Response
FFh	YES Response

Prompt is a pointer to a null-terminated message, which can be up to 60 characters long. If the character is a Y or y, Console Query returns 0FFh, otherwise, a zero is returned.

This call can be made from the VAP console handler or from the VAP initialization code (before calling Initialization Complete).

The NetWare C Interface format is:

```
int ConsoleQuery( char *prompt );
```

Console Read (07h)

This call enables the VAP console handler to read a string typed at the system keyboard.

Registers in:

DS:SI	Prompt
ES:BX	Input Buffer
DL	Input Buffer Length
DI	07h

Registers out:

AX	Input String Length

Prompt is a pointer to a null-terminated prompt message that can be up to 80 characters long.

Input Buffer is a pointer to a buffer up to 80 characters long which returns the string typed in by the user. The length of the input buffer must be specified in Input Buffer Length. The string returned is not null-terminated; the length is supplied in the Input String Length value.

This call can be made from the VAP console handler or from the VAP initialization code (before calling Initialization Complete).

The call returns when <ENTER> is pressed or the input buffer length is reached.

The NetWare C Interface format is:

```
int ConsoleRead( char *prompt, char *inputBuffer, BYTE bufferLength );
```

Get Screen Mode (09h)

This call enables a VAP to see who has control of the system console.

Registers in:

DI	09h

Registers out:

AX	Controlling Process

Controlling Process returns the VAP header segment of the VAP that has console control.

-1	0xFFFF	MONITOR has control of console
0	0x00	No process has control of console
positive		VAP header segment of VAP that has console control

This call can be made either from a VAP or from the VAP console handler.

This call should be made before calling In String or Out String.

The NetWare C Interface format is:

```
int GetScreenMode( void );
```

Set Screen Mode (08h)

This call clears the screen and gives control of the system console to the specified VAP.

Registers in:

AX	Requesting VAP
DI	08h

Requesting VAP is the header segment of the VAP that is requesting console control.

This call should only be made from the VAP console handler and should be made before any calls to In String or Out String.

The NetWare C Interface format is:

```
void SetScreenMode( WORD VAPHeaderSeg );
```

In String (0Bh)

This call enables the VAP console handler to read a string typed at the system keyboard.

Registers in:

AH	Row
AL	Column
DS:SI	Prompt
ES:BX	Input Buffer
DL	Input Buffer Length
DI	11h

Registers out:

AX	Input String Length

In String returns when either <ENTER> is pressed or the Input Buffer Length is reached. This call should be preceded by a call to Set Screen Mode to ensure that the caller has control of the system console.

Row and Column specify the cursor position at which In String is to display the prompt message. The Row parameter should not exceed 20.

Prompt is a pointer to a null-terminated prompt message that can be up to 80 characters long.

This call can be made from the VAP console handler or from the VAP initialization code (before calling Initialization Complete). Set Screen Mode should be called before this call is made.

The NetWare C Interface format is:

```
int InString( BYTE row, BYTE column, char *prompt, char *inputBuffer,
   BYTE bufferLength );
```

Out String (0Ah)

This call enables a VAP to display a message on the system console.

Registers in:

AH	Row
AL	Column
DS:SI	Message
DL	Message Length
DI	10h

Message Length specifies the character length of the message to be displayed. If Message Length is greater than the actual length of the message, the remaining spaces will be filled with blanks. If Message Length is set to 0xFFFF (-1), the actual length of the message is calculated and used.

This call can be made either from a VAP or from the VAP console handler. Set Screen Mode should be called before this call is made.

The NetWare C Interface format is:

```
void OutString( BYTE row, BYTE column, char *message, BYTE messageLength );
```

Print String (01h)

This call enables a VAP to print an ASCII string to the system console with cursor positioning.

Registers in:
DI 01h

Row and Column specify the screen coordinates of the string. Values for these coordinates can be specified explicitly, or the current values can be used. A value of FFFFh (-1) in both fields causes Print String to use the current Row or Column values.

String Offset and *String Segment* point to a null-terminated ASCII string.

String Length specifies the character length of the string to be printed. If String Length is actually greater than the length of the ASCII string, the remaining area on the system console is filled with blanks. String Length can be set to FFFFh to use the actual string length.

This call can be made from the VAP console handler or from within the VAP.

The NetWare C Interface format is:

```
void PrintString( WORD row, WORD column, char *message,
   WORD messageLength );
```

Read Keyboard (02h)

This call enables the VAP console handler to read command strings typed at the system keyboard.

Registers in:
DI 02h

Other parameters are passed on stack in the following order (all are WORD values): Buffer Length, Buffer Segment, and Buffer Offset.

Buffer Length is the length of the input buffer, and can not be greater than 80.

Input begins at the current cursor position. Keyboard input is returned in the buffer in the form of a complete command string.

This call can be made from the VAP console handler or from the VAP initialization code (before calling Initialization Complete).

The NetWare C Interface format is:

```
int ReadKeyboard( char *inputBuffer, WORD bufferLength );
```

DOS function calls available during normal operation

Set Disk Transfer Address	1Ah
Get Disk Free Space	36h
Create Subdirectory	39h
Remove Subdirectory	3Ah
Change Current Directory	3Bh
Create File	3Ch
Open a File or Device	3Dh
Close a Handle	3Eh
Write to a File or Device	40h
Delete a File	41h
Move Read/Write Pointer	42h
Change File Mode	43h
Get Current Directory	47h
Find First Matching File	4Eh
Find Next Matching File	4Fh
Rename a File	56h
Get a File's Date and Time	57h
Create Unique File	5Ah
Create New File	5Bh

Other Int 21h functions can be accessed before the VAP is fully loaded by using the Shell Pass Through Enable call. These functions can be performed until the Initialization Complete call is made.

NetWare Shell Services

These calls can be accessed like the Process and Console Services: Set up the call just as you would for DOS and instead of calling INT 21h, make a far call to the NetWare Shell Services offset in the VAP Header.

The following NetWare APIs are available from within a VAP:

- All Accounting Services
- All Bindery Services
- All Communications Protocols (IPX, SPX, and NetBIOS/INT 5Ch) except NetBIOS INT 2Ah

- All Connection Services except:
  - Attach To File Server (use VAP Attach To File Server instead)
  - Get Station Address
- All Diagnostic Services
- All Directory Services except:
  - Get Drive Information
  - Get Search Drive Vector
  - Set Drive Path
  - Set Search Drive Vector
- All File Server Environment Services
- All File Services
- All Message Services except:
  - Get Broadcast Mode
  - Set Broadcast Mode
- No Print Services
- All Queue Services
- All Synchronization Services except:
  - Get Lock Mode
  - Set Lock Mode
- All TTS Services
- All Workstation Environment Services except:
  - Get Number Of Local Drives
  - Get Shell Revision
  - Get Workstation Environment
  - Set End Of Job Status
  - Set NetWare Error Mode

Code Sample: ListUser.C, VHeader.Asm, VAP.Asm

ListUser is a short VAP that allows the system operator to list the users on the network and their stations. This can be useful for several reasons. First, it's often frustrating trying to figure out which user is logged into which station from the console. This utility will display that.

Also, when trying to bring down the file server, the supervisor may do a "monitor" at the console and see that two users are still in. This utility will tell which users are logged in. The supervisor can then decide whether to do a "clear station" or tell the user again to log out.

This VAP consists of three modules: VHeader.ASM is the assembly header file containing our VAP header and startup code, ListUser.C is our main code written in C, and VAP.ASM provides a library of C routines for accessing the VAP functions. You may wish to glance at all three before continuing.

When the file server is booted and wants to load in our VAP, it starts with the VAPStart procedure in the VHeader file. There we set up our segments and registers and call the main() function. (This VHeader file can be used as a template for your

VAPs. To get started right away, just change the references to ListUser to your program's name.)

When main() is begun, it calls VSpawnProcess(), passing the address of our start process procedure, ProcessStart(). ProcessStart() is defined in VHeader and is used to setup the data segment and other registers before calling our main process which we call Process(). Note that in the Process() function, we get our process id (into *ProcessID*) and call VInitializationComplete(); we need to do that for every new process (this one is new since it was spawned).

The second thing done in main() is we get the ID of our process through the VGetProcessID() function and store it in the *ConsoleProcess* variable.

Finally, we signal the file server that we've done all we're going to do (to initialize) and we call VInitializationComplete() and the file server continues its own loading and initialization.

When the file server comes up and schedules us to be run, it will execute our two processes: main() and Process(), executing on the next line after VInitialization-Complete(). What may seem perplexing is that, for both processes, the next command is a call to VSleepProcess() which puts them to sleep permanently!

What is actually happening is an interaction between main(), Process() and ConsoleHandler(). When main() and Process() go to sleep, they stay sleeping until the ListUser keyword is entered at the file server.

When the keyword is entered, the ConsoleHandler() is called. It wakes up the process stored in the *ConsoleProcess* variable. If you will remember, we saved this during the initialization of main() with a call to VGetProcessID(), so it's main() that is awakened. main() picks up processing with the while loop at the VWakeUp-Process() command, waking up *ProcessID*, which we saved in the Process() function. main() then goes back to sleep.

Meanwhile, Process() is now awakened by main(), and picks up after the VSleepProcess() call and runs ListUsers(), printing out the users on the screen. When it has finished this, Process() goes back to sleep.

Although this may be a complex means of accomplishing a simple task, it shows how multiple processes operate in a VAP.

To print to the screen, ListUsers() needs to make a call to Get Connection Information, but it first needs to be logged in. Therefore, the first action it performs is a call to LoginToFileServer, logging in as the user GUEST. If an error was encountered, the result is printed to the screen and the routine returns.

If the login was successful, we call Clear Screen and get our logical connection number in a variable called us and we start checking all of the connections (we assume no more than 100 for a 286 environment). The for loop scans all connections, and reports the users (except us) to the screen.

Note how the API calls are made: they are identical to the ones in previous code examples, except instead of interrupt 21h being called, we call ShellServices(). This routine is stored in the VAP module and makes a far call to the VAP header's NetWare Shell Services offset.

Note the makefile that was used to produce the VAP; remember that you have to rename the VAP to LISTUSER.VAP and place it in the SYS:SYSTEM directory.

ListUser.C

```
/*                                                                   */
/* ListUser - A sample VAP that lists currently logged in users from  */
/*            the file server console                                 */
/*                                                                   */
/* by Charles Rose                                                   */
/*                                                                   */

#include <stdio.h>
#include <dos.h>

#define BYTE unsigned char
#define WORD unsigned int

#define USER 0x0100

/* #define DEBUG */
/* Uncomment this line to debug or pass the define                        */
/* from the command-line compiler switch                                  */

/* Global variables                                                       */
extern int      Keyword;
unsigned        ConsoleProcess, ProcessID;

/* Local Prototypes */
void Process( void );
int ConsoleHandler( void );
int DownHandler( void );
void ListUsers( void );
int NCPGetOurStnNum( void );
int NCPGetConnInfo( BYTE connection, WORD *type, BYTE *name );
int LoginToFileServer( WORD type, char *name, char *password );

main()
{
        int     result, connID;
        void    ProcessStart();

        /* Get the Process ID of our Process */
        VSpawnProcess( ProcessStart );

        /* Get the current Process ID */
        ConsoleProcess = VGetProcessID();

        /* That's all we need to do until we receive the console command */
        VInitializationComplete();

        while (1)
        {
                VSleepProcess();
                VWakeUpProcess( ProcessID );
        }

}

void Process( void )
{
        ProcessID = VGetProcessID();
        VInitializationComplete();
        while (1)
        {
```

```
                VSleepProcess();
                ListUsers();
        }

}

int ConsoleHandler( void )
{
        VWakeUpProcess( ConsoleProcess );
        return (0);
}

int DownHandler( void )
{
        VPrintString( -1, -1, "ListUser VAP is down.\r\n\n", -1 );
        return (0);
}

void ListUsers( void )
{
        int x, status, type, result, us;
        BYTE name[48], message[80], msg[80];

#ifdef DEBUG
        VPrintString( -1, 1, "Just about to Login.\r\n", -1);
#endif

        result = LoginToFileServer( USER, "GUEST", NULL );
        if ( result )
        {
                VPrintString( -1, 1, "Error logging in to file server.", -1);
                strcpy( message, "Login failed, code = " );
                strcat( message, itoa( result, msg, 16 ) );
                strcat( message, "\r\n" );
                VPrintString( -1, 1, message, -1);
                return;
        }

#ifdef DEBUG
        VPrintString( -1, 1, "After login.\r\n", -1);
        VPrintString( -1, 1, "Login succeeded.\r\n", -1);
#endif

        VClearScreen();

        us = NCPGetOurStnNum();

        VPrintString( -1, 1, "\r\nUSERS CURRENTLY LOGGED IN:\n\n\r", -1 );
        for ( x = 0; x < 100 ; x++ )
        {
                status = NCPGetConnInfo( x, &type, name );

                if ( (!status) && ( type == 0x100 ) && ( x != us ) )
                {
                        strcpy( message, "   [" );
                        strcat( message, itoa( x, msg, 10 ) );
                        strcat( message, "]      " );
                        strcat( message, name );
                        strcat( message, "\r\n" );
                        VPrintString( -1, 1, message, -1 );
                }
        }
```

```
        VPrintString( -1, 1, "\r\n\n", -1 );
}

int NCPGetOurStnNum( void )
{
        _AH = 0xDC;
        ShellServices();
        return _AL;
}

int NCPGetConnInfo( BYTE connection, WORD *type, BYTE *name )
{

struct  ConnectionPacketRequest
{
        WORD     PacketLength;
        BYTE     Function;
        BYTE     ConnectionNumber;
} Request;

struct  ConnectionPacketReply
{
        WORD     ReturnLength;
        unsigned long   UniqueID;
        WORD     Type;
        BYTE     ObjectName[48];
        BYTE     LogTime[8];
} Reply;

        Request.PacketLength = 2;
        Request.Function = 22;
        Reply.ReturnLength = 62;

        _AH = 0xE3;
        _SI = (unsigned) &Request;
        _DI = (unsigned) &Reply;
        _ES = _DS;

        Request.ConnectionNumber = connection;

        ShellServices();

        strcpy( ( char * )name, ( char * )Reply.ObjectName );
        *type = Reply.Type;

        return _AL;
}


int LoginToFileServer( WORD type, char *name, char *password )
{
        BYTE Request[181];
        int Reply = 0;

        memset( Request, 0, 181 );

        Request[0] = 181;
        Request[2] = 0x14;
        *( (WORD *) (Request + 3) ) = type;
        Request[5] = strlen( name );
        strcpy( Request + 6, name );
        Request[ Request + 6 + Request[5] ] = strlen( password );
```

```
        strcpy( Request + 6 + Request[5] + 1, password );

        _AH = 0xE3;
        _SI = (unsigned)Request;
        _DI = (unsigned)&Reply;
        _ES = _DS;

        ShellServices();

        return _AL;
}
```

VHeader.Asm

```
;
; VAPHeader - This module contains the VAP Header and the routines necessary
;              to support the C code for the VAP
;
        name    VAPHeader

DGroup  GROUP   _DATA

PGROUP  GROUP   _TEXT
        assume cs:PGROUP

_TEXT   segment public 'CODE'

        ;VAP definitions
        public  _NetWareShellServices, _ProcessControlServices
        public  _ConsoleControlServices, _IPXSPXServices

        ;Handler routines
        extrn   _ConsoleHandler: near, _DownHandler: near

        ;VAP Header
        Signature                       db      'NWProc'
        _NetWareShellServices           dd      ?
        _ProcessControlServices         dd      ?
        _ConsoleControlServices         dd      ?
        _IPXSPXServices                 dd      ?
        VAPConsoleHandler               dd      ConsoleHandlerCALL
        VAPDownHandler                  dd      DownHandlerCALL
        VAPConsoleOrDownDataSegment     dw      DGroup
        VAPConnectionRequestFlag        dw      0       ;Require connection flag
        VAPNameString                   db 'ListUser', 64-($-VAPNameString)dup(0)
        VAPConsoleKeyWordCount          dw      1
        VAPKeyword1                     db 'LISTUSER', 16-($-VAPKeyword1) dup(0)
        VAPSignOnMessage                db      'ListUser VAP - Signing on.', 0
                                        db      500-($-VAPSignOnMessage) dup(0)


VAPStart proc    near
        mov     ax, DGroup
        mov     di, 1                   ;change segment to data (read/write)
        call    dword ptr cs:_ProcessControlServices
        cli
        mov     ax, DGroup
        mov     ds, ax
        mov     es, ax
        mov     ss, ax
```

```
        mov     ax, OFFSET DGroup:MainStackEnd
        mov     sp, ax
        sti
        call    _main
VAPStart endp

;
; This Process definition is called by NetWare.  We must
;  disable interrupts, setup the segments, the stack, enable
;  interrupts and call our C routine
;
        ;Process definitions
        public  _ProcessStart

        extrn   _main: near
        extrn   _Process: near

_ProcessStart   proc    near
        cli
        mov     ax, DGroup
        mov     ds, ax
        mov     es, ax
        mov     ss, ax
        mov     ax, OFFSET DGroup:FirstStackEnd
        mov     sp, ax
        sti
        call    _Process
_ProcessStart   endp

;
; Front-ends for the Console and Down Handler routines:
;
        assume  ds: DGroup

ConsoleHandlerCALL      proc    far
        mov     _Keyword, ax        ; If you have multiple keywords, this number
                                    ; can be used as an index to the
                                    ; keywords to tell which word was entered
        call    _ConsoleHandler
        ret
ConsoleHandlerCALL      endp

DownHandlerCALL         proc    far
        call    _DownHandler
        ret
DownHandlerCALL         endp

; This routine disables stack checking if Microsoft C is used
__CHKSTK proc   near
        pop     cx                  ; get return offset
        sub     sp,ax               ; allocate stack space
        jmp     cx                  ; return to cx
__CHKSTK endp

_TEXT   ends

;
; This section sets up the stack for our process and defines Keyword
_DATA   SEGMENT word public 'DATA'
        assume ds:DGroup
```

```
        ;Stacks
        dw      2000 dup (0)                    ; This is for main()
        MainStackEnd    label   word

        dw      2000 dup (0)                    ; This is for our other process
        FirstStackEnd   label   word

        ;Define Keyword
        public  _Keyword

        _Keyword dw     0

_DATA   ENDS

        end     VAPStart
```

VAP.Asm

```
;
; VAP Routines - callable from C
;               assumes small model
;
        name    VAPRoutines

PGroup  group   _TEXT
        assume cs: PGroup

_TEXT   segment public 'CODE'

        public  _VAllocateSegment
        public  _VChangeToDataSegment
        public  _VSpawnProcess
        public  _VInitializationComplete
        public  _VKillProcess
        public  _VChangeProcess
        public  _VDelayProcess
        public  _VSleepProcess
        public  _VWakeUpProcess
        public  _VConsoleError
        public  _VGetProcessID
        public  _SetEStoDS
        public  _VAPAttachToFileServer

        extrn   _ProcessControlServices: dword
        extrn   _NetWareShellServices: dword

AllocateSegment                 equu    0
ChangeToDataSegment             equ     1
ChangeSegmentToCode             equ     2
DeclareSegmentAsData            equ     3
DeclareExtendedSegment          equ     4
SpawnProcess                    equ     5
SetPassThroughShellMode         equ     6
InitializationComplete          equ     7
KillProcess                     equ     8
ChangeProcess                   equ     9
DelayProcess                    equ     10
GetProcessID                    equ     11
SleepProcess                    equ     12
```

```
WakeUpProcess                   equ     13
SetHardwareInterruptVector      equ     14
GetInterruptVector              equ     15
SetInterruptVector              equ     16
CalculateAbsoluteAddress        equ     17
SetExtendedProcessorError       equ     18
ConsoleError                    equ     19
GetFileServerName               equ     20
AttachToFileServer              equ     21
MapFileServerNameToNumber       equ     22

        public _ShellServices
_ShellServices proc near
        call    dword ptr cs:_NetWareShellServices
        ret
_ShellServices endp

_VAllocateSegment:
        push    bp
        mov     bp, sp
        mov     ax, [bp+4]              ; amount of paragraphs
        mov     di, AllocateSegment
        push    es
        jmp     ProcessControlServicesCALL

_VChangeToDataSegment:
        push    bp
        mov     bp, sp
        mov     ax, [bp+4]              ; segment value
        mov     di, ChangeToDataSegment
        push    es
        jmp     ProcessControlServicesCALL

_VSpawnProcess:
        push    bp
        mov     bp, sp
        mov     cx, [bp+4]                      ; process entry
        mov     dx, ds                          ; process data segment
        mov     bx, cs                          ; assume's near
        mov     bp, cs
        mov     di, SpawnProcess
        push    es
        jmp     ProcessControlServicesCALL

_VInitializationComplete:
        push    bp
        mov     di, InitializationComplete
        push    es
        jmp     ProcessControlServicesCALL

_VKillProcess:
        push    bp
        mov     di, KillProcess
        push    es
        jmp     ProcessControlServicesCALL

_VChangeProcess:
        push    bp
        mov     di, ChangeProcess
        push    es
        jmp     ProcessControlServicesCALL
```

```
_VDelayProcess:
        push    bp
        mov     bp, sp
        mov     dx, [bp+4]                  ;time to delay
        mov     di, DelayProcess
        push    es
        jmp     ProcessControlServicesCALL

_VSleepProcess:
        push    bp
        mov     di, SleepProcess
        push    es
        jmp     ProcessControlServicesCALL

_VWakeUpProcess:
        push    bp
        mov     bp, sp
        mov     bx, [bp+4]                  ; sleeping process ID
        mov     di, WakeUpProcess
        push    es
        jmp     ProcessControlServicesCALL

_VConsoleError:
        push    bp
        mov     bp, sp
        mov     si, [bp+4]                  ; show error on console
        mov     di, ConsoleError
        push    es
        jmp     ProcessControlServicesCALL


_VGetProcessID:
        push    bp
        push    es
        mov     di, GetProcessID

ProcessControlServicesCALL proc near
        call    dword ptr cs:_ProcessControlServices
        pop     es
        pop     bp
        ret
ProcessControlServicesCALL endp

_VAPAttachToFileServer  proc    near
        push    bp
        mov     bp, sp

        mov     ax, [bp+4]
        mov     si, ax
        mov     di, 15h
        call    dword ptr cs:_ProcessControlServices
        xor     ah, ah
        xor     dh, dh
        mov     si, [bp+6]
        mov     [si], dx

        pop     bp
        ret
_VAPAttachToFileServer  endp
```

```
;;;;;;;;;;;;;;;;;;;;;;;;;;;;;;;;;;;;;;;;;;;;;;;;;;;;;;;;;;;;;;;;;;;;;;;;;;;;
;       ConsoleControlServices Calls
;;;;;;;;;;;;;;;;;;;;;;;;;;;;;;;;;;;;;;;;;;;;;;;;;;;;;;;;;;;;;;;;;;;;;;;;;;;;

        public  _VClearScreen
        public  _VPrintString
        public  _VReadKeyboard
        public  _Interrupt3
        extrn   _ConsoleControlServices: dword

_Interrupt3     proc    near
        int     3
_Interrupt3     endp

_VClearScreen proc      near
        push    bp
        mov     bp, sp
        mov     di, 0                           ;0 = ClearScreen
        call    dword ptr cs:_ConsoleControlServices
        pop     bp
        ret
_VClearScreen   endp

_VPrintString proc      near
        push    bp
        mov     bp, sp
        mov     ax, [bp+10]
        push    ax
        push    ds
        mov     ax, [bp+8]
        push    ax
        mov     ax, [bp+6]
        push    ax
        mov     ax, [bp+4]
        push    ax
        mov     di, 1
        call    dword ptr cs:_ConsoleControlServices
        mov     sp, bp
        pop     bp
        ret
_VPrintString   endp

_VReadKeyboard  proc    near
        push    bp
        mov     bp, sp
        mov     ax, [bp+6]
        push    ax
        push    ds
        mov     ax, [bp+4]
        push    ax
        mov     di, 2

        call    dword ptr cs:_ConsoleControlServices
        mov     sp, bp
        pop     bp
        ret

_VReadKeyboard  endp
```

```
;;;;;;;;;;;;;;;;;;;;;;;;;;;;;;;;;;;;;;;;;;;;;;;;;;;;;;;;;;;;;;;;;;;;;;;;;;;
;       Misc Calls
;;;;;;;;;;;;;;;;;;;;;;;;;;;;;;;;;;;;;;;;;;;;;;;;;;;;;;;;;;;;;;;;;;;;;;;;;;;

_SetEStoDS      proc    near
        push    ds
        pop     es
        ret
_SetEStoDS      endp

_TEXT   ends
        end
```

Exercises

1. Install and run ListUser. Can you think of possible enhancements?

2. Construct you own VAP using a different API group. What issues do you run into? How is it different from the regular DOS, or client-side programming?

3. Use IPX-SPX and build a client-server application with some processing taking place at the server and presentation taking place at the workstation. The next chapter will discuss more about client-server development.

18 Microsoft Windows

The popularity of the Apple Macintosh has spurred a proliferation of workstation interfaces featuring windowed screens and a variety of engaging graphics with which to control programs. These bit-mapped graphical user interfaces (GUIs) appear to afford the user a quicker and clearer grasp of computing than do conventional character-based interfaces.

The LAN environment can be ideal for GUI-based applications. The network delivers far more information than most users have handled at their standalone workstations. And with that comes a flood of new concepts such as remote and local resources, users and user groups, volumes and file servers, and more. This increased complexity can readily be handled by the graphical user interface.

So, while at this writing only a small percentage of DOS applications employ GUIs, it is expected that eventually they will dominate the desktop computing world. With that in mind, this chapter will focus on development of GUI software for the NetWare environment. We'll develop a utility with a front end based on Microsoft Windows, explaining each step of development. The utility, ViewBind, will present the NetWare Bindery to the user and let the user examine objects, properties and values.

We assume that the reader has experience programming Microsoft Windows. If not, the reader should also read Charles Petzold's book *Programming Windows*.

It is important to remember that GUIs like Microsoft Windows use bit-mapped graphics for anything displayed on the screen. Text is written to the display by translating characters into bits that are drawn on the screen. This increases memory requirements substantially.

The GUI window is an area of the screen reserved for a particular purpose. When opened, it obscures anything beneath it; when closed, whatever was under the window is restored to view. Most files contain more information than can be displayed in a window. So windows usually have controls such as scroll bars to allow the windows to be scrolled horizontally or vertically over entire files.

When files are not documents but applications, windows can be used to present program options to the user. Most GUIs also feature pull-down menus for common user options, such as file operations.

Under NetWare, a developer may have to present a variety of network-related choices to the user. There are several ways to handle this with Microsoft Windows. A few examples follow.

Listing users and servers — and much more

If a network application allows one user to work with another, the application should provide a list of users. This could be quite clumsy in a text-based system; the list box control in Microsoft Windows, on the other hand, would fit the bill perfectly.

The list box control allows text strings to be placed in the list box where they can be sorted alphabetically. If the number of strings is larger than the number of lines in the box, vertical scroll bars allow the user to scroll through the list of users. If strings are wider than the list box, horizontal scroll bars can be employed. All the programmer has to do is place the strings in the box and let Windows indicate when a string has been chosen. Windows handles all string manipulation, scrolling, and selecting.

We'll demonstrate in our sample program, ViewBind, how to create list boxes, add information to them, and allow users to select from them.

As the average LAN gets larger and the technology is extended to broad, multiserver LANs, users may find data relevant to applications placed on different file servers and perhaps on different volumes on those file servers. List boxes could also list relevant file servers or those volumes. Users are also given a plethora of choices regarding where they want their document printed; that selection process too can easily be handled by list boxes.

Illustrations of buttons could also be clicked on or off to select printers. Buttons could also be used to toggle various print flags, such as whether or not to print the banner, expand tabs, suppress form feeds, etc.

The beauty of the graphical user interface is its extensibility; its functionality is a product of the creativity of the developer.

A utility based on Windows (Sample Code: ViewBind., ViewBind.RC, ViewBind.DLG, ViewBind.Def, ViewBind.H, ViewBind.C)

In this section we develop a utility for Microsoft Windows. ViewBind will provide the user with three list boxes: one listing the objects in the Bindery, one listing the properties belonging to a selected object and the last box listing the value(s) associated with a selected property. Though it is beyond the scope of this book to teach programming Windows, this example will illustrate how Windows can be combined with NetWare API programming.

The program was developed using the Microsoft C version 5.0 compiler and the Microsoft Windows Software Development Toolkit V2.0. Microsoft Windows 2.11 will be used to run the utility. The NetWare C Interface library routines were used to provide the Bindery access routines, although these could have been hand written.

The NetWare API programmer is advised to check thoroughly any NetWare C Interface code before using it in Windows programs. Some of the programming practices used in the NetWare C Interface libraries could cause Windows to hang. For instance, occasionally the libraries will place data in a code segment. This works fine under DOS, but Windows continually runs Cyclical Redundancy Checks (CRCs) on Windows code segments and if they change, Windows may believe the code was corrupted and halt the system.

ViewBind is a popup utility, a modeless dialog box. Modeless means that the user is free to work in other windows and switch back and forth to our dialog box. (Modal means the user can't do anything else until exiting the dialog box, by selecting OK or CANCEL, for example.)

We use the dialog box template because Windows does a lot of the processing for us and we're making the dialog box our main window (there's no parent window). This method conserves code space, takes advantage of Windows resources, and provides a flexible utility.

ViewBind's three list boxes are defined in the resource file ViewBind.RC with its associated header file ViewBind.H. The first line after the BEGIN statement identifies our three list boxes, their names, classes, flags, positions in the window, and sizes. After the boxes are defined, several text fields are created that will be displayed in the window.

The code for ViewBind begins by including the relevant files, providing a prototype for our Window procedure, WndProc, as well as the other local functions, and declaring the handles for our list boxes and radio buttons. Next, we define WinMain().

WinMain() first registers our window class, "ViewBind," with the RegisterClass() function. The class is fairly generic: standard style, WndProc for our window procedure, standard cursor and no icon. After we register our window class, we call CreateDialog().

CreateDialog() is usually used to create a modeless dialog box. In many Windows applications, we would call CreateWindow here to create the backdrop, or parent window for the application, but since we're just going to have one dialog box window, we call CreateDialog().

Next we need to get the window handles to our dialog boxes (which we will write to in the application). This is done with the GetDlgItem() call which retrieves the handle of a window given the parent window and the ID of the window in question. These handles are stored in our global variables *hList box1*, *hList box2*, and *hDisplayBox*, the handles for the list boxes, and *hUserButton*, *hGroupButton*, and *hFSButton*, the handles for the radio buttons.

After we have retrieved the handles we set the radio buttons to their start-up states. We want the User button on and the rest off so we use the SendMessage() call to send BM_SETCHECK messages, passing a 1 to turn the button on or 0 to turn it off.

Now we are ready to place the Bindery objects for type USER in the list box. This is accomplished through the UpdateObjectList box() routine. This routine, located near the end of the listing, begins by clearing all three list boxes out by sending them an LB_RESETCONTENT message. Next, a WM_SETREDRAW message is sent which tells the list box not to repaint itself after each new object is added.

The NetWare API call ScanBinderyObject() is called iteratively to get all Bindery objects. Before the call, *searchObjectType* is set to our global type variable, *objType* (which contains the current object type being scanned, either user, group, or file server).

The *completionCode* is checked for errors and, if one was encountered, a message box is displayed, providing an explanation, and some error handling.

Finally, when all of the objects are returned and added to the list box, we call InvalidateRect() which makes Windows redraw the list box with the new entries. We also turn the REDRAW flag back on with another SendMessage() call.

After we have initialized the list box, we call ShowWindow(), which displays the window on the screen for the first time. Finally, WinMain() enters the standard while loop that calls GetMessage() with the TranslateMessage() and DispatchMessage() calls. If the user quits the application, the window procedure WndProc() calls PostQuitMessage() which causes GetMessage() to return 0, the while loop falls through, and the application ends.

WndProc() processes the WM_COMMAND messages that occur when the user clicks on a list box and the WM_DESTROY message that is sent when the user double-clicks on the system menu box or chooses Close from the system menu.

A switch statement is used to check the value of *iMessage*. If a WM_COMMAND message is received, we check the *wParam* variable to see if it was List box_1, List box_2, USER_BUTTON, GROUP_BUTTON, or FS_BUTTON that sent the message.

If the first list box sent the message, we use the SendMessage() call to get first the index and then the value of the chosen object. Next, we get the properties associated with that object and use SendMessage() again to display the properties in the second window (we use an identical process to that used in UpdateObjectList box(), except we're scanning properties rather than objects).

If the second list box sent the message, SendMessage() is used to get the chosen property and the value is sent to the third box, DISPLAY_BOX. We check property to see if it is a set (of objects) or an item. Sets are displayed to the value box by looking up the object name and sending it to the list box. For item values that we do not explicitly handle, we print that the item was read but the format is unknown, since each item format is different.

However, for the NET_ADDRESS server property and the IDENTIFICATION properties, we do include routines to print their values. PrintNetAddress() uses sprintf() to print the 12-byte network address to a string and send it to the list box.

If a radio button was chosen, we turn it on and the other two off with SendMessage(). Next we set *objType*, the current object type, to USER, GROUP, or SERVER, depending on which button was hit. Finally, we call UpdateObjectList box() which clears the three list boxes and lists the objects of the new type.

The WM_SETFOCUS message is received when the window receives the input focus and we set it to the first dialog box. This is a start at keyboard handling, but one possible enhancement to ViewBind would be to include the capability to use the tab key to cycle from list box to list box and the arrow keys to move up and down in a list box. Other enhancements would include different buttons for other object types and other handlers for different property values.

If the user quit the application, the WM_DESTROY message is handled, calling PostQuitMessage() to end the application.

The default switch case sends processing of the message back to Windows.

There are two other files involved in creating ViewBind: the make file and the linker's DEF file. The make file first checks to see if ViewBind.OBJ is created and up to date. If not, the C compiler is called, passing the switches "-c -D LINT_ARGS -Gsw -Os -W2 and -Zp."

The "-c" argument tells the compiler to compile only (and not link); "-D LINT_ARGS" turns on type checking; and "-Gsw" removes stack checking and inserts Windows prologue and epilogue code. The "-Os" flag optimizes for size, "-W2" turns on more intensive, Level 2 warning messages, and, finally, "-Zp" packs structures on byte, rather than word, boundaries.

The DEF file, ViewBind.DEF is used by the Windows linker, LINK4.EXE, and defines the name and description of the program. The STUB is the program run when ViewBind is run from DOS (which says "This program needs Microsoft Windows to run." or some facsimile). The CODE and DATA statements tell Windows how it can manage the segments, the code, and data portions of ViewBind take up.

The HEAPSIZE and STACKSIZE statements define the sizes of the heap and stack, and the EXPORTS statement tells Windows the functions in the program that Windows will call (in this case, the only one is our windows procedure, WndProc()).

Will you do Windows?

The commitment to developing in the Windows environment should not be taken lightly. The ease with which information is presented to users is matched only in the complexity borne by the developer. Windows is not an environment for the developer faint of heart.

There are around 450 different function calls in the Windows environment and the developer must adapt to a radically different philosophy: passive programming, responding to the user's actions rather than active programming, the norm in most applications today. However, despite the complexities of Windows-based development, the rewards are apparent. The flexibility and therefore productivity to be gained are enormous.

```
          wndclass.hInstance      = hInstance;
          wndclass.hIcon          = NULL;
          wndclass.hCursor        = LoadCursor( NULL, IDC_ARROW );
          wndclass.hbrBackground  = GetStockObject( WHITE_BRUSH );
          wndclass.lpszMenuName   = NULL;
          wndclass.lpszClassName  = szAppName;

          if ( !RegisterClass( &wndclass ) )
               return FALSE;
     }

     hWnd = CreateDialog( hInstance, szAppName, 0, NULL );

     /* Get the window handles of our child windows */
     hListBox1 = GetDlgItem( hWnd, LISTBOX_1 );
     hListBox2 = GetDlgItem( hWnd, LISTBOX_2 );
     hDisplayBox = GetDlgItem( hWnd, DISPLAY_BOX );
     hUserButton = GetDlgItem( hWnd, USER_BUTTON );
     hGroupButton = GetDlgItem( hWnd, GROUP_BUTTON );
     hFSButton = GetDlgItem( hWnd, FS_BUTTON );

     /* Set our default button (User) and clear the others */
     SendMessage( hUserButton, BM_SETCHECK, 1, 0L );
     SendMessage( hGroupButton, BM_SETCHECK, 0, 0L );
     SendMessage( hFSButton, BM_SETCHECK, 0, 0L );

     /* List the objects in the bindery for the default type (User) */
     UpdateObjectListbox();

     /* Finally, display the main window and enter the message loop */
     ShowWindow( hWnd, nCmdShow );

     while ( GetMessage( &msg, NULL, 0, 0 ) )
     {
          TranslateMessage( &msg );
          DispatchMessage( &msg );
     }

     return msg.wParam;
}

long FAR PASCAL WndProc( HWND hWnd, unsigned iMessage, WORD wParam, LONG lParam
)
{
     char         szBuffer[50];
     char         szName[50];
     HDC          hDC;
     TEXTMETRIC   tm;
     static short xChar, yChar;
     static short xClient, yClient;
     PAINTSTRUCT  ps;
     WORD         x;
     BYTE         i;

     char         searchObjectName[48];
     WORD         searchObjectType;
     long         objectID = -1;
     char         objectHasProperties;
     char         objectFlag;
     char         objectSecurity;
```

```
int       completionCode;
char      objectName[48];
WORD      objectType;
char      searchPropertyName[16];
long      sequenceNumber = -1;
char      propertyName[16];
char      propertyFlags;
char      propertySecurity;
char      propertyHasValue;
char      moreProperties;

int       segmentNumber = 1;
BYTE      propertyValue[128];
BYTE      moreSegments;

switch ( iMessage )
{
     case WM_SETFOCUS:
               SetFocus( hListBox1 );
               break;

     case WM_COMMAND:
      /* If the first listbox was selected and the user selected an item */
    if ( ( wParam == LISTBOX_1 ) && ( HIWORD( lParam ) == LBN_SELCHANGE ) )
               {
   /* Get the pos. of the selected item, then place the item in szBuffer */
                    x = (WORD) SendMessage( hListBox1, LB_GETCURSEL, 0, 0L );
                      x = (WORD) SendMessage( hListBox1, LB_GETTEXT, x,
                         (LONG) szBuffer );

                      /* Clear the properties listbox */
                      SendMessage( hListBox2, LB_RESETCONTENT, 0, 0L );

                      /* Turn off box redrawing */
                      SendMessage( hListBox2, WM_SETREDRAW, FALSE, 0L );

                      /* And add the properties to it */
                      strcpy( objectName, szBuffer );
                      objectType = objType;
                      strcpy( searchPropertyName, "*" );
                      while ( 1 )
                      {
                        completionCode = ScanProperty( objectName,
                           objectType, searchPropertyName, &sequenceNumber,
                           propertyName, &propertyFlags, &propertySecurity,
                           &propertyHasValue, &moreProperties );

                           if ( completionCode == 0xFB )
                                break;

                  /* Use Windows message box facilities if there's an error */
                           if ( completionCode )
                           {
                   sprintf( szBuffer, "completionCode = %X", completionCode );
                                MessageBox( NULL, szBuffer, "ScanProperty",
                                     MB_OK | MB_ICONHAND );
                                break;
                           }

                           SendMessage( hListBox2, LB_ADDSTRING, 0,
                             (LONG) propertyName );
```

```
                    if ( !moreProperties )
                         break;

               }

               /* Update box and turn redrawing back on */
               InvalidateRect( hListBox2, NULL, TRUE );
               SendMessage( hListBox2, WM_SETREDRAW, TRUE, 0L );
          }

          /* If the property listbox was selected... */
if ( ( wParam == LISTBOX_2 ) && ( HIWORD( lParam ) == LBN_SELCHANGE ) )
          {
 x = (WORD) SendMessage( hListBox1, LB_GETCURSEL, 0, 0L );
      x = (WORD) SendMessage( hListBox1, LB_GETTEXT, x, (LONG) objectName );

               x = (WORD) SendMessage( hListBox2, LB_GETCURSEL, 0, 0L );
    x = (WORD) SendMessage( hListBox2, LB_GETTEXT, x, (LONG) propertyName );

               SendMessage( hDisplayBox, LB_RESETCONTENT, 0, 0L );

               SendMessage( hDisplayBox, WM_SETREDRAW, FALSE, 0L );

               objectType = objType;
               segmentNumber = 1;
               while ( 1 )
               {

   if ( ( completionCode == 0xEC ) || ( completionCode == 0xFB ) )
                         break;

                    if ( completionCode )
                    {
                  sprintf( szBuffer, "completionCode = %X", completionCode );
                         MessageBox( NULL, szBuffer, "ReadPropertyValue",
                              MB_OK | MB_ICONHAND );
                         break;
                    }

               /* If property was NET_ADDRESS, show it in the Display Box */
                    if ( !strcmp( propertyName, "NET_ADDRESS" ) )
                    {
                         PrintNetAddress( propertyValue );
                         break;
                    }

               /* If it was a Set (up to 32 4-byte values), show the names */
                    /* of the bindery objects they represent */
                    if ( propertyFlags && SET )
                         for ( x = 0; x < 32; x++ )
                         {
                  objectID = LongSwap( *((LONG *)(propertyValue + (x*4))) );

                              if ( !objectID )
                                   break;

 completionCode = GetBinderyObjectName( objectID, objectName, &objectType );
                              if ( completionCode )
                              {
                                sprintf( szBuffer,
                                "completionCode = %X", completionCode );
                                    MessageBox( NULL, szBuffer,
                                    "GetBinderyObjectName",
                                    MB_OK | MB_ICONHAND );
```

```
                        break;
                    }
                    strcpy( szBuffer, objectName );
                    GetAsciiObjectType( szName, objectType );
                    strcat( szBuffer, szName );
                    SendMessage( hDisplayBox,
                      LB_ADDSTRING, 0, (LONG) szBuffer );

                }
            else
                if ( !strcmp( propertyName,
                   "IDENTIFICATION" ) )
                    SendMessage( hDisplayBox,
                      LB_ADDSTRING, 0, (LONG) propertyValue );
                else
                    SendMessage( hDisplayBox,
                      LB_ADDSTRING, 0, (LONG) "Value read,
                      Unknown format" );

                /* Other cases would go here */

            segmentNumber++;
        }

        InvalidateRect( hDisplayBox, NULL, TRUE );
        SendMessage( hDisplayBox, WM_SETREDRAW, TRUE, 0L );
}

/* If a button was hit, set it to on and turn others off, */
/* set the new objectType and re-scan the bindery for the */
/* objects of this new type */
if ( wParam == USER_BUTTON )
{
        SendMessage( hUserButton, BM_SETCHECK, 1, 0L );
        SendMessage( hGroupButton, BM_SETCHECK, 0, 0L );
        SendMessage( hFSButton, BM_SETCHECK, 0, 0L );
        objType = USER;

        UpdateObjectListbox();
}

if ( wParam == GROUP_BUTTON )
{
        SendMessage( hUserButton, BM_SETCHECK, 0, 0L );
        SendMessage( hGroupButton, BM_SETCHECK, 1, 0L );
        SendMessage( hFSButton, BM_SETCHECK, 0, 0L );
        objType = GROUP;

        UpdateObjectListbox();
}

if ( wParam == FS_BUTTON )
{
        SendMessage( hUserButton, BM_SETCHECK, 0, 0L );
        SendMessage( hGroupButton, BM_SETCHECK, 0, 0L );
        SendMessage( hFSButton, BM_SETCHECK, 1, 0L );
        objType = SERVER;

        UpdateObjectListbox();
}

break;
```

```
          case WM_DESTROY:
                    PostQuitMessage( 0 );
                    break;

          default:
                    return DefWindowProc( hWnd, iMessage, wParam, lParam );
     }

     return 0L;
}

void UpdateObjectListbox( void )
{
     char           szBuffer[50];
     int            completionCode;
     char           searchObjectName[48];
     WORD           searchObjectType;
     long           objectID = -1;
     char           objectName[48];
     WORD           objectType;
     char           objectHasProperties;
     char           objectFlag;
     char           objectSecurity;

     /* Clear all three listboxes */
     SendMessage( hDisplayBox, LB_RESETCONTENT, 0, 0L );
     SendMessage( hListBox1, LB_RESETCONTENT, 0, 0L );
     SendMessage( hListBox2, LB_RESETCONTENT, 0, 0L );

     SendMessage( hListBox1, WM_SETREDRAW, FALSE, 0L );

     strcpy( searchObjectName, "*" );
     searchObjectType = objType;
     while ( 1 )
     {
          completionCode = ScanBinderyObject( searchObjectName,
              searchObjectType, &objectID, objectName, &objectType,
                  &objectHasProperties, &objectFlag, &objectSecurity );

          if ( completionCode == 0xFC )
              /* No Such Object, i.e. our scan is complete */
               break;

          if ( completionCode )
          {
               sprintf( szBuffer, "completionCode = %X", completionCode );
               MessageBox( NULL, szBuffer, "ScanBinderyObject",
                    MB_OK | MB_ICONHAND );
               break;
          }

          SendMessage( hListBox1, LB_ADDSTRING, 0, (LONG) objectName );
     }
     InvalidateRect( hListBox1, NULL, TRUE );
     SendMessage( hListBox1, WM_SETREDRAW, TRUE, 0L );
}

void GetAsciiObjectType( char *szBuffer, int objectType )
{
     *szBuffer = NULL;
     switch( objectType )
```

```
    {
         case 1:        strcpy( szBuffer, " (User)" );
                             break;
         case 2:        strcpy( szBuffer, " (Group)" );
                             break;
         case 3:        strcpy( szBuffer, " (Print Queue)" );
                             break;
         case 4:        strcpy( szBuffer, " (File Server)" );
                             break;
         default:       strcpy( szBuffer, " (Unknown)" );
                             break;
    }
}

void PrintNetAddress( BYTE *netAddress )
{
     int  i;
     char szAddress[50];

      sprintf( szAddress, "%02X%02X%02X%02X:%02X%02X%02X%02X%02X%02X:%02X%02X",
           netAddress[0], netAddress[1], netAddress[2], netAddress[3],
           netAddress[4], netAddress[5], netAddress[6], netAddress[7],
           netAddress[8], netAddress[9], netAddress[10], netAddress[11] );

     SendMessage( hDisplayBox, LB_ADDSTRING, 0, (LONG) szAddress );
}
```

Exercises

1. Run ViewBind. Use it to scan different types of objects. Notice how the different elements of the dialog box such as the buttons, list boxes, and other controls can be used to present Bindery information.

2. Modify ViewBind to handle property values other than IDENTIFICATION. Make a handler for other types of values that display in the lower box.

3. Create other buttons or dialog-box controls that can be used to enhance the program. Write code that uses these new controls.

4. Write a program similar to ViewBind that uses calls from a different API and uses Windows.

19 C-Worthy

For some environments, a graphical user interface such as Microsoft Windows puts too much of a demand on workstation hardware. A realistically minimal system for Windows, for example, includes at least a 286-based computer running at a good rate (such as 12 Mhz), a mouse, an EGA or VGA card and monitor, and enough memory to support the applications that will be running. (Often one to three megabytes of expanded memory are needed for increased performance and program storage.)

It is namely the bit-mapped graphics in the GUI that make such demands on the hardware. In a character-based environment, all one needs is a computer that will run DOS (an IBM XT will do just fine), and a display (monochrome without graphics is no problem); no mouse, or memory expansion beyond 640 kilobytes, is required. It is this flexibility that has sparked the popularity of character-based windowing environments.

Character-based environments are actually libraries linked to application code. They provide user interfaces with some appointments similar to the GUI's, such as windows, virtual window space, list boxes, standard, pull-down, and line menus, and context-sensitive help, among others. One such library, C-Worthy, also affords developers routines for background processing, list management, and editing, along with applications for creating error, help, and message libraries.

These applications let the developer store all error messages in one file, help screens in another, and other messages in yet another file. This feature alone provides tremendous organizing power, especially for large projects. Also, as in the Windows environment, because the errors, help screens and messages are stored in their own files, translation to other languages is much easier.

These benefits and others make C-Worthy the obvious choice in the NetWare environment for character-based windowing. C-Worthy, nee the C-Worthy Interface Library, is marketed by Solution Systems, but was created by Custom Design Systems of Orem, Utah.

The C-Worthy library is used by all of NetWare's major utilities such as SysCon, FConsole, Filer, etc., and has been since the earliest versions. Developers who want to create utilities and applications that look like Novell utilities must use C-Worthy.

In this chapter, we'll enumerate the ways C-Worthy can be used in the NetWare environment. Then we'll demonstrate a number of those techniques by adding C-Worthy to our IPXChat program. What we will end up with is a C-Worthy peer-to-peer chat program that looks like a Novell utility.

Naming conventions

When you start working with the C-Worthy library, you begin to see how the developers of this system thought through the user interface down to the most minute detail. As in Microsoft Windows, there is even a naming convention for functions and variables, which improves readability and consistency. Incidentally, the Novell NetWare C Interface libraries follow the same convention.

The naming convention is very simple: Function names start with capital letters, with each word starting with a capital letter, and variable names are the same except the first word starts with a lowercase letter. Thus the routine used to initialize most C-Worthy applications is called *InitUtility*. The name of the active window, on the other hand, is *currentPortal*.

Portals

The basic element of C-Worthy is the window, or portal. It affords the programmer a great degree of flexibility.

There are two types of portals: direct access and virtual. Direct access portals can be as small as a single character or as large as the entire screen (not including the header). Virtual portals can be up to 255 lines by 255 columns, assuming the total memory taken up (lines x columns x 2) is less than 64K. Changes that are made to the virtual portal are not shown on the screen until UpdatePortal() is called. Virtual portals can be scrolled to bring different parts of the virtual screen into view (on the real one).

Portals can be created with a "SAVE" flag which saves the screen information under the portal and restores it when the portal is closed. Developers have a variety of other options such as borders, headers, colors, and whether to save the screen the window overlays. A program may have up to 50 portals active at one time.

Menus in C-Worthy

A menu is built by creating a list of options and making a menu function call. There are three types of menus that may be presented to the user: pull down menus, bar menus (Lotus-style) and popup menus. The Novell utilities all use the popups.

The help system is tied closely to menus; help screens can be associated with menus, or with selections on the menus.

C-Worthy uses lists for building menu choices but it also provides list routines for other uses. Developers are given a group of routines for list management and display. For example, a menu presenting a list in a window could be used for selecting files.

An optional add-on to the C-Worthy library, the Form Interface Library is a powerful facility for generating forms, or data entry screens, for any type of application. The forms library provides a valuable tool for data acquisition, with features like data validation and programmer-defined routines for each field, and a long list of data types. Although the forms library is a formidable tool, we won't be covering it in our discussion of IPXChat because its function is not appropriate to that utility.

Compiling and linking

To include the C-Worthy routines in your software requires header files from the C-Worthy Interface Library. You must define a keyword to indicate which compiler you're using. (In our example, we'll use BTC200 for Turbo C 2.0.) As we'll see later, you must also link code files from the message, error and help librarians to the application code. These steps can be easily accomplished in a make file.

C-Worthy initialization

Initialization is quite easy. The InitUtility() routine calls several other routines and sets up the windowing environment for the high-level routines. RestoreUtility() should be called before exiting the application. It restores the PC to the environment it was in before InitUtility() was called. Several other routines are provided to modify the header at the top of the screen, to get system information, and to provide an alternate exit for the program.

Upon initialization, the programmer can use the virtual portal routines to write to memory, or the screen display routines to write directly to the screen. With these routines the programmer can initialize the display, control the cursor, manipulate the screen, use different colors, and get information about the display device.

Input handling

In C-Worthy, all input is collected in the input filter. The input filter can receive input from four sources: regular keystrokes, function keys, interrupt keys, or the mouse. Regular keystrokes are what a user would type normally. Function keys are the Escape key, Backspace, Enter, arrows, Insert, Delete, F1 through F10, ALT F1 through ALT F10, etc. Interrupt keys are those assigned to a particular interrupt routine; when the key is pressed, the routine is called (and the keystroke is not interpreted as another type of key). Mouse input is registered when the mouse moves or when a button is pressed. The input handling routines allow the programmer to poll for, get, or wait for input.

List-management routines

List-management routines manipulate groups of items, such as filenames. The list routines are used by the higher-level C-Worthy functions; they may also be used by programs. There are 46 routines available to manage and display these doubly-linked lists. Lists can be created, destroyed, saved, restored, manipulated, sorted, marked, and viewed.

Menu routines

A menu is simply a special kind of list. Usually, the list is shorter and the entries are specific to a task. The menu routines allow one to create, manage, display, and remove the three different types of menus.

Editing routines

One of the advantages of C-Worthy is its ability to easily present editable string portals (as for editing filenames) or buffer portals (for editing scripts, files, etc, up to 64K). A built-in editor allows for block editing, word-wrap, and other features.

The edit routines allow the programmer to provide string editing for lines that must be edited by the user, such as when entering file names or buffer editing for a buffer of up to 64K. The buffer editing is a full-screen editor providing block editing and word wrap. The simplicity with which a user can be presented with an editor for either of these functions makes them valuable tools. The buffer editing function is used by Novell's SysCon utility when editing the login script.

The C-Worthy Librarians

The messages that an application provides to the user are managed by the Message Librarian, a utility of C-Worthy that manages these messages for the programmer. The messages can be displayed to the user in various ways.

Similar to the message system, the error system places all error messages in a central area and the Error Librarian is used to manage them. Errors may be fatal, warnings, or informative. Fatal errors cause the program to exit once the error is displayed. Warnings should be displayed when the current operation cannot be performed but the rest of the application is okay. Informative errors are used when an error occurs that has no side effects on the program's operation.

The Error Librarian is linked with the Message Librarian such that the programmer sets up the names of calls and the error values in the former and stores the error messages in the latter.

For example, for the hypothetical routine PrintNumber(), the programmer makes an entry called PRINTNUMBER and two associated entries — a value of 255 with the token INV_NUM and a value of 254 with the token TOO_BIG — in the Error Librarian. In the Message Librarian, the programmer creates entries for INV_NUM and TOO_BIG associating them with messages like "Invalid Number" and "The Number given was too large for this function" respectively.

In the program code, the programmer would check the return value of Print-Number() and if nonzero, pass the value to the error system through the Display-

ErrorCondition() call. Assuming the error code was 255, the error system would look up the value in the error file, note that the associated error message was INV_NUM, go to the message file, get the message, and display "Invalid Number" in the error report. You'll see how this is used in more depth in our IPXChat program example.

The C-Worthy help system

C-Worthy stores help messages in its own central area. The Help Librarian manages help screens and establishes "help contexts" for applications. A help context is a name for a help screen that links it with the program. You can associate a help context with a menu, a list box, etc. Or you can just set a current help context for user input routines.

Background processing

Although it is not a real-time multitasking system, C-Worthy provides programmers with a way to incorporate nonpreemptive background processes. These processes are called in one of two ways: at least once between each input character, or only when a program is explicitly waiting for input. The routines can be chained, or a controlling routine can be used to call child processes.

Directory and file management

The C-Worthy Library contains a group of directory and file management routines that isolate the developer from lower-level DOS programming. Functions allow for such DOS management routines as get current or set current drive; get space; create, delete, change or get current directory; similar file operations; and directory searches, among others.

Memory management

Also built-in are high-level memory management routines for allocating, copying, and manipulating memory outside the program's address space.

Miscellaneous functions

The C-Worthy miscellaneous routines provide various useful functions such as debug trace, program delay, break status return, or DOS version identification, sound, and string functions.

Global variables

The C-Worthy documentation lists the global variables for use by programmers; some are read/write, others are read-only and some are nonuseable (for internal use only). One useful feature of the global variables for Novell programmers is that overlay files (files such as IBM$RUN.OVL which are loaded on demand) can be renamed so they don't conflict with the ones in the SYS:PUBLIC directory. If a Novell overlay files were read before yours, there could be a version conflict and the program might not run. This will be addressed in more detail in the explanation of IPXChat below.

Making IPXChat C-Worthy

In this section, we will discuss only those changes to IPXChat that are relevant to C-Worthy. For a complete discussion of IPXChat, see the IPX-SPX chapter.

The first step we take in building the C-Worthy interface is to include the message, error, and help header files. This is done with the include statements, including the files CHATMSG.MLH, CHATERR.ELH and CHATHLP.HLH. The file prefix names were chosen by the author, the three-character suffix names are assigned by C-Worthy.

We also define the widths and heights of our chat windows, PORTAL_WIDTH and PORTAL_HEIGHT.

Next we define prototypes for our three new routines: ProcessKeyInput(), Leave() and CleanUp(). We will discuss these routines below.

Just before we start main(), we define an external reference to the *currentPortal*, a global C-Worthy variable.

We let the user exercise command-line options, but if the user specifies no options, we present a menu. The first few lines after main() check the command line to see if a command line argument was specified. If it was, but was not /*r* for receive or /*s* for send, we abort the program, explaining the right syntax.

If there is no need to abort, the C-Worthy background screen is brought up and the C-Worthy environment is initialized with the InitUtility() routine. We pass PROGRAM_NAME which is a token for the long name of the program and is stored in the messages file. PROGRAM_VERSION and SHORT_PROGRAM_NAME are also in the messages file; all three tokens are placed in the header of the program. The last parameter in the routine is the name of our help file CHATHLP.HLP.

The next two lines disable mouse processing and remove the mouse pointer from the screen. There is no need for mouse processing in this utility and it was removed so the pointer would not be distracting.

Next we check to see if arguments were specified. If not, we display a menu that lists the choices of "Initiate a Chat Session" or "Listen for a Chat Request." We first must call InitList() to setup a new list (for the menu). Two calls to AppendToPopUpMenu() place our options in the menu list, passing the message file tokens for the list options, the value the menu choice will return, and the help context for the option. We define help contexts here.

A call to PopUpMenu() places the menu on the screen and solicits a response from the user. Once we've gotten a response DestroyList() removes the menu and we check the option variable, returned from PopUpMenu(). If it returned a -1, the ESC was pressed rather than the return key so we will have to ask if the user wants to quit. The Confirm() routine then presents a Yes/No menu and returns 1 for Yes, 0 for No. If Yes is returned, we call Leave() which runs RestoreUtility(), the C-Worthy main exit routine, and exit the program. If the user chose not to exit, we cycle back up to the top of the while loop and present the menu again.

If *option* is returned containing 1, we run MainSend() which sets up a chat request; otherwise, MainListen() is called, which waits for a chat request.

If correct command line arguments are specified, we call the appropriate routines.

MainSend()

We add two new variables to MainSend(), *element*, which is a pointer to a LIST structure and *someone*, a flag used in determining if anyone else is on the network. We start off with calls to PushList() and InitList() which saves any current list and initializes a new one.

In the loop that follows we iterate through each possible connection (0 through 99) to see if any other users are attached. If so, we append the name and station to the list and set the *someone* flag. Each list item contains a name and "secondary information" which is user-definable. We want to associate the connection number with each user so we first call malloc() to allocate space for the integer that will hold the connection number. Next we assign the value to the variable, *station*. Finally, we pass the *name* and the *station* variables to AppendToList() which adds them to our list.

When the loop is done, we check the value of *someone* to see if there were any other users. If not, we call the Alert() function which displays a message on the screen. The 0, 0 parameters mean to center the window vertically and horizontally. After displaying the Alert() message, we call Leave(), which shuts down the C-Worthy environment (RestoreUtility()) and exits the program.

The next step is to present the menu of users, so we set *element* to point to NULL. The element parameter tells where to place the selection bar on entering the List() routine and points to the option selected on exit. We then call PushHelpContext(), passing the name of the help context we have set up for this list box.

Next we call List() which will display our list and allow the user to select from it. Notice the M_SELECT value that is passed in List(). This value indicates that the return key is the only valid list-exit key, i.e., the user can't hit ESC, or DEL, or another key that would cause the list function to exit without returning a selected list element.

We set *targetConn* to the station of the selected user. We first cast the *otherInfo* structure to an int pointer and dereference it to obtain the value. Finally, we cast the value to a byte before we assign it to *targetConn*. Afterwards, we call DestroyList() and PopList() which deletes our current list and restores any old list to be the current one.

The next C-Worthy addition comes after we call IPXOpenSocket() to open the INVITE_SOCKET. If IPXOpenSocket() returned a value, indicating an error, we call DisplayErrorCondition(), passing the value returned from IPXOpenSocket(). Once you've set up the Error Librarian for each call, all you do is pass the name of the call and the error value it returned and C-Worthy displays the error associated with that returned value. This mechanism provides a clean, simple means of handling error messages.

We use DisplayErrorCondition() again after sending the chat request packet with IPXSendPacket(). Notice that the name of the call passed is in all uppercase — if we were to pass the name of the call, as called, the compiler would pass the address of the call, rather than our Error Library token. Also, FATAL indicates the program should terminate after displaying the error message.

After the program sends the request to Chat() it must wait for a response. C-Worthy provides a centered, blinking "Please wait..." box for just such an application. We call StartWait() just before our wait loop and pull down the wait box with EndWait().

If there was no response, we use an Alert message. If the returned ECB was bad, we call DisplayErrorCondition with a fatal message, and if the other user chose not to chat, we use an Alert message to convey that.

MainListen()

When MainListen() starts, we call StartWait() to put up a wait box. After that we need to create another window to indicate to the user that any key can be pressed to stop waiting for a chat request. We use ComputerPortalPosition() which tells us where to place a portal that we want to be centered, have its middle line on line 23, and be 28 characters wide.

We pass the line and column information to CreatePortal() which creates the portal structure in memory. SelectPortal() makes it the current portal, ExplodePortal() gives the effect of an exploding window, and DisplayTextInPortal() writes our message to the portal. No text is written, however, until we call UpdatePortal() which writes the virtual portal to the display.

DisplayErrorCondition() is used after we open the socket. After that, we enter a loop that checks for keyboard input or received packets. The part that checks for keyboard input first calls InputStatus() which looks to see if the input filter is empty. If it is, it returns zero and the program continues. InputStatus() returns nonzero if there is data in the input filter, and we call GetInput() to retrieve the data to the variable input, an instance of an INPUT_INFO structure.

There is no need to interpret the keystroke, since any key would have aborted, so we cancel the listen event, close the socket, and call Leave().

If a packet was received, we push a help context for the Confirm() statement and call Confirm() to see if the user wishes to chat. The response is placed in InitBuffer[0] and is sent back to the requesting user. If the user chose not to chat, Leave() is called and the program exits.

If the user chose to chat, we destroy the "Press any key..." portal with DestroyPortal() and close the wait box with EndWait(), before calling the main Chat() routine.

Chat()

The new variables for Chat() are *rcvCol*, *rcvRow*, *sendCol* and *sendRow* which are the column and row variables for the receive portal (the other user's transmissions) and the send portal (what we type). We set aside *portal1* and *portal2* for the portal numbers we will create and an INFO_INPUT structure, *input*, is created to hold our keyboard input.

All four column and row variables are initialized to 0 and we create and set up the portals for the two dialogues. Our portal is set up with the cursor on and the other is created with the cursor off. We select, explode, and update each portal.

When we exit from a routine in Chat(), such as from a fatal DisplayErrorCondition() call, we want to close the socket we have been using. We can have DisplayErrorCondition() make a call to a routine we specify before it exits. We install this routine with RegisterExitProcedure(), passing the name of our routine, CleanUp.

We also want to disable the help screens during our dialogue, because, since we're polling for packets, we don't want any to get lost while a user's help screen is up. There are several ways around this. Here we simply disable the function of the F1 key through the DisableFunctionKey() call.

When we enter our main loop, we check InputStatus() as in MainListen(), checking to see if it returned a nonzero value and, if so, calling GetInput() to get the input event. If the user pressed ESC, we set the *Finished* flag and quit.

For other keys, we call the ProcessKeyInput() routine, passing the character to display, the portal to send it to, and pointers to the current row and column for that portal.

ProcessKeyInput() first checks to see if the current portal is the one to write to; if not it highlights the appropriate portal. The routine checks the input to see if the Enter key, the Backspace key, or a regular keystroke was entered. If the Enter key was hit, the column is set to zero, and the line number is incremented. If this scrolls us past the bottom of the window, we scroll down with ScrollPortalZone().

The backspace handler decrements the column variable and prints a blank space over the current character. If a regular key was hit, the character is printed at the current cursor position, and the column is checked to see if it goes outside the width of the window. If so, the column is set back to zero, the line is incremented, and if necessary, the portal is scrolled.

Finally, for all of these routines, the cursor is moved and the screen is updated.

Back in Chat(), if the packet sent had an error, we use DisplayErrorCondition() to print the result.

If a new packet was received from the other user, we check the completion code and use DisplayErrorCondition() if necessary, or show an Alert() box if he or she requested to quit. Otherwise, we call ProcessKeyInput() to print the user's keystroke in the other user portal.

Finally, if we quit, we show an Alert() box saying so, we call CleanUp() and exit the program.

This program demonstrates just a few of the ways C-Worthy routines can be incorporated into a NetWare-aware program. Other features such as Forms, DOS calls, and other user options, such as background processing, have not even been covered. This should, however, provide a general introduction as to how C-Worthy can be used to enhance NetWare applications and make them blend more smoothly into the NetWare environment.

A last note about conflicts with overlay files: C-Worthy uses what it calls overlay files to handle the screen drivers for different kinds of machines. Under NetWare, these are called IBM$RUN.OVL or CMPQ$RUN.OVL. These names can be changed by altering global variables in C-Worthy. This is recommended because of potential conflicts with NetWare utilities.

Chaterr.elc

```
/* This PROGRAM file was generated by the Error Librarian. */
/* !!! DO NOT MODIFY !!! */

typedef struct
{
    int ccodeReturned;
    int errorMessageNumber;
} PROCERROR;

static
PROCERROR proc0[] =
{
    {240, 0x0006},
    {254, 0x0007},
    {255, 0x0008},
    {-1, -1}
};

static
PROCERROR proc1[] =
{
    {252, 0x0009},
    {253, 0x000a},
    {254, 0x000b},
    {255, 0x000c},
    {-1, -1}
};

static
PROCERROR proc2[] =
{
    {252, 0x0009},
    {253, 0x000a},
    {255, 0x000f},
    {-1, -1}
};

struct
{
    char *procedureName;
    PROCERROR *errorReturns;
} procedureErrorTable[] =
{
    {"IPXOPENSOCKET", proc0},
    {"IPXSENDPACKET", proc1},
    {"IPXLISTENFORPACKET", proc2}
};
```

Chatmsg.mlc

```
/* This PROGRAM file was generated by the Message Librarian. */
/* !!! DO NOT MODIFY !!! */

char *programMesgTable[] =
{
     "IPX Chat Utility",
     "V1.0",
     "IPXChat",
     "Other User's Text",
     "Your Text",
     "Do you wish to chat with other user?",
     "The Novell workstation shell has not been loaded.  Load IPX and NET3 for
       NetWare versions 2.1x or ANET3 for earlier versions. ",
     "The Socket Table is Full",
     "This Socket is already open",
     "The IPX Send request was cancelled by another process.",
     "The packet did not have a 30-byte header as the first fragment,
       or its total length exceeded 576 bytes.",
     "The Packet was not deliverable to the destination address.",
     "A Hardware Failure was encountered",
     "No response from target user",
     "The target user did not wish to chat",
     "A Listen request was posted for a socket that has not been opened.",
     "There are no other users logged in to the network",
     "Choose the user to chat with",
     "Initiate a Chat Session",
     "Listen for a Chat Request",
     "Available Options",
     "Other user quit",
     "Chat session cancelled - Other user has been notified",
     "Exit IPXChat?"
};
```

Esrhand.asm

```
        title   ESR Routines to C Functions
        name    ESRRoutines

DGroup  GROUP   _DATA
_DATA   segment word public 'DATA'
        assume  ds:DGroup

_DATA   ends

PGroup  GROUP   _TEXT
        assume  cs:PGroup

_TEXT   segment byte public 'CODE'

        extrn   _WaitESR:near
        extrn   _AdvertiseESR:near

        public  stacktop

        public  _WaitESRHandler
```

```
_WaitESRHandler proc    far
        mov     ax, DGroup
        mov     ds, ax

        push    es
        push    si
        call    _WaitESR
        add     sp, 4

        ret
_WaitESRHandler endp

        public  _AdvertiseESRHandler

_AdvertiseESRHandler    proc    far
        mov     ax, DGroup
        mov     ds, ax

        push    es
        push    si
        call    _AdvertiseESR
        add     sp, 4

        ret
_AdvertiseESRHandler    endp

_TEXT   ends
        END
```

IPXChat.C

```
/*                                                                        */
/* IPXChat - A true peer-to-peer chat utility                             */
/*          Using C-Worthy for its user interface                         */
/*                                                                        */
/*                                                                        */
/* by Charles Rose                                                        */
/*                                                                        */

typedef unsigned char BYTE;
typedef unsigned int WORD;
typedef unsigned long LONG;

#include <stdio.h>
#include <conio.h>
#include <string.h>
#include <mem.h>
#include <dos.h>
#include <time.h>
#include <cwuser.h>

#include "ipx.h"
#include "ncp.h"

#include "chatmsg.mlh"
#include "chaterr.elh"
#include "chathlp.hlh"

/* Definitions */

#define WAITMAX 15
```

```
#define PORTAL_WIDTH  70
#define PORTAL_HEIGHT 9

/* Foreign & domestic prototypes */

extern void SendESRHandler();
extern void ListenESRHandler();
void SendESR();
void ListenESR();

void Problem();
void SetupInitialPacket();

void MainSend();
void MainListen();

void ProcessKeyInput( int input, int portal, int *line, int *column );
void Leave();
void CleanUp();

/* Global data definitions */

int  NewPacket;
BYTE InitBuffer[49];

ECB InitialECB;
IPXPacket InitialIPXHeader;     /* Initial ECB/IPX for requesting chat */

BYTE targetNetwork[4] = { 0, 0, 0, 0 };
BYTE targetNode[6] = { 0xFF, 0xFF, 0xFF, 0xFF, 0xFF, 0xFF };

extern int currentPortal;

main( int argc, char *argv[] )
{
        int option;

        /* If they've used a parameter and it's wrong, show usage */
        if ( ( argc > 1 ) &&
             ( stricmp( argv[1], "/r" ) && stricmp( argv[1], "/s" ) ) )
        {
                printf( "Usage: IPXCHAT /s - to send a chat request or \n" );
                printf( "               /r - to wait to receive a chat request\n" );
                exit( 1 );
        }

        InitUtility( PROGRAM_NAME, PROGRAM_VERSION, SHORT_PROGRAM_NAME,
                HEADER_NORMAL, "chathlp.hlp" );

        DisableMouseUpdate();
        DisableMouseCursor();

        /* If they used no arguments, give them a menu */
        if ( argc == 1 )
        {
                while ( 1 )
                {
                        InitList();
                        AppendToPopUpMenu( SEND_OPTION, 1, SEND_HELP );
                        AppendToPopUpMenu( RECEIVE_OPTION, 2, RECEIVE_HELP );
                        option = PopUpMenu( CHOOSE_SEND_RECEIVE, 0, 0, DOUBLE,
                                        NullPointer( LIST ), MENU_NORMAL,
```

```
                                    NO_HELP_CONTEXT, NullProcedure( int ) );
                        DestroyList();
                        if ( option == -1 )
                        {
                                option = Confirm( EXIT_YES_NO, 0, 0, 0,
                                                NullProcedure( int ) );
                                if ( option )
                                        Leave();
                                else
                                        continue;
                        }
                        else
                                break;

                }

                if ( option == 1 )
                        MainSend();
                else
                        MainListen();
        }

        if ( !stricmp( argv[1], "/r" ) )
        {
                MainListen();
                exit(1);
        }

        if ( !stricmp( argv[1], "/s" ) )
        {
                MainSend();
                exit(1);
        }

}

void Chat()
{

        int                     rcvCol, rcvRow, sendCol, sendRow;
        /* int                  rcvHeight, rcvWidth, sendHeight, sendWidth; */
        int                     portal1, portal2;
        INPUT_INFO              input;

        ECB SendECB;
        IPXPacket SendIPXHeader;        /* Send ECB/IPX for outgoing packets */
        ECB RcvECB;
        IPXPacket RcvIPXHeader;         /* Rcv ECB/IPX for incoming packets */

        int Finished;                   /* If set, then communication is over */
        int FromHim;                    /* If set, the other guy terminated */

        BYTE SendBuffer;
        BYTE RcvBuffer;

        WORD                    targetSocket;

        char                    probdesc[80];
        int                     status, i;
```

```
/* Setup Send & Receive structures */
SetupSendPacket( &SendECB, &SendIPXHeader, targetNetwork,
        targetNode, CHAT_SOCKET, &SendBuffer, sizeof( SendBuffer ), 0 );

SetupRcvPacket( &RcvECB, &RcvIPXHeader, CHAT_SOCKET,
        &RcvBuffer, sizeof( RcvBuffer ), ListenESRHandler );

sendRow = rcvRow = 0;
sendCol = rcvCol = 0;

portal1 = CreatePortal( 4, 5, PORTAL_HEIGHT, PORTAL_WIDTH,
                PORTAL_HEIGHT, PORTAL_WIDTH, SAVE,
                GetMessage( PORTAL1_HEADER ), VINTENSE, SINGLE,
                VINTENSE, CURSOR_OFF, VIRTUAL );

portal2 = CreatePortal( 15, 5, PORTAL_HEIGHT, PORTAL_WIDTH,
        PORTAL_HEIGHT, PORTAL_WIDTH, SAVE, GetMessage( PORTAL2_HEADER ),
        VINTENSE, SINGLE, VINTENSE, CURSOR_ON, VIRTUAL );


SelectPortal( portal1 );
ExplodePortal( ' ', VINTENSE );
UpdatePortal();

SelectPortal( portal2 );
ExplodePortal( ' ', VINTENSE );
UpdatePortal();

RegisterExitProcedure( CleanUp );
DisableFunctionKey( I_F1 );

targetSocket = CHAT_SOCKET;

status = IPXOpenSocket( ( BYTE * ) &targetSocket, TEMPORARY_SOCKET );
if ( status )
        DisplayErrorCondition( IPXOPENSOCKET, status, FATAL );

/* Announce at the top who we're talking to */

IPXListenForPacket( &RcvECB );

NewPacket = 0;
SendBuffer = RcvBuffer = 0;
FromHim = Finished = 0;

while ( !(Finished) )
{
        if ( InputStatus() )
        {
                GetInput( &input );

                if ( ( input.type == FUNCTION_KEY_EVENT ) &&
                     ( input.info.key.value == I_ESC ) )
                        Finished++;
                else
                {
                        SendBuffer = input.info.key.value;
                        ProcessKeyInput( SendBuffer, portal2, &sendRow,
                          &sendCol );
                        IPXSendPacket( &SendECB );
                        while ( SendECB.InUseFlag != OKAY )
                                IPXRelinquishControl();
```

```
                                if ( SendECB.CompletionCode != OKAY )
                                        DisplayErrorCondition( IPXSENDPACKET,
                                                SendECB.CompletionCode, FATAL );
                        }
                }

                if ( NewPacket )
                {
                        NewPacket = 0;

        if ( RcvECB.CompletionCode != OKAY )
                                DisplayErrorCondition( IPXLISTENFORPACKET,
                                        RcvECB.CompletionCode, FATAL );

                        if ( RcvBuffer == 0xFF )
                        {
                                Alert( OTHER_USER_QUIT, 0, 0 );
                                Finished++;
                                FromHim++;
                        }
                        else
                        {
                                ProcessKeyInput( RcvBuffer, portal1, &rcvRow,
                                   &rcvCol );
                                IPXListenForPacket( &RcvECB );
                        }
                }
        }

        /* If we shut down, let him know */
        if ( !FromHim )
        {
                SendBuffer = 0xFF;
                IPXSendPacket( &SendECB );
                while ( SendECB.InUseFlag != OKAY )
                        IPXRelinquishControl();

                if ( SendECB.CompletionCode != OKAY )
                        DisplayErrorCondition( IPXSENDPACKET,
                                SendECB.CompletionCode, FATAL );

                Alert( WE_CANCELLED, 0, 0 );
        }

        CleanUp();
}

void SendESR( ECBptr )
ECB *ECBptr;
{
}

void ListenESR( ECBptr )
ECB *ECBptr;
{
        NewPacket++;
}

void Problem( char *prob )
{
```

```
        printf("%s\n", prob);
        exit(1);
}


void MainSend()
{
        int                     status, numrecs, x, ourstn = 0, *station;
        WORD                    select;
        char                    probdesc[80], reqtext[80];
        time_t                  wait_secs, start_secs;

        BYTE                    name[48], socket[2];
        WORD                    type;

        WORD                    targetSocket = INVITE_SOCKET;
        BYTE                    targetConn;
        IPXAddress              IPXaddr;

        LIST                    *element;
        char                    someone = 0;

        PushList();
        InitList();

        ourstn = NCPGetOurStnNum();

        targetConn = 0;
        for ( x = 0; x < 100 ; x++ )
        {
                status = NCPGetConnInfo( x, &type, name );

                if ( (!status) && ( type == 0x100 ) )
                {
                        /* Don't include ourselves in list */
                        if ( x == ourstn )
                                continue;

                        station = (int *) malloc( sizeof( int ) );
                        *station = x;
                        AppendToList( name, station );
                        someone++;


                }
        }

        if ( !someone )
        {
                Alert( WHEREDYAGO, 0, 0 );
                Leave();
        }

        element = NullPointer( LIST );
        PushHelpContext( CHOOSE_USER_HELP );
        List( CHOOSE_USER, 0, 0, 12, 30, M_SELECT, &element, 0,
                NullProcedure( int ), NullProcedure( int ) );
        PopHelpContext();

        targetConn = ( (BYTE) (* ( (int *) element->otherInfo ) ) );

        DestroyList();
        PopList();
```

```
/* Setup request window & get user to talk to */

/* Here's where you get the address & put it in targetNode */
NCPGetInterNetAddr( targetConn, targetNetwork, targetNode, socket );

/* Set InitBuffer[0] request class to 0 ( Chat request ) */
InitBuffer[0] = 0;

/* Open Socket */
status = IPXOpenSocket( ( BYTE * ) &targetSocket, TEMPORARY_SOCKET );
if ( status )
        DisplayErrorCondition( IPXOPENSOCKET, status, FATAL );

/* Now setup send packet */

SetupSendPacket( &InitialECB, &InitialIPXHeader, targetNetwork,
   targetNode, INVITE_SOCKET, InitBuffer, sizeof( InitBuffer ), 0 );

/* Send Initial Packet */

IPXSendPacket( &InitialECB );
while ( InitialECB.InUseFlag != OKAY )
        IPXRelinquishControl();

if ( InitialECB.CompletionCode )
        DisplayErrorCondition( IPXSENDPACKET, InitialECB.CompletionCode,
        FATAL );

/* Setup again and listen for response */

SetupRcvPacket( &InitialECB, &InitialIPXHeader, INVITE_SOCKET,
        InitBuffer, sizeof( InitBuffer ), 0 );

IPXListenForPacket( &InitialECB );

wait_secs = time( &start_secs );

StartWait( 0, 0 );
while ( ( InitialECB.InUseFlag != OKAY ) &&
         ( ( wait_secs - start_secs ) < WAITMAX ) )
{
        IPXRelinquishControl();
        time( &wait_secs );
}

EndWait();

if (  ( wait_secs - start_secs ) >= WAITMAX )
{
        Alert( NO_RESPONSE, 0, 0 );
        Leave();
}

if ( InitialECB.CompletionCode )
        DisplayErrorCondition( IPXLISTENFORPACKET,
        InitialECB.CompletionCode, FATAL );

if ( !(InitBuffer[0]) )
{
        Alert( NO_TALK, 0, 0 );
        Leave();
```

```
        }

        movmem( InitialECB.ImmediateAddress, IPXaddr.Node, 6 );
        movmem( targetNetwork, IPXaddr.Network, 4 );

        Chat();
}

void MainListen()
{
        WORD    targetSocket = INVITE_SOCKET;
        int     status;
        char    prob[80], chatMsg[48];
        BYTE    line, column;
        int     waitportal;
        INPUT_INFO input;

        StartWait( 0, 0 );

        status = ComputePortalPosition( 23, 0, 5, 28, &line, &column );
        waitportal = CreatePortal( line, column, 5, 28, 5, 28, SAVE, NOHEADER,
           VINTENSE, DOUBLE, VINTENSE, CURSOR_OFF, VIRTUAL );
        SelectPortal( waitportal );
        ExplodePortal( ' ', VINTENSE );
        status = DisplayTextInPortal( 1, 2, "Press any key to abort", VINTENSE );
        UpdatePortal();

        SetupRcvPacket( &InitialECB, &InitialIPXHeader, INVITE_SOCKET,
           InitBuffer, sizeof( InitBuffer ), 0 );

        status = IPXOpenSocket( ( BYTE * ) &targetSocket, TEMPORARY_SOCKET );
        if ( status )
                DisplayErrorCondition( IPXOPENSOCKET, status, FATAL );

        IPXListenForPacket( &InitialECB );

        while ( 1 )
        {
                if ( InputStatus() )
                {
                        GetInput( &input );
                        IPXCancelEvent( &InitialECB );
                        IPXCloseSocket( INVITE_SOCKET );
                        Leave();
                }

                if ( !InitialECB.InUseFlag )
                {
                        if ( !InitialECB.CompletionCode )
                        {

                                PushHelpContext( CONFIRM_CHAT_HELP );
                                InitBuffer[0] = Confirm( CONFIRM_CHAT_REQUEST, 0,
                                        0, 1, NullProcedure( int ) );
                                PopHelpContext();

                /* Place the immediate address returned into our new target node */
                   movmem( InitialIPXHeader.Source.Node,  targetNode, 6 );
                   movmem( InitialIPXHeader.Source.Network,  targetNetwork, 4 );
```

```
                                /* Setup to send the reply */
                                SetupSendPacket( &InitialECB, &InitialIPXHeader,
                                 targetNetwork, targetNode, INVITE_SOCKET,
                                 InitBuffer, sizeof( InitBuffer ), 0 );

                        /* Send the reply about whether we want to chat or not */
                                IPXSendPacket( &InitialECB );
                                while ( InitialECB.InUseFlag != OKAY )
                                        IPXRelinquishControl();

                                if ( InitialECB.CompletionCode )
                                        DisplayErrorCondition( IPXSENDPACKET,
                                        InitialECB.CompletionCode, FATAL );

                                /* If we didn't want to chat, then exit */
                                if ( !( InitBuffer[0] == 1 ) )
                                        Leave();

                                DestroyPortal( waitportal );
                                EndWait();
                                Chat();
                        }
                }
        }
}

void ProcessKeyInput( int input, int portal, int *line, int *column )
{
        if ( portal != currentPortal )
        {
                DeselectPortal();
                ReselectPortal( portal );
        }

        switch( input )
        {
                case I_ENTER:   *column = 0;
                                (*line)++;
                                if ( *line > PORTAL_HEIGHT - 5 )
                                {
                                        *line = PORTAL_HEIGHT - 5;
                                        ScrollPortalZone( 0, 0, 7, 70,
                                                VNORMAL, 1, V_UP );
                                }
                                break;

                case I_BACKSPACE:
                                (*column)--;
                                FillPortalZone( *line, *column, 1, 1,
                                        ' ', VNORMAL );

                                break;

                default :       FillPortalZone( *line, (*column)++, 1, 1,
                                        input, VNORMAL );

                                if ( *column == PORTAL_WIDTH - 2 )
                                {
                                        *column = 0;
                                        (*line)++;
                                        if ( *line > PORTAL_HEIGHT - 5 )
                                        {
```

```
                                                *line = PORTAL_HEIGHT - 5;
                                                ScrollPortalZone( 0, 0, 7, 70,
                                                 VNORMAL, 1, V_UP );
                                        }
                                }
                }

                PositionPortalCursor( *line, *column );
                UpdatePortal();
}

void Leave()
{
        RestoreUtility();
        exit( 1 );
}

void CleanUp()
{
        IPXCloseSocket( CHAT_SOCKET );
        Leave();
}
```

IPXChat.PRJ

```
ipxchat.c
ipxlib.c
chatmsg.mlc
chaterr.elc
ncplib.c
esrhand.obj
cwdoss.lib
cwusers.lib
```

IPXLib.C

```
/*      IPXLIB  -       Library of IPX functions                */
/*                                                              */
/*                                                              */

typedef unsigned char BYTE;
typedef unsigned int WORD;
typedef unsigned long LONG;

#include <stdio.h>
#include <dos.h>
#include "ipx.h"
#include "keys.h"

int  IPXOpenSocket(socketNumber,socketType)
BYTE socketNumber[2];
BYTE socketType;
{
        union REGS inregs,outregs;

        inregs.x.bx = 0;
        inregs.h.dl = socketNumber[0];
        inregs.h.dh = socketNumber[1];
        inregs.h.al = socketType;
        int86(0x7A,&inregs,&outregs);
        return(outregs.h.al);
```

```
}

void IPXCloseSocket(socketNumber)
WORD socketNumber;
{
        union REGS inregs,outregs;

        inregs.x.bx = 1;
        inregs.x.dx = (int) socketNumber;
        int86(0x7A,&inregs,&outregs);
}

int  IPXGetLocalTarget(networkAddress,immediateAddress,transportTime)
BYTE networkAddress[12];
BYTE immediateAddress[6];
WORD *transportTime;
{
        union REGS inregs,outregs;
        struct SREGS segregs;

        segread(&segregs);
        segregs.es = segregs.ds;

        inregs.x.bx = 2;
        inregs.x.si = (int) networkAddress;
        inregs.x.di = (int) immediateAddress;
        int86x(0x7A,&inregs,&outregs,&segregs);
        *transportTime = outregs.x.cx;
        return(outregs.h.al);
}

void IPXSendPacket(eventControlBlock)
ECB *eventControlBlock;
{
        union REGS inregs,outregs;
        struct SREGS segregs;

        segread(&segregs);
        segregs.es = segregs.ds;

        inregs.x.bx = 3;
        inregs.x.si = (int) eventControlBlock;
        int86x(0x7A,&inregs,&outregs,&segregs);
}

void IPXListenForPacket(eventControlBlock)
ECB *eventControlBlock;
{
        union REGS inregs,outregs;
        struct SREGS segregs;

        segread(&segregs);
        segregs.es = segregs.ds;

        inregs.x.bx = 4;
        inregs.x.si = (int) eventControlBlock;
        int86x(0x7A,&inregs,&outregs,&segregs);
}

void IPXScheduleIPXEvent(timeUnits,eventControlBlock)
WORD timeUnits;
ECB *eventControlBlock;
```

```
{
        union REGS inregs,outregs;
        struct SREGS segregs;

        segread(&segregs);
        segregs.es = segregs.ds;

        inregs.x.bx = 5;
        inregs.x.si = (int) eventControlBlock;
        inregs.x.ax = (int) timeUnits;
        int86x(0x7A,&inregs,&outregs,&segregs);
}

int  IPXCancelEvent(eventControlBlock)
ECB *eventControlBlock;
{
        union REGS inregs,outregs;
        struct SREGS segregs;

        segread(&segregs);
        segregs.es = segregs.ds;

        inregs.x.bx = 6;
        inregs.x.si = (int) eventControlBlock;
        int86x(0x7A,&inregs,&outregs,&segregs);
        return(outregs.h.al);
}

int  IPXScheduleSpecialEvent(timeUnits,eventControlBlock)
WORD timeUnits;
ECB *eventControlBlock;
{
        union REGS inregs,outregs;
        struct SREGS segregs;

        segread(&segregs);
        segregs.es = segregs.ds;

        inregs.x.bx = 7;
        inregs.x.si = (int) eventControlBlock;
        inregs.x.ax = (int) timeUnits;
        int86x(0x7A,&inregs,&outregs,&segregs);
        return(outregs.h.al);
}

int  IPXGetIntervalMarker()
{
        union REGS inregs,outregs;

        inregs.x.bx = 8;
        int86(0x7A,&inregs,&outregs);
        return(outregs.x.ax);
}

void  IPXGetInternetworkAddress(networkAddress)
BYTE networkAddress[10];
{
        union REGS inregs,outregs;
        struct SREGS segregs;

        segread(&segregs);
        segregs.es = segregs.ds;
```

```
        inregs.x.bx = 9;
        inregs.x.si = (int) networkAddress;
        int86x(0x7A,&inregs,&outregs,&segregs);
}

void IPXRelinquishControl()
{
        union REGS inregs,outregs;

        inregs.x.bx = 0xA;
        int86(0x7A,&inregs,&outregs);
}

void IPXDisconnectFromTarget(networkAddress)
BYTE networkAddress[12];
{
        union REGS inregs,outregs;
        struct SREGS segregs;

        segread(&segregs);
        segregs.es = segregs.ds;

        inregs.x.bx = 0xB;
        inregs.x.si = (int) networkAddress;
        int86x(0x7A,&inregs,&outregs,&segregs);
}

void IPXGetProcAddress(proc,addressField)
void (*proc)();
WORD addressField[2];
{
        struct SREGS segregs;

        segread(&segregs);
        segregs.es = segregs.ds;

        addressField[0] = (WORD) proc;
        addressField[1] = (WORD) segregs.cs;
}

void IPXGetDataAddress(data,addressField)
WORD *data;
WORD addressField[2];
{
        struct SREGS segregs;

        segread(&segregs);
        segregs.es = segregs.ds;

        addressField[1] = (WORD) segregs.ds;
        addressField[0] = (WORD) data;
}

void SetupSendPacket( ECBptr, IPXptr, Network, Node, Socket, Buffer, Buffsize,
ESR )
ECB *ECBptr;
IPXPacket *IPXptr;
BYTE Network[4];
BYTE Node[6];
WORD Socket;
char *Buffer;
WORD Buffsize;
void (*ESR)();
```

```
{
        WORD ttime;
        IPXAddress IPXaddr;

        movmem( Network, IPXaddr.Network, 4 );
        movmem( Node, IPXaddr.Node, 6 );
        movmem( Socket, IPXaddr.Socket, 2 );

        if ( ESR ) IPXGetProcAddress( ESR, ECBptr->ESRAddress );
        else memset( &ECBptr->ESRAddress,0,4 );

        ECBptr->InUseFlag = 0;
        ECBptr->ECBSocket = Socket;
        ECBptr->FragmentCount = 2;

        IPXGetDataAddress( (WORD *)IPXptr,
                           (WORD *)ECBptr->FragmentDescriptor[0].Address );
        ECBptr->FragmentDescriptor[0].Size = sizeof( *IPXptr );

        IPXGetDataAddress( (WORD *)Buffer,
                           (WORD *)ECBptr->FragmentDescriptor[1].Address );
        ECBptr->FragmentDescriptor[1].Size = Buffsize;

        IPXptr->PacketType = 0;

        IPXGetLocalTarget( &IPXaddr, ECBptr->ImmediateAddress, &ttime );
        movmem( Network, IPXptr->Destination.Network, 4);
        movmem( Node, IPXptr->Destination.Node, 6);
        movmem( &ECBptr->ECBSocket, IPXptr->Destination.Socket, 2);
}


void SetupRcvPacket( ECBptr, IPXptr, Socket, Buffer, Buffsize, ESR )
ECB *ECBptr;
IPXPacket *IPXptr;
WORD Socket;
char *Buffer;
WORD Buffsize;
void (*ESR)();
{
        if ( ESR ) IPXGetProcAddress( ESR, ECBptr->ESRAddress );
        else memset( &ECBptr->ESRAddress,0,4 );

        ECBptr->InUseFlag = 0;
        ECBptr->ECBSocket = Socket;
        ECBptr->FragmentCount = 2;

        IPXGetDataAddress( (WORD *)IPXptr,
                           (WORD *)ECBptr->FragmentDescriptor[0].Address );
        ECBptr->FragmentDescriptor[0].Size = sizeof( *IPXptr );

        IPXGetDataAddress( (WORD *)Buffer,
                           (WORD *)ECBptr->FragmentDescriptor[1].Address );
        ECBptr->FragmentDescriptor[1].Size = Buffsize;
}
```

Exercises

1. Run IPXChat. How is this different from the IPXChat without C-Worthy routines? How much work did it take to integrate this environment. How much more functional is the program?

2. Take advantage of other aspects of the C-Worthy environment. Integrate them into the IPXChat program. If you did the exercises in the IPX-SPX chapter and built a version of IPXChat for multiple callers, then extend it to include C-Worthy routines.

3. Use the tutorials provided in the C-Worthy manuals; they provide an excellent introduction to the features of C-Worthy and how to use them.

20 OOPS & C++

The last two chapters have covered techniques to make an application easier for the user; character and graphic windowing systems provide a clear, consistent means for the user to interact with an application. This chapter is devoted to making life easier for the programmer. Object-oriented programming (OOP) techniques enable the programmer to model a program much more closely to the task being accomplished.

The need for OOP originated in the 1960's when Norwegian computer scientists were trying to simulate and model real-world problems. They found that existing programming languages were clumsy and not suited for simulation. Those procedural languages were made for real-time or batch processing environments, not simulation, which is inherently data and event driven.

The first OOP language was Simula-67, developed in 1967 by Jens-Ole Dahl and Kristen Nygarrd. Since then, other languages have used the concepts from that language to form powerful OOP environments. Smalltalk, developed in 1980, has been extremely popular and is considered a "pure" OOP language. We will talk more about Smalltalk later in the chapter.

One of the most popular OOP languages today is C++, which is actually an extension of C. Developed in 1985 by Bjarne Stroustrup at AT&T, C++ provides a popular method of incorporating OOP techniques. Those already familiar with C may use as much or as little of the OOP part of the language as needed, providing a gradual introduction.

This chapter will provide an overview of OOP and C++ and discuss how NetWare software developers can incorporate these techniques to build more powerful, flexible programs. This chapter should be considered an introduction to the subject of OOP and C++. It provides a general discussion of the concepts surrounding OOP and C++ and will hopefully encourage the reader to learn more about these concepts. A list of other sources of information about OOP and C++ will be given after the concept discussion. As usual we will end the chapter with an example, combining C++ with NetWare API programming.

OOP and C++ Concepts

One of the most important aspects of OOP is the idea of having abstract data types, which are created by the programmer and consist of both data and functions. The internal details of these new types can be hidden from outside routines, giving them the ability to be changed without affecting other routines that use them.

Also central to the OOP philosophy is the idea of code re-use. Once these types, or objects, have been developed, they can be applied as tools in different applications. Also, through an idea called inheritance, new objects can inherit characteristics from others and simply extend the functionality of the previous object rather than starting over.

In this section we will discuss what abstract data types are and how they are expressed in C++. We will then explain how C++ extends the C language and talk about how it incorporates OOP features like classes, operator overloading, single and multiple inheritance, and polymorphism. Also covered are C++-specific items like constructors and destructors, type-safe linkage, I/O and Streams. But, we begin by defining what objects really are.

Abstract Data Types and Data Hiding

The central figure in object-oriented programming is the object. In a procedural programming language, such as C, programs are composed of functions that call other functions, passing data items. There is no relationship between functions and data except the functions operate on the data. Under OOP, the functions and data have been combined into one entity: the object.

An object is meant to model more closely the real world. An object has data and it has functions associated with that data. They are bound together as one.

To illustrate the difference, let's say you have a list of names that need to be sorted. In C, this could be illustrated as a list of strings, as in "char *list[]" and you might sort the list by passing the list variable to a sort() routine, as in sort(list);.

Under C++ the two would be combined into a list object. This list object could still be represented as a list of strings (we'll call the object strList), but the object would know how to sort itself. To do this you would have a line in the code like: strList.sort();.

The sort routine would be specific to the list object. You may have another object called numList that defined its internal list variable as a list of integers. Although the internals of your sort route would be different, you could still call it as numlist.sort();.

These two objects, strlist and numlist, are considered "abstract data types" because they allow programmers to create their own data type. The idea of not ever having to know about the list routine when you do a sort is called "data hiding" and is a feature of OOP.

The beauty of data hiding is that the implementation of a certain feature can be changed without changing the code in several places. In our example, only the sort() function in an object such as strlist would need to be changed, not the programs that used that object.

C++ Extensions to C

Programmers could use C++ without necessarily having to use any of the OOP concepts of C++. While they would miss the benefits of an object-oriented language, they would nonetheless profit from some of the ways that C++ extends C.

For instance, C++ imposes strict prototyping (optional in C), meaning that programs written in C++ must have prototypes defined before a function is called. When prototypes are used, the compiler detects when parameters of the wrong type (as well as too many or too few) are being passed.

Also, C++ implements reference variables. In C, all functions are call-by-value, meaning that they pass a copy of a variable to a function. The PASCAL language, for instance, implements call-by-reference, where you can pass the real variable to a function so it can modify the variable directly. C++ allows the programmer this freedom.

Variables can be defined in programs where they occur. If you haven't defined the variable x until you get to a for loop, you could use the following code for the loop:

```
for (int x = 0; x < 5; x++ )
```

This line would initialize a variable called x, set it to 0 and use it to count from 0 to 4.

Comments are also different with C++. The old style /* and */ operators are valid, but a new type involves two slashes: //. Anything on a line after the double slashes is considered a comment as in the following:

```
long compUBucks;              // Funds spent on hardware
```

Another extension to C involves the overloading of functions, so that the function behaves differently for different parameters passed to it. One might have a function that accepts an integer and another function by the same name that accepts a character string. The language would decide which function to call depending on what was passed.

When we look at classes in the next section, we will discover that operators such as plus (+) and minus (-) can be overloaded to perform differently with a specific class. For example, a class that had string members might overload the plus operator to concatenate the strings of two objects.

An important new operator is the scope resolution operator which is represented by two colons (::). The scope resolution operator is used in classes but can also be used in straight code to mean the outermost version of a variable. For instance, in the following code:

```
int x;
main()
{
        int x;
        x = 3;
        ::x = 4;
}
```

first the inner x is set to 3, then the outer x is set to 4.

Finally, C++ allows functions to have default arguments. For instance, function SetXY() and two examples of how it can be called are shown below:

```
void SetXY( int newX, int newY = 3 )
{
        x = newX;
        y = newY;
}

SetXY( 1, 5 );
SetXY( 4 );
```

The definition of SetXY() sets up newY as defaulting to 3. Therefore, when the first SetXY() is called, x is set to 1 and y is set to 5. In the second example, x is set to 4 and y defaults to 3.

Classes

The C++ class is central to its implementation of OOP features. In fact, when C++ was created, it was first called "C with classes." A class is a combination of data and programs (in OOP parlance, this would be considered an object) and looks similar to a C structure definition. Some of the internal variables and data can be private, meaning they can only be accessed by functions internal to the class, or they can be public, meaning any program can access them.

There is another security type called protected that works with derived classes and will be explained in the Inheritance/Derived Classes section later in the chapter.

Class members default to private, while structure members default to public. Structures and classes are similar except for this difference.

A sample class definition follows:

```
class testClass {
        int x;
        char *y;
public:
        testClass( int, char * );
        ~testClass();
        ShowX();
};
```

In this case, testClass is the name of the class and x & y are the local data. Note there is no private keyword because class members default to private (so x and y are private and the rest are public).

The next two functions are called constructors and destructors and are used in initializing the values of the internal variables and allocating memory for them. The destructor is used to free the memory. Also note that we specify them as public. Finally, ShowX() is a function that can be called to return the value of X.

In the class definition here, we define prototypes for all of our functions. We could list out the code for the constructor, destructor or ShowX() routine, but if we did, they would be considered in-line.

When functions are in-line the compiler treats them as a macro and copies their code to wherever they are called, rather than performing a jump. The benefit of this is mainly speed; in C one can create macros explicitly, but C++ provides the protection of a function call with local variables and prototyped parameters. An inline function can be created by including it in the class definition or by using the "inline" keyword in a function definition.

To define a function outside of the class, the following method is used (note how we use the scope resolution operator (::) to say what we are defining (the class is testClass, the specific data item/function is ShowX):

```
int testClass::ShowX( void )
{
        return x;
}
```

To define an instance of a class in a program, the format is similar to a structure definition:

```
testClass myClass( 1, "testing" );
```

This line would create an instance of testClass, calling it myClass. The constructor would then be called. Be aware that the names of structures in C++ are the name of the type. In C, this was not the case and the problem was worked around by using typedef; that method is no longer used in C++, so simply remove the typedef statement.

Constructors and Destructors

As stated in the last section, a constructor is used to initialize the contents and memory space for class variables. It may also be used to run certain machine- or device-specific start-up code, if necessary. The constructor is called when a class instance variable is initialized in the code. You can also have several different versions of constructors that accept different parameters.

Constructors are called by the same name for the class, so if the class is called testClass, then the constructor definition would look like:

```
testClass::testClass( int newX, char *newY  )
{
    x = newX;                       // set up x to value of newX
    int len = strlen( newY );       // get length of newY
    y = new char[len+1];  // allocate space, +1 for terminating 0
    strcpy( y, newY );              // initialize y to newY
}
```

The destructor is used to release the memory belonging to the internal class variables. It can also be used to call any machine- or device-specific exit code, the counterpart to what was called in the constructor.

A destructor is called when a class instance variable goes out of scope. For a local class variable this would happen when the routine was returned from; for a global one, it would go out of scope when the program terminated.

A destructor is given the same name as a constructor except it is precedeed by a tilde (~) character. The following code fragment illustrates how a destructor would be defined:

```
testClass::~testClass( void )
{
        delete y;
}
```

If no variable initialization was done in the constructor, no destructor may be needed.

Operator Overloading

As mentioned earlier, operators can be overloaded to perform functions specific to a certain class. For instance, we could overload the plus (+) operator to concatenate two classes. This provides the simplicity and real-world modeling we have been talking about. In C, you might add the elements in two structures with a statement like:

```
struct myStrings x, y, z;

z = AddMyStructs( x, y );
```

But it would be much simpler to use:

```
z = y + x;
```

C++ allows us to use the latter method by overloading the plus operator, which we will demonstrate for our test class example:

```
testClass operator+( const testClass &a, const testClass &b )
{
        testClass temp( ( a.x + b.x ), ( strcat( a.y, b.y ) );
        return temp;
}
```

The const keyword means we can't change the value of a or b in the function. The & keyword is used to pass by reference rather than value, so the actual parameters are passed, rather than copies of them. Finally, the function definition line begins with testClass, meaning this function will return an object of type testClass.

In our function, we define a new testClass instance, temp. We initialize temp by adding the x part of a and b. Similarly, we set the new y to the concatenated y's that belong to a and b. Finally, we return these to the caller. This function can be invoked with the following code:

```
c = a + b;
```

assuming a, b, and c are all instances of testClass. In this case, c would contain the added x components of a and b and the concatenated y components of a and b.

Inheritance/Derived Classes

Another one of the main strengths of OOP and C++ is the ability to build a class and then extended its functionality. The new extended class would be derived from the first; it would inherit all of the characteristics (functions, internal data) as the base class. Derived classes model life more closely, they provide for encapsulation of details, and they promote modularity of code.

The inheritance mechanism can be illustrated by the following example: A fish has certain characteristics: it is aquatic, it swims, etc. A Flying Fish is a derived class of fish in general: it inherits the characteristics of the common fish and it extends it with new attributes such as the ability to leap into the air for short periods.

This mechanism can be applied to programming where a class can perform certain functions. Later, new classes can be derived from previous ones, enhancing the functionality of the base classes. For instance, one could create a screen class that provided screen writing primitives. Later, someone could write a window class that inherited the screen writing functionality and added the new capability of windows.

In this way, significant code portions don't have to be re-written every time the function is needed. Using this philosophy of development usually means more time spent on design, but significantly less time spent on code writing.

To show how our testClass could be extended, we use the following code:

```
class newClass : public testClass {
        long z;
public:
        newClass( int, char *, long );
        long ShowZ();
}
```

Here we define newClass, derived from testClass. It inherits the x and y variables as well as the ShowXY() routine. The constructor has been redefined to include z and a new function, ShowZ() has been added. Our new testClass has been defined public so that the public parts of testClass will be public to newClass as well. If the public keyword is not used here, the public parts of testClass will become private when it is the base class.

Multiple Inheritance

In the previous discussion, we illustrated the concept of single inheritance, which is a new class that inherits characteristics from only one base class. Multiple inheritance is relatively new to C++ (version 2.0) and allows a new class to inherit from several base classes.

To inherit from several classes, our code would look like:

```
class bigClass: public testClass, public otherClass {

// Class code would go here

}
```

Here a new class, bigClass is formed from testClas and otherClass. Again we set testClass and otherClass as public so that the public part of the base becomes public to the new derived class.

Polymorphism and Virtual Functions

Another object-oriented concept is polymorphism, which is the ability of a function to act differently depending on what it is passed. If you defined a PrintIt() function for several different classes in a hierarchy (one derived from the other), you might have to use the scope resolution operator (::) to define which class the function should be called from. But that would create a chaotic mass of class references and require the programmer to keep track of the heirarchy while coding.

All that is necessary is to declare the base class function as virtual as in:

```
virtual void PrintIt();
```

This statement would declare a virtual function called PrintIt() that returned nothing. If you declared classes a, b and c, one derived from the other and each containing a PrintIt() function (you would only have to declare PrintIt virtual in the base class, a), when you called PrintIt(), the compiler would figure out which function to call (the one defined in a, b or c).

Type-safe linkage

In C, function prototypes are optional, but in C++, starting with AT&T version 2.0, prototypes are required. Functions declared without prototypes cause a compiler error message. While this ensures that functions called will match a declaration that has been made previously, it does not guarantee that the linker will link in the right function (if there are several by the same name).

To combat this situation, C++ uses a concept called type-safe linkage which is implemented by what is commonly referred to as name mangling. When the compiler finds a function prototype, it mangles the name, the return value, the arguments and the class name into one identifier that uniquely specifies the fuction.

I/O and Streams

The term stream originates with C which treats all I/O as character string manipulation. Files are essentially streams of characters. C++, as with operating systems like UNIX, models all I/O after the file model; even screen I/O is considered a stream.

The standard streams in C++ are cin, cout, and cerr which represent the standard input, output and error streams respectively. The streams can be redirected, closed and reopened, as well as combined with each other or with files.

C++ uses the input (>>) and output (<<) operator to channel data in and out of streams. For example, to print the ever popular "hello, world" message on the screen, use.

```
cout << "hello, world\n";
```

This statement redirects the string to the standard output device, namely the screen.

Programmers may overload the input and output operators to format and send specific classes through streams. The following example would overload the stream output operator (<<) for our testClass:

```
ostream& operator<<( ostream& stream, testClass test )
{
        char *temp = new char[80];
        sprintf( temp, "X = %d, Y: %s", test.x, test.y );
        return stream << temp;
}
```

Here we define an overloaded output operator (<<) that returns a reference to an ostream (the type for streams). The function is passed a reference to a stream and the value of a testClass instance. The following code would invoke this overloaded operator:

```
testClass myClass( 1, "hello" );

cout << myClass;
```

The previous code would print "X = 1, Y: hello" to the screen.

Future of OOP and C++

With constant conferences, seminars, articles, and books coming in, the popularity of OOP and C++ is on the rise. Since networks will play such an important role in the future, there will be some convergence between OOP and networking. The idea of distributed objects is just beginning. Under this new concept, objects don't all reside on one station. You may be able to share objects with a number of users and send messages to an object on another station.

Another concept that is slowly evolving is the idea of an object-oriented code server, one that provides code to client applications on other workstations and allows them to extend the functionality of their applications while applying the power and flexibility of the routines already developed.

Programming NetWare with OOP Techniques

Supporters of OOP and C++ contend that the concepts presented here can enrich and improve the productivity of the programming environment, whether it be on databases, spreadsheets, word processors, vertical applications, whatever. NetWare is no exception. In this section we will give several suggestions as to how one might incorporate the OOP philosophy into programming with the NetWare APIs, specifically by using C++.

Linking in C routines

The first hurdle in programming NetWare with C++ is getting C++ to link with external C routines. This can easily be accomplished through the extern "C" statement as shown below:

```
extern "C" {
        int function1( int, int );
        int function2( char * );
        int function3( char *, long );
}
```

When programmed as above, the functions will link to their external code. Using this mechanism we can incorporate NetWare calls.

Data Hiding

The data hiding mechanism can be used with NetWare API programming to hide the details of calls from the program. A class that included a group of records could simply issue a Lock() call and the routine would handle the details. If the programmer wanted to switch from logical locking to physical locking at a later date, this could be easily accomplished.

Further, if a call changed between two versions of NetWare, the details could be hidden from the program.

Using APIs as objects

When designing programs in C++, the question "What can be made viewed as an object?" comes up. The following examples provide several possibilities:

• Perhaps the most obvious is the bindery which calls its base entity an object. A program could define a class of type BindObject that contained a bindery object name and type (flags, etc.) as well as properties and values. When initializing the the class, the object name and type could be passed to the constructor which would allocate the appropriate memory and make an API call to get the object ID (which could be stored in a private variable).

The class could either be defined flat with properties and values on the same level as the object, or it could be defined as a hierarchy with properties derived from objects (a property is associated with an object) and values derived from properties.

• Another possibility is with the Queue Management System API. A queue job could be seen as an object. Queue functions such as Submit Job could be made as functions in the class that operate on the object. A job could be created, submitted, serviced, removed, etc.

• Also, the IPX-SPX mechanism lends itself to object orientation. The packet is the base item in any IPX conversation, so it could be the object. It would have an associated IPX header and an ECB structure associated with it (these could be internal variables) as well as functions to send it and receive it. The constructor could open a socket, and allocate space for it. Likewise the destructor could deallocate the space and close the socket (if it were the last packet to be sent on that socket).

• Another possibility is with the Print Services API. We use this idea in our example program and demonstrate how a network printer can be objectified. When we construct the object, the print flags are retrieved. Public functions allow a program to change the flags, turn capture on, or off, flush the buffer, or abort a capture. We hide the details of the calls and the structure from the program and allow for a simple, lucid means of network printing.

Sources of More Information

Although this is by no means a complete list of sources of information on C++, it can hopefully provide a start for those interested in learning more:

Conferences and workshops:
OOPSLA (Canada)
ECOOP (European Conference on Object Oriented Programming)
SCOOP (Seminars and Conference in OOP, Boston)
Miller-Freeman Software Development Conference
Usenix C++ Conference (San Francisco)

Magazines:
JOOP (The Journal of Object-Oriented Programming)
HOOT (The Hot-Line of Object-Oriented Technology)
The C++ Report
The Journal of Pascal, ADA and Modula-2

Books:
C++ Primer, by Stanley Lippman (Addison-Wesley, 1989).
Programming in C++, by Stephen Dewhurst and Kathy Stark (Prentice-Hall, 1989).
Using C++, by Bruce Eckel (Osborne/McGraw-Hill, 1989).
The C++ Answer Book, by Tony Hansen (Addison-Wesley, 1990).
C++ Programming, by John Berry (The Waite Group/SAMS, 1988).
C++ for C Programmers, by Ira Pohl (Benjamin/Cummings, 1989).
Object-Oriented Program Design, With Examples in C++, by Mark Mullin (Addison-Wesley, 1989).

Compilers:
Turbo C++ from Borland International, Inc.
C++ Compiler from Zortech, Inc.

Other instructional material:
Zortech C++ Video Course

I would like to add a note about the Borland and Zortech compilers. Both are powerful development environments for C++ programmers. I would recommend the Zortech C++ video course for anyone wanting live instruction. Those interested in learning and retaining the material must take the time to go through the exercises in the manual.

CODE EXAMPLE: NetTest

For our code example, we use the Print Services API to show how you can incorporate NetWare API calls into C++ programming. The compiler used is the Zortech C++ compiler. The following files make up the program:

NETPRT.HPP

This file defines the *captureInfo* structure which will be used in the Get Default Capture Flags call. Next, our extern "C" files are defined. These are the function prototypes to the assembly routines in PRTLIB.ASM. Finally, the captureBuffer class is defined.

The captureBuffer class consists of a private *captureInfo* structure, *info*, which will be used to get the default capture flags. We list a prototype for our constructor and a dummy destructor. The StartCapture(), FlushCapture(), CancelCapture(), and EndCapture() routines call their respective C counterparts.

NETPRT.CPP

This file defines the constructor for the *captureBuffer* class and the routines for starting, flushing, cancelling and ending the capture process. The constructor sets the target printer to zero and calls GetDefaultCaptureFlags(), passing the size of the structure containing the flags and its address.

PRTLIB.ASM

This file contains the assembly-level code that makes the Print Services API calls. We use the Zortech macros for function definition. The calls save the stack frame, manipulate the registers, call INT 21h, pop the bp register and return. GetDefaultCaptureFlags() gets the parameters off the stack and loads them into the appropriate registers before making the call.

NETTEST.CPP

This is the main body of our code, and as usual with C++ it is concise. The code starts with include statements that bring in the STDIO.H file as well as the

STREAM.HPP file. We also include our custom file NETPRT.HPP where we store our class definitions.

The function main() starts by defining an instance of the *captureBuffer* class. This line causes the constructor of *captureBuffer* to be called which gets the default print flags and stores them in the private structure.

Next, the StartCapture() function is called. In C++ this is referred to as "sending *buffer* a StartCapture message." This statement turns capture redirection on.

The next line uses the *cprn* stream, which is the standard printer device (which now is being redirected to the network). The string is redirected to the network printer.

Finally, we close by sending *buffer* an EndCapture message.

Although not necessarily complex, this sample program should provide a starting place for the programmer when implementing NetWare applications that use C++ code. The program was left lean so the developer can practice adding to it. The exercises provide some possible directions for enhancements.

NetPrt.HPP

```
typedef unsigned char BYTE;
typedef unsigned int WORD;

struct captureInfo
{
        BYTE Status;
        BYTE PrintFlags;
        BYTE Tabsize;
        BYTE TargetPrinter;
        BYTE Copies;
        BYTE Form;
        BYTE reserved;
        BYTE Banner[14];
        BYTE LocalPrinter;
        WORD Timeout;
        BYTE Endspool;
};

extern "C"
{
        void StartLPTCapture( void );
        void FlushLPTCapture( void );
        void CancelLPTCapture( void );
        void EndLPTCapture( void );
        void GetDefaultCaptureFlags( int, captureFlags * );
}

class captureBuffer
{
        captureInfo     info;
public:
        captureBuffer();
        ~captureBuffer(){};
```

```
        StartCapture();
        FlushCapture();
        CancelCapture();
        EndCapture();

        BYTE NetworkPrinter( BYTE printer = 0 );

};
```

NetPrt.CPP

```
#include "netprt.hpp"

captureBuffer::captureBuffer( void )
{
        info.TargetPrinter = 0;
        GetDefaultCaptureFlags( sizeof( flags), &flags );
}

captureBuffer::StartCapture( void )
{
        StartLPTCapture();
}

captureBuffer::FlushCapture( void )
{
        FlushLPTCapture();
}

captureBuffer::CancelCapture( void )
{
        CancelLPTCapture();
}

captureBuffer::EndCapture( void )
{
        EndLPTCapture();
}
```

PrtLib.ASM

```
include \zortech\include\MACROS.ASM
begcode prtlib

        c_public StartLPTCapture
func StartLPTCapture
        push    bp
        mov     bp, sp

        mov     ah, 0DFh
        xor     dl, dl
        int     21h

        pop     bp
        ret
c_endp StartLPTCapture

        c_public FlushLPTCapture
func FlushLPTCapture
```

```
        push    bp
        mov     bp, sp

        mov     ah, 0DFh
        mov     dl, 3
        int     21h

        pop     bp
        ret
c_endp FlushLPTCapture

        c_public CancelLPTCapture
func CancelLPTCapture
        push    bp
        mov     bp, sp

        mov     ah, 0DFh
        mov     dl, 2
        int     21h

        pop     bp
        ret
c_endp CancelLPTCapture

        c_public EndLPTCapture
func EndLPTCapture
        push    bp
        mov     bp, sp

        mov     ah, 0DFh
        mov     dl, 1
        int     21h

        pop     bp
        ret
c_endp EndLPTCapture

        c_public GetDefaultCaptureFlags
func GetDefaultCaptureFlags
        push    bp
        mov     bp, sp

        mov     ax, 0B800h
        mov     cx, [bp + 4]
        push    ds
        pop     es
        mov     bx, [bp + 6]
        int     21h

        pop     bp
        ret
c_endp GetDefaultCaptureFlags

endcode prtlib
end
```

NetTest.Cpp

```
#include <stdio.h>
#include <stream.hpp>

#include "netprt.hpp"

main()
{
        captureBuffer buffer;

        buffer.StartCapture();

        cprn << "Hi mom!\n";

        buffer.EndCapture();

}
```

Exercises

1. Study the sample program. Follow the execution before you run the program. You may have to modify the code for your C++ compiler. Get the program running.

2. Build more functionality into the program by allowing the flags to be changed. Don't allow the program to change them directly; rather, create public functions to access the private data.

3. Use derived classes; make captureBuffer the base class and create a new one derived from it. If you compiler supports it, create a program that uses multiple inheritance.

4. Create a new stream call netprt and overload the << operator. Programs should be able to redirect information to netprt and have it come out on the network printer.

5. List the output of the linker, the MAP file to see how the name-mangling works and how the functions are named.

6. Create default arguments for the captureBuffer class functions, including the constructor. Having default arguments for the constructor might allow you to declare an instance of the captureBuffer class and set the network printer number and possibly some flags, but give them default values.

Appendix A

Function Calls

Abort Sending Packets (04h) (Diagnostic Services API)

This call is supported in Advanced NetWare version 2.1 and will be supported in Novell's Network Management module.

Request Packet (44 bytes):

Offset	Content	Type
0	SPX Packet Header	BYTE[42]
42	Component Position	BYTE
43	04h	BYTE

Reply Packet
None

The NetWare C Interface format is:

```
void AbortSendingPackets( WORD connectionID, BYTE componentNumber );
```

Abort Servicing Queue Job and File (E3h 73h) (Queue Services API)

This call is supported in Advanced NetWare version 2.1, NetWare 386, and later versions.

Registers in:

AH	E3h
DS:SI	Request Packet Address
ES:DI	Reply Buffer Address

Registers out:

AL	Completion Code

Completion Codes:

00h	Successful
96h	Server Out Of Memory
D0h	Q Error
D1h	No Queue
D6h	No Job Rights
D9h	Stn Not Server

Request Packet (9 bytes):

Offset	Content	Type	Order
0	Request Packet Length-2	WORD	lo-hi
2	73h	BYTE	
3	Queue ID	LONG	hi-lo
7	Job Number	WORD	hi-lo

Reply Packet (2 bytes):

Offset	Content	Type	Order
0	0000h	WORD	lo-hi

The NetWare C Interface format is:

```
int AbortServicingQueueJobAndFile( long queueID, WORD jobNumber,
   int fileHandle );
```

Add Bindery Object To Set (E3h 41h) (Bindery Services API)

This call is supported in Advanced NetWare versions 1.0, 1.02, 2.0 and 2.1, and in NetWare 386 and later versions.

Registers in:

AH	E3h
DS:SI	Request Buffer Length
ES:DI	Reply Buffer Length

Registers out:

AL	Completion Code

Completion Codes:

00	Success
96h	Server Out Of Memory
E9h	Member Already Exists
EBh	Not Group Property
F0h	Wildcard Not Allowed
F8h	No Property Write Privileges
FCh	No Such Object
FEh	Server Bindery Locked
FFh	Bindery Failure

Request Packet (max size = 119 bytes):

Offset	Content	Type	Order
0	Request Buffer Length-2	WORD	lo-hi
2	41h	BYTE	
3	Object Type	WORD	hi-lo

5	Object Name Length	BYTE [1-47]	
6	Object Name	BYTE[LENGTH]	
?	Property Name Length	BYTE [1-15]	
?	Property Name	BYTE[*LENGTH*]	
?	Member Object Type	WORD	hi-lo
?	Member Name Length	BYTE [1-47]	
?	Member Name	BYTE[*LENGTH*]	

Reply Packet (2 bytes):

Offset	Content	Type	Order
0	0000	WORD	lo-hi

The NetWare C Interface format is:

```
int AddBinderyObjectToSet( char *objectName, WORD objectType,
    char *propertyName, char *memberName, WORD memberType );
```

AFP Alloc Temporary Directory Handle (23h 0Bh) (AppleTalk Filing Protocol Services API)

This call is supported in Advanced NetWare version 2.1, NetWare 386, and later versions.

Registers in:

AL	23h
DS:SI	Request Buffer Address
CX	Request Buffer Length
ES:DI	Reply Buffer Address
DX	Reply Buffer Length
AH	0Bh

Registers out:

AL	Completion Code

Completion codes:

00h	Successful
9Ch	Invalid Path

Request Buffer (maximum buffer length = 264 bytes):

Offset	Content	Type	Order
0	Request Buffer Length-2	WORD	lo-hi
2	0Bh	BYTE	
3	Volume Number	BYTE	
4	AFP Entry ID	LONG	hi-lo
8	AFP Directory Path Length	BYTE	
9	AFP Directory Path	BYTE[*LENGTH*]	

Reply Buffer (2 bytes):

Offset	Content	Type	Order
0	NetWare Directory Handle	BYTE	
1	Access Rights	BYTE	

The NetWare C Interface format is:

```
int AFPAllocTemporaryDirHandle( WORD connectionID, int volumeNum,
   long AFPEntryID, char *AFPPathString, BYTE *NetWareDirectoryHandle,
   BYT *accessRights );
```

AFP Create Directory (23h 01h) (AppleTalk Filing Protocol Services API)

This call is supported in Advanced NetWare version 2.1, NetWare 386, and later versions.

Registers in:

AL	23h
DS:SI	Request Buffer Address
CX	Request Buffer Length
ES:DI	Reply Buffer Address
DX	Reply Buffer Length
AH	01h

Registers out:

AL	Completion Code

Completion codes:

0h	Successful
9Ch	Invalid Path

Request Buffer (maximum buffer length = 297 bytes):

Offset	Content	Type	Order
0	Request Buffer Length	WORD	lo-hi
2	01h	BYTE	
3	Volume Number	BYTE	
4	AFP Entry ID	LONG	hi-lo
8	Reserved	BYTE	
9	Finder Information	BYTE[32]	
41	AFP Directory Path Length	BYTE (1-255)	
42	AFP Directory Path	BYTE[*LENGTH*]	

Reply Buffer (4 bytes)

Offset	Content	Type	Order
0	New AFP Entry ID	LONG	hi-lo

The NetWare C Interface format is:

```
int AFPCreateDirectory( WORD connectionID, int volumeNum,
   long AFPEntryID, BYTE *finderInfo, char *AFPPathString,
   long *newAFPEntryID );
```

AFP Create File (23h 02h) (AppleTalk Filing Protocol Services API)

This call is supported in Advanced NetWare version 2.1, NetWare 386, and later versions.

Registers in:

AL	23h
DS:SI	Request Buffer Address
CX	Request Buffer Length
ES:DI	Reply Buffer Address
DX	Reply Buffer Length
AH	02h

Registers out:

AL	Completion Code

Completion codes:

00h	Successful
9Ch	Invalid Path

Request Buffer (maximum buffer length = 297 bytes):

Offset	Content	Type	Order
0	Request Buffer Length - 2	WORD	lo-hi
2	02h	BYTE	
3	Volume Number	BYTE	
4	AFP Entry ID	LONG	hi-lo
8	Delete Existing File	BYTE	
9	Finder Information	BYTE[32]	
41	AFP File Path Length	BYTE	
42	AFP File Path	BYTE[*LENGTH*]	

Reply Buffer (4 bytes):

Offset	Content	Type	Order
0	New AFP Entry ID	LONG	hi-lo

The NetWare C Interface format is:

```
int AFPCreateFile( WORD connectionID, int volumeNum, long AFPEntryID,
  BYTE deleteExistingFile, BYTE *finderInfo, char *AFPPathString,
  long *newAFPEntryID );
```

AFP Delete (23h 03h) (AppleTalk Filing Protocol Services API)

This call is supported in Advanced NetWare version 2.1, NetWare 386, and later versions.

Registers in:

AL	23h
DS:SI	Request Buffer Address
CX	Request Buffer Length
AH	03h

Registers out:

AL	Completion Code

Request Buffer (maximum buffer length = 264 bytes):

Offset	Content	Type	Order
0	Request Buffer Length -2	WORD	lo-hi
2	03h	BYTE	
3	Volume Number	BYTE	
4	AFP Directory/File Path Length	BYTE	
5	AFP Directory/File Path	BYTE[*LENGTH*]	

Reply Buffer

none

Completion codes:

00h	Successful
9Ch	Invalid Path

The NetWare C Interface format is:

```
int AFPDelete( WORD connectionID, int volumeNum, long AFPEntryID,
   char *AFPPathString );
```

AFP Get Entry ID From Name (23h 04h) (AppleTalk Filing Protocol Services API)

This call is supported in Advanced NetWare version 2.1, NetWare 386, and later versions.

Registers in:

AL	23h
DS:SI	Request Buffer Address
CX	Request Buffer Length
ES:DI	Reply Buffer Address

DX	Reply Buffer Length
AH	04h

Registers out:

AL	Completion Code

Request Buffer (maximum buffer length = 264 bytes):

Offset	Content	Type	Order
0	Request Buffer Length - 2	WORD	lo-hi
2	04h	BYTE	
3	Volume Number	BYTE	
4	AFP Entry ID	LONG	hi-lo
8	AFP Directory/File Path Length	BYTE	
9	AFP Directory/File Path	BYTE[*LENGTH*]	

Reply Buffer (4 bytes):

Offset	Content	Type	Order
0	New AFP Entry ID	LONG	hi-lo

Completion codes:

00h	Successful
9Ch	Invalid Path

The NetWare C Interface format is:

```
int GetAFPEntryIDFromName( WORD connectionID, int volumeNum,
    long AFPEntryID, char *AFPPathString, long *newAFPEntryID );
```

AFP Get Entry ID From NetWare Handle (23h 06h) (AppleTalk Filing Protocol Services API)

This call is supported in Advanced NetWare version 2.1, NetWare 386, and later versions.

Registers in:

AL	23h
DS:SI	Request Buffer Address
CX	Request Buffer Length
ES:DI	Reply Buffer Address
DX	Reply Buffer Length
AH	06h

Registers out:

AL	Completion Code

Completion codes:

00h	Successful

Request Buffer (maximum buffer length = 9 bytes):

Offset	Content	Type	Order
0	Request Buffer Length - 2	WORD	lo-hi
2	06h	BYTE	
3	NetWare File Handle	BYTE[6]	

Reply Buffer (8 bytes):

Offset	Content	Type	Order
0	Volume Number	BYTE	
1	AFP Entry ID	LONG	hi-lo
5	Fork Indicator	BYTE	

The NetWare C Interface format is:

```
int AFPGetEntryIDFromNetWareHandle( int NetWareHandle, int volumeNum,
  long *AFPEntryID, BYTE *forkIndicator );
```

AFP Get Entry ID From Path Name (23h 0Ch) (AppleTalk Filing Protocol Services API)

This call is supported in Advanced NetWare version 2.1, NetWare 386, and later versions.

Registers in:

AL	23h
DS:SI	Request Buffer Address
CX	Request Buffer Length
ES:DI	Reply Buffer Address
DX	Reply Buffer Length
AH	0Ch

Registers out:

AL	Completion Code

Completion codes:

00h	Successful
9Ch	Invalid_Path

Request Buffer (maximum buffer length = 260 bytes):

Offset	Content	Type	Order
0	Request Buffer Length - 2	WORD	lo-hi
2	0Ch	BYTE	
3	NetWare Directory Handle	BYTE	

4	NetWare Directory/File Path Length	BYTE
5	NetWare Directory/File Path	BYTE[*LENGTH*]

Reply Buffer (6 bytes):

Offset	Content	Type	Order
0	AFP Entry ID	LONG	hi-lo

The NetWare C Interface format is:

```
int AFPGetEntryIDFromPathName( WORD connectionID,
   BYTE directoryHandle, char *pathName, long *AFPEntryID );
```

AFP Get File Information (23h 05h) (AppleTalk Filing Protocol Services API)

This call is supported in Advanced NetWare version 2.1, NetWare 386, and later versions.

Registers in:

AL	23h
DS:SI	Request Buffer Address
CX	Request Buffer Length
ES:DI	Reply Buffer Address
DX	Reply Buffer Length
AH	05h

Registers out:

AL	Completion Code

Completion codes:

00h	Successful
9Ch	Invalid Path

Request Buffer (maximum buffer length = 266 bytes):

Offset	Content	Type	Order
0	Request Buffer Length - 2	WORD	lo-hi
2	05h	BYTE	
3	Volume Number	BYTE	
4	AFP Entry ID	LONG	hi-lo
8	Request Bit Map	WORD	hi-lo
10	AFP Directory/File Path Length	BYTE	
11	AFP Directory/File Path	BYTE[*LENGTH*]	

Reply Buffer (116 bytes):

Offset	Content	Type	Order
2	AFP Entry ID	LONG	hi-lo
6	AFP Parent Entry ID	LONG	hi-lo
10	Attributes	WORD	hi-lo
12	Data Fork Length	LONG	hi-lo
16	Resource Fork Length	LONG	hi-lo
20	Number of Offspring	WORD	hi-lo
22	Creation Date	WORD	hi-lo
24	Access Date	WORD	hi-lo
26	Modify Date	WORD	hi-lo
28	Modify Time	WORD	hi-lo
30	Backup Date	WORD	hi-lo
32	Backup Time	WORD	hi-lo
34	Finder Information	BYTE[32]	
66	Long Directory/File Name	BYTE[32]	
98	Owner Object ID	LONG	hi-lo
102	Short Directory/File Name	BYTE[12]	
114	Access Rights	WORD	

The NetWare C Interface format is:

```
int AFPGetFileInformation( WORD connectionID, int volumeNum,
    long AFPEntryID, WORD requestBitMap, char *AFPPathString,
    WORD strucSize, AFPFileInfo *AFPFileInfo );
```

AFP Open File Fork (23h 08h)
(AppleTalk Filing Protocol Services API)

This call is supported in Advanced NetWare version 2.1, NetWare 386, and later versions.

Registers in:

AL	23h
DS:SI	Request Buffer Address
CX	Request Buffer Length
ES:DI	Reply Buffer Address
DX	Reply Buffer Length
AH	08h

Registers out:

AL	Completion Code

Completion codes:

00h	Successful
9Ch	Invalid_Path

Request Buffer (maximum buffer length = 266 bytes):

Offset	Content	Type	Order
0	Request Buffer Length -2	WORD	lo-hi
2	08h	BYTE	
3	Volume Number	BYTE	
4	AFP Entry ID	LONG	hi-lo
8	Fork Indicator	BYTE	
9	Access Mode	BYTE	
10	AFP File Path Length	BYTE	
11	AFP File Path	BYTE*[LENGTH]*	

Reply Buffer (14 bytes):

Offset	Content	Type	Order
0	AFP Entry ID	LONG	hi-lo
4	Fork Length	LONG	hi-lo
8	NetWare File Handle	BYTE[6]	

The NetWare C Interface format is:

```
int AFPOpenFileFork( WORD connectionID, int volumeNum,
    long AFPEntryID, BYTE forkIndicator, BYTE accessMode,
    char *AFPPathString, long *fileID, long *forkLength,
    BYTE *NetWareHandle, int *fileHandle );
```

AFP Rename (23h 07h) (AppleTalk Filing Protocol Services API)

This call is supported in Advanced NetWare version 2.1, NetWare 386, and later versions.

Registers in:

AL	23h
DS:SI	Request Buffer Address
CX	Request Buffer Length
ES:DI	Reply Buffer Address
DX	Reply Buffer Length
AH	07h

Registers out:

AL	Completion Code

Completion codes:

00h	Successful
9Ch	Invalid Path

Request Buffer (maximum buffer length = 524 bytes):

Offset	Content	Type	Order
0	Request Buffer Length-2	WORD	lo-hi
2	07h	BYTE	
3	Volume Number	BYTE	
4	Source AFP Entry ID	LONG	hi-lo
8	Destination AFP Entry ID	LONG	hi-lo
12	Source AFP Directory/File Path Length	BYTE	
13	Source AFP Directory/File Path	BYTE[*LENGTH*]	
?	Destination AFP Directory/File Path Length	BYTE	
?	Destination AFP Directory/ File Path	BYTE[*LENGTH*]	

Reply Buffer (2 bytes):

Offset	Content	Type	Order
0	0000h	WORD	lo-hi

The NetWare C Interface format is:

```
int AFPRename( WORD connectionID, int volumeNum,
    long AFPSourceEntryID, long AFPDestEntryID, char *AFPSourcePath,
    char *AFPDestPath );
```

AFP Scan File Information (23h 0Ah) (AppleTalk Filing Protocol Services API)

This call is supported in Advanced NetWare version 2.1, NetWare 386, and later versions.

Registers in:

AL	23h
DS:SI	Request Buffer Address
CX	Request Buffer Length
ES:DI	Reply Buffer Address
DX	Reply Buffer Length
AH	0Ah

Registers out:

AL	Completion Code

Completion codes:

00h	Successful
9Ch	Invalid_Path

ation (23h 09h)
rotocol Services API)

pported in Advanced NetWare version 2.1, NetWare 386, and

23h
Request Buffer Address
Request Buffer Length
Reply Buffer Address
Reply Buffer Length
09h

ut:

Completion Code

n codes:

Successful
Invalid Path

uffer (maximum buffer length = 312 bytes):

Content	Type	Order
Request Buffer Length - 2	WORD	lo-hi
09h	BYTE	
Volume Number	BYTE	
AFP Entry ID	LONG	hi-lo
Request Bit Map	WORD	hi-lo
Attributes	WORD	hi-lo
Creation Date	WORD	hi-lo
Access Date	WORD	hi-lo
Modify Date	WORD	hi-lo
Modify Time	WORD	hi-lo
Backup Date	WORD	hi-lo
Backup Time	WORD	hi-lo
Finder Information	BYTE[32]	
AFP Directory/File Path Length	BYTE	
AFP Directory/File Path	BYTE[*LENGTH*]	

y Buffer (2 bytes):

et	Content	Type	Order
	0000h	WORD	lo-hi

Request Bu

Offset	Co
0	Req
2	0Ah
3	Volu
4	AFP
8	AFP I
12	Desire
14	Search
16	Reques
18	AFP Di
19	AFP Dir

Reply Buffer (118

Offset	Content
0	Request B
2	Responses
4	AFP Entry
8	AFP Parent
12	Attributes
14	Data Fork Le
18	Resource For
22	Number Of O
24	Creation Date
26	Access Date
28	Modify Date
30	Modify Time
32	Backup Date
34	Backup Time
36	Finder Informatio
68	Long Directory/Fi
100	Owner Object ID
104	Short Directory/Fil
116	Access Rights

The NetWare C Interface for

```
int AFPScanFileInformation(
    long AFPEntryID, long *AF
    WORD requestBitMap, char
    AFPFileInfo *AFPScanFileIn
```


AFP Set File Inform (AppleTalk Filing P

This call is su later versions.

Registers in:

AL
DS:SI
CX
ES:DI
DX
AH

Registers o

AL

Completio

00h
9Ch

Request I

Offset	C
0	
2	
3	
4	
8	
10	
12	
14	
16	
18	
20	
22	
24	
56	
57	

Repl

Offs
0

The NetWare C Interface format is:

```
int AFPSetFileInformation( WORD connectionID, int volumeNum,
   long AFPEntryID, WORD requestBitMap, char *AFPPathString,
   WORD strucSize, AFPSETINFO *AFPSetInfo );
```

Allocate Segment (00h) (Value-Added Process Services API)

This call is supported in Advanced NetWare version 2.1.

Registers in:

AX	Segment Size
DI	00h

Registers out:

AX	Segment Value

The NetWare C Interface format is:

```
int AllocateSegment( int segmentSize );
```

Attach To File Server (F1h 00h) (Connection Services API)

This call is supported in Advanced NetWare versions 1.0, 1.02, 2.0 and 2.1, and in NetWare 386 and later versions.

Registers in:

AH	F1h
AL	00h
DL	Server Connection ID (1 to 8)

Registers out:

AL	Completion Code

Completion codes:

00h	Successful
F8h	Already Attached To Server
F9h	No Free Connection Slots at Server
FAh	No More Server Slots
FCh	Unknown File Server
FEh	Server Bindery Locked
FFh	No Response From Server (Server Address Illegal)

The NetWare C Interface format is:

```
int AttachToFileServer( char *serverName, WORD *connectionID );
```

Attach Queue Server To Queue (E3h 6Fh) (Queue Services API)

This call is supported in Advanced NetWare version 2.1, NetWare 386, and later versions.

Registers in:

AH	E3h
DS:SI	Request Buffer Address
ES:DI	Reply Buffer Address

Registers out:

AL	Completion Code

Completion Codes:

00h	Successful
96h	Server Out Of Memory
9Ch	Invalid Path
D0h	Queue Error
D1h	No Queue
D3h	No Queue Rights
DAh	Queue Halted
DBh	Max Queue Servers
FEh	Server Bindery Locked
FFh	Bindery Failure
	No Such Property
	No Such Member

Request Packet (7 bytes):

Offset	**Content**	**Type**	**Order**
0	Request Buffer Length-2	WORD	lo-hi
2	6Fh	BYTE	
3	Queue ID	LONG	hi-lo

Reply Packet (2 bytes):

Offset	**Content**	**Type**	**Order**
0	0000h	WORD	lo-hi

The NetWare C Interface format is:

```
int AttachQueueServerToQueue( long queueID );
```

Begin Logical File Locking (C8h) (Locking API)

This call is supported in NetWare versions 4.0 and 4.6, in Advanced NetWare versions 1.0, 1.02, 2.0 and 2.1, and in NetWare 386.

Under lock mode 0, the compatibility mode:

Registers in:

AH	C8h
DL	Mode (0 = No Wait, 1 = Wait)

Registers out:

AL	Completion Code

Completion Codes:

00h	Success
FFh	Failure

Under lock mode 1, the extended mode:

Registers in:

AH	C8h
BP	Timeout Limit (in 1/18th seconds, 0 = no wait)

Registers out:

AL	Completion Code

Completion Codes:

00h	Success
FEh	Timeout Failure
FFh	Failure

The NetWare C Interface format is not supported.

Broadcast To Console (E1h 09h) (Message Services API)

This call is supported in NetWare versions 4.0 and 4.6, in Advanced NetWare versions 1.0, 1.02, 2.0, and 2.1, and in NetWare 386; but will not be supported in NetWare 386 versions dated after 1990.

Registers in:

AH	E1h
DS:SI	Request Buffer Address
ES:DI	Reply Buffer Address

Registers out:

AL	Completion Code

Completion codes:

00h	Successful
FCh	Message Queue Full
FEh	I/O Failure; Lack Of Dynamic Workspace

Request Buffer (maximum buffer length = 64 bytes):

Offset	**Content**	**Type**	**Order**
0	Request Buffer Length- 2	WORD	lo-hi
2	09h	BYTE	
3	Message Length (1 to 60)	BYTE	
4	Message	BYTE[*LENGTH*]	

Reply Buffer (maximum buffer length = 2 bytes):

Offset	**Content**	**Type**	**Order**
0	0000	WORD	

The NetWare C Interface format is:

```
int BroadcastToConsole( char *message );
```

Calculate Absolute Address (11h) (Value-Added Process Services API)

This call is supported in Advanced NetWare version 2.1.

Registers in:

AX	Offset
BX	Segment
DI	11h

Registers out:

AX	Low Order Word
BL	High Order Byte

The NetWare C Interface format is:

```
long CalculateAbsoluteAddress( WORD segment, WORD offset );
```

Cancel LPT Capture (DFh 02h) (Print Services API)

This call is supported in NetWare versions 4.0 and 4.6, in Advanced NetWare versions 1.0, 1.02, 2.0 and 2.1, and in NetWare 386 and later versions.

Registers In:

AH	DFh
DL	02h

Registers Out:

AL	Completion Code

Completion Codes

00h	Successful

The NetWare C Interface format is:

```
int CancelLPTCapture( void );
```

Cancel Specific LPT Capture (DFh 06h) (Print Services API)

This call is supported in Advanced NetWare version 2.1, and in NetWare 386 and later versions.

Registers In:

AH	DFh
DL	06h
DH	LPT Device (0 = LPT1, 1 = LPT2, 2 = LPT3)

Registers Out:

AL	Completion Code

Completion Codes

00h	Successful

The NetWare C Interface format is:

```
int CancelSpecificLPTCapture( BYTE LPTDevice );
```

Change Bindery Object Password (E3h 40h) (Bindery Services API)

This call is supported in Advanced NetWare versions 1.0, 1.02, 2.0 and 2.1, and in NetWare 386 and later versions.

Registers in:

AH	E3h
DS:SI	Request Buffer Length
ES:DI	Reply Buffer Length

Registers out:

AL	Completion Code

Completion Codes:

00	Success
96h	Server Out Of Memory
F0h	Wildcard Not Allowed
FBh	No Such Property
FCh	No Such Object
FEh	Server Bindery Locked
FFh	No Such Object No Password Associated with Object or Old Password Invalid

Request Packet (max size = 309 bytes):

Offset	Content	Type	Order
0	Request Buffer Length-2	WORD	lo-hi
2	40h	BYTE	
3	Object Type	WORD	hi-lo
5	Object Name Length	BYTE [1-47]	
6	Object Name	BYTE[*LENGTH*]	
?	Old Password Length	BYTE [0-127]	
?	Old Password	BYTE[*LENGTH*]	
?	New Password Length	BYTE [0-127]	
?	New Password	BYTE[*LENGTH*]	

Reply Packet (2 bytes):

Offset	Content	Type	Order
0	0000	WORD	lo-hi

The NetWare C Interface format is:

```
int ChangeBinderyObjectPassword( char *objectName, WORD objectType,
  char *oldPassword, char *newPassword );
```

Change Bindery Object Security (E3h 38h) (Bindery Services API)

This call is supported in Advanced NetWare versions 1.0, 1.02, 2.0 and 2.1, and in NetWare 386 and later versions.

Registers in:

AH	E3h
DS:SI	Request Buffer Length
ES:DI	Reply Buffer Length

Registers out:

AL	Completion Code

Completion Codes:

00	Success
96h	Server Out Of Memory
F0h	Wildcard Not Allowed
F1h	Invalid Bindery Security
FCh	No Such Object
FEh	Server Bindery Locked
FFh	Bindery Failure

Request Packet (max size = 54 bytes):

Offset	**Content**	**Type**	**Order**
0	Request Buffer Length-2	WORD	lo-hi
2	38h	BYTE	
3	New Object Security	BYTE	
4	Object Type	WORD	hi-lo
6	Object Name Length	BYTE [1-47]	
7	Object Name	BYTE[*LENGTH*]	

Reply Packet (2 bytes):

Offset	**Content**	**Type**	**Order**
0	0000	WORD	lo-hi

The NetWare C Interface format is:

```
int ChangeBinderyObjectSecurity( char *objectName, WORD objectType,
  BYTE newObjectSecurity );
```

Change Password (E3h 01h) (Workstation Environment Services API)

This call is supported in NetWare versions 4.0 and 4.6, in Advanced NetWare versions 1.0, 1.02, 2.0 and 2.1, and in NetWare 386. It has been replaced by higher-level Bindery Services API calls such as Change Bindery Object Password, but is shown here for completeness.

Registers in:

AH	E3h
DS:SI	Address of Request buffer
ES:DI	Address of Reply buffer

Registers out:

AL	Completion Code

Completion codes:

00h	Successful

Request Packet (maximum buffer length = 307 bytes):

Offset	Content	Type	Order
0	Request Buffer Length-2	WORD	lo-hi
2	01h	BYTE	
3	User Name Length (1 to 47)	BYTE	
4	User Name	BYTE[*LENGTH*]	
?	User Password Length	BYTE (0-127)	
?	User Password	BYTE[LENGTH]	
?	User New Password Length	BYTE (0-127)	
?	User New Password	BYTE[*LENGTH*]	

Reply Buffer (2 bytes):

Offset	Content	Type	Order
0	0000h	WORD	lo-hi

The NetWare C Interface format is not supported.

Change Process (09h) (Value-Added Process Services API)

This call is supported in Advanced NetWare version 2.1.

Registers in:

DI	09h

The NetWare C Interface format is:

```
void ChangeProcess( void );
```

Change Property Security (E3h 3Bh) (Bindery Services API)

This call is supported in Advanced NetWare versions 1.0, 1.02, 2.0 and 2.1, and in NetWare 386 and later versions.

Registers in:

AH	E3h
DS:SI	Request Buffer Length
ES:DI	Reply Buffer Length

Registers out:

AL	Completion Code

Completion Codes:

00	Success
96h	Server Out Of Memory
F0h	Wildcard Not Allowed
F1h	Invalid Bindery Security
FBh	No Such Property
FCh	No Such Object
FEh	Server Bindery Locked
FFh	Bindery Failure

Request Packet (max size = 70 bytes):

Offset	Content	Type	Order
0	Request Buffer Length-2	WORD	lo-hi
2	3Bh	BYTE	
3	Object Type	WORD	hi-lo
5	Object Name Length	BYTE [1-47]	
6	Object Name	BYTE[*LENGTH*]	
?	New Property Security	BYTE	
?	Property Name Length	BYTE [1-15]	
?	Property Name	BYTE[*LENGTH*]	

Reply Packet (2 bytes):

Offset	Content	Type	Order
0	0000	WORD	lo-hi

The NetWare C Interface format is:

```
int ChangePropertySecurity( char *objectName, WORD objectType,
   char *propertyName, BYTE newPropertySecurity );
```

Change Queue Job Entry (E3h 6Dh) (Queue Services API)

This call is supported in Advanced NetWare version 2.1, NetWare 386, and later versions.

Registers in:

AH	E3h
DS:SI	Request Buffer Address
ES:DI	Reply Buffer Address

Registers out:

AL	Completion Code

Completion Codes:

00h	Success
96h	Server Out of Memory
D0h	Queue Error
D1h	No Queue
D5h	No Queue Job
D7h	Queue Servicing
FEh	Server Bindery Locked
FFh	Bindery Failure

Request Packet (263 bytes):

Offset	Content	Type	Order
0	Request Buffer Length-2	WORD	lo-hi
2	6Dh	BYTE	
3	Queue ID	LONG	hi-lo
7	Client Station	BYTE	
8	Client Task Number	BYTE	
9	Client ID Number	LONG	
13	Target Server ID Number	LONG	hi-lo
17	Target Execution Time	BYTE[6]	
23	Job Entry Time	BYTE[6]	
29	Job Number	WORD	hi-lo
31	Job Type	WORD	hi-lo
33	Job Position	BYTE	
34	Job Control Flags	BYTE	
35	Job File Name	BYTE[14]	
49	Job File Handle	BYTE[6]	
55	Server Station	BYTE	
56	Server Task Number	BYTE	
57	Server ID Number	LONG	
61	Text Job Description	BYTE[50]	
111	Client Record Area	BYTE[152]	

Reply Packet (2 bytes):

Offset	Content	Type	Order
0	0000h	WORD	lo-hi

The NetWare C Interface format is:

```
int ChangeQueueJobEntry( long queueID, JobStruct *job );
```

Change Queue Job Position (E3h 6Eh) (Queue Services API)

This call is supported in Advanced NetWare version 2.1, NetWare 386, and later versions.

Registers in:

AH	E3h
DS:SI	Request Buffer Address
ES:DI	Reply Buffer Address

Registers out:

AL	Completion Code

Completion Codes:

00h	Successful
96h	Server Out Of Memory
D0h	Queue Error
D1h	No Queue
D5h	No Queue Job
D6h	No Job Rights
FEh	Server Bindery Locked
FFh	Bindery Failure

Request Packet (10 bytes):

Offset	**Content**	**Type**	**Order**
0	Request Buffer Length-2	WORD	lo-hi
2	6Eh	BYTE	
3	Queue ID	LONG	hi-lo
7	Job Number	WORD	hi-lo
9	New Position	BYTE	

Reply Packet (2 bytes):

Offset	**Content**	**Type**	**Order**
0	0000h	WORD	lo-hi

The NetWare C Interface format is:

```
int ChangeQueueJobPosition( long queueID, WORD jobNumber,
   BYTE newPosition );
```

Change Segment To Code (02h) (Value-Added Process Services API)

This call is supported in Advanced NetWare version 2.1.

Registers in:

AX	Segment Value
DI	02h

The NetWare C Interface format is not supported.

Change Segment To Data (01h) (Value-Added Process Services API)

This call is supported in Advanced NetWare version 2.1.

Registers in:

AX	Segment Value
DI	01h

The NetWare C Interface format is:

```
int ChangeSegmentToData( WORD segment );
```

Change To Client Rights (E3h 74h) (Queue Services API)

This call is supported in Advanced NetWare version 2.1, NetWare 386, and later versions.

Registers in:

AH	E3h
DS:SI	Request Packet Address
ES:DI	Reply Buffer Address

Registers out:

AL	Completion Code

Request Packet (9 bytes):

Offset	Content	Type	Order
O	Request Packet Length-2	WORD	lo-hi
2	74h	BYTE	
3	Queue Object ID	LONG	hi-lo
7	Job Number	WORD	hi-lo

Reply Packet (2 bytes):

Offset	Content	Type	Order
0	0000h	WORD	lo-hi

Completion Codes

00h	Successful
96h	Server Out Of Memory
D0h	Q Error
D1h	No Queue
D6h	No Job Rights
D9h	Stn Not Server

The NetWare C Interface format is:

```
int ChangeToClientRights( long queueID, WORD jobNumber );
```

Check Console Privileges (E3h C8h) (File Server Environment Services API)

This call is supported in Advanced NetWare version 2.1, NetWare 386, and later versions.

Registers in:

AH	E3h
DS:SI	Request Buffer Address
ES:DI	Reply Buffer Address

Registers out:

AL	Completion Code

Completion codes:

00h	Successful
C6h	No Console Rights

Request Buffer (3 bytes):

Offset	Content	Type	Order
0	Request Buffer Length - 2	WORD	lo-hi
2	C8h	BYTE	

Reply Buffer (2 bytes):

Offset	Content	Type	Order
0	0000h	WORD	lo-hi

The NetWare C Interface format is:

```
int CheckConsolePrivileges( void );
```

Check Pipe Status (E1h 08h) (Message Services API)

This call is supported in NetWare versions 4.0 and 4.6, in Advanced NetWare versions 1.0, 1.02, 2.0, and 2.1, and in NetWare 386; but will not be supported in NetWare 386 versions dated after 1990.

Registers in:

AH	E1h
DS:SI	Request Buffer Address
ES:DI	Reply Buffer Address

Registers out:

AL	Completion Code

Completion codes:

00h	Successful

Request Buffer (maximum buffer length = 104 bytes):

Offset	Content	Type	Order
0	Request Buffer Length - 2	WORD	lo-hi
2	08h	BYTE	
3	Connection Count(1 to 100)	BYTE	
4	Connection List	BYTE[*COUNT*]	

Reply Buffer (maximum buffer length = 103 bytes):

Offset	Content	Type	Order
0	Reply Buffer Length - 2	WORD	lo-hi
2	Connection Count(1 to 100)	BYTE	
3	Pipe Status List	BYTE[*COUNT*]	

The NetWare C Interface format is:

```
int CheckPipeStatus( WORD *connectionList, BYTE *resultList,
   WORD connectionCount );
```

Clear Connection Number (E3h D2h) (File Server Environment Services API)

This call is supported in Advanced NetWare version 2.1, NetWare 386, and later versions.

Registers in:

AH	E3h
DS:SI	Request Buffer Address
ES:DI	Reply Buffer Address

Registers out:

AL	Completion Code

Completion code:

00h	Successful
C6h	No Console Rights

Request Buffer (4 bytes):

Offset	Content	Type	Order
0	Request Buffer Length - 2	WORD	lo-hi
2	D2h	BYTE	
3	Connection Number	BYTE	

Reply Buffer (2 bytes):

Offset	Content	Type	Order
0	0000h	WORD	lo-hi

The NetWare C Interface format is:

```
int ClearConnectionNumber( WORD connectionNumber );
```

Clear File (CEh) (FCB) (Locking API)

This call is supported in NetWare versions 4.0 and 4.6, in Advanced NetWare versions 1.0, 1.02, 2.0 and 2.1, and in NetWare 386. It will not be supported after 1990.

Registers in:

AH	CEh
DS:DX	Address of File Control Block

Registers out:

AL	Completion Code

Completion Codes:

00h	Success
FFh	Failure

The NetWare C Interface format is not supported.

Clear File (EDh) (ASCIIZ) (Locking API)

This call is supported in NetWare version 4.6, in Advanced NetWare versions 1.0, 1.02, 2.0 and 2.1, and in NetWare 386 and later versions.

Registers in:

AH	EDh
DS:DX	Request Buffer Address

Registers out:

AL	Completion Code

Completion Codes:

00h	Success
FFh	No Files Found

The NetWare C Interface format is:

```
int ClearFile( char *fileName );
```

Clear File Set (CFh) (Locking API)

This call is supported in NetWare versions 4.0 and 4.6, in Advanced NetWare versions 1.0, 1.02, 2.0 and 2.1, and in NetWare 386 and later versions.

Registers in:

AH	CFh

Registers out:
none

The NetWare C Interface format is:

```
void ClearFileSet( void );
```

Clear Logical Record (D4h) (Locking API)

This call is supported in NetWare versions 4.0 and 4.6, in Advanced NetWare versions 1.0, 1.02, 2.0 and 2.1, and in NetWare 386 and later versions.

Registers in:

AH	D4h
DS:DX	Request Buffer Address

Registers out:

AL	Completion Code

Completion Codes:

00	Success
FFh	No Record Found

Request Packet:

Logical Record Name Length(1-99)	BYTE
Logical Record Name	BYTE[*LENGTH*]

The NetWare C Interface format is:

```
int ClearLogicalRecord( char *logicalRecordName );
```

Clear Logical Record Set (D5h) (Locking API)

This call is supported in NetWare versions 4.0 and 4.6, in Advanced NetWare versions 1.0, 1.02, 2.0 and 2.1, and in NetWare 386 and later versions.

Registers in:

AH	D5h

Registers out:
none

The NetWare C Interface format is:

```
void ClearLogicalRecordSet( void );
```

Clear Physical Record (BEh) (Handle) (Locking API)

This call is supported in NetWare version 4.6, in Advanced NetWare versions 1.0, 1.02, 2.0 and 2.1, and in NetWare 386 and later versions.

Registers in:

AH	BEh
BX	File Handle
CX	High Record Offset
DX	Low Record Offset
SI	High Record Length
DI	Low Record Length

Registers out:

AL	Completion Code

Completion Codes:

00	Success
FFh	No Locked Record Found

The NetWare C Interface format is:

```
int ClearPhysicalRecord( int fileHandle, long recordStartOffset,
   long recordLength );
```

Clear Physical Record (C1h) (FCB) (Locking API)

This call is supported in NetWare version 4.6, in Advanced NetWare versions 1.0, 1.02, 2.0 and 2.1, and in NetWare 386.

Registers in:

AH	C1h
BX	High Record Offset
CX	Low Record Offset
DS:DX	Address of opened FCB (non-extended)

Registers out:

AL	Completion Code

Completion Codes:

00	Success
FFh	Invalid Record

The NetWare C Interface format is not supported.

Clear Physical Record Set (C4h) (Locking API)

This call is supported in NetWare version 4.6, in Advanced NetWare versions 1.0, 1.02, 2.0 and 2.1, and in NetWare 386 and later versions.

Registers in:

AH	C4h

Registers out:
none

The NetWare C Interface format is:

```
void ClearPhysicalRecordSet( void );
```

Clear Screen (00h) (Value-Added Process Services API)

This call is supported in Advanced NetWare version 2.1.

Registers in:

DI	00h

The NetWare C Interface format is:

```
void ClearScreen( void );
```

Close and Queue Capture File (E0h 01h) (Print Services API)

This call is supported in NetWare versions 4.0 and 4.6, in Advanced NetWare versions 1.0, 1.02, 2.0 and 2.1, and in NetWare 386. It has been replaced by higher-level functions, but is shown here for completeness.

Registers In:

AH	E0h
DS:SI	Request Buffer
ES:DI	Reply Buffer

Registers Out:

AL	Completion Code

Completion Codes

00h	Successful

Request Packet (4 bytes):

Offset	Content	Type	Order
0	Request Buffer Length-2	WORD	lo-hi
2	01h	BYTE	
3	Abort Flag	BYTE	

Reply Packet (2 bytes):

Offset	Content	Type	Order
0	0000	WORD	lo-hi

The NetWare C Interface format is not supported.

Close Bindery (E3h 44h) (Bindery Services API)

This call is supported in Advanced NetWare versions 1.0, 1.02, 2.0 and 2.1, and in NetWare 386 and later versions.

Registers in:

AH	E3h
DS:SI	Request Buffer Length
ES:DI	Reply Buffer Length

Registers out:

AL	Completion Code

Completion Codes:

00	Success

Request Packet (max size = 3 bytes):

Offset	Content	Type	Order
0	Request Buffer Length-2	WORD	lo-hi
2	44h	BYTE	

Reply Packet (2 bytes):

Offset	Content	Type	Order
0	0000	WORD	lo-hi

The NetWare C Interface format is:

```
int CloseBindery( void );
```

Close File and Start Queue Job (E3h 69h) (Queue Services API)

This call is supported in Advanced NetWare version 2.1, NetWare 386, and later versions.

Registers in:

AH	E3h
DS:SI	Request Buffer Address
ES:DI	Request Buffer Address

Registers out:

AL	Completion Code

Completion Codes:

00h	Success
96h	Server Out of Memory
D0h	Q Error
D1h	No Queue
D3h	No Q Rights
D5h	No Q Job
D6h	No Job Rights
FEh	Server Bindery Locked
FFh	Bindery Failure

Request Packet (9 bytes):

Offset	Content	Type	Order
0	Request Buffer Length-2	WORD	lo-hi
2	69h	BYTE	
3	Queue ID	LONG	hi-lo
7	Job Number	WORD	hi-lo

Reply Packet (2 bytes):

Offset	Content	Type	Order
0	0000h	WORD	lo-hi

The NetWare C Interface format is:

```
int CloseFileAndStartQueueJob( long queueID, WORD jobNumber,
   int fileHandle );
```

Close Message Pipe (E1h 07h) (Message Services API)

This call is supported in NetWare versions 4.0 and 4.6, in Advanced NetWare versions 1.0, 1.02, 2.0, and 2.1, and in NetWare 386; but will not be supported in NetWare 386 versions dated after 1990.

Registers in:

AH	E1h
DS:SI	Request Buffer Address
ES:DI	Reply Buffer Address

Registers out:

AL	Completion Code

Completion codes:

00h	Successful
FCh	Message Queue Full
FEh	I/O Failure; Lack Of Dynamic Workspace

Request Buffer (maximum buffer length = 104 bytes):

Offset	**Content**	**Type**	**Order**
0	Request Buffer Length - 2	WORD	lo-hi
2	07h	BYTE	
3	Connection Count(1 to 100)	BYTE	
4	Connection List	BYTE[*COUNT*]	

Reply Buffer (maximum buffer length = 103 bytes):

Offset	**Content**	**Type**	**Order**
0	Reply Buffer Length - 2	WORD	lo-hi
2	Connection Count (1 to 100)	BYTE	
3	Result List	BYTE[*COUNT*]	

The NetWare C Interface format is:

```
int CloseMessagePipe( WORD *connectionList, BYTE *resultList,
   WORD connectionCount );
```

Close Semaphore (C5h 04h) (Locking API)

This call is supported in NetWare version 4.6, in Advanced NetWare versions 1.0, 1.02, 2.0 and 2.1, and in NetWare 386 and later versions.

Registers In:

AH	C5h
AL	04h
CX,DX	Semaphore Handle

Registers Out:

AL	Completion Code

Completion Codes

00h	Successful
FFh	Invalid Semaphore Handle

The NetWare C Interface format is:

```
int CloseSemaphore( long semaphoreHandle );
```

Console Display (05h) (Value-Added Process Services API)

This call is supported in Advanced NetWare version 2.1.

Registers in:

DS:SI	Message
DI	05h

The NetWare C Interface format is:

```
void ConsoleDisplay( char *message );
```

Console Error (04h) (Value-Added Process Services API)

This call is supported in Advanced NetWare version 2.1.

Registers in:

DS:SI	Message
DI	04h

The NetWare C Interface format is:

```
void ConsoleError( char *message );
```

Console Message (03h) (Value-Added Process Services API)

This call is supported in Advanced NetWare version 2.1.

Registers in:

DS:SI	Message
DI	03h

This call may result in process rescheduling.
The NetWare C Interface format is:

```
void ConsoleMessage( char *message );
```

Console Query (06h) (Value-Added Process Services API)

This call is supported in Advanced NetWare version 2.1.

Registers in:

DS:SI	Prompt
DI	06h

Registers out:

AX	Completion Code

Completion Codes

00h	NO Response
FFh	YES Response

The NetWare C Interface format is:

```
int ConsoleQuery( char *prompt );
```

Console Read (07h) (Value-Added Process Services API)

This call is supported in Advanced NetWare version 2.1.

Registers in:

DS:SI	Prompt
ES:BX	Input Buffer
DL	Input Buffer Length
DI	07h

Registers out:

AX	Input String Length

The NetWare C Interface format is:

```
int ConsoleRead( char *prompt, char *inputBuffer, BYTE bufferLength );
```

Convert Novell Handle to DOS (B4h) (AppleTalk Filing Protocol Services API)

Registers in:

B4	E3h
DS:SI	Request Buffer Address
ES:DI	Reply Buffer Address

Registers out:
Carry flag set:
AX Completion Code (if no DOS file handle exists)
Carry flag clear:
AL DOS File Handle

Request Buffer (12 bytes):

Offset	Content	Type	Order
0	Connection ID	BYTE	
1	Access Mode	BYTE	
2	NetWare File Handle	BYTE[6]	
8	Fork Size	LONG	hi-lo

Reply Buffer

Offset	Content	Type	Order
0	0000	WORD	lo-hi

The NetWare C Interface format is not supported.

Create Bindery Object (E3h 32h) (Bindery Services API)

This call is supported in Advanced NetWare versions 1.0, 1.02, 2.0 and 2.1, and in NetWare 386 and later versions.

Registers in:
AH E3h
DS:SI Request Buffer Length
ES:DI Reply Buffer Length

Registers out:
AL Completion Code

Completion Codes:
00 Success
96h Server Out Of Memory
EEh Object Already Exists
EFh Invalid Name
F1h Invalid Bindery Security
F5h No Object Create Privileges
FEh Server Bindery Locked
FFh Bindery Failure

Request Packet (max size = 55 bytes):

Offset	Content	Type	Order
0	Request Buffer Length-2	WORD	lo-hi
2	32h	BYTE	
3	Object Flag	BYTE	
4	Object Security	BYTE	
5	Object Type	WORD	hi-lo
6	Object Name Length	BYTE [1-47]	
7	Object Name	BYTE[*LENGTH*]	

Reply Packet (2 bytes):

Offset	Content	Type	Order
0	0000	WORD	lo-hi

The NetWare C Interface format is:

```
int CreateBinderyObject( char *objectName, WORD objectType,
   BYTE objectFlag, BYTE objectSecurity );
```

Create Process (18h) (Value-Added Process Services API)

This call is supported in Advanced NetWare version 2.1.

Registers in:

AX	Connection Flag
BX	Code Segment
CX	Instruction Pointer
DX	Data Segment
DI	18h

Registers out:

AX	Process ID

The NetWare C Interface format is:

```
int CreateProcess( WORD connectionFlag, void (*)()codePtr,
   WORD dataSegment, WORD header );
```

Create Property (E3h 39h) (Bindery Services API)

This call is supported in Advanced NetWare versions 1.0, 1.02, 2.0 and 2.1, and in NetWare 386 and later versions.

Registers in:

AH	E3h
DS:SI	Request Buffer Length
ES:DI	Reply Buffer Length

Registers out:

AL	Completion Code

Completion Codes:

00	Success
96h	Server Out Of Memory
EDh	Property Already Exists
EFh	Invalid Name
F0h	Wildcard Not Allowed
F1h	Invalid Bindery Security
F7h	No Property Create Privileges
FCh	No Such Object
FEh	Server Bindery Locked
FFh	Bindery Failure

Request Packet (max size = 71 bytes):

Offset	Content	Type	Order
0	Request Buffer Length-2	WORD	lo-hi
2	39h	BYTE	
3	Object Type	WORD	hi-lo
5	Object Name Length	BYTE [1-47]	
6	Object Name	BYTE[*LENGTH*]	
?	Property Flags	BYTE	
?	Property Security	BYTE	
?	Property Name Length	BYTE[1..15]	
?	Property Name	BYTE[LENGTH]	

Reply Packet (2 bytes):

Offset	Content	Type	Order
0	0000	WORD	lo-hi

The NetWare C Interface format is:

```
int CreateProperty( char *objectName, WORD objectType,
    char *propertyName, BYTE propertyFlags, BYTE propertySecurity );
```

Create Queue (E3h 64h) (Queue Services API)

This call is supported in Advanced NetWare version 2.1, NetWare 386, and later versions.

Registers in:

AH	E3h
DS:SI	Request Buffer Address
ES:DI	Reply Buffer Address

Registers out:

AL	Completion Code

Completion Codes:

00	Success
96h	Server Out Of Memory
99h	Directory Full
9Bh	Bad Directory Handle
9Ch	Invalid Path
EDh	Property Already Exists
EEh	Object Already Exists
EFh	Invalid Name
F0h	Wildcard Not Allowed
F1h	Invalid Bindery Security
F5h	No Object Create Privilege
F7h	No Property Create Privilege
FCh	No Such Object
FEh	Server Bindery Locked
FFh	Bindery Failure

Request Packet (max = 173 bytes):

Offset	Content	Type	Order
0	Request Buffer Length-2	WORD	lo-hi
2	64h	BYTE	
3	Queue Type	WORD	hi-lo
4	Queue Name Length	BYTE (1-47)	
5	Queue Name	BYTE[*LENGTH*]	
?	Directory Handle	BYTE	
?	Path Name Length	BYTE (1-118)	
?	Path Name	BYTE	

Reply Packet (6 bytes):

Offset	Content	Type	Order
0	Reply Packet Length-2	WORD	lo-hi
2	Queue ID	LONG	hi-lo

The NetWare C Interface format is:

```
int CreateQueue( char *queueName, int queueType, char directoryHandle,
  char *pathName, long *queueID );
```

Create Queue Job and File (E3h 68h) (Queue Services API)

This call is supported in Advanced NetWare version 2.1, NetWare 386, and later versions.

Registers in:

AH	E3h
DS:SI	Request Buffer Address
ES:DI	Request Buffer Address

Registers out:

AL	Completion Code

Completion Codes:

00h	Success
96h	Server Out of Memory
99h	Directory Full
9Ch	Invalid Path
D0h	Q Error
D1h	No Queue
D2h	No Q Server
D3h	No Q Rights
D4h	Q Full
DAh	Q Halted
EDh	Property Already Exists
EFh	Invalid Name
F0h	Wildcard Not Allowed
F1h	Invalid Bindery Security
F7h	No property Create Privilege
FCh	No such Object
FEh	Server Bindery Locked
FFh	Bindery Failure

Request Packet (263 bytes):

Offset	**Content**	**Type**	**Order**
0	Request Buffer Length-2	WORD	lo-hi
2	6Dh	BYTE	
3	Queue ID	LONG	hi-lo
7	Client Station	BYTE	
8	Client Task Number	BYTE	
9	Client ID Number	LONG	
13	Target Server ID Number	LONG	hi-lo
17	Target Execution Time	BYTE[6]	
23	Job Entry Time	BYTE[6]	
29	Job Number	WORD	hi-lo
31	Job Type	WORD	hi-lo
33	Job Position	BYTE	
34	Job Control Flags	BYTE	
35	Job File Name	BYTE[14]	
49	Job File Handle	BYTE[6]	

55	Server Station	BYTE	
56	Server Task Number	BYTE	
57	Server ID Number	LONG	
61	Text Job Description	BYTE[50]	
111	Client Record Area	BYTE[152]	

Reply Packet (56 bytes):

Offset	**Content**	**Type**	**Order**
0	Reply Packet Length-2	WORD	lo-hi
2	Client Station	BYTE	
3	Client Task Number	BYTE	
4	Client ID Number	LONG	hi-lo
8	Target Server ID Number	LONG	hi-lo
12	Target Execution Time	BYTE[6]	
18	Job Entry Time	BYTE[6]	
24	Job Number	WORD	hi-lo
26	Job Type	WORD	hi-lo
28	Job Position	BYTE	
29	Job Control Flags	BYTE	
30	Job File Name	BYTE[14]	
44	Job File Handle	BYTE[6]	
50	Server Station	BYTE	
51	Server Task Number	BYTE	
52	Server ID Number	LONG	hi-lo

The NetWare C Interface format is:

```
int CreateQueueJobAndFile( long queueID, JobStruct *job,
   int *fileHandle );
```

Declare Extended Segment (04h) (Value-Added Process Services API)

This call is supported in Advanced NetWare version 2.1.

Registers in:

AX	Low Order Word
BL	High Order Byte
DI	04h

Registers out:

AX	Segment Value

The NetWare C Interface format is:

```
int DeclareExtendedSegment( WORD low, BYTE high );
```

Declare Segment As Data (03h) (Value-Added Process Services API)

This call is supported in Advanced NetWare version 2.1.

Registers in:

AX	Paragraph
DI	03h

Registers out:

AX Segment Value

The NetWare C Interface format is:

```
int DeclareSegmentAsData( WORD paragraph );
```

Delay Process (0Ah) (Value-Added Process Services API)

This call is supported in Advanced NetWare version 2.1.

Registers in:

DX	Delay
DI	0Ah

The NetWare C Interface format is:

```
void DelayProcess( WORD delay );
```

Delete Bindery Object (E3h 33h) (Bindery Services API)

This call is supported in Advanced NetWare versions 1.0, 1.02, 2.0 and 2.1, and in NetWare 386 and later versions.

Registers in:

AH	E3h
DS:SI	Request Buffer Length
ES:DI	Reply Buffer Length

Registers out:

AL	Completion Code

Completion Codes:

00	Success
96h	Server Out Of Memory
EFh	Invalid Name

F0h	Wildcard Not Allowed
F4h	No Object Delete Privileges
FCh	No Such Object
FEh	Server Bindery Locked
FFh	Bindery Failure

Request Packet (max size = 55 bytes):

Offset	Content	Type	Order
0	Request Buffer Length-2	WORD	lo-hi
2	33h	BYTE	
3	Object Type	WORD	hi-lo
5	Object Name Length	BYTE [1-47]	
6	Object Name	BYTE[*LENGTH*]	

Reply Packet (2 bytes):

Offset	Content	Type	Order
0	0000	WORD	lo-hi

The NetWare C Interface format is:

```
int DeleteBinderyObject( char *objectName, WORD objectType );
```

Delete Bindery Object From Set (E3h 42h) (Bindery Services API)

This call is supported in Advanced NetWare versions 1.0, 1.02, 2.0 and 2.1, and in NetWare 386 and later versions.

Registers in:

AH	E3h
DS:SI	Request Buffer Length
ES:DI	Reply Buffer Length

Registers out:

AL	Completion Code

Completion Codes:

00	Success
96h	Server Out Of Memory
EAh	No Such Member
EBh	Not Group Property
F0h	Wildcard Not Allowed
F8h	No Property Write Privileges
FBh	No Such Property
FCh	No Such Object
FEh	Server Bindery Locked
FFh	Bindery Failure

Request Packet (max size = 119 bytes):

Offset	Content	Type	Order
0	Request Buffer Length-2	WORD	lo-hi
2	42h	BYTE	
3	Object Type	WORD	hi-lo
5	Object Name Length	BYTE [1-47]	
6	Object Name	BYTE[*LENGTH*]	
?	Property Name Length	BYTE [1-15]	
?	Property Name	BYTE[*LENGTH*]	
?	Member Object Type	WORD	hi-lo
?	Member Name Length	BYTE [1-47]	
?	Member Name	BYTE[*LENGTH*]	

Reply Packet (2 bytes):

Offset	Content	Type	Order
0	0000	WORD	lo-hi

The NetWare C Interface format is:

```
int DeleteBinderyObjectFromSet( char *objectName, WORD objectType,
  char *propertyName, char *memberName, WORD memberType );
```

Delete Property (E3h 3Ah) (Bindery Services API)

This call is supported in Advanced NetWare versions 1.0, 1.02, 2.0 and 2.1, and in NetWare 386 and later versions.

Registers in:

AH	E3h
DS:SI	Request Buffer Length
ES:DI	Reply Buffer Length

Registers out:

AL	Completion Code

Completion Codes:

00	Success
96h	Server Out Of Memory
F0h	Wildcard Not Allowed
F1h	Invalid Bindery Security
F6h	No Property Delete Privileges
FBh	No Such Property
FCh	No Such Object
FEh	Server Bindery Locked
FFh	Bindery Failure

Request Packet (max size = 69 bytes):

Offset	Content	Type	Order
0	Request Buffer Length-2	WORD	lo-hi
2	3Ah	BYTE	
3	Object Type	WORD	hi-lo
5	Object Name Length	BYTE [1-47]	
6	Object Name	BYTE[*LENGTH*]	
?	Property Namc Length	BYTE [1-15]	
?	Property Name	BYTE[*LENGTH*]	

Reply Packet (2 bytes):

Offset	Content	Type	Order
0	0000	WORD	lo-hi

The NetWare C Interface format is:

```
int DeleteProperty( char *objectName, WORD objectType,
   char *propertyName );
```

Destroy Queue (E3h 65h) (Queue Services API)

This call is supported in Advanced NetWare version 2.1, NetWare 386, and later versions.

Registers in:

AH	E3h
DS:SI	Request Buffer Address
ES:DI	Reply Buffer Address

Registers out:

AL	Completion Code

Completion Codes:

00	Success
96h	Server Out Of Memory
9Ch	Invalid Path
D0h	Queue Error
D1h	No Queue
FFh	Hardware Failure

Request Packet (7 bytes):

Offset	Content	Type	Order
0	Request Buffer Length-2	WORD	lo-hi
2	65h	BYTE	
3	Queue ID	LONG	hi-lo

Reply Packet (2 bytes):

Offset	Content	Type	Order
0	0000	WORD	

The NetWare C Interface format is:

```
int DestroyQueue( long queueID );
```

Detach From File Server (F1h 01h) (Connection Services API)

This call is supported in Advanced NetWare versions 1.0, 1.02, 2.0 and 2.1, and in NetWare 386 and later versions.

Registers in:

AH	F1h
AL	01h
DL	Server Connection ID (1 to 8)

Registers out:

AL	Completion Code

Completion codes:

00h	Successful
FFh	Connection Does Not Exist

The NetWare C Interface format is:

```
int DetachFromFileServer( WORD connectionID );
```

Detach Queue Server From Queue (E3h 70h) (Queue Services API)

This call is supported in Advanced NetWare version 2.1, NetWare 386, and later versions.

Registers in:

AH	E3h
DS:SI	Request Buffer Address
ES:DI	Reply Buffer Address

Registers out:

AL	Completion Code

Completion Codes

00h	Successful
96h	Server Out Of Memory
9Ch	Invalid Path
D0h	Q Error
D1h	No Queue
D2h	No Q Server
FEh	Server Bindery Locked
FFh	Bindery Failure

Request Packet (7 bytes):

Offset	Content	Type	Order
0	Request Buffer Length-2	WORD	lo-hi
2	70h	BYTE	hi-lo
3	Queue ID	LONG	hi-lo

Reply Packet (2 bytes):

Offset	Content	Type	Order
0	0000	WORD	lo hi

The NetWare C Interface format is:

```
int DetachQueueServerFromQueue( long queueID );
```

Disable File Server Login (E3h CBh) (File Server Environment Services API)

This call is supported in Advanced NetWare version 2.1, NetWare 386, and later versions.

Registers in:

AH	E3h
DS:SI	Request Buffer Address
ES:DI	Reply Buffer Address

Registers out:

AL	Completion Code

Request Buffer (3 bytes):

Offset	Content	Type	Order
0	Request Buffer Length -2	WORD	lo-hi
2	CBh	BYTE	

Reply Buffer (2 bytes):

Offset	Content	Type	Order
0	0000h	WORD	lo-hi

Completion codes:

00h	Successful
C6h	No Console Rights

The NetWare C Interface format is:

```
int DisableFileServerLogin( void );
```

Disable Station Broadcasts (E1h 02h) (Message Services API)

This call is supported in NetWare versions 4.0 and 4.6, in Advanced NetWare versions 1.0, 1.02, 2.0, and 2.1, and in NetWare 386; but will not be supported in NetWare 386 versions dated after 1990.

Registers in:

AH	E1h
DS:SI	Request Buffer Address
ES:DI	Reply Buffer Address

Registers out:

AL	Completion Code

Completion codes:

00h	Successful

Request Buffer (3 bytes):

Offset	Content	Type	Order
0	Request Buffer Length - 2	WORD	lo-hi
2	2	BYTE	

Reply Buffer:

Offset	Content	Type
0	0000	WORD

The NetWare C Interface format is not supported.

Disable Transaction Tracking (E3h CFh) (File Server Environment Services API)

This call is supported in Advanced NetWare version 2.1, NetWare 386, and later versions.

Registers in:

AH	E3h
DS:SI	Request Buffer Address
ES:DI	Reply Buffer Address

Registers out:

AL	Completion Code

Completion code:

00h	Successful
C6h	No Console Rights

Request Buffer (3 bytes):

Offset	Content	Type	Order
0	Request Buffer Length - 2	WORD	lo-hi
2	CFh	BYTE	

Reply Buffer (2 bytes):

Offset	Content	Type	Order
0	0000h	WORD	lo-hi

The NetWare C Interface format is:

```
int DisableTransactionTracking( void );
```

Do Console Error (13h) (Value-Added Process Services API)

This call is supported in Advanced NetWare version 2.1.

Registers in:

DS:SI	Error Message
DI	13h

The NetWare C Interface format is:

```
void DoConsoleError( char *message );
```

Down File Server (E3h D3h) (File Server Environment Services API)

This call is supported in Advanced NetWare version 2.1, NetWare 386, and later versions.

Registers in:

AH	E3h
DS:SI	Request Buffer Address
ES:DI	Reply Buffer Address

Registers out:

AL	Completion Code

Completion code:

00h	Successful
C6h	No Console Rights
FFh	Open Files

Request Buffer (4 bytes):

Offset	**Content**	**Type**	**Order**
0	Request Buffer Length -2	WORD	lo-hi
2	D3h	BYTE	
3	Force Flag	BYTE	

Reply Buffer (2 bytes):

Offset	**Content**	**Type**	**Order**
0	0000h	WORD	lo-hi

The NetWare C Interface format is:

```
int DownFileServer( int forceFlag );
```

Enable File Server Login (E3h CCh) (File Server Environment Services API)

This call is supported in Advanced NetWare version 2.1, NetWare 386, and later versions.

Registers in:

AH	E3h
DS:SI	Request Buffer Address
ES:DI	Reply Buffer Address

Registers out:

AL	Completion Code

Completion code:

00h	Successful
C6h	No Console Rights

Request Buffer (3 bytes):

Offset	**Content**	**Type**	**Order**
0	Request Buffer Length - 2	WORD	lo-hi
2	CCh	BYTE	

Reply Buffer (2 bytes):

Offset	Content	Type	Order
0	0000h	WORD	lo-hi

The NetWare C Interface format is:

```
int EnableFileServerLogin( void );
```

Enable Station Broadcasts (E1h 03h) (Message Services API)

This call is supported in NetWare versions 4.0 and 4.6, in Advanced NetWare versions 1.0, 1.02, 2.0, and 2.1, and in NetWare 386; but will not be supported in NetWare 386 versions dated after 1990.

Registers in:

AH	E1h
DS:SI	Request Buffer Address
ES:DI	Reply Buffer Address

Registers out:

AL	Completion Code

Completion codes:

00h	Successful

Request Buffer (3 bytes):

Offset	Content	Type	Order
0	Request Buffer Length - 2	WORD	lo-hi
2	3h	BYTE	

Reply Buffer:

Offset	Content	Type
0	0000	WORD

The NetWare C Interface format is not supported.

Enable Transaction Tracking (E3h D0h) (File Server Environment Services API)

This call is supported in Advanced NetWare version 2.1, NetWare 386, and later versions.

Registers in:

AH	E3h
DS:SI	Request Buffer Address
ES:DI	Reply Buffer Address

Registers out:

AL	Completion Code

Completion code:

00h	Successful
C6h	No Console Rights

Request Buffer (3 bytes):

Offset	**Content**	**Type**	**Order**
0	Request Buffer Length - 2	WORD	lo-hi
2	D0h	BYTE	

Reply Buffer (2 bytes):

Offset	**Content**	**Type**	**Order**
0	0000h	WORD	lo-hi

The NetWare C Interface format is:

```
int EnableTransactionTracking( void );
```

End Logical File Locking (C9h) (Locking API)

This call is supported in NetWare versions 4.0 and 4.6, in Advanced NetWare versions 1.0, 1.02, 2.0 and 2.1, and in NetWare 386.

Registers in:

AH	C9h

Registers out:

AL	Completion Code

Completion Codes:

00h	Success
FFh	Failure

The NetWare C Interface format is not supported.

End LPT Capture (DFh 01h) (Print Services API)

This call is supported in NetWare versions 4.0 and 4.6, in Advanced NetWare versions 1.0, 1.02, 2.0 and 2.1, and in NetWare 386 and later versions.

Registers in:

AH	DFh
DL	01h

Registers out:

AL	Completion Code

Completion Codes:

00h	Successful

The NetWare C Interface format is:

```
int EndLPTCapture( void );
```

End Of Job (D6h) (Workstation Environment Services API)

This call is supported in NetWare versions 4.0 and 4.6, in Advanced NetWare versions 1.0, 1.02, 2.0 and 2.1, and in NetWare 386 and later versions.

Registers in:

AH	D6h
BX	Job Flag 00h (current process only) FFFFh (all processes on workstation)

The NetWare C Interface format is:

```
void EndOfJob( void );
```

End Specific LPT Capture (DFh 05h) (Print Services API)

This call is supported in Advanced NetWare version 2.1, and in NetWare 386 and later versions.

Registers in:

AH	DFh
DL	05h
DH	LPT Device (0 = LPT1, 1 = LPT2, 2 = LPT3)

Registers out:

AL	Completion Code

Completion Codes:

00h	Successful

The NetWare C Interface format is:

```
int EndSpecificLPTCapture( BYTE LPTDevice );
```

Enter Login Area (E3h 0Ah) (Connection Services API)

This call is supported in NetWare versions 4.0 and 4.6, in Advanced NetWare versions 1.0, 1.02, 2.0 and 2.1, and in NetWare 386 and later versions.

Registers in:

AH	E3h
DS:SI	Address of Request Buffer
ES:DI	Address of Reply Buffer

Completion codes:

00h	Successful

Request Buffer (maximum buffer length = 260 bytes):

Offset	Content	Type	Order
0	Request Buffer Length-2	WORD	lo-hi
2	0Ah	BYTE	
3	Number of Local Drives	BYTE	
4	Subdirectory Name Length	BYTE (0-255)	
5	Subdirectory Name	BYTE[*LENGTH*]	

Reply Buffer (2 bytes):

Offset	Content	Type	Order
0	0000h	WORD	lo-hi

The NetWare C Interface format is:

```
int EnterLoginArea( char *loginSubdirectoryName,
   int numberOfLocalDrives );
```

Erase Files (F2h 44h) (File Services API)

This call is supported in Advanced NetWare version 2.1 and in NetWare 386 and later versions.

Registers in:

AH	F2h
AL	44h
DS:SI	Request Buffer Length
ES:DI	Reply Buffer Length

Registers out:

AL	Completion Code

Completion Codes:

00	Success
98h	Volume does not exist
9Bh	Bad directory handle
9Ch	Invalid path
FFh	No files found error

Request Packet (max size = 258 bytes):

Offset	Content	Type
0	Directory Handle	BYTE
1	Search Attributes	BYTE
2	File Path Length(1-255)	BYTE
3	File Path	BYTE[*LENGTH*]

Reply Packet (2 bytes):

Offset	Content	Type	Order
0	0000	WORD	lo-hi

The NetWare C Interface format is:

```
int EraseFiles( BYTE directoryHandle, char *filePath,
   BYTE searchAttributes);
```

Examine Semaphore (C5h 01h) (Locking API)

This call is supported in NetWare version 4.6, in Advanced NetWare versions 1.0, 1.02, 2.0 and 2.1, and in NetWare 386 and later versions.

Registers in:

AH	C5h
AL	01h
CX,DX	Semaphore Handle

Registers out:

AL	Completion Code
CX	Semaphore Value
DL	Open Count

Completion Codes:

00h	Successful
FFh	Invalid Semaphore Handle

The NetWare C Interface format is:

```
int ExamineSemaphore( long semaphoreHandle, int *semaphoreValue,
   WORD *openCount );
```

File Server File Copy (E6h) (FCB) (File Services API)

This call is supported in NetWare versions 4.0 and 4.6, in Advanced NetWare versions 1.0, 1.02, 2.0 and 2.1, and in NetWare 386. It will not be supported after 1990.

Registers in:

AH	E6h
CX	Low order WORD Number of bytes to copy
DX	High order WORD Number of bytes to copy
DS:SI	Address of opened source FCB
ES:DI	Address of opened destination FCB

Registers out:

AL	Completion Code

Completion Codes:

00	Success

The NetWare C Interface format is not supported.

File Server File Copy (F3h) (Handle) (File Services API)

This call is supported in Advanced NetWare versions 2.0 and 2.1, and in Netware 386 and later versions.

Registers in:

AH	F3h
ES:DI	Request Buffer

Registers out:

AL	Completion Code
CX,DX	Number of Bytes Copied

Completion Codes:

00	Success

Request Packet:

Offset	Content	Type	Order
0	Source File Handle	WORD	lo-hi
2	Destination File Handle	WORD	lo-hi
4	Source File Offset	DWORD	lo-hi
8	Destination File Offset	DWORD	lo-hi
12	Number of Bytes to Copy	DWORD	lo-hi

The NetWare C Interface format is:

```
int FileServerFileCopy( int sourceFileHandle,
   int destinationFileHandle, long sourceFileOffset,
   long destinationFileOffset, long numberOfBytesToCopy,
   long *numberOfBytesCopied );
```

Finish Servicing Queue Job and File (E3h 72h) (Queue Services API)

This call is supported in Advanced NetWare version 2.1, NetWare 386, and later versions.

Registers in:

AH	E3h
DS:SI	Request Packet Address
ES:DI	Reply Buffer Address

Registers out:

AL	Completion Code

Completion Codes:

00h	Successful
96h	Server Out Of Memory
D0h	Q Error
D1h	No Queue
D6h	No Job Rights

Request Packet (13 bytes):

Offset	Content	Type	Order
0	Request Buffer Length -2	WORD	lo-hi
2	72h	BYTE	
3	Queue ID	LONG	hi-lo
7	Job Number	WORD	hi-lo
9	Charge	LONG	hi-lo

Reply Packet (2 bytes):

Offset	Content	Type	Order
0	000h	WORD	lo-hi

The NetWare C Interface format is:

```
int FinishServicingQueueJobAndFile( long queueID, WORD jobNumber,
   long charge, int fileHandle );
```

Flush LPT Capture (DFh 03h) (Print Services API)

This call is supported in Advanced NetWare versions 2.0 and 2.1, and in NetWare 386 and later versions.

Registers in:

AH	DFh
DL	03h

Registers out:

AL	Completion Code

Completion Codes:

00h	Successful

The NetWare C Interface format is:

```
int FlushLPTCapture( void );
```

Flush Specific LPT Capture (DFh 07h) (Print Services API)

This call is supported in Advanced NetWare version 2.1, and in NetWare 386 and later versions.

Registers in:

AH	DFh
DL	07h
DH	LPT Device (0 = LPT1, 1 = LPT2, 2 = LPT3)

Registers out:

AL	Completion Code

Completion Codes:

00h	Successful

The NetWare C Interface format is:

```
int FlushSpecificLPTCapture( BYTE LPTDevice );
```

Get Account Status (E3h 96h) (Accounting Services API)

This call is supported in Advanced NetWare version 2.1, NetWare 386, and later versions.

Registers in:

AH	E3h
DS:SI	Request Buffer Address
ES:DI	Reply Buffer Address

Registers out:

AL	Completion Code

Completion codes:

00h	Successful
C0h	No Account Privileges
C1h	No Account Balance

Request Buffer (maximum buffer length = 53 bytes):

Offset	**Content**	**Type**	**Order**
0	Request Buffer Length-2	WORD	lo-hi
2	96h	BYTE	
3	Bindery Object Type	WORD	hi-lo
5	Object Name Length (1 to 47)	BYTE	
6	Bindery Object Name	BYTE[*LENGTH*]	

Reply Buffer (256 bytes):

Offset	**Content**	**Type**	**Order**
0	Reply Buffer Length-2	WORD	lo-hi
2	Account Balance	LONG	hi-lo
6	Credit Limit	LONG	hi-lo
10	Reserved[120]	BYTE	
130	Server1 (ObjectID)	LONG	hi-lo
134	Server1 (Amount)	LONG	hi-lo
.			
.			
.			
248	Server 16 (Object ID)	LONG	hi-lo
252	Server 16 (Amount)	LONG	hi-lo

The NetWare C Interface format is:

```
int GetAccountStatus( WORD BinderyObjectType,
    char *BinderyObjectName, long *balance, long *limit,
    long *holds );
```

Get Banner User Name (B8h 08h) (Print Services API)

This call is supported in Advanced NetWare version 2.1, and in NetWare 386 and later versions.

Registers in:

AH	B8h
AL	08h
ES:BX	Reply Packet Address

Registers out:

AL	Completion Code

Completion codes:

0	Successful

Reply Packet (12 bytes):

Offset	Content	Type
0	Banner User Name	BYTE[12]

The NetWare C Interface format is:

```
int GetBannerUserName( char *userName );
```

Get Bindery Access Level (E3h 46h) (Bindery Services API)

This call is supported in Advanced NetWare versions 1.0, 1.02, 2.0 and 2.1, and in NetWare 386 and later versions.

Registers in:

AH	E3h
DS:SI	Request Buffer Length
ES:DI	Reply Buffer Length

Registers out:

AL	Completion Code

Completion codes:

00	Success

Request Packet (3 bytes):

Offset	Content	Type	Order
0	Request Buffer Length-2	WORD	lo-hi
2	46h	BYTE	

Reply Packet (7 bytes):

Offset	Content	Type	Order
0	Reply Buffer Length - 2	WORD	lo-hi
2	Access level	BYTE	
3	Object ID	LONG	hi-lo

The NetWare C Interface format is:

```
int GetBinderyAccessLevel( BYTE *securityAccessLevel,
   long *objectID );
```

Get Bindery Object Disk Space Left (E3h E6h) (File Server Environment Services API)

This call is supported in Advanced NetWare version 2.1, NetWare 386, and later versions.

Registers in:

AH	E3h
DS:SI	Request Buffer Address
ES:DI	Reply Buffer Address

Registers out:

AL	Completion Code

Completion code:

00h	Successful
C6h	No Console Rights

Request Buffer (7 bytes):

Offset	Content	Type	Order
0	Request Buffer Length - 2	WORD	lo-hi
2	E6h	BYTE	
3	Object ID	LONG	hi-lo

Reply Buffer (15 bytes):

Offset	Content	Type	Order
0	Reply Buffer Length - 2	WORD	lo-hi
2	System Elapsed Time	LONG	hi-lo
6	Object ID	LONG	hi-lo
10	Unused Disk Blocks	LONG	hi-lo
14	Restrictions Enforced	BYTE	

The NetWare C Interface format is:

```
int BinderyObjectDiskSpaceLeft( WORD connectionID,
   long binderyObjectID, long *systemElapsedTime,
   long *unusedDiskBlocks, int *restrictionEnforced );
```

Get Bindery Object ID (E3h 35h) (Bindery Services API)

This call is supported in Advanced NetWare versions 1.0, 1.02, 2.0 and 2.1, and in NetWare 386 and later versions.

Registers in:

AH	E3h
DS:SI	Request Buffer Length
ES:DI	Reply Buffer Length

Registers out:

AL	Completion Code

Completion codes:

00	Success
96h	Server Out Of Memory
EFh	Invalid Name
F0h	Wildcard Not Allowed
FCh	No Such Object
FEh	Server Bindery Locked
FFh	Bindery Failure

Request Packet (max size = 53 bytes):

Offset	Content	Type	Order
0	Request Buffer Length-2	WORD	lo-hi
2	35h	BYTE	
3	Object Type	WORD	hi-lo
5	Object Name Length	BYTE [1-47]	
6	Object Name	BYTE[*LENGTH*]	

Reply Packet (56 bytes):

Offset	Content	Type	Order
0	Reply Buffer Length - 2	WORD	lo-hi
2	Object ID	LONG	hi-lo
6	Object Type	WORD	hi-lo
8	Object Name	BYTE[48]	

The NetWare C Interface format is:

```
int GetBinderyObjectID( char *objectName, WORD objectType,
   long *objectID );
```

Get Bindery Object Name (E3h 36h) (Bindery Services API)

This call is supported in Advanced NetWare versions 1.0, 1.02, 2.0 and 2.1, and in NetWare 386 and later versions.

Registers in:

AH	E3h
DS:SI	Request Buffer Length
ES:DI	Reply Buffer Length

Registers out:

AL	Completion Code

Completion codes:

00	Success
96h	Server Out Of Memory
FCh	No Such Object
FEh	Server Bindery Locked
FFh	Bindery Failure

Request Packet (max size = 7 bytes):

Offset	Content	Type	Order
0	Request Buffer Length-2	WORD	lo-hi
2	36h	BYTE	
3	Object ID	LONG	hi-lo

Reply Packet (56 bytes):

0	Reply Buffer Length - 2	WORD	lo-hi
2	Object ID	LONG	hi-lo
6	Object Type	WORD	hi-lo
8	Object Name	BYTE[48]	

The NetWare C Interface format is:

```
int GetBinderyObjectName( long objectID, char *objectName,
   WORD *objectType);
```

Get Broadcast Message (E1h 01h) (Message Services API)

This call is supported in NetWare versions 4.0 and 4.6, in Advanced NetWare versions 1.0, 1.02, 2.0, and 2.1, and in NetWare 386; but will not be supported in NetWare 386 versions dated after 1990.

Registers in:

AH	E1h
DS:SI	Request Buffer Address
ES:DI	Reply Buffer Address

Registers out:

AL	Completion Code

Completion codes:

00h	Successful
FCh	Message Queue Full
FEh	I/O Failure; Lack Of Dynamic Workspace

Request Buffer (3 bytes):

Offset	**Content**	**Type**	**Order**
0	Request Buffer Length - 2	WORD	lo-hi
2	01h	BYTE	

Reply Buffer (maximum buffer length = 58 bytes):

Offset	**Content**	**Type**	**Order**
0	Reply Buffer Length - 2	WORD	lo-hi
2	Message Length (0 to 55)	BYTE	
3	Message	BYTE[*LENGTH*]	

The NetWare C Interface format is:

```
int GetBroadcastMessage( char *messageBuffer );
```

Get Broadcast Mode (DEh 04h) (Message Services API)

This call is supported in NetWare versions 4.0, and 4.6, in Advanced NetWare versions 1.0, 1.02, 2.0, and 2.1, and in NetWare 386; but will not be supported in NetWare 386 versions dated after 1990.

Registers in:

AH	DEh
DL	04h

Registers out:

AL	Message Mode

Completion codes:
None

The NetWare C Interface format is:

```
BYTE GetBroadcastMode( void );
```

Get Connection ID (EFh 03h) (Workstation Environment Services API)

This call is supported in Advanced NetWare versions 1.0, 1.02, 2.0 and 2.1, and in NetWare 386 and later versions.

Registers in:

AH	EFh
AL	03h

Registers out:

ES:SI	Pointer to Shell's Connection ID Table

The NetWare C Interface format is:

```
int GetConnectionID( char *fileServerName, WORD *connectionID );
```

Get Connection Information (E3h 16h) (Connection Services API)

This call is supported in Advanced NetWare versions 1.0, 1.02, 2.0 and 2.1, and in NetWare 386 and later versions.

Registers in:

AH	E3h
DS:SI	Address of Request Buffer
ES:DI	Address of Reply Buffer

Registers out:

AL	Completion Code

Completion codes:

00h	Successful

Request Buffer (4 bytes):

Offset	Content	Type	Order
0	Request Buffer Length-2	WORD	lo-hi
2	16h	BYTE	
3	Logical Connection Number	BYTE (1-100) for NetWare 286	

Reply Buffer (63 bytes):

Offset	Content	Type	Order
0	Reply Buffer Length-2	WORD	lo-hi
2	Object ID	LONG	hi-lo
6	Object Type	WORD	hi-lo
8	Object Name	BYTE[48]	
56	Login Time	BYTE[7]	

The NetWare C Interface format is:

```
int GetConnectionInformation( WORD connectionNumber,
  char *objectName, WORD *objectType, long *objectID,
  BYTE *loginTime );
```

Get Connection Number (DCh) (Connection Services API)

This call is supported in NetWare versions 4.0 and 4.6, in Advanced NetWare versions 1.0, 1.02, 2.0 and 2.1, and in NetWare 386 and later versions.

Registers in:

AH	DCh

Registers out:

AL	Logical Connection Number (1 to 100)
CH	Second digit of Logical Connection Number
CL	First digit of Logical Connection Number

The NetWare C Interface format is:

```
WORD GetConnectionNumber( void );
```

Get Connection's Open Files (E3h (DBh) (File Server Environment Services API)

This call is supported in Advanced NetWare version 2.1, NetWare 386, and later versions.

Registers in:

AH	E3h
DS:SI	Request Buffer Address
ES:DI	Reply Buffer Address

Registers out:

AL	Completion Code

Completion code:

00h	Successful
C6h	No Console Rights

Request Buffer (7 bytes):

Offset	Content	Type	Order
0	Request Buffer Length - 2	WORD	lo-hi
2	DBh	BYTE	
3	Logical Connection Number	WORD	hi-lo
5	Last Record Seen	WORD	hi-lo

Reply Buffer (maximum buffer = 512 bytes):

Offset	Content	Type	Order
0	Reply Buffer Length - 2	WORD	lo-hi
2	Next Request Record	WORD	hi-lo
4	Records	BYTE	

File Information (repeated Records times):

Offset	Content	Type	Order
?	Task Number	BYTE	
?	Lock Flag	BYTE	
?	Access Flag	BYTE	
?	Lock Type	BYTE	
?	Volume Number (0 to 31)	BYTE	
?	Directory Entry	WORD	hi-lo
?	File Name (ASCIIZ string)	BYTE[14]	

The NetWare C Interface format is:

```
int GetConnectionsOpenFiles( WORD connectionID,
   WORD connectionNumber, int *lastRecord, int *lastTask,
   int structSize, CON_OPEN_FILES *openFiles );
```

Get Connection's Semaphores (E3h E1h) (File Server Environment Services API)

This call is supported in Advanced NetWare version 2.1, NetWare 386, and later versions.

Registers in:

AH	E3h
DS:SI	Request Buffer Address
ES:DI	Reply Buffer Address

Registers out:

AL	Completion Code

Completion code:

00h	Successful
C6h	No Console Rights

Request Buffer (7 bytes):

Offset	Content	Type	Order
0	Request Buffer Length - 2	WORD	lo-hi
2	E1h	BYTE	
3	Logical Connection Number	WORD	hi-lo
5	Last Record Seen	WORD	hi-lo

Reply Buffer (maximum buffer length = 512 bytes):

Offset	Content	Type	Order
0	Reply Buffer Length - 2	WORD	lo-hi
2	Next Request Record	WORD	hi-lo
4	Records	BYTE	

File Information (repeated Records times):

Offset	Content	Type
?	Open Count	WORD
?	Semaphore Value (-127 to 128)	SIGNED BYTE
?	Task Number	BYTE
?	Lock Type	BYTE
?	Semaphore Name Length (1 to 127)	BYTE
?	Semaphore Name	BYTE[*LENGTH*]
?	File Name	BYTE[14]

The NetWare C Interface format is:

```
int GetConnectionsSemaphores( WORD connectionID,
   WORD connectionNumber, int *lastRecord, int lastTask,
   int structSize, CONN_SEMAPHORE *connectionSemaphores );
```

Get Connection's Task Information (E3h DAh) (File Server Environment Services API)

This call is supported in Advanced NetWare version 2.1, NetWare 386, and later versions.

Registers in:

AH	E3h
DS:SI	Request Buffer Address
ES:DI	Reply Buffer Address

Registers out:

AL	Completion Code

Completion code:

00h	Successful
C6h	No Console Rights

Request Buffer (5 bytes):

Offset	Content	Type	Order
0	Request Buffer Length - 2	WORD	lo-hi
2	DAh	BYTE	
3	Logical Connection Number	WORD	hi-lo

Reply Buffer (maximum buffer length = 512 bytes):

Offset	Content	Type	Order
0	Reply Buffer Length - 2	WORD	lo-hi
2	Connection's Lock Status	BYTE	

3	Status Information structure		
?	Records	BYTE	

Active task Information (repeated Records times):

Offset	Content	Type	Order
?	Task Number(1 to 225)	BYTE	
?	Task State	BYTE	

The NetWare C Interface format is:

```
int GetConnectionsTaskInformation( WORD connectionID,
   WORD connectionNumber, int *taskPointer, int structSize,
   CONN_TASK_INFO *connectionTaskInfo );
```

Get Connection's Usage Statistics (E3h E5h) (File Server Environment Services API)

This call is supported in Advanced NetWare version 2.1, NetWare 386, and later versions.

Registers in:

AH	E3h
DS:SI	Request Buffer Address
ES:DI	Reply Buffer Address

Registers out:

AL	Completion Code

Completion code:

00h	Successful
C6h	No Console Rights

Request Buffer (5 bytes):

Offset	Content	Type	Order
0	Request Buffer Length - 2	WORD	lo-hi
2	E5h	BYTE	
3	Logical Connection Number	WORD	

Reply Buffer (22 bytes):

Offset	Content	Type	Order
0	Reply Buffer Length - 2	WORD	lo-hi
2	System Elapsed Time	LONG	hi-lo
6	Bytes Read	BYTE[6]	
12	Bytes Written	BYTE[6]	
18	Total Request Packets	LONG	hi-lo

The NetWare C Interface format is:

```
int GetConnectionsUsageStats( WORD connectionID,
   WORD connectionNumber, int structSize,
   CONN_USAGE *connectionUsage );
```

Get Connections Using a File (E3h DCh) (File Server Environment Services API)

This call is supported in Advanced NetWare version 2.1, NetWare 386, and later versions.

Registers in:

AH	E3h
DS:SI	Request Buffer Address
ES:DI	Reply Buffer Address

Registers out:

AL	Completion Code

Completion code:

00h	Successful
C6h	No Console Rights

Request Buffer (maximum buffer length = 262):

Offset	Content	Type	Order
0	Request Buffer Length - 2	WORD	lo-hi
2	DCh	BYTE	
3	Last Record	WORD	hi-lo
5	Directory Handle	BYTE	
6	File Path Length (1 to 255)	BYTE	
7	File Path (ASCIIZ string)	BYTE[*LENGTH*]	

Reply Buffer (maximum buffer = 512 bytes):

Offset	Content	Type	Order
0	Reply Buffer Length - 2	WORD	lo-hi
2	Use Count	WORD	hi-lo
4	Open Count	WORD	hi-lo
6	Open For Read Count	WORD	hi-lo
8	Open For Write Count	WORD	hi-lo
10	Deny Read Count	WORD	hi-lo
12	Deny Write Count	WORD	hi-lo
14	Next Request Record	WORD	hi-lo
16	Locked	BYTE	
17	Records	BYTE	

File Usage Information (repeated Records times):

Offset	Content	Type	Order
?	Logical Connection Number	WORD	hi-lo
?	Task Number	BYTE	
?	Lock Flag byte	BYTE	
?	Access Flag	BYTE	
?	Lock Type	BYTE	

The NetWare C Interface format is:

```
int GetConnectionsUsingAFile( WORD connectionID, int *lastRecord,
   int *taskID, BYTE directoryHandle, char *filePath,
   int structSize, CONN_USING_FILE *fileUse );
```

Get Default Capture Flags (B8h 00h) (Print Services API)

This call is supported in Advanced NetWare versions 2.0 and 2.1, and in NetWare 386 and later versions.

Registers in:

AH	B8h
AL	00h
CX	Reply Buffer Length (1-63)
ES:BX	Reply Buffer

Registers out:

AL	Completion Code

Completion codes:

00h	Successful

Reply Packet (63 bytes):

Offset	Content	Type	Order
0	Status	BYTE	
1	Flags	BYTE	
2	Tab Size	BYTE (1-18)	
3	Server Printer	BYTE (0-4)	
4	Number of Copies	BYTE (0-255)	
5	Form Type	BYTE (0-255)	
6	Reserved	BYTE	
7	Banner Text (ASCIIZ)	BYTE[13]	
20	Reserved	BYTE	
21	Local LPT Device	BYTE	
22	Flush Capture Timeout	WORD	hi-lo
24	Flush Capture On Device Close	BYTE	

/* All fields below this are Adv. NetWare 2.1 and above compatible only. */

25	Max Lines	WORD	hi-lo
27	Max Chars	WORD	hi-lo
29	Form Name (ASCIIZ)	BYTE[13]	
42	LPT Capture Flag	BYTE	
43	File Capture Flag	BYTE	
44	Timing Out Flag	BYTE	
45	Printer Setup Buffer Address	LONG	hi-lo /*Different*/
49	Printer Reset Buffer Address	LONG	hi-lo ""
53	Connection ID Queue Print Job	BYTE	
54	Capture In Progress	BYTE	
55	Print Queue Flag	BYTE	
56	Print Job Valid	BYTE	
57	Print Queue ID	LONG	hi-lo
61	Print Job Number	WORD	hi-lo (1-999)

The NetWare C Interface format is:

```
int GetDefaultCaptureFlags( CAPTURE_FLAGS *captureFlags );
```

Get Default Connection ID (F0h 02h) (Workstation Environment Services API)

This call is supported in Advanced NetWare versions 1.0, 1.02, 2.0 and 2.1, and in NetWare 386 and later versions.

Registers in:

AH	F0h
AL	02h

Registers out:

AL	Connection ID of file server to which packets are currently being sent (1 to 8)

The NetWare C Interface format is:

```
WORD GetDefaultConnectionID( void );
```

Get Default Local Printer (B8h 04h) (Print Services API)

This call is supported in Advanced NetWare version 2.1, and in NetWare 386 and later versions.

Registers in:

AH	B8h
AL	04h

Registers out:

DH	Default LPT Device (0 = LPT1, 1 = LPT2, 2 = LPT3)

The NetWare C Interface format is:

```
int GetDefaultLocalPrinter( void );
```

Get Disk Cache Statistics (E3h D6h) (File Server Environment Services API)

This call is supported in Advanced NetWare version 2.1, NetWare 386, and later versions.

Registers in:

AH	E3h
DS:SI	Request Buffer Address
ES:DI	Reply Buffer Address

Registers out:

AL	Completion Code

Completion code:

00h	Successful
C6h	No Console Rights

Request Buffer (3 bytes):

Offset	Content	Type	Order
0	Reply Buffer Length - 2	WORD	lo-hi
2	D6h	BYTE	

Reply Buffer (80 bytes):

Offset	Content	Type	Order
0	Reply Buffer Length - 2	WORD	lo-hi
2	System Elapsed Time	LONG	hi-lo
6	Cache Buffer Count	WORD	hi-lo
8	Cache Buffer Size	WORD	hi-lo
10	Dirty Cache Buffers	WORD	hi-lo
12	Cache Read Requests	LONG	hi-lo
16	Cache Write Requests	LONG	hi-lo
20	Cache Hits	LONG	hi-lo
24	Cache Misses	LONG	hi-lo

28	Physical Read Requests	LONG	hi-lo
32	Physical Write Requests	LONG	hi-lo
36	Physical Read Errors	WORD	hi-lo
38	Physical Write Errors	WORD	hi-lo
40	Cache Get Requests	LONG	hi-lo
44	Cache Full Write Requests	LONG	hi-lo
48	Cache Partial Write Requests	LONG	hi-lo
52	Background Dirty Writes	LONG	hi-lo
56	Background Aged Writes	LONG	hi-lo
60	Total Cache Writes	LONG	hi-lo
64	Cache Allocations	LONG	hi-lo
68	Thrashing Count	WORD	hi-lo
70	LRU Block Was Dirty	WORD	hi-lo
72	Read Beyond Write	WORD	hi-lo
74	Fragmented Write Occurred	WORD	hi-lo
76	Cache Hit On Unavailable Block	WORD	hi-lo
78	Cache Block Scrapped	WORD	hi-lo

The NetWare C Interface format is:

```
int GetDiskCacheStats( WORD connectionID, int structSize,
   DISK_CACHE_STATS *cacheStats );
```

Get Disk Channel Statistics (E3h D9h) (File Server Environment Services API)

This call is supported in Advanced NetWare version 2.1, NetWare 386, and later versions.

Registers in:

AH	E3h
DS:SI	Request Buffer Address
ES:DI	Reply Buffer Address

Registers out:

AL	Completion Code

Completion code:

00h	Successful
C6h	No Console Rights

Request Buffer (4 bytes):

Offset	Content	Type	Order
0	Request Buffer Length - 2	WORD	lo-hi
2	D9h	BYTE	
3	Channel Number	BYTE	

Reply Buffer (170):

Offset	Content	Type	Order
0	Reply Buffer Length - 2	WORD	lo-hi
2	System Elapsed Time	LONG	hi-lo
6	Channel State	WORD	hi-lo
8	Channel Synchronization State	WORD	hi-lo
10	Driver Type	BYTE	
11	Driver Major Version	BYTE	
12	Driver Minor Version	BYTE	
13	Driver Description (ASCIIZ)	BYTE[65]	
78	First IO Address Used	WORD	hi-lo
80	First IO Address Length	WORD	hi-lo
82	Second IO Address Length	WORD	hi-lo
84	Second IO Address Length	WORD	hi-lo
86	First Shared Memory Address	BYTE[3]	
89	First Shared Memory Address Length	BYTE[2]	
91	Second Shared Memory Address	BYTE[3]	
94	Second Shared Memory Address Length	BYTE[2]	
96	First Interrupt Number In Use	BYTE	
97	First Interrupt Number Used	BYTE	
98	Second Interrupt Number In Use	BYTE	
99	Second Interrupt Number Used	BYTE	
100	First DMA Channel Used	BYTE	
101	First DMA Channel Used	BYTE	
102	Second DMA Channel Used	BYTE	
103	Second DMA Channel Used	BYTE	
104	Flag Bits	BYTE	
105	Reserved	BYTE	
106	Configuration Description	BYTE[80]	

The NetWare C Interface format is:

```
int GetDiskChannelStats( WORD connectionID, int channelNumber,
   int structSize, DISK_CHANNEL_STATS *channelStats );
```

Get Disk Utilization (E3h 0Eh)
(File Server Environment Services API)

This call is supported in Advanced NetWare 1.0 and later versions.

Registers in:

AH	E3h
DS:SI	Request Buffer Address
ES:DI	Reply Buffer Address

Registers out:

AL	Completion Code

Completion code:

00h	Successful
98h	Volume Does Not Exist
F2h	No Object Read Privileges

Request Buffer (8 bytes):

Offset	Content	Type	Order
0	Request Buffer Length - 2	WORD	lo-hi
2	0Eh	BYTE	
3	Volume Number (0 to 31)	BYTE	
4	Object ID	LONG	hi-lo

Reply Buffer (13 bytes):

Offset	Content	Type	Order
0	Reply Buffer Length - 2	WORD	lo-hi
2	Volume Number (0 to 31)	BYTE	
3	Object ID	LONG	hi-lo
7	Used Directories	WORD	hi-lo
9	Used Files	WORD	hi-lo
11	Used Blocks	WORD	hi-lo

The NetWare C Interface format is:

```
int GetDiskUtilization( long objectID, char volumeNumber,
   WORD *usedDirectories, WORD *usedFiles, WORD *usedBlocks );
```

Get Drive Connection ID Table (EFh 02h) (Workstation Environment Services API)

This call is supported in Advanced NetWare versions 1.0, 1.02, 2.0 and 2.1, and in NetWare 386 and later versions.

Registers in:

AH	EFh
AL	02h

Registers out:

ES:SI	Pointer to Shell's Drive Connection ID Table

The NetWare C Interface format is not supported.

Get Drive Flag Table (EFh 01h) (Workstation Environment Services API)

This call is supported in Advanced NetWare versions 1.0, 1.02, 2.0 and 2.1, and in NetWare 386 and later versions.

Registers in:

AH	EFh
AL	01h

Registers out:

ES:SI	Pointer to Shell's Drive Flag Table

The NetWare C Interface format is not supported.

Get Drive Handle Table (EFh 00h) (Workstation Environment Services API)

This call is supported in Advanced NetWare versions 1.0, 1.02, 2.0 and 2.1, and in NetWare 386 and later versions.

Registers in:

AH	EFh
AL	00h

Registers out:

ES:SI	Pointer to Shell's Drive Handle Table

The NetWare C Interface format is not supported.

Get Drive Mapping Table (E3h D7h) (File Server Environment Services API)

This call is supported in Advanced NetWare version 2.1, NetWare 386, and later versions.

Registers in:

AH	E3h
DS:SI	Request Buffer Address
ES:DI	Reply Buffer Address

Registers out:

AL	Completion Code

Completion code:

00h	Successful
C6h	No Console Rights

Request Buffer (3 bytes):

Offset	Content	Type	Order
0	Reply Buffer Length - 2	WORD	lo-hi
2	D7h	BYTE	

Reply Buffer (238 bytes):

Offset	Content	Type	Order
0	Reply Buffer Length - 2	WORD	lo-hi
2	System Elapsed Time	LONG	hi-lo
6	SFT Level	BYTE	
7	Logical Drive Count	BYTE	
8	Physical Drive Count	BYTE	
9	Disk Channel Table	BYTE[5]	
14	Pending IO Commands	WORD	hi-lo
16	Mapping Table	BYTE[32]	
48	Drive Mirror Table	BYTE[32]	
80	Dead Mirror Table	BYTE[32]	
112	Remirrored Drive	BYTE	
113	Reserved	BYTE	
114	Remirrored Block	LONG	hi-lo
118	SFT Error Table	WORD[60]	hi-lo

The NetWare C Interface format is:

```
int GetDriveMappingTable( WORD connectionID, int structSize,
   DRIVE_MAP_TABLE *driveMappingTable );
```

Get Extended File Attributes (B6h 00h) (File Services API)

This call is supported in Advanced NetWare 2.1, and in NetWare versions 386 and later.

Registers in:

AH	B6h
AL	0
DS:DX	File Path (ASCIIZ 1-255 bytes)

Registers out:

AL	Completion Code
CL	Extended File Attributes

Completion Codes:

00	Success
FFh	File Not Found — Carry flag is set.
FEh	No Search Rights — Carry flag is set.

The NetWare C Interface format is:

```
int GetExtendedFileAttributes( char *filePath,
   BYTE *extendedFileAttributes);
```

Get File Information (E3h 0Fh) (File Services API)

This call is supported in Advanced NetWare versions 1.0, 1.02, 2.0 and 2.1, and in NetWare 386 and later versions.

Registers in:

AH	E3h
DS:SI	Request Buffer Length
ES:DI	Reply Buffer Length

Registers out:

AL	Completion Code

Completion Codes:

00	Success
89h	No Search Privileges
FFh	No More Matching Files

Request Packet (max size = 263 bytes):

Offset	Content	Type	Order
0	Request Buffer Length - 2	WORD	lo-hi
2	0Fh	BYTE	
3	Sequence Number	WORD	hi-lo
5	Directory Handle	BYTE	
6	Search Attributes	BYTE	
7	File Path Length(1-255)	BYTE	
8	File Path	BYTE[*LENGTH*]	

Reply Packet (max size = 97 bytes):

Offset	Content	Type	Order
0	Reply Buffer Length - 2	WORD	lo-hi
2	Sequence Number	WORD	hi-lo
4	File Name	BYTE[15]	
19	File Attributes	BYTE	
20	Extended File Attributes	BYTE	
21	File Size	LONG	hi-lo
25	Creation Date	WORD	hi-lo
27	Last Access Date	WORD	hi-lo
29	Last Update Date & Time	LONG	hi-lo
33	Owner Object ID	LONG	hi-lo
37	Last Archive Date & Time	LONG	hi-lo
41	Reserved	BYTE[56]	

The NetWare C Interface format is:

```
int ScanFileInformation( BYTE directoryHandle, char *filePath,
   BYTE searchAttributes, int *sequenceNumber, char *fileName,
   BYTE *fileAttributes, BYTE *extendedFileAttributes,
   long *fileSize, char *creationDate, char *lastAccessDate,
   char *lastUpdateDateAndTime, char *lastArchiveDateAndTime,
   long *fileOwnerID );
```

Get File Server Date And Time (E7h)
(File Server Environment Services API)

This call is supported in NetWare 4.0 and later versions.

Registers in:

AH	E3h
DS:DX	Reply Buffer Address

Registers out:
None

Completion codes:
None

Reply Buffer (7 bytes):

Offset	Content	Type
0	Year (0 to 99)	BYTE
1	Month (1 to 12)	BYTE
2	Day (1 to 31)	BYTE
3	Hour (0 to 23)	BYTE
4	Minute (0 to 59)	BYTE

5	Second (0 to 59)	BYTE
6	Day Of Week (0 to 6) (0=Sunday)	BYTE

The NetWare C Interface format is:

```
int GetFileServerDateAndTime( BYTE *dateAndTime );
```

Get File Server Description Strings (E3h C9h) (File Server Environment Services API)

This call is supported in Advanced NetWare version 2.1, NetWare 386, and later versions.

Registers in:

AH	E3h
DS:SI	Request Buffer Address
ES:DI	Reply Buffer Address

Registers out:

AL	Completion Code

Completion code:

00h	Successful

Request Buffer (3 bytes):

Offset	Content	Type	Order
0	Request Buffer Length - 2	WORD	lo-hi
2	C9h	BYTE	

Reply Buffer (514 bytes):

Offset	Content	Type	Order
0	Reply Buffer Length - 2	WORD	lo-hi
2	Description Strings	BYTE[512]	

The NetWare C Interface format is:

```
int GetFileServerDescriptionStrings( char *companyName,
    char *revision, char *revisionDate, copyrightNotice );
```

Get File Server Information (E3h 11h) (File Server Environment Services API)

This call is supported in Advanced NetWare 1.0 and later versions.

Registers in:

AH	E3h
DS:SI	Request Buffer Address
ES:DI	Reply Buffer Address

Registers out:

AL	Completion Code

Completion code:

00h	Sucessful

Request Buffer(3 bytes):

Offset	Content	Type	Order
0	Request Buffer Length - 2	WORD	lo-hi
2	11h	BYTE	

Reply Buffer (130 bytes):

Offset	Content	Type	Order
0	Reply Buffer Length - 2	WORD	lo-hi
2	Server Name	BYTE[48]	
50	NetWare Version (1 to 255)	BYTE	
51	NetWare Subversion (0 to 99)	BYTE	
52	Connections Supported	WORD	hi-lo
54	Connections In Use	WORD	hi-lo
56	Max Connected Volumes	WORD	hi-lo
58	OS Revision Number	BYTE	
59	SFT Level	BYTE	
60	TTS Level	BYTE	
61	Peak Connections Used	WORD	hi-lo
63	Accounting Version	BYTE	
64	VAP Version	BYTE	
65	Queuing Version	BYTE	
66	Print Server Version	BYTE	
67	Virtual Console Version	BYTE	
68	Security Restrictions Level	BYTE	
69	Internetwork Bridge Version	BYTE	
70	Reserved	BYTE[60]	

The NetWare C Interface format is:

```
int GetServerInformation( int structSize,
   FILE_SERV_INFO *serverInfo );
```

Get File Server LAN IO Statistics (E3h E7h) (File Server Environment Services API)

This call is supported in Advanced NetWare version 2.1, NetWare 386, and later versions.

Registers in:

AH	E3h
DS:SI	Request Buffer Address
ES:DI	Reply Buffer Address

Registers out:

AL	Completion Code

Completion code:

00h	Successful
C6h	No Console Rights

Request Buffer (3 bytes):

Offset	Content	Type	Order
0	Request Buffer Length - 2	WORD	lo-hi
2	E7h	BYTE	

Reply Buffer (68 bytes):

Offset	Content	Type	Order
0	Reply Buffer Length - 2	WORD	lo-hi
2	System Elapsed Time	LONG	hi-lo
6	Configured Max Routing Buffers	WORD	hi-lo
8	Actual Max Used Routing Buffers	WORD	hi-lo
10	Currently Used Routing Buffers	WORD	hi-lo
12	Total File Service Packets	LONG	hi-lo
16	File Service Packet Buffered	LONG	hi-lo
18	Invalid Connection Packets	WORD	hi-lo
20	Bad Logical Connection Number Packets	WORD	hi-lo
22	Packets Received During Processing	WORD	hi-lo
24	Reprocessed Requests	WORD	hi-lo
26	Bad Sequence Number Packets	WORD	hi-lo
28	Duplicate Replies Sent	WORD	hi-lo
30	Acknowledgements Sent	WORD	hi-lo
32	Packets With Bad Request Type	WORD	hi-lo

34	Attach During Processing	WORD	hi-lo
36	Attach While Processing Attach	WORD	hi-lo
38	Forced Detach Requests	WORD	hi-lo
40	Detach For Bad Connection Number	WORD	hi-lo
42	Detach During Processing	WORD	hi-lo
44	Replies Cancelled	WORD	hi-lo
46	Packets Discarded By Hop Count	WORD	hi-lo
48	Packets Discarded Unknown Net	WORD	hi-lo
50	Incoming Packet Discarded No DGroup Buffer	WORD	hi-lo
52	Outgoing Packet Discarded No Buffer	WORD	hi-lo
54	IPX Not MY Network	WORD	hi-lo
56	NetBIOS Broadcast Was Propagated	LONG	hi-lo
60	Total Other Packets	LONG	hi-lo
64	Total Routed Packets	LONG	hi-lo

The NetWare C Interface format is:

```
int GetFileServerLANIOStats( WORD connectionID, int structSize,
   SERVER_LAN_IO *serverLANIOStats );
```

Get File Server Login Status (E3h CDh) (File Server Environment Services API)

This call returns the file server's login status.

Registers in:

AH	E3h
DS:SI	Request Buffer Address
ES:DI	Reply Buffer Address

Registers out:

AL	Completion Code

Completion code:

00h	Successful
C6h	No Console Rights

Request Buffer (3 bytes):

Offset	Content	Type	Order
0	Reply Buffer Length - 2	WORD	lo-hi
2	CDh	BYTE	

Reply Buffer (3 bytes):

Offset	Content	Type	Order
0	Reply Buffer Length - 2	WORD	lo-hi
2	Login Enabled Flag	BYTE	

The NetWare C Interface format is:

```
int GetFileServerLoginStatus( int *loginEnabledFlag );
```

Get File Server Misc Information (E3h E8h) (File Server Environment Services API)

This call is supported in Advanced NetWare version 2.1, NetWare 386, and later versions.

Registers in:

AH	E3h
DS:SI	Request Buffer Address
ES:DI	Reply Buffer Address

Registers out:

AL	Completion Code

Completion code:

00h	Successful
C6h	No Console Rights

Request Buffer (3 bytes):

Offset	Content	Type	Order
0	Request Buffer Length - 2	WORD	lo-hi
2	E8h	BYTE	

Reply Buffer (maximum buffer length = 58 bytes):

Offset	Content	Type	Order
0	Reply Buffer Length - 2	WORD	lo-hi
2	System Elapsed Time	LONG	hi-lo
6	Processor Type	BYTE	
7	Reserved	BYTE	
8	Number Of Service Processes	BYTE	
9	Server Utilization Percentage	BYTE	

10	Configured Max Bindery Objects	WORD	hi-lo
12	Actual Max Bindery Objects	WORD	hi-lo
14	Current Used Bindery Objects	WORD	hi-lo
16	Total Server Memory	WORD	hi-lo
18	Wasted Server Memory	WORD	hi-lo
20	Records	WORD	hi-lo

Dynamic memory information (repeated Records times):

?	Total Dynamic Space	LONG	hi-lo
?	Max Used Dynamic Space	LONG	hi-lo
?	Current Used Dynamic Space	LONG	hi-lo

The NetWare C Interface format is:

```
int GetFileServerMiscInformation( WORD connectionID, int structSize,
   SERVER_MISC_INFO *miscInformation );
```

Get File Server Name Table (EFh 04h) (Workstation Environment Services API)

This call is supported in NetWare versions 4.0 and 4.6, in Advanced NetWare versions 1.0, 1.02, 2.0 and 2.1, and in NetWare 386 and later versions.

Registers in:

AH	EFh
AL	04h

Registers out:

ES:SI	Pointer to Shell's Server Name Table

The NetWare C Interface format is:

```
void GetFileServerName( WORD connectionID, char *fileServerName );
```

Get File System Statistics E3h (D4h) (File Server Environment Services API)

This call is supported in Advanced NetWare version 2.1, NetWare 386, and later versions.

Registers in:

AH	E3h
DS:SI	Request Buffer Address
ES:DI	Reply Buffer Address

Registers out:

AL	Completion Code

Completion code:

00h	Successful
C6h	No Console Rights

Request Buffer (3 bytes):

Offset	Content	Type	Order
0	Request Buffer Length - 2	WORD	lo-hi
2	D4h	BYTE	

Reply Buffer (42 bytes):

Offset	Content	Type	Order
0	Reply Buffer Length - 2	WORD	lo-hi
2	System Elapsed Time	LONG	hi-lo
6	Configured Max Open Files	WORD	hi-lo
8	Actual Max Open Files	WORD	hi-lo
10	Current Open File	WORD	hi-lo
12	Total Files Opened	LONG	hi-lo
16	Total Read Requests	LONG	hi-lo
20	Total Write Requests	LONG	hi-lo
24	Current Changed FATS	WORD	hi-lo
26	Total Changed FATS	LONG	hi-lo
28	FAT Write errors	LONG	hi-lo
30	Fatal FAT Write Errors	WORD	hi-lo
32	FAT Scan Errors	WORD	hi-lo
34	Actual Max Indexed Files	WORD	hi-lo
36	Active Indexed File	WORD	hi-lo
38	Attached Indexed Files	WORD	hi-lo
40	Available Indexed Files	WORD	hi-lo

The NetWare C Interface format is:

```
int GetFileSystemStats( WORD connectionID, int structSize,
   FILE_SYS_STATS *fileSysStats );
```

Get Internet Address (E3h 13h) (Connection Services API)

This call is supported in Advanced NetWare 1.0 and later versions.

Registers in:

AH	E3h
DS:SI	Address of Request Buffer
ES:DI	Address of Reply Buffer

Registers out:

AL	Completion Code

Completion code:

00h	Successful

Request Buffer (4 bytes):

Offset	Content	Type	Order
0	Request Buffer Length-2	WORD	lo-hi
2	13h	BYTE	
3	Logical Connection Number	BYTE	

Reply Buffer (14 bytes):

Offset	Content	Type	Order
0	Reply Buffer Length-2	WORD	lo-hi
2	Network Number	BYTE[4]	
6	Physical Node Address	BYTE[6]	
12	Socket Number	BYTE[2]	

The NetWare C Interface format is:

```
int GetInternetAddress( WORD connectionNumber, char *networkNumber,
   char *physicalNodeAddress, int *socketNumber );
```

Get Interrupt Vector (0Fh) (Value-Added Process Services API)

This call is supported in Advanced NetWare version 2.1.

Registers in:

AL	Interrupt Vector
DI	0Fh

Registers out:

CX	ISR Segment
DX	ISR Offset

The NetWare C Interface format is:

```
void GetInterruptVector( BYTE vectorNum, WORD *ISRsegment,
   WORD *ISRoffset );
```

Get LAN Driver's Configuration Information (E3h E3h) (File Server Environment Services API)

This call is supported in Advanced NetWare version 2.1, NetWare 386, and later versions.

Registers in:

AH	E3h
DS:SI	Request Buffer Address
ES:DI	Reply Buffer Address

Registers out:

AL	Completion Code

Completion code:

00h	Successful
C6h	No Console Rights

Request Buffer (4 bytes):

Offset	Content	Type	Order
0	Request Buffer Length -2	WORD	lo-hi
2	E3h	BYTE	
3	LAN Board (0 to 3)	BYTE	

Reply Buffer (174 bytes):

Offset	Content	Type	Order
0	Reply Buffer Length - 2	WORD	lo-hi
2	Network Address	BYTE[4]	
6	Host Address	BYTE[6]	
12	LAN Driver Installed	BYTE	
13	Option Number	BYTE	
14	Configuration Text	BYTE[160]	

The NetWare C Interface format is:

```
int GetLANDriverConfigInfo( connectionID, BYTE LANBoardNumber,
   int structSize, LAN_CONFIG *LANConfiguration );
```

Get Lock Mode (C6h 00h) (Locking API)

This call is supported in NetWare version 4.6, in Advanced NetWare versions 1.0, 1.02, 2.0 and 2.1, and in NetWare 386 and later versions.

Registers in:

AH	C6h
AL	Function Code 00h = set to 4.0-style "compatibility mode" 01h = set to 4.6 and later "extended lock mode" 02h = return current lock mode

Registers out:

AL	Current lock mode

The NetWare C Interface format is:

```
int GetLockMode( void );
```

Get Logical Record Information (E3h E0h) (File Server Environment Services API)

This call is supported in Advanced NetWare version 2.1, NetWare 386, and later versions.

Registers in:

AH	E3h
DS:SI	Request Buffer Address
ES:DI	Reply Buffer Address

Registers out:

AL	Completion Code

Completion code:

00h	Successful
C6h	No Console Rights

Request Buffer (maximum buffer length = 105):

Offset	**Content**	**Type**	**Order**
0	Request Buffer Length - 2	WORD	lo-hi
2	E0h	BYTE	
3	Last Record Seen	WORD	hi-lo
5	Logical Record Name Length (1 to 99)	BYTE	
6	Logical Record Name	BYTE[*LENGTH*]	

Reply Buffer (maximum buffer = 514 bytes):

Offset	**Content**	**Type**	**Order**
0	Reply Buffer Length - 2	WORD	lo-hi
2	Use Count	WORD	hi-lo
4	Shareable Lock Count	WORD	hi-lo
6	Next Request Record	WORD	hi-lo
8	Locked	BYTE	
9	Records	BYTE	

Task information (repeated Records times):

Offset	**Content**	**Type**	**Order**
?	Logical Connection Number	WORD	hi-lo
?	Task Number	BYTE	
?	Lock Status	BYTE	

The NetWare C Interface format is:

```
int GetLogicalRecordInformation( WORD connectionID, int *lastRecord,
    int *list\ask, char *logicalRecordName, int structSize,
    LOGICAL_REC_INFO *logicalRecInfo );
```

Get Logical Records By Connection (E3h DFh) (File Server Environment Services API)

This call is supported in Advanced NetWare version 2.1, NetWare 386, and later versions.

Registers in:

AH	E3h
DS:SI	Request Buffer Address
ES:DI	Reply Buffer Address

Registers out:

AL	Completion Code

Completion code:

00h	Successful
C6h	No Console Rights

Request Buffer (7 bytes):

Offset	Content	Type	Order
0	Request Buffer Length - 2	WORD	lo-hi
2	DFh	BYTE	
3	Logical Connection Number	WORD	hi-lo
5	Last Record Seen	WORD	hi-lo

Reply Buffer (maximum buffer = 512 bytes):

Offset	Content	Type	Order
0	Reply Buffer Length - 2	WORD	lo-hi
2	Next Request Record	WORD	hi-lo
4	Records	BYTE	

Logical Lock Information (repeated Records times):

Offset	Content	Type
?	Task Number	BYTE
?	Lock Status	BYTE
?	Logical Lock Name Length	BYTE
?	Logical Lock Name	BYTE[*LENGTH*]

The NetWare C Interface format is:

```
int GetLogicalRecordLocksByConnection( WORD connectionID,
   WORD connectionNumber, int *lastRecord, int *lastTask,
   int structSize, LOGICAL_RECORD *logicalRecord );
```

Get LPT Capture Status (F0h 03h) (Print Services API)

This call is supported in Advanced NetWare versions 1.0, 1.02, 2.0 and 2.1, and in NetWare 386 and later versions.

Registers in:

AH	F0h
AL	03h

Registers out:

AH	Completion Code
AL	Connection ID (1-8)

Completion codes:

00h	Successful
FFh	Capture is Active

The NetWare C Interface format is:

```
int GetLPTCaptureStatus( WORD *serverNumber );
```

Get Member Set M of Group G (E3h 09h) (Workstation Environment Services API)

This call is supported in NetWare versions 4.0 and 4.6, in Advanced NetWare versions 1.0, 1.02, 2.0 and 2.1, and in NetWare 386. It has been replaced by higher-level Bindery Services API calls such as Scan Bindery Object and Read Property Value but is shown here for completeness.

Registers in:

AH	E3h
DS:SI	Address of Request buffer
ES:DI	Address of Reply buffer

Registers out:

AL	Completion Code

Completion codes:

00h	Successful

Request Packet (9 bytes):

Offset	Content	Type	Order
0	Request Buffer Length-2	WORD	lo-hi
2	09h	BYTE	
3	Group ID	LONG	hi-lo
7	Member Set	WORD	

Reply Buffer (202 bytes):

Offset	Content	Type	Order
0	Reply Buffer Length-2	WORD	lo-hi
2	Group Members	LONG[50]	hi-lo

The NetWare C Interface is not supported.

Get Number Of Local Drives (DBh) (Workstation Environment Services API)

This call is supported in NetWare versions 4.0 and 4.6, in Advanced NetWare versions 1.0, 1.02, 2.0 and 2.1, and in NetWare 386 and later versions.

Registers in:

AL	DBh

Registers out:

AL	Number of Local Drives

The NetWare C Interface format is:

```
int GetNumberOfLocalDrives( void );
```

Get Object Connection Numbers (E3h 15h) (Connection Services API)

This call is supported in Advanced NetWare versions 1.0, 1.02, 2.0 and 2.1, and in NetWare 386 and later versions.

Registers in:

AH	E3h
DS:SI	Address of Request Buffer
ES:DI	Address of Reply Buffer

Registers out:

AL	Completion Code

Completion codes:

00h	Successful

Request Buffer (maximum buffer length = 53 bytes):

Offset	Content	Type	Order
0	Request Buffer Length-2	WORD	lo-hi
2	15h	BYTE	
3	Object Type	WORD	hi-lo
5	Object Name Length (1 to 47)	BYTE	
6	Object Name	BYTE[*LENGTH*]	

Reply Buffer (maximum buffer length = 103 bytes):

Offset	Content	Type	Order
0	Reply Buffer Length-2	WORD	lo-hi
2	Number Of Connections	BYTE	
3	Logical Connection List	BYTE[*COUNT*](1-100) for 286	

The NetWare C Interface format is:

```
int GetObjectConnectionNumbers( char *objectName, WORD objectType,
   WORD *numberOfConnections, WORD *connectionList,
   WORD maxConnections );
```

Get Path From Directory Entry (E2h 1Ah) (File Server Environment Services API)

This call is supported in Advanced NetWare version 2.1, NetWare 386, and later versions.

Registers in:

AH	E2h
DS:SI	Request Buffer Address
ES:DI	Reply Buffer Address

Registers out:

AL	Completion Code

Completion code:

00h	Successful

Request Buffer (6 bytes):

Offset	Content	Type	Order
0	Request Buffer Length - 2	WORD	lo-hi
2	1Ah	BYTE	
3	Volume Number	BYTE	
4	Directory Entry	WORD	hi-lo

Reply Buffer (maximum buffer = 258 bytes):

Offset	Content	Type	Order
0	Reply Buffer Length - 2	WORD	lo-hi
2	Path	BYTE[256]	

The NetWare C Interface format is:

```
int GetFilePathFromDirectoryEntry( WORD connectionID,
   BYTE volumeNumber, WORD directoryEntry, char *path );
```

Get Personal Message (E1h 05h) (Message Services API)

This call is supported in NetWare versions 4.0 and 4.6, in Advanced NetWare versions 1.0, 1.02, 2.0, and 2.1, and in NetWare 386; but will not be supported in NetWare 386 versions dated after 1990.

Registers in:

AH	E1h
DS:SI	Request Buffer Address
ES:DI	Reply Buffer Address

Registers out:

AL	Completion Code

Completion codes:

00h	Successful
FEh	I/O Failure; Lack Of Dynamic Workspace

Request Buffer (3 bytes):

Offset	Content	Type	Order
0	Request Buffer Length - 2	WORD	lo-hi
2	05h	BYTE	

Reply Buffer (maximum buffer length = 130 bytes):

Offset	Content	Type	Order
0	Reply Buffer Length - 2	WORD	lo-hi
2	Source Connection	BYTE	
3	Message Length (0 to 126)	BYTE	
4	Message	BYTE[*LENGTH*]	

The NetWare C Interface format is:

```
int GetPersonalMessage( char *messageBuffer,
   WORD *sourceConnection );
```

Get Physical Disk Statistics (E3h D8h) (File Server Environment Services API)

This call is supported in Advanced NetWare version 2.1, NetWare 386, and later versions.

Registers in:

AH	E3h
DS:SI	Request Buffer Address
ES:DI	Reply Buffer Address

Registers out:

AL	Completion Code

Completion code:

00h	Successful
C6h	No Console Rights

Request Buffer (4 bytes):

Offset	Content	Type	Order
0	Request Buffer Length -2	WORD	lo-hi
2	D8h	BYTE	
3	Physical Disk Number	BYTE	

Reply Buffer (95 bytes):

Offset	Content	Type	Order
0	Reply Buffer Length - 2	WORD	lo-hi
2	System Elapsed Time	LONG	hi-lo
6	Physical Disk Channel	BYTE	
7	Drive Removable Flag	BYTE	
8	Physical Drive Type	BYTE	
9	Controller Drive Number	BYTE	
10	Controller Number	BYTE	
11	Controller Type	BYTE	
12	Drive Size	LONG	hi-lo
16	Drive Cylinders	WORD	hi-lo
18	Drive Heads	BYTE	
19	Sectors Per Track	BYTE	
20	Drive Definition String	BYTE[64]	
84	IO Error Count	WORD	
86	Hot Fix Table Start	LONG	hi-lo
90	Hot Fix Table Size	WORD	hi-lo
92	Hot Fix Blocks Available	WORD	hi-lo
94	Hot Fix Disabled	BYTE	

The NetWare C Interface format is:

```
int GetPhysicalDiskStatistics( WORD connectionID,
   BYTE physicalDiskNumber, int structSize,
   PHYS_DISK_STATS *physicalDiskStats, char *driveDefinition );
```

Get Physical Record Locks By Connection And File (E3h DDh) (File Server Environment Services API)

This call is supported in Advanced NetWare version 2.1, NetWare 386, and later versions.

Registers in:

AH	E3h
DS:SI	Request Buffer Address
ES:DI	Reply Buffer Address

Registers out:

AL	Completion Code

Completion code:

00h	Successful
C6h	No Console Rights
FFh	File Not Open

Request Buffer (24 bytes):

Offset	Content	Type	Order
0	Request Buffer Length -2	WORD	lo-hi
2	DDh	BYTE	
3	Logical Connection Number	WORD	hi-lo
5	Last Record Seen	WORD	hi-lo
7	Volume Number (0 to 31)	BYTE	
8	Directory Handle	WORD	hi-lo
10	File Path (ASCIIZ String)	BYTE[14]	

Reply Buffer (maximum buffer = 512 bytes):

Offset	Content	Type	Order
0	Reply Buffer Length -2	WORD	lo-hi
2	Next Request Record	WORD	hi-lo
4	Physical Record Lock Count	BYTE	
5	Records	BYTE	

Physical record lock information (repeated Records times):

Offset	Content	Type	Order
?	Task Number	BYTE	
?	LockStatus	BYTE	
?	Record Start	LONG	hi-lo
?	Record End	LONG	hi-lo

The NetWare C Interface format is:

```
int GetPhysRecLockByConnectAndFile( WORD connectionID,
   WOR connectionNumber, BYTE volumeNumber, WORD directoryHandle,
   char *filePath, int *lastRecord, int *lastTask, int structSize,
   SHORT_PHYS_REC_LOCK *recordLock );
```

Get Physical Record Locks By File (E3h DEh) (File Server Environment Services API)

This call is supported in Advanced NetWare version 2.1, NetWare 386, and later versions.

Registers in:

AH	E3h
DS:SI	Request Buffer Address
ES:DI	Reply Buffer Address

Registers out:

AL	Completion Code

Completion code:

00h	Successful
C6h	No Console Rights
FFh	File Not Open

Request Buffer (maximum buffer = 262 bytes):

Offset	Content	Type	Order
0	Request Buffer Length - 2	WORD	lo-hi
2	DEh	BYTE	
3	Last Record Seen	WORD	hi-lo
5	Directory Handle	BYTE	
6	File Path Length (1 to 255)	BYTE	
7	File Path (ASCIIZ String)	BYTE[*LENGTH*]	

Reply Buffer (maximum buffer = 512 bytes):

Offset	Content	Type	Order
0	Reply Buffer Length - 2	WORD	lo-hi
2	Next Request Record	WORD	hi-lo

4	Physical Record Lock Count	BYTE
5	Records	BYTE

Physical Record Lock (repeated Records times):

Offset	Content	Type	Order
?	Logged Count	WORD	hi-lo
?	Shareable Lock Count	WORD	hi-lo
?	Record Start	LONG	hi-lo
?	Record End	LONG	hi-lo
?	Logical Connection Number	WORD	hi-lo
?	Task Number	BYTE	
?	Lock Type	BYTE	

The NetWare C Interface format is:

```
int  GetPhysicalRecordLocksByFile( WORD connectionID,
   WORD directoryHandle, char *filePath, int *lastRecord,
   int *lastTask, int structSize, PHYS_REC_LOCK *recordLock );
```

Get Preferred Connection ID (F0h 01h) (Workstation Environment Services API)

This call is supported in Advanced NetWare versions 1.0, 1.02, 2.0 and 2.1, and in NetWare 386 and later versions.

Registers in:

AH	F0h
AL	01h

Registers out:

AL	Connection ID of the preferred file server (1 to 8) or a 0 if the preferred file server is not set

The NetWare C Interface format is:

```
WORD GetPreferredConnectionID( void );
```

Get Primary Connection ID (F0h 05h) (Workstation Environment Services API)

This call is supported in Advanced NetWare versions 2.0 and 2.1, and in NetWare 386 and later versions.

Registers in:

AH	F0h
AL	05h

Registers out:

AL	Connection ID of the primary file server (1 to 8), or 0 if the primary File Server is not set.

The NetWare C Interface format is:

```
WORD GetPrimaryConnectionID( void );
```

Get Printer Status (E0h 06h) (Print Services API)

This call is supported in NetWare versions 4.0 and 4.6, in Advanced NetWare versions 1.0, 1.02, 2.0 and 2.1, and in NetWare 386 and later versions.

Registers in:

AH	E0h
DS:SI	Request Packet Address
ES:DI	Reply Packet Address

Registers out:

AL	Completion Code

Completion codes:

00	Successful
FFh	No Such Printer

Request Packet (4 bytes):

Offset	Content	Type	Order
0	Request Buffer Length-2	WORD	lo-hi
2	06h	BYTE	
3	Printer Number	BYTE (0-4)	

Reply Packet (2 bytes):

Offset	Content	Type	Order
0	Reply Buffer Length - 2	WORD	lo-hi
2	Printer Halted	BYTE	
3	Printer Offline	BYTE	
4	Form Type	BYTE (0-255)	
5	Target Printer Number	BYTE (0-4)	

The NetWare C Interface format is:

```
int GetPrinterStatus( int printerNumber, BYTE *printerHalted,
   BYTE *printerOffLine, int *formType, int *targetPrinter );
```

Get Process ID (0Bh) (Value-Added Process Services API)

This call is supported in Advanced NetWare version 2.1.

Registers in:

DI	0Bh

Registers out:

AX	Process ID

The NetWare C Interface format is:

```
WORD GetProcessID( void );
```

Get Queue Job List (E3h 6Bh) (Queue Services API)

This call is supported in Advanced NetWare version 2.1, NetWare 386, and later versions.

Registers in:

AH	E3h
DS:SI	Request Buffer Address
ES:DI	Reply Buffer Address

Registers out:

AL	Completion Code

Completion codes:

00h	Success
96h	Server Out of Memory
9Ch	Invalid Path
D0h	Q Error
D1h	No Queue
D2h	No Q Server
D3h	No Q Rights
FCh	No Such Object
FEh	Server Bindery Locked
FFh	Bindery Failure

Request Packet (7 bytes):

Offset	Content	Type	Order
0	Request Buffer Length-2	WORD	lo-hi
2	6Bh	BYTE	
3	Queue ID	LONG	hi-lo

Reply Packet (504 bytes):

Offset	Content	Type	Order
0	Reply Packet Length-2	WORD	lo-hi
2	Job Count (1 to 250)	WORD	hi-lo
4	Job Number List	WORD[*Job Count*]	hi-lo
6	Max Job Numbers	WORD	hi-lo

The NetWare C Interface format is:

```
int GetQueueJobList( long QueueID, WORD *jobCount,
   WORD *jobNumberList, WORD maxJobNumbers );
```

Get Queue Job's File Size (E3h 78h) (Queue Services API)

This call is supported in Advanced NetWare version 2.1, NetWare 386, and later versions.

Registers in:

AH	E3h
DS:SI	Request Packet Address
ES:DI	Reply Buffer Address

Registers out:

AL	Completion Code

Completion codes:

00h	Successful

Request Packet (9 bytes):

Offset	Content	Type	Order
0	Request Packet Length-2	WORD	lo-hi
2	78h	BYTE	
3	Queue ID	LONG	hi-lo
7	Job Number	WORD	hi-lo

Reply Packet (12 bytes):

Offset	Content	Type	Order
0	Reply Packet Length-2	WORD	lo-hi
2	Queue Object ID	LONG	hi-lo
6	Job Number	WORD	hi-lo
0	File Size	LONG	hi-lo

The NetWare C Interface format is:

```
int GetQueueJobsFileSize( long queueID, int jobNumber,
   long fileSize );
```

Get Screen Mode (09h) (Value-Added Process Services API)

This call is supported in Advanced NetWare version 2.1.

Registers in:

DI	09h

Registers out:

AX	Controlling Process

The NetWare C Interface format is:

```
int GetScreenMode( void );
```

Get Shell Version Information (EAh 01h) (Workstation Environment Services API)

This call is supported in NetWare versions 4.6, in Advanced NetWare versions 1.0, 1.02, 2.0 and 2.1, and in NetWare 386 and later versions.

Registers in:

AH	EAh
AL	01h
BX	00h
ES:DI	Reply Buffer Address

Completion codes:
None

Registers out:

AH	Workstation Operating System (0=DOS)
AL	Customization Code
BH	Major NetWare Shell Version
BL	Minor NetWare Shell Version
CL	Shell Revision Number (1=A,2=B,etc.)

Reply Packet:

Offset	Content	Type
0	Operating System Type	BYTE
?	Operating System Version	BYTE
?	Hardware Type	BYTE
?	Short Hardware Type	BYTE

The NetWare C Interface format is:

```
int GetShellVersionInformation( BYTE *majorVersion,
   BYTE *minorVersion, BYTE *revisionLevel );
```

Get Specific Capture Flags (B8h 02h) (Print Services API)

This call is supported in Advanced NetWare version 2.1, and in NetWare 386 and later versions.

Registers in:

AH	B8h
AL	02h
CX	Reply Buffer Length (1-63)
ES:BX	Reply Buffer
DH	LPT Device (0 = LPT1, 1 = LPT2, 2 = LPT3)

Registers out:

AL	Completion Code

Completion codes:

00h	Successful

Reply Packet (63 bytes):

Offset	Content	Type	Order
0	Status	BYTE	
1	Flags	BYTE	
2	Tab Size	BYTE (1-18)	
3	Server Printer	BYTE (0-4)	
4	Number of Copies	BYTE (0-255)	
5	Form Type	BYTE (0-255)	
6	Reserved	BYTE	
7	Banner Text (ASCIIZ)	BYTE[13]	
20	Reserved	BYTE	
21	Local LPT Device	BYTE	
22	Flush Capture Timeout	WORD	hi-lo
24	Flush Capture On Device Close	BYTE	
25	Max Lines	WORD	hi-lo
27	Max Chars	WORD	hi-lo
29	Form Name (ASCIIZ)	BYTE[13]	
42	LPT Capture Flag	BYTE	
43	File Capture Flag	BYTE	
44	Timing Out Flag	BYTE	
45	Printer Setup Buffer Address	LONG	hi-lo /*Different*/
49	Printer Reset Buffer Address	LONG	hi-lo ""
53	Connection ID Queue Print Job	BYTE	
54	Capture In Progress	BYTE	
55	Print Queue Flag	BYTE	
56	Print Job Valid	BYTE	
57	Print Queue ID	LONG	hi-lo
61	Print Job Number	WORD (1-999)	hi-lo

The NetWare C Interface format is:

```
int GetSpecificCaptureFlags( BYTE localLPTDevice,
   CAPTURE_FLAGS *captureFlags );
```

Get Spool Queue Entry (E0h 04h) (Print Services API)

This call is supported in NetWare versions 4.0 and 4.6, in Advanced NetWare versions 1.0, 1.02, 2.0 and 2.1, and in NetWare 386. It has been replaced by higher-level functions, but is shown here for completeness.

Registers in:

AH	E0h
DS:SI	Request Buffer
ES:DI	Reply Buffer

Registers out:

AL	Completion Code

Completion codes:

00h	Successful

Request Packet (5 bytes):

Offset	Content	Type	Order
0	Request Buffer Length-2	WORD	lo-hi
2	04h	BYTE	
3	Printer Number	BYTE	
4	Job Number	BYTE	

Reply Packet (83 bytes):

Offset	Content	Type	Order
0	Reply Packet Length - 2	WORD	lo-hi
2	Job Number	BYTE	
3	Filler	BYTE[2]	
5	File Name	BYTE[14]	
19	Print Volume	BYTE	
20	Print Flags	BYTE	
21	Tab Size	BYTE	
22	Printer	BYTE	
23	Copies	BYTE	
24	Form Type	BYTE	
25	Station	BYTE	
26	Spool Time	BYTE[6]	
32	User Name	BYTE[15]	
47	Banner Name	BYTE[14]	
61	Path Name	BYTE[18]	
79	User ID	LONG	hi-lo /* only on NetWare 2.0 and above */

The NetWare C Interface format is not supported.

Get Station Address (EEh) (Connection Services API)

This call is supported in NetWare versions 4.6, in Advanced NetWare versions 1.0, 1.02, 2.0 and 2.1, and in NetWare 386 and later versions.

Registers in:

AH	EEh

Registers out:

CX, BX, AX	Physical Node Address

Completion codes:
None

The NetWare C Interface format is:

```
void GetStationAddress( BYTE *physicalNodeAddress );
```

Get Station's Logged Information (E3h 05h) (Workstation Environment Services API)

This call is supported in NetWare versions 4.0 and 4.6, in Advanced NetWare versions 1.0, 1.02, 2.0 and 2.1, and in NetWare 386. It has been replaced by higher-level calls such as Get Connection Information but is shown here for completeness.

Registers in:

AH	E3h
DS:SI	Address of Request buffer
ES:DI	Address of Reply buffer

Registers out:

AL	Completion Code

Completion codes:

00h	Successful

Request Packet (maximum buffer length = 51 bytes):

Offset	Content	Type	Order
0	Request Buffer Length-2	WORD	lo-hi
2	05h	BYTE	
3	Connection Number	BYTE	

Reply Buffer (max = 288 bytes):

Offset	Content	Type	Order
0	Reply Buffer Length-2	WORD	lo-hi
2	User Name	BYTE[16]	
18	Log Time	BYTE[7]	
25	Reserved	BYTE[9]	
34	Full Name	BYTE[30]	
64	User ID	LONG	
68	User Groups	LONG[32]	hi-lo
196	Home Directory	BYTE[64]	

The NetWare C Interface format is not supported.

Get VAP Header (17h) (Value-Added Process Services API)

This call is supported in Advanced NetWare version 2.1.

Registers in:

AX	VAP Number
DI	17h

Registers out:

AX	VAP Header Segment

The NetWare C Interface format is:

```
int GetVAPHeader( int VAPnumber );
```

Get Volume Information (E3h E9h) (Directory Services API)

This call is supported in Advanced NetWare 2.1 and in NetWare versions 386 and later.

Registers in:

AH	E3h
DS:SI	Request Buffer Address
ES:DI	Reply Buffer Address

Registers out:

AL	Completion Code

Completion codes:

00	Success

Request Packet (4 bytes):

Offset	Content	Type	Order
0	Request Buffer Length-2	WORD	lo-hi
2	E9h	BYTE	
3	Volume Number	BYTE	

Reply Packet (40 bytes):

Offset	Content	Type	Order
0	Reply Buffer Length-2	WORD	lo-hi
2	System Elapsed Time	WORD	hi-lo
6	Volume Number	BYTE	
7	Logical Drive Number	BYTE	
8	Sectors Per Block	WORD	hi-lo
10	Starting Block	WORD	hi-lo
12	Total Blocks	WORD	hi-lo
14	Available Blocks	WORD	hi-lo
16	Total Directory Slots	WORD	hi-lo
18	Avail. Directory Slots	WORD	hi-lo
20	Actual Max Used Dir Slots	WORD	hi-lo
22	Volume Is Hashed	BYTE	
23	Volume Is Cached	BYTE	
24	Volume is Removable	BYTE	
25	Volume is Mounted	BYTE	
26	Volume Name	BYTE[16]	

The NetWare C Interface format is:

```
int GetVolumeInformation( WORD connectionID, BYTE volumeNumber,
   int structSize, VOLUME_STATS *volumeStatistics );
```

Get Volume Info With Handle (E2h 15h) (Directory Services API)

This call is supported in NetWare versions 4.0 and 4.6, in Advanced NetWare versions 1.0, 1.02, 2.0 and 2.1, and in NetWare 386 and later versions.

Registers in:

AH	E2h
DS:SI	Request Buffer Address
ES:DI	Reply Buffer Address

Registers out:

AL	Completion Code

Completion codes:

00	Success

Request Packet (4 bytes):

Offset	Content	Type	Order
0	Request Buffer Length-2	WORD	lo-hi
2	15h	BYTE	
3	Directory Handle	BYTE	

Reply Packet (30 bytes):

Offset	Content	Type	Order
0	Reply Buffer Length-2	WORD	lo-hi
2	Sectors Per Block	WORD	hi-lo
4	Total Blocks	WORD	hi-lo
6	Available Blocks	WORD	hi-lo
8	Total Directory Slots	WORD	hi-lo
10	Available Directory Slots	WORD	hi-lo
12	Volume Name	BYTE[16]	
28	Volume Is Removable	WORD	hi-lo

The NetWare C Interface format is:

```
int GetVolumeInfoWithHandle( BYTE directoryHandle, char *volumeName,
    WORD *totalBlocks, WORD *sectorsPerBlock, WORD *availableBlocks,
    WORD *totalDirectorySlots, WORD *availableDirectorySlots,
    WORD *volumeIsRemovable );
```

Get Volume Info With Number (DAh) (Directory Services API)

This call is supported in NetWare versions 4.0 and 4.6, in Advanced NetWare versions 1.0, 1.02, 2.0 and 2.1, and in NetWare 386 and later versions.

Registers in:

AH	DAh
DL	Volume Number
ES:DI	Reply Buffer Address

Registers out:

AL	Completion Code

Completion codes:

00	Success

Reply Packet (28 bytes):

Offset	Content	Type	Order
0	Sectors Per Block	WORD	hi-lo
2	Total Blocks	WORD	hi-lo
4	Available Blocks	WORD	hi-lo
6	Total Directory Slots	WORD	hi-lo

8	Available Directory Slots	WORD	hi-lo
10	Volume Name	BYTE[16]	
26	Volume Is Removable	WORD	hi-lo

The NetWare C Interface format is:

```
int GetVolumeInfoWithNumber( BYTE volumeNumber, char *volumeName,
    WORD *totalBlocks, WORD *sectorsPerBlock, WORD *availableBlocks,
    WORD *totalDirectorySlots, WORD *availableDirectorySlots,
    WORD *volumeIsRemovable );
```

Get Volume Name (E2h 06h) (Directory Services API)

This call is supported in NetWare versions 4.0 and 4.6, in Advanced NetWare versions 1.0, 1.02, 2.0 and 2.1, and in NetWare 386 and later versions. It returns the volume name given the number of the volume.

Registers in:

AH	E2h
DS:SI	Request Buffer Address
ES:DI	Reply Buffer Address

Registers out:

AL	Completion Code

Completion codes:

00	Success
98h	Volume Does Not Exist

Request Packet (4 bytes):

Offset	**Content**	**Type**	**Order**
0	Request Buffer Length-2	WORD	lo-hi
2	06	BYTE	
3	Volume Number	BYTE	

Reply Packet (19 bytes):

Offset	**Content**	**Type**	**Order**
0	Reply Buffer Length-2	WORD	lo-hi
2	Volume Name Length(1-16)	BYTE	
3	Volume Name	BYTE[16]	

The NetWare C Interface format is:

```
int GetVolumeName( int volumeNumber, char *volumeName );
```

Get Volume Number (E2h 05h) (Directory Services API)

This call is supported in NetWare versions 4.0 and 4.6, in Advanced NetWare versions 1.0, 1.02, 2.0 and 2.1, and in NetWare 386 and later versions.

Registers in:

AH	E2h
DS:SI	Request Buffer Address
ES:DI	Reply Buffer Address

Registers out:

AL	Completion Code

Completion codes:

00	Success
98h	Volume Does Not Exist

Request Packet (20 bytes):

Offset	Content	Type	Order
0	Request Buffer Length-2	WORD	lo-hi
2	05	BYTE	
3	Volume Name Length(1-16)	BYTE	
4	Volume Name	BYTE[16]	

Reply Packet (3 bytes):

Offset	Content	Type	Order
0	Reply Buffer Length-2	WORD	lo-hi
2	Volume Number	BYTE	

The NetWare C Interface format is:

```
int GetVolumeNumber( char *volumeName, int *volumeNumber );
```

Initialization Complete (07h) (Value-Added Process Services API)

This call is supported in Advanced NetWare version 2.1.

Registers in:

DI	07h

The NetWare C Interface format is:

```
void InitializationComplete( void );
```

In String (0Bh) (Value-Added Process Services API)

This call is supported in Advanced NetWare version 2.1.

Registers in:

AH	Row
AL	Column
DS:SI	Prompt
ES:BX	Input Buffer
DL	Input Buffer Length
DI	11h

Registers out:

AX	Input String Length

The NetWare C Interface format is:

```
int InString( BYTE row, BYTE column, char *prompt,
   char *inputBuffer, BYTE bufferLength );
```

IPX Cancel Event (06h) (Communications Services API)

This call is supported in Advanced NetWare 1.02, 2.0 and 2.1, and in NetWare 386 and later versions.

Registers in:

BX	06h
ES:SI	ECB Address

Registers out:

AL	Completion Code

Completion codes:

00h	Successful
F9h	ECB Cannot Be Canceled
FFh	ECB Not In Use

The NetWare C Interface format is:

```
int IPXCancelEvent( ECB *eventControlBlock );
```

IPX Close Socket (01h) (Communications Services API)

This call is supported in Advanced NetWare 1.02, 2.0 and 2.1, and in NetWare 386 and later versions.

Registers in:

BX	01h
DX	Socket Number (hi-lo)

Registers out:
Nothing

Completion codes:
None

The NetWare C Interface format is:

```
void IPXCloseSocket( WORD socketNumber );
```

IPX Disconnect From Target (0Bh) (Communications Services API)

This call is supported in Advanced NetWare 1.02, 2.0 and 2.1, and in NetWare 386 and later versions.

Registers in:

BX	0BH
ES:SI	Request Buffer Address

Registers out:
Nothing

Completion codes:
None

Request Buffer (12 bytes):

Offset	Content	Type	Order
0	Destination Network	BYTE[4]	hi-lo
4	Destination Node	BYTE[6]	hi-lo
10	Destination Socket	BYTE[2]	hi-lo

The NetWare C Interface format is:

```
void IPXDisconnectFromTarget( BYTE *networkAddress );
```

IPX Get Internetwork Address (09h) (Communications Services API)

This call is supported in Advanced NetWare 1.02, 2.0 and 2.1, and in NetWare 386 and later versions.

Registers in:

BX	09h

Registers out:

ES:SI	Reply Buffer Address

Completion codes:
None

Reply Buffer (10 bytes):

Offset	Content	Type	Order
0	Network Address	BYTE[4]	hi-lo
4	Node Address	BYTE[6]	hi-lo

The NetWare C Interface format is:

```
void GetInternetworkAddress( BYTE *network Address );
```

IPX Get Interval Marker (08h) (Communications Services API)

This call is supported in Advanced NetWare 1.02, 2.0 and 2.1, and in NetWare 386 and later versions.

Registers in:

BX	08h

Registers out:

AX	Interval Marker

Completion codes:
None

The NetWare C Interface format is:

```
unsigned IPXGetIntervalMarker( void );
```

IPX Get Local Target (02h) (Communications Services API)

This call is supported in Advanced NetWare 1.02, 2.0 and 2.1, and in NetWare 386 and later versions.

Registers in:

BX	02h
ES:SI	Request Buffer Address
ES:DI	Reply Buffer Address

Registers out:

AL	Completion Code
CX	Transport Time

Completion codes:

00h	Successful
FAh	No Path to Destination Node Found

Request Buffer (12 bytes):

Offset	Content	Type	Order
0	Destination Network	BYTE[4]	hi-lo
4	Destination Node	BYTE[6]	hi-lo
10	Destination Socket	BYTE[2]	hi-lo

Reply Buffer (6 bytes):

Offset	Content	Type
0	Local Target	BYTE[6]

The NetWare C Interface format is:

```
int GetLocalTarget( BYTE *networkAddress, BYTE *immediateAddress,
   int transportTime );
```

IPX Listen For Packet (04h) (Communications Services API)

This call is supported in Advanced NetWare 1.02, 2.0 and 2.1, and in NetWare 386 and later versions.

Registers in:

BX	04h
ES:SI	ECB Address

Registers out:

AL	Completion Code

Completion codes:

FFh	Listening Socket Does Not Exist

The NetWare C Interface format is:

```
void IPXListenForPacket( ECB *eventControlBlock );
```

IPX Open Socket (00h) (Communications Services API)

This call is supported in Advanced NetWare 1.02, 2.0 and 2.1, and in NetWare 386 and later versions.

Registers in:

BX	00h
AL	Socket Longevity Flag
DX	Requested Socket Number (hi-lo)

Registers out:

AL	Completion Code
DX	Assigned Socket Number

Completion codes:

00h	Successful
FFh	Socket Already Open
FEh	Socket Table Is Full

The NetWare C Interface format is:

```
int IPXOpenSocket( BYTE *socketNumber, BYTE socketType );
```

IPX Relinquish Control (0Ah) (Communications Services API)

This call is supported in Advanced NetWare 1.02, 2.0 and 2.1, and in NetWare 386 and later versions.

Registers in:

BX	0Ah

Registers out:
None

Completion codes:
None

The NetWare C Interface format is:

```
void IPXRelinquishControl( void );
```

IPX Schedule IPX Event (05h) (Communications Services API)

This call is supported in Advanced NetWare 1.02, 2.0 and 2.1, and in NetWare 386 and later versions.

Registers in:

BX	05h
AX	Delay Time
ES:SI	ECB Address

Registers out:
Nothing

Completion codes:
None

The NetWare C Interface format is:

```
void IPXScheduleIPXEvent( WORD timeUnits, ECB *eventControlBlock );
```

IPX Send Packet (03h) (Communications Services API)

This call is supported in Advanced NetWare 1.02, 2.0 and 2.1, and in NetWare 386 and later versions.

Registers in:

BX	03h
ES:SI	ECB Address

Registers out:
Nothing

Completion codes:
None

The NetWare C Interface format is:

```
void IPXSendPacket( ECB *eventControlBlock );
```

Is Bindery Object In Set (E3h 43h) (Bindery Services API)

This call is supported in Advanced NetWare versions 1.0, 1.02, 2.0 and 2.1, and in NetWare 386 and later versions.

Registers in:

AH	E3h
DS:SI	Request Buffer Length
ES:DI	Reply Buffer Length

Registers out:

AL	Completion Code

Completion codes:

00	Success
96h	Server Out Of Memory
EAh	No Such Member
EBh	Not Group Property
F0h	Wildcard Not Allowed
F9h	No Property Read Privileges
FCh	No Such Object
FEh	Server Bindery Locked
FFh	Bindery Failure

Request Packet (max size = 119 bytes):

Offset	Content	Type	Order
0	Request Buffer Length-2	WORD	lo-hi
2	43h	BYTE	
3	Object Type	WORD	hi-lo
5	Object Name Length	BYTE [1-47]	
6	Object Name	BYTE[*LENGTH*]	
?	Property Name Length	BYTE [1-15]	
?	Property Name	BYTE[*LENGTH*]	
?	Member Type	WORD	hi-lo
?	Member Name Length	BYTE [1-47]	
?	Member Name	BYTE[*LENGTH*]	

Reply Packet (2 bytes):

Offset	Content	Type	Order
0	0000	WORD	lo-hi

The NetWare C Interface format is:

```
int IsBinderyObjectInSet( char *objectName, WORD objectType,
   char *propertyName, char *memberName, WORD memberType );
```

Kill Process (08h) (Value-Added Process Services API)

This call is supported in Advanced NetWare version 2.1.

Registers in:

DI	08h

The NetWare C Interface format is:

```
void KillProcess( void );
```

Lock File Set (CBh) (Locking API)

This call is supported in NetWare versions 4.0 and 4.6, in Advanced NetWare versions 1.0, 1.02, 2.0 and 2.1, and in NetWare 386 and later versions.

Under lock mode 0, the compatibility mode:

Registers in:

AH	CBh
DL	Mode (0 = No Wait, 1 = Wait)

Registers out:

AL	Completion Code

Completion codes:

00h	Success
FFh	Failure

Under lock mode 1, the extended mode:

Registers in:

AH	CBh
BP	Timeout Limit (in 1/18th seconds, 0 = no wait)

Registers out:

AL	Completion Code

Completion codes:

00h	Success
FEh	Timeout Failure
FFh	Failure

The NetWare C Interface format is:

```
int LockFileSet( WORD timeoutLimit );
```

Lock Logical Record Set (D1h) (Locking API)

This call is supported in NetWare versions 4.0 and 4.6, in Advanced NetWare versions 1.0, 1.02, 2.0 and 2.1, and in NetWare 386 and later versions.

Under lock mode 0, the compatibility mode:

Registers in:

AH	D1h
DL	Mode (0 = No wait, 1 = Wait)

Registers out:

AL	Completion Code

Completion codes:

00h	Success
FFh	Failure

Under lock mode 1, the extended mode:

Registers in:

AH	D1h
AL	Lock Directive
BP	Timeout Limit

Registers out:

AL	Completion Code

Completion codes:

00h	Success
FEh	Timeout Failure
FFh	Failure

The NetWare C Interface format is:

```
int LockLogicalRecordSet( WORD timeoutLimit );
```

Lock Physical Record Set (C2h) (Locking API)

This call is supported in NetWare version 4.6, in Advanced NetWare versions 1.0, 1.02, 2.0 and 2.1, and in NetWare 386 and later versions.

Registers in:

AH	C2h
AL	Lock Directive
BP	Timeout Limit (0 = no wait, -1 = wait forever)

Registers out:

AL	Completion Code

Completion codes:

00h	Success
FEh	Timeout Failure
FFh	Failure

The NetWare C Interface format is:

```
int LockPhysicalRecordSet( BYTE lockDirective, WORD timeoutLimit );
```

Log File (CAh) (FCB) (Locking API)

This call is supported in NetWare versions 4.0 and 4.6, in Advanced NetWare versions 1.0, 1.02, 2.0 and 2.1, and in NetWare 386.

Under lock mode 0, the compatibility mode:

Registers in:

AH	CAh
DS:DX	Address of File Control Block

Completion codes:

00h	No Error
FFh	Fail

Under lock mode 1, the extended mode:

Registers in:

AH	CAh
AL	Locking Directive
DS:DX	Address of FCB
BP	Timeout Limit

Registers out:

AL	Completion Code

Completion codes:

00	Success
96h	Server Out of Memory
FEh	Timeout Failure
FFh	Hardware Failure

The NetWare C Interface format is not supported.

Log File (EBh) (ASCIIZ) (Locking API)

This call is supported in NetWare versions 4.0 and 4.6, in Advanced NetWare versions 1.0, 1.02, 2.0 and 2.1, and in NetWare 386 and later versions.

Under lock mode 0, the compatibility mode:

Registers in:

AH	EBh
DS:DX	Request Buffer Address

Completion codes:

00h	No Error
FFh	Fail

Request Buffer:

File Path	1-255	ASCIIZ (max len is 255)

Under lock mode 1, the extended mode:

Registers in:

AH	EBh
AL	Locking Directive
DS:DX	Request Buffer Address
BP	Timeout Limit

Registers out:

AL	Completion Code

Completion codes:

00	Success
96h	Server Out of Memory
FEh	Timeout Failure
FFh	Hardware Failure

Request Buffer:

File Path	1-255	ASCIIZ (max len is 255)

The NetWare C Interface format is:

```
int LogFile( char *fileName, BYTE lockDirective,
  WORD timeoutLimit );
```

Login (E3h 00h) (Connection Services API)

This call is supported in NetWare versions 4.0 and 4.6, in Advanced NetWare versions 1.0, 1.02, 2.0 and 2.1, and in NetWare 386.

Registers in:

AH	E3h
DS:SI	Address of Request buffer
ES:DI	Address of Reply buffer

Registers out:

AL	Completion Code

Completion codes:

00h	Successful

Request Packet (maximum buffer length = 179 bytes):

Offset	Content	Type	Order
0	Request Buffer Length-2	WORD	lo-hi
2	00h	BYTE	
3	User Name Length	BYTE (1-47)	
4	User Name	BYTE[*LENGTH*]	
?	User Password Length	BYTE (0-127)	
?	User Password	BYTE[*LENGTH*]	

Reply Buffer (2 bytes):

Offset	Content	Type	Order
0	0000h	WORD	lo-hi

The NetWare C Interface format is not supported.

Login To File Server (E3h 14h) (Connection Services API)

This call is supported in Advanced NetWare 1.0 and later versions.

Registers in:

AH	E3h
DS:SI	Address of Request Buffer
ES:DI	Address of Reply Buffer

Registers out:

AL	Completion Code

Completion codes:

00h	Successful

Request Packet (maximum buffer length = 181 bytes):

Offset	Content	Type	Order
0	Request Buffer Length-2	WORD	lo-hi
2	14h	BYTE	
3	Object Type	WORD	hi-lo
5	Object Name Length (1 to 47)	BYTE	
6	Object Name	BYTE[*LENGTH*]	
?	Object Password Length	BYTE (0-127)	
?	Object Password	BYTE[*LENGTH*]	

Reply Buffer (2 bytes):

Offset	Content	Type	Order
0	0000h	WORD	lo-hi

The NetWare C Interface format is:

```
int LoginToFileServer( char *objectName, WORD objectType );
```

Log Logical Record (D0h) (Locking API)

This call is supported in NetWare versions 4.0 and 4.6, in Advanced NetWare versions 1.0, 1.02, 2.0 and 2.1, and in NetWare 386 and later versions.

Under lock mode 0, the compatibility mode:

Registers in:

AH	D0h
DS:DX	Request Packet Address

Registers out:

AL	Completion Code

Completion codes:

00h	Success
FFh	Failure

Under lock mode 1, the extended mode:

Registers in:

AH	D0h
AL	Locking Directive
DS:DX	Request Packet Address
BP	Timeout Limit

Registers out:

AL	Completion Code

Completion codes:

00	Success
FEh	Timeout Failure
FFh	Failure

Request Packet:

Logical Record Name Length(1-99)	BYTE
Logical Record Name	BYTE[*LENGTH*]

The NetWare C Interface format is:

```
int LogLogicalRecord( char *logicalRecordName, BYTE lockDirective,
   WORD timeoutLimit );
```

Log Network Message (E3h 0Dh) (Message Services API)

This call is supported in NetWare versions 4.0 and 4.6, in Advanced NetWare versions 1.0, 1.02, 2.0, and 2.15, and in NetWare 386; but will not be supported in NetWare 386 versions dated after 1990.

Registers in:

AH	E3h
DS:SI	Request Buffer Address
ES:DI	Reply Buffer Address

Completion codes:

00h	Successful

Request Buffer(maximum buffer length =84 bytes):

Offset	**Content**	**Type**	**Order**
0	Request Buffer Length - 2	WORD	lo-hi
2	0Dh	BYTE	
3	Message Length (0 to 80)	BYTE	
4	Message	BYTE[*LENGTH*]	

Reply Buffer (2 bytes):

Offset	**Content**	**Type**	**Order**
0	0000h	WORD	lo-hi

The NetWare C Interface format is:

```
int LogNetworkMessage( char *message );
```

Logout (D7h) (Connection Services API)

This call is supported in NetWare versions 4.0 and 4.6, in Advanced NetWare versions 1.0, 1,02, 2.0 and 2.1, and in NetWare 386 and later versions.

Registers in:

AH	D7h

Completion codes:
None

The NetWare C Interface format is:

```
void Logout( void );
```

Logout From File Server (F1h 02h) (Connection Services API)

This call is supported in Advanced NetWare versions 1.0, 1.02, 2.0 and 2.1, and in NetWare 386 and later versions.

Registers in:

AH	F1h
AL	02h
DL	Server Connection ID (1 to 8)

The NetWare C Interface format is:

```
int LogoutFromFileServer( WORD connectionID );
```

Log Physical Record (BCh) (Handle) (Locking API)

This call is supported in NetWare version 4.6, in Advanced NetWare versions 1.0, 1.02, 2.0 and 2.1, and in NetWare 386 and later versions.

Registers in:

AH	BCh
AL	Locking Directive
BX	File Handle
CX	High Record Offset (WORD)
DX	Low Record Offset (WORD)
BP	Timeout Limit
SI	High Record Length (WORD)
DI	Low Record Length (WORD)

Registers out:

AL	Completion Code

Completion codes:

00	Success
96h	Server Out of Memory
FEh	Timeout Failure
FFh	Failure

The NetWare C Interface format is:

```
int LogPhysicalRecord( int fileHandle, long recordStartOffset,
   long recordLength, BYTE lockDirective, WORD timeoutLimit );
```

Log Physical Record (BFh) (FCB) (Locking API)

This call is supported in NetWare version 4.6, in Advanced NetWare versions 1.0, 1.02, 2.0 and 2.1, and in NetWare 386. It will not be supported after 1990.

Registers in:

AH	BFh
AL	Locking Directive
BX	High Record Offset (WORD)
CX	Low Record Offset (WORD)
DS:DX	Address of opened File Control Block (non-extended)
BP	Timeout Limit
SI	High Record Length (WORD)
DI	Low Record Length (WORD)

Registers out:

AL	Completion Code

Completion codes:

00	Success
96h	Server Out of Memory
FEh	Timeout Failure
FFh	Failure

The NetWare C Interface format is not supported.

Map Number To Group Name (E3h 08h) (Workstation Environment Services API)

This call is supported in NetWare versions 4.0 and 4.6, in Advanced NetWare versions 1.0, 1.02, 2.0 and 2.1, and in NetWare 386. It has been replaced by higher-level Bindery Services API calls such as the Get Bindery Object Name call but is shown here for completeness.

Registers in:

AH	E3h
DS:SI	Address of Request buffer
ES:DI	Address of Reply buffer

Registers out:

AL	Completion Code

Completion codes:

00h	Successful

Request Packet (7 bytes):

Offset	Content	Type	Order
0	Request Buffer Length-2	WORD	lo-hi
2	08h	BYTE	
3	Group ID	LONG	hi-lo

Reply Buffer (8 bytes):

Offset	Content	Type	Order
0	Reply Buffer Length-2	WORD	lo-hi
2	Group ID	LONG	hi-lo
6	Group Name Length	BYTE	
7	Group Name	BYTE [1-47]	

The NetWare C Interface format is not supported.

Open Bindery (E3h 45h) (Bindery Services API)

This call is supported in Advanced NetWare versions 1.0, 1.02, 2.0 and 2.1, and in NetWare 386 and later versions.

Registers in:

AH	E3h
DS:SI	Request Buffer Length
ES:DI	Reply Buffer Length

Registers out:

AL	Completion Code

Completion codes:

00	Success

Request Packet (max size = 3 bytes):

Offset	Content	Type	Order
0	Request Buffer Length-2	WORD	lo-hi
2	45h	BYTE	

Reply Packet (2 bytes):

Offset	Content	Type	Order
0	0000	WORD	lo-hi

The NetWare C Interface format is:

```
int OpenBindery( void );
```

Map Number To Object (E3h 04h) (Workstation Environment Services API)

This call is supported in NetWare versions 4.0 and 4.6, in Advanced NetWare versions 1.0, 1.02, 2.0 and 2.1, and in NetWare 386. It has been replaced by higher-level Bindery Services API calls such as the Get Bindery Object Name call but is shown here for completeness.

Registers in:

AH	E3h
DS:SI	Address of Request buffer
ES:DI	Address of Reply buffer

Registers out:

AL	Completion Code

Completion codes:

00h	Successful

Request Packet (7 bytes):

Offset	Content	Type	Order
0	Request Buffer Length-2	WORD	lo-hi
2	04h	BYTE	
3	User ID	LONG	hi-lo

Reply Buffer (52 bytes):

Offset	Content	Type	Order
0	Reply Buffer Length-2	WORD	lo-hi
2	User Name	BYTE[16]	
18	Full Name	BYTE[30]	
48	User ID	LONG	

The NetWare C Interface format is not supported.

Map Object To Number (E3h 03h) (Workstation Environment Services API)

This call is supported in NetWare versions 4.0 and 4.6, in Advanced NetWare versions 1.0, 1.02, 2.0 and 2.1, and in NetWare 386. It has been replaced by higher-level Bindery Services API calls such as the Get Object Number call but is shown here for completeness.

Registers in:

AH	E3h
DS:SI	Address of Request buffer
ES:DI	Address of Reply buffer

Registers out:

AL	Completion Code

Completion codes:

00h	Successful

Request Packet (maximum buffer length = 51 bytes):

Offset	Content	Type	Order
0	Request Buffer Length-2	WORD	lo-hi
2	03h	BYTE	
3	User Name Length (1 to 47)	BYTE	
4	User Name	BYTE[*LENGTH*]	

Reply Buffer (6 bytes):

Offset	Content	Type	Order
0	Reply Buffer Length-2	WORD	lo-hi
2	Object ID	LONG	hi-lo

The NetWare C Interface format is not supported.

Map User to Station Set (E3h 02h) (Workstation Environment Services API)

This call is supported in NetWare versions 4.0 and 4.6, in Advanced NetWare versions 1.0, 1.02, 2.0 and 2.1, and in NetWare 386. It has been replaced by higher-level calls such as the Get Object Connection Numbers call but is shown here for completeness.

Registers in:

AH	E3h
DS:SI	Address of Request buffer
ES:DI	Address of Reply buffer

Registers out:

AL	Completion Code

Completion codes:

00h	Successful

Request Packet (maximum buffer length = 51 bytes):

Offset	Content	Type	Order
0	Request Buffer Length-2	WORD	lo-hi
2	02h	BYTE	
3	User Name Length (1 to 47)	BYTE	
4	User Name	BYTE[*LENGTH*]	

Reply Buffer (2 bytes):

Offset	Content	Type	Order
0	Reply Buffer Length-2	WORD	lo-hi
2	Station List Length	BYTE	
3	Station List	BYTE[*LENGTH*]	

The NetWare C Interface format is not supported.

Open Message Pipe (E1h 06h) (Message Services API)

This call is supported in NetWare versions 4.0 and 4.6, in Advanced NetWare versions 1.0, 1.02, 2.0, and 2.15, and in NetWare 386; but will not be supported in NetWare 386 versions dated after 1990.

Registers in:

AH	E1h
DS:SI	Request Buffer Address
ES:DI	Reply Buffer Address

Registers out:

AL	Completion Code

Completion codes:

00h	Successful
FEh	I/O Failure; Lack Of Dynamic Workspace

Request Buffer (maximum buffer length = 104 bytes):

Offset	Content	Type	Order
0	Request Buffer Length - 2	WORD	lo-hi
2	06h	BYTE	
3	Connection Count(1 to 100)	BYTE	
4	Connection List	BYTE[*COUNT*]	

Reply Buffer (maximum buffer length = 103 bytes):

Offset	Content	Type	Order
0	Reply Buffer Length - 2	WORD	lo-hi
2	Connection Count(1 to 100)	BYTE	
3	Result list	BYTE[*COUNT*]	

The NetWare C Interface format is:

```
int OpenMessagePipe( WORD *connectionList, BYTE *resultList,
   WORD connectionCount );
```

Open Semaphore (C5h 00h) (Locking API)

This call is supported in NetWare version 4.6, in Advanced NetWare versions 1.0, 1.02, 2.0 and 2.1, and in NetWare 386 and later versions.

Registers in:

AH	C5h
AL	00h
DS:DX	Request Buffer Address
CL	Semaphore Value (1-127)

Registers out:

AL	Completion Code
BL	Open Count
CX,DX	Semaphore Handle

Request Packet (Max - 128):

Semaphore Name Length (1-127)	BYTE
Semaphore Name	BYTE[*LENGTH*]

Completion codes:

00h	Successful
FEh	Invalid Semaphore Name Length
FFh	Invalid Semaphore Value

The NetWare C Interface format is:

```
int Open Semaphore( char *semaphoreName, int initialValue,
   long *semaphoreHandle, WORD *openCount );
```

Out String (0Ah) (Value-Added Process Services API)

This call is supported in Advanced NetWare version 2.1.

Registers in:

AH	Row
AL	Column
DS:SI	Message
DL	Message Length
DI	10h

The NetWare C Interface format is:

```
void OutString( BYTE row, BYTE column, char  *message,
   BYTE messageLength );
```

Print String (01h) (Value-Added Process Services API)

This call is supported in Advanced NetWare version 2.1.

Registers in:

DI	01h

The NetWare C Interface format is:

```
void PrintString( WORD row, WORD column, char *message,
   WORD messageLength );
```

Purge All Erased Files (E3h CEh) (File Services API)

This call is supported in Advanced NetWare 2.1 and NetWare 386. It purges all erased files of all workstations. To use it, the user must have console operator rights.

Registers in:

AH	E3h
DS:SI	Request Buffer Length
ES:DI	Reply Buffer Length

Registers out:

AL	Completion Code

Completion codes:

00	Succcss

Request Packet (max size = 3 bytes):

Offset	**Content**	**Type**	**Order**
0	Request Buffer Length-2	WORD	lo-hi
2	CEh	BYTE	

Reply Packet (2 bytes):

Offset	**Content**	**Type**	**Order**
0	0000	WORD	lo-hi

The NetWare C Interface format is:

```
int PurgeAllErasedFiles( void );
```

Purge Erased Files (E2h 10h) (File Services API)

This call is supported in NetWare versions 4.0 and 4.6, in Advanced NetWare versions 1.0, 1.02, 2.0 and 2.1, and in NetWare version 386.

Registers in:

AH	E2h
DS:SI	Request Buffer Length
ES:DI	Reply Buffer Length

Registers out:

AL	Completion Code

Completion codes:

00	Success

Request Packet (max size = 3 bytes):

Offset	Content	Type	Order
0	Request Buffer Length-2	WORD	lo-hi
2	10h	BYTE	

Reply Packet (2 bytes):

0	0000	WORD	lo-hi

The NetWare C Interface format is:

```
int PurgeErasedFiles( void );
```

Read Keyboard (02h) (Value-Added Process Services API)

This call is supported in Advanced NetWare version 2.1.

Registers in:

DI 02h

The NetWare C Interface format is:

```
int ReadKeyboard( char *inputBuffer, WORD bufferLength );
```

Read Property Value (E3h 3Dh) (Bindery Services API)

This call is supported in Advanced NetWare versions 1.0, 1.02, 2.0 and 2.1, and in NetWare 386 and later versions.

Registers in:

AH	E3h
DS:SI	Request Buffer Length
ES:DI	Reply Buffer Length

Registers out:

AL	Completion Code

Completion codes:

00	Success
96h	Server Out Of Memory
ECh	No Such Segment
F0h	Wildcard Not Allowed
F1h	Invalid Bindery Security
FBh	No Such Property
FCh	No Such Object
FEh	Server Bindery Locked
FFh	Bindery Failure

Request Packet (max size = 70 bytes):

Offset	Content	Type	Order
0	Request Buffer Length-2	WORD	lo-hi
2	3Dh	BYTE	
3	Object Type	WORD	hi-lo
5	Object Name Length	BYTE [1-47]	
6	Object Name	BYTE[*LENGTH*]	
?	Segment Number	BYTE	
?	Property Name Length	BYTE [1-15]	
?	Property Name	BYTE[*LENGTH*]	

Reply Packet (132 bytes):

Offset	Content	Type	Order
0	Reply Buffer Length-2	WORD	lo-hi
2	Property Value	BYTE[128]	
130	More Segments	BYTE	
131	Property Flags	BYTE	

The NetWare C Interface format is:

```
int ReadPropertyValue( char *objectName, WORD objectType,
   char *propertyName, int segmentNumber, BYTE *propertyValue,
   BYTE *moreSegments, BYTE *propertyFlags );
```

Read Queue Current Status (E3h 76h) (Queue Services API)

This call is supported in Advanced NetWare version 2.1, NetWare 386, and later versions.

Registers in:

AH	E3h
DS:SI	Request Buffer Address
ES:DI	Reply Packet Address

Registers out:

AL	Completion Code

Request Packet (7 bytes):

Offset	Content	Type	Order
0	Reply Packet Length -2	WORD	lo-hi
2	Queue ID	LONG	hi-lo
6	Queue Status	BYTE	
7	Number of Jobs	BYTE	
8	Number of Servers	BYTE	
9	Server ID List	LONG[25]	hi-lo
109	Server Stations List	BYTE[25]	
134	Max Number of Servers	BYTE	

Completion codes:

00h	Successful
96h	Server Out of Memory
9Ch	Invalid Path
D1h	No Queue
D2h	No Q Server
D3h	No Q Rights
F1h	Invalid Bindery Security
FCh	No Such Object
FEH	Server Bindery Locked
FFh	Bindery Failure

The NetWare C Interface format is:

```
int ReadQueueCurrentStatus( long queueID, BYTE *queueStatus,
   BYTE *numberOfJobs, BYTE *numberOfServers, long *serverIDList,
   WORD *serverStationList, WORD maxNumberOfServers );
```

Read Queue Job Entry (E3h 6Ch) (Queue Services API)

This call is supported in Advanced NetWare version 2.1, NetWare 386, and later versions.

Registers in:

AH	E3h
DS:SI	Request Buffer Address
ES:DI	Reply Buffer Address

Registers out:

AL	Completion Code

Completion codes:

00h	Success
96h	Server Out of Memory
D0h	Q Error
D1h	No Queue
D2h	No Q Server
D3h	No Q Rights
D5h	No Q job
FCh	No Such Object
FEh	Server Bindery Locked
FFh	Bindery Failure

Request Packet (9 bytes):

Offset	Content	Type	Order
0	Request Buffer Length-2	WORD	lo-hi
2	6Ch	BYTE	
3	Queue ID	LONG	hi-lo
7	Job Number	WORD	hi-lo

Reply Packet (258 bytes):

Offset	Content	Type	Order
0	Reply Packet Length-2	WORD	lo-hi
2	Client Station	BYTE	
3	Client Task Number	BYTE	
4	Client ID Number	LONG	hi-lo
8	Target Server ID Number	LONG	hi-lo
12	Target Execution Time	BYTE[6]	
18	Job Entry Time	BYTE[6]	
24	Job Number	WORD	hi-lo
26	Job Type	WORD	hi-lo
28	Job Position	BYTE	
29	Job Control Flags	BYTE	
30	Job File Name	BYTE[14]	
44	Job File Handle	BYTE[6]	
50	Server Station	BYTE	
51	Server Task Number	BYTE	
52	Server ID Number	LONG	hi-lo
56	Text Job Description	BYTE[50]	
106	Client Record Area	BYTE[152]	

The NetWare C Interface format is:

```
int ReadQueueJobEntry( long queueID, WORD jobNumber,
   JobStruct *job );
```

Read Queue Server Current Status (E3h 76h) (Queue Services API)

This call is supported in Advanced NetWare version 2.1, NetWare 386, and later versions.

Registers in:

AH	E3h
DS:SI	Request Packet Address
ES:DI	Reply Buffer Address

Registers out:

AL	Completion Code

Completion codes:

00h	Successful
96h	Server Out Of Memory
9Ch	Invalid Path
D1h	No Queue
D2h	No Q Server
D3h	No Q Rights
F1h	Invalid Bindery Security
FCh	No Such Object
FEh	Server Bindery Locked
FFh	Bindery Failure

Request Packet (12 bytes):

Offset	Content	Type	Order
0	Request Packet Length -2	WORD	lo-hi
3	Queue ID	LONG	hi-lo
7	Server ID Number	LONG	hi-lo
11	Server Station	BYTE	

Reply Packet (66 bytes):

Offset	Content	Type	Order
0	Reply Packet Length-2	WORD	lo-hi
2	Server Status Record	BYTE [64]	

The NetWare C Interface format is:

```
int ReadQueueServerCurrentStatus( long queueID, long serverID,
    char serverStation, char *serverStatusRecord );
```

Release File (CCh) (FCB) (Locking API)

This call is supported in NetWare versions 4.0 and 4.6, in Advanced NetWare versions 1.0, 1.02, 2.0 and 2.1, and in NetWare 386.

Registers in:

AH	CCh
DS:DX	Address of File Control Block

Registers out:

AL	Completion Code

Completion codes:

00h	Success
FFh	Failure

The NetWare C Interface format is not supported.

Release File (ECh) (ASCIIZ) (Locking API)

This call is supported in NetWare version 4.6, in Advanced NetWare versions 1.0, 1.02, 2.0 and 2.1, and in NetWare 386 and later versions.

Registers in:

AH	ECh
DS:DX	Request Buffer Address

Registers out:

AL	Completion Code

Completion codes:

00h	Success
FFh	No Files Found

Request Buffer:

File Path 1-255 ASCIIZ (max len is 255)

The NetWare C Interface format is:

```
int ReleaseFile( char *fileName );
```

Release File Set (CDh) (Locking API)

This call is supported in NetWare versions 4.0 and 4.6, in Advanced NetWare versions 1.0, 1.02, 2.0 and 2.1, and in NetWare 386 and later versions.

Registers in:

AH	CDh

Registers out:

none

The NetWare C Interface format is:

```
void ReleaseFileSet( void );
```

Release Logical Record (D2h) (Locking API)

This call is supported in NetWare versions 4.0 and 4.6, in Advanced NetWare versions 1.0, 1.02, 2.0 and 2.1, and in NetWare 386 and later versions.

Registers in:

AH	D2h
DS:DX	Request Packet Address

Registers out:

AL	Completion Code

Completion codes:

00	Success
FFh	No Record Found

Request Packet:

Logical Record Name Length(1-99)	BYTE
Logical Record Name	BYTE[*LENGTH*]

The NetWare C Interface format is:

```
int ReleaseLogicalRecord( char *logicalRecordName );
```

Release Logical Record Set (D3h) (Locking API)

This call is supported in NetWare versions 4.0 and 4.6, in Advanced NetWare versions 1.0, 1.02, 2.0 and 2.1, and in NetWare 386 and later versions.

Registers in:

AH	D3h

Registers out:

none

The NetWare C Interface format is:

```
void ReleaseLogicalRecordSet( void );
```

Release Physical Record (BDh) (Handle) (Locking API)

This call is supported in NetWare version 4.6, in Advanced NetWare versions 1.0, 1.02, 2.0 and 2.1, and in NetWare 386 and later versions.

Registers in:

AH	BDh
BX	File Handle
CX	High Record Offset
DX	Low Record Offset
SI	High Record Length
DI	Low Record Length

Registers out:

AL	Completion Code

Completion codes:

00	Success
FFh	No Locked Record Found

The NetWare C Interface format is:

```
int ReleasePhysicalRecord( int fileHandle, long recordStartOffset,
   long recordLength );
```

Release Physical Record (C0h) (FCB) (Locking API)

This call is supported in NetWare version 4.6, in Advanced NetWare versions 1.0, 1.02, 2.0 and 2.1, and in NetWare 386. It will not be supported after 1990.

Registers in:

AH	C0h
DS:DX	Address of opened File Control Block (non-extended)
BX	High Record Offset
CX	Low Record Offset

Registers out:

AL	Completion Code

Completion codes:

00	Success
FFh	Invalid record

The NetWare C Interface format is not supported.

Release Physical Record Set (C3h) (Locking API)

This call is supported in NetWare version 4.6, in Advanced NetWare versions 1.0, 1.02, 2.0 and 2.1, and in NetWare 386 and later versions.

Registers in:

AH	C3h

Registers out:
none

The NetWare C Interface format is:

```
void ReleasePhysicalRecordSet ( void );
```

Scan Property (E3h 3Ch) (Bindery Services API)

This call is supported in Advanced NetWare versions 1.0, 1.02, 2.0 and 2.1, and in NetWare 386 and later versions.

Registers in:

AH	E3h
DS:SI	Request Buffer Length
ES:DI	Reply Buffer Length

Registers out:

AL	Completion Code

Completion codes:

00	Success
96h	Server Out Of Memory
F1h	Invalid Bindery Security
FBh	No Such Property
FCh	No Such Object
FEh	Server Bindery Locked
FFh	Bindery Failure

Request Packet (max size = 73 bytes):

Offset	**Content**	**Type**	**Order**
0	Request Buffer Length-2	WORD	lo-hi
2	3Ch	BYTE	
3	Object Type	WORD	hi-lo
5	Object Name Length	BYTE [1-47]	
6	Object Name	BYTE[*LENGTH*]	
?	Sequence Number	LONG	hi-lo
?	Property Name Length	BYTE [1-15]	
?	Property Name	BYTE[*LENGTH*]	

Reply Packet (26 bytes):

Offset	**Content**	**Type**	**Order**
0	Reply Buffer Length-2	WORD	lo-hi
2	Property Name	BYTE[16]	
18	Property Flags	BYTE	
19	Property Security	BYTE	
20	Sequence Number	LONG	hi-lo
24	Property Has Value	BYTE	
25	More Properties	BYTE	

The NetWare C Interface format is:

```
int ScanProperty( char *objectName, WORD objectType,
   char *searchPropertyName, long *sequenceNumber,
   char *propertyName, char *propertyFlags, char *propertySecurity,
   char *propertyHasValue, char *moreProperties );
```

Remove Entry from Spool Queue (E0h 05h) (Print Services API)

This call is supported in NetWare versions 4.0 and 4.6, in Advanced NetWare versions 1.0, 1.02, 2.0 and 2.1, and in NetWare 386. It has been replaced by higher-level functions, but is shown here for completeness.

Registers in:

AH	E0h
DS:SI	Request Buffer
ES:DI	Reply Buffer

Registers out:

AL	Completion Code

Completion codes:

00h	Successful

Request Packet (min 5 bytes):

Offset	Content	Type	Order
0	Request Buffer Length-2	WORD	lo-hi
2	05h	BYTE	
3	Printer Number	BYTE	
4	Job Number	BYTE[1-99]	

Reply Packet (2 bytes):

Offset	Content	Type	Order
0	0000	WORD	lo-hi

The NetWare C Interface format is not supported.

Remove Job From Queue (E3h 6Ah) (Queue Services API)

This call is supported in Advanced NetWare version 2.1, NetWare 386, and later versions.

Registers in:

AH	E3h
DS:SI	Request Buffer Address
ES:DI	Request Buffer Address

Registers out:

AL	Completion Code

Completion codes:

00h	Success
96h	Server Out of Memory
D0h	Q Error
D1h	No Queue
D3h	No Q Rights
D5h	No Q Job
D6h	No Job Rights
FEh	Server Bindery Locked
FFh	Bindery Failure

Request Packet (9 bytes):

Offset	Content	Type	Order
0	Request Buffer Length-2	WORD	lo-hi
2	6Ah	BYTE	
3	Queue ID	LONG	hi-lo
7	Job Number	WORD	hi-lo

Reply Packet (2 bytes):

Offset	Content	Type	Order
0	0000h	WORD	lo-hi

The NetWare C Interface format is:

```
int RemoveJobFromQueue( long queueID, WORD jobNumber );
```

Rename Bindery Object (E3h 34h) (Bindery Services API)

This call is supported in Advanced NetWare versions 1.0, 1.02, 2.0 and 2.1, and in NetWare 386 and later versions.

Registers in:

AH	E3h
DS:SI	Request Buffer Length
ES:DI	Reply Buffer Length

Registers out:

AL	Completion Code

Completion codes:

00	Success
96h	Server Out Of Memory
EFh	Invalid Name

F0h	Wildcard Not Allowed
F3h	No Object Rename Privileges
FCh	No Such Object
FEh	Server Bindery Locked
FFh	Bindery Failure

Request Packet (max size = 57 bytes):

Offset	Content	Type	Order
0	Request Buffer Length-2	WORD	lo-hi
2	34h	BYTE	
3	Object Type	WORD	hi-lo
5	Object Name Length	BYTE[1-47]	
6	Object Name	BYTE[*LENGTH*]	
?	New Object Name Length	BYTE[1..47]	
?	New Object Name	BYTE[*LENGTH*]	

Reply Packet (2 bytes):

Offset	Content	Type	Order
0	0000	WORD	lo-hi

The NetWare C Interface format is:

```
int RenameBinderyObject( char *objectName, char *newObjectName,
   WORD objectType );
```

Restore Queue Server Rights (E3h 75h) (Queue Services API)

This call is supported in Advanced NetWare version 2.1, NetWare 386, and later versions.

Registers in:

AH	E3h
DS:SI	Request Packet Address
ES:DI	Reply Buffer Address

Registers out:

AL	Completion Code

Completion codes:

00h	Successful
96h	Server Out Of Memory
9Ch	Invalid Path
D0h	Q Error
D1h	No Queue
D3h	No Q Rights

D5h	No Q Job
D9h	Stn Not Server
DAh	Q Halted
FEh	Server Bindery Locked
FFh	Bindery Failure

Request Packet (3 bytes):

Offset	Content	Type	Order
0	Request Packet Length-2	WORD	lo-hi
2	75h	BYTE	

Reply Packet (2 bytes):

Offset	Content	Type	Order
0	000h	WORD	lo-hi

The NetWare C Interface format is:

```
int RestoreQueueServerRights( void );
```

Return All Known Networks (02h) (Diagnostic Services API)

This call is supported in Advanced NetWare version 2.1 and will be supported in Novell's Network Management module.

Request Packet (46 bytes):

Offset	Content	Type	Order
0	SPX Packet Header	BYTE[42]	
42	Component Position	BYTE	
43	02h	BYTE	
44	Next Set Starting Point	WORD	lo-hi

Reply Packet (53 bytes):

Offset	Content	Type	Order
0	SPX Packet Header	BYTE[42]	
42	Completion Code	BYTE	
43	Interval Marker	LONG	lo-hi
47	Number Of Network Addresses	WORD	lo-hi
49	Network Address 0	BYTE[4]	

The NetWare C Interface format is:

```
int GetAllKnownNetworks( WORD connectionID, BYTE connectionNumber,
  AllResponseData *response, AllKnownNetworksStruct *responseData );
```

Return All Known Servers (04h) (Diagnostic Services API)

This call is supported in Advanced NetWare version 2.1 and will be supported in Novell's Network Management module.

Request Packet (46 bytes):

Offset	Content	Type	Order
0	SPX Packet Header	BYTE[42]	
42	Component Position	BYTE	
43	04h	BYTE	
44	Next Set Starting Point	WORD	lo-hi

Reply Packet (99 bytes):

Offset	Content	Type	Order
0	SPX Packet Header	BYTE[42]	
42	Completion Code	BYTE	
43	Interval Marker	LONG	lo-hi
47	Number Of Servers	WORD	lo-hi
49	Server Type 0	WORD	lo-hi
51	Server Name 0	BYTE[48]	

The NetWare C Interface format is:

```
int GetAllKnownServers( WORD connectionID, BYTE connectionNumber,
    WORD numberServersToSkip, AllResponseData *response,
    AllKnownServersStruct *responseData );
```

Return Bridge Driver Configuration (01h) (Diagnostic Services API)

This call is supported in Advanced NetWare version 2.1 and will be supported in Novell's Network Management module.

Request Packet (45 bytes):

Offset	Content	Type
0	SPX Packet Header	BYTE[42]
42	Component Position	BYTE
43	01h	BYTE
44	Bridge Driver	BYTE

Reply Packet (269 bytes):

Offset	Content	Type	Order
0	SPX Packet Header	BYTE	
42	Completion Code	BYTE	
43	Interval Marker	LONG	lo-hi
47	Network Address	BYTE[4]	

51	Node Address	BYTE[6]	
57	LAN Mode	BYTE	
58	Node Address Type	BYTE	
59	Maximum Data Size	WORD	lo-hi
61	Reserved	BYTE[2]	
63	LAN Hardware ID	BYTE	
64	Transport Time	WORD	lo-hi
66	Reserved	BYTE[9]	
75	Ethernet Type	BYTE[2]	
77	Major Version	BYTE	
78	Minor Version	BYTE	
79	Misc Flags	BYTE	
80	Selected Configuration	BYTE	
81	LAN Description	BYTE[80]	
161	I/0 Address 1	WORD	lo-hi
163	Decode Range 1	WORD	lo-hi
165	I/0 Address 2	WORD	lo-hi
167	Decode Range 2	WORD	lo-hi
169	Memory Address 1	BYTE[3]	
172	Decode Range 1	WORD	lo-hi
174	Memory Address 2	BYTE[3]	
177	Decode Range 2	WORD	lo-hi
179	Interrupt Is Used 1	BYTE	
180	Interrupt Line 1	BYTE	
181	Interrupt Is Used 2	BYTE	
182	Interrupt Line 2	BYTE	
183	DMA Is Used 1	BYTE	
184	DMA Line 1	BYTE	
185	DMA Is Used 2	BYTE	
186	DMA Line 2	BYTE	
187	Microchannel Flags	BYTE	
188	Reserved	BYTE	
189	Text Description	BYTE[80]	

The NetWare C Interface format is:

```
int GetBridgeDriverConfiguration( WORD connectionID,
    BYTE connectionNumber, BYTE LANBoardNumber,
    AllResponseData *response,
    DriverConfigurationStruct *responseData );
```

Return Bridge Driver Diagnostic Statistics (02h) (Diagnostic Services API)

This call is supported in Advanced NetWare version 2.1 and will be supported in Novell's Network Management module.

Request Packet (45 bytes):

Offset	Content	Type
0	SPX Packet Header	BYTE[42]
42	Component Position	BYTE
43	02h	BYTE
44	Bridge Driver	BYTE

Reply Packet (maximum packet size = 576 bytes):

Offset	Content	Type	Order
0	SPX Packet Header	BYTE[42]	
42	Completion Code	BYTE	
43	Interval Marker	LONG	lo-hi
47	Reserved	BYTE[2]	
49	Statistics Version	BYTE[2]	
51	Total TX Packet Count	LONG	lo-hi
55	Total RX Packet Count	LONG	lo-hi
59	No ECB Available Count	WORD	lo-hi
61	Packet TX Too Small Count	WORD	lo-hi
63	Packet TX Too Small Count	WORD	lo-hi
65	Packet RX Overflow Count	WORD	lo-hi
67	Packet RX Too Big Count	WORD	lo-hi
69	Packet RX Too Small Count	WORD	lo-hi
71	Packet TX Misc Error Count	WORD	lo-hi
73	Packet RX Misc Error Count	WORD	lo-hi
75	Retry TX Count	WORD	lo-hi
77	Checksum Error Count	WORD	lo-hi
79	Hardware RX Mismatch Count	WORD	lo-hi
81	Number of Custom Variables	WORD	lo-hi
83	Custom Variable 0	WORD	lo-hi
?	Text 0	BYTE[?]	
?	Text Delimiter(0000h)	BYTE[2]	

The NetWare C Interface format is:

```
int GetBridgeDriverStatus( WORD connectionID, BYTE connectionNumber,
AllResponseData *response, BridgeDriverStatusStruct *responseData );
```

Return Bridge Driver Status (00h) (Diagnostic Services API)

This call is supported in Advanced NetWare version 2.1 and will be supported in Novell's Network Management module.

Request Packet (44 bytes):

Offset	Content	Type
0	SPX Packet Header	BYTE[42]
42	Component Position	BYTE
43	00h	BYTE

Reply Packet (51 bytes):

Offset	Content	Type	Order
0	SPX Packet Header	BYTE[42]	
42	Completion Code	BYTE	
43	Interval Marker	LONG	lo-hi
47	LAN Board 0 Status	BYTE	
48	LAN Board 1 Status	BYTE	
49	LAN Board 2 Status	BYTE	
50	LAN Board 3 Status	BYTE	

The NetWare C Interface format is:

```
int GetBridgeDriverStatus( WORD connectionID, BYTE connectionNumber,
  AllResponseData *response, DriverStatisticsStruct *responseData );
```

Return Bridge Statistics (00h) (Diagnostic Services API)

This call is supported in Advanced NetWare version 2.1 and will be supported in Novell's Network Management module.

Request Packet (44 bytes):

Offset	Content	Type
0	SPX Packet Header	BYTE[42]
42	Component Position	BYTE
43	00h	BYTE

Reply Packet (69 bytes):

Offset	Content	Type	Order
0	SPX Packet Header	BYTE[42]	
42	Completion Code	BYTE	
43	Interval Marker	LONG	lo-hi
47	Too Many Hops Count	WORD	lo-hi
49	Unknown Network Count	WORD	lo-hi
51	No space For Service Count	WORD	lo-hi
53	No Receive Buffers Count	WORD	lo-hi
55	Reserved	WORD	lo-hi
57	NetBIOS Propagate Count	LONG	lo-hi
61	Total Packets Serviced	LONG	lo-hi
65	Total Packets Routed	LONG	lo-hi

The NetWare C Interface format is:

```
int GetBridgeStatistics( WORD connectionID, BYTE connectionNumber,
  AllResponseData *response, BridgeStatisticsStruct *responseData );
```

Return Connection ID Table (03h) (Diagnostic Services API)

This call is supported in Advanced NetWare version 2.1 and will be supported in Novell's Network Management module.

Request Packet (44 bytes):

Offset	Content	Type
0	SPX Packet Header	BYTE[42]
42	Component Position	BYTE
43	03h	BYTE

Reply Packet (303 bytes):

Offset	Content	Type	Order
0	SPX Packet Header	BYTE[42]	
42	Completion Code	BYTE	
43	Interval Marker	LONG	lo-hi
47	Server Used 0	BYTE	
48	Order Number 0	BYTE	
49	Server Network 0	BYTE[4]	lo-hi
53	Server Node 0	BYTE[6]	
59	Server Socket 0	BYTE[2]	
61	Receive Timeout 0	WORD	lo-hi
63	Immediate Node 0	BYTE[6]	
69	Sequence Number 0	BYTE	
70	Connection Number 0	BYTE	
71	Connection OK 0	BYTE	
72	Maximum Timeout 0	WORD	lo-hi
74	Reserved 0	BYTE[5]	

.
.
.

(The entire response packet is 303 bytes long consisting of the following: (47) bytes of overhead + [8 * 32 bytes of server information].)

The NetWare C Interface format is:

```
int GetServerAddressTable( WORD connectionID, BYTE connectionNumber,
AllResponseData *response, ServerAddressTableStruct *responseData );
```

Return IPX/SPX Version (00h) (Diagnostic Services API)

This call is supported in Advanced NetWare version 2.1 and will be supported in Novell's Network Management module.

Request Packet (44 bytes):

Offset	**Content**	**Type**
0	SPX Packet Header	BYTE[42]
42	Component Position	BYTE
43	00h	BYTE

Reply Packet (51 bytes):

Offset	**Content**	**Type**	**Order**
0	SPX Packet Header	BYTE[42]	
42	Completion Code	BYTE	
43	Interval Marker	LONG	lo-hi
47	IPX Major Version	BYTE	
48	IPX Minor Version	BYTE	
49	SPX Major Version	BYTE	
50	SPX Minor Version	BYTE	

The NetWare C Interface format is:

```
int GetIPXSPXVersion( WORD connectionID, BYTE connectionNumber,
    AllResponseData *response, IPXSPXVersion *responseData );
```

Return IPX Statistics (01h) (Diagnostic Services API)

This call is supported in Advanced NetWare version 2.1 and will be supported in Novell's Network Management module.

Request Packet (44 bytes):

Offset	**Content**	**Type**
0	SPX Packet Header	BYTE[42]
42	Component Position	BYTE
43	01h	BYTE

Reply Packet (81 bytes):

Offset	**Content**	**Type**	**Order**
0	SPX Packet Header	BYTE[42]	
42	Completion Code	BYTE	
43	Interval Marker	LONG	lo-hi
47	Send Packet	LONG	lo-hi
51	Malformed ECBs	WORD	lo-hi
53	Inbound Packets	LONG	lo-hi
57	Lost Packets	LONG	lo-hi
61	AES Events	LONG	lo-hi
65	Postponed AES Events	WORD	lo-hi
67	Max Possible Sockets	WORD	lo-hi
69	Max Open Sockets	WORD	lo-hi

71	Open Socket Failures	WORD	lo-hi
73	Listen ECBs	LONG	lo-hi
77	Cannot Cancel ECBs	WORD	lo-hi
79	Cannot Find Route	WORD	lo-hi

The NetWare C Interface format is:

```
int GetIPXStatistics( WORD connectionID, BYTE connectionNumber,
   ALLResponseData *response, IPXStatisticsStruct *responseData );
```

Return Local Tables (01h) (Diagnostic Services API)

This call is supported in Advanced NetWare version 2.1 and will be supported in Novell's Network Management module.

Request Packet (44 bytes):

Offset	Content	Type
0	SPX Packet Header	BYTE[42]
42	Component Position	BYTE
43	01h	BYTE

Reply Packet (239 bytes):

Offset	Content	Type	Order
0	SPX Packet Header	BYTE[42]	
42	Completion Code	BYTE	
43	Interval Marker	LONG	lo-hi
47	Network Number 0	BYTE[4]	
.			
.			
.			
111	Node Addresses 0	BYTE[8]	
.			
.			
.			

(The total length of the reply packet is 239 bytes. The packet includes 16 Network Number fields and 16 Node Address fields.)

The NetWare C Interface format is:

```
int GetLocalTables( WORD connectionID, BYTE connectionNumber,
   AllResponseData *response, LocalTablesStruct *responseData );
```

Return OS Version (00h) (Diagnostic Services API)

This call is supported in Advanced NetWare version 2.1 and will be supported in Novell's Network Management module.

Request Packet (44 bytes):

Offset	Content	Type
0	SPX Packet Header	BYTE[42]
42	Component Position	BYTE
43	00h	BYTE

Reply Packet (maximum packet size = 88 bytes):

Offset	Content	Type	Order
0	SPX Packet Header	BYTE[42]	
42	Completion Code	BYTE	
43	Interval Marker	LONG	lo-hi
47	Machine ID	BYTE	
48	OS Text	ASCIIZ	
??	OS Version Text	ASCIIZ	
??	Hardware Type Text	ASCIIZ	

The NetWare C Interface format is:

```
int GetOSVersionInfo( WORD connectionID, BYTE connectionNumber,
   AllResponseData *response, OSVersionStruct *responseData );
```

Return Primary Server Number (05h) (Diagnostic Services API)

This call is supported in Advanced NetWare version 2.1 and will be supported in Novell's Network Management module.

Request Packet (44 bytes):

Offset	Content	Type
0	SPX Packet Header	BYTE[42]
42	Component Position	BYTE
43	05h	BYTE

Reply Packet (48 bytes):

Offset	Content	Type	Order
0	SPX Packet Header	BYTE[42]	
42	Completion Code	BYTE	
43	Interval Marker	LONG	lo-hi
47	Server Position Number	BYTE	

The NetWare C Interface format is:

```
int GetPrimaryServerNumber( WORD connectionID,
   BYTE connectionNumber, AllResponseData *response,
   PrimaryServerStruct *responseData );
```

Return Received Packet Count (06h) (Diagnostic Services API)

This call is supported in Advanced NetWare version 2.1 and will be supported in Novell's Network Management module.

Request Packet (44 bytes):

Offset	Content	Type
0	SPX Packet Header	BYTE[42]
42	Component Position	BYTE
43	06h	BYTE

Reply Packet (49 bytes):

Offset	Content	Type	Order
0	SPX Packet Header	BYTE[42]	
42	Completion Code	BYTE	
43	Interval Marker	LONG	lo-hi
47	Reserved	BYTE[4]	

The NetWare C Interface format is:

```
int ReturnReceivedPacketCount( WORD connectionID,
   BYTE connectionNumber, AllResponseData *response,
   ReturnReceivedPacketStruct *responseData );
```

Return Server Name Table (04h) (Diagnostic Services API)

This call is supported in Advanced NetWare version 2.1 and will be supported in Novell's Network Management module.

Request Packet (44 bytes):

Offset	Content	Type
0	SPX Packet Header	BYTE[42]
42	Component Position	BYTE
43	04h	BYTE

Reply Packet (431 bytes):

Offset	Content	Type	Order
0	SPX Packet Header	BYTE[42]	
42	Completion Code	BYTE	
43	Interval Marker	LONG	lo-hi

47	Server Name 0	BYTE[48]
95	Server Name 1	BYTE[48]
43	Server Name 2	BYTE[48]
191	Server Name 3	BYTE[48]
239	Server Name 4	BYTE[48]
287	Server Name 5	BYTE[48]
335	Server Name 6	BYTE[48]
383	Server Name 7	BYTE[48]

The NetWare C Interface format is:

```
int GetServerNameTable( WORD connectionID, BYTE connectionNumber,
   AllResponseData *response, ServerNameTableStruct *responseData );
```

Return Shell Address (01h) (Diagnostic Services API)

This call is supported in Advanced NetWare version 2.1 and will be supported in Novell's Network Management module.

Request Packet (44 bytes):

Offset	Content	Type
0	SPX Packet Header	BYTE[42]
42	Component Position	BYTE
43	01h	BYTE

Reply Packet (59 bytes):

Offset	Content	Type	Order
0	SPX Packet Header	BYTE[42]	
42	Completion Code	BYTE	
43	Interval Marker	LONG	lo-hi
47	Local Network	BYTES [4]	
51	Local Node	BYTES [6]	
57	Local Socket	BYTES [2]	

The NetWare C Interface format is:

```
int GetShellAddress( WORD connectionID, BYTE connectionNumber,
  AllResponseData *response, ShellStatisticsStruct *responseData );
```

Return Shell Driver Configuration (00h) (Diagnostic Services API)

This call is supported in Advanced NetWare version 2.1 and will be supported in Novell's Network Management module.

Request Packet (44 bytes):

Offset	Content	Type
0	SPX Packet Header	BYTE[42]
42	Component Position	BYTE
43	00h	BYTE

Reply Packet (269 bytes):

Offset	Content	Type	Order
0	SPX Packet Header	BYTE[42]	
42	Completion Code	BYTE	
43	Interval Marker	LONG	lo hi
47	Reserved	BYTE[4]	
51	Node Address	BYTE[6]	
57	Reserved	BYTE	
58	Node Address Type	BYTE	
59	Maximum Data Size	WORD	lo-hi
69	Reserved	BYTE	
63	LAN Hardware ID	BYTE	
64	Transport Time	WORD	lo-hi
66	Reserved	BYTE[9]	
75	Ethernet Type	BYTE[2]	
77	Major Version	BYTE	
78	Minor Version	BYTE	
79	Misc Flags	BYTE	
80	Selected Configuration	BYTE	
81	LAN Description	BYTE[80]	
161	I/O Address 1	WORD	lo-hi
163	Decode Range 1	WORD	lo-hi
165	I/O Address 2	WORD	lo-hi
167	Decode Range 2	WORD	lo-hi
169	Memory Address 1	BYTE[3]	
172	Decode Range 1	WORD	lo-hi
174	Memory Address 2	BYTE[3]	
177	Decode Range 2	WORD	lo-hi
179	Interrupt Is Used 1	BYTE	
180	Interrupt Line 1	BYTE	
181	Interrupt Is Used 2	BYTE	
182	Interrupt Line 2	BYTE	
183	DMA Is Used 1	BYTE	
184	DMA Line 1	BYTE	
185	DMA Is Used 2	BYTE	
186	DMA Line 2	BYTE	
187	Microchannel Flags	BYTE	
188	Reserved	BYTE	
189	Text Description	BYTE[80]	

The NetWare C Interface format is:

```
int GetShellDriverConfiguration( WORD connectionID,
   BYTE connectionNumber, AllResponseData *response,
   DriverConfigurationStruct *responseData );
```

Return Shell Driver Diagnostic Statistics (01h) (Diagnostic Services API)

This call is supported in Advanced NetWare version 2.1 and will be supported in Novell's Network Management module.

Request Packet (44 bytes):

Offset	Content	Type
0	SPX Packet Header	BYTE[42]
42	Component Position	BYTE
43	01h	BYTE

Reply Packet (maximum packet size = 576 bytes):

Offset	Content	Type	Order
0	SPX Packet Header	BYTE[42]	
42	Completion Code	BYTE	
43	Interval Marker	LONG	lo-hi
47	Reserved	BYTE[2]	
49	Statistics Version	BYTE[2]	
51	Total Tx Packet Count	LONG	lo-hi
55	Total Rx Packet Count	LONG	lo-hi
59	No ECB Available Count	WORD	lo-hi
61	Packet Tx Too Big Count	WORD	lo-hi
63	Packet Tx Too Small Count	WORD	lo-hi
65	Packet Rx Overflow Count	WORD	lo-hi
67	Packet Rx Too Big Count	WORD	lo-hi
69	Packet Rx Too Small Count	WORD	lo-hi
71	Packet Tx Misc Error Count	WORD	lo-hi
73	Packet Rx Misc Error Count	WORD	lo-hi
75	Retry Tx Count	WORD	lo-hi
77	Checksum Error Count	WORD	lo-hi
79	Hardware Rx Mismatch Count	WORD	lo-hi
81	Number of Custom Variables	WORD	lo-hi
83	Custom Variable 0	WORD	lo-hi
.			
.			
.			
?	Text 0	BYTE[?]	
.			
.			
.			
?	Text Delimiter (0000h)	BYTE[2]	

The NetWare C Interface format is:

```
int GetShellDriverStatistics( WORD connectionID,
    BYTE connectionNumber, AllResponseData *response,
    DriverStatisticsStruct *responseData );
```

Return Shell Statistics (02h) (Diagnostic Services API)

This call is supported in Advanced NetWare version 2.1 and will be supported in Novell's Network Management module.

Request Packet (44 bytes):

Offset	Content	Type
0	SPX Packet Header	BYTE[42]
42	Component Position	BYTE
43	02h	BYTE

Reply Packet (85 bytes):

Offset	Content	Type	Order
0	SPX Packet Header	BYTE[42]	
42	Completion Code	BYTE	
43	Interval Marker	LONG	lo-hi
47	Shell Requests Count	LONG	lo-hi
51	Operator Aborts Count	WORD	lo-hi
53	Operator Retries Count	WORD	lo-hi
55	Timeouts Count	WORD	lo-hi
57	Write Error Count	WORD	lo-hi
59	Invalid Reply Header Count	WORD	lo-hi
61	Invalid Slot Count	WORD	lo-hi
63	Invalid Sequence Number Count	WORD	lo-hi
65	Error Receiving Count	WORD	lo-hi
67	No Router Found Count	WORD	lo-hi
69	Being Processed Count	WORD	lo-hi
79	Unknown Error Count	WORD	lo-hi
73	Invalid Server Slot Count	WORD	lo-hi
75	Network Gone Count	WORD	lo-hi
77	Reserved	WORD	lo-hi
79	Allocate Cannot Find Route	WORD	lo-hi
81	Allocate No Slots Available	WORD	lo-hi
83	Allocate Server Is Down	WORD	lo-hi

The NetWare C Interface format is:

```
int GetShellStatistics( WORD connectionID, BYTE connectionNumber,
    AllResponseData *response, ShellVersionStruct *responseData );
```

Return Shell Version (06h) (Diagnostic Services API)

This call is supported in Advanced NetWare version 2.1 and will be supported in Novell's Network Management module.

Request Packet (44 bytes):

Offset	Content	Type
0	SPX Packet Header	BYTE[42]
42	Component Position	BYTE
43	06h	BYTE

Reply Packet (49 bytes):

Offset	Content	Type	Order
0	SPX Packet Header	BYTE[42]	
42	Completion Code	BYTE	
43	Interval Marker	LONG	lo-hi
47	Major Version	BYTE	
48	Minor Version	BYTE	

The NetWare C Interface format is:

```
int GetShellVersionInfo( WORD connectionID, BYTE connectionNumber,
   AllResponseData *response, ShellVersionStruct *responseData );
```

Return Specific Network Information (03h) (Diagnostic Services API)

This call is supported in Advanced NetWare version 2.1 and will be supported in Novell's Network Management module.

Request Packet (48 bytes):

Offset	Content	Type
0	SPX Packet Header	BYTE[42]
42	Component Position	BYTE
43	03h	BYTE
44	Specific Network Address	BYTE[4]

Reply Packet (75 bytes):

Offset	Content	Type	Order
0	SPX Packet Header	BYTE[42]	
42	Completion Code	BYTE	
43	Interval Marker	LONG	lo-hi
47	Network Address	BYTE[4]	
51	Route Hops	BYTE	
52	Reserved	BYTE[7]	
59	Route Time	WORD	lo-hi
61	Number Of Known Routes	WORD	lo-hi

63	Router 0 Node Address	BYTE[6]	
69	Router 0 Next Board Position	BYTE	
70	Reserved 0	BYTE[2]	
72	Route 0 Hops	BYTE	
73	Route 0 Time	WORD	lo-hi

.
.
.

The NetWare C Interface format is:

```
int GetSpecificNetworkInfo( WORD connectionID,
   BYTE connectionNumber, AllResponseData *response,
   SpecificServerInfoStruct *responseData );
```

Return Specific Server Information (05h) (Diagnostic Services API)

This call is supported in Advanced NetWare version 2.1 and will be supported in Novell's Network Management molule.

Request Packet (94 bytes):

Offset	Content	Type	Order
0	SPX Packet Header	BYTE[42]	
42	Component Position	BYTE	
43	05h	BYTE	
44	Server Type	WORD	lo-hi
46	Server Name	BYTE[48]	

Reply Packet (115 bytes):

Offset	Content	Type	Order
0	SPX Packet Header	BYTE[42]	
42	Completion Code	BYTE	
43	Interval Marker	LONG	lo-hi
47	Server Type	WORD	lo-hi
49	Server Name	BYTE[48]	
97	Server Address	WORD[6]	lo-hi
189	Route Hops	WORD	lo-hi
111	Reserved	BYTE[2]	
113	Number Of Known Routes	WORD	lo-hi
115	Router 0 Node Address	WORD [3]	lo-hi
121	Route 0 Hops	BYTE	
122	Reserved 0	BYTE[2]	

.
.
.

The NetWare C Interface format is:

```
int GetSpecificServerInfo( WORD connectionID, BYTE connectionNumber,
AllResponseData *response, SpecificServerInfoStruct *responseData );
```

Return SPX Statistics (02h) (Diagnostic Services API)

This call is supported in Advanced NetWare version 2.1 and will be supported in Novell's Network Management module.

Request Packet (44 bytes):

Offset	Content	Type
0	SPX Packet Header	BYTE[42]
42	Component Position	BYTE
43	02h	BYTE

Reply Packet (91 bytes):

Offset	Content	Type	Order
0	SPX Packet Header	BYTE[42]	
42	Completion Code	BYTE	
43	Interval Marker	LONG	lo-hi
47	Max Possible Connections	WORD	lo-hi
49	Max Open Connections	WORD	lo-hi
51	Establish Connection Requests	WORD	lo-hi
53	Establish Connection Failures	WORD	lo-hi
55	Listen For Connection Requests	WORD	lo-hi
57	Listen For Connection Failures	WORD	lo-hi
59	Send Packet Requests	LONG	lo-hi
63	No Listen Failures	LONG	lo-hi
67	Bad Send Requests	WORD	lo-hi
69	Send Failures	WORD	lo-hi
71	Abort Connections	WORD	lo-hi
73	Listen Packet Requests	LONG	lo-hi
77	Malformed Listen ECBs	WORD	lo-hi
79	Incoming Packets	LONG	lo-hi
83	Bad Incoming Packets	WORD	lo-hi
85	Duplicate Packets	WORD	lo-hi
87	No Listen ECBs	WORD	lo-hi
89	Watchdog-Destroyed Connections	WORD	lo-hi

The NetWare C Interface format is:

```
int GetSPXStatistics( WORD connectionID, BYTE connectionNumber,
    AllResponseData *response, SPXStatisticsStruct *responseData );
```

Return VAP Shell Address (01h) (Diagnostic Services API)

This call is supported in Advanced NetWare version 2.1 and will be supported in Novell's Network Management module.

Request Packet (44 bytes):

Offset	Content	Type
0	SPX Packet Header	BYTE[42]
42	Component Position	BYTE
43	01h	BYTE

Reply Packet (59 bytes):

Offset	Content	Type	Order
0	SPX Packet Header	BYTE[42]	
42	Completion Code	BYTE	
43	Interval Marker	LONG	lo-hi
47	Local Network	BYTES [4]	
51	Local Node	BYTES [6]	
57	Local Socket	BYTES [2]	

The NetWare C Interface format is:

```
int GetShellAddress( WORD connectionID, BYTE connectionNumber,
    AllResponseData *response, ShellStatisticsStruct *responseData );
```

Return VAP Shell Statistics (02h) (Diagnostic Services API)

This call is supported in Advanced NetWare version 2.1 and will be supported in Novell's Network Management module.

Request Packet (44 bytes):

Offset	Content	Type
0	SPX Packet Header	BYTE[42]
42	Component Position	BYTE
43	02h	BYTE

Reply Packet (85 bytes):

Offset	Content	Type	Order
0	SPX Packet Header	BYTE[42]	
42	Completion Code	BYTE	
43	Interval Marker	LONG	lo-hi
47	VAP Shell Requests Count	LONG	lo-hi
51	Operator Aborts Count	WORD	lo-hi
53	Operator Retries Count	WORD	lo-hi
55	Timeouts Count	WORD	lo-hi
57	Write Error Count	WORD	lo-hi
59	Invalid Reply Header Count	WORD	lo-hi
61	Invalid Slot Count	WORD	lo-hi
63	Invalid Sequence Number Count	WORD	lo-hi

65	Error Receiving Count	WORD	lo-hi
67	No Router Found Count	WORD	lo-hi
69	Being Processed Count	WORD	lo-hi
71	Unknown Error Count	WORD	lo-hi
73	Invalid Server Slot Count	WORD	lo-hi
75	Network Gone Count	WORD	lo-hi
77	Reserved	WORD	lo-hi
79	Allocate Cannot Find Route	WORD	lo-hi
81	Allocate No Slots Available	WORD	lo-hi
83	Allocate Server Is Down	WORD	lo-hi

The NetWare C Interface format is:

```
int GetShellStatistics( WORD connectionID, BYTE connectionNumber,
   AllResponseData *response, ShellVersionStruct *responseData );
```

Return VAP Shell Version (06h) (Diagnostic Services API)

This call is supported in Advanced NetWare version 2.1 and will be supported in Novell's Network Management module.

Request Packet (44 bytes):

Offset	Content	Type
0	SPX Packet Header	BYTE[42]
42	Component Position	BYTE
43	06h	BYTE

Reply Packet (49 bytes):

Offset	Content	Type	Order
0	SPX Packet Header	BYTE[42]	
42	Completion Code	BYTE	
43	Interval Marker	LONG	lo-hi
47	Major Version	BYTE	
48	Minor Version	BYTE	

The NetWare C Interface format is:

```
int GetShellVersionInfo( WORD connectionID, BYTE connectionNumber,
   AllResponseData *response, ShellVersionStruct *responseData );
```

Scan Bindery Object (E3h 37h) (Bindery Services API)

This call is supported in Advanced NetWare versions 1.0, 1.02, 2.0 and 2.1, and in NetWare 386 and later versions.

Registers in:

AH	E3h
DS:SI	Request Buffer Length
ES:DI	Reply Buffer Length

Registers out:

AL	Completion Code

Completion codes:

00	Success
96h	Server Out Of Memory
EFh	Invalid Name
FCh	No Such Object
FEh	Server Bindery Locked
FFh	Bindery Failure

Request Packet (max size = 57 bytes):

Offset	Content	Type	Order
0	Request Buffer Length-2	WORD	lo-hi
2	37h	BYTE	
3	Last Object ID	LONG	hi-lo
7	Object Type	WORD	hi-lo
9	Object Name Length	BYTE [1-47]	
10	Object Name	BYTE[*LENGTH*]	

Reply Packet (59 bytes):

Offset	Content	Type	Order
0	Reply Buffer Length-2	WORD	lo-hi
2	Object ID	LONG	hi-lo
6	Object Type	WORD	hi-lo
8	Object Name	BYTE[48]	
56	Object Flag	BYTE	
57	Object Security	BYTE	
58	Object Has Properties	BYTE	

The NetWare C Interface format is:

```
int ScanBinderyObject( char *searchObjectName,
   WORD searchObjectType, long *objectID, char *objectName,
   WORD *objectType, char *objectHasProperties, char *objectFlag,
   char *objectSecurity );
```

Send Broadcast Message (E1h 00h) (Message Services API)

This call is supported in NetWare versions 4.0 and 4.6, in Advanced NetWare versions 1.0, 1.02, 2.0, and 2.15, and in NetWare 386; but will not be supported in NetWare 386 versions dated after 1990.

Registers in:

AH	E1h
DS:SI	Request Buffer Address
ES:DI	Reply Buffer Address

Registers out:

AL	Completion Code

Completion codes:

00h	Successful
FEh	I/O Failure; Lack Of Dynamic Workspace

Request Buffer (maximum buffer length = 160 bytes):

Offset	Content	Type	Order
0	Request Buffer Length - 2	WORD	lo-hi
2	00h	BYTE	
3	Connection Count (1 to 100)	BYTE	
4	Connection List	BYTE[*COUNT*]	
?	Message Length (1 to 55)	BYTE	
?	Message	BYTE[*LENGTH*]	

Reply Buffer (maximum buffer length = 103 bytes):

Offset	Content	Type	Order
0	Reply Buffer Length - 2	WORD	lo-hi
2	Connection Count(1 to 100)	BYTE	
3	Result List	BYTE[*COUNT*]	

The NetWare C Interface format is:

```
int SendBroadcastMessage( char *message, WORD *connectionList,
   BYT *resultList, WORD connectionCount );
```

Send Console Broadcast (E3h D1h) (File Server Environment Services API)

This call is supported in Advanced NetWare version 2.1, NetWare 386, and later versions.

Registers in:

AH	E3h
DS:SI	Request Buffer Address
ES:DI	Reply Buffer Address

Registers out:

AL	Completion Code

Completion code:

00h	Successful
C6h	No Console Rights

Request Buffer (maximum buffer length = 164 bytes):

Offset	Content	Type	Order
0	Request Buffer Length - 2	WORD	lo-hi
2	D1h	BYTE	
3	Connection Count (1 max)	BYTE	
4	Connection List	BYTE[*COUNT*]	
?	Message Length (1)	BYTE	
?	Message	BYTE[*LENGTH*]	

Reply Buffer (2 bytes):

Offset	Content	Type
0	0000	WORD

The NetWare C Interface format is:

```
int SendConsoleBroadcast( char *message, WORD connectionCount,
   WORD *connectionList );
```

Send Personal Message (E1h 04h) (Message Services API)

This call is supported in NetWare versions 4.0 and 4.6, in Advanced NetWare versions 1.0, 1.02, 2.0, and 2.15, and in NetWare 386; but will not be supported in NetWare 386 versions dated after 1990.

Registers in:

AH	E1h
DS:SI	Request Buffer Address
ES:DI	Reply Buffer Address

Registers out:

AL	Completion Code

Completion codes:

00h	Successful
FEh	I/O Failure; Lack Of Dynamic Workspace

Request Buffer (maximum buffer length = 231 bytes):

Offset	Content	Type	Order
0	Request Buffer Length - 2	WORD	lo-hi
2	04h	BYTE	
3	Connection Count (1 to 100)	BYTE	

4	Connection List	BYTE[*COUNT*]
?	Message Length (1 to 126)	BYTE
?	Message	BYTE[*LENGTH*]

Reply Buffer (maximum buffer length = 103 bytes):

Offset	**Content**	**Type**	**Order**
0	Reply Buffer Length - 2	WORD	lo-hi
2	Connection Count (1 to 100)	BYTE	
3	Result List	BYTE[*COUNT*]	

The NetWare C Interface format is:

```
int SendPersonalMessage( char *message, WORD *connectionList,
   BYTE *resultList, WORD connectionCount );
```

Service Queue Job and Open File (E3h 71h) (Queue Services API)

This call is supported in Advanced NetWare version 2.1, NetWare 386, and later versions.

This call is supported in Advanced NetWare version 2.1, NetWare 386, and later versions.

Registers in:

AH	E3h
DS:SI	Request Buffer Address
ES:DI	Reply Buffer Address

Registers out:

AL	Completion Code

Completion codes:

00h	Successful
96h	Server Out of Memory
9Ch	Invalid Path
D0h	Q Error
D1h	No Queue
D3h	No Q Rights
D5h	No Q Job
D9h	Stn Not Server
DAh	Q Halted
FEh	Server Bindery Locked
FFh	Bindery Failure

Request Packet (9 bytes):

Offset	Content	Type	Order
0	Request Packet Length-2	WORD	lo-hi
2	71h	BYTE	
3	Queue ID	LONG	hi-lo
7	Target Job Type	WORD	hi-lo

Reply Packet (56 bytes):

Offset	Content	Type	Order
0	Reply Packet Length -2	WORD	lo-hi
2	Client Station	BYTE	
3	Client Task Number	BYTE	
4	Client ID Number	LONG	hi-lo
8	Target Server ID Number	LONG	hi-lo
12	Target Execution Time	BYTE[6]	
18	Job Entry Time	BYTE[6]	
24	Job Number	WORD	hi-lo
26	Job Type	WORD	hi-lo
28	Job Position	BYTE	
29	Job Control Flags	BYTE	
30	Job File Name	BYTE[14]	
44	Job File Handle	BYTE[6]	
50	Server Station	BYTE	
51	Server Task Number	BYTE	
52	Server ID Number	LONG	hi-lo

The NetWare C Interface format is:

```
int ServiceQueueJobAndOpenFile( long queueID, WORD targetJobType,
   JobStruct *job, int *fileHandle );
```

Set Banner User Name (B8h 09h) (Print Services API)

This call is supported in Advanced NetWare version 2.1, and in NetWare 386 and later versions.

Registers in:

AH	B8h
AL	09h
ES:BX	Request Packet Address

Registers out:

AL	Completion Code

Completion codes:

0	Successful

Request Packet (12 bytes):

Offset	Content	Type
0	Banner User Name	BYTE[12]

The NetWare C Interface format is:

```
int SetBannerUserName( char *userName );
```

Set Broadcast Mode (DEh) (Message Services API)

This call is supported in NetWare versions 4.0 and 4.6, in Advanced NetWare versions 1.0, 1.02, 2.0, and 2.1, and in NetWare 386; but will not be supported in NetWare 386 versions dated after 1990.

Registers in:

AH	DEh
DL	Target Message Mode

Registers out:

AL	Message Mode

Completion codes:
None

The NetWare C Interface format is:

```
void SetBroadcastMode( BYTE broadcastMode );
```

Set Capture Print Job (B8h 07h) (Print Services API)

This call is supported in Advanced NetWare version 2.1, and in NetWare 386 and later versions.

Registers in:

AH	B8h
AL	07h
DH	LPT Device (0 = LPT1, 1 = LPT2, 2 = LPT3)
BX	Job Number
SI,DI,CX	NetWare File Handle

Registers out:

AL	Completion Code

Completion codes:

00	Successful
FFh	Print Job Already Queued

The NetWare C Interface format is:

```
int SetCapturePrintJob( BYTE LPTDevice, WORD jobNumber,
   BYTE *jobFileHandle );
```

Set Capture Print Queue (B8h 06h) (Print Services API)

This call is supported in Advanced NetWare version 2.1, and in NetWare 386 and later versions.

Registers in:

AH	B8h
AL	06h
DH	LPT Device (0 = LPT1, 1 = LPT2, 2 = LPT3)
BX,CX	Queue ID

Registers out:

AL	Completion Code

Completion codes:

00	Successful
FFh	Print Job Already Set

The NetWare C Interface format is:

```
int SetCapturePrintQueue( BYTE LPTDevice,
   BYTE serverNumberConnectionID, long QueueID );
```

Set Default Capture Flags (B8h 01h) (Print Services API)

This call is supported in Advanced NetWare versions 2.0 and 2.1, and in NetWare 386 and later versions.

Registers in:

AH	B8h
AL	01h
CX	Request Buffer Length (1-63)
ES:BX	Request Buffer

Registers out:

AL	Completion Code

Completion codes:

00h	Successful

Reply Packet (63 bytes) :

Offset	Content	Type	Order
0	Status	BYTE	
1	Flags	BYTE	
2	Tab Size	BYTE (1-18)	
3	Server Printer	BYTE (0-4)	
4	Number of Copies	BYTE (0-255)	
5	Form Type	BYTE (0-255)	
6	Reserved	BYTE	
7	Banner Text (ASCIIZ)	BYTE[13]	
20	Reserved	BYTE	
21	Local LPT Device	BYTE	
22	Flush Capture Timeout	WORD	hi-lo
24	Flush Capture On Device Close	BYTE	

/* All fields below this are Adv. NetWare 2.1 and above compatible only. */

25	Max Lines	WORD	hi-lo
27	Max Chars	WORD	hi-lo
29	Form Name (ASCIIZ)	BYTE[13]	
42	LPT Capture Flag	BYTE	
43	File Capture Flag	BYTE	
44	Timing Out Flag	BYTE	
45	Printer Setup Buffer Address	LONG	hi-lo /*Different*/
49	Printer Reset Buffer Address	LONG	hi-lo ""
53	Connection ID Queue Print Job	BYTE	
54	Capture In Progress	BYTE	
55	Print Queue Flag	BYTE	
56	Print Job Valid	BYTE	
57	Print Queue ID	LONG	hi-lo
61	Print Job Number	WORD (1-999)	hi-lo

The NetWare C Interface format is:

```
int SetDefaultCaptureFlags( SET_CAPTURE_FLAGS *captureFlags );
```

Set Default Local Printer (B8h 05h) (Print Services API)

This call is supported in Advanced NetWare version 2.1, and in NetWare 386 and later versions.

Registers in:

AH	B8h
AL	05h
DH	LPT Device (0 = LPT1, 1 = LPT2, 2 = LPT3)

Registers out:

AL	Completion Code

Completion codes:

00	Successful

The NetWare C Interface format is:

```
int SetDefaultLocalPrinter( BYTE LPTDevice );
```

Set End Of Job Status (BBh) (Workstation Environment Services API)

This call is supported in NetWare version 4.6, in Advanced NetWare versions 1.0, 1.02, 2.0 and 2.1, and in NetWare 386 and later versions.

Registers in:

AH	BBh
AL	End Of Job Flag (0 = Disabled, 1 = Enabled)

Registers out:

AL	Previous End Of Job Flag (0 = Disabled, 1 = Enabled)

The NetWare C Interface format is:

```
BYTE SetEndOfJobStatus( BYTE endOfJobFlag );
```

Set Extended File Attributes (B6h 01h) (File Services API)

This call is supported in Advanced NetWare 2.1, and in NetWare versions 386 and later.

Registers in:

AH	B6h
AL	1
DS:DX	File Path (ASCIIZ 1-255 bytes)
CL	Extended File Attributes

Registers out:

AL	Completion Code

Completion codes:

00	Success
FFh	File Not Found - Carry flag is set if this code obtains
FEh	Insufficient Access Privileges

The NetWare C Interface format is:

```
int SetExtendedFileAttributes( char *filePath,
   BYTE extendedFileAttributes);
```

Set External Process Error (12h) (Value-Added Process Services API)

This call is supported in Advanced NetWare version 2.1.

Registers in:

CX	Error Handler Segment
DX	Error Handler Offset
BX	Data Segment
DI	12h

The NetWare C Interface format is:

```
int SetExternalProcessError( void (*)()codePtr, WORD dataSegment );
```

Set File Information (E3h 10h) (File Services API)

This call is supported in Advanced NetWare versions 1.0, 1.02, 2.0 and 2.1, and in NetWare 386 and later versions.

Registers in:

AH	E3h
DS:SI	Request Buffer Length
ES:DI	Reply Buffer Length

Registers out:

AL	Completion Code

Completion codes:

00	Success

Request Packet (max size = 339 bytes):

Offset	Content	Type	Order
0	Request Buffer Length - 2	WORD	lo-hi
2	10h	BYTE	
3	File Attributes	BYTE	
4	Extended File Attributes	BYTE	
5	Reserved	LONG	hi-lo
9	Creation Date	WORD	hi-lo
11	Last Access Date	WORD	hi-lo
13	Last Update Date & Time	LONG	hi-lo

17	Owner Object ID	LONG	hi-lo
21	Last Archive Date & Time	LONG	hi-lo
25	Reserved	BYTE[56]	
81	Directory Handle	BYTE	
82	Search Attributes	BYTE	
83	File Path Length (1-255)	BYTE	
84	File Path	BYTE[*LENGTH*]	

Reply Packet (2 bytes):

0	0000	WORD	lo-hi

The NetWare C Interface format is:

```
int SetFileInformation( BYTE directoryHandle, char *filePath,
   BYTE searchAttributes, BYTE fileAttributes,
   BYTE extendedFileAttributes, char *creationDate,
   char *lastAccessDate, char *lastUpdateDateAndTime,
   char *lastArchiveDateAndTime, long fileOwnerID );
```

Set File Server Date And Time (E3h CAh) (File Server Environment Services API)

This call is supported in Advanced NetWare version 2.1, NetWare 386, and later versions.

Registers in:

AH	E3h
DS:SI	Request Buffer Address
ES:DI	Reply Buffer Address

Registers out:

AL	Completion Code

Completion codes:

00h	Successful
C6h	No Console Operator

Request Buffer (9 bytes):

Offset	Content	Type	Order
0	Request Buffer Length - 2	WORD	lo-hi
2	CAh	BYTE	
3	Year (0 to 99)	BYTE	
4	Month (1 to 12)	BYTE	
5	Day (1 to 31)	BYTE	
6	Hour (0 to 23)	BYTE	
7	Minute (0 to 59)	BYTE	
8	Second (0 to 59)	BYTE	

Reply Buffer:

Offset	Content	Type	Order
0	0000h	WORD	lo-hi

The NetWare C Interface format is:

```
int SetFileServerDateAndTime( WORD year, WORD month, WORD day,
   WORD hour, WORD minute, WORD second );
```

Set Hardware Interrupt Vector (0Eh) (Value-Added Process Services API)

This call is supported in Advanced NetWare version 2.1.

Registers in:

AL	Hardware Interrupt Number
SI	ISR Segment
BX	ISR Offset
DI	0Eh

Registers out:

AL	EOI Flag

The NetWare C Interface format is:

```
BYTE SetHardwareInterruptVector( BYTE interruptNumber, WORD *ISRseg,
   WORD *ISRoffset );
```

Set Interrupt Vector (10h) (Value-Added Process Services API)

This call is supported in Advanced NetWare version 2.1.

Registers in:

AL	Interrupt Vector Number
CX	ISR Segment
DX	ISR Offset
DI	10h

The NetWare C Interface format is:

```
void SetInterruptVector( BYTE vectorNumber, WORD ISRseg,
   WORD ISRoffset );
```

Set Lock Mode (C6h 01h) (Locking API)

This call is supported in NetWare version 4.6, in Advanced NetWare versions 1.0, 1.02, 2.0 and 2.1, and in NetWare 386 and later versions.

Registers in:

AH	C6h
AL	Function Code
	00h = set to 4.0-style "compatibility mode"
	01h = set to 4.6 and later "extended lock mode"
	02h = return current lock mode

Registers out:

AL	Current lock mode

The NetWare C Interface format is:

```
int SetLockMode( BYTE lockMode );
```

Set NetWare Error Mode (DDh) (Workstation Environment Services API)

This call is supported in NetWare versions Advanced NetWare versions 2.0 and 2.1, and in NetWare 386 and later versions.

Registers in:

AH	DDh	
DL	Error Mode:	00h
		01h
		02h

Registers out:

AL	Previous Error Mode

The NetWare C Interface format is:

```
int SetNetWareErrorMode( BYTE errorMode );
```

Set Preferred Connection ID (F0h 00h) (Workstation Environment Services API)

This call is supported in Advanced NetWare versions 1.0, 1.02, 2.0 and 2.1, and in NetWare 386 and later versions.

Registers in:

AH	F0h
AL	00h
DL	Connection ID of the preferred file server (1 to 8), or 0 (if the preferred server is not set)

The NetWare C Interface format is:

```
void SetPreferredConnectionID( BYTE connectionID );
```

Set Primary Connection ID (F0h 04h) (Workstation Environment Services API)

This call is supported in Advanced NetWare versions 1.0, 1.02, 2.0 and 2.1, and in NetWare 386 and later versions.

Registers in:

AH	F0h
AL	04h
DL	Connection ID of the primary file server (1 to 8), or 0 (if the Primary file server is not set)

The NetWare C Interface format is:

```
void SetPrimaryConnectionID( int primaryConnectionID );
```

Set Queue Current Status (E3h 67h) (Queue Services API)

This call is supported in Advanced NetWare version 2.1, NetWare 386, and later versions.

Registers in:

AH	E3h
DS:SI	Request Buffer Address
ES:DI	Request Buffer Address

Registers out:

AL	Completion Code

Completion codes:

00h	Success
96h	Server Out Of Memory
9Ch	Invalid Path
D0h	Q Error
D1h	No Queue

D3h	No Q Rights
FEh	Server Bindery Locked
FFh	Bindery Failure

Request Packet (8 bytes):

Offset	Content	Type	Order
0	Request Buffer Length-2	WORD	lo-hi
2	67h	BYTE	
3	Queue ID	LONG	hi-lo
7	Queue Status	BYTE	

Reply Packet (2 bytes):

Offset	Content	Type	Order
0	0000h	WORD	lo-hi

Only a station with operator privileges can make this call.
The NetWare C Interface format is:

```
int SetQueueCurrentStatus( long queueID, BYTE queueStatus );
```

Set Queue Server Current Status (E3h 77h) (Queue Services API)

This call is supported in Advanced NetWare version 2.1, NetWare 386, and later versions.

Registers in:

AH	E3h
DS:SI	Request Packet Address
ES:DI	Reply Buffer Address

Registers out:

AL	Completion Code

Completion codes:

00h	Successful
96h	Server Out Of Memory
9Ch	Invalid Path
D0h	Q Error
D1h	No Queue
FEh	Server Bindery Locked
FFh	Bindery Failure

Request Packet (71 bytes):

Offset	Content	Type	Order
0	Request Packet Length-2	WORD	lo-hi
2	77h	BYTE	
3	Queue ID	LONG	hi-lo
7	Server Status Record	BYTE [64]	

Reply Packet (2 bytes):

Offset	Content	Type	Order
0	0000h	WORD	lo-hi

The NetWare C Interface format is:

```
int SetQueueServerCurrentStatus( long queueID,
   BYTE *serverStatusRecord );
```

Set Screen Mode (08h) (Value-Added Process Services API)

This call is supported in Advanced NetWare version 2.1.

Registers in:

AX	Requesting VAP
DI	08h

The NetWare C Interface format is:

```
void SetScreenMode( WORD VAPHeaderSeg );
```

Set Specific Capture Flags (B8h 03h) (Print Services API)

This call is supported in Advanced NetWare version 2.1, and in NetWare 386 and later versions.

Registers in:

AH	B8h
AL	03h
CX	Request Buffer Length (1..63)
ES:BX	Request Buffer
DH	LPT Device (0 = LPT1, 1 = LPT2, 2 = LPT3)

Registers out:

AL	Completion Code

Completion codes:

00h	Successful

Reply Packet (63 bytes):

Offset	Content	Type	Order
0	Status	BYTE	
1	Flags	BYTE	
2	Tab Size	BYTE (1-18)	
3	Server Printer	BYTE (0-4)	
4	Number of Copies	BYTE (0-255)	
5	Form Type	BYTE (0-255)	
6	Reserved	BYTE	
7	Banner Text (ASCIIZ)	BYTE[13]	
20	Reserved	BYTE	
21	Local LPT Device	BYTE	
22	Flush Capture Timeout	WORD	hi-lo
24	Flush Capture On Device Close	BYTE	
25	Max Lines	WORD	hi-lo
27	Max Chars	WORD	hi-lo
29	Form Name (ASCIIZ)	BYTE[13]	
42	LPT Capture Flag	BYTE	
43	File Capture Flag	BYTE	
44	Timing Out Flag	BYTE	
45	Printer Setup Buffer Address	LONG	hi-lo /*Different*/
49	Printer Reset Buffer Address	LONG	hi-lo ""
53	Connection ID Queue Print Job	BYTE	
54	Capture In Progress	BYTE	
55	Print Queue Flag	BYTE	
56	Print Job Valid	BYTE	
57	Print Queue ID	LONG	hi-lo
61	Print Job Number	WORD	hi-lo (1-999)

The NetWare C Interface format is:

```
int SetSpecificCaptureFlags( BYTE LPTDevice,
   SET_CAPTURE_FLAGS *setCaptureFlags );
```

Set Spool Flags (E0h 02h) (Print Services API)

This call is supported in NetWare versions 4.0 and 4.6, in Advanced NetWare versions 1.0, 1.02, 2.0 and 2.1, and in NetWare 386. It has been replaced by higher-level functions, but is shown here for completeness.

Registers in:

AH	E0h
DS:SI	Request Buffer
ES:DI	Reply Buffer

Registers out:

AL	Completion Code

Completion codes:

00h	Successful

Request Packet (23 bytes):

Offset	Content	Type	Order
0	Request Buffer Length-2	WORD	lo-hi
2	02h	BYTE	
3	Print Flags	BYTE	
4	Tab Size	BYTE (1-20)	
5	Target Printer	BYTE (1-5)	
6	Copies	BYTE (0-255)	
7	Form Type	BYTE (0-255)	
8	Reserved	BYTE	
9	Banner	BYTE[13]	
22	Terminator (00h)	BYTE	

Reply Packet (2 bytes):

Offset	Content	Type	Order
0	0000	WORD	lo-hi

Print Flags:

0x08	Suppress automatic form feed at end of print job
0x20	Delete spool file after printing
0x40	Enable tab expansion
0x80	Print banner page

The NetWare C Interface format is not supported.

Shell Pass Through Enable (06h) (Value-Added Process Services API)

This call is supported in Advanced NetWare version 2.1.

Registers in:

AL	Enable Flag
DI	06h

The NetWare C Interface format is:

```
void ShellPassThroughEnable( BYTE enable );
```

Signal Semaphore (C5h 03h) (Locking API)

This call is supported in NetWare version 4.6, in Advanced NetWare versions 1.0, 1.02, 2.0 and 2.1, and in NetWare 386 and later versions.

Registers in:

AH	C5h
AL	03h
CX,DX	Semaphore Handle

Registers out:

AL	Completion Code

Completion codes:

00h	Successful
01h	Semaphore Overflow (Value was increased over 127)
FFh	Invalid Semaphore Handle

The NetWare C Interface format is:

```
int SignalSemaphore( long semaphoreHandle );
```

Sleep Process (0Ch) (Value-Added Process Services API)

This call is supported in Advanced NetWare version 2.1.

Registers in:

DI	0Ch

The NetWare C Interface format is:

```
void SleepProcess( void );
```

Spawn Process (05h) (Value-Added Process Services API)

This call is supported in Advanced NetWare version 2.1.

Registers in:

BX	Code Segment
CX	Instruction Pointer
DX	Data Segment
BP:0	VAP Header
DI	05h

Registers out:

AX	Process ID

The NetWare C Interface format is:

```
int SpawnProcess( void (*)()childCodePtr, WORD childDataSegment,
   WORD header );
```

Specify Capture File (E0h 09h) (Print Services API)

This call is supported in NetWare versions 4.0 and 4.6, in Advanced NetWare versions 1.0, 1.02, 2.0 and 2.1, and in NetWare 386 and later versions.

Registers in:

AH	E0h
AL	09h
DS:SI	Request Packet Address
ES:DI	Reply Packet Address

Registers out:

AL	Completion Code

Completion codes:

00	Successful
9Ch	Invalid Path

Request Packet (max = 260 bytes):

Offset	**Content**	**Type**	**Order**
0	Request Buffer Length-2	WORD	lo-hi
2	09h	BYTE	
3	Directory Handle	BYTE	
4	File Path Length	BYTE (1-255)	
5	File Path	BYTE[*LENGTH*]	

Reply Packet (2 bytes):

Offset	**Content**	**Type**
0	0000	WORD

The NetWare C Interface format is:

```
int SpecifyCaptureFile( BYTE driveHandle, char *filePath );
```

Spool Data to a Capture File (E0h 00h) (Print Services API)

This call is supported in NetWare versions 4.0 and 4.6, in Advanced NetWare versions 1.0, 1.02, 2.0 and 2.1, and in NetWare 386.

Registers in:

AH	E0h
DS:SI	Request Buffer
ES:DI	Reply Buffer

Registers out:

AL	Completion Code

Completion codes:

00h	Successful

Request Packet (max 258 bytes):

Offset	Content	Type	Order
0	Request Buffer Length-2	WORD	lo-hi
2	00h	BYTE	
3	Data to Send	BYTE (1-256)	

Reply Packet (2 bytes):

Offset	Content	Type	Order
0	0000	WORD	lo-hi

The NetWare C Interface format is not supported.

Spool Existing File (E0h 03h) (Print Services API)

This call is supported in NetWare versions 4.0 and 4.6, in Advanced NetWare versions 1.0, 1.02, 2.0 and 2.1, and in NetWare 386.

Registers in:

AH	E0h
DS:SI	Request Buffer
ES:DI	Reply Buffer

Registers out:

AL	Completion Code

Completion codes:

00h	Successful

Request Packet (max 261 bytes):

Offset	Content	Type	Order
0	Request Buffer Length-2	WORD	lo-hi
2	03h	BYTE	
3	Directory Handle	BYTE	
4	File Path Length	BYTE	
5	File Path	BYTE[*LENGTH*]	

Reply Packet (2 bytes):

Offset	Content	Type	Order
0	0000	WORD	lo-hi

The NetWare C Interface format is not supported.

SPX Abort Connection (14h) (Communications Services API)

This call is supported in Advanced NetWare 2.1 and in NetWare 386 and later versions.

Registers in:
BX 14h
DX Connection ID

Registers out:
Nothing

Completion codes:
None

The NetWare C Interface format is:

```
void SPXAbortConnection( WORD connectionIDNumber );
```

SPX Establish Connection (11h) (Communications Services API)

This call is supported in Advanced NetWare 2.1 and in NetWare 386 and later versions.

Registers in:
BX 11h
AL Retry Count
AH SPX Watchdog Flag
ES:SI ECB Address

Registers out:
AL Completion Code
DX Connection ID

Completion codes:
00h SPX Attempting To Contact Destination Socket
EFh Local Connection Table Full
FDh Fragment Count Not 1; Buffer Size Not 42
FFh Send Socket Not Open

The NetWare C Interface format is:

```
int SPXEstablishConnection( BYTE retryCount, BYTE watchDog,
   WORD *connectionID, ECB *eventControlBlock );
```

SPX Get Connection Status (15h) (Communications Services API)

This call is supported in Advanced NetWare 2.1 and in NetWare 386 and later versions.

Registers in:

BX	15h
DX	Connection ID
ES:SI	Address of Reply Buffer

Registers out:

AL	Completion Code

Completion codes:

00h	Connection Is Active
EEh	No Such Connection

Reply Buffer (46 bytes):

Offset	**Content**	**Type**	**Order**
0	Connection State	BYTE	hi-lo
1	Watchdog Is On	BYTE	hi-lo
2	Local Connection ID	WORD	hi-lo
4	Remote Connection ID	WORD	hi-lo
6	Sequence Number	WORD	hi-lo
8	Local Acknowledge Number	WORD	hi-lo
10	Local Allocation Number	WORD	hi-lo
12	Remote Acknowledge Number	WORD	hi-lo
14	Remote Allocation Number	WORD	hi-lo
16	Local Socket	BYTE[2]	hi-lo
18	Immediate Address	BYTE[6]	hi-lo
24	Remote Network	BYTE[4]	hi-lo
36	Retransmission Count	WORD	hi-lo
38	Estimated Roundtrip Delay	WORD	hi-lo
40	Retransmitted Packets	WORD	hi-lo
42	Suppressed Packets	WORD	hi-lo

The NetWare C Interface format is:

```
int SPXGetConnectionStatus( WORD connectionIDNumber,
  CONNECTION_INFO_STRUCT *connectionInfo );
```

SPX Initialize (10h) (Communications Services API)

This call is supported in Advanced NetWare 2.1 and in NetWare 386 and later versions.

Registers in:

BX	10h
AL	00h

Registers out:

AL	SPX Installation Flag
BH	SPX Major Revision Number
BL	SPX Minor Revision Number
CX	Maximum SPX Connections Supported
DX	Available SPX Connection Count

Completion codes:
None

The NetWare C Interface format is:

```
BYTE SPXInitialize( BYTE *majorRevisionNumber,
   BYTE *minorRevisionNumber, WORD *maxConnections,
   WORD *availableConnections );
```

SPX Listen For Connection (12h) (Communications Services API)

This call is supported in Advanced NetWare 2.1 and in NetWare 386 and later versions.

Registers in:

BX	12h
AL	Retry Count
AH	SPX Watchdog Flag
ES:SI	ECB Address

Registers out:
Nothing

Completion codes:
None

The NetWare C Interface format is:

```
void SPXListenForConnection( BYTE retryCount, BYTE watchDog,
   ECB *eventControlBlock );
```

SPX Listen For Sequenced Packet (17h) (Communications Services API)

This call is supported in Advanced NetWare 2.1 and in NetWare 386 and later versions.

Registers in:

BX	17h
ES:SI	ECB Address

Registers out:
Nothing

Completion codes:
None

The NetWare C Interface format is:

```
void SPXListenForSequencedPacket( ECB *eventControlBlock );
```

SPX Send Sequenced Packet (16h) (Communications Services API)

This call is supported in Advanced NetWare 2.1 and in NetWare 386 and later versions.

Registers in:

BX	16h
DX	Connection ID
ES:SI	ECB Address

Registers out:
Nothing

Completion codes:
None

The NetWare C Interface format is:

```
void SPX SendSequencedPacket( WORD connectionIDNumber,
   ECB *eventControlBlock );
```

SPX Terminate Connection (13h) (Communications Services API)

This call is supported in Advanced NetWare 2.1 and in NetWare 386 and later versions.

Registers in:

BX	13h
DX	Connection ID
ES:SI	ECB Address

Registers out:
Nothing

Completion codes:
None

The NetWare C Interface format is:

```
int SPXTerminateConnection( WORD connectionIDNumber,
   ECB *eventControlBlock );
```

Start Counting Packets (05h) (Diagnostic Services API)

This call is supported in Advanced NetWare version 2.1 and will be supported in Novell's Network Management module.

Request Packet (44 bytes):

Offset	Content	Type
0	SPX Packet Header	BYTE[42]
42	Component Position	BYTE
43	05h	BYTE

Reply Packet (49 bytes):

Offset	Content	Type	Order
0	SPX Packet Header	BYTE[42]	
42	Completion Code	BYTE	
43	Interval Marker	LONG	lo-hi
47	Destination Socket	BYTE[2]	

The NetWare C Interface format is:

```
int StartCountingPackets( WORD connectionID, BYTE connectionNumber,
   AllResponseData *response,
   StartCountingPacketsStruct *responseData );
```

Start LPT Capture (DFh 00h) (Print Services API)

This call is supported in NetWare versions 4.0 and 4.6, in Advanced NetWare versions 1.0, 1.02, 2.0 and 2.1, and in NetWare 386 and later versions.

Registers in:

AH	DFh
DL	00h

Registers out:

AL	Completion Code

Completion codes:

C0	Successful

The NetWare C Interface format is:

```
int StartLPTCapture( void );
```

Start Sending Packets (03h) (Diagnostic Services API)

This call is supported in Advanced NetWare version 2.1 and will be supported in Novell's Network Management module.

Request Packet (70 bytes):

Offset	Content	Type	Order
0	SPX Packet Header	BYTE[42]	
42	Component Position	BYTE	
43	03h	BYTE	
44	Destination Network	BYTE[4]	
48	Destination Node	BYTE[6]	
54	Destination Socket	BYTE[2]	
56	Immediate Address	BYTE[6]	
62	Number Of Packets	WORD	lo-hi
64	Send Interval	BYTE	
65	Packets Per Send Interval	BYTE	
66	Packet Size	WORD	lo-hi
68	Change Size	WORD	lo-hi

Reply Packet (49 bytes):

Offset	Content	Type	Order
0	SPX Packet Header	BYTE[42]	
42	Completion Code	BYTE	
43	Interval Marker	LONG	lo-hi
47	Transmit Errors	WORD	lo-hi

The NetWare C Interface format is:

```
int StartSendingPktsTimed( WORD connectionID, BYTE connectionNumber,
  SendPacketsRequestStrruct *requestData, AllResponseData *response,
  SendPacketsResponseStruct *responseData );
```

Start Specific LPT Capture (DFh 04h) (Print Services API)

This call is supported in Advanced NetWare version 2.1, and in NetWare 386 and later versions.

Registers in:

AH	DFh
DL	04h
DH	LPT Device (0 = LPT1, 1 = LPT2, 2 = LPT3)

Registers out:

AL	Completion Code

Completion codes:

00	Successful

The NetWare C Interface format is:

```
int StartSpecificLPTCapture( BYTE LPTDevice );
```

Submit Account Charge (E3h 97h) (Accounting Services API)

This call is supported in Advanced NetWare version 2.1, NetWare 386, and later versions.

Registers in:

AH	E3h
DS:SI	Request Buffer Address
ES:DI	Reply Buffer Address

Registers out:

AL	Completion Code

Completion codes:

00h	Successful
C0h	No Account Privileges
C1h	No Account Balance
C2h	Credit Limit Exceeded

Request Buffer (maximum buffer length = 321):

Offset	Content	Type	Order
0	Request Buffer Length-2	WORD	lo-hi
2	97h	BYTE	
3	Service Type	WORD	hi-lo
5	Charge Amount	LONG	hi-lo

9	Cancel Hold Amount	LONG	hi-lo
13	Bindery Object Type	WORD	hi-lo
15	Comment Type	WORD	hi-lo
17	Object Name Length (1 to 47)	BYTE	
18	Bindery Object Name	BYTE[*LENGTH*]	
?	Comment Length	BYTE	
?	Comment	BYTE[*LENGTH*]	

Reply Buffer (2 bytes):

Offset	Content	Type	Order
0	0000h	WORD	lo-hi

The NetWare C Interface format is:

```
int SubmitAccountCharge( WORD BinderyObjectType,
   char *BinderyObjectName, WORD serviceType, long chargeAmount,
   long cancelHoldAmount, WORD commentType, char *comment );
```

Submit Account Hold (E3h 98h) (Accounting Services API)

This call is supported in Advanced NetWare version 2.1, NetWare 386, and later versions.

Registers in:

AH	E3h
DS:SI	Request Buffer Address
ES:DI	Reply Buffer Address

Registers out:

AL	Completion Code

Completion codes:

00h	Successful
C0h	No Account Privileges
C1h	No Account Balance
C2h	Account Credit Limit Exceeded
C3h	Account Too Many Holds

Request Buffer (maximum buffer length = 57 bytes):

Offset	Content	Type	Order
0	Request Buffer Length-2	WORD	lo-hi
2	98h	BYTE	
3	Reserve Amount	LONG	hi-lo
7	Bindery Object Type	WORD	hi-lo
9	Object Name Length (1 to 47)	BYTE	
10	Bindery Object Name	BYTE[*LENGTH*]	

Reply Buffer (2 bytes):

Offset	Content	Type	Order
0	0000h	WORD	lo-hi

The NetWare C Interface format is:

```
int SubmitAccountHold( WORD BinderyObjectType,
    char *BinderyObjectName, long reserveAmount );
```

Submit Account Note (E3h 99h) (Accounting Services API)

This call is supported in Advanced NetWare version 2.1, NetWare 386, and later versions.

Registers in:

AH	E3h
DS:SI	Request Buffer Address
ES:DI	Reply Buffer Address

Registers out:

AL	Completion Code

Completion codes:

00h	Successful
C0h	No Account Privileges

Request Buffer (maximum buffer length = 313):

Offset	Content	Type	Order
0	Request Buffer Length	WORD	lo-hi
2	99h	BYTE	
3	Service Type	WORD	hi-lo
5	Bindery Object Type	WORD	hi-lo
7	Comment Type	WORD	hi-lo
9	Object Name Length	BYTE	
10	Bindery Object Name (1 to 47)	BYTE[*LENGTH*]	
?	Comment Length	BYTE	
?	Comment	BYTE[*LENGTH*]	

Reply Buffer (2 bytes):

Offset	Content	Type	Order
0	0000h	WORD	lo-hi

The NetWare C Interface format is:

```
int SubmitAccountNote( WORD BinderyObjectType,
    char *BinderyObjectName, WORD serviceType, WORD commentType,
    char *comment );
```

TTS Abort Transaction (C7h 03h) (Transaction Tracking System)

This call is supported in SFT Level II NetWare, System Fault Tolerant Netware 286 and NetWare 386.

Registers in:

AH	C7h
AL	3

Registers out:

AL	Completion Code

Completion codes:

Carry flag cleared:

00h	Successful

Carry flag set:

FDh	Transaction Tracking Disabled (No backout performed)
FEh	Transaction Ended, Records Locked
FFh	No Explicit Transaction Active

The NetWare C Interface format is:

```
int TTSAbortTransaction( void );
```

TTS Begin Transaction (C7h 00h) (Transaction Tracking System)

This call is supported in SFT Level II NetWare, System Fault Tolerant Netware 286 and NetWare 386.

Registers in:

AH	C7h
AL	0

Registers out:

AL	Completion Code

Completion codes:

Carry flag cleared:

00h	Successful

Carry flag set:

96h	Out of Dynamic Workspace
FEh	Implicit Transaction Already Active (active implicit transaction now converted to an explicit transaction)
FFh	Explicit Transaction Already Active (existing explicit transaction continues normally)

The NetWare C Interface format is:

```
int TTSBeginTransaction( void );
```

TTS End Transaction (C7h 01h) (Transaction Tracking System)

This call is supported in SFT Level II NetWare, System Fault Tolerant Netware 286 and NetWare 386.

Registers in:

AH	C7h
AL	1

Registers out:

AL	Completion Code

Completion codes:

Carry flag cleared:

00h	Successful
FDh	Transaction Tracking Disabled
FEh	Transaction Ended Records Locked

Carry flag set:

FFh	No Explicit Transaction Was Active

The NetWare C Interface format is:

```
int TTSEndTransaction( long *transactionNumber );
```

TTS Get Statistics (E3h D5h) (File Server Environment Services API)

This call is supported in Advanced NetWare version 2.1, NetWare 386, and later versions.

Registers in:

AH	E3h
DS:SI	Request Buffer Address
ES:DI	Reply Buffer Address

Registers out:

AL	Completion Code

Completion code:

00h	Successful
C6h	No Console Rights

Request Buffer (3 bytes):

Offset	Content	Type	Order
0	Request Buffer Length - 2	WORD	lo-hi
2	D5h	BYTE	

Reply Buffer (maximum buffer length = 446 bytes):

Offset	Content	Type	Order
0	Reply Buffer Length - 2	WORD	lo-hi
2	System Elapsed Time	LONG	hi-lo
6	Transaction Tracking Supported	BYTE	
7	Transaction Tracking Enabled	BYTE	
8	Transaction Volume Number	WORD	hi-lo
10	Configured Max Simultaneous Transactions	WORD	hi-lo
12	Actual Max Simultaneous Transactions	WORD	hi-lo
14	Current Transaction Count	WORD	hi-lo
16	Total Transactions	LONG	hi-lo
20	Total Write Transactions Performed	LONG	hi-lo
24	Total Transactions Backed Out	LONG	hi-lo
28	Total Unfilled Backout Requests	WORD	hi-lo
30	Transaction Disk Space	WORD	hi-lo
32	Transaction FAT Allocations	LONG	hi-lo
36	Transaction File Size Changes	LONG	hi-lo
40	Transaction Files Truncated	LONG	hi-lo
44	Records	BYTE	

Active Transaction (repeated Records times):

Offset	Content	Type
?	Logical Connection Number	BYTE
?	Task Number	BYTE

The NetWare C Interface format is:

```
int TTSGetStats( WORD connectionID, int structSize,
   TTS_STATS *TTSStats );
```

TTS Is Available (C7h 02h) (Transaction Tracking System)

This call is supported in SFT Level II NetWare, System Fault Tolerant Netware 286 and NetWare 386.

Registers in:

AH	C7h
AL	2

Registers out:

AL	Completion Code (carry flag is unaffected)

Completion codes:

00h	Transaction Tracking Not Available
01h	Transaction Tracking Available
FDh	Transaction Tracking Disabled

The NetWare C Interface format is:

```
int TTSIsAvailable( void );
```

TTS Get Application Thresholds (C7h 05h) (Transaction Tracking System)

This call is supported in SFT Level II NetWare, System Fault Tolerant Netware 286 and NetWare 386.

Registers in:

AH	C7h
AL	5

Registers out:

AL	Completion Code
CL	Logical Record Lock Threshold (0 to 255)
CH	Physical Record Lock Threshold (0 to 255)

Completion codes:

00	Successful

The NetWare C Interface format is:

```
int TTSGetApplicationThresholds( BYTE *logicalRecordLockThreshold,
  BYTE *physicalRecordLockThreshold );
```

TTS Get Workstation Thresholds (C7h 07h) (Transaction Tracking System)

This call is supported in SFT Level II NetWare, System Fault Tolerant Netware 286 and NetWare 386.

Registers in:

AH	C7h
AL	7

Registers out:

AL	Completion Code
CL	Logical Record Lock Threshold (0 to 255)
CH	Physical Record Lock Threshold (0 to 255)

Completion codes:

00	Successful

The NetWare C Interface format is:

```
int TTSGetWorkstationThresholds( BYTE *logicalRecordLockThreshold,
  BYTE *physicalRecordLockThreshold );
```

TTS Set Application Thresholds (C7h 06h) (Transaction Tracking System)

This call is supported in SFT Level II NetWare, System Fault Tolerant Netware 286 and NetWare 386.

Registers in:

AH	C7h
AL	6
CL	Logical Record Lock Threshold (0 to 255)
CH	Physical Record Lock Threshold (0 to 255)

Registers out:

AL	Completion Code

Completion codes:

00	Successful

The NetWare C Interface format is:

```
int TTSSetApplicationThresholds( BYTE logicalRecordLockThreshold,
   BYTE physicalRecordLockThreshold );
```

TTS Set Workstation Thresholds (C7h 08h) (Transaction Tracking System)

This call is supported in SFT Level II NetWare, System Fault Tolerant Netware 286 and NetWare 386.

Registers in:

AH	C7h
AL	8
CL	Logical Record Lock Threshold (0 to 255)
CH	Physical Record Lock Threshold (0 to 255)

Registers out:

AL	Completion Code

Completion codes:

00	Successful

The NetWare C Interface format is:

```
int TTSSetWorkstationThresholds( BYTE logicalRecordLockThreshold,
   BYTE physicalRecordLockThreshold );
```

TTS Transaction Status (C7h 04h) (Transaction Tracking System)

This call is supported in SFT Level II NetWare, System Fault Tolerant Netware 286 and NetWare 386.

Registers in:

AH	C7h
AL	4
CX, DX	Transaction Number

Registers out:

AL	Completion Code

Completion codes:
Carry flag cleared:

00h	Successful
FFh	Transaction Not Yet Written To Disk

The NetWare C Interface format is:

```
int TTSTransactionStatus( long transactionNumber );
```

VAP Attach To File Server (15h) (Value-Added Process Services API)

This call is supported in Advanced NetWare version 2.1.

Registers in:

DS:SI	Server Name
DI	15h

Registers out:

AL	Completion Code
DL	Server Number

Completion codes:

00h	Successful
01h	Already Attached to File Server
03h	No Attachment Slot Available
04h	File Server Name Too Long

The NetWare C Interface format is:

```
int VAPAttachToFileServer( char serverName, int *connectionID );
```

VAP Get Connection ID (16h) (Value-Added Process Services API)

This call is supported in Advanced NetWare version 2.1.

Registers in:

DS:SI	Server Name
DI	16h

Registers out:

AL	Completion Code
DL	Connection ID

Completion codes:

00h	Already Attached to Server
nonzero	Not Attached to Server

The NetWare C Interface format is:

```
itn VAPGetConnectionID( char *serverName, int *connectionID );
```

VAP Get File Server Name (14h) (Value-Added Process Services API)

This call is supported in Advanced NetWare version 2.1.

Registers in:

ES:SI	Buffer
DI	14h

Registers out:

AL	Completion Code

Completion codes:

00h	VAP Resides With a File Server
01h	VAP Resides With a Bridge

The NetWare C Interface format is:

```
int VAPGetFileServerName( char *serverName );
```

Verify Bindery Object Password (E3h 3Fh) (Bindery Services API)

This call is supported in Advanced NetWare versions 1.0, 1.02, 2.0 and 2.1, and in NetWare 386 and later versions.

Registers in:

AH	E3h
DS:SI	Request Buffer Length
ES:DI	Reply Buffer Length

Registers out:

AL	Completion Code

Completion codes:

00	Success
96h	Server Out Of Memory
F0h	Wildcard Not Allowed
FBh	No Such Property
FCh	No Such Object
FEh	Server Bindery Locked
FFh	Bindery Failure (No such object or bad password)

Request Packet (max size = 181 bytes):

Offset	Content	Type	Order
0	Request Buffer Length-2	WORD	lo-hi
2	3Fh	BYTE	
3	Object Type	WORD	hi-lo
5	Object Name Length	BYTE [1-47]	
6	Object Name	BYTE[*LENGTH*]	
?	Password Length	BYTE [1-127]	
?	Password	BYTE[*LENGTH*]	

Reply Packet (2 bytes):

Offset	Content	Type	Order
0	0000	WORD	lo-hi

The NetWare C Interface format is:

```
int VerifyBinderyObjectPassword( char *objectName, WORD objectType,
   char *password );
```

Wake Up Process (0Dh) (Value-Added Process Services API)

This call is supported in Advanced NetWare version 2.1.

Registers in:

BX	Process ID
DI	0Dh

The NetWare C Interface format is:

```
void WakeUpProcess( WORD processID );
```

Wait On Semaphore (C5h 02h) (Locking API)

This call is supported in NetWare version 4.6, in Advanced NetWare versions 1.0, 1.02, 2.0 and 2.1, and in NetWare 386 and later versions.

Registers in:

AH	C5h
AL	02h
CX,DX	Semaphore Handle
BP	Timeout Limit

Registers out:

AL	Completion Code

Completion codes:

00h	Successful
FEh	Timeout Failure
FFh	Invalid Semaphore Handle

The NetWare C Interface format is:

```
int WaitOnSemaphore( long semaphoreHandle, WORD timeoutLimit );
```

Write Property Value (E3h 3Eh) (Bindery Services API)

This call is supported in Advanced NetWare versions 1.0, 1.02, 2.0 and 2.1, and in NetWare 386 and later versions.

Registers in:

AH	E3h
DS:SI	Request Buffer Length
ES:DI	Reply Buffer Length

Registers out:

AL	Completion Code

Completion codes:

00	Success
96h	Server Out Of Memory
E8h	Not Item Property
ECh	No Such Segment
F0h	Wildcard Not Allowed
F1h	Invalid Bindery Security
F8h	No Property Write Privileges
FBh	No Such Property
FCh	No Such Object
FEh	Server Bindery Locked
FFh	Bindery Failure

Request Packet (max size = 199 bytes):

Offset	Content	Type	Order
0	Request Buffer Length-2	WORD	lo-hi
2	3Eh	BYTE	
3	Object Type	WORD	hi-lo
5	Object Name Length	BYTE [1-47]	
6	Object Name	BYTE[*LENGTH*]	
?	Segment Number	BYTE	
?	Erase Remaining Segments	BYTE	
?	Property Name Length	BYTE [1-15]	
?	Property Name	BYTE[*LENGTH*]	
?	Property Value Segment	BYTE[128]	

Reply Packet (2 bytes):

Offset	Content	Type	Order
0	0000	WORD	lo-hi

The NetWare C Interface format is:

```
int WritePropertyValue( char *objectName, WORD objectType,
   char *propertyName, int segmentNumber, BYTE *propertyValue,
   BYTE moreSegments );
```

Appendix B

NetWare Fields

Appendix B: The NetWare Fields

Fields employed in NetWare calls — except for those which are self-explanatory, such as file or record offsets — are listed here in alphabetical order. (APIs where more information may be found are listed in parentheses.)

Abort Connections (Diagnostic Services API) is the number of times (since SPX was loaded) that applications have called SPX Abort Connection.

Abort Flag (Print Services API), if nonzero, deletes a capture file rather than queuing it for printing.

Access Date (AppleTalk Filing Protocol Services API) returns the date the target AFP file was last accessed. If the AFP Directory/File Path specifies an AFP directory, the Creation Date field returns a zero.

Access Flag (File Server Environment Services API) contains bit flags indicating a connection's access rights for the file, as shown below.

0x01	Open For Read by this Station
0x02	Open For Write by this Station
0x04	Deny Read Requests from Other Stations
0x08	Deny Write Requests from other stations
0x10	File Detached
0x20	TTS Holding Detach
0x40	TTS Holding Open

Access Mode (AppleTalk Filing Protocol Services API) defines how the call opens a target file. The following bits are defined:

0x01	Read Access
0x02	Write Access
0x04	Deny Read Access to Others
0x08	Deny Write Access to Others

Access Rights (AppleTalk Filing Protocol Services API) returns a one-word bit mask of the calling station's privileges for accessing the specified file or directory.

The *Access Privileges* field contains the following bits:

High Byte	
0x01	Read
0x02	Write
0x04	Open
0x08	Create

0x10	Delete
0x20	Parental
0x40	Search
0x80	Modify

Acknowledgments Sent (File Server Environment Services API) is a count of acknowledgments sent by a server. An acknowledgment is sent when a workstation repeats a request that is being serviced.

Acknowledge Number (Communication Services API) is the Sequence Number of the next packet SPX expects to receive. SPX manages this field; clients needn't worry about it.

Active Indexed Files (File Server Environment Services API) contains the count of files that are currently active, open and indexed.

Actual Maximum Bindery Objects (File Server Environment Services API) is the maximum number of Bindery objects that have been used concurrently since the file server came up. This field is only meaningful if the previous field is set.

Actual Maximum Indexed Files (File Server Environment Services API) contains the number of indexed files the server has had active simultaneously since it was brought up.

Actual Maximum Open Files (File Server Environment Services API) contains the number of files open simultaneously since the server was brought up.

Actual Maximum Simultaneous Transactions (File Server Environment Services API) is the highest number of transactions that have occurred simultaneously since the server was brought up.

Actual Maximum Used Directory Slots (Directory Services API) is the most directory slots ever used at one time on a volume.

Actual Maximum Used Routing Buffers (File Server Environment Services API) is the maximum number of routing buffers that have been in use simultaneously since the server was brought up.

AES Events (Diagnostic Services API) is the number of times (since IPX was loaded) that IPX has used the AES to schedule an event.

AFP Directory Path (AppleTalk Filing Protocol Services API) specifies at least the target AFP directory name, and optionally the names of one or more parent directories. The field is 1 to 255 bytes long.

AFP Entry ID (AppleTalk Filing Protocol Services API) is the four-byte Apple equivalent of a NetWare directory handle, with one exception: A NetWare directory handle points to a file server volume or directory and an AFP entry ID points to a file server volume, directory, or file.

Allocate Cannot Find Route (Diagnostic Services API) is the number of times (since the shell was activated) that the shell, asked by an application to establish a connection with a file server, could not find a route to the destination network.

Allocate No Slots Available (Diagnostic Services API) is the number of times (since the shell was activated) that the shell, asked by an application to establish a connection with a file server, could not because the file server's connection table was full.

Allocate Server Is Down (Diagnostic Services API) is the number of times (since the shell was activated) that the shell, asked by an application to establish a connection with a file server, could not establish the connection because the target file server was down.

Allocation Number (Communication Services API) is the number of listen buffers outstanding in one direction on the connection. SPX manages this field; clients need not be concerned with it.

Amount (Accounting Services API) if positive is a charge, if negative a credit.

Attached Indexed Files (File Server Environment Services API) contains the count of indexed files ready for indexing but not ready for use.
Attach During Processing (File Server Environment Services API) is the number of requests to establish connections from workstations for which the server is currently processing requests.

Attach While Processing Attach (File Server Environment Services API) is the number of times a request to establish a connection from a workstation was received when the server was already processing a request to establish a connection with that workstation.

Available Blocks (Directory Services API) is the number of unused blocks on a volume.

Available Directory Slots (Directory Services API) is the number of unused directory slots on a volume.

Available Indexed Files (File Server Environment Services API) contains the count of file indexes that are available for use.

Available SPX Connection Count (Communication Services API) is how many SPX connections are available to an application.

Background Aged Writes (File Server Environment Services API) is the number of times the background disk write process wrote a partially filled cache block to disk.

Background Dirty Writes (File Server Environment Services API) is the number of times a cache block that was written to disk was completely filled with information.

Backup Date (AppleTalk Filing Protocol Services API) returns the date of the last backup of the specified directory or file.

Backup Time (AppleTalk Filing Protocol Services API) returns the time of the last backup of the specified directory or file.

Bad Incoming Packets (Diagnostic Services API) is the number of times (since SPX was loaded) that SPX has received and discarded a packet because the connection ID in the packet was wrong.

Bad Logical Connection Number Packets (File Server Environment Services API) is the count of all request packets with invalid logical connection numbers, which are those numbers not supported by a file server (such as 573).

Bad Send Requests (Diagnostic Services API) is the number of times (since SPX was loaded) that applications have incorrectly called SPX Send Sequenced Packet by passing an invalid connection ID, or bypassing the address of an ECB that indicates a packet header size of less than 42 bytes.

Bad Sequence Number Packets (File Server Environment Services API) is a count of request packets the server received from a connection where the sequence number in the packet did not match the current sequence number or the next sequence number. (Packets with bad sequence numbers are discarded.)

Balance (Accounting Services API) contains an object's account balance.

Banner Text (Print Services API) is a flag that contains the text of the bottom half of a banner. This is an uppercase, 13-character ASCIIZ string. The default is the name of the file to be printed.

Being Processed Count (Diagnostic Services API) is the number of times (since the shell was activated) that the shell has received a "being processed" reply from a file server. A file server sends this reply to a shell when the server, while processing the shell's request, receives duplicate requests from the shell for the same service.

Bridge Driver (Diagnostic Services API) specifies the target bridge driver (0,1, 2,or 3) within the target node. The target bridge driver corresponds to the target LAN board (0,1,2,or 3).

Buffer (Value-Added Process Services API) is a pointer to a 48-byte buffer that will receive a file server name if the VAP is on a file server.

Buffer Length (Value-Added Process Services API) is the length of an input buffer and can not be greater than 80.

Bytes Read (File Server Environment Services API) is the number of bytes a logical connection has read since the workstation logged in.

Bytes Written (File Server Environment Services API) is the number of bytes a logical connection has written since the workstation logged in.

Cache Allocations (File Server Environment Services API) is the number of times a cache block was allocated for use.

Cache Block Scrapped (File Server Environment Services API) contains the number of times a cache block is scrapped due to the following scenario: A process was put to sleep because it needed a cache block and the Least-Recently-Used block had to be written to disk before it could be reused. When the process awoke after the block had been written and freed, the process checked and discovered that while it was asleep another process had come in, allocated a different block, and read into it the information that the sleeping process was seeking. In this case, the newly awakened process must free the cache block, and use the block that already contains the sought information.

Cache Buffer Count (File Server Environment Services API) is the number of cache buffers in a server.

Cache Buffer Size (File Server Environment Services API) is the number of bytes in a cache buffer.

Cache Full Write Requests (File Server Environment Services API) is the number of times the cache software was instructed to write information that exactly filled one or more sectors.

Cache Get Requests (File Server Environment Services API) is the number of times the cache software was requested to read information from the disk.

Cache Hit On Unavailable Block (File Server Environment Services API) is number of times a cache request could be serviced from an available cache block but the cache buffer could not be used because it was in the process of being written to or read from disk.

Cache Hits (File Server Environment Services API) is the number of times cache requests were serviced from existing cache blocks.

Cache Misses (File Server Environment Services API) is the number of times cache requests could not be serviced from existing cache blocks.

Cache Partial Write Requests (File Server Environment Services API) is the number of times cache software was instructed to write information that did not exactly fill a sector.

Cache Read Requests (File Server Environment Services API) is the number of times the cache software was asked to read data.

Cache Write Requests (File Server Environment Services API) is the number of times the cache software was asked to write data.

Cancel Hold Amount (Accounting Services API) should be the same as the amount specified in the corresponding Submit Account Hold call. If no Submit Account Hold call was made prior to providing the service, the hold amount should be zero.

Cannot Cancel ECBs (Diagnostic Services API) is the number of times (since IPX was loaded) that IPX has been unable to cancel an ECB.

Cannot Find Route (Diagnostic Services API) is the number of times (since IPX was loaded) that IPX has been unable to find a route to a requested network address.

Capture In Progress (Print Services API) is a flag set when the first character is sent to the specified LPT device. The flag is cleared when the capture is ended, canceled, or flushed.

Change Size (Diagnostic Services API) specifies a value to increase or decrease the size of the next packet. This feature allows a packet size to vary during a diagnostic test.

Channel Number (File Server Environment Services API) is the number of the disk channel to be queried.

Channel State (File Server Environment Services API) is the state of a disk channel:

00h	Channel running
01h	Channel being stopped
02h	Channel stopped
03h	Channel nonfunctional

Channel Synchronization State (File Server Environment Services API) is the control state of the disk channel. In nondedicated versions of NetWare, the disk channel may be used by more than one piece of software, and control of the channel must be synchronized. This field can have the following values:

0	Channel is not being used.
2	NetWare is using the channel; no one else requests it.
4	NetWare is using the channel; someone else requests it.
6	Someone else is using the channel; NetWare does not need it.
8	Someone else is using the channel; NetWare needs it.
10	Someone else has released the channel; NetWare should use it.

Charge (Queue Services API) is an accounting information field not used in the current queue-management system but provided to allow job servers to charge their customers and to log accounting information in future NetWare releases.

Charge Amount (Accounting Services API) is the amount a server charges for the service it provides.

Checksum (Communication Services API) was used for compatibility with the original Xerox packet header. Now it is always set to 0xFFFF by IPX; LAN cards do hardware checksums on entire IPX packet frames, so this field is unnecessary.

Checksum Error Count (Diagnostic Services API) specified the number of checksum errors that have occurred while receiving packets (since the last reset or initialization).

Client ID (Accounting Services API) is the Bindery object ID of the client being charged for a service.

Client ID Number (Queue Services API) returns the object ID number of the station that placed a job in a queue.

Client Record Area (Queue Services API) contains additional information passed to a job server by the client. The information can take any format agreed upon by both. This field must be supplied by the client creating the queue job.

Client Station (Queue Services API) is the connection number of the station that placed a job in a queue. This station has read-write access to the Job Entry's associated file.

Client Task Number (Queue Services API) is a field containing the number of the task active on the workstation when the job was placed in the queue.

Code Segment (Value-Added Process Services API) is the code segment of a new process.

Comment (Accounting Services API) is an entry that the server makes in the audit record in the SYS:SYSTEM\NET$ACCT.DAT file.

Comment Type (Accounting Services API) is one of six different types defined by Novell or created by developers.

Component Position (Diagnostic Services API) is the position of the target component within the IPX Configuration Response Packet (00h = first position, 01h = second position, etc.).

Configuration Description (File Server Environment Services API) contains an ASCIIZ string indicating the channel's current I/O driver configuration.

Configured Maximum Bindery Objects (File Server Environment Services API) is the maximum number of Bindery objects that the file server will track (0 = unlimited).

Configured Maximum Open Files (File Server Environment Services API) contains the number of files the server can open simultaneously.

Configured Maximum Simultaneous Transactions (File Server Environment Services API) is the most transactions the server can track simultaneously. It is set with the Install/Netgen utility.

Connection/Address Mismatch Count (Diagnostic Services API) is the number of times (since the shell was activated) that the shell has received an error code from a server indicating that the connection number in a shell's request packet did not match the shell's connection number in the server's tables.

Connection Control (Communication Services API) contains four single-bit flags used by SPX to control the bidirectional flow of data across a connection:

1-8	(Undefined) These bits are undefined in the Xerox Sequenced Packet protocol, and NetWare's SPX dutifully ignores them.
10h	(End-Of-Message) A client sets this flag to signal to its partner an end of connection. SPX ignores it, passing it on unaltered.
20h	(Attention) A client sets this flag if a packet is an attention packet. This feature has not been implemented, so SPX ignores this bit, too.
40h	(Acknowledgment Required) SPX sets this bit if an acknowledgment packet is needed. Because SPX handles acknowledgment requests and responses, clients need not be concerned with it.

80h (System Packet) SPX sets this bit if the packet is a system packet. Such packets are not delivered to clients.

Connection Count (Message Services and File Server Environment Services APIs) contains the number of logical connections to receive a message (0 = broadcast to all workstations).

Connection Flag (Value-Added Process Services API) determines whether the created process is to be connected with a file server. If zero, then the created process receives a default connection with a file server; if nonzero, then no connection is established.

Connection ID Queue Print Job (Print Services API) is a flag containing a value (1-8) indicating the position in the workstation's Connection ID Table of the server receiving a print job.

Connection List (Message Services API) field specifies the connection number of each station to which a message is sent. Each byte in a connection list field has a corresponding byte in a Result List field.

Connection Number (Workstation Services API) is assigned by a file server to a workstation.

Connection's Lock Status (File Server Environment Services API) is:

0 = Normal (connection free to run)
1 = Connection waiting on physical record lock
2 = Connection waiting on file lock
3 = Connection waiting on logical record lock
4 = Connection waiting on a semaphore

Connection State (Communication Services API) is the state of the specified connection. Four possible states are defined:

01h *Waiting*. SPX is listening (SPX Listen For Connection) on the connection, waiting to receive an Establish Connection packet.

02h *Starting*. SPX is attempting to create (SPX Establish Connection) a full connection with a remote workstation by sending Establish Connection packets on its half of the connection.

03h *Established*. SPX has established a connection with a remote workstation, and the connection is open for two-way packet transmission.

04h *Terminating*. The remote SPX has terminated the connection (SPX Terminate Connection). However, the local SPX has not yet terminated its half of the connection.

Connection Status (Workstation Services API) contains 0xFF when the connection is active.

Controller Drive Number (File Server Environment Services API) is the drive number of a disk unit relative to a controller number.

Controller Number (File Server Environment Services API) contains the address on a physical disk channel of the controller that controls the disk.

Controller Type (File Server Environment Services API) contains the number identifying the type (make and model) of a disk controller.

Controlling Process (Value-Added Process Services API) returns the VAP header segment of a VAP that has console control.

-1	0xFFFF	MONITOR has control of console
0	0x00	No process has control of console
positive	VAP header segment of VAP that has console control	

Creation Date (File Services and Directory Services APIs) and Last Access Date are specified in two bytes. Last Update Date and Time and Last Archive Date and Time are in four-byte format.

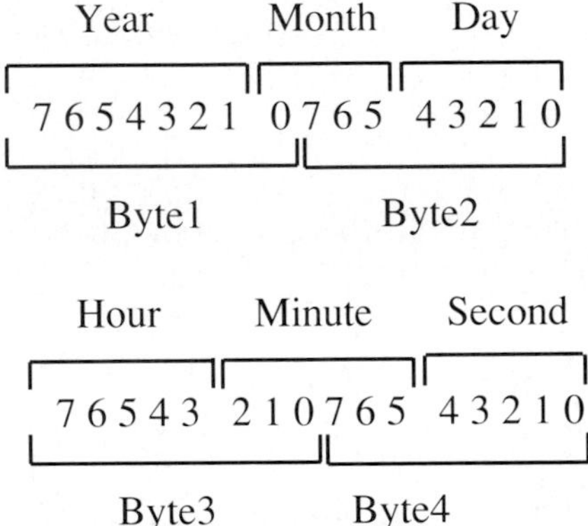

Credit Limit (Accounting Services API) is a minimum balance that must be maintained in an account.

Current Changed FATS (File Server Environment Services API) contains the number of current FAT sectors the file system has modified.

Current Charge Rate Multiplier (Accounting Services API) is multiplied by units of service (connect time, requests made, blocks read or written), then the result is divided by the Current Charge Rate Divisor to calculate a charge against a user's account.

Current Charge Rate Divisor (Accounting Services API) is used after the Current Charge Rate Multiplier is applied to units of service (connect time, requests made, blocks read or written) to calculate a charge against a user's account.

Current Entries (Queue Services API) is a count (0-250) of the jobs in a queue.

Currently Used Routing Buffers (File Server Environment Services API) is the number of routing buffers that are being used by a server.

Current Open Files (File Server Environment Services API) contains the number of files the server has open. It reflects files workstations have open and any internal files, such as the Bindery, that the file server has open.

Current Servers (Queue Services API) is the number (0-25) of currently attached job servers that can service a queue.

Current Transaction Count (File Server Environment Services API) is the number of transactions in progress.

Current Used Bindery Objects (File Server Environment Services API) is the number of Bindery objects currently in use on the server.

Current Used Dynamic Space (File Server Environment Services API) is the amount of memory in the dynamic memory area that is currently in use.

Custom Variable (Diagnostic Services API) is a WORD-length field that specifies information pertinent to the particular driver. These fields are optional.

Data Fork Size (AppleTalk Filing Protocol Services API) is the data size of a target AFP file. If the AFP Directory/File Path specifies an AFP directory, the Data Fork Size field returns a zero.

Data Segment (Value-Added Process Services API) is the data segment of a new process, or designates a segment to be used by the error handler.

Datastream Type (Communication Services API) is a one-byte flag that indicates the type of data found in the packet. Possible values and definitions for the field are:

0-FDh	(Client Defined) This field is defined by the application and ignored by SPX.

FEh	(End-of-Connection) SPX generates this packet when a client calls for termination of an active connection; it is the last message delivered on the connection.
FFh	(End-of-Connection acknowledgment) SPX generates this system packet; it is not delivered to the connected clients.

Data Type (Accounting Services API) contains the data types of a record. Data types larger than a LONG should be described as series of BYTE, WORD, and LONG fields. Valid types are:

Value	**Type**
1 (BYTE)	An 8-bit value
2 (WORD)	A 16-bit value, hi-lo order
3 (LONG)	A 32-bit value, hi-lo order
4 (TEXT)	A length byte followed by a string of printable characters

Days Charge Occurs Mask (Accounting Services API) is a field that contains a bit mask that specifies the days of the week for which a charge rate applies. If the bit corresponding to the day of the week is set (bit 0 = Sunday, bit 6 = Saturday) the charge is made during that day at the half hour specified in Time Change Occurs. If this field is 0, no charges are made.

Dead Mirror Table (File Server Environment Services API) is a 32-byte table containing the secondary physical drive that each logical drive was last mapped to (FFh = logical drive was never mirrored). The Dead Mirror Table is used in conjunction with the Drive Mirror Table. If the Drive Mirror Table shows that a drive is not currently mirrored, this table can be used to determine the drive that previously mirrored the logical drive. This table is used to remirror a logical drive after a mirror failure.

Decode Range (Diagnostic Services API) following a Memory Address is the number of paragraphs in the block. Decode Range following an I/O Address is the number of ports to be decoded.

Delay (Value-Added Process Services API) specifies the length of a delay interval in 1/18-second ticks.

Deny Read Count (File Server Environment Services API) is the number of logical connections that have denied other stations read privileges.

Deny Write Count (File Server Environment Services API) is the number of logical connections that have denied other stations write privileges.

Description Strings (File Server Environment Services API) contains the following four ASCIIZ strings:

Company Name: Name of the company that distributed this copy of NetWare
Revision: NetWare version and revision
Revision Date: Revision date in the form of mm /dd/yy
Copyright Notice: Copyright notice

Desired Response Count (AppleTalk Filing Protocol Services API) specifies the number of subdirectories or files (1-4) for which the calls return reply buffers.

Destination Connection ID (Communication Services API) is a number assigned by SPX at the packet's destination.

Destination Network (Communication Services and Diagnostic Services APIs) contains the number of the network on which the Destination Node resides. NetWare network numbers are four-byte values given to servers on the same network segment.

Destination Node (Communication Services and Diagnostic Services APIs) is a six-byte field that specifies the physical address of the Destination Node. The number of bytes depends on the LAN hardware used. Ethernet cards use all six, Omninet cards just one. A node address of FFh FFh FFh FFh FFh FFh (all six set to FFh) sets IPX to broadcast mode, sending the packet to all nodes on the Destination Network.

Destination Socket (Communication Services and Diagnostic Services APIs) is the socket address of the packet's destination process. Sockets route packets to different processes within each node. Xerox has reserved the following socket numbers:

1	Routing Information Packet
2	Echo Protocol Packet
3	Error Handler Packet
20h-3Fh	Experimental
1h-BB8h	Registered with Xerox
BB9h-	Dynamically assignable

Xerox has assigned Novell the following sockets for NetWare:

451h	File Service Packet
452h	Service Advertising Packet
453h	Routing Information Packet
455h	NetBIOS Packet
456h	Diagnostic Packet

Detach During Processing (File Server Environment Services API) is the number of requests to terminate a connection from a workstation that were received while previous requests were still being processed for that connection.

Detach For Bad Connection Number (File Server Environment Services API) is a count of requests to terminate a connection where the connection number is not supported by the server.

Directory Entry (File Server Environment Services API) is an offset into the file server's Directory Entry Table for the volume.

Directory Handles (Directory Services and Queue Services APIs). Directory handles are used in most calls. A handle is simply the index into the Directory Handle Table, which contains a pointer to the Directory Table and a pointer to the Volume Table. So when we have a directory handle, we know it describes a volume and a directory, such as "SYS:PUBLIC".

If no directory handle is used in a call, the programmer must specify the full path name, including the volume, directory and subdirectory names, in the format VOLUME:DIRECTORY\SUBDIRECTORY\SUBDIRECTORY.

If a directory handle is used, it may specify a full path; if so, then no path need be included in the function call.

A third variation is to use a directory handle as the base of the path and send the remainder of the path as an offset. For example, if our directory handle pointed to "SYS:DATA\" and our path was "DBDATA" then the final directory would be "SYS:DATA\DBDATA".

The directory handles calls are used find handles given drive numbers, to set handles to different directories, and to save and restore handles.

Directory Name (Directory Services API) is a regular DOS file or directory name (up to an eight-character name and three-character extension, separated by a period). The Directory Name cannot include the following characters: *, ?, :, \, /. Directory names longer than 14 characters get truncated.

Directory Path (Directory Services and Queue Services APIs) can be the full path itself or an offset to a directory handle. If no handle is specified, the volume name must be specified in the format "VOLUME:DIRECTORY\SUBDIRECTORY". If a directory handle is specified, the path can be used as an offset to it.

Dirty Cache Buffers (File Server Environment Services API) is the number of cache buffers containing data that has not been written to disk.

Disk Channel Table (File Server Environment Services API) is a five-byte table showing which disk channels exist on a server and what their drive types are. (Each channel is 1 byte.) A nonzero value in the disk channel table means that the corresponding disk channel exists in the file server (1 = XT drive type, 2 = AT drive type, 3 = SCSI drive type, 4 = disk coprocessor drive type, 50 to 255 = value-added disk drive types).

DMA Is Used (Diagnostic Services API) tells whether the value in the following DMA Line field is valid. The following values can appear in a DMA Is Used field:

00h	No DMA line defined
FFh	DMA line defined for exclusive use
FEh	DMA line defined for a particular LAN board, but can be shared by others of the same type

DMA Line (Diagnostic Services API) returns the value of the DMA line used by the LAN board. Zeros returned in the second DMA Line field indicate that the LAN board does not use the field.

Drive Cylinders (File Server Environment Services API) is the number of physical cylinders on the drive.

Drive Definition String (File Server Environment Services API) contains the make and model of a drive (ASCIIZ string).

Drive Heads (File Server Environment Services API) is the number of disk heads on the drive.

Drive Mapping Table (File Server Environment Services API) is a 32-byte table containing the primary physical drive that each logical drive is mapped to (FFh = no such logical drive exists on the server).

Drive Number (Directory Services API) corresponds to an index into the Drive Handle Table (0 to 31) for permanent drives (A..Z)(0..25) and temporary drives ([,\,],^,_,')(26..31). Drive A is 0, drive F is 5, etc.

Drive Removable Flag (File Server Environment Services API) indicates whether a disk is removable (0 = nonremovable).

Driver Mirror Table (File Server Environment Services API) is a 32-byte table containing the secondary physical drive that each logical drive is mapped to (FFh = no such logical drive exists on the server).

Driver Type (File Server Environment Services API) contains a number indicating the type of disk driver software installed on a disk channel.

Driver Workspace (Communication Services API) is a 12-byte field reserved for the network driver whenever IPX is using an ECB. It can be used by applications any other time.

Drive Size (File Server Environment Services API) is the size of the physical drive in blocks (1 block = 4,096 bytes). The drive size does not include the portion of the disk reserved for Hot Fix redirection in the event of media errors.

Duplicate Replies Sent (File Server Environment Services API) is a count of request packets for which a server had to send duplicate replies. Duplicate replies are only sent for requests the server cannot process.

Duplicate Packets (Diagnostic Services API) is the number of times (since SPX was loaded) that SPX has discarded inbound packets because they were duplicates of previously received packets.

ECB Address (Communication Services API) points to an IPX Event Control Block.

Enable Flag (Value-Added Process Services API) is set to 00h to disable pass-through mode, and to nonzero to enable pass-through mode.

Error Message (Value-Added Process Services API) is a pointer to a null-terminated error message.

Error Receiving Count (Diagnostic Services API) is the number of times (since the shell was activated) that IPX has indicated an error even though a packet was received on the socket. This usually indicates an "Overrun" error.

ESR Address (Communication Services API), if it is used at all, contains the address of an application-defined event service routine (ESR) IPX can call when it's done sending or receiving. If the ESR is not used, this field should be a null pointer (four bytes or zero).

Establish Connection Failures (Diagnostic Services API) is the number of times (since SPX was loaded) that calls to SPX Establish Connection have failed because the SPX Packet Header was too small, the SPX Connection Table was full, or no router was found to a target network.

Establish Connection Requests (Diagnostic Services API) is the number of times (since SPX was loaded) that applications have issued calls to SPX Establish Connection.

Estimated Roundtrip Delay (Communication Services API) indicates in clock ticks the time that the local SPX waits. (Eighteen clock ticks equal approximately 1 second.)

Ethernet Type (Diagnostic Services API) is significant only for Ethernet drivers using the Ethernet protocol (not the IEEE 802.3 protocol). Xerox assigned a value of 8137h to Novell where 81 is the high-order byte and 37 is the low-order byte. Only drivers with identical Ethernet Types can communicate.

Extended File Attributes (File Services API). In DOS, File Attributes are bit fields in a byte that resides in the directory entry of each file. The DOS File Attributes are read-only, hidden, system or archive. NetWare extends the DOS File Attributes to include four network-specific ones: the Transaction Bit, the Index Bit, and the Read and Write Audit Bits.

The Transaction Bit, bit 4 (08h), is set to work with Novell's Transaction Tracking System (TTS, see Chapter 5). If this bit is set, the TTS will track all writes to this file during a transaction. Also, if this bit is set, it cannot be deleted or renamed until the bit is cleared by the Set Extended File Attributes call.

When the Index Bit, bit 5 (10h), is set, NetWare will index the file's File Allocation Tables (FATs), which will speed file access. Novell recommends setting this bit for files that are randomly accessed and are larger than 2MB.

The Read and Write Audit Bits, bit 6 (20h) and bit 7 (40h) are not yet used.

Fatal FAT Write Errors (File Server Environment Services API) contains the number of disk write errors that occurred in both the original and mirrored copies of a FAT sector.

FAT Scan Errors (File Server Environment Services API) contains the number of times an internally inconsistent state existed in the file system.

FAT Write Errors (File Server Environment Services API) contains the number of disk write errors that have occurred when writing FAT sectors to the disk.

Field Count (Accounting Services API) contains the number of fields in a record type.

File Attributes (File Services API) contains information about a directory entry. A user must have modify rights to change these bits:

01h	Read-Only Bit (File may be read but not written to.)
02h	Hidden Bit (File will not be shown in directory listing.)
04h	System Bit (File will not be shown in directory listing.)
08h	Execute Only Bit (File can be executed, but not read or written to; once set, this bit cannot be cleared.)
10h	Subdirectory Bit (Entry is a subdirectory.)

20h Archive Bit
(Bit is set if file has changed since last backup.)

40h Shareable Bit
(Set if more than one user can access this file at once.)

File Capture (Print Services API) is a flag set when a capture filename has been specified. Data to be printed is then sent to the file, rather than being queued for printing.

File Handle (Locking and File Services APIs) is the DOS file handle of the target file. The programmer can obtain it through the DOS Create File call or the DOS Open File call.

File Path (Locking and File Services APIs) is a null-terminated string (ASCIIZ) that specifies the full pathname of the target file. Full paths may be specified as in SYS:USER\DJT\MYFILE.DAT or paths may extend the default directory. Assuming the default directory is SYS:APPS, setting File Path to WP\TEST.DAT would make the target file SYS:APPS\WP\TEST.DAT.

File Service Packets Buffered (File Server Environment Services API) is the number of times file service request packets were stored in routing buffers.

File Size (Queue Services API) returns the size of the file associated with a specified job.

Finder Information (AppleTalk Filing Protocol Services API) returns the 32-byte Finder Information structure associated with each AFP directory or file.

First DMA Channels Used (File Server Environment Services API) lists the DMA controllers a disk driver uses to control a disk channel.

First DMA Channels Used In Use Flag (File Server Environment Services API) is a flag for a DMA Channels Used field.

First Interrupt Numbers Used (File Server Environment Services API) contains interrupt numbers a disk driver uses to communicate with a disk channel.

First Interrupt Numbers Used In Use Flag (File Server Environment Services API) is a flag for the First Interrupt Numbers Used.

First IO Address Used (File Server Environment Services API) contains addresses a disk driver uses to control a disk channel.

First IO Address Used Length (File Server Environment Services API) contains the lengths of the addresses a disk driver uses to control a disk channel.

First Shared Memory Address (File Server Environment Services API) is a field a disk driver uses to control a disk channel.

First Shared Memory Address Length (File Server Environment Services API) contains the length of a shared memory addresses.

Flush Capture Timeout Count (Print Services API) is a flag (0-65535) that starts counting down when an application prints any data (INT 17 is called).

Flush Capture On Device Close (Print Services API) is a flag that tells whether (any value) or not (0 — the default) to flush a capture.

Force Flag (File Server Environment Services API) indicates whether the file server should force itself down even when files are open. Placing 00 in this field will cause the call to abort if files are open; 1 will down the server.

Forged Detach Requests (File Server Environment Services API) is a count of requests to terminate connections where the source addresses did not match the address the server had assigned to the connection. The detach request is ignored.

Fork Indicator (AppleTalk Filing Protocol Services API) tells whether the returned AFP Entry ID points to a data fork (0) or to a resource fork (1).

Format Length (Accounting Services API) contains the length of the format control string used to print comment records associated with the Charge or Note Record.

Form Name (Print Services API) is a flag containing the name of a form to be mounted in a file server. This field is only for reference.

Form Type (Print Services API) is a flag that tells which of 256 (0-255) forms to use. The default form is 0.

Fragment Count (Communication Services API) is the number of buffers from which a packet is formed for sending or into which it is split when received; it must be greater than zero.

Fragment Descriptor (Communication Services API) contains the address and size of the buffer to or from which a packet is sent or received.

Fragmented Write Occurred (File Server Environment Services API) is the number of times a dirty cache block contained noncontiguous sectors of information to be written, and the skipped sectors were not preread from the disk.

Function Code (File Services API) indicates the current lock mode or the mode to be set with Get Lock Mode and Set Lock Mode.

> 00h = set to 4.0-style "compatibility mode"
> 01h = set to 4.6 and later "extended lock mode"
> 02h = return current lock mode

Grant Rights Mask (Directory Services API) contains the rights to be granted to a directory's Maximum Rights Mask.

Hardware Interrupt Number (Value-Added Process Services API) can range from 0 to 15, and specifies which hardware interrupt is to be installed.

Hardware Rx Mismatch Count (Diagnostic Services API) specifies the number of times (since the last reset or initialization) that the hardware has received more or less bytes than expected.

Hardware Type Text (Diagnostic Services API) identifies the target machine (e.g., IBMPC, SAMSUNG 286A).

High Record Offset (Locking API): Record Offset is a LONG (unsigned long) value expressed in two WORDs (unsigned ints) containing the offset from the beginning of the file where the record begins. The programmer must place the more significant WORD in High Record Offset and less significant WORD in Low Record Offset.

Hot Fix Blocks Available (File Server Environment Services API) is the number of redirection blocks that are still available. This field is only meaningful with SFT NetWare Level I or above.

Hot Fix Disabled (File Server Environment Services API) indicates whether Hot Fix is enabled or disabled (0 = enabled). This field is only meaningful with SFT NetWare Level I or above.

Hot Fix Table Size (File Server Environment Services API) is the total number of redirection blocks set aside on the disk for Hot Fix redirection. Some or all of these blocks may be in use. This field is only meaningful with SFT NetWare Level I or above. To determine the number of redirection blocks still available for future use, see the Hot Fix Blocks Available field.

Hot Fix Table Start (File Server Environment Services API) indicates the first block of the disk Hot Fix Redirection Table. This field is only meaningful with SFT NetWare Level 1 or above. The redirection table is used to replace bad disk blocks with usable blocks in the event that a media failure occurs on the disk.

Immediate Address (Communication Services and Diagnostic Services APIs) is a six-byte field containing the address of a node to which a packet is sent or from which it arrived, or the address of an internetwork bridge on the local network. In IPX, an application must initialize this field before an ECB is sent. In SPX, the field is filled during creation of a connection for ECBs. In diagnostics, it specifies the node address of the first bridge a packet encounters as it travels from a source node to a socket node. If the application sets this field to FFFFFFFFFFFFh (-1), IPX chooses a bridge.

Inbound Packet (Diagnostic Services API) is the number of times (since IPX was loaded) that a node's driver has given an incoming packet to IPX.

Incoming Packets (Diagnostic Services API) is the number of times (since SPX was loaded) that a node's driver has given an incoming packet to SPX.

Incoming Packet Discarded No DGroup Buffer (File Server Environment Services API) is the number of incoming packets that were received in a routing buffer that needed to be transferred to a DGroup buffer so the socket dispatcher could transfer the packet to the correct socket. If no buffers are available, such packets are lost.

Input Buffer (Value-Added Process Services API) is a pointer to a buffer up to 80 characters long which returns the string typed in by the user. The length of the input buffer must be specified in Input Buffer Length. The string returned is not null-terminated; the length is supplied in the Input String Length value.

In String (Value-Added Process Services API) returns either when <ENTER> is pressed or the Input Buffer Length is reached.

Instruction Pointer (Value-Added Process Services API) is a created process's instruction pointer.

Intermediate Networks (Service Advertising Protocol) shows the number of hops a server ID packet is required to make traveling from a value-added server to a querying process. Initially, the field is set to 1; each time the packet passes through an intermediate network, the field is incremented. When this field is set to 0x10, the ID packet is a server shutdown packet and recipient file servers and bridges respond by purging the server from their Binderies.

Internetwork Address (Connection Services API) is composed of the server's Network Number and the Physical Node Address.

Interrupt Is Used (Diagnostic Services API) indicates whether the value in the following Interrupt Line field is valid. The following values can appear in an Interrupt Is Used field:

00h	No Interrupt line defined
FFh	Interrupt line defined for exclusive use
FEh	Interrupt line defined for a particular LAN board, but can be shared by others of the same type

Interrupt Line (Diagnostic Services API) returns the value of the interrupt used by the LAN board. Zeros returned in the second Interrupt Line field indicate that the LAN board does not use the field.

Interrupt Vector (Value-Added Process Services API) contains the interrupt vector number (0 to 255).

Interval Marker (Communication Services and Diagnostic Services APIs) is a value between 0 and 65,535 (0000h and FFFFh), representing one clock tick (1/18th of a second).

In Use Flag (Workstation Services and Communications Services APIs). In workstation calls, this flag displays the state of whatever activity the shell is performing and its possible values are:

0xE0	AES Temporary Indicator
0xF8	Critical Holding (IPX in critical process)
0xFA	Processing
0xFB	Holding (in processing after an event occurred)
0xFC	AES Waiting
0xFD	Waiting
0xFE	Receiving
0xFF	Sending

In communications calls, the flag is reset to zero when IPX is done with an ECB. When the ECB is in use, possible values are:

0xF8	A send was attempted while IPX was busy, so the send packet and ECB have been queued for later processing.
0xFA	The ECB is being processed by IPX.
0xFB	A send or receive has occurred, but the ECB is in a holding queue waiting to be processed.
0xFD	An event is scheduled and IPX awaits expiration of its time interval.
0xFE	IPX is listening on a socket for incoming packets.
0xFF	The ECB is in use for sending a packet.

Invalid Connection Packets (File Server Environment Services API) is the count of all request packets with invalid logical connection numbers. A connection packet is invalid if it contains a logical connection number that has not been allocated or a source address that does not match the address the file server has assigned to the logical connection.

Invalid Reply Header Count (Diagnostic Services API) is the number of times (since the shell was activated) that the shell has received a reply packet header whose Checksum field was -1 or whose Packet Type field indicated that the packet was not a file server reply.

Invalid Sequence Number Count (Diagnostic Services API) indicates the number of times (since the shell was activated) that the shell has received a file server reply packet specifying an incorrect sequence number. This usually indicates that the reply was unnecessary.

Invalid Slot Count (Diagnostic Services API) indicates the number of times (since the shell was activated) that the shell has received a file server reply packet specifying an incorrect connection ID.

I/O Address (Diagnostic Services API) is the address of a block of I/O addresses to be decoded by a LAN board.

IO Error Count (File Server Environment Services API) is the number of times I/O errors have occurred on the disk since the server was brought up.

IPX Major Version (Diagnostic Services API) is which IPX major version is installed on a responding node.

IPX Minor Version (Diagnostic Services API) is which IPX minor version is installed on a responding node.

IPX Not My Network (File Server Environment Services API) is a count of packets received that were destined for the B, C, or D side drivers.

IPX Workspace (Communication Services API) is a four-byte field reserved for IPX whenever IPX is using an ECB. When IPX is not using the ECB, an application may use this field.

ISR Offset (Value-Added Process Services API) is the offset of an interrupt.

ISR Segment (Value-Added Process Services API) is either a real-mode segment value or a protected-mode segment descriptor, depending upon the processor mode in use.

Job Control Flags (Queue Services API) indicate the status of a job. Bits in the field are set as follows.

When bit 08h (the Service Auto-Start flag) is set, the job will be serviced if a job server connection is broken, even if the client has not explicitly started the job. If the bit is cleared when a server connection is broken, and the client has not yet released the job to the queue, QMS removes the job from the queue.

When bit 10h (the Service Restart flag) is set, the job remains in the queue (in its current position) after a job server has aborted the job. If this bit is cleared when a server aborts the job, QMS removes the job from the queue.

QMS sets bit 20h (the Entry Open flag) to indicate that the client has not filled the associated job file. Close File And Start Queue Job clears this bit, indicating that the job is ready for service if the User Hold flag and Operator Hold flag are clear.

When bit 40h (the User Hold flag) is set, the job continues to advance in the queue, but cannot be serviced until the client who placed the job, or the operator, clears the flag.

Bit 80h (the Operator Hold Flag) prevents the job from being serviced, as does the User Hold flag; only operators can clear or set the Operator Hold flag.

Job Count (Queue Services API) returns the number of job entries in a queue.

Job Entry (Queue Services API) is a number the Queue Management System assigns to a job when the job first enters a queue.

Job Entry Time (Queue Services API) is when the job entered the queue, according to the system clock of the file server. The format is year, month, day, hour, minute, second (one byte each).

Job File Handle (Queue Services API) is a handle created by the Queue Management System for a corresponding Job Entry.

Job File Name (Queue Services API) is the name of a file created by the Queue Management System for a corresponding Job Entry.

Job Number (Queue Services API) returns the Job Entry number the Queue Management System assigned to a job when the job first entered the queue.

Job Numbers (Queue Services API) returns an array containing Job Entry numbers the Queue Management System assigned to jobs when they entered the queue, listed according to their positions in the queue.

Job Position (Queue Services API) returns Job Entry's position within a queue.

Job Type (Queue Services API) is a number specifying the type of a Job Entry; this field should be set to 0 if not used, and should never be set to -1 (wildcard).

LAN Board Status (Diagnostic Services API) returns one of the following values to indicate the status of the corresponding LAN board:

00h	The board is alive and running.
01h	The board does not exist.
02h	The board is dead.

LAN Description (Diagnostic Services API) returns a null-terminated text string of not more than 69 bytes listing LAN hardware supported by a driver.

LAN Hardware ID (Diagnostic Services API), hard-coded into the Master Configuration Table, uniquely identifies the LAN hardware. The OEM/Driver Support Group Manager at Novell assigns this ID.

LAN Mode (Diagnostic Services API) is a one-byte field with the following bits defined:

bits 0-7

bit 0:

off(0)	Place-holding dummy driver
on (1)	Real Driver

bit 1:

off	Not 100% guaranteed driver
on	100% guaranteed driver

bit 7:

off	Driver does not use DMA
on	Driver uses DMA; no receive block straddles 64k physical address boundary

Last Access Date (File Services API) and Creation Date are specified in two bytes. Last Update Date and Time and Last Archive Date and Time are in four-byte format.

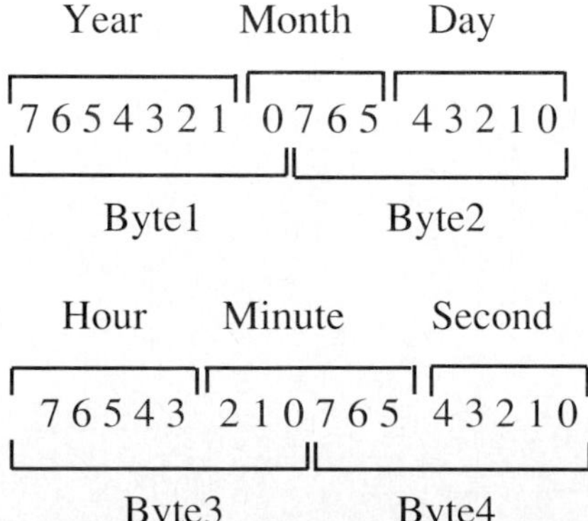

Last Archive Date (File Services API). Last Access Date are and Creation Date are specified in two bytes. Last Update Date and Time and Last Archive Date and Time are in four-byte format.

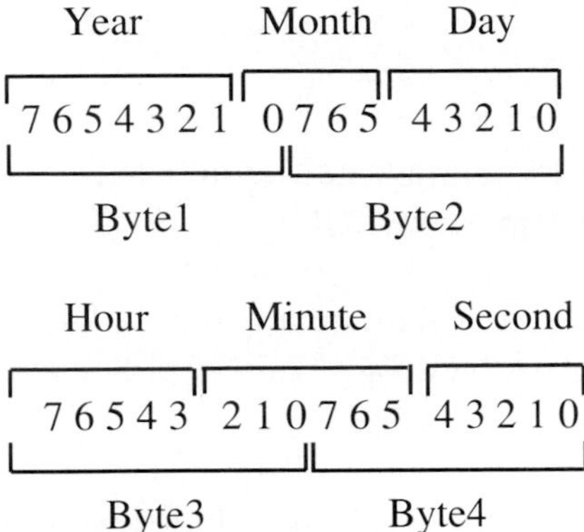

Last Archive Date (File Services API). Last Access Date are and Creation Date are specified in two bytes. Last Update Date and Time and Last Archive Date and Time are in four-byte format.

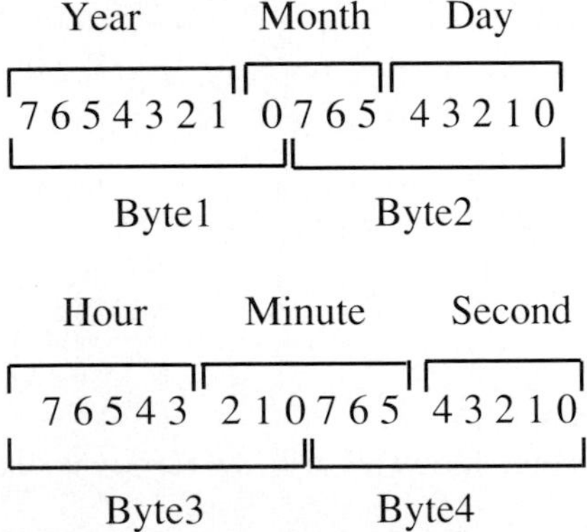

Last Archive Time (File Services API). Last Access Date are and Creation Date are specified in two bytes. Last Update Date and Time and Last Archive Date and Time are in four-byte format.

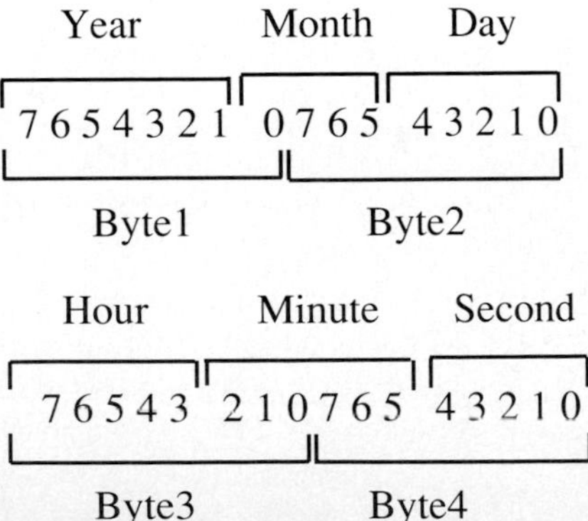

Last Record Seen (File Server Environment Services API) indicates the last record seen. On the first call, it must be set to zero; on subsequent calls it should receive the value in the Next Request Record field until it returns zero.

Last Update Date (File Services API). Last Access Date are and Creation Date are specified in two bytes. Last Update Date and Time and Last Archive Date and Time are in four-byte format.

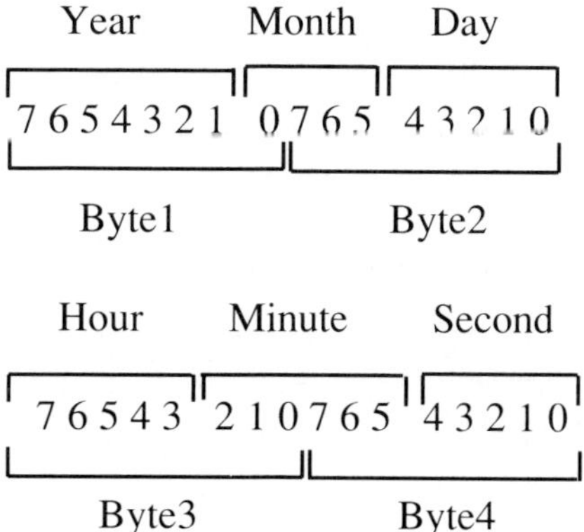

Last Update Time (File Services API). Last Access Date are and Creation Date are specified in two bytes. Last Update Date and Time and Last Archive Date and Time are in four-byte format.

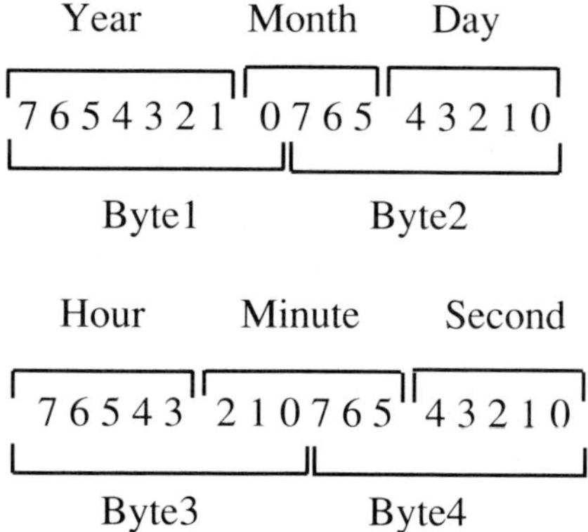

Link Address (Communication Services API) is a field maintained by IPX while an ECB is in use and is available to the application when the ECB is not in use.

Listen ECBs (Diagnostic Services API) is the number of times (since IPX was loaded) that applications have given IPX a listen ECB.

Listen For Connection Failures (Diagnostic Services API) is the number of times (since SPX was loaded) that calls to SPX Listen For Connection have failed because the SPX Connection Table was full.

Listen For Connection Requests (Diagnostic Services API) is the number of times (since SPX was loaded) that applications have issued calls to SPX Listen For Connection.

Listen Packet Requests (Diagnostic Services API) is the number of times (since SPX was loaded) that applications have given listen ECBs to SPX.

Local Allocation Number (Communication Services API) is the number of outstanding packet receive buffers (posted listens) available for an SPX connection.

Local Connection ID (Communication Services API) is the number of the specified SPX connection from the local workstation's point of view.

Local LPT Device (Print Services API) is a flag that specifies which LPT device is the default. 0 = LPT1, 1 = LPT2, 2 = LPT3.

Local Socket (Communication Services API) is the Socket Number the local SPX is using to send and receive packets.

Locked (File Server Environment Services API) is whether the file is locked exclusively (0 = not locked exclusively).

Locking Directive (Locking API) directs the call to either log or log and lock the file. It may have one of two values with Log File:

00 Log file
01 Log and lock file

Locking Directive has three possible values with Log Physical Record and Log Logical Record:

00	Log record
01	Log and lock record with an exclusive lock
03	Log and lock record with a shareable, read-only lock

And with Lock Logical Record Set it specifies the type of lock. The options are:

00	Lock with an exclusive lock
01	Lock record with a shareable lock

Lock Flag (File Server Environment Services API) contains bit flags indicating the file's lock information, as shown below.

0x01	Locked
0x02	OpenShareable

0x04	Logged
0x04	Open Normal
0x40	TTS Holding Lock
0x80	Transaction Flag Set on this File

Lock Status (File Server Environment Services API) contains bit flags indicating a file's lock status, as shown below.

0x01	Locked Exclusive
0x02	Locked Shareable
0x04	Logged
0x40	Lock is held by TTS

Lock Type (File Server Environment Services API) contains a flag indicating the type of lock, if any, on a file, as shown below.

00h	Not Locked
FEh	Locked by a File Lock
FFh	Locked by Begin Share File Set

Logical Connection Number (Connection Services API) is the position of an attached workstation in the File Server Connection Table, or (File Server Environment Services API) the logical connection involved in a transaction.

Logical Drive Count (File Server Environment Services API) is the number of logical drives attached to a server. If disks are mirrored, the logical drive count will be lower than the actual number of physical disks attached because a set of mirrored disks is considered to be one logical drive.

Logical Record Lock Threshold (Transaction Tracking System API) is the number (0 to 255) of logical record locks that may be set before a transaction is begun.

Login Enabled Flag (File Server Environment Services API) indicates whether login is enabled (1) or disabled (0).

Login Subdirectory Name (Connection Services API) is an ASCII string containing the name of the subdirectory below SYS:LOGIN where the file LOGIN.EXE can be executed.

Login Time (Connection Services API) format is:

Byte	**Content**	
0	Year	(0 to 99, where a value of 80 = 1980, 81 = 1981, etc.; however, if the value is less than 80, the year is considered to be in the twenty-first century.)

1	Month	(1 to 12)
2	Day	(1 to 31)
3	Hour	(0 to 23)
4	Minute	(0 to 59)
5	Second	(0 to 59)
6	Day	(0 to 6, where a value of 0 = Sunday, 1 = Monday, etc.)

Long Directory/File Name (AppleTalk Filing Protocol Services API) returns the AFP directory or file name of the specified directory or file. An AFP directory or file name must be 32 characters long.

Lost Packets (Diagnostic Services API) is the number of times (since IPX was loaded) that IPX has been unable to supply a receive ECB for an incoming packet.

Low Record Offset (Locking API). Record Offset is a LONG (unsigned long) value expressed in two WORDs (unsigned ints) containing the offset from the beginning of the file where the record begins. The programmer must place the more significant WORD in High Record Offset and less significant WORD in Low Record Offset.

LPT Capture (Print Services API) is a flag that indicates whether (any value) or not (0) capture of a specified LPT device is taking place.

LRU Block Was Dirty (File Server Environment Services API) is the number of times the Least-Recently-Used cache block allocation algorithm reclaimed a dirty cache block.

Machine ID (Diagnostic Services API) returns a value of 00h if the target machine is an IBM PC computer or compatible.

Major Version (Diagnostic Services API) identifies the major version of a driver release.

Malformed ECBs (Diagnostic Services API) is the number of times (since IPX was loaded) that applications have passed malformed ECBs to IPX. An ECB is considered malformed if the value in its Fragment Count field is 0, or if the value in its first Fragment Descriptor field's Size field is less than 30 bytes.

Malformed Listen ECBs (Diagnostic Services API) is the number of times (since SPX was loaded) that applications have given malformed ECBs to SPX. An ECB is malformed if the value in its Fragment Count field is 0, if the value in its first Fragment Descriptor field's Size field is less than 42, or if the listen socket is not open.

Maximum Characters (Print Services API) is a flag that specifies the maximum characters per line, up to 65535; default is 132.

Maximum Data Size (Diagnostic Services API) is the maximum size of a packet's data portion for the target driver. It is always 64 bytes less than the packet size advertised by a LAN board.

Maximum Lines (Print Services API) is a flag that tells the maximum lines per page, up to 65535; default is 66.

Maximum Number of Servers (Queue Services API) is the maximum number of connections to be returned.

Maximum Open Connections (Diagnostic Services API) is the maximum number of SPX connections that have been open simultaneously since IPX was loaded.

Maximum Open Sockets (Diagnostic Services API) is the maximum number of sockets that have been open simultaneously since IPX was loaded.

Maximum Possible Connections (Diagnostic Services API) is the maximum number of SPX connections possible on the target node. (This value is configurable.)

Maximum Possible Sockets (Diagnostic Services API) is the maximum number of open sockets possible on a target node. (This value is configurable.)

Maximum Rights Mask (Directory Services API) is a byte containing bit fields specifying privileges. The bit assignments are:

0x01	Read	- may read files
0x02	Write	- may write to files
0x04	Open	- may open files
0x08	Create	- may create files
0x10	Delete	- may delete files
0x20	Parental	- may create or delete subdirectories and trustee rights can be granted or revoked
0x40	Search	- may search directory
0x80	Modify	- may change file attributes

The Maximum Rights Mask determines the absolute maximum privileges that anyone could have in a directory area. If someone had trustee rights that gave them all rights to the area, but the directory's maximum rights mask was "Read, Open, and Search," then that would be all the user could do (except for the Supervisor or Supervisor equivalent users, who have all rights to everything).

Maximum SPX Connections Supported (Communication Services API) is the maximum number of SPX connections set up in the SHELL.CFG file.

Maximum Timeout (Workstation Services API), the most clock ticks a Receive Timeout is allowed, is set by a shell when it attaches to a file server.

Maximum Used Dynamic Space (File Server Environment Services API) is the maximum amount of memory in the dynamic memory area that has been in use since the server was brought up.

Member Name (Bindery Services API) is the name of an object in a Property Name set.

Memory Address (Diagnostic Services API) identifies the address of a block of memory address space to be decoded by a LAN board.

Message (Message Services and Value-Added Process Services APIs), in Message Services contains a message to be sent. It can be from 1 to 60 bytes long and cannot contain ASCII characters less than 20h or greater than 7Eh. For VAPs, it is a pointer to a null-terminated message which can be up to 80 characters long.

Message Length (Value-Added Process Services API) specifies the character length of the message to be displayed. If Message Length is greater than the actual length of the message, the remaining spaces will be filled with blanks. If Message Length is set to F (-1), the actual length of the message is calculated and used.

Message Mode (Message Services API) tells whether attached file servers store or reject messages sent to a workstation, and whether a workstation should be notified of messages.

00h Attached servers store both user and server messages intended for the workstation. The shell automatically retrieves and displays each message.

01h The server stores server messages but discards user messages intended for this station. The shell automatically retrieves and displays each console vmessage.

02h The server stores server messages but discards user messages intended for this station. The shell ignores the file server's notification that a message exists in the message buffer. Applications can poll for and retrieve the most recently stored message by calling Get Broadcast Message.

03h The server stores both user and server messages intended for this station. The shell ignores the file server's notification that a message exists in the message buffer. Applications can poll for and retrieve the most recently stored message by calling Get Broadcast Message.

The default is 00h.

Microchannel Flags (Diagnostic Services API) describe microchannel support for configurations. The following bits are defined:

for bits 0-7

bit 0:

on (1)	The configuration does not use microchannel.
off(0)	The configuration uses microchannel but cannot be combined with other configurations that do not use microchannel.

bit 1:

on	This configuration uses microchannel and can be combined with other configurations regardless of whether they use microchannel.

Minor Version (Diagnostic Services API) identifies minor version of a driver release.

Miscellaneous Flags (Diagnostic Services API) is a one-byte field with the following bits defined:

For bits 0-7:

bit 4:

off(0)	NonEthernet or nonconfigurable board drive
on(1)	Configurable Ethernet board driver

bit 0:

off	IEEE 802.3 protocol
on	Ethernet protocol

bit 2:

off	Driver can run in protected mode.
on	Driver runs only in real mode on 286-based machines.

Modify Date (AppleTalk Filing Protocol Services API) returns the date a target AFP file was last modified.

Modify Time (AppleTalk Filing Protocol Services API) returns the time of the last modification of a target AFP file.

More Properties (Bindery Services API) is a flag set (FFh) if more properties exist for this object, or to zero if not.

More Segments (Bindery Services API) is a flag set to true (FFh) if there are more 128-byte value segments for a property, to false (00) if not.

Net BIOS Broadcast Was Propagated (File Server Environment Services API) is a count of NetBIOS packets propagated through this network.

NetBIOS Propagate Count (Diagnostic Services API) is the number of times the bridge has received NetBIOS broadcasts since it was initialized.

NetWare File Handle (AppleTalk Filing Protocol Services API) field specifies a six-byte NetWare file handle.

NetWare Version (File Server Environment Services API) (1 to 255) is the version of NetWare running on the default server (2 = Advanced NetWare 2.x).

Network (Service Advertising Protocol) field is the network address of the LAN on which the value-added server resides.

Network Addresses (Diagnostic Services API) is how many Network Address (0 to 128) the call is returning in the current set.

Network Gone Count (Diagnostic Services API) indicates the number of times (since the shell was activated) that the shell has received a packet from a file server indicating the target network has gone away. Only a 68000 file server can generate this kind of packet.

Network Number (Workstation Services and Connection Services APIs) is a server's four-byte network address.

New AFP Entry ID (AppleTalk Filing Protocol Services API) is an AFP entry ID that points to the newly created AFP directory.

Next Set Starting Point (Diagnostic Services API) is set to 0 for the first call for all known networks or servers. If that call returns a full set of 128, the application should set this field to 128 for the next call, 256 for the one after that, and so on until the call returns only a partial set.

Node (Service Advertising Protocol) is the node on which the value-added server resides.

Node Address (Workstation and Diagnostic Services APIs) is a server's six-byte node address in Workstation Services; in diagnostics, it returns the six-byte node address of a LAN board installed in a workstation. The node address uniquely identifies the driver and board on the network. If the node address is less than six bytes long (for example, 24E0h), the address appears as: 00 00 00 00 24 E0.

Node Address Type (Diagnostic Services API) indicates who records a node address in a driver to match the node address setting of the LAN board; and how and when the node address is recorded. The following values are defined:

00h	The driver dynamically reads and records the node address by calling Driver Initialize.
01h	The developer hard codes the node address in the driver code Master Configuration Table.
02h	A configuration utility assigns the node address.

No ECB Available Count (Diagnostic Services API) specifies the number of packets the driver has received (since the last reset or initialization) for which there was no listening ECB.

No Listen ECBs (Diagnostic Services API) is the number of times (since SPX was loaded) that SPX was forced to discard an inbound SPX Establish Connection packet because SPX lacked a corresponding SPX Listen For Connection ECB.

No Listen Failures (Diagnostic Services API) is the number of times (since SPX was loaded) that SPX has failed to send a packet because a target station had not allocated a receive buffer.

No Receive Buffers Count (Diagnostic Services API) is the number of times (since the bridge was initialized) that the bridge could not receive inbound packets because of inadequate buffer space. These packets are lost.

No Router Found Count (Diagnostic Services API) is the number of times (since the shell was activated) that the shell has tried and failed to find a route to a destination node. The shell attempts to reroute a packet when a connection seems to fail and the user requests a "Retry."

No Space For Service Count (Diagnostic Services API) is the number of times (since the bridge was initialized) that the bridge has received internetwork packets that it could not accommodate because the router did not have enough space in its DGroup area to copy the packets. These packets are lost.

Number of Copies (Print Services API) is flag set at a number from 0 to 255. The default is 1; 0 means don't print anything.

Number of Custom Variables (Diagnostic Services API) field specifies the number of Custom Variables that will follow.

Number of Known Routes (Diagnostic Services API) is the number of routes between the source bridge and the destination network or server. If only one route exists, this field returns a value of 0001h.

Number of Local Drives (Connection Services API) is used to determine the workstation drive ID to assign to a server's SYS volume.

Number of Offspring (AppleTalk Filing Protocol Services API) field returns the number of files and subdirectories contained within the specified directory.

Number of Operator Retries (Diagnostic Services API) is the number of times (since the shell was activated) that the user has instructed the shell to retry an operation.

Number of Packets (Diagnostic Services API) is the total number of packets to be sent to a destination node during a diagnostic test.

Number of Servers (Diagnostic Services API) is how many server types and name combinations the call is returning in the current set. The maximum value this field returns is 10.

Number Of Service Processes (File Server Environment Services API) is the number of service processes in the server. A service process handles incoming service requests.

Object Flag (Bindery Services API) is one byte identifying an object as either static (0) or dynamic (1).

Object Name (Bindery Services API) is up to 47 uppercase characters long. Only printable ASCII characters 21h through 7Dh may be used; excluded are control characters, spaces, slashes, backslashes, colons, semicolons, commas, asterisks, question marks, and tildes.

Object Name Length (Bindery Services API) is the number of characters in a Bindery object's name.

Object Security (Bindery Services API) is a single byte, with the high-order four-bit nibble defining write privileges and the low-order nibble defining read privileges.

Hex	Access	Explanation
0	Anyone	Any object has access, whether or not it is logged into the file server.
1	Logged	Access is granted to any object logged into the file server.
2	Object	Access is granted only to objects logged into the file server with their names, types and passwords.

3	Supervisor	Access is granted only to the supervisor or an object that is supervisor-equivalent. An object is supervisor-equivalent if its SECUR - ITY_EQUALS property contains the object ID of the supervisor.
4	NetWare	Only NetWare can access an object or property with this security level.

Thus, access 0x31 is supervisor write, logged read; access 0x33 is supervisor read and write, etc.

Object Type (Bindery Services API) is a two-byte value. It can be set to 0 if the object's type is not known, or it can be set to -1 (Wild) when scanning for an object whose type is unknown or irrelevant. The types from 1 to 0x8000 have been reserved by Novell for such common objects as users and servers. All other numbers are available for assignment by developers, and developers may have their object types registered by Novell if required.

The object types currently assigned by Novell are:

Type	Value
Unknown	0h
User	1h
User Group	2h
Print Queue	3h
File Server	4h
Job Server	5h
Gateway	6h
Print Server	7h
Archive Queue	8h
Archive Server	9h
Job Queue	Ah
Administration	Bh
Remote Bridge Server	24h
Advertising Printer Server	47h
Reserved up to	8000h
Wild	FFFFh (-1)

Open Count (Locking and File Server Environment Services APIs) is the number of stations that have opened a semaphore. This number is incremented when the station uses Open Semaphore and decremented when the station calls Close Semaphore.

Open Socket Failures (Diagnostic Services API) is the number of times (since IPX was loaded) that applications have unsuccessfully called the IPX Open Socket call. IPX cannot open a socket if the socket table is full or if the socket is already open.

Operator Aborts Count (Diagnostic Services API) is the number of times (since the shell was activated) that the user has aborted the shell-server connection by entering "A" in reply to a "Network Error" message.

Order Number (Workstation Services API) is a field that shows the order of the server's network/node address relative to the others in the table. An order of 1 indicates the server has the lowest network/node address, 2 indicates the next lowest, etc.

OS Text (Diagnostic Services API) identifies the operating system (e.g., DOS).

OS Version Text (Diagnostic Services API) identifies the operating system version (e.g., v3.1).

Outgoing Packet Discarded No Buffer (File Server Environment Services API) is the number of packets the server attempted to send which were lost because no routing buffers were available.

Owner Object ID (File Services, Directory Services and AppleTalk Filing Protocol Services APIs) is the Bindery object identification of the user that created a file or directory.

Packets Discarded By Hop Count (File Server Environment Services API) is the number of packets that were discarded because they had passed through more than 16 bridges without reaching their destinations.

Packets Discarded Unknown Net (File Server Environment Services API) is the number of packets that were discarded because their destination networks were unknown to the server.

Packets Received During Processing (File Server Environment Services API) is the number of times a new request was received while a previous request was still being processed.

Packet Rx Misc Error Count (Diagnostic Services API) specifies the number of miscellaneous errors that have prevented the driver from receiving a packet (since the last reset or initialization).

Packet Rx Overflow Count (Diagnostic Services API) specifies the number of times (since the last reset or initialization) that the driver has received a packet larger than the buffer space allocated for the packet.

Packet Rx Too Big Count (Diagnostic Services API) specifies the number of times (since the last reset or initialization) that the driver has received a packet that has over the maximum legal size.

Packet Rx Too Small Count (Diagnostic Services API) specifies the number of times (since the last reset or initialization) that the driver has received a packet that has under the minimum legal size.

Packet Sequence Number (Workstation Services API) contains the sequence ID number for the current request to the file server.

Packet Size (Diagnostic Services API) is the size of the first packet to be sent. The size must be between 30 and 512 bytes inclusive. If the packet size shrinks below 30 bytes or grows beyond 512, IPX automatically adjusts the size to a valid value.

Packets Per Send Interval (Diagnostic Services API) is how many packets a source node should send to a destination node as each send interval expires. (For example, if the send interval is 3 and the Packets Per Send Interval is 5, a source node sends 5 packets every 3/18 of a second.)

Packets Received (Diagnostic Services API) is the number of point-to-point test packets that actually arrived at the destination node during a diagnostic test.

Packet Tx Misc Error Count (Diagnostic Services API) specifies the number of miscellaneous errors that have prevented the driver from transmitting a packet (since the last reset or initialization).

Packet Tx Too Big Count (Diagnostic Services API) specifies the number of times (since the last reset or initialization) that applications have asked the driver to send a packet that has over the maximum legal size.

Packet Tx Too Small Count (Diagnostic Services API) specifies the number of times (since the last reset or initialization) that applications have asked the driver to send a packet that has under the minimum legal size.

Packet Type (Communication Services API) indicates the type of service offered or required by the packet. Xerox has defined the following values:

0	Unknown Packet Type
1	Routing Information Packet
2	Echo Packet
3	Error Packet
4	Packet Exchange Packet
5	Sequenced Packet Protocol Packet
16-31	Experimental Protocols
17	NetWare Core Protocol

IPX users should set the Packet Type to 0 or 4, SPX users set it to 5.

Packets With Bad Request Type (File Server Environment Services API) is a count of request packets containing invalid request types.

Paragraph (Value-Added Process Services API) contains the real-mode paragraph value of a memory address.

Password (Bindery Services API) of a Bindery object must be uppercase; the field can be NULL if there is no password.

Pending IO Commands (File Server Environment Services API) is the number of outstanding disk controller commands.

Physical Disk Channel (File Server Environment Services API) is the disk channel to which the disk unit is attached.

Physical Drive Count (File Server Environment Services API) is the number of physical disk units attached to a server.

Physical Drive Type (File Server Environment Services API) is the type of drive (1 = XT, 2 = AT, 3 = SCSI, 4 = disk coprocessor, 5 = PS/2 MFM Controller, 6 = PS/2 ESDI Controller, 7 = Convergent Technology SBIC, 50 to 255 = value-added disk drive).

Physical Node Address (Connection Services API) is the address of the workstation's LAN board.

Physical Read Errors (File Server Environment Services API) is the number of times the cache software received an error from the disk driver on a read request.

Physical Read Requests (File Server Environment Services API) is the number of times cache software issued a physical read request to a disk driver.

Physical Record Lock Count (File Server Environment Services API) is a count of the number of physical record locks.

Physical Record Lock Threshold (Transaction Tracking System API) is the number (0 to 255) of logical record locks that may be set before a transaction is begun.

Physical Write Errors (File Server Environment Services API) is the number of times the cache software received an error from the disk driver on a write request.

Physical Write Requests (File Server Environment Services API) is the number of times cache software issued a physical write request to a disk driver.

Pipe Status List (Message Services API) returns a pipe status code for each connection number contained in the Connection List field. The following codes are defined:

00h	Open.	The message pipe is complete at both ends.
FEh	Incomplete.	The target connection's half of the message pipe does not exist.
FFh	Closed.	The calling client's half of the message pipe does not exist, or the connection number is not in use or is invalid.

Postponed AES Events (Diagnostic Services API) is the number of times (since IPX was loaded) that IPX has been unable to service an AES event on time. For example, IPX cannot send an outgoing packet to a driver that is busy with another packet.

Print Job Number (Print Services API) is a flag containing a number (1-999) the Queue Management System assigns to a print queue job entry.

Print Job Valid (Print Services API) is a flag set while a capture file is open to receive captured characters. When the capture is ended, canceled, or flushed, the flag is cleared.

Print Queue (Print Services API) is a flag set when a job entry is placed in a print queue. When the capture is ended or cancelled, the flag is cleared.

Print Queue ID (Print Services API) is a flag containing the Bindery object ID (four bytes) of the print queue on the target server.

Print Volume (Print Services API) is the number of a volume where a print job is stored.

Printer Reset Buffer Address (Print Services API) is a flag containing a long pointer to a buffer containing the printer reset string.

Printer Setup Buffer Address (Print Services API) is a flag containing a long pointer to a buffer that contains a printer setup string.

Print Flags (Print Services API) is byte containing four bit fields that control a print job. The default value for this field is 0x80. Possible values are:

0x04 Print job is released to be printed if the capture is interrupted by a breach of connection with the file server.

0x08 Automatic form feed is suppressed after the document is printed.

0x40 Tabs are converted to spaces (and other control characters are converted). Tab size is specified in the next field.

0x80 Banners are printed before documents.

Process ID (Value-Added Process Services API) is the ID of a created process or a calling process.

Prompt (Value-Added Process Services API) is a pointer to a null-terminated message, which can be up to 60 characters long.

Property Has Value (Bindery Services API) is a flag that tells (0 = False, FFh = True) whether a property contains a value.

Property Name (Bindery Services API) is a property containing a set to be searched in the call Is Bindery Object In Set.

Query Type (Service Advertising Protocol) is set to 1 for a "general service" query or a 3 for a "nearest server" query.

Queue ID (Queue Services API) is the Bindery object ID of a queue.

Queue Status (Queue Services API) is a byte showing with bits set as follows. 01h means the operator does not want new jobs added to the queue. 02h means the operator does not want additional job servers attaching to the queue. 04h means the operator does not want job servers servicing jobs in the queue. Clearing a bit has the opposite meaning.

Queue Type (Queue Services API) is the Bindery object type of a queue.

Queue Name (Queue Services API) is 1-47 characters long.

Read Beyond Write (File Server Environment Services API) is the number of times a file read request was made when file write requests had not yet filled the cache block.

Read Queue Server Current Status (Queue Services API) returns the Server Status Record of a job server attached to a queue.

Receive Timeout (Workstation Services and Connection Services APIs) is the number of clock ticks the workstation will wait for a response from a file server before timing out. This field is used in the shell's retry-management scheme; it changes to adapt to differing traffic levels on the network.

Record Offset (Locking API) is a LONG (unsigned long) value expressed in two WORDs (unsigned ints) containing the offset from the beginning of the file where the record begins. The programmer must place the more significant WORD in High Record Offset and less significant WORD in Low Record Offset.

Record Length (Locking API) is a LONG value expressed in two WORDs (High and Low) containing the length of the record. The programmer must place the more significant WORD in High Record Offset and less significant WORD in Low Record Offset.

Records (File Server Environment Services API) is the number of dynamic areas used by the server (1 to 3), or the number of transactions to be performed.

Record Type (Accounting Services API) is type1 for a Charge, type2 for a Note.

Remirrored Block (File Server Environment Services API) contains the block number that is being remirrored.

Remirrored Drive (File Server Environment Services API) is the physical drive number of the disk currently being remirrored (FFh = no disk being remirrored).

Remote Acknowledge Number (Communication Services API) is the Sequence Number of the next packet that the remote SPX expects to receive from the local SPX. When this Sequence Number reaches FFFFh, it wraps to 0000h. This field is not valid if the connection state is waiting.

Remote Connection ID (Communication Services API) indicates the number of the specified SPX connection from the remote workstation's point of view.

Remote Network (Communication Services API) returns the number of the network on which the remote workstation resides.

Remote Node (Communication Services API) returns the node address of the destination node. This field is not valid if the connection state is waiting.

Remote Socket (Communication Services API) is the number of the socket that the remote SPX is using to send and receive packets. This field is not valid if the connection state is waiting.

Replies Canceled (File Server Environment Services API) is the number of replies that were canceled because a connection was reallocated while a request was being processed.

Reprocessed Requests (File Server Environment Services API) is the count of requests that were reprocessed by a server.

Requested Socket Number (Communication Services API) is the socket to open. If you pass 0000h in this field, IPX will assign you a socket dynamically.

Reserve Amount (Accounting Services API) is the amount that the account server expects to charge for a service it is about to provide.

Resource Fork Size (AppleTalk Filing Protocol Services API) returns the size of a target AFP file's resource portion. If the AFP Directory/File Path specifies an AFP directory, the Resource Fork Size field returns a zero.

Responses Found (AppleTalk Filing Protocol Services API) indicates how many sets of information (1-4) a call is returning.

Response Type (Service Advertising Protocol) is set to 2 for general service or to 4 for nearest service when the server responds to the query packet. It is also set to 2 for initialization and periodic broadcasts.

Restrictions Enforced (File Server Environment Services API) tells whether limits were placed upon use of disk resources (00h = enforced, FFh = not enforced) when the network was installed.

Result List (Message Services API) field returns a result code for each connection number contained in the Connection List field. The following result codes are defin-ed:

00h	Successful.	The server stored the message in the target connec tion's message buffer. (It is the target connec-tion's responsibility to retrieve and display the message.)
FCh	Rejected.	The target connection's message buffer is already holding a message.
FDh	Invalid Connec-tion Number.	The specified connection number is unknown.
FFh	Blocked.	The target connection's message mode is set to block messages, or the target connection is not is use.

Retransmission Count (Communication Services API) is the number of times since SPX was loaded that SPX attempts to retransmit an unacknowledged packet before it decides that the remote SPX has become inoperable or unreachable.

Retransmitted Packets (Communication Services API) is the number of times (since SPX was loaded) that the local SPX has had to retransmit a packet on a connection before receiving the expected acknowledgment.

Retry Count (Communication Services API) specifies how many times SPX will resend unacknowledged packets before concluding that the destination node is not functioning properly. This field should be set 00h, instructing SPX to use its own internal retry count. A value of 1 through 255 (inclusive) indicates that SPX should resend packets the specified number of times.

Retry Tx Count (Diagnostic Services API) specifies the number of times (since the last reset or initialization) that the driver resent a packet. For example, when the driver detects a collision, the driver resends a packet.

Revoke Rights Mask (Directory Services API) contains the rights to be removed from a directory's Maximum Rights Mask.

Route Hops (Diagnostic Services API) returns the number of hops (between the source bridge and the destination network or server) of the most efficient route. The value in this field and the value returned in the Route 0 Hops field are the same.

Router 0 Next Board Position (Diagnostic Services API) indicates the position of the LAN board (inside Router 0) that receives packets from the LAN board mentioned in the preceding field. A value of 00h indicates LAN A; a value of 01h indicates LAN B, etc.

Router 0 Node Address (Diagnostic Services API) is the node address of the LAN board inside Router 0 that receives packets from the source bridge.

Route Time (Diagnostic Services API) returns the route time (between the source bridge and the destination network or server) of the most efficient route. The value in this field and the value returned in the Route 0 Time field are the same.

Route 0 Hops (Diagnostic Services API) returns the number of hops a packet makes traveling between the source bridge and the destination network or server on route 0.

Route 0 Time (Diagnostic Services API) returns the time it takes a packet to travel between the source bridge and the destination network or server on route 0.

Routing Node (Workstation Services API) is the address of the preferred bridge to route through if a connection is not direct (on the same network).

Save Buffer (Directory Services API) is 16-byte buffer that contains information on the volume and directory pointed to by a directory handle.

Search Attributes (File Services API) is a bit field that specifies the type of file to be returned:

00	Normal Files
02	Normal and hidden files
04	Normal and system files
06	Normal, hidden and system

Search Bit Map (AppleTalk Filing Protocol Services API) determines what kinds of subdirectories and/or files to search for. The following bits are defined:

Low Byte

0x01	Hidden files and Directories
0x02	System files and Directories
0x04	Subdirectories
0x08	Files

Second DMA Channels Used (File Server Environment Services API) lists the DMA controllers a disk driver uses to control a disk channel.

Second DMA Channels Used In Use Flag (File Server Environment Services API) is a flag for a DMA Channels Used field.

Second Interrupt Numbers Used (File Server Environment Services API) contains interrupt numbers a disk driver uses to communicate with a disk channel.

Second Interrupt Numbers Used In Use Flag (File Server Environment Services API) is a flag for the Second Interrupt Numbers Used.

Second IO Address Used (File Server Environment Services API) contains addresses a disk driver uses to control a disk channel.

Second IO Address Used Length (File Server Environment Services API) contains the lengths of the addresses a disk driver uses to control a disk channel.

Second Shared Memory Address (File Server Environment Services API) is a field a disk driver uses to control a disk channel.

Second Shared Memory Address Length (File Server Environment Services API) contains the length of a shared memory addresses.

Sectors Per Block (Directory Services API) is the number of 512-byte sectors in each block of a volume.

Sectors Per Track (File Server Environment Services API) is the number of sectors on each disk track (1 sector = 512 bytes).

Segment (Value-Added Process Services API) is the memory segment for which an absolute address is to be calculated.

Segment Number (Bindery Services API) is a counting field used with Read Property Value and Write Property Value.

Segment Size (Value-Added Process Services API) is specified in 16-byte paragraphs.

Segment Value (Value-Added Process Services API) is either a real-mode segment or a protected mode segment descriptor, depending on the mode at the time. If zero, no memory was available.

Selected Configuration (Diagnostic Services API) returns a value indicating which hardware configuration in the Hardware Configuration Table the driver is using.

Semaphore Handle (Locking API) is a two-word value returned by the call Open Semaphore; it is used in all of the subsequent semaphore calls.

Semaphore Value (Locking and File Server Environment Services APIs) must start as a positive number, the number of available openings in the semaphore. When it goes negative, the value is the number of stations in the queue waiting for semaphores to become available. The number of available slots is between -127 and 127 if Semaphore Value >= 0; if Semaphore Value <0, it is the number of users queued up to access the semaphore.

Send Failures (Diagnostic Services API) is the number of times (since SPX was loaded) that SPX has been unable to send a packet across an SPX connection and receive acknowledgment. In such a case, SPX aborts a connection and informs the calling application.

Send Interval (Diagnostic Services API) indicates how often a source node should send a specified number of packets to a destination node. Send Interval is measured in units of 1/18 of a second.

Send Packet (Diagnostic Services API) is the number of times (since IPX was loaded) that applications have called IPX to send a packet.

Send Packet Requests (Diagnostic Services API) is the number of times (since SPX was loaded) that applications have issued calls to SPX Send Sequenced Packet.

Sequence Number (File Services, Bindery Services and Communications Services APIs). This field is used for counting and reiterating calls. Initial settings are specified with the individual calls.

Server Address (Diagnostic Services API) is the destination server's 12-byte internetwork address.

Server ID (Bindery and Accounting Services APIs) is the Bindery object ID of a server.

Server ID List (Queue Services API) contains the object IDs of job servers servicing a queue.

Server ID Number (Queue Services API) contains the ID number of a job server servicing a job.

Server Name (Service Advertising Protocol) is a 48-byte null-terminated string that is the server's unique name within the internetwork. Any character between 21h (!) and 7Fh (DEL) may be used, except the following:

/ (slash)
\ (backslash)
: (colon)
; (semicolon)
, (comma)
* (asterisk)
? (question mark)
+ (plus)
- (minus)

Server Order Number (Connection Services API) indicates the order number (1 through 8) assigned to the corresponding server. The lowest order number indicates the server with the lowest network/node address. The second lowest number indicates the second lowest address, etc.

Server Printer (Print Services API) is a flag holding the number (0-4) of the printer to which a job will be sent. The default is 0.

Server Station (Queue Services API) contains the station number of the job server servicing a job.

Server Stations (Queue Services API) are the station attachments of the job servers servicing a queue.

Server Status Record (Queue Services API) is a 64-byte field that can contain any information useful to job servers and queue users.

Server Task Number (Queue Services API) contains the task number of the job server servicing a job.

Server Type (Diagnostic Services and Service Advertising Protocol APIs), in diagnostics, returns the object type of the server whose name appears in the following field; in advertising it is the type of server that should respond to a query. A file server's object type is 0004h. A print server's object type is 0003h. FFFFh is wild and causes all server types to respond. The wildcard is good only for general service queries. Other well-known object types appear in the introductory section to Bindery Services.

Server Utilization Percentage (File Server Environment Services API) is the current server utilization percentage (0 to 100). The field is updated once a second.

Service Type (Accounting Services API) specifies type of service for which a charge is being made.

SFT Error Table (File Server Environment Services API) is a 60-byte table containing SFT internal error counters.

SFT Level (File Server Environment Services API) is the SFT level offered by the file server. SFT Level I offers hot disk error fix. SFT Level II offers disk mirroring and transaction tracking. SFT Level III offers physical file server mirroring.

Shareable Lock Count (File Server Environment Services API) is the number of logical connections that have a shareable lock.

Shell Requests Count (Diagnostic Services API) is the number of times (since the shell was activated) that the shell has made requests to a file server.

Short Directory/File Name (AppleTalk Filing Protocol Services API) field returns the NetWare directory or file name of the specified directory or file.

Slot in Use (Connection Services API) indicates whether a slot in the Connection ID Table is in use.

Socket (Service Advertising Protocol) is the socket number on which a value-added server accepts queries and delivers services.

Socket Longevity Flag (Communication Services API) specifies how long a socket should remain open. Setting this field to 00h specifies that the socket will remain open until closed with the IPX Close Socket call or until the application is terminated. A value of FFh indicates that the socket will remain open until it is explicitly closed with IPX Close Socket.

Socket Number (Workstation Services, Connection Services and Communications Services APIs) is the number of the socket on which a server will receive requests, or the socket associated with an ECB.

Source Connection (Message Services API) returns the connection number of a sending station.

Source Connection ID (Communication Services API) is a number assigned by SPX at a packet's source.

Source Network (Communication Services API) is the network number of a station sending an IPX packet. NetWare network numbers are four-byte values given to servers on the same network segment. IPX sets this field to the network number of the station making the request; if zero, the physical network is unknown.

Source Node (Communication Services API) is set by IPX to the physical address of the source node.

Source Socket (Communication Services API), set by IPX, is the socket address of the process sending a packet.

Spool Time (Print Services API) is when a job was spooled to a print queue.

SPX Installation Flag (Communication Services API) indicates whether SPX is installed (00h = not installed; FFh = installed).

SPX Major Revision Number (Communication Services API) indicates which SPX revision is installed.

SPX Major Version (Diagnostic Services API) is which SPX major version is installed on a responding node.

SPX Minor Revision Number (Communication Services API) indicates which SPX revision is installed.

SPX Minor Version (Diagnostic Services API) is which SPX minor version is installed on a responding node.

SPX Packet Header (Diagnostic Services API) is a 42-byte field containing information specific to SPX.

SPX Watchdog (Communication Services API) is a flag that monitors an SPX connection, ensuring that the connection is functioning properly when traffic is not passing through the connection. The application should initialize the SPX Watchdog Flag field to 01h, which enables the feature (0 disables it).

Starting Block (Directory Services API) is the number of the first block of a volume.

Statistics Version (Diagnostic Services API) field returns a major and minor version number that a developer assigns and updates each time the developer modifies the Driver Diagnostic Table.

Status (Print Services API) is a flag used internally by the shell to indicate whether capture is enabled (0) or disabled (any other value) for the default LPT device.

Status Information (File Server Environment Services API) contains information about the lock state of the connection. If the connection is waiting on a lock request, the Status Information field contains information about the resource the connection is waiting for. Therefore, the Status Information structure varies depending on which lock status is returned. If lock status = 0, the Status Information field receives no information.

If lock status = 1, the Status Information field receives information on the physical record lock.

Offset	Content	Type
?	Waiting task number	BYTE
?	Begin address	LONG
?	End address	LONG
?	Volume number	BYTE
?	Directory Entry	WORD
?	File name (ASCIIZ string)	BYTE[14]

If lock status = 2, the Status Information field receives information on the file lock.

Offset	Content	Type
?	Waiting task number	BYTE
?	Volume number	BYTE
?	Directory Entry	WORD
?	File name (ASCIIZ string)	BYTE[14]

If lock status = 3, the Status Information field receives information on the logical record lock.

Offset	Content	Type
?	Waiting task number	BYTE
?	Record name length	BYTE
?	Record name (ASCIIZ string)	BYTE[*LENGTH*]

If lock status = 4, the Status Information field receives information on the semaphore lock.

Offset	Content	Type
?	Waiting task number	BYTE
?	Semaphore name length	BYTE
?	Semaphore name (ASCIIZ string)	BYTE[*LENGTH*]

String Length (Value-Added Process Services API) specifies the character length of a string to be printed.

Subdirectory Name (Directory Services API) is a regular DOS file/directory name (up to an eight-character name and three-character extension, separated by a period).

Suppressed Packets (Communication Services API) is the number of times (since SPX was loaded) that the local SPX has received and discarded a packet because the packet was a duplicate of a previously received packet or because the packet was out-of-bounds for the current receive window.

System Elapsed Time (Directory Services API) is the file server's interval marker, a count of the number of ticks (18 per second) on its clock at the time of a call. This field can be used to measure time between calls. System Elapsed Time (File Server Environment Services API) is the time since the server was brought up.

Tab Size (Print Services API) is a flag holding a number from 1 to 18 that determines how many spaces each tab contains. The default is 8.

Target Execution Time (Queue Services API) is the earliest a job can be serviced. The format is year, month, day, hour, minute, second. If this field is set to FFFFFFFFFFFFh, the job is serviced at the first opportunity.

Target Job Type (Queue Services API) contains a number specifying the job type a station will accept for service If this field is set to FFFFh, the job server will accept any job in the queue.

Target Message Mode (Message Services API) specifies the message mode.

Target Server ID Number (Queue Services API) is the Bindery object ID of a queue server that can service a job. If this field is set to FFFFFFFFh, any job server can service the job.

Task Number (File Server Environment Services API) is which task within a logical connection is involved in a transaction.

Task State (File Server Environment Services API) is the state of the task for which information is to be returned:

01h = TTS Explicit transaction in progress
02h = TTS Implicit transaction in progress
04h = Shared file set lock in progress

Text (Diagnostic Services API) is a null-terminated string that describes the corresponding Custom Variable field and each Text field.

Text Delimiter (Diagnostic Services API) is the end of the Text fields.

Text Description (Diagnostic Services API) returns a null-terminated text string not more than 69 bytes summarizing configuration information in preceding fields.

Text Job Description (Queue Services API) is a null-terminated ASCII description of the content or purpose of a job. The client creating the queue job must supply this field.

Thrashing Count (File Server Environment Services API) is the number of times a cache block was not available when a cache block allocation was requested.

Time Charge Occurs (Accounting Services API) contains the half hour (12am = 0, 11:30pm = 47) during which a charge rate takes effect.

Time of Next Charge (Accounting Services API) contains the time of the next charge, measured in minutes since January 1, 1985.

Time of Previous Charge (Accounting Services API) contains the time of the previous charge, measured in minutes since January 1, 1985.

Timeout Limit (Locking API) is the time the program will wait for a file to become available if another station has it locked. It is measured in clock ticks, where a tick is an eighteenth of a second (1/18), and may be set to 0 if no wait is desired.

Timeouts Count (Diagnostic Services API) is the number of times (since the shell was activated) that the shell has sent a request to a server and then timed out without receiving a reply. (Normally, the shell sends another request packet.)

Time Stamp (Accounting Services API) holds the date and time the server submitted the charge. The format is year (where year = current year - 1900), month, day, hour, month, second, where each is a byte-sized integer.

Timing Out (Print Services API) is a flag set to FFh when the Flush Capture Timeout is decrementing, to 0 when no timeout count is under way.

Too Many Hops Count (Diagnostic Services API) is the number of times (since the bridge was initialized) that the bridge has received packets on their fifteenth hop across an internetwork bridge. These packets are discarded.

Total Blocks (Directory Services API) is the total number of blocks on the volume.

Total Cache Writes (File Server Environment Services API) is the total number of cache buffers written to disk.

Total Changed FATS (File Server Environment Services API) contains the number of FAT sectors the file system has modified since it was brought up.

Total Directory Slots (Directory Services API) is the maximum number of slots on a volume. These slots correspond to entries in the Directory Table (i.e., a new file will take up space as well as a directory slot).

Total Dynamic Space (File Server Environment Services API) is the amount of memory in the dynamic memory area.

Total File Service Packets (File Server Environment Services API) is the number of request packets serviced by a file server.

Total Files Opened (File Server Environment Services API) contains the number of files the server has opened since the server was brought up. If this number reaches FFFFFFFFh, it wraps back to zero.

Total Other Packets (File Server Environment Services API) is a count of all packets received that are not requests for file services.

Total Packets Routed (Diagnostic Services API) is the total number of packets that the router actually routed.

Total Packets Serviced (Diagnostic Services API) is the total number of packets that the bridge has serviced since the bridge was initialized.

Total Read Requests (File Server Environment Services API) contains the number of file read requests a server has received since it was brought up.

Total Request Packets (File Server Environment Services API) is the number of request packets a logical connection has sent to a server since the workstation attached.

Total Routed Packets (File Server Environment Services API) is a count of all packets routed by the server.

Total Rx Packet Count (Diagnostic Services API) specifies the number of packets the driver has successfully received and passed into the system since the last reset or initialization.

Total Server Memory (File Server Environment Services API) is the total amount of memory the server has installed (1KB units).

Total Transactions Performed (File Server Environment Services API) is the number of transactions performed by the server since it was brought up.

Total Transactions Backed Out (File Server Environment Services API) is the number of transactions backed out since the file server was brought up. Backouts occur upon workstations requests or if a workstation fails during a transaction. The value in this field includes backout requests the file server could not perform because transaction tracking was disabled.

Total Tx Packet Count (Diagnostic Services API) specifies the number of packets the driver has successfully transmitted since the last reset or initialization.

Total Unfilled Backout Requests (File Server Environment Services API) is the number of backouts that failed because transaction tracking was disabled.

Total Write Requests (File Server Environment Services API) contains the number of write requests the server has received since it was brought up.

Total Write Transactions Performed (File Server Environment Services API) is the number of transactions that required the file server to track file changes. If a workstation requests a transaction but does not actually modify (write) a file during the transaction, the transaction tracking software will ignore the transaction.

Transaction Disk Space (File Server Environment Services API) is the number of disk blocks being used by the transaction tracking software (1 block = 4,096 bytes).

Transaction FAT Allocations (File Server Environment Services API) is the number of blocks that have been allocated for FATs of files being tracked since the server was brought up.

Transaction File Size Changes (File Server Environment Services API) is the number of times files being tracked changed their sizes within transactions since the server was brought up.

Transaction Files Truncated (File Server Environment Services API) is the number of times files being tracked have been truncated within a transaction since the server was brought up.

Transaction Tracking Supported (File Server Environment Services API) tells whether the server supports TTS. If this field is zero, the server does not support TTS and the rest of the fields are undefined.

Transaction Volume Number (File Server Environment Services API) identifies the volume used for the transaction work file.

Transmit Errors (Diagnostic Services API) is the number of errors that occur during transmission of diagnostic packets.

Transport Control (Communication Services API) is used by internetwork bridges; IPX sets this field to zero before transmission.

Transport Time (Diagnostic Services API) returns a value indicating the speed of the LAN associated with a target driver and board. Speed is measured by the amount of time it takes a 576-bye packet to travel from one node on the LAN to another node. Time is measured in units of 1/18 of a second and rounded to the next highest 1/18.

Trustee Object ID (Directory Services API) is the Bindery object identification of the trustee that will be placed in the directory's trustee list with the rights specified in its Trustee Rights Mask.

Trustee Path (Directory Services API) is the path of a directory for which a Trustee Access Mask applies.

Trustee Rights Mask (Directory Services API) contains the rights a user or users may enjoy in a directory if the Maximum Rights Mask concurs.

Unknown Error Count (Diagnostic Services API) is the number of times (since the shell was activated) that the shell has received a packet containing an undefined error value.

Unknown Network Count (Diagnostic Services API) is the number of times (since the bridge was initialized) that the bridge has received packets bound for an unknown network. These packets are discarded.

Unused Disk Blocks (File Server Environment Services API) is the number of remaining blocks the Bindery object can allocate.

Use Count (File Server Environment Services API) is the number of logical connections that have used a logical record logged, or the number of tasks that have opened or logged a file.

Used Directories (File Server Environment Services API) are the number of directories owned by a Bindery object.

Used Files (File Server Environment Services API) are the number of files created by a Bindery object.

VAP Header (Value-Added Process Services API) is a pointer to a VAP header.

Volume Is Cached (Directory Services API) shows whether a volume is cached. Caching is the process of storing the most recent reads and writes to memory so that subsequent requests may read from memory instead of the drive. It is used to improve performance on the drive.

Volume Is Hashed (Directory Services API) shows whether a volume's Directory Table is stored in file server memory, which improves performance.

Volume Is Mounted (Directory Services API) tells whether a volume is mounted in the file server.

Volume Is Removable (Directory Services API) is a bit field for the flag showing whether a volume can be physically removed from the file server (such as in a removable hard disk cartridge-type drive). A value indicates the volume is removable, zero indicates it is not.

Volume Name (Directory Services API) must be no longer than 16 characters and must not contain spaces, asterisks, question marks, colons, backslashes or forward slashes. If a wildcard is used for the name, the first name found is returned.

Volume Number (Directory Services API) is a volume's offset into the Volume Table.

Wasted Server Memory (File Server Environment Services API) is the amount of memory in the server that is not being used (1KB units). The Wasted Server Memory will normally be 0. If this field is nonzero, the file server has more memory installed than can be used. Usually all extra memory is used for cache blocks.

Watchdog-Destroyed Connections (Diagnostic Services API) is the number of times (since SPX was loaded) that the watchdog process destroyed a connection because the connection was no longer valid.

Watchdog Is On (Communication Services API) is a field whose second bit, if set (0x02), indicates that the watchdog process is monitoring local SPX proceedings.

Write Error Count (Diagnostic Services API) is the number of times (since the shell was activated) that the driver has been unable to send a request to a file server (after repeated retries). In this case, the shell displays the message "Error writing to network" on the workstation screen. The shell does not increment this counter if, after repeated retries, the driver is able to send the request.

Appendix C

NetWare 286/386 Differences

There are several differences in the programming environments of NetWare 286 and NetWare 386.

Name spaces and data streams

In NetWare 286, the filing system recognized only DOS filenames — eight characters, a dot, and a three-character suffix. To let different operating systems coexist on a heterogeneous network, NetWare 386 allows for multiple name spaces. Currently, there are only two. Space zero is used by the operating system to store DOS file information, space one to store Macintosh file information. In the future, however, spaces are planned such environments as OS/2 and UNIX.

In NetWare 286, the data portion of a DOS file was stored in a data fork, and the data portion of a Macintosh file was stored in a resource fork. In NetWare 386, these forks give way to data streams. Data stream zero corresponds to name space zero and is where DOS files are stored. Similarly, data stream one corresponds to name space one and is where the data for Macintosh files are stored (the old resource fork).

This system allows for NetWare 386 to grow to house any number of diverse filing systems under one roof. See the New Calls section below for names of the new calls that manage name space and data stream information.

Salvageable file options

When a file in NetWare 286 version 2.15 or earlier is deleted, it is purged the next time an application writes to its disk. Once purged, the file is lost forever. A Salvage command could save the file if it were issued before that writing, but only rarely do users remember that files must be recovered immediately after deletion.

When a file is deleted in NetWare 386, it is salvageable until free disk space becomes so low that salvageable files must be purged to make room for new data. At any point up until this time, salvageable files may be recovered. Files may still be explicitly purged.

Trustee rights amendments

NetWare 286 version 2.15 trustee rights are as follows:

0x01	Read (file reads allowed)
0x02	Write (file writes allowed)
0x04	Open (files can be opened)
0x08	Create (files can be created)
0x10	Delete (files can be deleted)
0x20	Parental (subdirectories can be created and deleted and trustee rights can be granted or revoked)
0x40	Search (directory can be searched)
0x80	Modify (file attributes can be modified)

In NetWare 386, open is implied when read and write are granted. The create right allows users to create directories as well as files in 3.0. Also, in NetWare 3.0, trustee rights can be granted or revoked with the modify right. NetWare 386 trustee rights are held in two bytes instead of one and are defined as follows:

Byte 1 (Least Significant Byte)

0x01	Read (open and read allowed)
0x02	Write (open and write allowed)
0x04	Reserved (must be set to 0)
0x08	Create (files and directories can be created)
0x10	Erase (files and directories can be deleted)
0x20	Access (may set and delete trustees)
0x40	File Scan (if the trustee applies to a directory, that directory may be scanned; when applied to a file, it is visible on the scan)
0x80	Modify (file attributes can be modified)

Byte 2 (Most Significant Byte)

0x01	Supervisor (has supervisor rights to file or directory; does not apply to inherited rights — NetWare 3.x ONLY.)

The remaining bits are reserved and must be set to 0.

New shells

In 1990, Novell released new workstation shells (called version 3.01) "to more fully support" NetWare 386 and Microsoft Windows 3.0, and to provide a variety of memory schemes. Three new versions of the shell were released using: conventional, expanded (EMS) and extended memory (XMS). Several new configuration parameters and command-line options were added to the SHELL.CFG file.

New parameters

ALL SERVERS = ON/OFF

This option determines whether the End Of Task is sent to all connected servers (ON) or only those involved in the task (OFF). The default is off.

SHOW DOTS = ON/OFF

Because the NetWare file server does not have directory entries for "." and "..", the DOS symbols for current and parent directories, the shell emulates these entries in the Find First Matching File and Find Next Matching File calls. Programs, such as Microsoft Windows, which use these entries to traverse directory trees assume in the absence of these directories that the program is at the root of a drive. This option defaults to off.

MAX CUR DIR LENGTH = 64-255 (Maximum Current Directory Length)

DOS defines the Get Current Directory Call to return a 64-byte pathname. The old NetWare shell allowed for 128 bytes to be returned. For compatibility, this parameter is now configurable. The default is 64.

SET STATION TIME = ON/OFF

This option allows a user to avert updating a workstation's time when the shell loads. With this option on, the shell will synchronize the workstation's time with that of the file server it attaches to. Default is on.

SPECIAL UPPERCASE = ON/OFF

This option determines how the shell translates ASCII characters above 127 into uppercase characters. With this option off, no translation is performed on these characters. With this option on, the shell asks the resident DOS to do the translation. Default is off.

PREFERRED SERVER = <server name> [48 characters maximum, including one character for null terminator]

This option allows the user to specify a preferred server. When the shell loads, it will attempt to establish its first connection to this server, rather than just the first server that responds. If this option is used, the shell will also attempt up to five different server connections before returning the message "Server has no available slots". The server name must be a valid server name. If the shell can't connect to the preferred server but can connect to one of the other five servers, it will. Default is none.

ENTRY STACK SIZE = 5-40 [EMS shell version only]

This option lets the user configure the size of the internal stack the expanded memory shell uses. When the shell is busy and an interrupt handler makes a shell request, the shell must get and save the current page mapping more than is usual. Some programs also change the size of this save array; this requires additional space for second and succeeding re-entries into the shell. Default is 10.

New command-line options

'I' displays version, type, and copyright information. Around since version 2.1, this option has not been documented until now. It displays the information, but does not attempt to establish a server connection or load the shell.

'U' attempts to unload the (3.01) shell from memory. To succeed, the shell attempting the unload must be the same one that is currently resident. If any programs that Terminate and Stay Resident (TSRs) are loaded between the unloading and the resident shell, the unload will terminate with an error message, as it will if any of the shell's interrupts have been grabbed by some other program.

'PS=<*server name*>' loads the(3.01) shell and attempts to connect to the specified server. The server name must be that of a valid server on the network with connection slots available for the connection to succeed. If the connection does not succeed, the shell establishes a connection to the closest server it can.

APIs obsolete in NetWare 386

The following APIs are obsolete in NetWare 386. If a call is made to one of these APIs, an error code will result.

File Services:

Purge Erased Files
Purge All Erased Files
Restore Erased Files

These calls have been replaced in the NetWare 386 environment by the Purge Salvageable File and Recover Salvageable File calls. The disk space recovery algorithm has also changed in NetWare 386. At press time, Novell had not yet published the Assembler or C documentation, however.

File Server Services:

Get Disk Channel Statistics
Get Connection's Task Information
Get List of Connections Using a File
Get Physical Record Locks By Connection and File
Get Physical Record Locks By File
Get Logical Record Locks By Connection
Get Server LAN IO Statistics
Get Server Miscellaneous Information
Clear Connection Number
Get File System Statistics
Get Transaction Tracking Statistics
Read Disk Cache Statistics
Get Drive Mapping Table
Read Physical Disk Statistics
Get Logical Record Information
Get Connection's Semaphores
Get Semaphore Information
Get LAN Driver's Configuration Information
Get Connection's Usage Statistics

These calls are not in NetWare 386. Novell says similar calls will again be available when the Network Management module for NetWare 386 is released, though the company doesn't say just when that will be.

Message Services:

Send Personal Message
Get Personal Message
Open Message Pipe
Close Message Pipe
Check Pipe Status
Log Network Message

These calls are not included in NetWare 386 because they are not needed thanks to the IPX-SPX calls.

Directory Services:

Get Volume Information

The information returned by this call can be returned with the NetWare 386 call Get Volume Usage which will also work on NetWare 286, returning a subset of the fields.

Calls introduced in NetWare 386

The following calls were introduced in the NetWare 386 programming environment. At press time, Novell had not yet released documentation on these calls.

Name space and data stream information:

Fill Name Space Buffer
Get Data Stream Info
Get Name Space Info
Get Number of Name Space and Data Streams

NetWare 3.0 file system:

Scan File Entry
Scan File Physical
Get Name Space Entry
Scan Directory Entry
Get Directory Entry
Set Entry
Move Entry
AFP Open File Fork

Disk space restriction:

Scan Directory Restrictions
Scan Volume For Restrictions
Clear Volume Restrictions
Get Object Disk Restrictions
Set Directory Restrictions
Set Volume Restrictions

The following new calls have been documented by Novell. They became available with version 3.00 of the NetWare workstation shell.

Task mode calls:

Get Task Mode
Get Task Mode Pointer

In the past, the workstation shell performed cleanup operations such as closing files for programs found in unallocated memory. This has caused problems with program shells, memory swapping programs and other memory-resident software. The cleanup operation can be checked and optionally disabled with these calls.

Get Task Mode (B5h 03h)

This call returns the current task mode.

Registers in:

AH	B5h
AL	03h

Registers out:

AH	0
AL	Task Mode Setting

Task Mode Setting defines the mode of the Task flag. Values 0-3 are are reserved; if this value is set to 4, no task cleanup is performed.

Get Task Mode Pointer (B5h 04h)

This call returns the address of the current task mode byte.

Registers in:

AH	B5h
AL	04h

Registers out:

ES:BX	Pointer to the Task Mode byte

Warning: Defined use of this byte is reserved, and may change in the future without prior notice. It is recommended that this value be left to the default setting to prevent files being left open by abnormally terminated programs. However, if a program absolutely must have task cleanup disabled, it is up to the programmer to maintain the version information necessary to ensure compatibility with future use of this value.

Enhancing Microsoft Windows usage

Shell functions have been added for fake roots and the shell show dots parameter. These functions were added to enhance the use of Microsoft Windows. Fake roots allow a directory on a mapped drive to appear to Windows as the root directory. The shell's "show dots on" parameter causes the single dot "." and double dot ".." directory names to be recognized by the shell in directory search calls. Windows uses the double dot to allow the user to select the parent directory.

Map a Fake Root (E9h 05h)

If a specified drive is not currently mapped, a drive mapping will be created, and a fake root will be set.

Registers in:

AH	E9h
AL	05h
BL	Drive Number (0 = current, 1 = A, 26 = Z)
DS:DX	Pointer to ASCII path (may include [server/][volume:][path] and may be NULL length)

Registers out:

Carry flag cleared:
Successful

Carry flag set:

AL	Completion Code

Completion Codes

3	Invalid Path
0Fh	Invalid Drive
11h	Not same device

Delete a Fake Root (E9h 06h)

This call deletes a fake root.

Registers in:

AH	E9h
AL	06h
BL	Drive Number

Registers out:
none

Get Relative Drive Depth (E9h 07h)

This call returns the number of directories below the fake root for the drive mapping of the specified drive.

Registers in:

AH	E9h
AL	07h
BL	Drive Number

Registers out:

AL	Relative Depth (Number of directories below the fake root) FFh indicates to fake root assigned.

For example, if a drive is mapped to SERVER/SYS:USERS/NAME and the fake root is set to SERVER/SYS:USERS. The prompt (if set to PG) would show F:\NAME>. This function would return 1 as the relative depth.

Set Show Dots Parameter (E9h 08h)

This call sets the show dots parameter.

Registers in:

AH	E9h
AL	08h
BL	Directive (set to 0 for Show Dots off, non-zero for on)

Registers out:

BL	Previous Show Dots setting

Extended shell call:

Get Shell Version and Type.

With release 3.00 of the workstation shell, there can be three different types: conventional, EMS, and XMS, depending on the kind of memory used (conventional, expanded, or extended). This new call tells which type of shell is being used.

Get Shell Version and Type (EAh)

Registers in:

AH	EAh
AL	Directive (set to 0 to not return a string in ES:DI describing the shell version, non-zero to do so)

Registers out:

ES:DI	Workstation Environment String (only filled in if Directive is non-zero)
AH	Workstation Shell OS (0 = MSDOS)
BH	Major NetWare Shell Version
BL	Minor NctWare Shell Version
CH	Shell Type (0 = conventional, 1 = expanded, 2 = extended)
CL	Shell Revision Number

The CH parameter is new for this call.

Appendix D

Further Information

Further information on programming to the NetWare environment can be obtained from the following sources:

Magazines/Newsletters

NetWare Technical Journal

The Journal is a quarterly publication that contains informative, technical discussions aimed at the developer. Source code examples can be found in every issue.

For subscription info call: 1-800-433-0880

Subscription rate: $34.95 for one year, $65.00 for two years

The NetWare Programmer's Newsletter

Published by RoseWare, 8515 Cyrus Place, Alexandria, VA 22308. (703) 799-2509. A newsletter for programmers developing to the NetWare environment. Provides thorough code examples, new API call explanations, and discussions of the topics that face NetWare programmers.

PDS Bullets

(Published by Novell and sent to registered developers. Contact the Novell, Austin office for further information.)

Third-Party Books

NetWare User's Guide by Ed Liebing (1989, M&T Publishing, Inc.). This book provides a good starting place for someone completely new to NetWare. Taking the reader by the hand, it provides a good user-oriented background.

NetWare Supervisor's Guide by John T. McCann (1989, M&T Publishing, Inc.). This book provides a good supervisor-level framework for the details surrounding the NetWare environment that a programmer should be aware of, such as the inner workings of the workstation and the file server.

Novell Manuals/Development Kits NetWare 286 and General Development Tools:

NetWare System Interface Technical Overview

The technical overview serves as an explanatory text to the System Calls for DOS manuals. Included with the purchase of either the System Calls for DOS or the C Interface for DOS manuals, it provides conceptual information and prototypes for C Library manuals. (These concepts are covered in this book.)

NetWare System Calls for DOS vols. 1 & 2

These manuals document the assembler-level calls to the NetWare APIs. (The information contained in them is covered in this book.) Both manuals: $195.00

NetWare C Interface for DOS vols. 1 & 2

The C Interface is actually a library of calls and two manuals that document them. Both manuals: $195.00

C Network Compiler NetWare 386 Development Tools:

C Network Compiler/386

The C Network Compiler/386 allows developers to create NetWare Loadable Modules for NetWare 386 as well as client applications for 386 PCs.

NLM Developer's Kit (only to registered developers)

It includes the C Network Compiler/386 and the SDK version of NetWare 386 3.1.

NetWare RPC DOS

A set of development tools that allow the programmer to create client-server applications. Includes the RPC Compiler, Network and Runtime Libraries, Server Control Procedures, and pre-written RPC Specifications.

NetWare RPC 386

Allows a NetWare 386 server to act as the server part of a client-server relationship in a distributed application environment.

NetWare Btrieve 386

Novell's database management module that runs on a NetWare 386 server.

Phar Lap 386/ASM Assembler

A 386 assembler that can be used in the development of NetWare Loadable Modules. Produces 386-specific code.

NetWare 386 Client APIs

A C library for 386 NetWare that replaces the NetWare 2.*x* C libraries.

NetWare Print Server APIs

The APIs to support the NetWare Print Server which allows up to four queue service modes and up to 16 printers on a single print server.

NetWare 386 v3.1 Software Developer's Kit (SDK) (only to registered devs)

This package includes the NLM C Interface library which allows developers to create Netware 386 server-based applications. NetWare STREAMS, which is a UNIX System 5.3-standard environment for concurrently supporting multiple protocol stacks is also incorporated.

STREAMS gives developers Inter-Process Communication (IPC) support to enable writing applications that support multiple communications interfaces such as Named Pipes and Transport Level Interface (TLI). Currently supported is the IPX/SPX protocols but support is planned for AppleTalk, TCP/IP, NetBEUI/DLC, SNA, X.25, and OSI.

TLI Documentation

Describes the NetWare 386 Transport Layer Interface (TLI) for developing client-server applications.

Directory Services Documentation

Future versions of NetWare 386 will replace local file server binderies with a network-wide security database and resource directory. This document describes the following component services: Authentication Services, Authorization Services, Directory Services, Directory Management, Notification Services and Authentication Time Services.

AT&T STREAMS Documentation

STREAMS provides a protocol-independent protocol stack support infrastructure for NetWare 386. This document outlines developing user-level applications and the STREAMS kernel facilities for development of modules and drivers. Includes discussions of basic and advanced operations, multiplexed streams, and message handling interfaces.

Database development products:

XQL

Provides the Application Program Interfaces to Novell's NetWare SQL (a database-server package).

XQL for OS/2

XTrieve Plus

Querying facility and report writer for Btrieve/NetWare XQL databses

Other development products:

MHS Interface Guide

Provides programmer documentation on the Application Program Interface for the MHS.

TCPort Developers Kit

Allows the programmer to develop applications for the TCP/IP networking platform on the Apple Macintosh. The Kit provides: an interface for Berkeley socket emulation (UNIX 4.3 BSD-compatible), the TCPort driver library, and Apple's MacTCP driver library.

Macintosh Client APIs

Provides the Client APIs for developing NetWare-compatible applications on an Apple Macintosh.

LANAlyzer Group

Services/Programs

NetWire

Based on CompuServe, NetWire provides a host of topics on three different forums: NOVA, NOVB and NOVC. There are two developer topics on the NOVC forum. Contact Novell, Austin for information on subscribing to NetWire.

The Strategic Relations Program

Novell offers this program to developers who wish to create software for the NetWare environment. The program is free to qualified developers and provides support to the following categories of developers: Independent Software Vendor (ISV), Peripheral Vendor, Corporate MIS, Government, and Education.

Several levels of support are offered in the program depending on the needs and eligibility of the developer:

Bronze - available to those who create NetWare-compatible software.

Silver - available to those developers whose products use IPX/SPX and a suite of Novell APIs. This level includes developers creating LAN drivers and disk drivers as well as server-based applications (both VAPs and NLMs).

Gold - available to developers who are creating NetWare Loadable Modules for 386 versions of NetWare.

Each level provides increased support from Novell. Bronze level developers benefit from Novell's Direct Connect Service, LANSWER phone support, inclusing in the Strategic Relatios mailing list, and notification of the Professional Developers' Forum and Novell Developers' Conference. The Silver and Gold levels expand upon the Bronze offering based on the developer's committment to Novell.

Software Development Kits (SDKs) are available only to qualified registered developers. Kits are available for Macintosh, OS/2 and NetWare 386.

The Strategic Relations group also offers training for NetWare 386 developers; call 1-800-233-EDUC for more information. A brochure (which includes an application) is available from the Strategic Relations Group about their program. Call 1-800-767-4787.

Appendix E

Completion Codes

Appendix E: Completion Codes

Throughout this book, completion codes documented by Novell have been listed for each call. In some cases, there may be a completion code returned that is not listed in the call reference. The following list provides a comprehensive presentation of the completion codes returned by NetWare function calls. A completion code of zero usually means that no error occurred during a call.

Hex	Dec	Meaning
0	0	SPX Not Installed
		SPX Connection OK
		SPX Connection Started
		SPX Connection Established
		SPX Packet Successful
		Server Not In Use
		TTS Not Available
1	1	DOS Invalid Function Number
		Server In Use
		Semaphore Overflow
		TTS Available
2	2	DOS File Not Found
3	3	DOS Path Not Found
4	4	DOS Too Many Open Files
5	5	DOS Access Denied
6	6	DOS Invalid File Handle
7	7	DOS Memory Blocks Destroyed
8	8	DOS Insufficient Memory
9	9	DOS Invalid Memory Block Address
A	10	DOS Invalid Environment
B	11	DOS Invalid Format
C	12	DOS Invalid Access Code
D	13	DOS Invalid Data
F	15	DOS Invalid Drive Specified
10	16	DOS Attempt To Delete Current Directory
11	17	DOS Not Same Device
12	18	DOS No More Files
20	32	DOS Sharing Violation
21	33	DOS Lock Violation
80	128	File In Use Error
81	129	No More File Handles
82	130	No Open Privileges
83	131	IO Error Network Disk
84	132	No Create Privileges
85	133	No Create Delete Privileges

86	134	Create File Exists Read Only
87	135	Wild Cards In Create File Name
88	136	Invalid File Handle
89	137	No Search Privileges
8A	138	No Delete Privileges
8B	139	No Rename Privileges
8C	140	No Modify Privileges
8D	141	Some Files Affected In Use
8E	142	No Files Affected In Use
8F	143	Some Files Affected Read Only
90	144	No Files Affected Read Only
91	145	Some Files Renamed Name Exists
92	146	No Files Renamed Name Exists
93	147	No Read Privileges
94	148	No Write Privileges Or Read Only
95	149	File Detached
96	150	Server Out Of Memory Out of Dynamic Workspace
97	151	No Disk Space For Spool File
98	152	Volume Does Not Exist
99	153	Directory Full
9A	154	Renaming Across Volumes
9B	155	Bad Directory Handle
9C	156	Invalid Path No More Trustees
9D	157	No More Directory Handles
9E	158	Invalid Filename
9F	159	Directory Active
A0	160	Directory Not Empty
A1	161	Directory IO Error
A2	162	Read File With Record Locked
C0	192	No Account Privileges
C1	193	Login Denied - No Account Balance No Account Balance
C2	194	Account Credit Limit Exceeded Login Denied - No Credit
C3	195	Account Too Many Holds
C5	197	Intruder Detection Lock
C6	198	No Console Operator
D0	208	Queue Error
D1	209	No Queue
D2	210	No Queue Server
D3	211	No Queue Rights
D4	212	Queue Full
D5	213	No Queue Job
D6	214	No Job Rights

D7	215	Password Not Unique
		Queue Servicing
D8	216	Password Too Short
		Queue Not Active
D9	217	Login Denied - No Connection
		Station Not Server
DA	218	Unauthorized Login Time Queue Halted
DB	219	Unauthorized Login Station
		Max Queue Servers
DC	220	Account Disabled
DE	222	Password Has Expired No Grace
DF	223	Password Has Expired
E8	232	Not Item Property Write Property To Group
E9	233	Member Already Exists
EA	234	No Such Member
EB	235	Not Group Property
EC	236	No Such Segment
		SPX Terminated Poorly
ED	237	Property Already Exists
		SPX No Answer From Target
		SPX Connection Failed
		SPX Connection Terminated
EE	238	Object Already Exists
		SPX Invalid Connection
EF	239	Invalid Name
		SPX Connection Table Full
F0	240	Wild Card Not Allowed
		IPX Not Installed
F1	241	Invalid Bindery Security
F2	242	No Object Read Privilege
F3	243	No Object Rename Privilege
F4	244	No Object Delete Privilege
F5	245	No Object Create Privilege
F6	246	No Property Delete Privilege
		Not Same Local Drive
F7	247	No Property Create Privilege
		Target Drive Not Local
F8	248	Already Attached To Server
		No Property Write Privilege
		Not Attached To Server
F9	249	No Free Connection Slots
		No Property Read Privilege
FA	250	No More Server Slots
		Temp Remap Error

FB	251	Invalid Parameters
		No Such Property
		Unknown Request
FC	252	Internet Packet Request Cancelled
		Unknown File Server
		Message Queue Full
		SPX Listen Cancelled
		No Such Object
FD	253	Bad Station Number
		Invalid Packet Length
		Unknown Request
		SPX Malformed Packet
		SPX Packet Overflow
		Field Already Locked
		TTS Disabled
FE	254	Bindery Locked
		Directory Locked
		Invalid Semaphore Name Length
		Packet Not Deliverable
		Server Bindery Locked
		Socket Table Full
		Spool Directory Error
		Supervisor Has Disabled Login
		Timeout Failure
		Transaction Ends Record Lock
		Implicit Transaction Active

FF	255	Bad Printer Error
		Bad Record Offset
		Close FCB Error
		File Extension Error
		File Name Error
		Hardware Failure
		Invalid Drive Number
		Invalid Initial Semaphore Value
		Invalid Semaphore Handle
		IO Bound Error
		No Files Found Error
		No Response From Server
		No Such Object Or Bad Password
		Path Not Locatable
		Queue Full Error
		Request Not Outstanding
		Socket Already Open
		Transaction Not Yet Written
		No More Matching Files
		Bindery Failure
		SPX Is Installed
		SPX Socket Not Opened
		Explicit Transaction Active
		No Explicit Transaction Active
		Transaction Not Yet Written
		No More Matching Files
		No Record Found

Index

A

B

C

D

E

F

G

H

I

Q

R

S

T

U

V

W

X